DEMOCRACY BY PETITION

DANIEL CARPENTER

Democracy by Petition

Popular Politics in Transformation, 1790–1870

HARVARD UNIVERSITY PRESS
Cambridge, Massachusetts, and London, England
2021

Printed in the United States of America

Publication of this book has been supported through the generous provisions of the Maurice and Lula Bradley Smith Memorial Fund.

FIRST PRINTING

Library of Congress Cataloging-in-Publication Data

Names: Carpenter, Daniel P., 1967– author.
Title: Democracy by petition : popular politics in transformation, 1790–1870 / Daniel Carpenter.
Description: Cambridge, Massachusetts : Harvard University Press, 2021. | Includes index.
Identifiers: LCCN 2020042416 | ISBN 9780674247499 (cloth)
Subjects: LCSH: Petitions—North America—History—19th century. | Democracy—North America—History—19th century. | Political participation—North America—History—19th century.
Classification: LCC JF799 .C3698 2021 | DDC 322.40973/09034—dc23
LC record available at https://lccn.loc.gov/2020042416

To Laurel and Leo

Contents

Preface

"Democracy" and "petition" are concepts that seem, at first glance, utterly unfit for each other. Democracy proclaims the people as sovereign, its constituent citizens as equals. Those who rule in a representative democracy do so by holding offices to which citizens alone elect them or, for many administrators and judges, by having been appointed by the elected. Democratic government derives its authority from laws passed by those elected officials. Petitioning, on the other hand, evokes a humble approach on bended knee to a ruler—in the premodern notion, a monarch—asking for something only the sovereign can grant. So conceived, the petition seems to presume a form of abasement, the supplicant rendered as subject, every aspiration converted into a meek request whose fulfillment is a matter of the ruler's whim.

For much of a century, though, petitioning and democracy ran together as never before and never since. In nineteenth-century North America, petitioning became truly explosive and starkly radical. It became more democratic in its aspirations, its proliferating masses of signatures, and its connection of one petition to another in the architecture of a campaign. Petitioning had broken from the monarchical model of supplication before, especially during the American Revolution, but never with such audacity or scale. Few corners of the continent's far-flung populations appear to have been untouched by this revolution. From Indigenous villages in the Saint Lawrence valley and from pueblos in Nuevo México, from women and men of color in Barbados and Trinidad and from Black communities in Boston, New York, and Philadelphia, from tenant farmers and from urban artisans, from politicians like Thomas Jefferson, Henry Clay, Louis-Joseph Papineau, and William Lyon Mackenzie, from eight-year-old boys and twelve-year-old female canvassers and from aging widows who wanted to vote—from these and from thousands of other authors, both individual and collective, new petitions surged.

The democracy portrayed in the pages that follow is not our mothers' democracy or our fathers' democracy or our own. Yet it might well have been our ancestors' democracy, albeit a partial one, some five to ten generations back. It is a democracy in a different imaginary. The story of American democratization we have been taught is not false. It is one of revolutions, assemblies, and legislatures; the torturous evolution of voting rights for men, for African Americans, and for women; the organization of mass parties; the abolition of slavery; and the enshrining of civil equality in constitutional text. An appreciation of petitioning, however, deepens and changes this story in important ways.

First, crucial dimensions of democratization—the expansion of suffrage rights, the empowering of representative bodies, the freeing of lands from feudal tenure, the abolition of slavery, and the expansion of civil rights and preliminary equality—depended as much on petitioning campaigns as on voting and parties themselves. In these developments, petitioning shifted agendas and coordinated popular pressure. Petitions helped bring us the hallmarks of the democracy we know.

Second, much of the development of organized civil society in North America—the fundaments of the democracy that Alexis de Tocqueville saw and admired in voluntary associations—happened by petition. In a virtuous cycle, petitioning campaigns were often sponsored by organizations, which themselves may have been started by petitions for incorporation or of protest. Time and again in the antebellum period, petitioning campaigns left organizational legacies, including the building blocks of new political parties, that were far larger and more capacious than the groups that had initially sponsored them.

Third, the petitioning authors of democratization encompass peoples and places different from those centered in customary narratives. These different peoples include not only American free Black communities but also women and men of color in the British West Indies whose activity alarmed slaveholding interests in the American South. The different peoples include thousands of petitioning Indigenous women and men who reshaped legislative and bureaucratic agendas from Canada through Massachusetts and

New York to the Great Lakes to Mexico and the Pacific Coast. The different peoples include women, who revolutionized the petition canvass and seeded many thousands of deliberative conversations on Indigenous dispossession, slavery, war and imperialism, temperance, and the rights of their sex.

The different peoples of this story also inhabited different spaces, including those outside the boundaries and sovereignties of the United States. They include French Canadians who deposed a powerful colonial governor and whose activity inspired the English Chartists, American settlers in what is now Ontario, alliances of pueblo Natives, *genízaros* and Hispanos in Nuevo México, Catholic women during Mexico's La Reforma, men and women of color in the Caribbean, and women and men in Indigenous villages across the continent.

Finally, a more democratic reading of petitions—interpreting them as alliances and organizations emergent on paper—permits a rereading of the role of those who have figured centrally in existing stories of democratization. Henry Clay, Louis-Joseph Papineau, and Robert Gourlay built the fundaments of opposition parties in part through petitioning campaigns. The views of leaders ranging from Thomas Jefferson to Abraham Lincoln were shaped and reshaped by democratic petitioning campaigns. William Lloyd Garrison, Angelina Grimké, Maria Stewart, and many others harnessed petitioning to build a multiracial coalition behind the immediate abolition of slavery. City artisans and distant farmers united in signing for tariff protection and antimonopoly initiatives. The petitioning campaigns of Black and Indigenous peoples were highly successful in part because they successfully courted White allies.

The inseparability of petitioning and democratization forms the central work of this study. Unpacking that claim necessitates thinking of democracy not only as institutions of voting and parties but also as a work of agendas, of dialogue between government and citizen, of civic organizations, and of cultural transformation. It also requires a modernization in how we regard the petition, as only in part the supplication of yesteryear but also a modern technology of text and testimony.

DEMOCRACY BY PETITION

INTRODUCTION

ONE

Signature Moments, 1846–1849

Ka tshishe utshimauin takuikan ka itikuin, niran Shatshekuriniuiatsh, ishkuamishkuriniuatsh, uauiapikuriniuiatsh kie uashauriniuiatsh shuk stamiskatinan

In the powerful words of an enduring language, on April 8, 1847—at the moon of the geese, on the northern shore of the great seaward flow of North America's dawnland—did the chiefs *rui paku, pat shetus, shapatits eltiru, misher ashini, rui minik, aripic mistikutiae,* and 125 other men of the Innu nation address the governor general of Canada. "O Great Chief who we call the captain of the ship of state," they wrote, "we the Indians of Tadoussac, of the Isles de Jeremie of the Godebou River and of Sept-Îles salute you respectfully."[1]

The Innu had come to the governor with complaints and requests. They began to make their case:

at mak shashies utshiparu shuriau nitishinats uets tats atauirinuts, uets itauanuts mistikuts ka mirushits, uets manikashuts nitisshinats ka issiitsets mauats esku peik tshistapashun nuts uapitenan, eku etsheskaki-uats esku mauats pek shipu nika ianan tshe pistuaiats. miam uepastits eku tshetiats eka tsispeuasiats. Sas nipetenan tshe mijikats ua mani-kashuts nitissinats nete kamiruarits aetshiru

For a long time now the Province has derived its annual revenues from our lands, by the commercial posts as much as by woodcutting, and thereby our hunting grounds have vanished in conversion to farming, and still we have received absolutely no compensation. Thus are we thrown back into the forests. Soon we will not even have a river in which to cast our nets. We will vanish like the sand carried by the wind if You do not take up our cause. We have learned that new settlers are coming to stay on our productive lands.

. . .

iterimiiats iriniuiats tshika uitamatinau iteritamats.

If you want us to be able to live, we are going to let you know what we think.

. . .

tshima mirikuiats tshe mirikuiats ute pretipistikuts aitukan ruas pestsamits nitukam.

tshima tiperitamats e nutimeshanuts niran muk eriniuiats nissashits shipu: uapitshiuapui, mak minikuakanistuk mak eshipu, mak pretipistikut, mak kamenishuts, mak kamishinaskuiatsh, mak mistisin, mak usiku shipu, mak pestsamits;

That you reserve to us the land stretching from the Outardes River including its two banks, all the way to the Betseamis River, including its two banks as well.

That you leave us with exclusive rights to fish in the Outardes River, and the Papinachois, and the Great and small Escoumain, and the Mistashini, and the Betsi, and the Romaine, and the Betseamis.

. . .

eku tsek kutakats uiruau maniteuts katsi iatuau nistastsinaru tshimimiskuts tshiskakuiats usam nipa mirueritenan

That, finally, you give us indemnities for the lands that the whites occupy in our homeland, and we will be satisfied.

eka mak tshekuan mirikuiats ekun tshe ishinakushiats ka ishinakaishinakusits ka tshimikatets

If on the other hand you give us nothing, then will we soon resemble those dead of hunger.

The Innu have millennia of history in what is now known as the Saint Lawrence River, but in the 1840s, their already difficult plight became truly dire. As British and French settlers crowded onto lands they had inhabited for generations—but which the Canadian government had recently opened as part of the King's Domain—the Innu watched traditional fishing runs dwindle and saw their hunts come up empty. The British hatched proposals to relocate them, but the Innu knew that the new lands would not be as good as those they currently occupied. They began hearing of new settlers coming, and they realistically feared death as a people.

In a bilingual petition to the colonial governor Lord Elgin, the Innu made an appeal to justice and to the heart. On the left side of three successive sheets of paper were arranged phrases in transliterated Innu language, while on the right side ran a French translation, performed by Catholic missionary Flavien Durocher. In return for the demands made, what Canadians called "the petition of the Montagnais Indians" tendered no benefits, promised no cooperation, advanced no threats to the welfare of the settlers around them.

The Innu had petitioned Canada's government before, many times over. Yet they changed their approach on this occasion. Having learned of reserves created to the west and the south for other tribes, they asked for lands and associated rights of their own. This reserve would include not only land but also water and, crucially, exclusive fishing and hunting privileges on those waters. As the Innu listed river after river, bay upon bay, island after island in the gulf of the Saint Lawrence from which they wanted other hunters and fishers excluded, they mapped the waterscapes that sustained a people.[2]

The Innu emphasized waters in the very month when they would depend most greatly on them. During their migration south from winter hunting lands to the river coast, as supplies of hunting meat dwindled in March and April and before fishing picked up, the Innu relied heavily on bird meat harvested from geese and ducks. The first bugling of the goose signaled the end of a habitual winter hunger, one converted into ever more systemic famine by settler encroachment.[3]

That these new demands came in a petition signed by more Innu men than usual was no accident. Innu historians and elders today regard the 1847 petition, along with several that followed, as a moment of renewed political clarity for their nation, when claims to tribal sovereignty emerged more lucidly and consciously than before, when territorial and waterscape claims became more integral than ever to Innu survival, and when chiefs and elders set aside earlier factions to advance a vision of their future.

The Innu petition of 1847, followed by seven others, thrust the plight of the Saint Lawrence's Indigenous communities on the colonial agenda. In 1850 and 1851, the government created a series of reserves totaling 230,000 acres, some of which persist to this day. Viewed in 1847, however, the document raises as many questions as it resolves. Why had an oppressed people chosen to express themselves in language that their imperial governors would not understand? A decade after religious and linguistic tensions boiled over into a civil war in the Rebellion of 1837, killing hundreds, why entrust a Catholic priest to convey a French language translation to an English colonial official? Of what possible use were the 125 signatures that followed those of the chiefs? And at a time of such weakness, why did the Innu petition with such bold demands?

* * *

> The present government of this state has widely departed from the true democratic principles upon which all just governments must be based by denying to the female portion of community the right of suffrage and any participation in forming the government and laws under which they live.

Eight months before six Innu chiefs and their nation had appealed to Canada, six women sat down at a table in a town hundreds of miles upstream on the Saint Lawrence, in Jefferson County, New York, and composed a radical proposal to the New York Constitutional Convention. Reminding the convention of the proper form of "civil government," Eleanor Vincent, Susan Ormsby, Lydia A. Williams, Amy Ormsby, Lydia Osborn, and Anna Bishop contrasted the status quo in New York State with that of a proper democracy. "All governments must derive their just powers from the consent of the governed," they wrote in August 1846, but quoting the celebrated James Madison, they argued that the governed must be composed "from the great body of society, and not from a favored class, although that favored class may be even a majority of the inhabitants."[4]

New York had failed these minimal tests of popular government, the women concluded. A population laboring under the laws and the taxes of the state had no representation at the polls by which those who governed were selected. Such a right of representation composed the "only safeguards of their individual and personal liberties." After laying out a grievance about inequality based on sex and framing these laments in the language of the American founding, the six women put forth a simple but radical proposal before the convention: "Your Memorialists therefore ask your honorable body to remove this just cause of complaint, by modifying the present Constitution of this State, so as to extend to women equal, and civil political rights with men."[5]

The origins of the American woman suffrage movement have often been placed at Seneca Falls, New York, about a hundred miles from the homestead in Jefferson County where this six-woman petition was probably written. At that now celebrated convention, on July 19, 1848, the assembled Woman's Rights Convention proclaimed that "woman is man's equal—was intended to be so by the Creator, and the highest good of the race demands that she should be recognized as such." The following day, Elizabeth Cady

Stanton read a proposed Declaration of Sentiments to the convention. Echoing Thomas Jefferson's Declaration of Independence line by line in its list of grievances, the 1848 Declaration of Sentiments advanced women's political and legal equality as a value and precept founded in nature and insisted on the American woman's "immediate admission to all the rights and privileges which belong to them as citizens of these United States." [6]

Stirrings of discontent and visions of equality had begun much earlier among American women. New ideas and templates of action emerged in the decades before Seneca Falls. Whether in petitioning for divorce or property rights, building new organizations, or taking up the cause of displaced Native Americans or enslaved African Americans, women crossed lines of race and class and began to question established institutions, to enter the public and political spheres in much more direct and assertive ways. Before and as they did so, they had taken note of the political and legal authority of Native American women in the Seneca and Cherokee tribes. By the 1830s some of these women had become public figures, including the antislavery activist Angelina Grimké, who gave the first address of a woman before a North American legislature in 1837, while introducing hundreds of petitions with thousands of signatures.

Even in light of these earlier developments, however, the Jefferson County women's petition of 1846 stands out. Far more than attempted by earlier activists, the six women of Jefferson County mounted a direct attack on sexual inequality in law and politics. Like the Declaration of Sentiments that followed it but unlike the longer essays and treatises of the Grimké sisters and others, the Jefferson County petition was brief, more philosophical in its argumentation. Distinctly untethered to evangelical Protestant arguments, it not only appealed to values of the American republic but extended its vision to the "true democratic principles upon which all just governments must be based."

The Jefferson county petition of 1846 raises a set of different puzzles, historical knots that have occupied scholars elsewhere but which remain hard to untangle fully. Why did such a radical proposal come from so small a network? Why did the women use the arguments of Madison and not the arguments of Thomas Jefferson or of another renowned thinker, even Angelina Grimké? Why hadn't the six women of Jefferson County launched a campaign to get others, including their husbands, to join them? Why hadn't they canvassed their document, as had hundreds of women in New York State with antislavery petitions in the decades before, to add more names to the document? Why hadn't they petitioned the state legislature or the governor, either before or after 1846? Finally, is it at all noteworthy that a "petition" of six women came two years before a "declaration" signed by sixty-eight women and thirty-two men?

* * *

Eighteen years before Gettysburg, Pennsylvania, became the site of mass carnage and a presidential speech forever etched in American memory, a thirty-six-year-old Black fence maker named Aaron Constant put his witness to a petition from that town's African American community. Expressing themselves "earnestly desirous to free this Commonwealth from all connection with Slavery," Constant and 110 other Black women and men sent an appeal to the Pennsylvania state legislature.[7] Their petition of January 1847 called for organized, institutional resistance to fugitive slave recapture. Shrewdly recognizing the shifting sentiments among Pennsylvania's political elite, Gettysburg's Black petitioners asked the following of the legislature:

1. That you will repeal all laws which permit the holding of slaves for any length of time within the limits of this State.
2. That you will repeal all laws of this Commonwealth which direct or authorize our judges, magistrates, sheriffs, constables, jailors, or other officers, to aid in the capture and removal from this State of persons claimed as fugitive slaves.
3. That you will propose such measures to Congress as will have the effect either to abolish Slavery in the United States, or release this Commonwealth from the legal obligation to aid in its continuance.[8]

Constant and his community printed and signed their requests at a time when national and state politics mixed turbulence with hope. As an increasingly sophisticated underground railroad transported Black women, men, and children northward into freedom—often ending in failure and violence but with enough success to hold out promise for many enslaved—southern slaveholders and politicians began to engineer coercive national solutions to shut down the incipient machinery of liberation. Living in southern Pennsylvania meant that Constant and his community were less than ten miles away from slave territory and well-organized kidnappers in Maryland. Drawing on the 1793 Fugitive Slave Act, which permitted slaveholders to employ agents to search out and hunt down escaped slaves, slaveholders redoubled their efforts to surveil and retrieve the free bodies they regarded as their stock. They were aided by the Supreme Court's 1842 decision in

Prigg v. Pennsylvania that state laws on slavery were precluded by the 1793 act and Article VI of the Constitution, which sanctified the contracts that converted souls into chattel.

The 1847 petition insightfully drew on the growing antislavery sentiment in Pennsylvania, a sentiment shared across lines of ideology, county, class, sex, and race. The efforts of southern politicians to extend their system of bondage farther west, even north, helped build a reputation for the South as a "Slave Power" that threatened to conquer the North and the West as well as the South, and antislavery sentiment began to spread even among those who could never imagine political and legal equality for Black women and men. Constant and his fellow petitioners were shrewd not to mistake antislavery sentiment for racial harmony. No White men or women signed their petition, just as the other antislavery petitions sent to Harrisburg and Washington, D.C., displayed no Black signatures.[9]

Yet Aaron Constant and his fellow Black Gettysburg residents had skills, advantages, and contacts at their disposal. Constant had experience in organizing, having cofounded the town's first temperance society in 1840 at the age of thirty and having traveled to Philadelphia to do so. The group also knew that their effort was joined by others. In the twelve months following their January petition, Pennsylvania's eastern counties sent fifty-four petitions to the state's legislature. Many of these echoed the demands for "personal liberty" for Black residents of Pennsylvania.[10]

In the ensuing years, northern states seized on an ironic opening in the *Prigg* decision to disallow their state officials—courts, marshals, and representatives—any role in the capture of fugitive slaves. If the *Prigg* decision had declared federal law superior to that of states regarding slavery, then northerners reasoned that their legal apparatus could not be compelled to assist in enforcing slavery's reach: that job would have to fall to the federal government. The weak administrative and coercive force of the federal government before the Civil War undoubtedly assisted these calculations.

The petition of Aaron Constant and 110 other Gettysburg Black women and men participated in a larger foment. Starting with the Great Massachusetts Petition of 1842 (signed by nearly sixty thousand individuals), then extending through the Pennsylvania personal liberty law campaign of 1847 and into the following decade with a multistate reaction to the Fugitive Slave Act of 1850, antislavery activists focused on what they could accomplish in ideologically more supportive northern states, pushing their elected officials to buck the U.S. Congress and the administration of President Franklin

Pierce. In 1847 alone, these campaigns sent forty-four petitions with over twenty-eight hundred signatures to the Massachusetts legislature, calling on the state to secede from the Union based on antislavery principles.[11]

Expressing an alliance with the state's Quaker elite, the petition of the Gettysburg Black community joined and impelled a movement for "personal liberty" that spanned states and national boundaries. The petition met with success, and Pennsylvania passed a new antislavery law in 1847 guaranteeing further personal liberties. As testimony to its triumph, southern congressmen viewed the law with contempt. Only later would slaveholders and their legislators raise the stakes to a national, and much more coercive, level by enlisting the federal government itself in slave recapture, passing the Fugitive Slave Act of 1850.

* * *

> You are aware that from ½ past 4 in the morning until within ¼ of 8 in the Evening is too long to be withstood at hard labour, and for men who have got to stand it in a hot climate and in a sickly state and for month after month.

Toiling in Indiana in the summer of 1847, sixty-one Irish workers went on strike and set their names to a remarkable document that expressed their solidarity in labor, in citizenship, and in whiteness.[12]

In the harried enterprise of building waterways, roads, and rail lines that remapped the North American landscape, construction companies relied heavily on the raw expenditure of immigrant labor. The flux of men, both young and middle aged, from Ireland in the 1840s provided a ready supply of mechanical power for "grubbing," digging, loading and unloading wagons, teaming horses, cleaning, and moving equipment.[13]

In their petition, the Irish workers drew attention not only to their roughly fifteen-hour days but also to the fact that they remained on their feet for almost all that time. Canal construction demanded that its workers stand far more than they kneel, and newly arrived superintendents to the Illinois and Michigan Canal Company coercively saw to it that their underlings "stood at hard labor." Above these superintendents was Colonel Charles Oakley, resident trustee for the State of Illinois, and it was to Oakley that the Irish workers petitioned. Charles Vassar, James Loftus, and the other men first asked for "time for sleep." Beyond that, they wanted regulations for their work and an increase in pay, from $1.00 per day to either $1.25 or one dollar plus boarding included.[14]

Nasty, brutish, and short-lived by design, the canal company was that species of corporation spawned by states through the early nineteenth century to advance the project of civilization and commerce. Deriving their monopolies and limited liabilities from corporate charters granted by one or more state legislatures, they mixed the public and the private. They allocated capital and derived profit, some of which went back into capital outlays. They had corporate directors and used wage laborers just as other companies did, yet they also employed managers under the auspices of state governments. State officials always held the last word on managerial affairs, however, and with apprehension about the pace of the project, Illinois superintendents took over canal construction in the summer of 1847.

The rapid settlement of Indiana proved both boon and bane to the Illinois and Michigan Canal Company. The blessing came from the influx of men, creating a ready supply of willing labor. The curse came when White farm families, who were participating in an ever more commercial agriculture, began to hire more laborers of their own. The very anxiety that drove canal proprietors to newly exploit their workers also meant that they could little afford the siphoning off of their men. The Irish were working the Summit Division, spatially central and politically critical to the entire canal. The stiff competition for workers gave the Irish an opening, and in July 1847 they seized it.

In their petition, however, Vassar and his compatriots displayed none of this bargaining power. Rather, they appealed to Oakley's sense of justice and the racial citizenship they shared with him: "Yet We hope it will be taken into consideration by You, whom we believe to [be] both Humane and Gentleman[l]y. Beside[s] being an independent, born American, who should abhor oppression in Any form[,] To take the matter into your own hands. So as not to have white Citizens, drove Even worse than Common Slave Negroes."[15]

The American "free soil" debate of the 1840s often drew on binary contrasts between the unfree South and the free North. Both celebrating and taking aim at industrial capitalism itself, voices across the continent decried the institutions and practices of slavery as well as that system's hell-bent expansion. Freedom could be defined, visualized, and lived in contrast to the experience of a Black slave. And the society of slavery could be defined by its opposition to the society of free citizens. Alexis de Tocqueville had rendered just such a contrast to his readers in *Democracy in America* a decade earlier (1835) as he journeyed down the Ohio River, the liberated energies of free-state Ohio on his right, the sluggish desolation of slave-state Kentucky on his left.

The Irish petitioners took this black-and-white contrast and weaved it directly into the text of their prayer. In doing so, they rehearsed a metaphor that echoed throughout North America at the time. Critical voices of the time took aim not only at slavery but at the system of wage labor that had displaced more autonomous, independent forms of work in the previous decades. To work with dignity was to be a citizen and, in the Irishmen's imagination, to be White. To work without dignity was to be a slave, to be Black, to be anything but a citizen. These were not portraits fashioned from scratch by sixty-one Irish workers in the summer of 1847 but the symbols and tropes of a spiritual and political argument that spanned the Atlantic Ocean. In 1847, neither Oakley nor his petitioners could have possibly lived in ignorance of these currents of imagery and debate.[16]

The petition of the Irish canal workers was sent not to a legislature or a governor, nor to a court or an office, but to a company trustee. Vassar and his fellow strikers knew that Oakley would be the most likely to give them a hearing, even though he lacked the authority to grant their requests unilaterally.

Another set of changes afoot in 1847 provides further context to the Irish petition. As wave upon monthly wave of Irish and German immigrants, most of them Catholic, crashed ashore to flee the potato blight, economic crisis, or revolution, White Protestant majorities began to express their discomfort and to organize nativist organizations and parties. A May 1844 riot in the Kensington neighborhood of Philadelphia saw thousands of nativists face off against Irish Catholic families. Surely aware of these tensions, Vassar and his Irish compatriots petitioned Charles Oakley at the very moment when they found themselves becoming ever less welcome in North America. Faced with these currents of religious and racial vitriol, they responded with simile and contrast, claiming membership in the citizenship of White workers while marking themselves distinct from the Black bodies they located at the bottom of the North American order of labor, citizenship, and race.

* * *

> The Petition of Harriet, a woman of color states, that she is claimed as a slave by one Irene Emerson, of the County of St. Louis in the State of Missouri. . . . The said Irene, claims property in her as a slave but believing, that under this state of facts, that she is entitled to freedom, she prays your

> honor to allow her to sue in said Court the said Irene Emerson in order to establish her right to freedom and she will pray be.
>
> **—Harriet X of Color**

Harriet Scott's petition of April 1846 has largely been eclipsed by that of her husband, Dred.[17] The two of them are better known in American law and much of history as the plaintiffs of a U.S. Supreme Court case with national and continental implications. Yet before their case could be considered by judge and jury, Harriet and her husband had to petition for the standing to sue their legal owner for their freedom.

Harriet's petition—an appeal to a court—was a document substantively and procedurally different from that of Aaron Constant and the African Americans of Gettysburg. In Missouri, governed by laws covering the Louisiana Territory from 1807, the petitions of Harriet and Dred Scott qualified as legal instruments. These appeals aimed to launch a court-based procedure of adjudication rather than a sequence of lawmaking. Once granted standing to sue—based on the finding by the court that they were, in all plausibility, being wrongfully held—they would be entitled to rights and constraints that did not bind a legislature, namely due process: the right to counsel, trial by jury, and proscriptions on any punishment from having brought the suit.[18]

In two ways, however, the Scott petitions joined a broader mobilization. First, there were thousands upon thousands of other "freedom suits" during the period. Where the laws permitted freedom suits, a petition to a judge usually launched the process, and Black women and men inundated southern courts with these suits in antebellum America. Second, these freedom suits coevolved with a range of other Black petitioning strategies. Especially where freedom suits were unlikely to proceed successfully, slaves and their allies deployed freedom petitions to state legislatures. In what amounts to a skillful exploitation of the private bill system in the United States at the time, thousands of these manumission and freedom petitions were in fact sent to legislatures in the decades before Harriet and Dred Scott petitioned the courts of Missouri. By the 1840s, in fact, they had begun to decline in the United States from the peak they had reached in the 1820s and 1830s. Like other southern legislatures, the Missouri General Assembly became an ever more aggressively racist institution after 1830. The year of Harriet's petition, Missouri legislators granted a slave owner's petition for importation of their human property and passed another law prohibiting Black education and gatherings (including religious services) and the emigration of free people of color. In the midst of this legislative brutality, Black women and men took their claims to another venue.[19]

Dred Scott's name would, of course, become known for other reasons. His case wound its way through the Missouri and federal court systems and ended up at the Supreme Court, where in 1857 Justice Roger Taney upended the Missouri Compromise and authored perhaps the most aggressive judicial defense of American racial hierarchy ever penned. Thus did Dred Scott become synonymous with the Supreme Court decision that represents either a stark departure from the jurisprudence of American liberty or the embodiment of the original evil embedded in the U.S. Constitution. Those legal debates often elide or ignore Dred Scott's own words, to say nothing of his wife's. But eight years before that decision, their own voices emerged in their respective prayers to the St. Louis Circuit Court.[20]

* * *

> We, the people of New Mexico, respectfully petition Congress for the speedy organization by law of a territorial government for us.
>
> We respectfully petition Congress to grant us a government purely civil in its character. . . .
>
> We respectfully but firmly protest against the dismemberment of our territory in favor of Texas, or for any cause.
>
> We do not desire to have domestic slavery in our borders, and until the time shall arrive for our admission into the Union as a State, we desire to be protected by Congress against their introduction amongst us. . . .
>
> In consideration of the fact that New Mexico contains from 75,000 to 100,000 souls, we believe that we have made no unreasonable requests, and we confidently rely upon Congress to provide for us laws as liberal as those enjoyed by any of her Territories.
>
> **Santa Fe, October 14, 1848**
> **José Antonio Martínez**
> **Presidente de la Condado de Santa Fe**[21]

In the aftermath of the imperial conquest and bloody rebellion that shook New Mexico in the 1840s, Don José Antonio Martínez is as unlikely as anyone to have emerged as Santa Fe's shrewdest politician, but a politician he was, one whose work inspired admiration and bitterness.

As the United States waged war with Mexico from 1846 to 1848, the lands known as Nuevo México were some of the first to fall into American hands. In June 1846, General Stephen Watts Kearny marched his Army of the West into Santa Fe and proclaimed New Mexico part of the United States. By August the annexation was official, but the fighting was yet to begin. An alliance of Hispano citizens and Pueblo Indians, uneasy about the intrusion of Anglo-Americans into the world they knew and unwilling to give up the independent Republic of Mexico, plotted a revolt and, in January 1847, carried it out. Together, Hispanos and Taos Pueblo Natives sacked the house of Governor Charles Bent, shot him with arrows, and scalped him in front of his family. A force of five hundred later attacked the Arroyo Hondo mill nearby. Fifteen Americans (including Bent) would perish in the violence, all of them men, many scalped. U.S. troops arrived within the month, armed with cannons. What is known as the Taos Rebellion was put down and its leaders executed.

Not without some reason, U.S. officials suspected Martínez of engineering the Taos Rebellion. To the Hispanos and Indians of Taos, Don José Antonio Martínez was better known as Padre Martínez. Born in Abiquiú in 1791, he married at age eighteen but lost his wife during childbirth a year later. He entered the seminary in Durango in 1817 and became fascinated by the ideas of Mexican reform liberals, including Manuel Hidalgo. When he came to Taos in 1826, his family was already well known as the most powerful and wealthy Hispano family of the area. The padre imported New Mexico's first printing press, publishing *El crepúsculo de la libertad* (The dawn of liberty), and began to introduce a legal curriculum to his seminary.

Padre Martínez lived in and between two New Mexican worlds, one Hispano, the other Indigenous. His ties to those who proclaimed themselves *indio naturales* and those who claimed Mexican citizenship as *vecinos* had economic, spiritual, and even carnal intimacy. Historians now believe he fathered as many as a dozen children with the women of his parish. The worlds that Padre Martínez personally spanned had slowly and partially merged for two centuries—a fusion rife with violence and enslavement—but in the aftermath of Mexican independence in 1821, they did so in new and deeply reinforcing ways. Indians and Hispanos contested lands and resources even as they united to defend in common what they often held separately.[22]

After Taos, Martínez found himself something of a marked man. Given his prominence, the loyalty of his Hispano and Indigenous parishioners, and

Americans' suspicion of Catholics in postwar New Mexico, American officials both doubted and sought his loyalty. So it was that in December 1847, Padre Martínez put his name first and highest on the signatory list of the petition of the citizens of New Mexico territory to the United States Congress, asking for the immediate formation of a territorial government.

Territorial petitions marked a common mode of transition by which the subjects and settlers on annexed lands could form new governments, but Martínez's came much quicker than expected and differed in its rhetoric and tone from the customary form. With Martínez signing in the lead, New Mexicans in 1847 leapt into the arms of their conqueror and declared their fidelity. "New Mexicans, not through fear, but for the sake of their well-being, avail themselves of the opportunity to seek the good will of the American government of the north . . . asking . . . to be numbered among its citizens, with all the privileges and rights awarded to its people."[23]

Padre Martínez's literal leadership among the territorial petition signers prefigured his role in organizing New Mexico's territorial government. In October 1848, New Mexicans amassed in convention to draw up a constitution and apply for statehood or territorial status in the United States. At that gathering, Martínez again placed his name at the head of signatories to a document asking something of the U.S. Congress. The appeal of October 14 from Santa Fe qualifies as much as remonstrance as petition, and it shocked southern senators.[24]

Having embraced membership in the United States, Padre Martínez and his territorial flock now wanted everything they saw bundled with citizenship, including rights and the ability to organize their laws and lands as they saw fit. It was the second time in a year that Martínez emphasized the language of rights in his petition to the U.S. Congress. New Mexicans wanted membership in the United States and wanted its republican institutions—but on their own terms.

Padre Martínez found it easy, almost natural, to resort to a petition to advance his people's aims. His ecclesiastical and political career had been made by political and legal petitioning. In the previous decades, he had repeatedly used petitions and exploited legal and political processes in different venues to defend lands and natural resources for members of his parish, which included both Taos Pueblo Indians and Hispanos. The defeat of Spain in 1821 had opened the Santa Fe Trail, and trade and immigration flourished accordingly. Wealthy Hispano settlers from the South and Anglo-Americans descended on the region and made vast claims on lands that pressed up against the fields and folkways of his parishioners. In a petition of August 1836, Martínez drew on his position at the interstices of Pueblo Indian society and Hispano farmers. The powerful Vigil family had advanced a claim for land whose cultivation would draw from the Río Lucero. The system of acequias that drew water from that river and another had been expanded greatly in the previous decade, and Martínez's makeshift coalition put aside past divisions to fight the Vigil family claim. The claim was denied. In the 1840s, Martínez would use petitions to seek other lands for colonization purposes and to push rival families out of the expansion business.[25]

Padre Martínez had more than one enemy to worry about. His superiors in the Catholic Church saw in his officeholding and his liberal views a threat not so much to their past as to their future. With the American regime came a young French archbishop named Jean-Baptiste Lamy and pressures to render the Catholic culture of New Mexico more "modern," which meant in part undermining the hybrid practices of worship that the padre had encouraged in Taos. Tensions mounted quickly between the two men. When Lamy removed Martínez's priest José Manuel Gallegos in 1852, Martínez and his allies launched another petition, this time to Rome, to protest. The petition, signed by at least 950 parishioners, mixed the voices of the Taos Pueblo Indians and the Hispanos who worshipped alongside them. Lamy not only rejected the petition but moved to excommunicate Martínez entirely, completing the process in 1857. Yet the parishioners of Taos paid little if any attention and, in the years immediately following Lamy's move, not only celebrated Mass with Martínez but elected him three times to their territorial assembly.[26]

The more durable legacy of Padre Martínez—and that of his petitions of 1847 and 1848—came in his territory's popular sovereignty and nominally slave-free status. In the Compromise of 1850, New Mexico received just about everything for which Martínez and his territorial flock had asked. Texas surrendered its claim to New Mexico, and the territory would decide by popular sovereignty whether African slaveholding would be permitted.[27]

* * *

> The undersigned, making use of the right of petition bestowed upon us by law, raise today our weak and humble voices toward the prime minister of the Republic, to show him, with all sincerity and good faith, the sentiments that animate our heart, about a measure that has come to be proposed for

> deliberation in our distinguished chambers, yet which is in clear opposition to our customs, to basic law, and most of all, to our religious beliefs.[28]

While New Mexicans resigned themselves to Anglo-American rule, saving their energies for slavery and other battles, and a new regime emerged in a jittery environment of religious tension in Santa Fe, the citizens of Guadalajara, Mexico, confronted a different multireligious environment, seeking to make sense of it and to protect what they knew.

Nineteenth-century Mexico was buffeted and reshaped by revolution, war, constitutional reform, and—perhaps most of all—trade and migration. A rapidly growing economy pushed settlement into previously depopulated regions, and the supply of work brought Germans practicing Lutheranism as well as Freemasons and other Protestant faiths. These peoples were in an abject minority position, but from the 1820s forward, liberal currents of thought gained popularity and respectability in Mexico. With the fetters of Spanish colonialism formally cast off and with a new constitution in 1824, Mexican intellectuals began to imagine a different world, one that looked somewhat more like the multicultural and industrially progressive northern United States, even as the Mexican regime retained much of the detritus of the Spanish past.[29]

Preoccupied with constitutional reform issues in the 1820s, Mexican *liberalismo* was led almost entirely by Hispano men, most notably José María Luis Mora. In the 1830s, Mora and his collaborators turned to the issue of land monopolies, targeting not only the corporate privileges (*fueros*) of the Catholic Church but also the communal property granted to indigenous Mexicans, who made up the vast majority of the country's population. Liberating these lands from their unproductive possessors would invigorate the economy, and as the liberals vouched in the 1840s, immigration and religious toleration would further the enterprise.[30]

War with the United States converted the American exemplar into the Anglo-Protestant aggressor, and it reconfigured Mexican reform politics. When in October 1848 the *diputados* of the Mexican national assembly proposed a law that would protect minority faiths, the *vecinos* of Guadalajara and Puebla sent large petitions to the national assembly excoriating the measure. So too did the women of Orizaba, whose town had been occupied by an American brigade during the war. The arguments used in these petitions differed rather starkly from those sent by Catholic parishioners, not least because they invoked a majoritarian, nationalist logic. They claimed that

Catholic supremacy represented "the true interests of the Mexican nation" and implored their representatives to obey the will of the country's majority (*la voluntad de los mas*).[31]

So began a much wider movement that would attract thousands of signatures, especially those of women, in the 1850s. In the constitutional reform project of 1855, the constituent congress met to consider a proposed revision of the Mexican constitution. Article 15 of that proposed constitution, which had in mind to grant equal protection of the law to all religions, occasioned the largest outpouring of women's petitions in Mexican history up to that time. Petitions with vast signatory lists—sequences of hundreds upon hundreds of names that induced a mixture of shock and doubt among Mexican deputies and newspaper editors—came not only from Mexico City (with over one thousand signatures) but also from townships and cities far and wide, from Etzatlán, Guadalajara, Morelia, Pátzcuaro, and San Luis Potosí.[32]

That Mexican women petitioned in league with Catholic priests is not in doubt. Yet the women broke gender roles as much as they embraced them. Their repeated reminders that they were entering the realm of politics in their role as mothers and not as citizens belied the fact that their petitions challenged not only political but also ecclesiastical roles. With these documents and other actions, Mexican women began to lay claim to the role of more authentic protectors of the traditions and communities of the Mexican faith.[33]

In the midst of constitutional reform, an anomalous, oddly democratic moment brought an antiliberal outcome. What the *señoras mexicanas* petitioned for—the continued constitutional supremacy of Roman Catholicism—was kept in the new constitution, the liberal proposal for *tolerancia de cultos* jettisoned during debate. On the issues where these women remained silent—namely the land monopolies of the church—the reformers won lasting victories. Newly vocal in the wake of the American invasion, Mexican women formed the backbone of a conservative democratic majority, a petitioning majority, and, on one issue, a winning majority.

* * *

These moments of prayer and of signature—glimpses viewed from East to West—compose but a tendril flow of the vast waves of petitions surging toward legislatures, governors, companies, courts, churches, and other venues in the late 1840s. Planters and freedmen in Jamaica had launched a petition campaign to end slavery in Brazil. Ojibwe Indians near present-day Minnesota sent a pictorial petition to the U.S. president. The U.S. Congress was flooded with petitions calling for an end to the Mexican War. The Hudson's Bay Company petitioned the English crown for monopoly rights to Vancouver Island, indigenous peoples on Rupert's Land counterpetitioned, and soon gold beckoned settlers to a new Pacific Republic in California, prompting a deluge of petitions to the region's courts and new assembly.[34]

From the Atlantic dawnland of a continent through its interior to the Pacific Coast, these petitions coursed. Prayers signed by six, by dozens, by hundreds, and by thousands came from vastly different contexts, different peoples, different languages, different struggles. They flowed from Indigenous nations, White women and men rethinking who they were, African Americans under threat of restriction and reenslavement, many thousands of religiously motivated souls seeking to restrict an evil system, Spanish-speaking parishioners of a world undone by the U.S. Army, *vecinas* aspiring to greater voice in their towns and their churches, new California settlers desiring land and gold, a company requesting monopoly of an island it barely knew. They sought liberty, they sought money, they sought land and protection, and, often enough, they sought the oppression of others. They introduced bills to legislatures, complaints to agencies, lawsuits to courts.

The energies common to these prayers beckon as much for study as do their differences and their tensions. They were all appeals to those in power, offering not threats but reasons, emotions, and grievances. They all participated in a structure of expectations about petition and response, one with ambiguities yet also criteria and obligations.

Each of the petitions bespoke a moment of political stirring. The Innu pushed back against settler encroachment; alerted a government to their slow death as a people; and proposed exclusive spaces, waters, and rights. The women of Jefferson County, New York, touted the ideals of democracy and claimed that absent full citizenship, New York violated those standards. As Harriet and Dred Scott sued for freedom, the African Americans of Gettysburg petitioned for more than freedom.[35] The Irish canal workers in Indiana sketched out a vision of hell at work, a state of diligence that undermined their promised land of labor, citizenship, and Whiteness. Hispanos and Pueblo Indians in New Mexico allied with a priest-politician to reject Anglo land claims and to carve out a space apart from slavery in the republic that had just conquered them. The women of Mexico pushed back against that conqueror, entering the public arena to protect the religious world they knew even as they remade it.

The signature moments of 1846 to 1849 represent less a novelty than an emergent politics coming into full bloom. The efflorescence of North American petitioning had begun three decades earlier. Indeed, this glimpse of petitions from the late 1840s could, in theory, have been sampled from the revolutionary 1770s and the founding decade of the 1780s, the war-struck 1810s and 1820s, the industrializing and evangelical 1820s and 1830s, or the wars and national reconfigurations of the 1860s. Any number of historical and political moments might suffice to view petitions at work. Yet the late 1840s offer a remarkable apex and comparison point.

As religious and class tensions in Europe boiled over into revolutions that shook an entire continent, a different kind of revolution was underway in North America: a revolution in claims and in signatures. As the United States finished a war with Mexico, as the discovery of gold triggered a flood of Americans to settle California, as Frederick Douglass began publishing the *North Star*, as women's rights movements became more formally structured than ever before, as Whig Zachary Taylor defeated Democrat Lewis Cass and Martin Van Buren's Free-Soil Party in the pivotal election of 1848, and before the political crisis of the 1850s unfolded, these documents and their signatories enacted older rites and created new apertures—and they did so on a scale grander than ever before or since. The Thirty-First Congress (1849–1850) concluded two decades of the highest sustained petitioning in American history to the U.S. House of Representatives and many state legislatures.

We can read these petitions as successes, or we can read them as failures. In the larger arc of history and politics, they were both and neither. They represent moments of awakening, of agenda setting, of the emergence of a form of democracy.

TWO

Eruptions and Democracies

Democracy wants a hearing, expects an answer.

For centuries, humans have justly tied democracy to elections. Only when the subjects choose their sovereigns does the rule of the people become any sort of reality. Philosophers attach other conditions to democracy, as in when they insist that true popular government requires that citizens deliberate before and beyond voting. Other observers demand the centrality of rights, such as freedom of speech and the press, touting "liberal democracy." Still others call for "social democracy," with regimes that support the material and bodily welfare of citizens. Whatever these modern variants, free and competitive elections are considered both the benchmark and the bedrock of democracy virtually everywhere.[1]

Absent a quotidian technology linking citizens to their government, however, a democracy founded on elections alone remains an impoverished regime and a dangerous form of rule. No democracy can flourish without institutions that encourage and embed the voices of its people directly and regularly—not just at the time of election—in government and its operations. Nor can any story of the coming of democracy dispense with these technologies and their transformation. In North America, petitioning provided this institutional technology and figured centrally in the long and tortuous development of the continent's democracies. In petitioning, North Americans found and remade a technology that conveyed the grievances of oppression, that induced citizens to organize their claims and to oppose state action, that allowed inhabitants to shape the agenda of government, that preserved and advanced a basic equality of voice, and that carried the expectation of government response. In fashioning the new, North America's democrats reinvented the ancient. In both its orderly operation and its many disruptions, the reinvented petition powered many of the democratic transformations of the nineteenth century.

Petitions transform the raw pain and outrage of human subjects into the textual grievances and accompanying testimony of plaintive communities. As an institutional technology of representation, the petition converts the grievances external to government office into expressed rhetoric, to which is attached an array of names. In its modern form, the rhetorical statement (called the *prayer*) is written and is often accompanied by a list of those assenting to the prayer's claims (the *signatory list*). Through procedures of official receipt, the text and the testimony—the prayer and the signatures—are together rendered visible in the organizations of government. The grievances of the people "out of doors," as early American colonists described them, reappear "within doors." The resulting indoor re-presentation of the people can take many forms, from the simplest printed and rehearsed apparition of a population's laments in a government edifice (recorded in journals and archives and, for legislatures, often printed in official proceedings), to the introduction of a bill or an administrative proposal pursuing the petition's aims, to a hearing or committee report on the matter, and possibly to a law or ruling addressing the sufferers' laments. The rhetoric and names combine to portray a community ("We the Undersigned"), one united in its exclamation of suffering and its appeal for redress.[2]

The transformation of grievance into text is both powerful and incomplete. Petitions record and reframe the bodily pain and emotional anguish of a people, trying to render them worthy of empathy. Yet much of that trauma is lost in translation, perhaps even betrayed to a degree. No document sufficed to carry the full weight of the creeping dispossession and anxious hunger of the Innu. No memorial could altogether convey the simultaneous aspirations and indignation of the women of Jefferson County. Aaron Constant and Harriet Scott had far more in mind and heart—visions more grand, trauma more brutal—than they had put to paper. The sweat, toil, and self-understanding of Indiana's Irish canal laborers were only partially legible in ink. Mexico's *señoras católicas* expressed only a tendril of their anxiety, greatly heightened by the recent American invasion, in their published memorials.

What petitions did commit to ink, however, conveyed voices that elections and parties sometimes represented well but often represented quite poorly. As people repurposed them, leveraging them for ends they had never quite been designed for, petitions complemented elections and parties in North American democratization but also did things that elections and parties could not. In their daily practice of making claims and canvassing, in their combination of radicalism and ubiquity, in their shaping of agendas in administrative and elective offices, in their mobilization of the disenfranchised and their alliance building outside partisan auspices—in all these domains and more, petition democracy transcended the limits of electoral democracy. While legal claims have always offered a more daily communicative technology—the chance to bring a grievance before a judge or jury—access to courts was not nearly as universal as access to the petition, and judicial access was then, as it is now, both mediated and restricted through the strictures of legal doctrine and its practitioners. More often, as with African Americans and Native Americans, the use of the petition to convert grievances into written expression went hand in hand with emerging new strategies of individual and collective legal action. Nor could the more traditional rites and practices of petitioning have sufficed to advance democracy as much. Democratization by petition required, in some sense, the remaking of the petition by the populace.[3]

Democratization cannot advance without the evolution of an electoral realm, yet a developed electoral system falls far short of a representative democracy. Representative elections are highly blunt instruments, often between just a few candidates. Voters' choices are not specific to particular policies or laws; they are often driven by judgments on the incumbent. Elections are episodic, whereas the voice of the people needs to be heard and integrated constantly into democratic government. Modern political parties would emerge to do some of the necessary connective work of representative democracy by connecting one kind of citizen (as voter of a particular faction) to allied politicians, and by nominating candidates for office and agreeing on platforms that might guide electoral competition. Yet political parties are subject to their own forms of oligarchy, and majoritarian competition creates weak incentives for the winners to listen to most, much less all, of the losers. As antislavery forces learned in the antebellum United States, even tense two-party competition excludes and suppresses critical issues. Finally, in plebiscitary systems, where the electorate chooses policy directly, a new form of popular sovereignty emerges but one that packs popular sovereignty into a single moment and carries immense jeopardy to minorities, as the American Federalists feared. In summary, elections are insufficient for democracy, as they can coexist with, even enable, authoritarian, monarchical, and tyrannical governments.[4]

In its deliberative and contestatory manifestations, modern democracy evolved with a preexisting, even assumed institutional technology for disputing government action and, in so doing, connecting citizens regularly to their government and to one another: the petition. In regimes ranging from empires to monarchies to parliamentary republics and democracies, the petition's receipt by the occupant of a sovereign office—a monarch, a legislature, certain courts, an administrative official—triggers a response. The response could be outright rejection, the pronouncement of an edict or a law (by a monarch) or the introduction of a bill (in a legislature) to address the petition's grievances, or the tabling of a petition due to questions about its relevance to the powers of the sovereign recipient. Yet petitioning systems, even in decidedly nondemocratic regimes, carry the expectation of a response, even when that response is negative. For millennia, petitions have brought rulers into dialogue with their supplicants. Before and after they were democratized, petitions created a literal accountability that stands aside any theoretical accountability dreamt in democracy.[5]

The nineteenth century in North America was a democratizing age and a new petitioning age. The coevolution of these trajectories forms the narrative and the analytic labor of this book. Petitioning democratized as it moved from the individual and supplicative to the public and aspirational—a movement of degrees more than of absolutes—and began to involve claimants from virtually every part of the population. In turn, this new and more democratic petitioning played a central role in the development of different dimensions of democracy—what I call institutional democracy, procedural democracy, organizational democracy, and cultural democracy.

In using and transforming the petition, citizens and their rulers created new forms of democracy in nineteenth-century North America. These nascent forms fell far short of creating a full democratic regime with basic protections and minority rights. Yet the democratic spaces they fashioned were real, more equitable than the politics they replaced, and long lasting. Many endured for decades, some for a century or more. Sometimes democratic petitioners rendered existing institutional and organizational spaces—churches, civic associations, tribes, city governments, banks—more egalitarian. Sometimes they created new organizations that beckoned and mobilized the participation of many hundreds of thousands of souls. Often enough, they used the petition in combination with other strategies to give to citizens rights of voting, property, speech, and representation that either had not existed before or had been weakly enforced. Much of the petition's democratizing force came from embedded and evolving norms of government response.

As much as anything else, petitioning and its transformations democratized vast spheres of life, both public and private. Those women and men previously excluded from debates could introduce proposals and grievances on a scale far grander than before. Their claims were not just printed and circulated widely but heard and debated in the chambers of power. Even as settler governments largely dispossessed them, bands of Indigenous peoples could launch public debates about their removal. In selected but critical cases, as this volume shows, they employed the petition to protect lands and even to gain back some of what they had lost. Artisan workers could contest the terms of their employment—and organize anew by doing so—even as capital and factory systems weakened their bargaining power and their autonomy. Women could impel legislators to think about changing the population of the American and Canadian electorates as well as the character of constitutions. Free people of color could create new advocacy organizations calling for legal equality; voices more radical still could call for constitutional amendment and even the impeachment and removal of racist politicians. White landholders could decry corruption in feudal tenure systems, in banking, or in government administration. Vast multiracial coalitions of women and men utterly changed the debate over slavery and, with it, America's party system. Efforts like these brought people into politics in new ways and left them more organized than before. In terms of changing laws and policy, however, these petitioning efforts failed more than they succeeded. Their triumphs lay not only, or even primarily, in near-term statutes and decrees but in the twin legacies of agenda setting and citizen mobilization.

It was in the agenda of government that, as much as anything else, petitioning and democracy ran together. The deliberative and contestatory features of these North American democratic spaces depended not just on citizens making claims but on the aperture of institutions (legislatures and committees, governors, administrative offices). When women, tenant farmers, Indigenous communities, people of color, artisans, and shopkeepers could not only discuss among themselves but appear before hearings or compel governments to investigate an issue, democracy took on flesh and assumed a new form. Petitions thus fashioned a minimal equality on the matters before government decision-makers—the agenda of rule. They also created a platform on which aspirations of equality could be realized. As much as any other form of politics, petitioning permitted claims of equality to reach those in power—as audiences, as decision-makers—and compelled rulers to respond.

* * *

The Innu of the Saint Lawrence River, the White women of Jefferson County, the free Black people of Gettysburg, the Irish laborers of Indiana, Harriet and Dred Scott in St. Louis, the momentarily allied Hispanos and Pueblo Indians of Santa Fe and Taos, the *vecinas* of Orizaba, Etzatlán, Guadalajara, and Mexico City—the voices echoing in memorials across the continent in the late 1840s represent, in some ways, scattered, momentary outcries in the ceaseless back and forth between the petitioner and the powerful. Petitions had long contested and softened the rule of European monarchies and empires, poured into English colonial legislatures and new state assemblies, and inundated the early U.S. Congress to the point of procedural rupture, contesting and affirming government and law.

From roughly 1810 to the 1850s, however, petitioning in North America reached a voice and volume to which it would never again return. From peoples poor and rich, Indigenous, settler and enslaved, Black and White, grievances and memorials issued forth with mass and frequency that awed their recipients and observers. The result was a continuous torrent of activity whose everyday flows overwhelmed legislatures, offices, and courts, and whose surges transformed democracy in North America.

Something else changed, too, in the years between the War of 1812 and the American Civil War, something for which sheer numbers cannot serve as adequate witness. Petitions themselves became more democratic, more accessible, than in previous centuries. From Montréal through western New York to the western plains to urban and rural Mexico, girls and boys as young as eight to twelve years old broke with precedents and expectations, not only by signing memorials and grievances but by circulating and canvassing them. Women signed and circulated alone or with their daughters. Men signed alongside women. Religious minorities signed with establishment figures. Many of these patterns had surfaced occasionally before 1800, but they became far more common in nineteenth-century North America.[6]

For sender as well as recipient, both in their rhetoric and in the masses of names attached to them, North American petitions became imposing, demanding, weighty. The prayers of these documents became ever less supplicating and deferential, ever more declaratory. Petitions that had attracted a handful or dozens—occasionally hundreds—of affiliated names in the eighteenth century now amassed thousands and tens of thousands. As these petitions were drawn up, signed, circulated, and sent to resistant officials or welcomed by officeholders, they articulated a logic of greater equality, asking that voice and power be meted out more evenly, more fairly, more humanely. They placed these claims and sketches not just in front of nations, states, colonies, and towns but also before tribes, corporations, churches, and associations. And while most failed to change law or policy, many thousands of these petitions realized their aims in different ways. Petitioning expanded suffrage rights for White men, ended the last vestiges of feudalism in the North, advanced personal liberty laws for Black men and women, secured hard-won territories and fairer treaties for Indigenous peoples, expanded access to capital, and opened new space for technological innovation. Even when achievement of their immediate aims lay decades in the future, petitioners used memorials and grievances to launch and sustain transformative new movements, ranging from antislavery to woman suffrage to labor activism. Activists used petitions to build new party structures and networks of resistance and opposition, whether Henry Clay in opposition to Andrew Jackson, free Blacks and Angelina Grimké in opposition to slaveholders, Louis-Joseph Papineau in opposition to English lords, or Indigenous and Hispano alliances against Anglo-American settler capitalists.

Democracy by petition, like democracy itself, could suffocate as well as unshackle. Petitions and the energies of a new electoral politics animated and legitimated the vast dispossession of Indigenous peoples in North America. Slaveholders large and small relied on petitions to protect property in persons, to clear paths for expanding their system, and to defeat attempts to limit or regulate it. Petitions were used to secure and maintain economic monopolies; to exclude competitors from markets; to discriminate against Catholics, Jews, Mormons, and other religious minorities; to sustain the hierarchy of man over woman, of White over Black, of slaveholder over slave, of settler over Native. Petitioners and their documents had always carried these oppressive possibilities, yet the relative balance shifted toward democracy in antebellum North America.

* * *

The massive swell in North American petitioning resists a simple summary. Most of the petitions were English-language documents drawn up in the United States, but if there was an epicenter of the surge, it was probably located in French Canada in the 1820s, or among dozens of Indigenous communities scattered from Saguenay to Cattaraugus to Red Clay to Taos, or within networks of free Black men in the Caribbean. Men made up the majority of petitioners, but it was women who, by revolutionizing canvassing practices in the 1830s, most thoroughly remade the North American petition. By the 1850s, petitioning had exploded across the continent, but it was rapidly declining in much of the southern United States, where the breadth of issues became circumscribed by state governments that verged on the authoritarian.

Why the surge? North American petitioning flourished as a range of social, political, economic, and religious transformations and upheavals shaped and scarred the continent. Those changes brought pestilence, war, enslavement, torture, and death on a grand scale. They also brought a degree of democracy in official and unofficial politics that had never before been witnessed. Many of these forces contributed to the continent-wide efflorescence of petitioning: literacy and print culture; publishing and communications technology (especially the American postal system); religious revivals among Protestants, Catholics, and Indigenous peoples; industrial change and transformations in women's and men's labor; and the combined forces of Indigenous dispossession and the expansion of the slave system, an interconnected web of forced removal, enslavement, immigration, and settlement by tens of millions of souls.

Among these forces, however, two stand out: venues and aspirations. The revolutions of the late eighteenth century toppled monarchies and empires, converted colonies into states, and left thousands dead in their wake. Yet they also laid the foundations for a veritable explosion of new offices and governing bodies. With these vessels of power—legislatures, executives, courts, county seats, religious councils, freshly incorporated associations—people felt that their voices would be heard even when their wishes were rejected.

The diffusion and population of venues was accompanied by a second force: a change in expectations attached to these sites of power. A culture of aspiration, of possible equality, took root. In the midst of so much carnage there arose the possibility that someone, somewhere, would listen; that a hearing would be as available and open to women as it would be to men, to Africans and Indigenous North Americans as to Europeans, to laborers as to the landed.

Neither the venues nor the aspirations were entirely new. The American Revolution and its aftermath had, in particular, built new governments and catalyzed a pervasive new sense of equality. Yet the way office and expectation combined—especially after the War of 1812, the death of the American Federalists after 1815, the Mexican rebellion of 1821, the failure of the provincial union in Canada in 1822, and the explosion of White settlement and the violence it wrought on Native North Americans and African slaves—meant that millions of souls turned to grievances and memorials as a way of crying out for their own and for others, and indeed as a way of making and conveying their sense of the disrupted worlds around them.

The many documents that fell under the category of "petition" differed enormously and visibly from one another.[7] In the early nineteenth century, citizens filed petitions as complaints about another person's behavior or as claims against the government for damages, claims that approximate the form of contemporary lawsuits. Self-styled inventors used petitions to obtain protection for their intellectual property in ways that we would now classify as a patent application. Women filed for divorce by submitting petitions to courts and often to legislatures. In other petitions, citizens wrote remonstrances against the behavior of officeholders. Veterans of wars and their widows and children demanded benefits owed to them alone in petitions that became "private bills" in the legislature. Compared to English, North America's two other main European tongues—French with *supplique, plainte,* and *requête* and Spanish with *solicitud, demanda,* and *representación*—often provided more linguistic room for these conceptual distinctions.

These differences complicate any attempt to compare these documents, whether numerically or in a narrative. Whether a pardon petition from the antebellum South, a product of its legal culture, is at all commensurable with an autochthonous complaint to a Canadian governor or a Mexican *representación* in the same year is certainly questionable. Petitions represent claims advanced within the understanding (and often misunderstanding) of political regimes, cultures, and legal systems. These documents also represent moving targets for those who read them today. What surged in so many contexts and spaces was not a changeless entity. Their meaning, their power, and their implications all morphed into new forms as the century progressed.[8]

Despite massive differences among these documents, people of the time did not blunder in describing them commonly as petitions. What united these forms was the combination of directed claim, signature list, and expected response. All these claims and communities rendered in print targeted those who held some kind of power. While petitions had many audiences—allies and opponents; community members; readers who would sign and those who would not; ancestors, spirits, and gods—they fixed upon those with political, legal, ecclesiastical, or even economic authority. Overlapping somewhat with letters but differing enormously from tracts, pamphlets, and broadsides, petitions attracted the signatures of a handful or of tens of thousands. The harvest of names converted the petition into a technology of recruitment and organization, one that became increasingly more systematic, refined, and planned in nineteenth-century North America. Finally, and perhaps most important, a divorce petition shared with a pension claim what an Indigenous complaint about treaty violations had in common with an African American freedom suit: a firm expectation that duty compelled the petition's recipient, or someone else in power, to read the document, possibly refer it to an office or committee more appropriate for its consideration, grant its claims or reject them, and offer a response explaining the action taken.

People in quite different legal, cultural, political, and economic contexts learned about petitioning from one another. Citizens in one area read through newspapers of debates and petitioning campaigns in another. The reactions ranged from admiration and emulation to outright mockery and disdain, yet the petitioning template diffused nonetheless. In part through missionaries and religious allies such as Catholic priests and Quakers, petitioning practices that were already well embedded in Native North American communities began to be directed to new ends. The Innu knew that Indigenous communities to their west and south in Canada had petitioned successfully for reservation lands and water. Black and White peoples in Gettysburg did not sign each other's personal liberty law appeals, but they clearly knew of each other's efforts. In Massachusetts, meanwhile, Black and White antislavery activists actively collaborated in petition work. In England, the Chartists took cues from democratic energies in French Canada, which were marked far more by petitioning than by electoral activity.

The illumination to be gained from comparison outweighs the risks of anachronism.

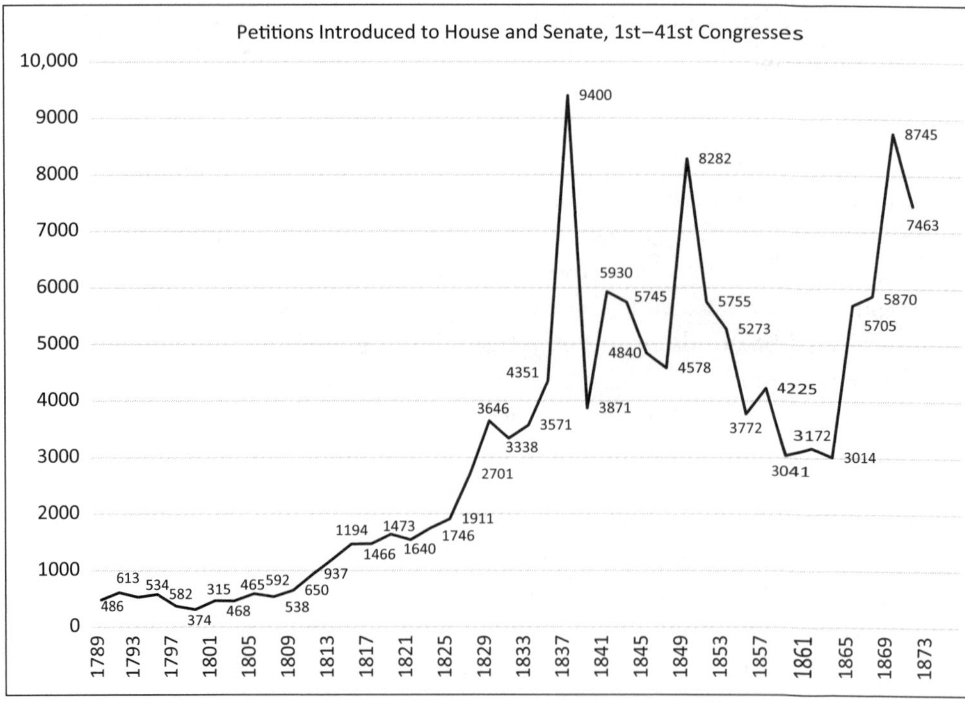

FIGURE 2.1. Annual Petitions to Congress, 1789–1871

* * *

North America's petitioning explosion remains visible on canvasses small and large, in individual acts as well as in monster petitions rolled and carted to legislatures. Yet at a time when officeholders and citizens began to fixate on numbers in political rhetoric, the evidence for democracy by petition is seen first in the masses of petitions that descended on the venues that would receive them. While the eighteenth century saw several petitioning surges of its own—including a multidimensional pouring forth of grievance in the American Revolution that was itself connected to energies of democratization (see Chapter 3)—the mass and form of the nineteenth-century North American petitioning explosion were unprecedented.

In the United States, the First Congress wrote into the First Amendment to the new national Constitution a "right to petition the Government for redress of grievances." Both reflecting that right and the cultures that gave rise to it, the two chambers of Congress received petitions from its incep-

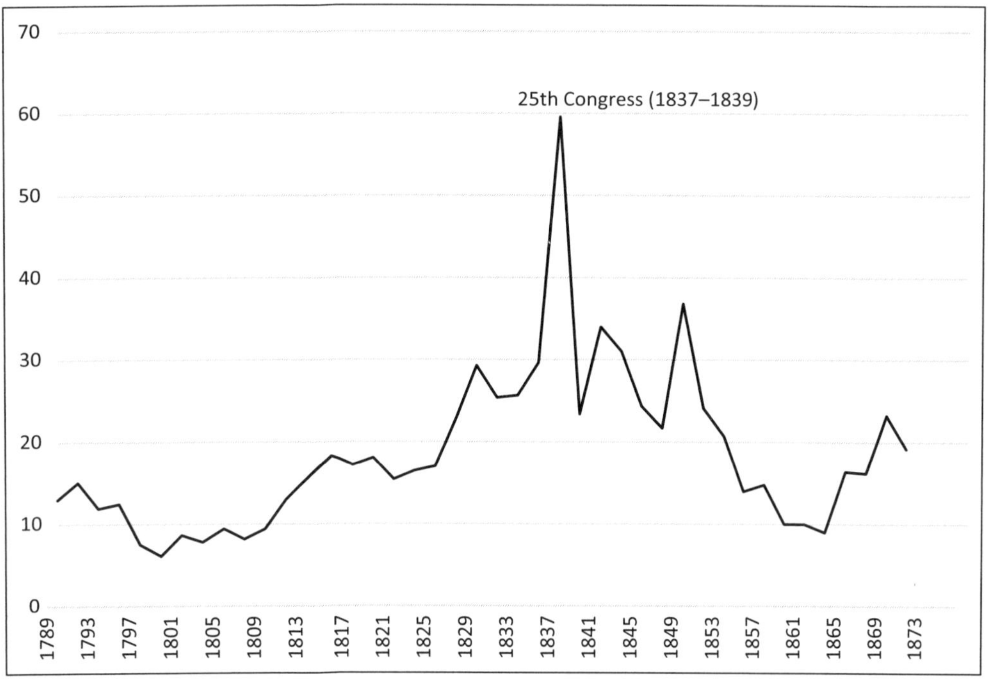

FIGURE 2.2. Annual Petitions to Congress per 100,000 U.S. Population, 1789–1871.

tion, usually four hundred to five hundred per two-year session for the first twenty years of its existence.[9] Beginning in the late 1810s, the House began to receive over one thousand petitions per session, and in the late 1820s, over two thousand. On a population-adjusted basis, the decades from the 1820s through the 1840s comprise the historical peak of petitioning in the United States, with over twenty petitions per 100,000 national population.[10] The peak of American national petitioning came with the Twenty-Fifth Congress (1837–1839), in the midst of agitation over the gag rule enacted to prevent the hearing of antislavery petitions, and in the wake of the continent-wide economic crisis that followed the Panic of 1837. The House of Representatives had never before received, and would never again receive, when accounting for population, as many petitions as it did during the late 1830s.

Similar patterns were observed in American state legislatures. In Virginia—the largest and most influential state of the early republic—

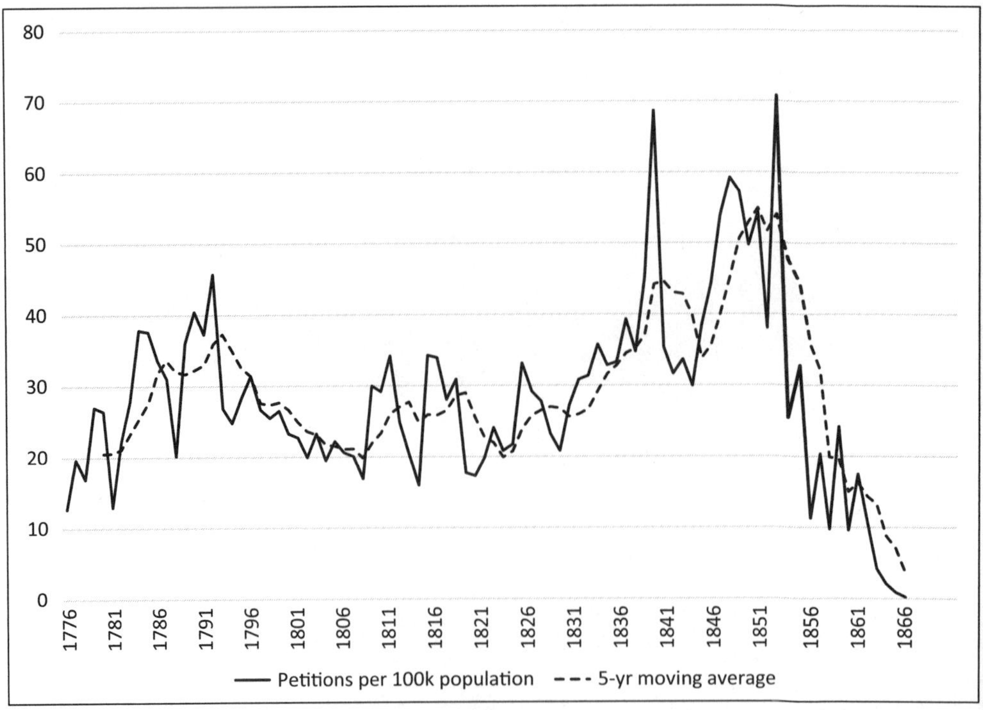

FIGURE 2.3. Annual Petitions to Virginia House of Delegates per 100,000 state population, 1776–1865.

petitioning continued its notable pace from the colonial and revolutionary period. Yet the volume of petitioning in Virginia also rose consistently in the 1820s through the 1840s, and from 1839 to 1855, petitioning in Virginia attained a population-adjusted intensity greater than at any time during either the Revolution or the early Republic, before dropping precipitously in the 1850s and then cratering during the Civil War. Similar patterns were witnessed in other American states, including Tennessee, where the period 1820 to 1835 saw the largest population-adjusted peak of petitioning to the assembly.[11]

In British Canada, the flow of memorials, complaints, propositions, and grievances overwhelmed the small, largely nonprofessional legislatures that received them. The 1791 Constitutional Act split the British space north of the United States into two colonies, one (Lower Canada) largely French speaking and corresponding in part to Québec, the other more English (Upper Canada), much of which became present-day Ontario. Following the

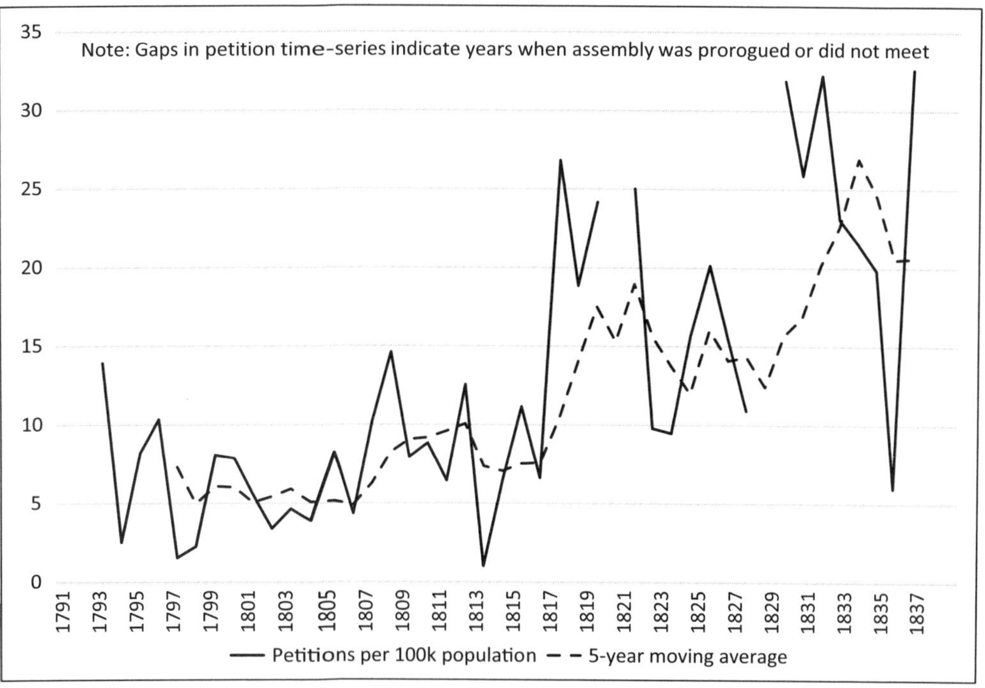

FIGURE 2.4. Annual Petitions to the *Chambre d'Assemblée du Bas-Canada* per 100,000 Colony Population, 1791–1837.

Constitutional Act, a burst of petitions flooded the new legislature, but then petitioning sank to a trickle for the coming two decades. In the legislative journals of the representative chamber of Lower Canada, the 1820s and 1830s also witnessed a much higher frequency of petition mentions than in the 1790s and early 1800s, with peaks in 1818 and 1829.

Legislative records for the Upper Canadian province are scarce before the 1830s, making comparison with the post-1791 period impossible. Yet one careful study of the colony concludes that from the 1820s onward, even as Upper Canadian men obtained the right to vote, petitioning was more common than voting, and by a fair margin.[12]

Institutions in Spanish-speaking regimes of North America have left us with the most scattered archives of petitions for the nineteenth century, not least because of the many disruptions brought on Mexico by wars of independence and American imperialism. Yet telling clues come from the archives that remain, for instance in New Mexico during the Spanish period (through 1821) and the Mexican period (1821–1846), and from legislative compilations from the *congresos* of independent Mexico. These sources also display a clear rise in petitioning and noncriminal complaints occurring in the 1820s in New Mexico, with legislative petitioning recorded more prominently in the 1840s and 1850s in the national congress.[13]

These statistical comparisons are possible only because many legislatures, governors, councils, and assemblies in North America systematically tracked the petitions coming into them, a practice I will discuss further in Chapter 3. Other petitions were sent to overseas authorities—England, France, Spain, the Vatican. Perhaps countless other petitions were sent to county and township governments that either did not have clerical operations or did not publish their records.[14] Unless petitions have been cataloged by a clerk and published in a record of proceedings, scholars and students must today rely on archives, many of which are incomplete or whose records are lost due to deterioration, fire, and periodic destruction of what were considered at another time to be records of little value.[15] These weaknesses of the archive call for multiple strategies of aggregation: using published journals of proceedings where they exist; consulting archives; and scouring contemporary reports in newspapers, tracts, and diaries. Working back and forth among these sources—that is, performing a cross-check by comparing proceedings, archives, and reports—better establishes the validity of the estimates from any one source.

* * *

Because they count documents and not the signatures upon them, these aggregate numbers greatly understate the continental explosion of petitioning. Legislatures and governments rarely kept track of how many signatures appeared on these petitions. What evidence remains available suggests that the phenomenon of large petitions—signed by the hundreds in small communities to the thousands and tens of thousands in cities and over broader geographical spaces—reached exceptional height and breadth from the 1820s through the 1850s. In the two decades before Chartist petitions in England attracted over a million signatures, and continuing a decade after, mass petitions began to appear throughout North America.

While mass petitions had appeared in earlier centuries, something extending far beyond the tumults of the 1770s and 1780s was afoot after 1820. The departures from those earlier times were more differences of degree and scale than of kind, but a new scale and regularity of mass petitioning had crystallized.

Table 2.1 Notable Mass Petitions and Petitioning Campaigns in Antebellum North America

Anti-fusion petition, Lower Canada, 1822: 69,404 signatures

Petitions for legal equality from "free men of color," 1823–1826 (Jamaica, Grenada, Dominica, Trinidad, etc.): over 1,000 signatures

Anti-Dalhousie petition, Lower Canada, 1827–1828: 87,090 signatures (17.5% of population)

- *comté* of Trois-Rivières: 10,660 signatures (50.6% of *comté* population)

Anti-auction petition, New York City, 1828: over 10,000 signatures

Anti-Jackson, pro-Bank petition campaign, 1833–1834: over 150,000 signatures

Cherokee petition against the Treaty of New Echota, 1836: 3,352 Cherokee signatures

Cherokee petition against the Treaty of New Echota, 1838: ~15,000 signatures

Antislavery petitioning campaign to 25th Congress, U.S. House, 1837–1839: at least 5,421 petitions, 598,066 signatures

Women's antislavery petitions to Massachusetts legislature, 1838: over 20,000 signatures

- Presented by Angelina Grimké in the first invited address by a woman before an American legislature, 1838

Mormon scroll petition from Nauvoo, 1838: 3,419 signatures

Great Latimer Petition (Massachusetts), 1843: over 65,000 signatures (many African American)

Petition against the Kansas-Nebraska Act, 1850: 3,050 clergymen, reportedly over 200 feet long

Parishioners' petition in defense of Father José Manuel Gallegos, Santa Fe, 1852, ~950 signatures

Temperance petitions, 1853

- New York State, over 130,000 signatures
- Michigan, over 70,000 signatures

Representaciones católicas against Project 15 of the 1856 Constitutional Project of Mexico, 1856: over 6,000 signatures.

Petition for abolition amendment, to Charles Sumner, 1864–100,000 signatures (65,601 women, 34,399 men)

Sources: Anti-fusion petition, 1822—Chapter 7; Petitions from free men of color—Chapter 6; Anti-Dalhousie petition, 1827–1828—Chapter 7; Anti-auction petition, New York, 1828—Chapter 8; Anti-Jackson and pro-Bank petitions—Chapter 9; Antislavery petitions of 25th Congress—Chapter 10; Cherokee petition against the Treaty of New Echota, 1836, and Cherokee anti-removal petition, 1838—Chapter 5; Mormon scroll petition—Chapter 3; Great Latimer Petition—Chapter 10; Petition against Kansas-Nebraska Act—Chapter 10; Petition in defense of Gallegos—Ray John De Aragon, *Padre Martinez and Bishop Lamy* (Santa Fe: Sunstone Press, 2006), 64; Temperance petitions, Chapter 11; *Representaciones católicas*—Chapter 11; Petition for abolition amendment; Chapter 15.

The raw signature counts of these memorials do not signify any unique world-historical peak mass of names rendered in ink. Compared to some of the monster petitions that emerged under English Chartism (in which single petitions were accompanied by one or two million signatures) or set against the large memorials of the late nineteenth-century United States, the mass petitions of the antebellum period appear smaller. Yet there are important differences. For one, European mass petitions of the period were sent largely to a crown or a single lower parliamentary chamber to which national political energies could be focused, whereas in North America, the thousands of venues to which these petitions were sent meant that the experience of canvassing for hundreds to tens of thousands of signatures was repeated many times over and in quite diverse places. Beyond decentralized venues, North American mass petitions often issued from local contexts where neither print technology nor economic development was especially advanced. Among the tens of thousands of French Canadian names on petitions in the 1820s, a disproportionate number came from rural villages with low literacy. In cases such as the Canadiens at Trois-Rivières, the Latter-day Saints at Nauvoo, or the Cherokee at Red Clay, the names of half to over 80 percent of an entire population appeared as colossal scrolls were unfurled.

Such aggregates inevitably raise questions of authenticity and legitimacy. Did signatures represent the identities of persons without the ability to write, much less read? If so, could these people possibly have assented to the petition's requests or grievances? Whether signed by themselves or not, did the names of some "signatories" appear in contradiction to their wishes or their understanding of the petition? Did they fully embrace the entire meaning of the prayer when signing it? These questions must be answered with skeptical realism. Examination of signatory lists reveals that signatures often appeared in identical handwriting, particularly when organized by family name. Fathers often penned the names of each and every member of their family (including infants), mothers often signed for daughters, friends often signed their associates' names, and while the stories are often not verifiable, many narratives of outright fraud spread about the continent. In what amounts to deep testimony to the ethical basis of the petition culture of the time, accusations of fraudulent or nonconsensual signatures abounded in nineteenth-century North America, and petitioners contested these accusations ferociously, yet none of the political regimes examined here had systematic laws, regularly enforced, that prohibited misrepresentation.[16]

The doubt we properly attach to some petition signatures should not, however, blind us to the earnestness, honesty, and energy with which tens of millions of nineteenth-century North Americans raised their prayers to sovereign powers. Once the questions of authenticity and legitimacy are raised, we can and should ask them of any form of political activity. There is little reason to believe that mass petitions were any less representative of their signatories' wishes than were the many thousands of ballots cast by drunken voters who were bribed with liquor at the very saloon where they registered their votes, or were the steps of those marchers whose attendance and energy responded as much to community norms and social pressure as to their own will, or were the punches, stabs, and shots of those who engaged in political violence. Indeed, once we cast off the lens of contemporary individual choice and autonomy, we can see in the petition, as well as in elections and assemblies, the unit of volition not only as the individual but also as the networked voices to which the petition gave expression.[17]

The North American age of mass petitions offers a rich irony, however, in the contrast of individual signatures and communal activity. Even as political activity followed the organization of local cultures and social networks, the petitions presented a public list of single names attached to a prayer. Neither ballots nor letters nor tracts nor assemblies took this form. The sequential array of individual assent bespoke a countability of voice, the idea that one thousand signatures were more formidable, conveyed greater legitimacy, than a dozen or a hundred. This countability of voice, in turn, embedded an ethic and an arithmetic of equality. As with elections, each name contributed identically to the total accounting of souls in prayer.

Because petitioning was available to those without the vote, moreover, the equality of prayer diffused much further than did the equality of ballots. To be sure, petitions had their own gradations of power, sometimes encoded in the list of signatories, whereby local notables were encouraged to affix their names first to the petition. In other cases, norms of exclusion, both visible and implicit, shaped the petition. Women and men often signed in separate columns, African Americans and Native Americans were regularly excluded from signing memorials also signed by Whites, and certain groups (especially women) were expected to petition only on matters spiritual and personal, not "political." Still, every one of these norms was contested and broken in antebellum North America. And in contrast to the exclusions of the electoral arena—where democracy was mainly a construct for White males—the public space of petitioning remained vastly more accessible.

Women, free Blacks, Indigenous peoples, and religious minorities sent petitions by the thousands, petitions that were attended to and that provided an opportunity for organization and expression even when tabled or rejected. In hundreds upon hundreds of cases, these minority petitions found occasional if limited success.

* * *

> Bureaucratic rule, the anonymous rule of the bureaucrat, is no less despotic because "nobody" exercises it. On the contrary, it is more fearsome still, because no one can speak with or petition this "nobody."
>
> —**Hannah Arendt**[18]

For good reason has the nineteenth century been called the age of democracy. In the United States, the world's broadest suffrage constituency arose in the years following the War of 1812 as state after state abolished property qualifications for voting, creating a White male electorate unlike any the Atlantic world had ever known. America's mass political parties emerged in the wake of these openings, including the two that survived the U.S. Civil War and remain in the twenty-first century: the Democrats and the Republicans.

Only the United States and its constituent states can appropriately be classified as a democratic regime, albeit a highly limited one, during this period. Yet the development of more democratic institutions and cultures was common to Canada and Mexico as well, if highly variegated. Even as Canada remained a British colony, representation by elected officials advanced in both its French- and English-speaking regions. Well beyond the electoral realm, democracy appeared in other North American spaces as well. Scholars have adduced evidence for the democratization of American Protestantism; the democratization of voluntary organizations; the democratization of scientific and medical knowledge, and the democratization of access to capital, land, and information.[19]

Did the age of democracy and the age of petitioning happen separately, carried along by currents of industry, modernity, and religious revival, and a culture of equality? If not, what relationship prevailed between electoral democracy and petition democracy?

The answer to these puzzles depends on how we understand democracy. Democracy—a system of self-ruling popular government protecting liberty and advancing political equality—implies both a formal regime (including electoral competition with universal suffrage and parties) and a mix of institutions and cultures of operation (including expanded access to material goods and norms of equality). In his influential nineteenth-century treatise *Democracy in America* (1835), Alexis de Tocqueville saw these different dimensions at work. A political regime that rests formal authority on the assent of the people can be nonetheless populated by deeply hierarchical associations and infused by cultures that reinforce privilege. Four facets or dimensions of democracy—institutional, procedural, organizational, and cultural—can be brought to bear in evaluating whether and how petitioning advanced North American democratization.

INSTITUTIONAL DEMOCRACY

The political regimes that emerged in Mexico and the United States both claimed to be republics. By this they meant that they were no longer monarchies, that important offices (usually legislative) were filled by election, and that the governments had a mixed regime separating executive, legislative, and judicial powers in different offices and sometimes entire branches. Even as Canada remained a colony of the English Crown, its leaders embraced and deployed a republican idiom. Nearly the entirety of North America had known or felt the bloody imprint of rule by European monarch from the sixteenth through the eighteen centuries. In contrast to government by crown, republics promised to found regimes and their laws on the sovereignty of the people, who would rule by their representatives both elected and appointed. Even where voters had ultimate say, these voices were refracted through federalism and staggered in a republic of time, with lower chambers (a house of representatives as opposed to a senate) standing for election most frequently, and occupants of more legal and technical offices serving for longer tenures.

In the early nineteenth-century world of republics, including republics with monarchs, many self-styled democrats aspired to what John Adams (and later Thomas Jefferson) would call a "representative democracy" as opposed to a "pure" one.[20] It meant in part what James Madison pointed to in *Federalist* no. 39 when he remarked that it would be "*essential* to such a government that it be derived from the great body of the society, not from an inconsiderable proportion, or a favored class of it; otherwise a handful of tyrannical nobles, exercising their oppressions by a delegation of their powers, might aspire to the rank of republicans, and claim for their government the honorable title of republic."[21] In that essay, Madison envisioned a world in which the legislature was legitimated by the votes of the broadest corpus of citizens. Scholars now regard this criterion of democracy as competitive elections with universal suffrage.[22]

For nineteenth-century North Americans, democracy did not generally imply government by referendum. With important exceptions for certain structural reforms, such as Massachusetts' ratification of its 1780 Constitution, legal and policy decisions were not left to voters but rather to their representatives; democracy thus referred to the mode of selecting those representatives. Even the Jefferson County women's radical vision of democracy did not suggest plebiscitary rule, or direct votes on policy. French Canadians, on the other hand, used petitions to defend and expand the power of their elected representatives.

Petitioning advanced both suffrage reform and party formation. Petitions for expanded suffrage flowed by the hundreds into the various state constitutional conventions of the post–War of 1812 period, making its way into numerous state constitutions drafted in the North and South before the Civil War. Organizers also harnessed popular petitioning in the development of mass parties in the United States and Canada.[23]

Institutional democracy, though, means more than parchment regime forms sketched out in constitutions and voting laws. A society can acquire the formal trappings of democracy without having a set of complementary institutions and cultures that support it. The institutions supporting and constituting democracy require in part the dismantling of older forms of political institutions, not least aristocracy and seigneurial rights. This reduced role for aristocratic forms—sometimes an abolition of the aristocracy itself—induces greater access to land and capital, property and bodily rights independent of the realm, and, not least, civic and educational institutions. In the late nineteenth and early twentieth centuries, thinkers expanded these notions to include state-supported minimal standards of living, what we might refer to today as social democracy.

Viewed through the prism of contemporary political equality and inequality, the developments of early nineteenth-century North America seem small, diffuse, only budding. Even as the American founders instituted a mixed regime with elements of aristocratic forms of government, they could not have known that some aspects of aristocratic rule would be undone by petition. American states and French Canada both abolished forms of feudal land tenure, and in both cases petitions were as consequential as elections in doing so. Petitions figured prominently in the construction and placement of county seats, townships, libraries and colleges, and schools—all institutions that brought representative government and civic institutions closer to the citizen.[24]

To be clear, at no time before the U.S. Civil War did anything like a social democracy exist in North America. Even the vast expansion of veterans' benefits after the Revolutionary War, the War of 1812, and the Civil War fell far short of the universality and procedural regularity of twentieth-century programs in the United States. Among the kinds of benefit claims that were made in the early nineteenth century, many of them leading to laws for adjudication, petitions played a surprisingly expansive and durable role in claims-making and political pressure. The fact that nineteenth-century officeholders converted veterans' benefits and other programs into petition-like processes in administrative procedures only testifies further to their prayerful, supplicative origins. In the United States, petitions democratized access to national state resources and rendered welfare more equitable as or before elections began to do so.[25]

PROCEDURAL DEMOCRACY, OR THE DEMOCRACY OF AGENDAS

The insufficiency of representative elections for democracy rests in two understandings about what democracy implies for the everyday practice of politics. The informal underpinnings of institutional democracy require a procedural democracy, or what one might call *a democracy of agendas:* the ability of the people (and the myriad subpopulations that compose it) to place issues of importance on the calendar of the government for deliberation and possible action. In a robust democratic agenda politics, the set of politically accepted issues up for debate is shaped not by a menu-restricting oligarchy but by the people and its diverse parts. Democracy in this sense enables not just the equality of final decisions but the equality of participation in lawmaking (what ancient Athenians called *isonomia*) and the counterpart of equality in access to public forums (*isegoria*).[26]

Democratization in this reading means that the agenda of sovereign possibilities is increasingly shaped by the ruled, by the humblest who can bring a prayer to the seat of authority. Features of monarchical and imperial petitioning contained this possibility, but usually for individual supplicants. What the age of mass petitioning campaigns advanced was a more egalitarian politics of collective claims-making. The instantiation of this new politics took different forms. Indigenous tribes could publicly call into question a treaty or an administrative action, alerting allies. Nonvoting women could gain legislative hearings across the northern United States. Tenant farmers could place debt enforcement and rent taxation on legislative agendas. Free Black petitioners could induce legislatures to take up legal equality bills and consider the impeachment of executive branch officials. In these and myriad other moments, a kind of democracy distinctly outside the electoral realm had emerged.[27]

The quotidian character of the petition stands in sharp contrast with the episodic nature of elections. The second dimension of electoral insufficiency comes in the infrequency of elections, an infrequency that makes it impossible for elections alone to shape a democracy of agendas. Elections for state and national offices in the nineteenth century occurred every few months, once a year, or (for many legislative and executive offices) every two to four years. Even the vaunted equality of the common man at the polls translated into a legal parity that crystallized only once in a while. It would be naïve to believe that perfect equality in electoral participation once every few years would somehow suffice to bring about equality before the lawmaking and administrative organs of government. To be sure, the democracy of agendas achieved by petitioning and other forms of influence rested to some degree on electoral calculations. Petitioning campaigns reminded officeholders that votes—many thousands of them—lay behind particular grievances and demands. Yet repeatedly in nineteenth-century North America, petitioning campaigns from electorally negligible minorities still engendered changes in law and administration. Petition generation observed a rhythm—following legislative sessions, for instance—but happened far more commonly than elections. The democracy of agendas involved the everyday activity of government.

ORGANIZATIONAL DEMOCRACY

Democracy develops with the capacity of citizens to collaborate on common problems and contest government agendas and laws. North America witnessed a veritable explosion of such forms in the nineteenth century: women's benevolent societies, trade unions and labor associations, temperance and antislavery societies, farmers' organizations, new groups organized among people of color, new forms of tribal government, and Indigenous lobbies. The surge of organizations came about for many reasons, yet the entrepreneurs and radicals who founded new organizations—in French Canada, along the Erie Canal in the "burned-over district," in U.S. cities stretching from Boston to Cincinnati to Charleston, among tenant farmers and religious opponents of slavery, and among religiously inspired women from western Massachusetts to Guadalajara—knew intimately the powerful feedback between petitioning and organization building. Organizational leaders ranging from John Ross to Lucy Stone to William Lloyd Garrison recognized and even exploited the rich recruitment possibilities embedded in mass petitioning campaigns. By helping organization builders find those with common cause, by advertising an organization's values and desires to a broader audience, and by legitimating an organization before sovereign assemblies and executives, a more democratic petitioning allowed activists to build new associations without as much reliance as before on elites. Petitions helped democratic aspirants build not just any organizations but their own organizations.[28]

In ways recognized by the U.S. Constitution's First Amendment right to peaceful assembly, a democratic republic requires the ability of citizens to join continually with others in common cause and to establish incorporated organizations that seek out new members, and in ways that do not merely reinforce existing hierarchies outside the group. Organizational democracy requires not only the diversity and vibrancy of nongovernmental organizations but a level of democracy within those organizations. The coevolution of petitioning and organization management embedded vast tensions, yet popular petitioning often strengthened political organizations while also democratizing them. The ability of any organization's member to draft and circulate a petition and to represent a collective will separate from its leadership placed constraints on those who managed civil society.

CULTURAL DEMOCRACY

Cultural democracy calls for forms of engagement, autonomy, and equality. Ideal democratic societies have citizens with capabilities for public involvement. The mutually reinforcing feedback of education and citizenship results, aspirationally, in a government whose laws and policies are more responsive to the engaged citizens who live under them and reshape them through responsible politics. One might say it is the job not only of an education system but of a political system and its workings to ready citizens for participation. The very institutions of democracy depend to a degree on this cultural democracy. Accountability cannot prevail without democratic cultures and aspirations. Passive citizens will not effectively monitor officeholders; citizens must scrutinize officeholders by thinking about what they, were they officeholders, would decide or how they would behave. Self-rule needs to be actualized and choices visualized, which requires a certain imagination, even a certain confidence in equality.[29]

Few other practices or institutions matched the effect of popular petitioning in the democratizing formation of citizens and their capabilities in nineteenth-century North America. Canvassing campaigns fostered an awareness of politics, spread information, and, beyond that, sparked argumentation, often face to face in dialogue. When girls and boys aged eight to twelve began to circulate and sign petitions in the 1820s and 1830s, entire new apertures of political possibility, literacy, and consciousness were created in ways that could not have happened through elections, churches, or labor unions. Petitions occasioned new debates in North American legislatures, executive councils and offices, and courts; they placed the evils of Indigenous dispossession and African slavery on national agendas. They represented new mechanisms by which Indigenous languages were written and articulated. Those who sent memorials saw in them the possibility that previously ignored voices might be heard in the halls of power. To those who received them, petitions represented an array of human concerns far broader than what they could have possibly learned from their social circles or their newspapers.

Accountability in a democracy also has a cultural dimension. It means not merely that officeholders suffer negative consequences from untoward actions but also that they be required to give an "account"—aural, verbal, textual, symbolic—of what they did and why they did it. The notion of the petition of grievance embedded exactly this understanding, and many thousands of nineteenth-century "surge" petitions took this form, not merely complaints about laws passed but also complaints about the behavior of administrative and judicial officials who applied the law.[30]

Finally, democracy in its liberal and republican forms often implies an equality of certain minima, certain baselines such as property, privacy, opportunity, education, basic resources, political voice, and human capacities. Democracy in this sense is as much aspirational as it is a binding institutional constraint on the way regimes operate. Yet the tension between majority-driven popular sovereignty and individual human rights is profound and lasting, and it threatens to undermine democracy itself. Democracy requires, at some level, that those who lose democratic contests do not, by virtue of those defeats, lose everything they have and are. Even as petitions advanced the politics of numbers and the countability of voice, they remained an instrument of remonstrance and grievance. Using patterns of complaint along with other legal instruments, minorities in the age of democratization often had no better tool than the petition to protect their lives, bodies, lands, and interests.[31]

To be sure, other political practices flourished during these periods—marches, campaigns, pamphlets and broadsides, and voting in a new party world. The bourgeoning of the petition drew on these influences and also fed back into them. Yet none of these practices amounted to the quotidian technology of representation and voice that was provided by the petition, especially to those millions of souls who neither owned nor published a newspaper. And neither marches nor pamphlets put citizens in direct dialogue with government officials; only petitions came with the widely observed norm of response.[32]

It is important, moreover, to understand what made petitioning separable if not unique. Pamphlets, broadsides, and newspapers brought—along with the postal system that ferried them far-flung through a continent's interior and along its coasts—vast new spaces of communication and statements of philosophy. Yet those who could neither read nor write made far less use of these technologies, and these documents were not ritually canvassed and, more important, signed. Marches and "commons democracy" had wide individual participation, but not participation that explicitly connected itself to other campaigns, especially in rural places where most North Americans lived and where local landscapes shaped their identities. While control over news production and ownership of print in early America was broader than ever before, it was still rather narrowly distributed among those with land, capital, or power, or some combination of the three. Petitioning needed no printer. And while print technology subsidized and assisted petitioning, the range of voices who could sign was much greater than in published forums.

More than other technologies of politics, petitions existed in a deep feedback relationship with venues: the assemblies and offices that were expected to respond to them. Among the various technologies of North American politics, only petitions allowed citizens to put a matter on the agenda of elected and appointed officeholders and require an answer to their specific claims. Claims that were adjudicated at court constituted only a partial exception to this rule. Petitioning claims met with responses more often negative than positive, and the dynamic was rife with inequalities. Yet no pamphlet, no newspaper editorial, no collection of essays, no march or riot, no party platform, no election, could, by itself, change the particular administrative or legislative agenda of those who held the levers of republican power. Even when these other tools contributed to agenda change, they rarely did so without involving petitions.

* * *

Many of the waves of petitioning that reshaped North American politics were preceded and in some cases shaped by earlier swells in Europe, especially in Britain. These movements often drew additional inspiration from revolutionary activity in the Caribbean and South America—including Haiti and Bolivarian Venezuela. Indeed, there is a larger book to be written on the transatlantic petitioning explosion of the early nineteenth century—in England, France, Portugal, the Netherlands, Spain, Ireland, and other nations, as well as in North America and extending into the global South.

For reasons theoretical and empirical, however, there is ample justification to focus on North America. The first is that the petitioning explosion in Europe has, to a degree, been better narrated—especially in England, where historians have puzzled over the rise of the Chartist movement, but also in France and other continental nations, where scholars have made great strides documenting the breadth of petitioning. Before scholars turn to a transatlantic study of petitioning, the largely unexplored mobilizations of North America must be better understood.

Second, Indigenous and African peoples contributed far more to North American petitioning, as well as democratization by petition, than they did in Europe. The transformative shape of Native North American petitioning included an enhanced role for women; the skilled targeting of administrative venues; embassy-based transport, which opened offices of lobbying; and deeply embedded arguments about law and diplomacy. While free Blacks certainly contributed to and took cues from transatlantic antislavery, a range of other African American petitioning practices—especially those taking aim at racial hierarchy and segregation laws and advocating personal liberty—owed far less to metropolitan British campaigns than to developments in the Caribbean and the United States. Accordingly, this study places Indigenous people and North Americans of color at the center of the narrative in ways that would not be possible in a narrative centered on Europe.

Petitioning in nineteenth-century North America diverged most from European forms in its contours and its legacies. A third rationale for the North American focus in this volume comes from the fact that petitioning enabled a set of partial democratizations in North America to a greater and quicker degree than in Europe. In the United States and Canada, petitioning both helped establish and partially rested on a much broader electorate than elsewhere. Aristocracy's persistence in Britain and other European nations also subdued democratic politics. Vestiges of feudal privilege remained in Canada and New York, but they were undone in large measure by popular petitioning. Electorally and politically marginalized and oppressed populations, such as African Americans, Indigenous North Americans, and women, more quickly ignited and sustained petitioning's energy. Before 1850, no setting in Europe experienced anything like the explosion of women's canvassing and petitioning that came in the United States in the 1830s. Petitioning by Catholic women in 1840s and 1850s Mexico exceeded any such contemporary movement in Europe. To be sure, these minority laments often fell on deaf ears, and their requests were more often refused than granted. Yet they achieved some small and meaningful triumphs and, more important, fashioned an agenda for debate, movement, and legal change for decades to come. In Canada, Mexico, and the United States, petitioning also helped democratize a wider set of social, ecclesiastical, economic, and other institutions of the period.

By contrast, petitioning surged in early nineteenth-century Europe but often met with suppression, including heavy restrictions imposed after the Chartist movement of the 1840s. Aristocratic elements endured in Britain as the petition's democratizing force was stunted. In France, the restricted nature of venues induced a relatively weak petitioning culture in the early nineteenth century, in part because of the chronic instability of institutions and the reappearance of the imperial government, in part because one of the most important participants in, and venues for, petitioning (the Catholic Church) had been weakened by disassembly.[33]

* * *

A focus on North America as opposed to Europe begs the question of extension: Why examine anything other than the United States at all?

Even as a limited realm of White male democracy, the nineteenth-century United States provided a model for other nations and publics to emulate, a sketch of the possible. Woman suffragists, the freed Blacks of the antebellum North and the post–Civil War South, Indigenous aspirants to citizenship—they all wanted, at least in part, what the United States had built for adult White men.

In democratizing political culture, however, the United States was far from the only exemplary space of the nineteenth century. With asset requirements for suffrage remarkably low and property so broadly distributed in 1820s British Canada, voting was more widespread there than in Britain, and as widespread as it was in much of the United States. Developments in political culture among French Canadian men—including party organization, literature, Jacksonian assemblies and marches, and especially petitioning—rivaled those of White Americans, coming as they did at the same time as (or even earlier than) those in the United States.[34] French Canadians were petitioning for woman suffrage roughly two decades before their American counterparts did so. Free Black men in the Caribbean islands developed practices of democratized petitioning and political pressure that rivaled those of their counterparts in North American towns and cities. The United States provided far less political voice for Indigenous North Americans than did Canada or Mexico. Even as the Mexican republic and its successors bulldozed Indigenous people aside in the name of industrial progress, it left residual mission lands and spaces of Hispano-Indian collaboration—albeit limited and with abundant opportunities for settler coercion—that often surpassed what Anglo-American governments in Canada and the United States had created. Beyond this, Mexican debates over religion in La Reforma (1849–1856) provided a space for women's political participation in national debates that surely rivaled if not surpassed anything observed in the U.S. South at the time.

The focus of this book is on the United States, Canada, the Caribbean, and selected developments in Mexico. I offer limited exposure to Mexican developments outside the internal provinces (Saltillo, Guadalajara) and California, New Mexico, and Texas. In part this is because important features of popular petitioning in 1840s and 1850s Mexico were driven by interaction with the United States. The United States dominated nineteenth-century North America not just in size and economic production but also in reputation, the diffusion of its settlements, and the threat of conquest. Neither Canada nor Mexico ever witnessed full democratization in the nineteenth century, but then again, neither did the United States. Nor is it an original claim that the nineteenth century saw surges of republicanism or democratizing tendencies in Canada and Mexico. Nor is it original for the studies and writings making this observation to include petitions as part of, if not the center of, their evidence base.[35]

Indeed, a re-visioning of petitioning beyond U.S. borders is important not least to place what we might otherwise read as merely "American" developments in spatial context. American contemporaries knew at the time that non-English petitioning flourished well beyond the United States of White and Black. Elite American observers ranging from New York political elites to frontiersman politician Henry Clay to Southern state legislators took note of French Canadian petitioning campaigns, of massively signed free Black memorials in the West Indies, and of Native American mobilizations. American soldiers and journalists writing from 1840s Mexico puzzled at the widespread participation of women in the country's resistance, including petitioning.

* * *

To a far greater extent than in Europe but well beyond the United States, petitioning in antebellum North America carved out new democratic spaces—a democracy of aspirations and energies, of claims, of presence. Even as it progressed only incrementally, even as it enabled oppressions that undid many of its advances, the North American democracy of petitions developed across lines of color, class, gender, ethnicity, and indigeneity.

What was this North American democracy of petitions? The narrative and argument comprise three interrelated developments.

First, petitioning of many forms surged numerically and was transformed organizationally and rhetorically. A more individual and supplicative practice of petitioning, often used to acquire the benefits distributed by settler societies, slowly (sometimes dramatically) gave way to more coordinated petitioning campaigns that placed not merely individual but more commonly collective grievances before governments. The petitioning campaign—premised on canvassing, recruitment into new forms of activity, and the gathering of masses of signatures—became a durable repertoire of citizens across the continent.

Second, petitioning became more democratic, in part because its more egalitarian aspects came to the fore, in part because other features of egalitarianism were grafted on to it. Precisely because petitioning was so widespread, democratization over the *longue durée* required, in some sense, the democratization of petitioning.

Third, petitioning moments partially democratized different realms in North America. In the United States, this happened in multiple registers, with suffrage extensions and the commencement of campaigns for wider suffrage, the campaign against enslavement (setting an agenda for the eventual abolition of slavery), the development of labor and party organizations, legal changes to property regimes, and greater autonomy for minorities. Democratization by petition happened more organizationally and culturally in Canada and the Caribbean, where colonial systems remained in place but representation was extended and protected, and where minorities occasionally won important legal and policy victories that stabilized their communities. In Mexico, neither democratization nor republicanism took stable root, but petitioning campaigns engendered the reorganization of Indigenous communities, of local autonomy movements, and of women. The end of the period saw a stark decline in petitioning, especially popular petitioning, in the U.S. South, just as a party-state apparatus dedicated to racial dominance and chattel slavery began to consolidate its power.

A republic cannot reduce its citizens to episodic partisan voters and fulfill its democratic aspirations. The coming of North American democracy, in all its forms, transcended and surpassed the story of elections and parties. Democratization is not reducible to a narrative of "movements," with the thinly descriptive attribution of energy and direction to humans, riven of communicative structures with officeholders, too often implied by that term. Even constitutional reforms so critical to democratization must be read in the longer history of those who complained and appealed for them. In Europe, democratization and the slow unraveling of political hierarchy would await the late nineteenth and early twentieth centuries for their fruition. In North America, from the age of revolution through the U.S. Civil War, the democratized petition in turn helped to democratize vast spaces of a continent. It became what neither aristocracy nor empire nor demagoguery could break.

STIRRINGS

THREE

Petitions, Prayers, and Their Venues

In the years of tumult that followed Britain's abolition of slavery in 1833, two women who lived an ocean away from each other engaged in a similar political strategy: searching for a new audience that would hear their claims. In 1835, Mary Venus of Trinidad "heard the negroes were free" but was still working fourteen-hour days, enslaved on the Bonne Aventure estate.[1] Unable to work extra hours in the field once she reached her sixth month of pregnancy, she suddenly learned she had been sold and was to be immediately separated from her husband, Auguste. This she was unwilling to bear. "I cannot go away from my garden and my husband," she said.[2] She approached her master's brother-in-law, a member of the island's council, who told her to speak to her new owner. Instead, "fearful of being taken away by violence," she walked "one day and three nights" in order to take her case to the Government House, where she conveyed her petition to Lieutenant Governor Sir George Hill.[3] Other Black women of Trinidad had also taken their complaints and requests—in the form of what they called "petitions"—to Hill that year. They followed a common strategy among people of color in alternating their appeals between island councils and British commissioners and magistrates.[4]

Angelina Grimké found a different door closed, one shut by the political concert of the slave system that had shackled Venus. In 1836, southern Democrats in the U.S. House of Representatives placed a procedural gag on any petition concerning slavery. Citizens could send their memorials, but the House would not hear them. Memorials about slavery would not receive the customary acknowledgment and reading on the floor that was traditionally granted under Anglo-American parliamentary procedure. Legislators would refuse, on a categorical basis, to convert them into bills or to refer them to a committee for further consideration. American women found myriad ways around the gag to place slavery on the national agenda, but in 1837 and 1838, Grimké took her petitions along with her person to the Massachusetts General Court, the state legislature of the commonwealth. On February 21, 1838, she became the first woman recognized to speak before a U.S. legislature.[5]

Mary Venus, a young, pregnant, and enslaved woman of color, and Angelina Grimké, an older, wealthy, free White woman, whose family of origin had owned slaves, lived in fundamentally distinct worlds. Their pathways were linked, however, by debates over slavery and by something else: a fluidity and multiplicity of sites to which they could take a grievance. For Mary Venus, it was a matter of life and death, and freedom for self and family. She approached a local venue (the island council and her ally on it) and then a colonial venue, the island magistrate (a British imperial appointee). Angelina Grimké's memorials had been silenced in the chambers of a national sovereignty, and she sought to shift the debate to a more proximate seat of power: a prominent state legislature. The Massachusetts General Court had created a special joint committee to respond to petitions that had amassed more than twenty thousand names. Mary Venus took her appeal from the local to the more encompassing, while Grimké moved her court from a national to a local audience. Both carried their petitions and their person to a seat of authority that was not in the habit of recognizing their persons. That they could do so testified to an emerging reality.

All over the continent, legislatures, councils, courts, administrative and ecclesiastical offices, committees, and other sites of sovereignty had proliferated in the previous half century. Even as these venues contested one another's power, they multiplied biblically. Important as it is to recognize the vast differences among them, these sites of audience and power grew by the thousands and tens of thousands. The disintegration of empires and the decentralization of the American and Mexican republics meant that these venues had greater autonomy from one another than would prevail in the late nineteenth and early twentieth centuries. The emergence of these venues, combined with the various norms and procedures of petition and response, laid the foundation for the democratization of petitioning and the petition-shaped democratization of societies more generally.

A range of historical, political, and economic forces contributed to the upsurge of a more democratized petitioning in nineteenth-century North America. Literacy rose to a level never before witnessed as schools, societies, and missions taught European languages to the millions. Newspapers and other print outlets proliferated widely, in part because of cheaper printing machines but even more so because, especially in the United States, a vast and highly efficient postal system ferried and subsidized print materials. These newspapers carried petition prayers in cut-out form as well as news of other petitioning campaigns and issues arising before offices and councils of state. Among Christian faiths, especially American Protestantism, a contentious stew of dissenting and egalitarian religious cultures boiled over, creating new fault lines in established churches. Movements for local autonomy also appeared in Catholic cultures, including in French Canada and Mexico, where forces of nationalism and parish independence combined to create abiding tensions between local clergy and laity on one side and bishops on the other. Further egalitarian energies flowed from the revolutions of the late 1700s. The American independence campaign and France's toppling of its king and its feudal society advanced the idea of the citizen as ruler, the growing antipathy toward monarchies and colonial forms of rule, and commitments to rid societies of vested interests (including clergy privileges and the trappings of nobility).[6]

Far more than in Europe at the time, however, the propagation of venues drove North America's petitioning surge. Literacy figured centrally in the eruption of nineteenth-century petitioning, but the signatures of many an adherent to a petition's prayers—including the majority of those on the largest petition of its time, a French Canadian petition amassing over eighty-seven thousand names in 1827—came from those who could neither read nor write anything other than their own name. Newspapers and printing machines were vital technologies in the realm of nineteenth-century grievances, but petitioners continued to write a surprisingly large fraction of their documents by hand. Over a third of the slavery-related petitions sent to the Massachusetts General Court from 1800 to 1870 offered manuscript prayers, a proportion that remained statistically invariant from 1800 to 1860 and indeed rose to over one-half of the nearly nine hundred slavery-related petitions received by Massachusetts lawmakers after 1860. Other legislatures and bureaus in North America with well-preserved archival collections, including the legislatures of Tennessee and Lower Canada, exhibit similar patterns. Even as religious ferment and a rising ethic of equality fueled many of the petitions, these moments of spiritual fervor and egalitarian striving often asserted the primacy and responsibility of more proximate governments. Contemporaries and students alike knew that the revolutions of the previous century had, as Jefferson had memorialized in the Declaration of Independence, relied heavily on "humble petitions" to reigning monarchs, petitions whose rejection or dismissal bred enormous currents of discontent and violence. Republicans wanted governments closer to them, governments with separated powers and branching offices.[7]

Without attention to the astounding range of venues responding to petitions, the contours and content of the North American petitioning explosion become essentially invisible. If one looks only at the U.S. Congress, one would conclude that free Blacks participated little in the U.S. antislavery petition movement. One would conclude that the Cherokee petitioned heavily but most other Indigenous tribes did not. Free Blacks spent much more time petitioning state legislatures in the United States than Congress and, in the British Caribbean, approached colonial commissions more than the House of Commons. In the United States, Natives often petitioned administrators at various levels of the office hierarchy, from the U.S. president through the secretary of war to dozens of Indian agents and offices scattered across the settlement frontier. Similar dynamics unfolded in Canada and Mexico, where Indigenous communities approached governors, various colonial offices, local councils (including *ayuntamientos*), and religious offices. A range of economic and governmental issues—from battles over the rights of lord versus tenant to debates over women's property and political liberties, from the abolition of imprisonment for debt to the restriction of alcohol, from slavery to bank incorporation and regulation—were debated largely outside the central national or imperial bodies that officially ruled a space.

* * *

The political saga of North American petitioning can be written neither from above nor from below. The vast energies thrown into petitioning came from every corner of North America and its societies. Leaders and elites harnessed these energies but never controlled them. Enormous movements of ideas, hopes, resentments, and human bodies mobilized Black women and men (slave and free), Indigenous tribes, clans and alliances, White working-class democrats, and parvenu merchants and investors. Petitions flowed from many peoples.

Yet petitions coursing through the continent did not end up just anywhere. They were sent to vessels of power and authority—legislatures, governors, presidents, courts, assemblies and councils, bureaus and offices, bishops and synods, tribes and clans, and associations. In these vessels, citizens placed their hopes; to these vessels, they directed their anger. An economy of grievances, proposals, and aspirations took root, founded on the norm of petition and response.

Petitions often met with rejection, but whether these documents met with affirmation or denial, petitioners expected an answer. They followed governmental developments closely, tracking the passage of their signed documents from a representative to the floor of a chamber to a committee, from governor to department head to lower office. When the residents of Indiana Territory (then governed by William Henry Harrison, the future president) petitioned the U.S. Congress in September 1814, they reminded the House and Senate that they had been tracking how those chambers dealt with previous memorials. An earlier petition, they wrote, "was referred to a committee appointed by the House of Representatives in Congress who reporting among other things, that the Memorialists did not designate the particular companies of militia, and failing therein the committee could not say whether the companies of militia had been paid or not."[8] In the midst of the War of 1812, with the Old Northwest highly contested territory, the alliances and fidelities of these settlers carried weight far beyond their votes. Both sovereign and subject learned from these exchanges. From this discussion, congressmen knew that Indiana settlers were closely watching the procedural progress of their petitions. And the Indiana settlers learned that there were particular standards of evidence that, when met, improved the chances of a successful memorial.

In the committee systems of legislatures and assemblies, in the filing and reply routines of administrative offices, in the back-and-forth of bishop and tribe, the norm of petition and response became real. In these exchanges lay the bones and sinew of bodies politic, with their vitality and their disease, their injuries and recoveries, their perpetual imperfection.

Well beyond just receiving them, politicians and government officials actively encouraged petitions. In the parliamentary traditions of the English colonies, petitions could form the basis for bills and eventual legislation. In many legal systems—not just the English but also the French, Spanish, and Indigenous—petitions communicated grievances and could serve as a record of wrongs, of debts to be claimed, of insults and wounds that required diplomatic mediation or reconciliation, of contracts broken and treaties ruptured. Revolt-wary rulers, whether monarchs, governors, chiefs, bishops, or occupants of other offices, often preferred to learn of these grievances in the form of a petition in lieu of letting them fester to the point of an open rebellion or social violence.

As either movements from below or elite parchment economies from above, single-sided understandings of the petition mislead us. The aperture must be widened to capture a dual reflection, a feedback between people and situated power.

PETITIONS EVERYWHERE

By 1800, cultures of supplication and grievance were deeply ingrained in North America. When Americans founded their national government in 1789, they could assume that their new Article I vessel, the U.S. Congress, would receive petitions much as the state legislatures created in 1776 and 1777 were already doing, and not unlike the colonial assemblies under British rule had done. Mexicans declaring independence from Spain created many new vessels of government, including *congresos* and provincial deputations, but also relied heavily on a range of local offices to receive petitions in accordance with earlier precepts of Spanish law. French-speaking subjects in Canada had become accustomed to a parliamentary petitioning model through which they could approach the monarch of the Parliament, but they had also grafted previous understandings of ancien régime French practices of claims-making (*requêtes*) onto British colonial practices. Indigenous communities had been petitioning for centuries, in a slow transformation of diplomatic practices whereby diplomatic councils governed by the spoken word became accompanied and partially replaced by deputations to national and provincial capitals or, just as commonly, colonial and military bureaus, with written petitions and complaints.[9]

Every petition was a supplication of sorts, and the text of appeal, complaint, and persuasion that preceded any signature was called the petition's "prayer." The rules for writing a petition varied, but wherever European laws and institutions were involved, they descended heavily from premodern practices of *ars dictaminis,* with its formulary of *salutatio, exordium, narratio, petitio,* and *conclusio.* These were standardized by clerks in the twelfth century as a means of writing prose but gradually made their way into letters and supplications. In a striking example of historical continuity, soldier's petitions for benefits or pardons, whether in fifteenth-century Europe or in the late eighteenth-century United States, often followed a common form: an introductory *exordium,* a narrative of military service (*narratio*), a presentation of their deservingness or pitiable state (*narratio* or *argumentatio*), a request for aid (*petitio*), and then a gracious ending (*conclusio*). Petitioners who neglected or defied these conventions—whose approach lacked appropriate deference to authority, failed to establish the merits of the supplicant, or offered weak evidence for their claims—could expect a dismissal of their appeal. The norm of petition and response did not compel the sovereign to deliberate on a poorly prepared petition, though many legislatures and governors still did so.[10]

The emergence of parliaments and other conciliar bodies in medieval and early-modern Europe brought vast changes to Western models of petitioning. The idea of the parliament as an alternative source of authority led subjects to petition assemblies as well as monarchs. In France and other settings, these assemblies were often regional gatherings of estates (clergy, nobility, and the commoner), as in the Languedoc assemblies over which Alexis de Tocqueville reminisced in *The Old Regime and the French Revolution* (1856). Whether in the House of Lords or the Parliament of Paris, bodies of assembled lords and jurists often heard petitions for grace, acting in an adjudicative manner. Starting with the Tudor period in England, Parliament collectively petitioned the monarch itself in an institution called a "petition of right." Whether in the Petition of Right of 1628 (in which Parliament, led by Sir Edward Coke, advanced a widely held set of grievances about kingly taxation without accountability) or the manifold petitions that accompanied the English Civil War (1641–1649), many English petitioners of the Stuart period called for more parliamentary authority and the weakening—in some cases the outright abolition—of the monarchy. Especially in the eighteenth century, English Parliaments began to spawn committees and special commissions of inquiry, and these subordinate vessels became themselves target and audience for many a petitioner.[11]

No later than the sixteenth century, large signatory lists of several dozen to several hundred names began to appear with petitions to monarchs and estates. Whether among Protestants in France or combatants in the English Civil Wars, these petitioners forged communities of subscription, whose practices also borrowed from medieval precedents. Medieval and early modern Europeans had long signed conventions and covenants pledging mutual assistance, and a range of documents—not just petitions but also addresses and open letters—began to attract multiplying numbers of signatures. Nowhere was this accumulation of names more apparent than seventeenth-century England, where petitions signed by the hundreds, and some signed by the thousands, burst forth during the Civil Wars and the battles over the Restoration. So disruptive of English political stability had mass petitioning become that upon the arrival of Charles II to the throne in 1660, the Cavalier Parliament quickly passed the Act Against Tumultuous Petitioning (1661), limiting not the set of claims that could be made but the number of signatures permitted on any petition. While thought to have been superseded by the Bill of Rights, the act remained ambiguously on the books well into the nineteenth century, so much so that English parliamentary clerks wondered in print whether mass petitions from the 1820s through the 1840s were violating the old statute. The assemblies and offices of colonial North America emerged in a world where multiply signed petitions were already known, though most petitions received by these venues remained signed by one or a handful of men.[12]

By 1791, the Anglo-American model of government and assembly governed much of petitioning in North America—in Lower and Upper Canada, in the United States and its territories, and in the British West Indies. The fifth article of the English Bill of Rights declared it the right of every English subject to petition the king and outlawed any prosecution for such activity. North American constitutions and governments, whether they ruled colonies, states, or smaller governments still, followed this lead. The First Congress acted quickly to enshrine the right "to petition the government for redress of grievances" into the First Amendment of the U.S. Constitution. That "petition clause" of the First Amendment itself was as much a symptom of the Revolution's heady petitioning culture as it was the cause of anything that followed. Pennsylvania's radical legislature-centered Constitution of 1776 established the right of "the people" to "apply to the legislature for redress of grievances, by address, petition, or remonstrance," while John Adams's more executive-leaning Massachusetts Constitution of 1780 held it the people's right to "request of the legislative body, by the way of addresses, petitions, or remonstrances, redress of the wrongs done them, and of the grievances they suffer." Exactly what these constitutional protections for petitioning would have proscribed was not clear, yet two likely aims were, first, to prohibit anything like the 1661 Act Against Tumultuous Petitioning and, second, to outlaw what the House of Commons had done for most of the eighteenth century—namely to ban all petitions against intended new taxation by the Crown.[13]

Petitions dominated the life and work of early Anglo-American legislatures. From year to year, generally more than half of the statutes passed by Virginia's House of Burgesses in the 1700s started as petitions, a pattern that continued in early national Virginia, when fifty-six of the ninety-nine laws passed by the 1790 House of Delegates started as petitions. Article I of the U.S. Constitution of 1787 gave each chamber of the nation's new Congress the discretion to organize its proceedings as it saw fit. Following examples in the Virginia House of Delegates and other state assemblies, the House of Representatives from its earliest days of operation would develop a set of procedures for receiving, debating, and referring petitions. These petitions—and the responses to them—were carefully recorded in docket books. As early as Congress's second session, after members spent eight days debating three antislavery petitions, writers alternately lamented or defended the meticulous attention to such "trifling memorials." By the 1820s, these procedures had become standardized in the institution of "petition days." On each of the first thirty days of a session, the House would call the roll of states for presentation of petitions. (Thirty days consumed a third to half of the session, as both the House and the Senate met for just a few months per year at the time.) After that calling of the states, every other Monday in the chamber's session was considered a petition day. In the legislative councils of Lower and Upper Canada, similar patterns held. Immediately upon the resolution of the speakership and organization of Lower Canada's assembly, in January 1793, the chamber started hearing and processing petitions.[14]

Nowhere on the continent was petitioning more common than in colonial Spanish America. Spanish law governed petition and response systems in New Spain, and descending from medieval practices, regal and viceregal authorities entertained a range of petitions that crossed the boundaries between judicial, administrative, and legislative. Paperwork in New Spain followed the categories of *justicia* (court cases), *gracia* (privileges), and *gobierno* (administrative legislation). The first two categories emphasized, respectively, casuistic jurisprudence and bestowals of grants, pardons, and pensions. Critical to imperial governance were *gobierno* petitions that led imperial officials to issue edicts with the force of law; there were tens (perhaps hundreds) of thousands of such petition-induced rulings for Spanish colonies in the sixteenth and seventeenth centuries. *Gobierno* petitions were sent to the Council of the Indies or to viceregal officials and high courts in Mexico. Indigenous people and mestizos used them regularly and with some success; even as their rights and land claims changed dramatically, and even as dispossession continued apace, petitioning led to Spanish creation of new Indigenous entitlements, a system of rights that created pathways and agendas for further empowerment by petitioning.[15]

EQUALITY AND SELF-RULE: DISRUPTIONS OF THE AMERICAN REVOLUTION AND EARLY REPUBLIC

Petitioning had never been a static reality, but the rebellion of the American colonies against Britain from 1776 to 1783 brought forth new egalitarian visions and transformed the way that petitions expressed and organized them. From the ideology of republicanism—especially its contrast of freedom to slavery, virtue to corruption, republic to monarchy—came the twin liberation and burdening of the citizen. The citizen now shared in government as never before. Extending colonial freedom, Revolution-era Americans engaged in practices of self-government ranging from militia and grand jury service to engagement in town meetings to the petitioning and instruction of representative assemblies, which, from 1776 onward, were transformed into ruling legislatures. New Americans expected that they would take part in governing and in the making of laws and their administration. Yet Americans also shared in the burdens of government and virtue. In the nineteenth query of his *Notes on the State of Virginia* (1785), Thomas Jefferson portrayed the ideal citizen as a farmer idyllically removed from the tempest and corruptions of city commerce, a man whose virtue lay in his earthly labor and his militancy at the ready: his watchful eye on liberty's enemies foreign and domestic. Jefferson's portrait was undermined, as he wrote, by a burgeoning commercial sector that generated growing economies and popular energies in cities and port towns.[16]

The entwined aspirations of liberty and equality spread widely, including in ways that would undermine the assumed White and male character of American citizens. Women shared in revolutionary notions of virtue and self-government as they began to vote in selected elections, to petition collectively, and to canvass subscribers for thousands of dollars in contributions to the Patriot cause in 1780. African Americans steadily claimed a notable place in this new citizen order: as military and civilian contributors to the

Patriot cause and, with ever greater frequency in the 1770s, as petitioners for freedom. Nor were these transformations limited to the United States. The antislavery cause in England took energy and inspiration from the American Revolution. In economic matters, Americans could inherit, purchase, and dispose of their land more securely and equitably than before. Yet freer access to property ran alongside the imperative to regulate economies for the common good. As in the Declaration of Independence, liberty meant, in part, the ability of communities to freely govern their affairs by laws of their choosing.[17]

A fresh energy of more egalitarian petitioning swelled in matters of religion, and nowhere more than in Virginia. Thomas Jefferson's doctrine of disestablishment came in part from his own thinking and reading but also from petition-based drives in Virginia against Anglican dominance. He found himself fascinated by these "dissenters," whose mass, he would write in query seventeen of *Notes on the State of Virginia,* reached two-thirds of the commonwealth's citizens. Thousands of dissenters seized on the disruption of proclaimed independence to demand reform of vestries (those boards of local parishioners who chose ministers) and disestablishment. In its first session in October 1776, Virginia's new House of Delegates received more petitions on religion than on any other subject. In one impressive demonstration, the dissenters stitched over one hundred signature pages together and bound them with waxen seals. So constructed, the "ten-thousand name" petition came to the House on October 16, 1776. Jefferson, who had not sat on the Committee *for* Religion in the House of Burgesses, served on the new Committee *of* Religion in the Delegates. Jefferson and dissenters combined to craft a new language of religious liberty, one that informed the commonwealth's Bill for Establishing Religious Freedom in 1786 and, eventually, the First Amendment to the United States Constitution.[18]

The Revolution and the new Constitution furnished as much enigma as it did threat. Some, like Benjamin Rush, claimed that the sovereign people made their appearance on election day and immediately surrendered power to their representatives on all others. Thousands upon thousands of Americans thought otherwise and methodically reenacted their existence as a people in marches, processions, pageants, and assemblies. Extending colonial practices, Revolution-era Americans instructed their representatives on matters ranging from taxation to religion to slavery. They formed new organizations both incipient and durable, from rebellious gatherings to hinder tax and debt enforcement to benevolent associations and antislavery societies. To counter the abuses of Federalist administrations in the 1790s, over forty Democratic-Republican Societies emerged as an oppositional force. By continual petitioning as well as assembly, the Democratic-Republicans joined hundreds of other societies and tens of thousands of other Americans in enacting the people outside elections.[19]

The democratic moment of the American Revolution was also a petitioning moment, which both harnessed and transformed colonial institutions and practices to create a world of ubiquitous petitioning by the end of the eighteenth century. Nary an officeholder in the antebellum United States—essentially all White men—lacked intimate firsthand experience with petitions. They prepared them, signed them, received them, and deliberated on them. The leaders of the founding era—Samuel Adams, John Adams, John Jay, Patrick Henry, George Washington—had all been active in petitioning the Crown before and during the Revolution. In 1776 and after, Thomas Jefferson's work to disestablish the Anglican Church in Virginia was spurred by the petitions of Anglican dissenters to the Virginia House of Delegates, which structured his work on the Committee of Religion. In the months before his death in April 1790, Benjamin Franklin signed a congressional petition calling for the gradual abolition of slavery, a document sponsored more by other activists than by the aging statesman but whose signing brought Franklin the enmity of southern representatives. Alexander Hamilton sponsored petitions for New York City bank charters. Henry Clay led a petitioning campaign to defend the Bank of the United States.[20]

The culture of petitioning ranged far beyond elite White men. Women petitioned all over the continent from the late eighteenth century onward. Since state legislatures were the adjudicators of marriage, women in the fledgling United States inundated their newly empowered assemblies with divorce petitions. Women's petitions in North and South Carolina rose tenfold from 1775 to 1800. And women petitioned the U.S. Congress, too, with at least 246 women submitting petitions to the House and Senate from 1789 to 1820. Widows requesting pensions for their husbands' military service constituted more than four out of five of these female congressional petitioners, and while they largely petitioned alone, the aggregation of their efforts placed the welfare of family matrons regularly on the congressional calendar. In Lower Canada, too, widows (who enjoyed expansive property rights under the Custom of Paris, which still reigned in the French-speaking colony) petitioned widely, as did women in Catholic religious orders. By the 1820s, in fact, women appeared more commonly on petitions to the legislature in Lower Canada than they did in neighboring Maine.[21]

Petitions flowed abundantly from people of color in the post-Revolution world. Chiefs, warriors, and clan mothers in Indigenous cultures signed and sponsored petitions as part of diplomatic traditions extending back centuries. In the flurry of treaty making with the new American nation in the 1790s, leaders of the Cherokee, Oneida, Seneca, and other nations repeatedly petitioned the U.S. president. Leaders among free Blacks as well as slaves had petitioned in the eighteenth century and beyond. Free men of color in Saint Domingue (now Haiti) petitioned the new French National Assembly in 1791, complaining of their treatment by White colonists and administrators on the island. Slaves and free Blacks throughout the new southern states, women and men alike, petitioned their new legislatures, asking for freedom and complaining of restrictions on court testimony. Slaves in Massachusetts petitioned in 1773 and 1774 for freedom and in 1777 for legal abolition of their servitude, while in 1783 Belinda Royall requested a portion of her deceased master's estate on the basis of the labor she had rendered as a slave.[22]

Literary and spiritual leaders in America also embraced and harnessed the petition for ends spiritual, personal, and collective. President George Washington's famous 1790 letter to the Hebrew congregation at Touro, Rhode Island—declaring that "the Government of the United States gives to bigotry no sanction, to persecution no assistance"—came in response to an epistolary petition from that town asking protection for its congregation. Writing anxiously from 1839 to 1843, the fledgling Church of Jesus Christ of Latter-day Saints launched one of the largest religious liberty petitioning campaigns of the century. The sequence of three appeals to Congress culminated in a memorial to the Senate that amassed 3,419 names, including the signatures of Joseph Smith and Brigham Young. They asked for reparations for the violence and dispossession visited on them from their brief time in northeastern Missouri, when Governor Lilburn Boggs issued an "extermination order" requiring that Mormons leave the state or be killed. Mormons would continue petitioning through the nineteenth century. Mark Twain initiated a petition during the Civil War on behalf of the besieged schoolteacher Prudence Crandall, who had founded a school for girls of color in Rhode Island. In 1861, friends and allies of Herman Melville, a decade past his publication of *Moby Dick*, petitioned President Abraham Lincoln for a consular post for Melville in Florence, on the Italian peninsula. Melville then petitioned Lincoln himself.[23]

Every one of Lincoln's predecessors in the presidency knew petitions personally, having authored their prayers alone or with others, affixed their name to one or more, or examined them in preparation of a response in their earlier officeholding. These intimate, tangible experiences happened before, during, and after their time in executive office. Washington, Adams, and Jefferson petitioned in their lives as British colonial subjects. In the midst of the Seven Years' War, Washington (then in command of the Virginia Regiment) wrote movingly of the "supplicating tears of the women; and moving petitions from the men, [which] melt me into such deadly sorrow."[24] Washington then petitioned George III on behalf of the regiment in 1762. When John Adams began to contest the Stamp Act in 1765, he did so with a petition to the selectmen of Braintree. In an appeal to the North Carolina legislature in 1796, Andrew Jackson, later the first president of the Democratic Party, joined with other piedmont landholders to claim the equality of their land titles when a set of earlier claims threatened to dislodge their own. In the midst of the debate over slavery and the gag rule in the 1830s, James Madison (one of the few founding-era men still living) reflected on the right of petition, revising a speech he had given almost five decades prior in the First Congress. William Henry Harrison, later the first Whig president, read petitions from Detroit-area settlers as a member of Congress and signed his own land petitions to the New Jersey legislature. In 1837, twenty-three years before he became the first Republican president, Abraham Lincoln chaired a select committee in the Illinois General Assembly that reviewed a petition of 1,437 names favoring the creation of new counties from Sangamon County, comparing the document with a remonstrance of 2,213 names against any county division. Nineteenth-century American presidents knew petitioning as well as they knew voting.[25]

In a world with so many sovereigns, petitions made and unmade careers. As Alexander Hamilton knew when he embedded a plan for petitioning into the constitution of the Bank of New York in 1784, a skillful petition for a bank charter could launch a vocation, a fortune, and eventually the fundaments of a political machine. Early nineteenth-century banks, it turned out, could not survive without petitions. In a career at once ecclesiastical, commercial, and legal, Padre José Antonio Martínez of Santa Fe navigated the petitioning worlds of Spanish law and the institutions of independent Mexico. Martínez's ally Padre José Manuel Gallegos of Santa Fe used petitions to build local alliances and contest the church hierarchy; by 1853, he had become New Mexico's territorial delegate to the U.S. Congress, the first Hispanic to serve in that position. *Alcaldes* in New Spain and Mexico relied on petitions to cement alliances in other local governments. French Canadian leaders Pierre-Stanislas Bédard, Louis-Hippolyte LaFontaine, and Louis-Joseph Papineau, among many others, all took part in extended monster petitioning campaigns to launch and support crusades for provincial autonomy. These leaders, whose names remain engraved in national memories and local monuments, built and protected their power through skilled petitioning.

* * *

These continuities of grievance and proposal mask a set of abiding transformations. While men from Jefferson and Washington through Garrison and Lincoln all petitioned, the petition had become a different thing by the time of Lincoln's presidency. Especially from the 1820s onward, petitioning verged toward the more democratic, widespread, popular, radical, and massive. In their regularly amassed signatures, the boldness of their claims, their connection to other petitions in coordinated campaigns, and their recruitment of new voices into public spheres, the kinds of petitions written by the Innu, the women of Jefferson County, Aaron Constant and his fellow men of color, the Irish canal workers of Indiana, and the *señoras* of Orizaba in the late 1840s were ever more emblematic of their time, and ever less expressive of the deferential and more diplomatic styles that had reigned before 1815. The democratization of petitioning that occurred from the 1820s to the 1850s stemmed from a congeries of intersecting and often reinforcing developments.

A massive economy of paper and print emerged in the late eighteenth and early nineteenth century, and it fueled much of the petitioning explosion. The proliferation of literacy, in part through public and religious schools, permitted the kind of public awareness that enabled women and men to read petition prayers and write their name on documents. Newspapers spread rapidly through the continent. In 1788, the United States had 93 newspapers with roughly four million annual copies printed; by 1828, 863 newspapers were in business and over sixty-eight million copies were printed annually. These increases were three or more times greater than the population growth at the time. In both the United States and Canada, newspapers were often tied explicitly to factional and partisan organizations—for example, Noah Webster's Federalist daily *Minerva* (founded 1793) in New York, the more Jeffersonian *Aurora General Advertiser* (1794) in Philadelphia, Pierre Bédard's *Le Canadien* (1810) in Québec City, and William Lyon Mackenzie's *Colonial Advocate* (1824) in York. Thurlow Weed began his political career in the Anti-Masonic Party in 1828 after having both worked for and owned a range of newspapers. In 1829 he launched the *Albany Evening Journal*, one of the most influential newspapers of the century, which served as a mouthpiece for New York Whigs and Republicans. Newspapers in Mexico also proliferated after independence, mainly those in the federal district in Mexico City (including the *Aguila Mexicana,* founded in 1823) but also a number of shorter-lived papers in the various *estados*. Padre Martínez, who drew on his legal training to spread new juridical doctrines in New Mexico, introduced the first printing press to the Mexican province in 1830s. The activity of the Cherokee in petitioning went hand in hand with the tribe's operation of newspapers (the *Cherokee Phoenix,* 1828, and later the *Cherokee Advocate,* 1844), while in other tribes, missionary journals carried not only Bible translations but also news.[26]

The emergence of the penny press in New York and Boston—newspapers that cost one penny per day, at a time when the cheapest were six cents per day, and that carried stories of crime, politics, and gossip, as well as outright fiction—leveraged high-speed printing machines that could kick out tens of thousands of newspapers per day. William Lloyd Garrison's the *Liberator* transformed antislavery politics, and a range of newspapers only slightly more expensive than the penny news emerged in rural America. These newspapers reprinted speeches from legislative and executive proceedings, which permitted their readers to scrutinize petitions and their disposition by governments. And these newspapers did not confine their attention to matters immediately local. As early as 1820, 20 percent of the political content (and as much as 50 percent of the articles) in American newspapers concerned national politics, as contrasted with state and local affairs, and after 1840, national politics dominated most American newspapers for the remainder of the century. Beyond their informational role, newspapers literally carried petitions to their readers. They published the petitions of others and printed mass-manufactured prayers that could be clipped and pasted to blank sheets of paper, ready for the canvass.[27]

No force contributed more mightily to this print and political revolution in the United States than the largest administrative organization, public or private, of the time: the United States Post Office Department. The Postal

Service Act of 1792 established a system of debt-fueled postal system growth and a distributive politics that favored the spread of the network across the Appalachian divide. From 1792 until Andrew Jackson's election in 1828, Congress added 2,476 postal routes to the American mail network; the number of post offices grew from 75 in 1790 to 8,450 by 1830. By 1828, the United States had almost double the number of post offices as Britain, and five times as many as the French system. The smaller U.S. population rendered even this comparison misleading; Americans could count seventy-four post offices for every 100,000 inhabitants, while Great Britain had seventeen and France, just four. While rural areas in Canada and Mexico saw nothing quite like the American postal explosion, these countries also witnessed dramatic growth in postal operations, linking their cities in particular. Daily mail service between Montréal and Québec was a regularity by 1820, and by 1831, Niagara in Upper Canada had been added to the five-days-per-week network. In 1824, independent Mexico had 17 "principal" (coordinating) post offices with 338 branch offices, and by 1846, it had 45 principal offices with 440 branches.[28]

A world of print and mail facilitated the writing and transmission of grievances, yet the grievances themselves were also transformed. More radical egalitarian forms of petitioning often arose from the growing consciousness of those who saw their fate as bound to that of others and who saw themselves and others as deserving of participation in popular sovereignty. The advent of industrial capitalism in the early nineteenth century, nowhere more visible than in the global cotton market and the advance of textile manufacturing in the United States, set laborers against owners of factory, mine, and machine in new ways, and also created more homogeneous forms of work that, even as they blunted the artisan skill of many workers, lay the template for the awareness of workers as producers. The Anglo-American and Mexican settler republics created new pressures and logics for the conversion of space into commodified land, and the organization of these lands under new governments backed by local and metropolitan forces. Settler pressure generated political contests and petitions among White men and families, among governments, and among the souls of those whom settlement displaced, enslaved, and disrupted.[29]

Embracing equality, North Americans also targeted corruption, hierarchy, and privilege. Even after eighteenth-century revolutions toppled empires and monarchs, many forms of hereditary and corporate privilege remained in the United States and Canada in 1810. Voting rights were still premised on property (though Canadian requirements were so low as to distribute the ballot widely among men, more so than much of the early republic of the United States), and landed gentry still possessed extra representation in senates, executive councils, or councils of revision. Forms of manorial land tenure, with tenant farmers answering to landlords, remained in New York and the Canadian lands abutting the Saint Laurence River. A vast intercontinental economy of chattel slavery shackled millions of Black men and women; even the northern states and Canada were webbed to its capital and commodity flows. The profits and consumed space of the American and Caribbean slave system, fueled by the global cotton boom, continued to expand, and its architects and justifiers in the southern U.S. states set their gaze on spaces to the south and west for its expansion.[30]

The War of 1812—which pitted Britain and its allies against the fledgling and militarily inchoate United States—set in motion cultural changes that began to undermine these bastions of privilege and domination. In the United States, the Federalist Party and its networks allied with those who favored accommodation with Britain, so much so that some Federalist newspapers openly advocated regional secession (or the expulsion of western states from the Union). The scale of the conflict, the recruitment of tens of thousands of men (many without voting rights) into voluntary and professional military service, the symbolic burning of Washington in 1814, the celebrated victory of Brevet Major General Andrew Jackson at the Battle of New Orleans but two weeks after the conclusion of the Federalists' Hartford Convention of 1814–1815—all of these events and their narration combined to both poison the Federalists' strategic wager and sully their professed and suspected loyalties. The party collapsed everywhere outside New England. Within a decade it would die there, too. Less immediate and less perceptible changes were occurring in American and Canadian political culture, changes that vaulted equality as a political ideal more than at any time since the 1770s. The rise of equality as a White male ethic came hand in hand with the war's devastation of Native American autonomy east of the Mississippi River.

It is impossible now to comprehend the antipathy so many North Americans felt and expressed in both the midst and the aftermath of that war to all things British and aristocratic. The War of 1812 engendered a newfound celebration of what was American, of what was revolutionary and French, and a reembrace of the Declaration of Independence as a kind of scripture. When the French officer Marquis de Lafayette, who had led American troops in the War of Independence and later fought in the French Revolution as well, returned to the United States in 1824 (invited by President James Madison), he was greeted with near-universal acclaim and by massive and adoring crowds. A throng ranging from fifty to eighty thousand New Yorkers (roughly a quarter to two-fifths of the city's population) amassed to salute his ship as it arrived in New York harbor; twenty thousand others pressed upon his appearance in Philadelphia. And at the Richmond convention in 1828, conservatives decried the foment of popular discourse, where they heard "so large a dose of French rights of man." In Lower Canada, a British colony, the perception of the Americans grew steadily more positive, and French Canadians increasingly read and cited French authors (Rousseau, Voltaire, Montesquieu, and Madame de Staël). After the war, news of the Bolivarian revolutions (1817–1822) and of Mexican independence (1821) also spread widely in the United States and Canada and captivated aspiring republicans and citizens. Growing nationalism reinforced an aspiration to equality as participants in self-rule.[31]

The new cultures of petitioning, then, relied on technology and print; policy and post; hatred of redcoats and everything they defended; and new tensions between worker and owner, woman and man, slave and sovereign, settler and Indigenous. Yet as much as anything else, they came from a transformed culture of prayer and audience, of earnest supplication and split sovereignties.

PRAYER, FERVENT

Petitions entail prayer. John Quincy Adams and Charles Grandison Finney lived vastly different experiences, inhabiting distinct spiritualities and social classes, but both men recognized this simple fact. Adams—the son of the second U.S. president, a Harvard College graduate, and himself a one-term president (1825–1829)—served as a member of the U.S. House in the 1830s, representing Massachusetts' Twelfth Congressional District (Plymouth); while there, he defended antislavery petitioners against the gag rule. In the midst of a chamber debate in 1837, Adams defended petitioning as every bit as sacrosanct as religious faith: "Petition is supplication—it is entreaty—it is prayer," he intoned. In an argument about whether slaves' petitions belonged before the chamber, he inverted the logic of proslavery legislators who wanted them excluded, reasoning that since slaves were petitioning (which they had done for many years), then this practice stood as additional evidence of their humanity.

Finney was the firebrand Presbyterian minister whose revival-based, itinerant preaching spawned many an emulator and whose meetings revolutionized Christian practice in America, with women speaking aloud at religious gatherings, unrehearsed sermons, and Gospel preaching connected to social and political issues of the day that discomfited more established preachers and their churches. As much or more than any other radical preacher of his day, Finney used the terms "petition" and prayer" almost interchangeably. He regarded the Lord's Prayer (usually referring to the version of Matthew 6:10) as a petition par excellence. Finney also knew well the massive petitioning campaigns surrounding him from the 1820s to the 1850s, whether in ecclesiastical struggles or slavery politics. He and his biographers remembered the petitions requesting his presence in Auburn (Cayuga County), New York, in 1826, whose five hundred signatories had, Finney believed, been converted to the worship of Jesus and thereby saved from damnation.[32]

The vast majority of humans in nineteenth-century North America believed in one form or another of an otherworldly spiritual realm, to the occupants of which (whether a single Creator or God, saints, ancestors, or spirits) a prayer could be raised. Dominated by different forms of Christian belief and by Indigenous faiths, the continent's religious worlds were greatly in flux, and these transformations both shaped and were shaped by petitioning. Petitioning waxed with a set of religious energies that, in all their diversity, spanned millions of souls. Members of established Protestant churches such as Anglicans, Episcopalians, and Congregationalists sparred with upstart communities like Free Baptists, Methodists, and American Presbyterians over questions of separation of religion and government and, beyond that, the authority of trained and licensed preachers of scripture. African American preachers started new Baptist and Methodist churches that appealed to Black converts. Philadelphia's Black communities erected no less than fourteen churches (twelve being Baptist or Methodist) in Philadelphia from 1800 to 1833, with roughly four thousand worshippers by 1837. Indigenous communities split over the rise of new actors, such as the Seneca's Handsome Lake or Tenskwatawa—some of whom became known as "prophets"—and just how much, if at all, they should accept the help or tutelage of Christian missionaries. In the diverse Catholic worlds of North America, which ranged from French Canada to wide expanses of the former

Louisiana Territory to Mexico and parts of the Caribbean, congregants and clergy battled over the direct and daily life of parish buildings and communities. Indigenous women in Canada wrested partial control of their Catholic parishes from priests and bishops, while in other cases pro-papacy Catholics launched offensives against liberal reformers. Men and women calling themselves "liberals" and "free thinkers" laid claim to alternative spiritualities in which they rejected church authority and religious faith itself.[33]

A more general democratization of American Christianity followed from late eighteenth-century disruptions. A new generation of preachers whose currency came not from college training in ministry but from personal popularity—Billy Hubbard, Lorenzo Dow, Freeborn Garrettson, and Black preachers Richard Allen and Daniel Coker—began to range around the American states and spread a passion for religious equality, the prerogative of every worshipper to interpret scripture for himself (and, often enough, herself). Everywhere, it seemed, the authority of trained ministers was under attack. Even Catholic priests in the United States complained of the unwillingness of ordinary men (and some ordinary women) to defer to ecclesiastical judgment on matters of doctrine and scriptural interpretation. The many new churches that budded from this broad transformation in American Christianity included African Methodist Episcopal (AME) congregations; the Mormons; and Calvinist dissidents who launched new Methodist churches, Universalist communities, and the Christian Connection.[34]

These religious movements and egalitarian forces both fueled and ran alongside another revolution in American Christianity. What is known as the Second Great Awakening shook the United States as religious outsiders made innovations in religious organization, doctrine, and the habits of individual and communal faith. Symbolized and partly led by Finney, preachers started campaigns of lectures and sermons that obeyed neither the calendars nor the doctrinal restrictions of established churches. Conversion and salvation happened not according to the auspices of ministerial authority or churches but meeting by meeting, revival by revival, proselytizing pitch by proselytizing pitch. Emotion began to accompany reason as legitimate inspiration, as spontaneous outbursts of prayer, song, crying, physical trembling, and falling became regular, even expected, events at revivals. Even as Finney believed that emotional sources of faith needed harnessing by the force of Gospel preaching, he recognized them as legitimate. The awakening newly recruited women into the ranks of those who could speak, pray, and even preach. Areas of western New York State were so heavily affected that they became known as the "burned-over district," and the area remained a hotbed of social, cultural, religious, and political innovation and controversy for decades. The awakening emphasized a woman's or man's personal relationship to God, ever less mediated—for some, entirely unmediated—by preachers, priests, and ecclesiastical office.[35]

Yet the liberation that accompanied the Second Great Awakening also placed new burdens of conscience on the believer. The idea of "testimony"—of the individual's need to affirm the truth before God and the community—took root and transformed individual and communal behavior. Protestant believers increasingly felt that God was watching each person individually. The prayers of an earlier age would have characterized the aspirations and appeals of a community, a church, conveyed in the name of collectivity by an ordained leader. Now that the relationship to God was more individualized, an individual's political and social activities became meaningful and observable in ways that melted earlier distinctions. Signing a petition became a form of testimony, a proof of salvation. The irony of salvation in this individualized view—emphasizing a person-by-person interpretation of Paul's insistence on faith-based conversion in Ephesians 2:8 or Galatians 3:10—was that it had been obtained not through works but through God's grace. Following the New Testament letter of James (2:14–26), however, awakened American Christians also tended to believe that once possessed, salvation needed to be demonstrated: "For as the body without the spirit is dead, so faith without works is dead also." And in the increasingly melded worlds of church and political affairs, petition signing became a key mode of showing conversion. God watched the signature, and God watched the refusal to sign. God also watched the canvasser.[36]

In ways more subtle and less visible, Catholicism also changed. Claiming the allegiance of peoples inhabiting vast swaths of North America—much of Canada (including present-day Québec and the maritime regions but also large parts of what is now Ontario and Manitoba), the United States and its territories (ranging from Louisiana through Missouri to plains and mountain territories), and the vast spaces claimed by Mexico before the war with the United States—the Catholic Church was in reality a remarkably decentralized organization, delegating authority heavily to bishops and missionaries. Rural communities in turn-of-the-century French Canada increasingly refused deference to bishops and freshly organized against parish reforms and closures. In late colonial Mexico, young women began to pour into ministry in greater numbers in the late eighteenth century, so much so that internecine struggles and what observers called "rebellions" occurred in some Mexican convents as these new generations clashed with elders. Women in colonial New Spain defied the older binary vision of marriage or convent, and laywomen increasingly aspired to a community reputation for piety, hoping to become known for a combination of *honor, vergüenza* (modesty), and *recogimiento*. In the 1830s, a decade after Mexican independence, bishoprics in Guadalajara and Michoacán encouraged lay devotional associations, and the strategy appears to have brought swelling numbers of women into these groups. When Mexican liberals began to attack the Catholic Church, women did not take orders from bishops to challenge them but took the lead in launching new organizations and petitions to combat what they perceived as anti-Catholic and anti-Mexican initiatives coming from Mexico City.[37]

The manifold religious worlds of Indigenous North America resist a simple summary, yet in many communities that had extended contact with British or American missionaries, Native autonomy movements emerged in the late eighteenth and early nineteenth centuries. Whether in the form of cross-tribal, cross-village leaders such as Tecumseh, Tenskwatawa, and Handsome Lake, or in more local but still concerted refusals to receive missionaries, many Indigenous communities began to reject Christian religions, however much they had been hybridized by missionaries and cultural accommodations. Increasingly, these alternative religious movements organized themselves as political bodies, becoming known as parties (pagan versus Christian) and factions within linguistic or tribal communities. In worlds where Indigenous and Catholic beliefs merged, there arose Indigenous pressures for parochial autonomy that ranged from villages such as Kahnawá:ke and Odanak in French Canada to pueblos in New Mexico. Nineteenth-century leaders, such as Denis-Benjamin Viger in Lower Canada or Padre Martínez in New Mexico, emerged in part because they could attract Indigenous loyalties in the multicultural worlds they inhabited.

These spiritual energies collided as much or more than they reinforced one another. Protestants suppressed minority churches from New England to the Mississippi Valley, Catholic and Protestant missionaries battled over the size of their congregations, and one community's awakening became another's suppression. Yet the stirrings of the early nineteenth century provided a common template for a spiritual realm characterized by greater equality of prayers and claims. All these movements brought new audiences to watch the petitioner. Many of them brought new venues, or new claims to old venues (bishops' offices, synods). What they shared was the decline, in some cases the annihilation, of deference to older authority and the recognition that spiritual energy, wisdom, truth, and multiplying prayer could come from below.

VENUES

From the spread of discretionary settler governments and the belief in separation of powers came a swelling population of government organizations: legislatures, councils, committees, executives, bureaus, offices, courts, and commissions to which petitions could be sent. At all these venues petitioners wanted some sort of hearing and expected a response even when it amounted to a refusal to grant the supplicant's request.

Compared to earlier imperial regimes and to Europe, government in nineteenth-century North America was remarkably decentralized. New political jurisdictions proliferated, each claiming a measure of sovereignty. Aside from avowing independence, the decisive revolutionary break with Great Britain came when the thirteen colonies declared themselves states and wrote fresh constitutions that placed their new legislatures at the center of government. Colonial assemblies already differed markedly from Parliament, having disbursement and military planning functions that Parliament never held. The new American states increased these powers greatly, placing all manner of taxation and war powers in their arsenal. By vesting legislatures with sovereignty and by championing the rights of petition and assembly, the early American states vaulted a model of representation that harnessed elections, instructions, and petitions. The exemplar of legislative supremacy came in Pennsylvania's constitution of 1776, with its unicameral legislature and its eviscerated governorship, the office replaced by a council of twelve. As in Pennsylvania, new American states designed executive weakness into their new constitutions, some being appointed by the legislature, some being plural.[38]

The American founding brought even more plurality in office. Even as the American states adopted a unified national government by ratifying the Constitution of 1787, they altered their own institutions in ways that reinforced divided powers. By the late 1780s, states had rejected the Pennsylvania model of unicameralism and a weak executive branch to embrace the

Massachusetts Constitution of 1780, drafted by John Adams and inspired by Montesquieu's model of the English constitution in his *Spirit of the Laws* (1756). Massachusetts' legislature (the Massachusetts General Court) had two chambers, whose concurrence was necessary for new legislation, as well as an independently elected governor endowed with broad appointment powers and a legislative veto. By the time of their adoption of the new U.S. Constitution, these thirteen states generally had combinations of a lower chamber, a governorship, and one more upper councils or a senate. Many would convert their upper councils into a senate in the early nineteenth century. These legislative chambers generally spawned committees, just as their executives branched into new agencies and their court systems multiplied.[39]

The growth of the American republic brought new states and territories, new bureaus and outposts for the federal government's Post Office Department and War Department, and new courts to which an array of claims could be taken. The admission of Missouri as a state in 1821 raised the number of states to twenty four, and that same year, New York's Constitutional Convention abolished its elite-leaning Council of Revision. As states and territories proliferated, so too did lower houses, more accessible upper chambers, and elective governors. Territorial legislatures also organized on a bicameral model—Indiana Territory having a general assembly and a legislative council (appointed until 1809 and elected after that)—usually well before they became states. As the national government tried to regulate settlement according to a more rationalized model, settlers themselves petitioned for more proximate governments that would bend more to their wishes. They asked Congress for territorial governments, and territories petitioned to become states. Once new states were created, settlers petitioned their legislatures for the creation of new counties and townships, each of which could house courts, municipal councils, and other offices. In the southern states after the Revolution, county courts created localized systems of law that limited the purview of state legislatures. The same 1821 New York Constitutional Convention that abolished the Council of Revision and broadened White voting rights (while effectively denying them to Black men) also created the Canal Board to govern the state's new infrastructure system. The board soon found itself inundated with petitions.[40]

American legislatures everywhere began to operate more and more by committee and to create fresh executive agencies to carry out provisions of law. Virtually every one of these bodies became the explicit or implicit target of petitioning. Some of the committees were ad hoc groups designed to address a particular item in a president's annual message or, just as commonly, a petition. Their work and status would officially expire with each session. Congress also created standing committees, which were expected to renew each session and which began to acquire a semblance of property rights over certain areas of law and administration. The House created twelve of these by the end of the Thirteenth Congress (1813–1815), including Claims, Commerce and Manufactures, Ways and Means, Post Offices and Post Roads, Public Lands, and Public Expenditures. By the day of President Andrew Jackson's inauguration in March 1829, the House had twenty-eight standing committees, including an Agriculture Committee and one on Indian Affairs. Committee proliferation redirected rather than solved the workload problem induced by petitioning. Committee investigations of petitions provided the basis for early American legislative hearings. These events included invited testimony from the petitioners, attorneys, and executive branch officials who could speak to the matter at hand. Newspapers, in turn, often published full or partial proceedings of these committee investigations. Much like Indiana Territory legislators wrote the House and Senate in 1814, petitioners often knew of the committees to which their documents were referred. Even with emerging legislative party organizations headed by the Speaker, the U.S. House found that the fact of committee referral made supplicants more likely, not less, to send additional petitions.[41]

Even as the U.S. House and other legislatures groaned under the burden of their petition-based workload, these bodies still regarded the presentation and reading of petitions, their introduction to the chamber, their induced debate, and their referral as necessary if not sacrosanct features of legislative procedure. By the Second Congress, the U.S. House had begun reading petitions as early as the second day of the session, the same day that the address of the president was read. This is surprisingly early given that the first day was, by necessity, devoted to selecting a Speaker and arranging rules for the upcoming session. By the 1810s, petitions would be read and referred to a set of committees, generally as soon as the very day after committee appointments were announced on the floor. The time spent on individual petitions was sufficiently demanding that members complained from the very first congressional sessions. As the writer Candidus wondered aloud in the *Gazette of the United States* in 1790, "Why is so much attention paid to trifling memorials?" He quickly supplied his own answer: "The answer to questions of this kind is obvious. Justice is uniform. It is the same when

TABLE 3.1 Petitions, Bills, and Roll Calls in the Early U.S. House

Congress	Petitions Introduced to the House Floor	Bills Introduced
5th (1797–1799)	328	178 (155 roll call votes taken)
10th (1807–1809)	495	173 (237)
15th (1817–1819)	1,263	331 (106)
20th (1827–1829)	2,067	462 (233)

administered to an individual, a state or a nation. . . . In order to gain the confidence of the people they must be fully convinced that their memorials and petitions will be duly attended to when they are not directly repugnant to the interest and welfare of the community."[42]

Norms of procedure like this made for arduous work. Compared to other indices of legislative activity, such as the introduction of bills and the calling of the roll, petitions and their introduction were far more common occupants of the legislative calendar in the early nineteenth century.

In the Fifth Congress starting in 1797, the number of petitions introduced to the floor of the House of Representatives stood at roughly double the number of bills introduced. By the conclusion of the Twentieth Congress in 1829, House petition introductions had grown to almost five times the number of bills and nine times the number of roll calls taken. These comparisons must be considered in the historical context of legislative activity: many votes were taken viva voce in the early Congress, so more votes occurred than these figures suggest, but many bills also came from petitions in the first place.[43]

In part because petitioners approached them with such heady aspirations, new legislatures found themselves receiving far more petitions in their first sessions than they would five to ten years afterward. Such first-session surges were witnessed in the U.S. House (1789–1791), the Virginia House of Delegates (1789), and the Legislative Assembly of Lower Canada (1791). Virginia started its House of Delegates with a standing committee system broader than that of the U.S. Congress, and the petitions were quickly referred to many of these standing bodies as well as to ad hoc committees designed to respond to only a single or a small set of petitions. Lower Canada's assembly was dominated numerically by the French speakers who called themselves *Canadiens,* and because these men knew that royal authority was concentrated in the hands of the province's upper chamber (legislative council) and in the governor and his executive council, they petitioned with abandon their assembly, the one representative institution they had. In turn, the assembly took up a disproportionate share of its time and its journals discussing these petitions. When these expectations for representation, and especially the receipt of petitions, were dashed, collective anger ensued. Men calling themselves the "*gens de couleur*" from Saint-Domingue (soon to become Haiti) petitioned the new National Assembly of France in 1789, and the assembly's tepid reaction to the petition and resistance to Black delegates engendered a bitter remonstrance on the part of the Saint-Domingue men and their representatives in 1791.[44]

Petition-receiving routines were not confined to national and state governments. City councils and mayors governed much of their affairs by responding to petitioning and writing memorials themselves. Philadelphia launched its elective city council in 1789, with fifteen aldermen and thirty common councilors from the city at large. In 1796, Philadelphia opted for a bicameral arrangement, converting its single body into a twenty-member common council and adding a special council of twelve members more. For much of the nineteenth century, it was the largest municipal legislature in the United States, and its archives suggest that it was regularly inundated with petitions signed from a broad sampling of the city's denizens (including women). In New York, the common council served as a way station or launching post for many of the city's most storied nineteenth-century politicians, including Mayor Stephen Allen (who represented the city's Tenth Ward). Municipal agencies and boards, whether the New York Board of Supervisors (petitioned by Allen himself in the 1840s) or the Philadelphia Common Council's Paving Committee, became targets of petitioning in their own right. In blooming Cincinnati, by 1850 the fifth largest city in the United States, petitions to the city council led town leaders to build some of the earliest public health infrastructure in the country, including public health boards with broad regulatory powers.[45]

Organizations of government, economy, and society received petitions. Like other fraternal societies, the Independent Order of Odd Fellows had a mechanism for petition receipt and disposition.[46] Synods of ministers received petitions, and Catholic bishops throughout the continent could expect to receive petitions from priests, missionaries, and parishioners, even as the bishops themselves repeatedly petitioned Rome. The petition of Indiana's Irish canal workers to their company gestured to a much broader pattern. As railroad companies burgeoned in the antebellum period and grappled with high injury rates, petitions to company officials from workers and even passengers and pedestrians flooded company offices, each claim seeking gratuities for injuries or hardship. The social expectation of responses, coupled with the advantages of a casuistic system that did not create costly precedents for companies, overwhelmed railroad owners and their burgeoning classes of managers.[47]

PROVINCES, PRONUNCIAMIENTOS, PETITIONS

Mexico's federal republic—with a mix of state governments and territories, and legislative institutions in each jurisdiction—emerged in the 1820s. Would-be emperors and invading powers contested this decentralization, yet the system of states stubbornly resisted national instability. Mexican federalism had roots that predated the independence campaign, issuing from Spain's reaction to the Napoleonic invasion of 1808. A meeting of the Spanish Cortes from 1810 to 1813 in Léon (one attended by twenty-two Mexican deputies) produced a new constitution in 1812. The constitution granted Mexico six "provincial deputations" for the internal governance of its provinces. Spanish deputies to the Cortes saw the deputations as administrative bodies, but because the deputations were elected, Mexicans saw potential legislatures. When Ferdinand VII returned to the Crown in 1814, he abrogated the Cortes rulings, and absolutism reigned again. When the independence campaign acquired new life in 1819, Ferdinand reinstated the 1812 constitution, the Cortes passed new enabling acts in 1820 and 1821, and by November 1820, Mexico again had six deputations. The successful independence campaign led by Agustín de Iturbide created a new provisional governing junta in the autumn of 1821. Iturbide himself authorized the new provincial deputation in Puebla in August 1821, and by October, independent Mexico had eight provincial deputations: Guadalajara, the Eastern Interior Provinces, the Western Interior Provinces, México, San Luis Potosí, Yucatán, Puebla, and Chiapas. Six other jurisdictions known as intendancies from the colonial period—Arispe (the provinces of Sinaloa and Sonora), Guanajuato, Michoacán, Oaxaca, Veracruz, and Zacatecas—were given the authority to form provincial deputations, and they did so immediately. Mexico had fourteen provincial deputations before it had settled on a national congress. In a pattern that would persist through the early independence period, other intendancies and localities (including Sonora, Chihuahua, Nuevo Mexico, and Coahuila y Texas) petitioned for deputations.[48]

Agustín de Iturbide's victory in September 1821 engendered forces for regional autonomy and independence far more vexing than he or his allies had anticipated. The third and twelfth articles of Iturbide's Plan de Iguala guaranteed political equality to Mexicans and abolished the prevailing caste system. Elections for the new national congress were held in January 1822, and by March, Mexico had a national legislature whose members were chosen from the various provinces. The provincial deputations would, however, serve as far more than conduits for local representation to a central sovereignty; they would claim a measure of rule in their own right. The struggle over central rule versus provincial autonomy would define Mexico's nineteenth century, and it would doom the plans and the life of Iturbide himself. Iturbide seized power from the Mexican congress in May 1822 and declared himself Emperor Agustín I. Ramos Arizpe's Plan de Casa Mata, drafted both as a blueprint to eject Iturbide from rule and as a guarantee of provincial autonomy for Veracruz, quickly gained support across the provinces and major cities. Iturbide abdicated his perch in March 1823 and left for exile two months later. A new constituent congress, commencing work in November, created the Mexican Constitution of 1824, which made broader guarantees of provincial self-rule and created a pathway for the provinces to become states in a partial mimicry of American federalism. When Iturbide returned to Mexico in 1824, it was the legislature of Nuevo Santander that tried him and the national congress that authorized his execution in July. For a moment, regional autonomy and legislative supremacy seemed triumphant. By January 1825, Mexico had nineteen constituent congresses and five territories (including Nuevo Mexico and California).[49]

Early independent Mexico swung between consolidating and diffusive tendencies, yet even when centralizers had an upper hand, popular pressure and organized coalitions for self-rule at the state level remained formidable. In the late 1820s and early 1830s, Mexican state constituent congresses used petitions to bring issues before the national congress, and the congress, in turn, often used petitions as a means of allying the different states with one another. In the repeated battles over state autonomy and the role of the Catholic Church in the 1820s, the powerful *estado de México* petitioned the national congress for rights over ecclesiastical appointments and the disposition of church properties, and the state's petition was joined by Jalisco and Guanajuato. Meanwhile, friars displaced by the state of

Mexico's 1827 seizure of their missions ran around the state legislature and took their petitioning appeals directly to the national congress. Local governments, especially *ayuntamientos* (town councils), both received and sent petitions, as when over six thousand artisans signed a petition to Mexico City's *ayuntamiento* in 1851 calling for regulation of illicit trade, or when Puebla's *ayuntamiento* in 1845 petitioned former president Manuel Gómez Pedraza, then a deputy to the constituent congress, for the restoration of independence-era laws.[50]

Independent Mexico also gave rise to a form of request and complaint quite unlike anything regularly performed elsewhere in North America—the *pronunciamiento.* Mexicans used the term contemporaneously to describe a range of actions, including assemblies of armed supplicants who gathered before a government office, an *ayuntamiento*'s declaration of principles or call for a reform plan, or a peaceful petition (called a *representación* as readily as a *pronunciamiento*) of a town leader and his allies. Whether the *pronunciamiento* qualifies as a petition to be compared readily with other forms of complaint and supplication remains unclear, yet its use overlapped with more formal petitions, the assembly of men called *pronunciados* usually brought with them a text, and the text often had signatories (and others who accompanied the text to its place of delivery, often with firearms visible). The frequently armed presentation of complaints and requests simultaneously recognized the sovereignty of their audience yet reminded that audience of its fragility and the rough equality of the supplicant. *Pronunciamientos* were widely used in nineteenth-century Mexico, and not only by military officers or armed groups. Indigenous peoples sponsored them in the 1830s, and there is evidence that women may have authored one or more.[51]

The expectations attached to petitioning remain difficult to observe, yet telltale legal reforms gesture to the fact that a widespread culture of supplication and grievance remained. When a conservative resurgence in the early 1830s destabilized the federal republic and ushered in a new period of instability—marked by a nineteenth-century peak of *pronunciamientos*—the Mexican chamber of deputies felt it important enough to deputize a committee to both establish and regulate petitioning rights. In some ways, the chamber's work was merely symbolic, yet petitioning continued to course through Mexican politics in the 1830s, establishing precedents and patterns that could be observed in the ensuing decades. The fact that the state of Puebla's 1861 constitution explicitly protected *ayuntamientos*' right to petition the state congress gestured to the prohibitions on local supplication in the previous decade but also to the cultural expectation that channels of complaint and request should be facilitated.[52]

* * *

Despite vast institutional differences among the governments of North America, then, petitioners confronted and exploited a bewildering array of authorities to whom they could take their appeals. Local and state assemblies in Mexico, Canada, and the United States both received petitions and petitioned higher authorities. Revolutions, independence campaigns, and new constitutions created more comprehensive legislatures and executive offices, which themselves opened new questions regarding the location of power—in the American presidency, in the Mexican national congress, or in the Legislative Assembly of Lower Canada. For British colonies in Canada and the Caribbean, the House of Commons and, through the Colonial Office, the Crown retained ultimate authority. Yet the highly decentralized character of North American government meant that petitioning remained a deeply local act, often displaying grievances and directing appeals to nearby audiences alongside memorials sent to more encompassing offices.

FOUR

Petitioning in the Settler Republic

Space, Capital, Soldiers

A volatile mix of nations, empires, villages, cities, and colonies, nineteenth-century North America promised heaven to millions of settlers, most of them of European descent. Those same promises delivered hell to millions of other souls. The dreamt paradise bundled a mix of republican visions and realities—rapidly expanding spaces for agriculture and industry, for worshipping Christian communities, and for new forms of popular government ever less tethered to European empires. Hell on earth came with the mass death and dispossession of various Indigenous peoples, an expanding slave system that shackled Black women and men, vast environmental degradation, and lost voting rights and property claims for women. The aspiration of freedom coupled tightly to the threat of empire, dislocation, and slavery. Increasingly dominated by English and American settlement but profoundly shaped by Native North American cultures, French colonial legacies, and Spanish institutions, North America housed an abiding struggle over newly opened territories, waterscapes, and the disposition of both.

Settlers and both their allies and their adversaries fought many thousands of battles over spaces both solid and fluid. They brandished weapons of steel, leather, lead, fire, wood, and flint, and they deployed petitions by the many thousands. Beyond the machineries that pierced and shackled skin, crushed skulls, and removed bodies and their kin, petitions figured centrally in settlement politics. Settlers and their political representatives relied heavily on petitions for land and water rights. Men aspiring to charter banks, to build canals and roads, or to launch new industries petitioned for capital and for the rights only a legislature or governor could give. As they created new societies, these men (occasionally joined by women) asked for military protection or action against the enemies of settlement. As much as anything, settlers voracious for space, capital, and statehood petitioned for new venues—new legislatures and councils; offices and county seats; and courts that could more favorably adjudicate their claims, become targets of their political pressure, and receive their future petitions. Settler petitioners often wanted new, more intimate sovereigns constructed in their midst.

Politics and petitioning intertwined in ways that marked an older world of monarchical supplication and networked advocacy, a world in transition to an industrial republican dream. These dynamics gave rise to two kinds of petitioning: the petitions of settler interests, and the petitions of networked elites. Settlers sought the goods and rights of landed citizenship, often gained at the expense of others: Natives, slaves, and—not least—other settlers and development interests. These claims ranged from petitions for land grants, to petitions for postal routes and offices, to petitions asking for new governments, to which, if fulfilled, the petitioners would next turn their endeavors of influence. Competing coalitions of connected local elites practiced a second kind of petitioning, through which they sought appointments, charters, incorporations, and the intervention of whatever sovereign they could invoke to secure and stabilize their projects. Both modes of petitioning thrived at the intersection of rapidly propagating venues and the politics of development.

The abrasions of settlement created an early but radically inchoate democratic moment. Craftsmen and mechanics called for more equal tax burdens. Soldiers lay claim to benefits, to bounty lands acquired in military campaigns, and to a reduction of their debt burdens. Many of these petitioners had fought long before they petitioned, whether in the American Revolution, the War of 1812, the Mexican independence campaign, or the many "Indian wars" fought by settler governments. And many of these petitioners were widows and daughters marking a resurgent women's presence before officeholders. In other ways, petitions from coalitions of investors promised, for a time, to open the development of capital-intensive industries to anyone who could make the case before a legislature. Petitions for appointment to government office offered, at least in principle, the same leveling potential.

Yet much remained undemocratic, even deeply inegalitarian, about this mode of petitioning. Incorporation petitions, once successful, often established monopolies; these corporate charters were tightly guarded by their possessors, who blocked the petitions of competitors in the legislature. Chartered monopolies confined market and capital access to a select few, namely those most intimately connected with the dominant legislative faction or party. Similarly, appointment petitioning often generated a restricted network of government officeholding. Early nineteenth-century petitioning advanced White men's political citizenship, but it also widely restricted that of Black men. These colonial models of petitioning mobilized women very little except as widows, women desiring divorce, and, for a brief time, those who joined the patriot cause. Even as the language of republicanism suffused North American politics, especially in the United States, petitioners to Congress rarely identified themselves as "producers," "laborers," or even carpenters and workmen as they would, much more commonly, after the War of 1812.[1]

In the years after the epic pivots of 1787 to 1791—the Confederation Congress's Northwest Ordinance, the French Revolution and its destabilization of Atlantic politics, the new U.S. Constitution, the Spanish royal Plan de Pitic in 1789 creating new settlement models in Mexico, and Britain's 1791 Constitution Act for Canada—there was no more common subject of petitioning in North America than space, and especially its solid variant: land. In law and practice, petitions created a formal claim for resources or a grievance. They enabled a paper record, allowing different bodies—whether classified as "legislative," "judicial," "gubernatorial," "administrative," "governmental" or other—to adjudicate these claims. As political instruments, however, petitions of the time did far more than create a legal record. They knit together constituencies of investors, settlers, laborers, and merchants; they coalesced opponents of settlement, dispossession, encroachment, and slavery.

In the United States, the Louisiana Purchase and the War of 1812 together wrought the canvas for Thomas Jefferson's vast inland "empire of liberty." The purchase made it clear that America's designs were cast well beyond the Appalachian mountain range and indeed well past the Mississippi. The war with the British cemented American claims to those spaces, opened the way for dispossession of the Indians who lived on them, and created a template whereby Indigenous occupants would often be replaced by smaller farmers, plantation societies, and African American slaves. The visions of an American settler republic came from Jefferson and his dream of an agrarian society (rendered most starkly in query nineteen in *Notes on the State of Virginia*), but also from Hamilton, who in *Federalist* no. 17 and elsewhere worried about the effect of institutional instability on the value of improved land.

As the specter of American domination crystallized, the imperial holds of Britain on Canada and of Spain on Mexico became ever more tenuous. The Mexican war for independence created its own republic, one in which the population broke dramatically with earlier colonial institutions even as many legacies of Spanish law remained. Meanwhile, in both French-speaking Lower Canada as well as more English-friendly Upper Canada, changing dynamics of settlement and weariness over colonial administration engendered growing efforts to reform British colonial institutions toward a republican model. These struggles eventually spawned mass violence.

In aspiration as much as in reality, North American societies from the 1820s onward embraced a republican model. Settler republics cast their designs on the conquest of space, both animating and limiting settlement by popular sovereignty, states with enforcement capacity over statutes, and the rule of law. The fundamental struggle was one over land and resources, spaces over which settlers and investors had grand designs. These mass transformations can only partially be understood through the lenses of settlement and colonialism, by which colonies were hatched as extensions of empire, preexisting Indigenous peoples were dispossessed, and, in their place, settler regimes inserted new, more extractive forms of production and discipline—most notably slavery. To view settlement as "colonial" only is to miss the popular energy—indeed, the republican energy—that gave rise to, energized, and legitimated it. The idea of the sovereignty of peoples fueled and justified the expansion of North American society. So, too, a colonial understanding of settlement misses the deep engagement of Native peoples with settler governments, much of it performed through petitions.[2]

THE FLUID AND SOLID SETTLER REPUBLIC: PETITIONS AND THE EARLY EMPIRE STATE

Settler republics sought fluid and solid space. Farmer-citizens in the Jeffersonian mold needed land. Transportation and land companies wanted river and lake access and the ability to build bridges. These spaces were prized by Native Americans for some of the very reasons that land companies sought them: the prospects of easier portage. Industrial settlers sought to incorporate towns and monopolies near rivers with particulars kinds of rapids—Lowell, Springfield, Worcester, and others in Massachusetts; Harper's Ferry in Virginia; Hartford and New Haven in Connecticut; Saco and Biddeford in Maine; Trois-Rivières in Canada; Cincinnati and Wheeling in Ohio; Pittsburgh in Pennsylvania; and later Eau Claire in Wisconsin.[3]

The political realities of settlement unfolded heterogeneously across a continental canvas, but New York State functioned as exemplar for many patterns elsewhere. Antebellum New York showcased the continent's most explosive industrial city, a burgeoning financial sector, a canal network and steamboat economy that pierced the Appalachian barrier and opened the Great Lakes to fresh development, a pernicious model of Indian removal, and a budding party system. Every one of these elements—industry, finance, infrastructure, dispossession, and politics—became a model for practices elsewhere on the continent. And every element was deeply interconnected.

The great city was a creature of New York State, literally a chartered incorporation of its legislature and structurally a beneficiary of its many endowed advantages. New York's industry and financial capital depended heavily on a network of transportation that allowed agricultural and raw materials to flow from the interior while rural settlers could purchase finished goods manufactured in cities. The roads, bridges, turnpikes, and canals in central and western New York depended, in turn, on the loans and backing provided by New York's banks and by its state government. Much of the state's cheap and remarkably fertile land was largely occupied and claimed by Indigenous peoples. The investors who projected their capital and settlement dreams over New York's forests and fields worked with, and sometimes were themselves, the very politicians and officeholders who dragooned the Onondaga, Oneida, and Seneca. These mixed energies of settlement, industry, finance, infrastructure, and Indian removal came together in the state legislature at Albany and the city's common council.[4]

With Virginia ceding its western lands to the federal government in 1784, followed by North Carolina in 1790, New York cemented its status as the American state that contained within its borders the richest development and settlement opportunities. Unlike so much of the Ohio valley and Great Lakes region, New York's policy would be driven as much or more by its state government than by national imperatives. This localism reflected the reach and capacity of New York's institutions—its Assembly and Senate, its capital resources, its position in networks of international commerce, and its powerful governor and Council of Revision.

The dreams of the Empire State's settler republic extended only so far as the region's Native inhabitants could be vanquished. Preserving as they could a linguistic federation many centuries old, the Six Nations of the Haudenosaunee (or Iroquois) occupied most of the lands in what became New York and the upper Ohio valley at the time of the American Revolution. The dispossession of eastern Indians combined with the ravages of pestilence and war had created a world of refugees in the seventeenth and eighteenth centuries. As a result, many Natives who belonged to Haudenosaunee tribes and clans were the descendants of other linguistic groups—Anishinaabe-speaking populations of Ottawa and Ojibwe, as well as Iroquoian groups of Huron and Neutral. As American elites from Benjamin Franklin to George Washington recognized, the robust institutions and diplomatic models of the Haudenosaunee enhanced their stability.[5]

American independence and the crystallization of New York's settler dreams undid this tenuous equilibrium. In an earlier time, the Iroquois were allies and trading partners as well as objects of imperial fascination. Up against the dreamt expansionary republic, however, they became only roadblocks. Settlers, speculators, capitalists, and lawmakers saw in Haudenosaunee lands a bounty of fertility and forests beyond anything remaining in New England. In those lands they also saw access to the vast networks and freshwater resources of the Great Lakes region. The development of this complex would require investments of resources material and spiritual, not only banks and industrial companies but new Christian communities. Yet capital was scarce, tied up in battles between Whigs and Tories, and fastened to war debt. The locus of republican settlement work—capital bundling, Indian removing, land acquiring, infrastructure building—became the state capitol at Albany.[6]

An American state legislature had sovereignty over lands and economic activity within its domain. The New York State Assembly and Senate sought to extend those lands and to encourage the energetic Christian, republican settlement of those lands. New York's powerful governors, who held positions of influence in early state parties, who had appointment and veto power, and who until 1821 sat on the state's Council of Revision, became rhetorical and political architects of republican settlement. The opening of interior markets and settlement lands in New York State targeted foremost the spaces occupied by the Oneida, the People of the Standing Stone, who occupied more than five million acres of land. What the Oneida called their "carrying place"—where canoes could be hauled on land between the Mohawk River and an inlet to Oneida Lake—lay at the center of New York's industrial vision. New York politicians, capitalists, and settlers aligned over a period of four decades to wrest these spaces from the Oneida.[7]

In the twin projects of Indigenous removal and settlement, governors and lawmakers in Albany saw their task as twofold. The first was to channel energies voiced in petitions and lobbying initiatives to developmental imperatives. The second, and every bit as important, was to keep the national government out of New York affairs, especially when it came to Indian removal and infrastructure. In both of these tasks, settler interests in the Empire State drew on the model of insider petitioning. When they allied with Oneida who were willing to sell, settlers used petitions to ask the state legislature to appoint a commission for the purpose of conducting treaty negotiations. Land companies—first the Holland Land Company and later the Ogden Land Company—also used petitions to call for policy making by the legislature. Beyond this, New York politicians used petitions to shift venues or to call in political reinforcements when necessary. As the Ogden Land Company set its sights on Buffalo after the War of 1812, and as the Seneca began to divide on the question of land sales and resist encroachments, David Ogden sent a petition to President James Monroe in 1819 calling for the removal of the Senecas from New York, based on the model of ongoing Oneida removal. An emerging industrial vision for New York—one that embedded its sprawling canal network—assumed the clearance of Indigenous peoples.[8]

Petitions for Incorporated Capital—Banks and Their Charters

Early American elites regarded the establishment of banking systems as some of their first tasks. In an attempt to moderate tensions between Whigs and Tories and to build a new political economy for the city, men such as Robert Livingston and Alexander Hamilton sought to create new banks. These city elites disagreed over whether the proper bank should hold its primary assets in land (Livingston's model) or money (Hamilton's). The city's merchants, believing themselves sidelined in these debates, coalesced to form a bank of their own, the Bank of New York. The merchants' campaign acquired enough momentum that Hamilton left another coalition and joined it.[9]

Hamilton and his merchant allies founded the Bank of New York in 1784 on hard coin and on a plan of petitioning. The bank held its reserves in gold and silver coin, or specie. And the bank's very constitution—which bore Hamilton's influence—embedded the obligation that "the President and Directors shall Petition the Legislature" for incorporation and "to pass Laws for inflicting the most exemplary punishment" on any who would commit fraud, embezzlement, or counterfeiting of bank notes or checks. The centrality of petitioning in Hamilton's new bank was no accident. As he helped his allies draft their charter and approach the legislature, Hamilton had just petitioned New York lawmakers for debts owed from the Revolution, and he watched anxiously as Livingston and other backers of a land bank were actively petitioning the legislature for an exclusive charter of their own.[10]

The Bank of New York implanted petitioning in its 1784 constitution because its existence would depend on the state assembly and senate. Banks in the dawning republic could open as partnerships or as unchartered entities, yet early American capitalists prized the model of a limited liability chartered corporation. Those who stored their assets in a bank without a limited liability charter risked everything if the institution failed. A limited liability charter constrained claims on investors to what they had deposited. In the United States, would-be bankers could get these protective corporate charters only from legislative sovereigns. The formal and the informal approach to the sovereign required a petition.[11]

Like other incorporation initiatives of the time, the Bank of New York's requests were carefully prepared documents, not only in their prayers but also in their signatory lists. Those who signed the petition pledged their name, their respectability, their capital, and their political energy. Signatories were expected to act not merely as investors and managers but as lobbyists in the complex factional politics of city and state. Headlining the signatory list in the bank's 1784 petition was Jacobus Van Zandt, a prominent merchant, a former leader of the Sons of Liberty, and uncle to Peter Van Zandt, who had just been elected to the assembly. Other directors of the bank also signed, and the bank's petitioning effort in 1785 attracted radical merchants like John Lamb, Isaac Sears, and Melancton Smith, who would, at other times and in other places, oppose Hamilton's vision and the projects of the Federalists.[12]

New York's assembly and senate constituted the main field of battle between Livingston's and Hamilton's banks. In the city's burgeoning newspaper field, backers of a new bank issued an open call for allies and investors and rendered arguments about the insufficiency of existing capital institutions in the city. Further petitioning efforts by Bank of New York allies beginning in July 1789 and continuing for another eighteen months resulted in a legislative charter in March 1791.[13]

Each pro-bank mobilization became a petition campaign in miniature, a canvassing of capital. In many cases, these petitions harnessed preexisting networks, but as the Bank of New York mobilization shows, incorporation initiatives and their petition processes could draw together new, unexpected coalitions from cross-cutting elements of post-Revolution New York politics, uniting Whigs with Tories, incipient anti-Federalists with Federalists, radical merchants with parvenu shopkeepers. These petitioning coalitions often required allies well beyond the number and breadth any one capitalist could marshal through his personal network. As the parties developed organizationally, incorporation petitions required cross-factional alliances, bridging splits among the three blocs of Republicans: one led by Aaron Burr, another by DeWitt Clinton, the third by Livingston. Incorporation petitions and mobilizations built new networks as much as they relied on old ones.[14]

The coalitions that petitioned for and against corporate charters would meld with others to shape the parties of the early national Empire State, with Federalists opposing Jeffersonian Republicans. These dynamics became evident in the rise of New York's alternative bank, the Manhattan Company. In the wake of yellow fever epidemics that wracked New York City in the summer of 1798, prominent city elites called for enhancements to the city's freshwater infrastructure. A coalition of elites that included Hamilton and Burr petitioned the New York state legislature to incorporate a water company in New York City.[15]

In 1799, the city's two existing banks (the Bank of New York and the Bank of the State of New York) served not in formality but in social fact as Federalist institutions through and through. Their networks of shareholders were Federalist partisans, and their loan-making practices also favored Federalist constituencies to the extent possible. In contrast, Burr's proposed Manhattan Company appeared bipartisan on its face. The coalition that sought the city's common council to launch a petition was led by Hamilton and Burr and was composed of three Federalists and three Republicans. Subscribers to the Manhattan Company were also signatories to the petition and eventually shareholders who would be called on to petition yet again. They sought a corporate charter for an independent water company that would draw fresh water from the East River, one chartered by the state as opposed to one operated by the state-chartered city itself.[16]

Once awarded a corporate charter, Burr transformed a water company into a bank. He inserted a provision into the company's charter that would allow the firm to dispose freely of its surplus capital, opening the way for loan making. The Manhattan Company began investing in a range of capital projects, usually with the aim of supporting Republican allies, especially those in the Burr faction. Detecting themselves outwitted in 1799, the Federalists counterattacked in that year's municipal elections, making Burr and the Manhattan Company their principal target and coordinating an onslaught in print with an electoral campaign. This task proved easier editorialized than accomplished; three Federalists served as directors of the Manhattan Company. The May 1799 city elections proved a temporary rebuke for the Republicans, but the battle soon became one fought through petitions in Albany more than through votes in the city. The Bank of Albany petitioned to restrict the Manhattan Company's charter, while the Bank of New York's directors took a different tack, asking for a revision of their own charter for repealing the clauses limiting the duration of their enterprise and constraining the range of assets in which they could invest. The Bank of New York's petition ran into Federalist opposition in committee and was refused.[17]

Surviving these challenges, the Manhattan Company would begin investing in the state's exploding infrastructure sector, especially turnpike roads and bridges. Turnpike roads in New York had grown immensely in activity, with sixty-seven companies receiving charters from 1800 to 1807. The Manhattan Company would enter into the business of building, most of it well outside the confines of the city. The Manhattan Company increasingly became a thoroughly Republican instrument, one capable of bestowing favors on linked partisans.[18]

The Manhattan Company's first loan demonstrated the fraught politics of corporate chartering by petition. The company invested in the Cayuga Bridge Company to build what was, at a length of over a mile in 1800, the longest bridge in the Western Hemisphere at its time. The 1799 loan served to enrich Burr's ally John Swartwout, who directed the bridge company. The Cayuga Bridge functioned as one of the primary routes for freight and personal transport between the city and the central and western reaches of the state. Yet as an infrastructure project, it became an emblem of failure and corruption. The Cayuga Bridge was badly weakened in the winter of 1807 and collapsed in 1808. The company built another bridge a mile north of the original, a much smaller conduit traversing the outlet of Cayuga Lake.

When in 1811 Abraham Dox petitioned to start a new enterprise, funded by lottery, to build a bridge across the middle of Cayuga Lake, the Cayuga Bridge Company protested in a remonstrance of its own. The battle of petition and remonstrance pitted newcomer against incumbent and set Burr's old allies against settlers in the western reaches of the state. Here the westerners won. The committee that deliberated on the matter was stacked with western interests, led by Robert S. Rose of Seneca County (which abutted the Cayuga outlet). Reviewing the "facts connected with the prayer of the petitions," Rose's committee announced in favor of the "principle of construction that incorporated companies should be held strictly to their charters," concluding that the Cayuga Bridge Company had "failed to perform the express condition of their charter." When it came to rendering a decision, Rose noted "the number and respectability of the petitions" as the first reason for deciding in Dox's favor.[19]

The incorporation petition had proved a double-edged weapon. The very advantages that had served the Burr faction so well—petitioning and the lobbying connections to Republican elites in 1799 and 1800—now occasioned its temporary defeat. Western New York politicians—Dox was connected to Augustus Porter, Benjamin Walker, and John Devereaux—took up the same petitions to evident effect. While corporate charters often created and protected monopolies, the assembly committee in 1811 called for the provision of explicit competition. The company regrouped and met with Dox's outfit, which agreed to withdraw its petitions if the Cayuga Bridge Company would rebuild the bridge and would agree to three new stipulations to its charter, one limiting rate differentials between the long and short bridges, the other committing to forfeit the charter if either bridge became impassable for more than thirty days, and the third committing to rebuild any bridge that collapsed within eighteen months. The rechartering passed the legislature in 1812, and the Cayuga Bridge was relaunched in 1813 and would persist into the 1850s, when its traffic was largely displaced to ferries and the state's canal system. The Cayuga Bridge battle lay bare the stakes of early New York State political economy, wherein the essential assets for profit making—monopolies and limited liability corporate charters—were gained via memorials to state legislatures.[20]

Not just any petition would do. Even as incorporation petitioning in the early U.S. republic relied on networks of investors, landed gentry, and elites, it also bespoke an emerging politics of numbers. Contracts for the construction of important infrastructure—such as the steamboat *Washington* in

1824—and incorporation petitions gathered not only large numbers of signatories but a diversity of capital holders and elites. The petitions presented the portfolio of investors in such a way as to render the ensuing legislative "investment" in a corporate charter seem worth the evident risk. Bank and corporate charter petitions in early national New York failed far more often than they met with success. Yet they coursed into the assembly and senate nonetheless. Their persistent flow despite long odds expressed the reality every aspiring banker knew: that petitions were essential to the process of capital formation, and that the charter petitioning process was governed and limited by elite networks.[21]

As power in the state edged westward, incumbents and Republican elites discovered that as with the Cayuga Bridge affair, petition-based advocacy could be turned against them through manipulation of the same legislative machinery they had used to gain their positions.

THE FLUID STATE OF EMPIRE: PETITIONS FOR BOATS AND CANALS

Water's centrality in New York's political development stemmed from its advantages as a medium of transport. Stagecoaches were constrained by what limited axles and wheels (many still wooden) could bear. Only after the Civil War would railroads massively displace waterborne freight shipping. Settlement of land and connectivity to global trade placed literal and symbolic weight, as well as a monetary premium, on carriage by water.[22]

The emergence of steam-based boiler engines transformed New York's water world, and the steamboat industry's rise came in a battle of petitions, as the team of Robert Fulton and Robert R. Livingston skillfully managed legislative processes in New York and Washington. The two men petitioned for an incorporated monopoly and the police powers to enforce it, and after New York's legislature granted their petition, the first Fulton-Livingston steamboat launched in August 1807. The men quickly established a thriving monopoly and sought to extend their patent rights in Congress, stoking challenges from resentful and aspiring steamboat interests in Albany and New Jersey. Petitioning Albanians harnessed the growing antimonopoly sentiment in Congress to stymie the Livingston-Fulton patent extension bill, while in February 1814, former New Jersey governor Aaron Ogden petitioned Albany for a repeal of the forfeiture and enforcement provisions benefiting the company. The assembly would pass the relevant bill, but the senate narrowly rejected the legislation. Livingston had died, and the firm's political work was then being performed by his son-in-law Edward. But the Fulton-Livingston monopoly had scraped by.[23]

Fulton and Livingston then counterattacked, petitioning New Jersey for a repeal of Ogden's charter there, and petitioning the New York State Assembly for a strengthening of their monopoly in that state. In New Jersey, they marshaled lawyers and Republican allies—newly emboldened and numerous due to recent election wins—to put Ogden on the defensive. They secured a party-line vote for the repeal of Ogden's monopoly in New Jersey. The petition had become a forcing tool, opening a partisan venue of advantage for one monopolist against another. The persistence of their monopoly owed much to petitioning politics.[24]

David Ogden took his next battles to different venues—state and federal courts—and in doing so both exposed and undermined the primacy of state legislative incorporation petitions. Having joined with the volatile Republican Daniel Tompkins to buy the rights to a ferry between Staten Island and Manhattan, he found himself in a fray with the former Georgia congressman Thomas Gibbons, to whom Tompkins sold the ferry rights in 1817, a year after being elected vice president. Gibbons turned on his partner and bought rights to a line from New Jersey to Staten Island. Ogden sued in New York chancery courts under the 1811 law giving him his monopoly. Gibbons's appeal made its way to the Supreme Court, and the resulting decision—*Gibbons v. Ogden* (1824), authored by Chief Justice John Marshall—drew on the U.S. Constitution's supremacy clause to invalidate New York's statutes. Marshall acknowledged that, within their proper domains, state legislatures had ultimate authority to grant petitions for "an exclusive property." Yet as Marshall knew, that very power entailed the specter of anarchy, carrying "embarrassing and destructive consequences."[25] In the American world of multiple sovereignties, incorporation petitioning led almost inevitably to conflicting rights and turf claims. This "war of legislation" led to initiatives to redirect conflict to new venues and to calls that courts, especially federal courts, "interpose [their] friendly hand."[26] The decision blunted the utility of the state legislature as a venue and induced a range of capitalists to take their claims, and their aspirations, to the U.S. Congress.[27]

DeWitt Clinton's "Memorial" and the Making of the Erie Canal

The ultimate fantasy of New York's capitalists was to break the Appalachian land barrier and bypass the Niagara Gorge. Designs on a canal connecting the Mohawk River (and thereby the Hudson) to Lake Erie came in the form of pamphlets, essays, and petitions from the late 1700s onward. Observers suspected that an American canal connecting the Great Lakes with the Atlantic would be built through New York State or would not be built at all. New York was the only state that touched the Atlantic, Lake Ontario, and Lake Erie. Moreover, the difficulties of building cross-state coalitions precluded a meaningful national role for cross-state infrastructure programs on the scale of a massive canal. Legislators in the Empire State considered a range of proposals, but not until 1791 did the legislature pass the first general canal law, leading to the creation of the Western Inland Lock Navigation Company, or Western Company, in 1792. Canal dreams linked settlement interests and opportunists, banks in the city and in Albany, merchants and farmers—essentially all the industrial players in early national New York.[28]

These dreams soon ran up hard against the realities of state politics. City politicians showed tepid interest in a canal to Lake Erie. They worried about the displacement of power to the west, about the infirmities of capital projects, about money wasted. The Western Company was justifiably regarded as a Federalist project. Among those who did favor a canal to Lake Erie, differences of judgment and interest split over whether to place the terminus at Buffalo or Black Rock. Treasury Secretary Albert Gallatin's 1808 proposal—for a congressionally funded system that linked the Hudson to Lake Champlain and ultimately Lake Ontario, with an upstream bypass around Niagara Falls—introduced the possibility of a new funder and a new venue, yet the possibility of a Jeffersonian project made New York Federalists uneasy.[29]

The New York legislature relaunched a grand canal vision in 1810. Thomas Eddy, the city Quaker who served as the Western Company's treasurer, approached Federalist senator Jonas Platt with an idea to create a commission to oversee a more extensive canal than had been envisioned, an "internal route" connecting the Hudson to Lake Erie. To dilute the company's reputation as a Federalist venture, the seven-seated Board of Canal Commissioners would include prominent Republicans, most notably state treasurer Simeon De Witt, state senator DeWitt Clinton (nephew of Governor

George Clinton), and Peter B. Porter of the Tammany bloc. The Erie Canal project and the Western Company had always been political creatures, but the commission idea now transformed them into a vehicle for cross-partisan hopes and an institution of the state with the imprimatur of credible experts and engineers. The canal commission became an important player in its own right, proposing a project far more expensive than originally envisioned, initiating a lobbying trip to Washington to rally support from affected congressmen, and addressing petitions to western state and territorial governors to gain their backing. These initiatives met with defeat, and the onset of war with Britain in 1812 cast doubt over the entire enterprise. By 1814, Delaware County Republican Erastus Root had built a small but effective anti-commission movement in the legislature, one that attracted the political prodigy Martin Van Buren, then state senator. The senate followed the assembly in stripping the commission of its ability to issue reports (thereby crippling its ability to shape public opinion through print) and to pay engineers and surveyors. Joseph Ellicott of the Holland Land Company wrote that the "Canal bubble it appears, has at length exploded."[30]

Backers of the canal and its commission realized they needed a political strategy. Their essential political work would begin in the city, where politicians and interests were doubtful both of the canal's merits and the commission's credibility, due not least to an abiding distrust of anything Federalist stoked by the war. Simeon De Witt called on Thomas Eddy, now a corporate officer in the Western Company, who convinced his old ally Jonas Platt to call a meeting of the canal's backers to draft a petition to Albany. Eddy united DeWitt Clinton with an old enemy—John Swartwout, former head of the Cayuga Bridge Company—to appear publicly and jointly behind the canal project. Clinton and Swartwout had fallen out since the bridge endeavor, aligning themselves with rival banks, even facing off in a duel. Yet the meeting galvanized a new alliance, and Clinton carefully drafted a petition calling on the legislature to resurrect the commission and the canal. Clinton's advocacy brought city merchants into the fold of the coalition by promising them expanded markets. It also promised benefits for agricultural and manufacturing interests. And Clinton's petition embedded a financing and organizational proposal that appealed to doubtful investors and elites. Clinton concluded his prayer with a stirring call "to erect a work more stupendous, more magnificent and more beneficial than has hitherto been achieved by the human race," one that marked the state's "character" and the "glory of a republic."[31]

The pro-canal petition drawn up and assembled in New York City became a cultural object in its own right, soon known as "the Memorial." Clinton's draft of February 1816 served as the rhetorical and organizational glue by which canal backers put together a coalition. A comprehensive signature-gathering campaign in Manhattan followed, and the "Memorial of the Citizens of New York" arrived in Albany on February 16, 1816, with more than one thousand signatures. Other petitions flowed from Buffalo, Seneca, Reading, and Geneva on February 21. Legislators then observed an onslaught of memorials from throughout the Empire State. By late March, the mass of names had reportedly surpassed one hundred thousand signatures.[32]

These petitions proved remarkably forceful. They helped to knit together an alliance of city interests with western and central state townships, and of Federalists with Republicans. They placed the canal idea in the minds of hundreds of thousands of men and women. These petitions were drawn up at a propitious time for those seeking charters and infrastructure grants, as the legislature's 1816 session saw a boom in charter requests. State lawmakers chartered two additional banks in 1816, four more in 1817, and another four in 1818. Upon their delivery to Albany, moreover, the petitions' sheer weight overwhelmed the politicians who saw them.[33] Martin Van Buren, earlier opposed to the canal, would remark that "our tables have groaned with the petitions of the people from every section of our country in favor of it. And not a solitary voice has been raised against it."[34] The state senate reporter documented his change of volition: "He considered it the most important vote he ever gave in his life. . . . He repeated that we were bound to consider that the people have given their assent. Twelve thousand men of wealth and respectability in the city of New York, last year petitioned for the canal."[35]

With the votes of Van Buren and others, the legislature passed a canal law in 1817. The canal was finally completed in 1825. Its construction spelled doom for the Oneida in New York.[36]

Citizens, engineers, scholars, and students have learned of the Erie Canal as a monumental advance in American transportation, an exemplar of the state-funded infrastructure drive of the early nineteenth century. As a political project, the canal owed its life to the incipient culture of popular petitioning, albeit one still tethered to insider advocacy. The city's backers chose as their political instrument a massively canvassed documentary appeal to the state legislature. DeWitt Clinton's 1816 "Memorial" joined cross-factional coalition building with popular boosterism, and it amounted to a rather limited triumph of democracy. In part, the Clinton memorial aimed at the very kind of monopoly chartering that banks and turnpike companies desired. The pivotal signatures for Van Buren came not from Buffalo, Reading, or Rome but from "men of wealth and respectability in the city of New York."[37] Even in those towns to the west, such as Batavia and Canandaigua, local notables such as Robert Troup, Gideon Granger, and Nathaniel Howell led the pro-canal petition meetings. Soon the canal commission itself became the preferred venue for settlement and industrial battles.[38]

SETTLER PETITIONING IN THE AMERICAN WEST AND SOUTH

The states and territories west and south of New York had neither the capital nor the strength of party organization found in the Empire State, and their petitioning politics differed considerably. Incorporated land companies had served as a staple feature of British colonies in the eighteenth century. Yet the American Revolution unsettled the business of settlement and reshaped its terms, compelling land companies to appeal to state legislatures. Where territorial governments in the Old Northwest and Old Southwest were forming, the locus of authority for land access, chartering, and Indian removal was far less certain. It often fell to the federal government to sort out a welter of conflicting claims. Land companies, settlers, and other interests, including Native Americans, appealed to Congress and to its claims system. The reality of multiple venues both complicated and advanced the world of insider petitioning and occasionally created broad counterpetitioning movements that claimed a republican mantle.[39]

Republicans against Land Companies—the Contest of Petitions at Yazoo

Among its first acts as a state in the new nation, Georgia in 1789 recognized the claims of several land companies to a vast tract of land in what is now Alabama and Mississippi. Settlers named these the Yazoo lands after the river that ran through them, whose mouth at the Mississippi River (at present-day Vicksburg) offered a highly desired site for development. The South Carolina Yazoo Company had begun a small settlement there in the years before and now petitioned the Georgia legislature to confirm the company's interest. Other land companies—the Virginia Yazoo Company and the Tennessee Company—added petitions of their own.[40]

Georgia's claim on these spaces was anything but firm. Both settler communities and land companies who desired these lands regarded them indisputably as places occupied past and present by Indigenous peoples—Choctaw, Chickasaw, Creek, and Cherokee. And aside from Georgia, the state of South Carolina, the federal government, and the Spanish also asserted jurisdiction over Yazoo. Georgia worried that its western lands were a drag on the state, indefensible given the state's meager resources, and outside the ambit of its republican model. The state approved the claims in 1789. The land companies, for their part, had not planned on immediately colonizing and settling the lands but instead expressing their claim and conveying a series of payments. Their failure to meet the terms and schedule of payments invalidated the project and left the Yazoo lands in further limbo after 1791.[41]

In 1795, the land companies returned with more powerful lobbies and allies, and a bill passed by the Georgia legislature would precipitate a crisis of state and nation. Georgia sold the western lands to four companies—the Georgia Company, the Georgia Mississippi Company, the Upper Mississippi Company, and the Tennessee Company. The Georgia Company was headed by Senator James Gunn, who had been reelected the year before to the U.S. Senate by the very legislature he now petitioned and lobbied aggressively. With his company partners, Gunn submitted a proposal to the Georgia legislature: $500,000 for an estimated 21.4 million acres of land. He then defeated rival bidders, eased his bill past a gubernatorial veto, spiced his measure with reserve lands for militia members and Georgia citizens, and fended off a rival proposal that offered $800,000 to the state and left millions more acres to Georgia citizens. The Yazoo Act of 1795 left Gunn and his associates with about half the land—10,762,000 acres—purchased at a price of 2.33 cents an acre. The state legislature had just sold off spaces whose size equaled that of Great Britain.[42]

Gunn's enmeshment with the legislature, the favorable terms his company received, and his defeat of more generous proposals all combined to create the case for corruption on a vast geographic and financial scale. Protests ensued, charged both philosophically and emotively, and they resulted in one of the most democratic petitioning and pamphleteering moments of the early Republic. Georgia's other senator, James Jackson, led the agitation over the Yazoo sale. Jackson attacked its squandering of public resources and, most centrally, its undermining of republican government. Whereas the Georgia state constitution "breathes Republican & equality principles," Jackson lamented, the legislature in the Yazoo Act "establishes Aristocratic Bodies, in those Speculating Companies."[43]

Petitions by the dozens, signed by thousands, targeted the state constitutional convention of May 1795. Listing seven grievances against the Yazoo Act, the petitions focused on violations of the state constitution, the lack of necessity for such a giant measure, and a more generous deal foregone. The act was "obtained by fraud, collusion and corruption" and surrendered vast spaces and sovereignties. It raised the specter of "a military government, and all the arbitrary concomitants thereof," including titles of nobility, "enormous and unequal possessions," and an abandonment of republican principles. The petitioners, writing as "We the People (from whom all power originates)," instructed the legislature to render "utterly null and void, and of none effect" the 1795 law and the claims granted under it.[44]

The anti-Yazoo petitions advanced not merely an argument but a portrait of a coalition in formation. They flowed heavily from two regions in the state: Chatham and Effingham Counties near Savannah, and Burke, Elbert, Oglethorpe, and Washington Counties near Augusta and the upper Savannah River watershed. In Burke County, which likely provided more signatories (over seven hundred) than any other, petition signers often included Revolutionary War veterans who had just recently come into new lands—such as Daniel Boatwright, Jonathan Coleman, Levi Emanuel, Elijah Sapp, and James Young—and their families. Some members of these families, such as David Emanuel, who represented Burke County at the constitutional convention of 1795 and in the Georgia senate after 1796, would soon become leading officeholders of the anti-Yazoo revolution.[45]

While the convention of 1795 declined to nullify the Yazoo sale, it regarded the petitions and memorials as evidence of the public's will and transmitted them to the next meeting of the Georgia General Assembly. Many of the newly elected legislators had pledged to undo the Yazoo Act, and immediately upon taking office they established a committee to investigate the sale. James Jackson chaired this committee, which also included Burke County's David Emanuel. The committee regarded the petitions (along with accompanying grand jury presentments) as the core of their evidence on public welfare. The rescinding act, almost certainly authored by Jackson, figuratively erased the putative aristocracy and corruption embedded in the 1795 legislature. Upon the rescinding law's passage, the Jackson committee called for the expunging of the 1795 law from the books and a public burning of the offending pages. Drawing inspiration from "the said petitions and remonstrations of the good people composing the state" and from the French Revolution, anti-Yazoo legislators proclaimed the true form of Georgia's government a "republican democracy": "a government founded on equality of rights; and which is totally opposed to all proprietary grants or monopolies in favor of a few, which tend to build up that destructive aristocracy in the new, which is tumbling in the old world."[46]

Georgia's reversal of the Yazoo Act sent shock waves through surrounding states and into northern investor networks. In the evanescent moment they held the Yazoo lands, Gunn's Georgia Company and the other companies had sold many claims to other speculators, including northern land companies existing and in formation. When the Yazoo land sale collapsed, the fate of these speculators took two different but intertwined paths. Some, like Bostonian James Greenleaf and Gideon Denison of the North American Land Company, fell deeply into debt and thereby into ill health or prison. Other investors, like the youthful proprietor John Peck of Boston, survived and turned to politics and to petitioning. Investors joined with Georgia Company principals to form a coalition of Yazoo claimants, and they repeatedly petitioned Congress in the years after 1796.[47]

Yazoo claimants turned to petitioning and lobbying because they needed to coordinate and because they were desperate for a change in venue. The concatenating networks of claimants would not organize themselves, and congressional petitioning and lobbying provided a synchronizing vehicle. And the beneficiaries of 1795 wanted to shift the turf from Georgia in its Jeffersonian democratic moment to a federal government where a different audience, as well as the debt and supremacy clauses of the Constitution, might change the game.

Peck and his New England land company allies knew that they were unlikely to see the lands returned. In 1798, Congress established the Mississippi Territory, and in 1802, Georgia ceded the lands to the federal government for a per-acre value over twice that of the 1795 law. In lieu of land, they wanted a monetary settlement from Congress. Their petitions therefore targeted not the body in general but the Claims Committee, strongly hinting at a suit in federal court to resolve the issue of title. After rejecting a set of Virginia claims in 1804, the House received so many in 1805 that it charged the Claims Committee with bundling petitions and examining them in a summary report. The report proposed the creation of a commission to resolve the claims, which produced a partial compromise in 1808. John Peck's petitions eventually triggered a court case that wound its way to John Marshall's Supreme Court. The court's decision in *Fletcher v. Peck* (1810) found in favor of Peck and the land company claimants and established an important precedent for the inviolability of contract and judicial review of state statutes. In the decades following *Fletcher v. Peck*, Yazoo claimants continued to petition Washington for recognition or benefits, stoking a debate in the Senate about just how much Congress could serve as an alternative venue to the federal courts. The American culture of petitioning flourished under the uncertainty that any one venue had the final word.[48]

Further north and west, the federal government took a more prominent role in adjudicating claims. In the Ohio Valley, upper Mississippi Valley, and Great Lakes regions, larger Native populations lived in the midst of French settlers and incoming Anglo-American migrants. The U.S. settlement model focused on treaty-based Indian removal; economic development premised on farming and the construction of roads, bridges, canals, and water transport; the creation of new states (and, within them, counties); and the peopling of "the West" with White settlers who would multiply themselves and the adherents of the Christian (especially Protestant) faith.[49]

The War of 1812 had extinguished British aspirations to these lands and weakened the already tenuous hold of Indigenous communities on them. Before, during, and after the war, American settlers mounted regular attacks on Indigenous villages and tribes, relying on the hastily organized militia systems and the U.S. Army. The war combined with a resurgence of Indigenous nationalism and religious movements—led most notably by the prophets Tecumseh and Tenskwatawa—to induce Native Americans to take up arms against settler communities, to disengage from the treaty-making process, and to resist settler encroachment.[50]

The resulting contests—of settler versus Indian, old settler versus new, migrant Native versus existing Native, territory versus state versus militia—were also games of petitioning. Territorial and state legislatures provided one set of venues, while the various organs of the federal government—Congress, the War Department, commissions established for treaty making or land disposition, and the federal court system—offered another. In part because jurisdictions remained both unclear and unstable, none of these venues offered a sure victory. Political success would depend on the allies recruited and on the audiences that heard them—especially governors and legislatures. Petition provided a common approach to all of them, though less so in courts.

William Henry Harrison made his career in these spaces and practices. As sovereign and as supplicant, he built a living and a reputation at the boundaries of jurisdictions, roles, and loyalties. Harrison served as governor of Indiana Territory from 1800 to 1812 and as a general in the war from 1812 to 1814. His legislative connections and his loyalty to the Jefferson and Madison administrations would position him well to approach Congress. In the midst of the multinational Native mobilization by Tecumseh, Harrison began receiving petitions for protection from settlers in the Indiana Territory. They asked for information and for reinforcements, including an occasional display of force by militia.[51]

Harrison instigated petitions not only for Indian removal but for Indian war. In 1811, he lobbied a group of Protestant ministers to advance their claim on the lands of the Old Northwest as sacred places, and to do so in a petition to President Madison. The preachers' petition decried "the impunity" and the "insolence" of "these savages [who] have been so long suffered to commit crimes." Presenting themselves as sober ministers of the Gospel, they cast their request as an act not of belligerence but of necessity: "Our object is peace—but we are fully persuaded that that blessing can now only be secured to us by the exertion of some rigor."[52] Another petition to Madison came from settlers in Knox County, and it framed Prophetstown as a British endeavor, maintaining that "the safety of the persons and property of this frontier can never be effectually secured" but by an attack on the village.[53] These appeals openly invited the U.S. government into war against "the Prophet" Tenskwatawa, and Madison responded as Harrison and the ministers wished. Harrison led militia forces in a November assault on Tenskwatawa at Prophetstown. The ensuing battle became inscribed in American national memory as "Tippecanoe." It remapped the American political imaginary for at least a generation.[54]

Right after Harrison's battle with the Native prophets, settlers in his region began asking the U.S. government for a more extensive military presence. Residents of Michigan Territory, organizing themselves as a committee of public safety, called for permanently stationed army troops. "An increase of military force is necessary," they pleaded, "sufficient to man the works, and afford a body to march out, in aid of the militia; a part cavalry." They asked for garrisons on "points of the Northwestern frontier," near Detroit; at the mouth of the Wisconsin River; and another on the Missouri River.

On this petitioning committee sat the most notable men of the Jeffersonian settlement regime in Michigan, including Augustus Woodward, then chief justice of the territory, and Solomon Sibley, soon to serve as its congressional representative. Settlers in St. Clair County in Illinois Territory petitioned Madison in the same month, calling for garrisons at Peoria and on the Mississippi, as well as the provision of rifles and muskets.[55]

During and after the war with Britain, Harrison and his Indiana Territory allies both used and responded to petitions to define and consolidate a settlement regime. Many of the lands in the territory were set aside for militia members who served in the war. When citizens of Wayne County petitioned the legislature of the territory for benefits to compensate for losses of farm product during their militia service, the houses took the petition to Congress. When Congress returned the petition without action, reporting that the memorial had not specified the members of the militia companies, the legislature transmitted a second petition complete with muster rolls documenting the service of the company members.[56]

The petitions of state and territorial legislatures converted the federal government into an on-demand military authority, an insurance organ, and ultimately a land enterprise of its own. As sovereign, the territorial legislature received petitions from settlers but in many cases lacked the money, arms, or clear legal authority to act on them. The legislature thus became the supplicant, which begged the national sovereign for troops and guns. The supplicant pleaded for the nation to pay off settlers' losses due to service rendered against the British and against Indians. The supplicant then demanded, with ever greater assertiveness after the war, to speed the process of extinguishing Indian title and move forward with surveying, sale, and settlement.

These petitions undermine the narrative of Indian removal in the United States as primarily a story of Andrew Jackson and his allies. There is truth in this, but a partial one. Jackson's actions in the late 1820s and 1830s met long-standing wishes of the settler republic—wishes expressed, refined, communicated, and ultimately achieved through petitions for dispossession, removal, and acquisition. And no petitioner for Indian removal appeared as commonly before Congress as the state or territorial legislature. Whether the Georgia legislature in 1817, Georgia and the Arkansas territorial assembly in 1823, or, most elaborately, the North Carolina legislature in 1827, state assemblies harnessed the most robust and intricate of their procedures for preparing these appeals. They often created select committees to draft these memorials and placed some of their most talented legal minds and preeminent elites on them. Thereby carefully drawn up, pro-removal memorials wrought a vivid portrait of the American racial imaginary and the necessary Whiteness of the spaces they desired. North Carolina legislators proposed that "the fertility of soil, the extent and value of territory, are sufficient inducements to urge the extinguishment of [Cherokee] Indian title. . . . These are not the only inducements; the red men are not within the pale of civilization, they are not under the restraints of morality, nor the influence of religion; and they are always disagreeable and dangerous neighbors to a civilized people. The proximity of those red men to our white population, subjects the latter to depredations and annoyance, and is a source of perpetual and mutual irritation."[57]

Settler petitioning thus embedded the invective of an avowed racism into the routines and rhetoric of early America's principal instrument of popular sovereignty: the state legislature.

So well-honed had the legislative petition mechanism become by the 1820s and 1830s that incipient settler republics turned these parchment weapons on each another. Before its admission to the union, Michigan Territory repeatedly advanced claims over lands at its border with Ohio. Michigan Territory residents had been using petitions to advance claims on lands in Ohio since the end of the war. Continued friction from settlement and claims of trespassing would reach levels of hostility in 1831, when the Ohio legislature petitioned Congress to resolve the matter, to no avail. Matters reached a boiling point when, in its statehood petition of 1835, Michigan declared jurisdiction over the "Toledo Strip," a small piece of land over which existing claims of Ohio were not settled. Parrying this assertion, the Ohio congressional delegation held up Michigan's admission to the union. Michigan officials' attempted enforcement of their claims led to the Toledo War of 1835, involving mildly violent confrontations between Michigan's self-styled settlers and their "trespasser" adversaries from Ohio. A slew of settlers' protests, including court presentments and petitions to the Legislative Council of Michigan, resulted in a convention in Ann Arbor, at which Michigan reluctantly agreed to Ohio's claims in order to enter the union.[58]

As in antebellum New York State, the settlement models of the American interior prized canals and water transport. Robert Livingston and Robert Fulton would not confine their imperial visions to a linkage between the Atlantic Ocean and the Great Lakes. In 1809 and 1810 they flooded state and territorial authorities with petitions for monopolies—the legislatures of Kentucky and Ohio; the governor of Tennessee; and governors and lawmakers in the territories of Indiana, Michigan, Orleans, Upper Louisiana, and Mississippi. These overtures largely failed, often on the grounds of antimonopoly sentiment. In 1810, Livingston traveled to Orleans Territory and sought the alliance of Governor William C. C. Claiborne, who was at the time presenting a statehood petition for Louisiana to Congress. After plying the spendthrift Claiborne with favors and inviting him for a ride on one of the Fulton's steamboats, Claiborne joined the steamboat regime. The territorial legislature obliged in April 1811, and the Fulton-Livingston steamboat monopoly—fueled as much by insider lobbying and petitioning as by anthracite—became an object of industrial fascination, commercial jealousy, and political suspicion.[59]

Thus did the early American nation and its settler republics in states and territories build a century's economy on the basis of settlement and dispossession, slavery and capital, and statutory privileges. The world of petitioning occasionally opened itself to a greater equality of claims—as in the Yazoo crisis—but more often it rewarded advantages in factional rivalries and elite networks. Insider petitioning never unfolded with clean predictability. Monopolies, land claims, and settlement dreams were just as often undone by petitions as they were made through them. Yet petitioning formed the necessary turf on which battles for early American settlement dreams were fought.

SETTLEMENT PETITIONING IN MEXICAN SPACES

Spain claimed vast spaces in early nineteenth-century North America. In governing this area, the Crown developed a settlement regime that melded colonial institutions of control with reliance on custom and Indigenous alliances. As in British Canada and the United States, petitions for land functioned to encourage and regulate settlement according to an ideal settler model. Imperial Spain did not permit land grants to foreigners, and Catholics were heavily favored. The land grant system relied heavily on petitions as legal devices that both channeled and subordinated local politics. At the close of the nineteenth century, the imperial government began to implement agricultural, town-based settlement visions, most notably in the Plan de Pitic of 1789. The Plan de Pitic covered the "internal provinces" of New Spain: Sonora, California, Nueva Vizcaya (contemporary Chihuahua), and

Nuevo México. Water, especially in permanent streams, figured every bit as much as land in these farming visions. Diversion of these waters into *acequia* systems (ditches and canals) required a petitioning process of its own.[60]

In the internal provinces and other areas removed from Mexico City, men with arms figured centrally in these settlement plans. Late imperial Spain and Mexico both relied on military forces to wrest spaces from Natives and to defend them from attack. Settlement interests in these Spanish-governed spaces contended with Indigenous peoples and existing Hispanos. As in the Old Northwest and Old Southwest in the United States, dominant models of settlement favored those who combined habitation with armed protection. As they retired or left existing positions, military men petitioned for benefits, promotions, or legal powers (*fueros* or *licencias absolutas*) from the imperial governor, and when army captains relayed these requests, they often featured tales of heroism in fighting Indians. One captain from the colonial province of New Santander conveyed the 1808 petition of his sergeant, who, "having found himself in many a battle against the barbarous Indians who attack this province, . . . endeavored with his intrepid spirit to kill with his own hand four of the barbarous aggressors." Other requests noted the successful Indian-removing activity of settler communities and proposed rewarding and sustaining these populations with land grants and other benefits. Veterans' petitions for benefits were moderated by the imperial hierarchy, and they created resources for armed settlers. After independence, the Mexican regime would similarly reward army veterans and militia members with land grants by welcoming their land petitions and inducing them to settle.[61]

In the complicated terrain of colonial Nuevo México, land grant petitioners sought both to dispossess Indigenous peoples and to gain their alliance. The racial landscape of Nuevo México separated Hispanos, Pueblo Indians, and mixed-race *genízaros* (non-Pueblo Indian captives owned by Hispanos or sometimes Pueblos, as well as their descendants). *Genízaros* moved between worlds of Indigenous and Spanish, slave and free. Their existence at cultural boundaries positioned them as negotiators across cultures, and they frequently signed land grant petitions.

Two turn-of-the-century petitions to Nuevo México governor Fernando Chacón illustrate the unsettled dynamics of settlement by petition. When fifty-two inhabitants of Santa Fe petitioned Chacón in 1794 for a plot on the Pecos River, thirteen *genízaro* family heads were among the petitioners.

Chacón granted the petition but only on the stipulation that the residents possess firearms. Six years later a land grant petition at Cebolleta by elite settler families brought an immediate counterpetition by Río Puerco Navajos who countered that the Cebolleta grant would cut into their grazing lands. Chacón rejected the Navajo protest and granted the petition. The Navajo responded with an attack on the settlement, killing all its stock and twelve shepherds, and forcing the Hispano families to abandon the grant. In the ensuing decades, *genízaro* men would consistently accompany Hispano land petitioners in appeals to colonial governors.[62]

The war for independence and the Mexican victory in 1821 transformed the stakes and the process of land acquisition. Mexico's more liberal model opened settlement and trade to non-Spaniards, and the expansion of American activity in the Mississippi River basin accentuated the pressure on its government to encourage settlement. Mexico's Colonization Law of 1824 allowed grants of eleven square leagues, or about 48,000 acres, and the government opened land acquisition to foreigners in the Regulations of 1828. Procedurally, the Mexican government delegated important decisions to territorial governors and to local *alcaldes*, the mayoral officials who governed townships. Land grants required a petition to the territorial governor detailing the lands sought, the qualifications of the claimant, and documentation of the absence of competing claims and uses of the land. The governor often relayed the petition to the *alcalde*, who weighed in with his recommendation. The *alcalde*'s role was officially advisory but in New Mexico, California, and other internal provinces, the *alcaldes* carried significant weight, given their legitimacy in local networks. In many but not all cases, the *alcalde* would solicit responses from Pueblo Indians or Hispano settlers who might have interests in the land.[63]

Mexican land petitions had both legal and political features. Spanish and Mexican land law generally distinguished between private grants and community grants, the essential difference being that community land grants both set aside a commons (immune from settlement) and listed the prospective settlers in the grant petition. In New Mexico and other internal provinces of the Mexican regime, most of the land grants were community grants, and these required a principal petitioner (*principal solicitante* or *poblador principal*) to represent the settler group. A successful grant required persuading the *alcalde* of the petitioner's need for the land, a settlement plan, the suitability of the *poblador* and his group, and the absence or paucity of competing claims.[64]

Far beyond their legal status, however, Spanish-regime land petitions expressed, even impelled, the local politics of mass settlement. They frequently set in motion a set of protests and counterpetitions that could not have been predicted beforehand. These political contests would mobilize various interests, sometimes Hispanos versus Natives, sometimes older claim holders against new petitioners who drew on their military service to invalidate claims granted under the Spanish regime. Moreover, the uncertainty of legal claims and the dominance of custom and gubernatorial discretion opened space for competition between elite families and new-settler versus old-settler interests. Though the land grant process officially reserved a voice for Indigenous people (communally and individually), wealthy, well-connected claimants could override the claims of Natives. Despite persistent petitioning from *genízaros* at Abiquiú pueblo seeking to preserve their community lands, a number of Hispano settlers carved out land tracts from individual sales in the Mexican period, especially after the Spanish Cortes declared in favor of privatization of unused pueblo lands in 1812 and 1813, a decree that remained in force well into the 1820s.[65]

After Mexican independence, these petitioning battles would involve the full range of political and legal institutions governing the internal provinces. From the early nineteenth century onward, settlers in Nuevo México cast their eyes on the lands at the confluence of the east and west branches of the Rio Chama, known as Tierra Amarilla (yellow earth). In 1814, 1820, and again in 1824, settlers asked for community grants on these lands, but all these petitions were refused by the governor. When in 1832 Manuel Martinez sought a land claim at Tierra Amarilla, his petition was referred not to the *alcalde* but to the local council, the *ayuntamiento* of Abiquiú. The *ayuntamiento* approved Martinez's grant as a community grant, but Martinez quickly petitioned the governor in protest, arguing that he had wanted a private grant. Governor Santiago Abreú then referred the matter to the provincial deputation of Nuevo México, which appointed a three-man commission to decide the question. Martinez received a community grant, which was converted to a private claim by the U.S. government in 1860. The shifting of venues and the flurry of petitions had involved two legislative bodies and an ad hoc commission as well as the governor.[66]

While land institutions and law were ever changing, the regulations imposed real limits on claims. The contesting aspirations of two Hispano settlers—Captain Bartolomé Baca and Don Antonio Sandoval—and their descendants lay bare these constraints. The scion of a Spanish aristocratic family, Baca petitioned Governor Facundo Melgares for a land grant in 1819, drawing on his connections to Spanish elites and his reputation as a militia leader at Albuquerque a decade before. The governor granted the petition and left to José Garcia de la Mora, *alcalde* of Tome, the transfer of land, conditioned on fulfillment of criteria observed by the *alcalde*. Baca took hold of a vast tract of land in present-day Torrance County. Baca would soon become governor and captain general of New Mexico. He occupied only a small part of the land granted to him, and frequent Navajo raids compelled him to abandon the tract. In 1845, the Mexican government carved from the Baca grant a new tract of about 400,000 acres—containing two artesian water sources—and awarded it to Don Antonio Sandoval for his "services to the Mexican government." The amount of land was well in excess of the eleven leagues per settlement permitted by the colonization regulations of 1828, and the Congreso Nacional never ratified the grant. Like Baca before him, Sandoval soon left the property, and the grant lands shuffled among various owners until the late nineteenth century, when Baca's and Sandoval's descendants faced off in federal court over the claim. In 1897 (*Bergere v. United States*) and again in 1901 (*Whitney v. United States*), the U.S. Supreme Court would sort out these titles based on a reading of Spanish and Mexican law. The Baca descendants eventually won, in part because the Sandoval grant of 1845 was too large and had never been confirmed by the Congreso Nacional. As Justice Rufus Peckham and his cosigners resolved the Baca-Sandoval contest, they cited a congeries of faded institutions—the enormous discretion of Spanish governors, the authority that Mexican governments delegated to provincial governors and further to *alcaldes*, the necessary approval of the provincial land grants by the Mexican legislature—that had left a durable imprint on New Mexican geography.[67]

The formal openness of Mexico's land petition system—the fact that foreigners could request land, that Indigenous communities had an aperture for protest and claims of their own, that multiple venues were brought into play—disguised some harder realities of power. Elites under the Mexican regime often sat as arbiters on one petition while, in a neighboring vicinity, they applied for land with petitions of their own. Mexican regime elites had sprawling families with marriage and patronage links to *alcaldes*, governors, judges, and priests. The Beaubien family and the Martínez family were active in New Mexican land petitioning as speculators from the 1820s through the 1840s, not least because they correctly foresaw the influx of settlement after 1821, when the Santa Fe Trail opened and patterns of St. Louis–Santa

Fe–Chihuahua trade crystallized. Padre Martínez not only applied for land in the 1830s and 1840s but also persuaded allies to request federal subsidies for the region in 1832. Elite petitioning crossed boundaries of land and water, church and state, legislative and judicial, Hispano and Anglo. Not unlike the settler republics of the United States, independent Mexico favored a certain model of citizenship, one that prized Catholicism, respectability, prior service to the Mexican cause, and the wherewithal to spur economic development. Soon the contests would involve debates over slavery and venue.[68]

* * *

The seemingly relentless expansion of North American societies after 1789 cloaked a massive institutional friction. The building blocks of a settler republic often required a labor of supplication for things only a legislative or an administrative sovereign could deliver. Settlers, speculators, and would-be rulers had to ask not merely for land and water but also for bridges, canals, transport companies, banks, monopolies, organs of government and justice, rights to slaves, and the removal of Indigenous peoples. Whether in Spanish and Mexican law or in Canada, with its mix of British imperial and French seigneurial institutions, or in the United States, with its distributed legislative and administrative sovereigns, building expansive societies required petitioning.[69]

The insatiable demands of settler interests ran up against the gatekeeping of sovereigns. The petitioning politics that ensued had democratic moments but remained a world of insider advocacy, of networked claims. Even as new political models of republics, democracies, unions, and breakaway churches emerged, the model of insider petitioning expressed an older logic of monarchs and empires, in which an approach on bended knee to a sovereign could grant supremely powerful goods—such as monopolies, charters, and the protection of the state—to those whose humility remained a fiction.

FIVE

First Nations, First Wave Petitioners

> These [white men] ought to be our truest friends but prove to be our worst enemies. They seem to be only concerned how to increase their riches, but do not care what becomes of our Nation.
>
> —**Cherokee women's petition, 1818**

> Oh White man, white man, the blood of our fathers spilt in the Revolutionary War from the ground of our native soil. . . . Brake the chains of oppression & let our children go free—.
>
> —**Mashpee Revolt petition, 1834**

> Such is the language of the Indians: what they say is true; what they forebode seems to me inevitable. From whichever side one considers the fate of the indigenous of North America, one sees nothing but irreparable evils.
>
> —**Alexis de Tocqueville, *Democracy in America***

In 1835, John Ross—leader of the Cherokee Nation—sketched out an essay that cast his people's predicament in global, historical, and spiritual relief. In "The Contrast," he juxtaposed two moments: one sacred, the other utterly unholy. Before traversing the Atlantic, the Quakers had sent "addresses and prayers soliciting relief for their sufferings" to their English king, who, "needless of their supplications, ran on his career of luxury, mocking at the disquietude of his petitioners."[1] They left for "America, the land of Religious Tolerance," Ross wrote, where they met "not only the good will, but the confidence of the Indians."[2] Together, Quaker and Indian engaged in a policy of mutual toleration and liberty. Yet even as the Friends "acknowledged the validity of the Indians' title to the land," other Christian denominations repeatedly betrayed Indigenous Americans' trust over centuries of colonization.[3] Now, with Andrew Jackson as president, the ultimate infidelity came in the federal government's policy of removing all tribes west of the Mississippi River. Indian removal busted older agreements and substituted a new covenant, the Treaty of New Echota—"this instrument of fraud"—which rendered in ink a fictional assent by the Cherokee, having been signed by a distinct minority of tribal members and not its acknowledged leadership.[4]

John Ross wrote with despair and determination. Beyond dispossession, Cherokee removal was spiritual warfare. In the ejection of communities from sacred spaces, Georgians and the U.S. government had mounted an attack on soul and soil, on a people's hallowed link with their ancestors. These spiritual and earthly linkages defined what Ross consciously termed a "nation." The Cherokee lay claim to their land based "on the ties of patriotism which bound them to their Country." As he poured his laments into "The Contrast," Ross had just led a campaign that delivered petitions with thousands of Cherokee signatures to the U.S. Congress. Yet "to all remonstrances came the stern reply 'it is the settled policy—you must go.'" The American government had forsaken the example of the Quakers, behaving instead like the seventeenth-century English monarchy in both visiting evil upon a minority and refusing to hear its just complaints.[5]

Alexis de Tocqueville noted these petitions, too, in 1835, and felt himself moved to a mix of pity and resignation. The ethicist in the French aristocrat acknowledged the truth in the Cherokees' grievances. Injustice was being performed on them. The prognosticator in Tocqueville foresaw nothing short of extinction. Not only did he, like other Europeans, view Indigenous North Americans as racially inferior, but he also saw the relentless machineries of settlement and "civilization" at work. Tocqueville wrote at a time when Indigenous resistance to these machineries was emerging all around him. He saw these iniquities unfold on a continent-wide canvas, not just in the United States but in North America more generally, including the Canadian colonies he had just toured.

That Indigenous North Americans would remain at all—battered, traumatized, split from kin, and evicted from their homeland—is due in part to the political alliances, legal and ethical claims, and spiritual counterattack that they mounted through petitions. Men like Ross and the Seneca orator Sagoyewatha and women such as Nancy Ward and Jenny McIntosh exercised new forms of minority politics and Indigenous diplomacy through written appeals backed by the signatures of dozens, hundreds, even thousands. The most famous interpreter of American democracy reflected at length on these documents, focusing his reading on petitions, just as he had analyzed signed grievances in his study of the French Revolution, which had shaken his motherland a generation before. The Indigenous words Tocqueville found "true" had not just been uttered anywhere but been inscribed and distributed in petitions.[6]

John Ross wrote in the midst of, and about, this Native petitioning moment. The Quakers he praised had served as among the most active allies in the Cherokee Nation's fight against removal, and they had also assisted other tribes to the north, including the Haudenosaunee in New York. Ross himself had launched several petitioning campaigns in the 1820s and 1830s. In ways that he knew, and in ways no one fully recognized at the time, his writings marked a longer moment of Indigenous voice. In the early nineteenth century, Native North Americans began to petition at much higher rates, and in different modes, in a wave of activity that would endure through the century. Because they assisted in recruiting tribal communities and allies to Indigenous causes, these petitioning moments enhanced organizational democracy. They also advanced procedural democracy by effectively placing Indigenous issues on local, ecclesiastical, tribal, state, and national agendas.

These memorials—thousands upon thousands of them—call for anything but simplistic celebration or crude appraisals. Despite their surge in petitioning, Indigenous North Americans saw White settlers wrest from them millions of acres of land, and they lost invaluable human communities and traditions in the process. Native petitioning also surged as an older dynamic of treaty councils waned; the reduction of Indigenous military power compelled Native North Americans to pursue a different strategy, one that partook of diplomatic traditions among equal nations but also recognized the sovereignty of settler governments. The documents that remain require cautious readings. Those who claimed to speak in the name of a tribe or a village were often advancing their own aims. A translator or scribe could render Native appeals inaccurately or simplistically based on outdated understandings of Indigenous politics from a previous century or on brute settler mentalities that continued to portray Natives as "savages"—as incorrigibly "wild" and "hostile." Natives' self-styled allies were often grasping for their own stake in Indian lands or maneuvering for their continued perch as privileged and governmentally paid religious overseers. In other cases, petitions played out in factional splits between villages and pueblos. Those who claimed to speak for a people in fact represented one bloc, one "party," one clan, or one phratry in a contentious alliance whose internal bouts spanned from just a few years to decades or centuries.

Yet the transformation was real. Native North American petitioning has a history as old as Indigenous diplomacy itself, but early nineteenth-century Native petitioning took on new force and frequency. The first sign is that writer after writer, minister after priest, politician after politician began to remark upon these petitions and began to puzzle over them, asking themselves and others how to read them and what to do with them. From Alexis de Tocqueville to Henry Clay and Lewis Cass, from newspaper editors to legislators, elite White men wrestled with the petitions of Indigenous North Americans. So did Native leaders and orators, some of whom, like the Shawnee Prophet Tenskwatawa, openly disdained the petitioning movement. The second is that Indigenous petitions met with counterpetitioning movements, attempts at suppression, or cessation of settlement initiatives. Allies and opponents of Native communities recognized that they needed to act in response to these memorials, and they often did so by organizing petition campaigns of their own. The third sign of Native petitioning vitality is that these memorials began to upend politics within and among Indigenous villages and tribes. Petitions allowed women and warriors and those in a less privileged clan or family to take their case outside older diplomatic channels and address settler governments directly. The fourth sign is that, in some cases, Native petitions met with limited but appreciable success. Some of these partial triumphs came in the 1820s and 1830s. Still others would await the 1840s and 1850s but would rest on earlier mobilizations.

Indigenous North Americans were leading actors in the institutional conversion of the petition to a democratizing instrument. They petitioned to consolidate political community and build organizations, to shape and maintain alliances, to perform administrative and judicial work along with legislative advocacy, and to claim (and occasionally advance) their equal sovereignty. To observe this is neither to claim that they were somehow "the first petitioners" nor to claim that important developments in petitioning, including Indigenous petitioning, had not preceded this moment. To ask who authored the first petition is akin to asking who uttered the first prayer. The practice remains so ubiquitous in human history that the question begs reformulation. Indigenous North Americans, like White settlers and free and enslaved Blacks, had petitioned repeatedly in the centuries before 1800. They had taken their supplications, requests, and complaints to French, English, and Spanish monarchs; to British, French, and Spanish colonial governors; and to colonial legislatures and courts.

The Native North American petitioning moment of the early nineteenth century unfolded in ways both similar to and different from previous waves. In a vein of continuity, Indigenous petitioners grafted new modes of minority politics onto an ancient instrument of diplomacy and rule. They also harnessed and repurposed diplomatic practices honed over many centuries of experience with imperial governments. The surge was different in that whereas other minority petitioning connected deeply with national and state-granted citizenship, Native petitioning surged in a more liminal space of ambiguity and continuance, somewhere between formal citizenship and complete exclusion. Many Native petitions claimed neither and both, asking for the rights of legal citizens and White men even as they called for the ejection of Whites from their spaces, proclaiming their membership in nations from time immemorial.

In the millennial timescale of Indigenous North America, these petitions also marked a conscious and collective reassertion of nationality. In an earlier time, colonial powers had acknowledged the nation-state status of these alternative powers. Yet now North American governments were confining the identity of Indigenous communities to that of "tribe," a pattern etched into constitutional law in the McIntosh decision with the description of tribes as "domestic dependent nations." Indigenous petitioning communities declared themselves originary nations. Indeed, they invoked concepts of "nation" even when representing the identity of one village among others in a larger tribal population.

Why the surge? Too often at the brutal end of settlers' cannons, Indigenous North Americans petitioned en masse because their lands, lives, and traditions were under imperial threat. Anti-removal petitioning often changed venues and sought to remind recipients of treaty obligations, the dictates of law, and, where possible, the Christian spirit and charity to which White governments purportedly subscribed. Yet while dispossession and Indian removal occasioned many hundreds of Indigenous North American petitions, other energies were also at work. Indigenous communities petitioned even when their communities had long since been reduced to small and scattered villages, as in the Saint Lawrence valley, New England, and Nuevo México. Their grievances were real, so too their radicalism, yet the organized threat of government removal was not among their list of threats or appeals. In some cases, they sought to build new governments. In other cases, they sought new lands. Petitions served diplomatic purposes at a time when (after the War of 1812) other modes of diplomacy and political action were no longer as efficacious to Indigenous North Americans. Petitions also helped Native North Americans stitch together alliances among tribes and with committed White allies.

Beyond the structural forces impelling the documentation of Indigenous voices, Native communities took note of one another's petitioning practices. Villages in Canada and New England knew of one another's petitions through travel, kinship networks, and shared missionaries. The Cherokee in the 1830s took note of the petitioning and memorializing of the Seneca. The Wampanoag community at Mashpee in Massachusetts would point to the Cherokee example when writing their petitions, as did a subsequent generation of Seneca trying to protect Haudenosaunee lands.

No petitioning moment in global history was more distinctively North American than this one. British activists harnessed petitions for antislavery causes in ways that profoundly shaped the American contest, and European developments in religious liberty; free banking; and suffrage extension to women, free Blacks and the unpropertied ran alongside petitioning campaigns for these causes in British Canada, the United States, the Caribbean, and Mexico. The pouring forth of Indigenous memorial marked a distinctive fusion of asserted spaces and projected voices.

DAWNLAND PETITIONERS AT ODANAK, KAHNAWÁ:KE, AND MASHPEE

Indigenous North American grievance surged far and wide from 1800 through the 1820s, as villages and reorganized tribes petitioned dozens of different venues. Some of the earliest transformations in petitioning arose among small Native villages in the Saint Lawrence valley, often in their approaches to Canadian governors. These multitribal and multilingual communities stretched their membership and alliances across the Canada-U.S. border. Among the most actively petitioning villages were Odanak (also known as Saint François), the Iroquois community at Kahnawá:ke, and the Wampanoag village at Mashpee in Massachusetts.[7]

Natives at Odanak petitioned as Abenakis, and many of them were. Yet the village was a historical composite, the result of successive waves of migration from the south and the west. Many Indigenous families from Massachusetts fled to the region in King Philip's War (1675–1678) and during the waves of violence that followed. The Western Abenaki population came

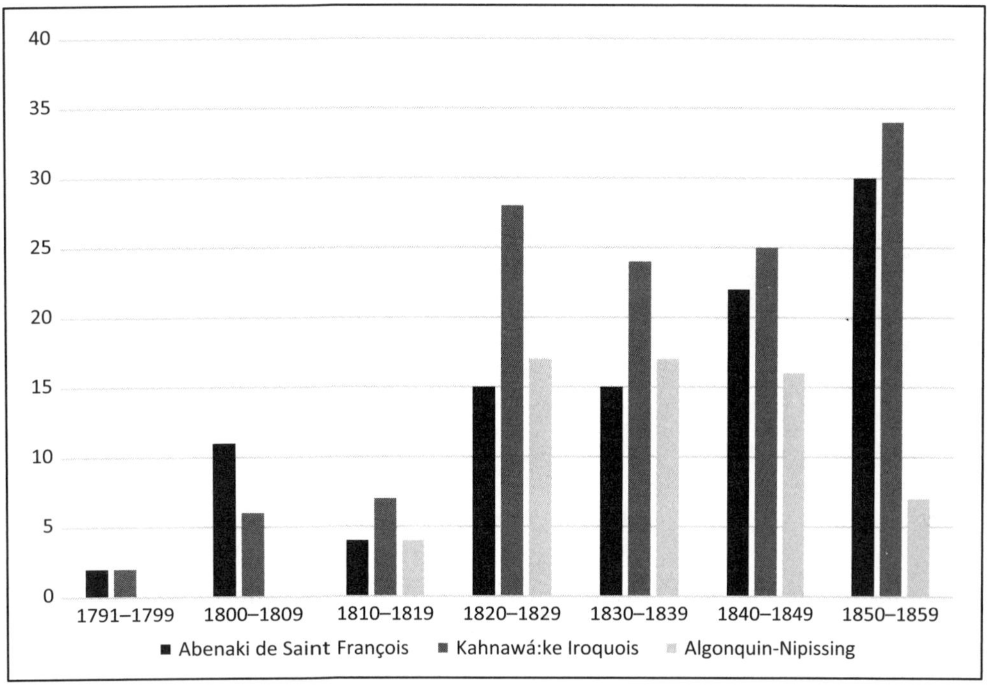

FIGURE 5.1. Total Petitions Sent by Three Indigenous Communities in Canada, 1791–1859.

from diverse places, especially southward from Missisquoi on the northern end of Lake Champlain, and the village included Eastern Abenaki, Schaghticoke, Penacook, and Amonoscoggin families and others who had arrived in the mid-1700s, as well as Sokwaki, Algonquin, and Loup families that had migrated in the seventeenth century. Odanak's population had grown after the American Revolution and had, according to ethnographic accounts, settled and stabilized by 1800.[8]

It was in the midst of this stabilization that "the Abenakis of Saint Francis" began to approach the governor of Canada and the colonial administration with claims about their land, their community, and their rights. Like other villages in the Saint Lawrence valley, such as the Huron community at Lorette, they began to represent themselves more commonly as a "nation," a self-identification that would only grow in the 1810s and 1820s. Yet unlike many other petitioning communities in North America, Indigenous women actively joined in these expressions; a 1799 petition expressed the concord of the women and children of the tribe. In 1802, the village sent a petition written entirely in phoneticized Abenaki to the governor general. The petition was prepared by the village's Catholic missionary—Louis-Gabriel-Roland Lenoir—but was also signed by some of its leading and rising elders and leaders, including the young François Annance. In this petition, the Saint François Natives protested a series of incursions on their lands from white settlers. Petitions in the ensuing years asked for land on which they had settled. The complaints in 1802 marked a period of territorial consolidation and even expansion for the Odanak Natives, who were granted additional land at Durham in 1805 and who in 1809 successfully petitioned for rights to an island in the Saint-François River. More so than Iroquoian villages, Abenakis and other Algonquian communities tended to emphasize sovereignty over fluid spaces.[9]

A new generation came to leadership at Odanak in the early nineteenth century, including the chiefs Louis De Gonzague, Pierre M'Sadoques, Louis Portneuf, Amable Pelicane (Pakikan), Joseph Obomsawin, and François Annance. Over sixty men in this cohort had fought in the War of 1812 on the British side, thereby gaining a debt of service and legitimacy from which they could make more credible claims on the imperial Crown. Even before the war, Annance was well known to senior British administrators, such as Lord Dorchester. Lower Canadian Whites referred to François Annance as the "chief of the Abenakis" at Odanak even as others also occupied those roles within the community. His son Noel would serve as a captain among the "Indian Warriors" during the War of 1812 and would follow in his father's leadership of the tribe.[10]

On behalf of "the Abenaki tribe at Saint François Mission," Odanak war veterans began to make claims to liberties, benefits, and lands that were far more extensive than any petitions before the war. From 1819 to 1833, they sent a series of memorials to various offices in Lower Canada. After a fire destroyed the mission church, seventeen elders of the tribe petitioned Bishop Joseph Octave Plessis in July 1819. The lead signatures were those of the chiefs and war chiefs, including some in phoneticized Abenaki, led by Louis De Gonzague, Pierre M'Sadoques, Augustin Guille, and Louis Pakikan, along with war chief Joachim Penedis (signing as "minrddu8" before marking his name), but the final signature came from François Annance, one of the few to sign without making a mark. The petitioners referred repeatedly to the "nation at Saint François." In 1821, the men relayed a similar petition to the assembly of Lower Canada. The Odanak Natives' 1821 request for an appropriation was the only one they made to the assembly before the chamber's dissolution in 1838. Guille and an interpreter presented the petition in person before the assembly, where they emphasized the past military service of the village's warriors and elders, as well as the Odanak Natives' centrality in the Indigenous networks of the region. The "maintaining and preserving of this Nation is highly important to the Government of this Province," they argued, warning that Odanak families might depart for their lands in the United States were they not to receive the appropriation.[11] The petition for a new church stretched across two sessions of the assembly, but the chamber eventually voted 500 pounds of appropriation for a new church building in stone. The leaders of the legislative effort to advance the appropriation were some of the same Lower Canadian men who were then transforming provincial politics—Louis Bourdages, Jean-Baptiste Proulx, and John Neilson. The upper chamber in Canada at the time, the legislative council, rejected these bills, underscoring tensions between the chambers that would only grow over the ensuing decade. Guille's family would fund the construction of a new mission church in the early 1830s.[12]

Odanak petitions of the 1820s became more structured and more strident, with more forceful claims and longer signatory lists. In 1824, Abenaki leaders sent a petition signed by forty-four of their members to Superintendent of Indian Affairs John Johnson, denouncing their missionary. Two other petitions, sent to Colonial Governor Lord Dalhousie in 1826, advanced broad new claims over the spaces of Odanak. In February of that year, they requested a new law that no White person be permitted to purchase property in the village of Saint-Francois. In September, they complained to the governor about the encroachment of white settlers on their lands at Odanak. Even as Dalhousie tabled or openly refused these appeals, Odanak Natives began to press for permanent recognition of hunting rights on the other (north) shore of the Saint Lawrence, both as an extension of customary practices and from the perceived imperative to claim identity as an Indigenous community.[13]

So it was that a village of captives and refugees, one reshaped continuously over the previous centuries, began to assert a more homogeneous identity as a "nation." The village at Saint François had become a space where the community of "Abenaquis" increasingly claimed a political community, to the point that they functioned as a sort of constituency for the provincial assembly. Elders' status as British war veterans, especially that of François and Noel Annance, gave organization, legitimacy, and purpose to this effort. The emergence of a political identity in petitioning came in part from critical families such as the Annances—in Abenaki, the word for "nation" corresponds roughly to "the families come together"—drawing on connections, education, identity claims, and military experience.[14]

Like the village at Odanak, the community at Kahnawá:ke (who call themselves the Kahnawakehro:non) was attached to a Catholic mission and included in its membership families and clans who crossed a border that Natives regarded as artificial. The community's founding members left the Mohawk valley in the seventeenth century and settled near Montréal at the Sault-Saint-Louis seigneury, which had been given to the Jesuits by the French Crown in 1680. After the British conquest, General Thomas Gage in 1762 granted seigneurial title to the Kahnawá:ke Iroquois—another seigneury (La Prairie) on Kahnawá:ke's eastern boundary remained with the Jesuits—stating that no White settler could henceforth purchase property in the seigneury, and that any existing White settler could not enlarge his property. As late as 1810, seigneurial status conferred suffrage on the Kahnawakehro:non. By the 1830s, the Kahnawá:ke occupied land totaling over forty thousand acres at Sault-Saint-Louis, in part by having used petitions and lawsuits in the 1790s to parry Jesuit and settler incursions over the preceding decades.[15]

Kahnawá:ke's entwined histories of Mohawk nationality and Catholic alliance combined to create a platform for women's voice and governance, a perch of power articulated in women's petitions. In 1809, women cantors of the Holy Family of Sault-Saint-Louis sent a memorial to Plessis, asking him to constrain their missionary at the time, Antoine Rinfret, who had restricted their access to the Holy Family Church and had "broken" their organization. "It's the women who run this village," griped Rinfret to his superiors.[16] In 1816, Kahnawá:ke women calling themselves the woman chiefs (*chefferesses*) of the village sent a petition, along with the warriors, to Colonel Louis-Joseph Fleury Deschambault, lamenting that the chiefs "won't let us have access to their council."[17] This complaint harked back to a much older pattern—one contested during the era of colonialism—of women and warriors participating in the council of the chiefs. The chiefs, for their part, argued that "the voice of women does not deserve to be heard."[18] In the complicated Catholic legacy at Kahnawá:ke, the Jesuit-inspired cult of Saint Kateri Tekakwitha and the strength of women's organization at the Holy Family parish provided space for women's voice and governance, even as later missionaries like Marcoux tried to control the village.[19] Women's voice in governance matters at Kahnawá:ke emerged nowhere more starkly than in episcopal petitions.[20]

Kahnawá:ke Mohawks began making more assertive claims to nationhood in the 1820s, after the 1819 arrival of Catholic missionary Paul Marcoux and, separately, the appointment of Lord Dalhousie as governor general of British North America in 1820. Their grievances centered on several issues: the status of the eastern boundary with the Jesuits, the presence of White men marrying Kahnawá:ke women and thereby claiming land, and the incursions of other White settlers on lands and hunting and fishing spaces.[21]

Nationalism at Kahnawá:ke long preceded the arrival of Marcoux and Dalhousie, but new petitioning struggles of the 1820s and 1830s sharpened the village's posture. The Kahnawakehro:non began battling with Marcoux, who assisted the tribe in relaying complaints about land issues but also tried domineering the souls under his care. Marcoux prepared an Iroquois dictionary for his mission but used it only for the priests, steadfastly refusing to offer linguistic education or to make scriptures available to the Kahnawakehro:non for fear they would become independent of the clergy. The chiefs at Kahnawá:ke detected Marcoux's ruse and began petitioning his superiors as well as colonial officials in an attempt to have him disciplined or even removed.[22] In an 1825 petition to Bishop Joseph-Octave Plessis, Louis Garoniatsigowa—who called himself "principal chief and Christian Captain of the Iroquois tribe settled at the village of Sault Saint-Louis"—joined with two other chiefs to advance two complaints at Marcoux: "He meddles in the affairs of the chiefs concerning the rents of the seigneury, after having himself established a revenue collector unbeknownst to the same chiefs, and what is more, he addressed in his way a petition to his excellence without having spoken to a single one of the chiefs who lead the village of Sault St. Louis. The trust that the Iroquois had in their missionary was lost."[23] Garoniatsigowa's telling lament demonstrated not only that the Kahnawá:ke chiefs valued their seigneurial rights and the developing agricultural economy of their village but that they considered petitioning to be central to their sovereignty. Like other tribes, the Kahnawakehro:non regularly involved missionaries in the preparation of petitions, not merely for their clerical and legal skills but also because missionaries provided crucial alliances and linkages to ecclesiastical and colonial elites. Yet to construct and send a petition without consultation with chiefs, as Marcoux had, was a violation of the basic constitution of the Kahnawakehro:non.[24]

The decline of the fur trade after the War of 1812 hastened a transition to farming by the village's families, who raised a variety of crops and also kept cattle, hogs, and poultry. White settlers began to crowd Kahnawá:ke, coveting the rich alluvial lands there. As Lower Canadian White men began to intermarry with Kahnawá:ke women, they became eligible under Canadian property law for property rights in the village. Kahnawá:ke residents viewed these developments with unease. These traditionalists focused their anxieties on George de Lorimier, a mixed-race man who owned the ferry license for the lucrative passage between Kahnawá:ke and Lachine on the other side of the Saint Lawrence. Lorimier struck an alliance with Father Marcoux, while a Kahnawá:ke faction emerged to oppose the priest and ferry captain, joined by British colonial administrator James Hughes and interpreter Bernard St. Germain.[25]

The dispute over White presence in Kahnawá:ke become a battle of petitions. Wary of Lorimier's influence and frustrated by repeated battles with Marcoux, Mohawk chiefs advanced bold new claims of territorial sovereignty. A group of Kahnawakehro:non calling themselves "the Red Children of the Iroquois Tribe of the Village of Sault Saint Louis" petitioned Lord Gosford in 1835 with a radical demand, namely the racial purification of their village: "Thus do we the Red Children pray to our Father, as the only way of bestowing peace and concord upon the village, to establish and enforce our ancient laws and customs, to send away from us the Whites and Foreigners, and to prevent them from coming here again. And we ask you, too . . . to give orders . . . to return to us all of our property, that has been so unjustly taken from us by our ignorance and imbecility by people who know that the Red Children have no authority or right to alienate them."[26]

In the midst of the battle over race, women of Kahnawá:ke sided with Marcoux and the Catholic faith. In June 1835, sixty-three women signatories calling themselves "women of the Holy Family" at Kahnawá:ke approached the bishop with a petition asking about the reestablishment of payments to Father Marcoux by the special council of the village. And in the religious conflicts of the 1830s, many women sided not with their chiefs but with Father Marcoux, petitioning for his retention.[27]

Further anti-White petitions at Kahnawá:ke followed from 1836 to 1840, prompting Marcoux and his allies to launch a counterattack. Marcoux argued that the number of Whites in the village was quite small, "basically a half-dozen," and he and his allies warned that to empty the village of all mixed-race inhabitants would risk depopulating it entirely. The Rebellions of 1837–1838 brought charges on both sides that their enemies had conspired with the Patriote rebels against the queen. The thrust and parry of petitions, slanders, and insults continued until a peace treaty between the two factions was signed in December 1840. Battles over land would last throughout the century, but the nationalism at Kahnawá:ke had crystallized in new ways.[28]

Village-based Indigenous petitioning grew in the United States as well, even as legal institutions differed significantly. Sachems of the Wampanoag tribe near present-day Cape Cod had approached colonial authorities in Massachusetts repeatedly in the seventeenth and eighteenth centuries, occasionally taking their complaints and requests to the Crown. By the late 1700s, the Wampanoag were concentrated in several village settlements, one at Gay Head (Aquinnah) on Martha's Vineyard, another near Mashpee on the Cape, and still others in southeastern Massachusetts. From 1763 onward, the Wampanoag at Mashpee had exercised the right to elect their own officers and to manage the village commons, but after 1789, they were governed by a board of five overseers, who appointed one or more guardians to carry out state policies. The overseers were charged with protecting Mashpee Natives and their property rights from trespassers and were also responsible for religious education.[29]

Wampanoag petitioners at Mashpee saw their continuance as a project involving space, autonomy, and spirit. In a budding conflict with the overseer Gideon Hawley, which lasted from 1789 to 1807 (Hawley's death) and then beyond with Hawley's son, Mashpee Natives began to challenge the system of overseers and to demand their "ancient liberties" under the 1763 colonial regulations. A series of Mashpee petitions in 1789, 1794, and 1796 underscored the villagers' frustration with Hawley, who doubted the Wampanoag's capacity for self-government even as he aggressively sought to protect the tribe's property from incursions. Many Mashpee Natives had started following the sermons of another preacher, the Baptist Thomas Jeffers, who had Wampanoag or Massachusetts ancestry and a more charismatic style.[30]

Upon Hawley's death in 1807, Mashpee men and women sent a new petition proposing reform of the overseer system. Under the 1763 regulations, "we had the liberty of choosing our Masters," while under the 1789 regulations "even this small portion of Liberty is taken away."[31] The new system was too unwieldy, encompassing too many officials, none of whom were regularly present. Governing in absentia, "the overseers are too remote and scattered for the Indians to repair to, in times of distress, with their complaints."[32] The 1807 petition to the Massachusetts General Court came, in part, due to the lack of someone more proximate to whom the Wampanoag could carry their grievances. Of the petition's seventy-two signatories, fully forty-three were women of Mashpee, whose names appeared amid and alongside those of Mashpee men. A document proclaiming Revolution-era ideals of rights to property and self-governance presented a subscriber list that re-expressed the interchangeability, the rough equality, of a village's citizens both female and male.[33]

Detecting both the jeopardy posed by Hawley's death and the persuasiveness of the 1807 Mashpee memorial, Mashpee's overseers tried to launch a counterpetitioning campaign of their own. In an 1807 countermemorial purportedly signed by seventy-eight Mashpee Natives, overseers painted the Wampanoag as divided internally, but the Natives successfully convinced the court that the signatures on these counterpetitions were fraudulently obtained. Whereas the memorials of the 1790s had been rejected by the General Court, the 1807 mixed-gender petition met with an appreciative hearing and some success, as the Court legislated in 1808 to reduce the number of overseers to three and the guardians to only one. Overseers had felt it necessary to combat an effective Indigenous petition by synthesizing another Indigenous petition, and the General Court's committees had enough capacity to sniff out the ruse.[34]

Wampanoag at Mashpee and Gay Head would continue to approach the general court after 1810. Gay Head Wampanoag petitioned in 1811, 1815, and 1816 asking for a reversal of regulations that limited their village autonomy, and while the petitions were never officially granted, the state eventually stopped renewing overseer appointments, which gave the Gay Head Wampanoag much greater discretion. Meanwhile, eight Mashpee elders approached the court in 1817 and requested far more than they had asked just a decade earlier: the certain ability to elect their overseers. Another memorial soon arrived signed by eighty Mashpee Natives, claiming that the current system was "the best ever tried," and the investigative committee sided in this case with the overseers. Yet the continued petitioning placed Indigenous governance squarely on the state's legislative agenda, leading to

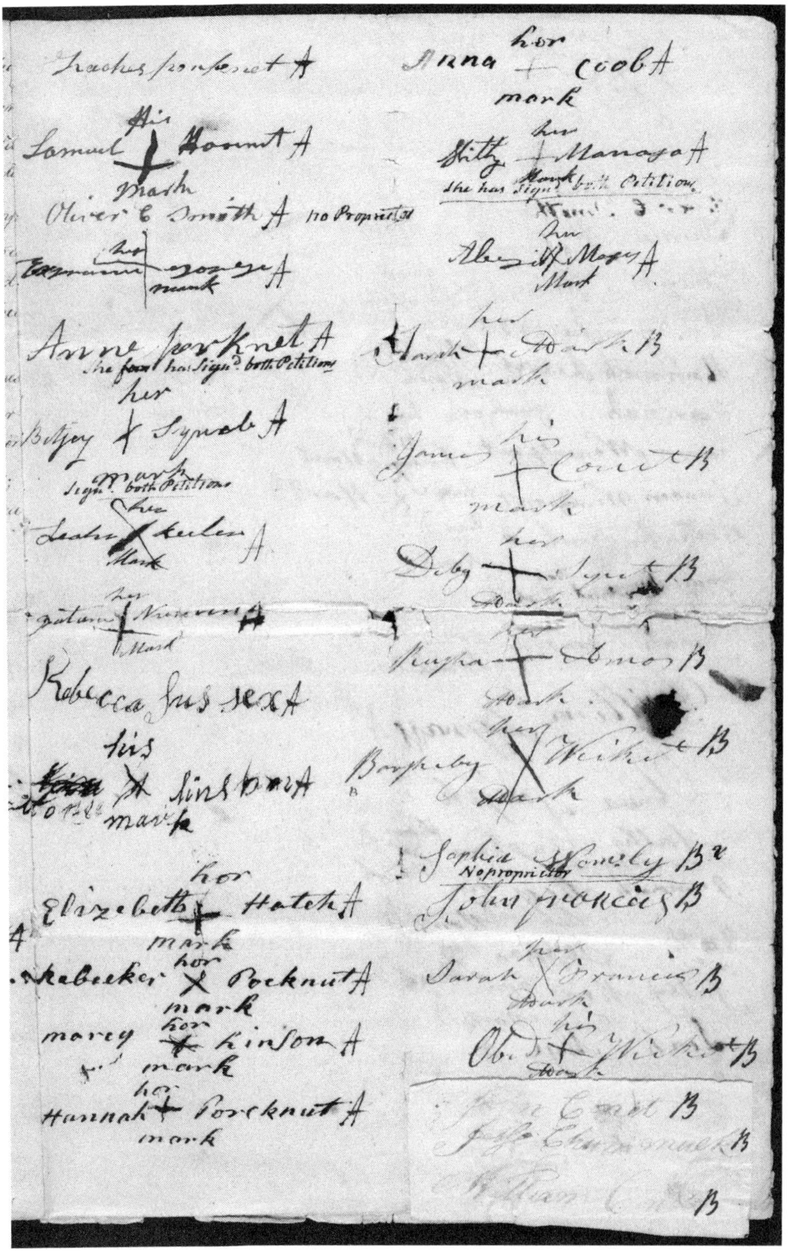

FIGURE 5.2. Signatory List from Mashpee Protest Petition, 1807.
Credit: Massachusetts Archives of the Commonwealth.

a series of state reports and investigations throughout the 1820s and 1830s. A starker confrontation was yet to come.[35]

The trajectories of claims-making at Odanak, Kahnawá:ke, and Mashpee echo broader developments among Native petitioners in the early nineteenth century. In the Saint Lawrence valley and New England, Indigenous petitions of the early nineteenth century came from villages (the primary geographic unit of organization) but more often spoke as nations and tribes. The fact that these national claims came in part from a position of structural weakness via-à-vis the colonial and settler states pressing on them undermines neither the sincerity nor the occasional effectiveness of the assertions. Chiefs used national identity to remind colonial officers of treaty obligations; to rally women, warriors, and elders to a cause; to alloy one faction; and to remind colonial authorities that Indigenous peoples were not just any supplicants but petitioners that had preceded them in space and time on the continent. Indigenous petitioners buttressed themes of nationalism by attaching distinctively Indigenous language and symbolism to their petitions. The Abenaki language petition of 1802 and the Abenaki expressions on the episcopal petition of 1819 pointed not to a dying pattern but to a reawakening. Totemic signatures and Indigenous language expressions became if anything *more* common, not less, in the nineteenth century as compared to the late eighteenth century.[36]

As elsewhere in North America, Indigenous petitions to Canadian authorities differed from the petitions of White North Americans in ways both stark and subtle. First, to a much greater degree than other petitioners, Natives carried their laments to administrative offices. This pattern reflected in part the elaborated architecture of colonial governance that Anglo-Americans in particular had created to manage relationships with Native peoples and often to subjugate and remove them. In the Saint Lawrence valley, over half of Indigenous petitions from 1791 to 1859 were addressed to the head of colonial administration (the governor general, the lieutenant governor, or the acting administrator), while less than 10 percent were sent to legislative bodies. So, too, in the United States, more and more Native petitions would target administrative authorities in the Department of War and later the Department of the Interior.[37]

Second, Native women appear to have signed separate petitions earlier and more frequently than White women of the period, and Indigenous women's practice of signing memorials alongside men was quite rare among White North Americans until the 1830s. The Kahnawá:ke petitions in Canada were emblematic of a broader pattern, one that was most pronounced at the Huron village of Lorette, where women sent at least five petitions to colonial authorities from 1823 to 1850. Native women's participation in petitioning stemmed in part from their earlier involvement in Indigenous diplomacy. In both Algonquian and Iroquoian worlds, clan and family mothers often attended diplomatic conferences and presented wampum in their own name. Colonial authorities tried to restrict this practice, in part out of patriarchal beliefs, in part out of a failure to recognize the multiple sources of authority within Indigenous nations, in part as a way to simplify the organization of the counterparties to treaties and agreements. Even as colonial practices muted it, women's activity in petitioning—both separately as "mothers of the nation" or "singers of Holy Family Parish" and alongside chiefs and warriors—would survive colonial restrictions.[38]

In some ways, this heightened role of women in Indigenous North American petitioning represented the documentary residue of a clash of worlds. As the appetites of the American settler republic ran up against many matrilineal societies of Native Americans, Native women took on a far more prominent and regular role in petitioning than in perhaps any other society of the time. An important force animating Native petitioning was the defense and management of land, eagerly sought after by White settlers. Matrilineal legacies in Native American communities put women in ownership, partial or full, of much of this land. When it came to defending these lands by petition, women thus took on a role that was less commonly witnessed in White society. Where women exercised a more prominent role in tribal and community governance, as with the Cherokee or the Ojibwe, the petitioning contributions of women were all the greater.

None of these developments went unnoticed by colonial and ecclesiastic authorities in Canada and New England. Both newspapers and legislative assemblies began to publish Indigenous petitions in the 1820s. Just as Father Rinfret complained about the women of Kahnawá:ke in 1809, priests and ministers elsewhere tried to resist, harness, assist, and occasionally redirect the petitioning activities of their villages. Men like François Annance, Louis Garoniatsigowa, and others represented a new, educated, and multilingual elite among First Nations villages, and neither priests nor Indian agents nor land company officials could effectively constrain them. These families—their women and their men—formed the basis of political community in petitioning villages, inscribing on paper the Abenaki concept of nation as "the families come together."[39]

THE CONTEST AGAINST AMERICAN REMOVAL—FROM STOCKBRIDGE TO WISCONSIN

In the stories that remain with us, anti-removal endeavors focus on particular tribes, especially the Cherokee and the Iroquois (Haudenosaunee). These tribally specific stories, while essential, can obscure a wider reality. Native Americans challenged removal on a continent-wide basis, adopting and refining strategies that other tribes had used with success or failure and calling in allies among churches and humanitarian Whites, acutely conscious of stakes both local and global. Anti-removal petitions authored by Natives and their allies functioned far beyond their contributions to a movement. Anti-removal petitions recorded an alternative history, reminded the organs of state of past agreements, and created a record of Native continuance.[40]

Compared to Saint Lawrence valley and New England natives, the Iroquois and other western tribes were petitioning to defend much larger spaces—lands and waterscapes they had not yet entirely lost to colonial regimes. As in the East, however, colonial settlement and its disruptions had created a multitribal and often multilingual world of Native villages. Iroquoia already included a large number of adopted Natives from its Algonquian neighbors as well as the Tuscarora Nation, which had joined the Iroquois confederacy in 1722. The fate of the Oneida was interlinked with that of Christian Indians from New England, including a variegated group known as the Stockbridge Indians, named after the Mohhekonnuck (Mohican) village that had welcomed Indigenous migrants in the 1730s. Harassed by west-bound settlers after the Revolution, the Stockbridge struck an agreement with the Oneida to form a new community at New Stockbridge in New York in the 1780s.

Indigenous Christians populated much of both Stockbridge village and the Oneida space to which the Stockbridge moved. This religious similarity both aided the immigration of the Stockbridge and led to enduring splits in and among the villagers and tribes. The Oneida came under increasing pressure after 1789 and divided into the Christian Party and the Pagan Party, a rupture formalized in 1805 when each party took possession of separate tracts of land. New York officials desirous of land cessions now had two Indigenous communities to target and play against each other. In the decade after the split, the parties would turn to the legislature to warn Albany officials about the intentions and past deeds of their Oneida rivals. The question of representation played out in a contest of memorials. The Pagans warned the assembly in an 1810 petition that "Our Brothers the Christian Partie inclines to sell . . . a goar of Land" that actually ran into the Pagan Party's partition holdings, while the Christians insisted in their own 1810 petition that any treaty negotiations occur at the council fire and not by delegations sent to Albany. In this older model of diplomacy, both New York State and the Oneida held "council fires," and any alienation of lands had to occur at the seller's diplomatic center.[41]

Renewed pressure for removal after the war induced both Oneida parties to solicit the legislature for protection. In 1814, a group of mixed Oneidas requested Assembly compensation for what they saw as a swindle of their lands in 1809. Another 1814 petition of twenty-six Christian Oneida "chiefs and warriors"—accompanied by a concurring statement from the wives and widows of the chiefs—alerted the assembly of a Pagan Party deputation headed to Albany, arguing that further land sales were not acceptable. The legislature concluded a deal with the Pagan Party leader anyway the following year. With Albany newly aware of the weight of settler encroachment on the Oneida and the decline of Indigenous military independence east of the Mississippi, land appetites combined with a perverse paternalism to forge a new rationale for programmed removal. When in his 1818 address to the New York State Assembly DeWitt Clinton called for the forcible migration of the Haudenosaunee to "an extensive territory remote from the white population," he crystallized in words what land company officials had long sought and what the Haudenosaunee had rumored among themselves for decades: that the Americans desired not just parts of their land but their complete erasure from their ancestral spaces.[42]

The stark visibility of New York State's removal agenda spurred new and anxious political action. Pagan and Christian party leaders briefly united, and the Oneida turned to two venues at once. Thirty-two leading Oneida sent memorials to the New York legislature and President Monroe in November 1818, urging them to abandon the removal project. The 1818 petitions brought Pagan Cornelius Sagoyountha and Christians Peter Bread and Paul Powlis together in rhetoric and in signatures. They implored Monroe to deal with the Oneidas as a sovereign unity, reminding him of the "obligations we humbly conceive the American people are under to this nation." Invocations of nationhood came in part from the strategic necessity to parry the "divide and entreat" tactic of the Ogden Land Company and New York State, whereby anyone claiming Oneida authority was deemed a suitable subject for land cession negotiations. These laments fell on unsympathetic ears, not least because John Calhoun, newly arrived as the secretary of war, gave federal support to the project of Clinton and the Ogden Land Company. In a fashion piecemeal, fraudulent, and brutal, New York settler interests joined with the Kahnawá:ke mixed-blood clergyman Eleazar Williams and carved up Oneida lands. The tribe split again in the 1820s, with a more traditional Second Christian Party splitting from the first. The Second Christian Party contested a fraudulent 1826 treaty ceding over sixteen hundred acres to the state, while the First Christian Party demanded fair price for its already ceded lands. While many Oneida would move to Seneca lands near Buffalo Creek, removal created a new settlement at Green Bay. The Stockbridge soon followed. As their alliance despairingly began plans to migrate west, the hopes of the Stockbridge for a settlement in Indiana were dashed by Delaware land sessions in the Treaty of St. Mary (1818). Still calling themselves the Mohhekonnuck, Stockbridge chiefs and headmen petitioned in 1820 for an allotment of western lands. An accompanying petition reminded Congress of the Stockbridge's service in "the late war with Great Britain." Negotiations with Wisconsin-based tribes (the Ho-Chunk and the Menominee) were undertaken in 1821 and 1822, after which the Stockbridge moved to a settlement on the Fox River near Green Bay.[43]

Because New York's imperial visions extended to Buffalo and beyond, the battle of removal next turned to the Seneca. The Keepers of the Western Door had already lost all but a small set of eleven land tracts in the Treaty of Big Tree (1797), yet White settlers pouring into the region coveted ever more of the little that remained. New York set into motion its apparatus of removal. In part because of the skill with which Seneca leaders deployed petitions to unite their members, build alliances with concerned Whites, and induce the entry of the federal government into New York removal politics, the men aiming to oust the Seneca from their lands would express growing frustration. In the eyes of Democratic leader Peter B. Porter and land magnate David Ogden, the Seneca would prove a more formidable object of removal resistance than their eastern neighbors. Seneca leaders—especially the Pagan Party chief Big Kettle and the orator Sagoyewatha, nicknamed "Red Jacket" because of the vestment he wore to diplomatic engagements—had cultural and political resources that were in shorter supply for the Oneida.[44]

Sagoyewatha and his allies would represent the chief symbolic and political obstacle to Seneca removal in the decade after the War of 1812. The way Sagoyewatha came to prominence, mixed with the diplomatic and political tools he used, gestured to a wider political transformation in Indigenous North America. In the midst of the war, the area spanning western New York south through the Ohio valley and into the western Great Lakes was rocked by radical spiritual movements, a growing rejection of Western and American religious and political models, and a pan-Indian revolt. The leaders' names have since become etched in legend—Tecumseh, Tenskwatawa (the Prophet), Handsome Lake. Tecumseh and Tenskwatawa counseled mistrust of the White man and a return to traditional ways (including rejection of alcohol and intermarriage with Whites). The Prophet in particular abhorred the petition-based diplomatic appeals of his brethren to the U.S. president. He decried the false leaders who "had abandoned the Interests of their respective nations and sold all the Indians land to the united states and requested the president to take care of them and appoint masters over them to make them work." To petition was to recognize an alternative sovereignty, to wander meekly into negotiations with an implacable and deceptive enemy. The death of Tecumseh in the Battle of the Thames, the death of Handsome Lake in 1815, and the decline of the Prophet left a gaping vacuum of symbolic and relational authority in Indigenous life near the Great Lakes.[45]

The demise of separatism transferred power not only to settler interests but also to Red Jacket and to Indigenous petitioning as a strategy. Big Kettle and Sagoyewatha had been active in Haudenosaunee circles and in New York politics before 1810, but the war and the slow decline of the Oneida enhanced their leadership position among the Seneca and the remaining Haudenosaunee migrants. Famed for his oratorical skills and centering his politics at the multinational Buffalo Creek reservation, Sagoyewatha turned increasingly to petitions as diplomatic instruments after the war. In October 1813, he wrote to remind Indian agent Erastus Granger of the Seneca's loyalty to the American side during the war and of their continued claims on the spaces they occupied and hunted, reminding Granger that "we are an Independent nation" and that "this Country belongs to us and the U States."[46]

Like other Indigenous petitioners before him, Sagoyewatha took his grievances and requests to administrators both high and low. Colonial agents had received these claims for centuries, yet the development of more refined Indian affairs organizations in the United States (Department of War) and British Canada (Indian Affairs) gave Indigenous communities clear and stable venues in a world otherwise muddled by revolutions, the proliferation of new settler governments, and partisan turnover. In approaches to the national government, petitioning the Indian agent as a first approach became something of a recognized protocol.[47] The pace of petitioning to Indian agents rose perceptibly after the war, so much so that Lewis Cass, then governor of Michigan Territory, complained about their concomitant burden. "I do not think that there is an officer in the Union, who has more or importunate calls upon him, than I have," lamented Cass to Secretary of War John Calhoun in 1820.[48] "I have frequently to resist great claims, which are urged with great force. Poverty, nakedness, hunger & wretchedness in every shape are importunate applicants, & they appear in all sexes and ages."[49] Two years later, Cass appealed to Congress for more funds for his bureau, describing both the weight of Indigenous claims and the duty of the state under law and justice to respond to them:

> There are other indispensable objects which can never be avoided.
>
> We must have officers upon the frontier, charged with the management of Indian affairs, to license traders, to keep improper persons from the Indian Country, to see that the laws upon this subject are executed, to pay the annuities, to listen to and redress the complaints of the Indians, to serve as the medium of communication & generally to perform the infinite variety of duties, which our anomalous connection with the Indians requires.[50]

At one level, Cass's remarks merely reflected the views of a functionary eager for a larger budget. His career, moreover, reflected an organized inhumanity toward the Native peoples in his midst. Yet the surge of Indigenous claims to Indian offices was no less real for these facts, and Cass recognized that Indigenous petitioners expected Indian agents, as well as legislatures, governors, presidents and others, to respond to their complaints and grievances.

Richly aware that Indian agents participated in a larger organization dedicated to clearing them from their existing and ancestral spaces, Native petitioners approached them nonetheless—and continually. They knew that by recruiting federal officials into local conflicts, they could delay and sidetrack removal plans, and they could place their concerns at the seat of the government with which they had struck treaties. Thus did the Indian agent, and the U.S. government more generally, become a venue for partially deflecting the initiatives of states and their governors and settler-dominated legislatures. Among the many reasons behind settlers' constant petitions for new state governments was a wish to transfer the site of Indian affairs from Washington and its scattered offices to a more proximate, favorable audience.

The Seneca were thus dismayed when Erastus Granger retired in 1818 after the new statute governing Indian affairs made no provision for an agent for the Six Nations. Exploiting the hiatus in agents, Sagoyewatha and the assembled council fire at Buffalo met in December 1817 and opted to take their case directly to the top.[51] In January 1818, the Seneca transmitted a petition to President Monroe and Secretary Calhoun, offering what was to date the firmest disavowal of a dislocated future. They stated their refusal to move along with a request for an Indian agent, which would legitimize their presence in western New York. Merging the council fire oration and the petition form, Sagoyewatha waxed supplicatory and defiant:

> *Father:*
> From the fatherly care the Presidents of the United States have exercised towards their Red Children, we speak to our father in confidence, believing he will not turn away his ears from his Red Children. Having no agent through whom we might speak, we are persuaded that our father will not be displeased that we speak directly to him, as it were, face to face. . . .
>
> *Father:*
> We are alarmed lest we lose our seats. Those men that say they have a right to purchase our lands, have been distressing us for a number of years with their plans to possess our lands; offering us in exchange lands to the westward. . . .
>
> *Father:*
> We declare to you, we desire you to publish to all our white brothers, that it is our fixed and determined purpose to live and die on our present seats. It is sealed to us by the bones of our fathers. They obtained it by their blood. Our bones shall be beside theirs. It is the heritage of the Almighty. He gave it us. He it is [who] must take it from us.[52]

Sagoyewatha's imploring rhetoric reflected a transformation from earlier modes of oral and in-person diplomacy in which Natives held significant advantages, but it also performed a manifold political strategy. By taking his tribe's case to Monroe and Calhoun, he and Big Kettle parried the initiative of Clinton and the Ogden Land Company to schedule removal. They also joined with the Seneca Christian Party and sent a memorial to

Governor Clinton, asking for protection against further encroachment. An avowed adherent to the Seneca Pagan Party, Sagoyewatha deployed ominous tones, warning of the wrath of God who is "terrible in judgment."[53] Just as he said that Six Nations' lands were not the Senecas' to alienate, he also appealed to the mercy of the governments around him.

The starkness of New York's removal project complicated the Senecas' task. The new Indian subagent Jasper Parrish allied with Ogden Land Company interests to assist some Seneca in organizing a pro-removal party. Big Kettle and Sagoyewatha began a search for new allies, and they relied increasingly on Seneca women. Compared to other tribes petitioning in this period, Seneca women did not appear as commonly as signatories. Yet through their traditional leadership in clans and through the property they controlled through intermarriage, Seneca women remained important participants in Indigenous land politics. In the 1797 Treaty of Big Tree, the Seneca and the United States had set apart a four-square-mile tract for two daughters (Mary Allen and Chloe Allen) of the clan mother Kyendanenthan. By the 1820s, land company interests (Robert Morris) began to lay claim to the land and began settling there. Sagoyewatha brought the Allen women's complaint to the council and helped draft a petition to the secretary of war. Morris soon backed off and described the affair as a misunderstanding. Sagoyewatha would continue allying with women at councils and would continue pressing this case before the president and the secretary of war. In his view—one widely shared among the Seneca—the fundamental treaty governing their spaces was the 1797 Treaty of Canandaigua, which gave them federal recognition of their lands but also "the right . . . to lay our complaint before our Great Father."[54]

Recognizing the progress that Big Kettle and Sagoyewatha, the Pagan Party, and anti-removal Senecas had made, Jasper Parrish joined with the Christian Party and its chiefs—Tall Peter, Young King, White Seneca, Little Billy, Destroy Town, and others—and began to petition Washington more regularly. The Pagan Party leaders pronounced their harmony with some of the removal plans ("we have a great deal of good land . . . which we cannot improve for a great many years") and effusively praised Parrish.[55] By 1826, in a clear effort to portray themselves with greater authority, Pagan Party petitioners began to write two names alongside every signature: an English name and a phoneticized Seneca name. Ogden Land Company interests also turned to the federal government, writing to the secretary of war in the summer of 1825 and asking for federal pressure on the Seneca for more land cessions. The company's turn to Washington and its recruitment of the pro-removal party's petitioning reflected the changed terms of land battles as well as the partial success of Big Kettle and Sagoyewatha's petition in shifting the venue of adjudication. Yet the Senecas' procedural victories were short lived. In March 1826, the company got what it wanted from the War Department. Secretary James Barbour appointed Oliver Forward (an Ogden Land Company business associate) as treaty commissioner for a proposed Seneca land sale. By August, the Seneca had "agreed" to sell four of its reservations as well as substantial portions of the Buffalo Creek, Tonawanda, and Cattaraugus reservations for the paltry sum of $2,583.

Sagoyewatha signed the 1826 "treaty" but did so in seething protest, and his manifold counterattack took shape in a petition to DeWitt Clinton, his recruitment of allies among nearby Quakers, and another petition to President John Quincy Adams. In March 1828, Sagoyewatha and two other Seneca visited with President Adams at the White House. They asked for the dismissal of Parrish, stated their abject refusal to move to Green Bay, and asked Adams to appoint a special investigator to examine their charges of fraud in the 1826 agreement. Seneca and Quaker protest swelled in tandem, and Senate action on the treaty stalled. Secretary of War Peter Buell Porter then appointed Richard Livingston to investigate the 1826 deal.

Livingston's report of December 1828, published widely, vindicated Sagoyewatha and the anti-removal Seneca. Livingston found that the Ogden Land Company had bribed the War Department's interpreters and agents over many years, that many of the chiefs who had signed the false treaty of 1826 did so under a company-inspired misunderstanding, and that Forward had wrongly and illegally threatened the Seneca with removal to Green Bay if they did not agree to land cessions. The false treaty of 1826 would never be submitted to the president, and the reversal of many chiefs' positions on the 1826 deal helped restore Sagoyewatha's reputation. With Sagoyewatha's death in January 1830, the Seneca would refract and face new challenges from a presidential administration bent on making removal a nationwide policy. Settlers began to pour into the lands ceded in the 1820s, especially near the Genesee River, rendering de facto the results of a fraudulent and never-ratified treaty.[56]

Less visibly, the legacy of early Seneca anti-removal efforts, especially their calculated and spirited risk, would endure. The battles of the 1820s had left a newly organized and legitimized anti-removal network. Sagoyewatha's petitions and approaches to Washington had changed the venue of land politics, and in their memorials and protests with the Quakers, the Seneca had now mobilized White supporters as never before. In collaboration on parchment, a budding alliance had emerged.

AGAINST ERASURE AND ENCROACHMENT: INDIGENOUS PROTEST IN NEW MEXICO

In the early nineteenth-century spaces claimed by Spain and then Mexico, new energies of nationalist settlement and Native protest petitioning unfolded in illuminating ways in the borderlands of New Mexico. At least a decade before Mexico's war for independence, Spain began to target Indigenous lands for settlement. In April 1821, General Alejo García Conde sent the 1813 decree to New Mexico governor Facundo Melgares, instructing Melgares to implement it. The 1813 decree authorized the Spanish regime to facilitate land grants to unpropertied settlers and military veterans. In 1823, King Ferdinand annulled the 1821 Cortes decision in Spain, but Mexican independence rendered that decision irrelevant for Native pueblos. Mexican liberalism put Natives further on the defensive, as it prized individual, private land ownership, viewing collective ownership patterns among pueblos as doubly regressive. With the opening of the Santa Fe Trail linking St. Louis to Chihuahua, and with the Mexican government encouraging Hispano settlement in borderlands out of fear of American incursions, land pressure on the pueblos surged.[57]

Indigenous governments immediately perceived a threat, and they petitioned a range of offices and councils. The pueblo of San Juan de los Caballeros petitioned in 1821 for a statement of its rights under the "four square leagues" (or "pueblo league") policy dating from the Ordinance of May 1567, under which each pueblo was entitled to lands extending one league in each of the four cardinal directions (north, south, east, and west) from the pueblo center. While San Juan Pueblo took its case to the commanding general in Chihuahua, another pueblo, San Lorenzo, took a similar petition to the territorial deputation in Santa Fe. Residents of another pueblo (Santa Clara) had taken their complaints nearly one thousand miles south to Durango in 1815 and 1816.[58]

Hispano settlers, along with some Anglo-American families, targeted certain pueblos before others, notably San Lorenzo Pueblo near El Paso, Pecos Pueblo, and the *genízaro* pueblo at Abiquiú. What counted as "unused" land in the Cortes' decrees of 1811 through 1813 remained ambiguous, but where Indigenous populations had dwindled (San Lorenzo counted a single Indian in 1823, Pecos but several) or where Indigenous alliances were less clear (as with *genízaros*), settlers detected better opportunities for land acquisition.

The pueblos' petitions thereby countered a settler narrative of Indian disappearance. These complaints often surprised Hispano interests. When New Mexico deputation member Domingo Fernandez asked Governor Bartolome Baca for "surplus" Pecos Pueblo land in 1823, the remaining Pecos Indians sprang into action. In March 1825, the Pecos Indians filed a complaint with the territorial deputation asserting broad rights to the "four square leagues." Their prospects at first looked bleak. The deputation advised the Pecos Indians that, due to the Cortes' policy as adopted in Mexico, the deputation could dispose of unused land and, beyond that, authorize individual land sales within the pueblo league. The September 1825 arrival of a new governor, Antonio Narbona, changed the stakes, the rhetoric, and Indigenous fortunes. Despite his past in military campaigns against Native populations, campaigns that led to his appointment as *jefe politico* of New Mexico, Narbona lent a responsive ear to Indigenous complaints. Narbona took over the territorial deputation, clouding the future of the privatization initiative in Mexican New Mexico.[59]

Acting anew, as much from opportunity as from threat, Pecos Indians sent a petition to Narbona just one month after his arrival, in October 1825. They asserted their rights to what Narbona would call their "immemorial property, which has been considered as belonging to each pueblo in their territory." By this he meant the "pueblo league" of five thousand Spanish *varas* (about 2.6 miles) from the center of the pueblo in each of the cardinal directions. The Pecos petition caught the provincial deputation unawares and rendered the body uncertain of its prerogatives, resulting in a consultation to Mexico City. As news of this consultation quickly spread, Hispano land requests in pueblo spaces came to an abrupt halt. The former *regidor* and now *alcalde* of Pecos Pueblo, Rafael Aguilar, authored a new petition for the pueblo in May 1826. Aguilar's petition mixed wrath and delicacy, directing anger at the former secretary of the deputation in Santa Fe while also genuflecting to the powers of the new deputation. If the Hispanos in their midst were so hungry for land, the Pecos Natives wrote, "let don Juan Vigil [the previous deputation head] donate to them and help them with his own money." Aguilar also asserted the full and unambiguous citizenship of his fellow *pecoseños* in the "republic of Mexico." In response, Governor Narbona again asked the national government in Mexico City for clarification on the pueblo privatization policy. The machinery of land sales and grants become clogged by the Pecos Pueblo's petitions.[60]

Pecos Indians, for their part, wanted not only the cessation of land sales in their midst but also the reversal of previous sales that had permitted Hispanos to occupy and farm what they considered the best of their lands. The Santa Fe deputation appointed a committee to look into the Pecos petition and Narbona's report to Mexico City. Pecos Indians petitioned the deputation again in May 1829, targeting this committee. The committee noted that Narbona's reassurances to the Pecos were premised on thin facts and recommended the reversal of any and all land grants to Hispanos within the pueblo that were awarded in 1825. Implementing the vision of Mexican liberalism, however, the committee recognized individual Pecos Indians as Mexicans and upheld their right to sell land without the consent of the pueblo community. By their petitioning, the *pecoseños* had attained a form of citizenship, yet their recognition as Mexicans also opened the way for further individual land sales and the decline of the Indigenous community at Pecos.[61]

A similar petitioning battle played out among *genízaro* Indians at Abiquiú some sixty miles northwest of Pecos Pueblo. As in Pecos, settlers sought lands less by establishing new grants than by inducing individual *genízaros* to part with their lands inside the pueblo league. In one of the earliest attempted privatization sales in New Mexico after the imperial decrees of 1811 and 1812, Teresa Cortés sold her pueblo league lands in 1812 to a Hispano named José Velarde. The pueblo sent a protest in 1815 to Governor Alberto Maynez. Maynez reversed the sale, declaring that pueblo land could not be sold. By 1821 and the transition to Mexican rule, the Velarde land had yet to be returned to the Abiquiú pueblo. The *genízaros* at Abiquiú found only erstwhile allies, if not enemies, in priests and government officials. A prominent *alcalde* of the region, José Garcia de la Mora, openly campaigned for pueblo privatization from 1818 onward and was supported in his push by Governors Facundo Melgares (1818–1822) and Bartolomé Baca (1823–1825), as well as by the resident priest, Fray Teodoro Alcina.[62]

Beginning in 1820, Abiquiú *genízaros* parried this dispossessive thrust in a series of petitions. They first sought the removal and replacement of Fray Alcina, ostensibly on doctrinal grounds, in an 1820 petition to the *ayuntamiento* of Santa Fe. Another pueblo protest of 1822 to the territorial deputation rebuked an attempt by Fray Alcina to commandeer the pueblo's lands. Then in April 1824, Abiquiú *alcalde* Francisco Trujillo joined with four other *genízaro* petitioners to contest the Cortés land sale and *alcalde* Garcia de la Mora's initiatives. This petition took the *genízaros'* case to the constitutional *alcalde* of Santa Fe and referred to the 1754 pueblo land grant at Abiquiú. Ignacio María Sánchez Vergara, protector of Indians for Abiquiú, followed with another petition in May. Garcia de la Mora was sufficiently incensed by Vergara's petition that he sent a long missive to Governor Baca lamenting the faulty legal reasoning of the pretended "Protector of the Indians."[63]

Genízaros had joined land grant petitions for centuries, but the Abiquiú *genízaro* petitions of the early 1820s were different in critical ways. First, these were petitions of protest and grievance, not the grant petitions in which *genízaros* played the role of mediator among Hispano and Indigenous interests. The complaints targeted bishops, *alcaldes, ayuntamientos,* and governors. They functioned as lawsuits only in part; the documents also served to represent, delay, and render an array of nonlegal claims. Second, Abiquiú petitioning of the 1820s explicitly claimed a *genízaro* identity, stepping beyond the allied Indigenous petitioning of earlier generations. The Abiquiu *genízaros* had adopted a more distinctive religious identity, and the 1824 petitioners referred to themselves as the "principal men" of the Abiquiú "congregation."[64] The repeated claim that Teresa Cortés, though an Abiquiú *genízaro,* could not alienate lands held in common precisely because she was a pueblo member marked an innovative assertion in *genízaro* protest. Finally, a wider array of signatures was represented than in some other pueblo cases, including not only educated *alcalde* representatives but also other heads of families, who signed with their marks. The petitions of the 1820s successfully impeded Fray Alcina from taking possession of pueblo common lands and halted further individual land sales. Although the population of the Abiquiú pueblo would wither, *genízaros* and descendant families would remain in possession of the property into the twentieth century.

New Mexican pueblos soon took petition-based resistance to new issues and new forms of organization. Having tired of their corrupt *alcalde* Marcos Baca, petitioners calling themselves "the people" of the pueblo San Jose de la Laguna sent a long petition to Governor José Antonio Chaves in 1830 detailing Baca's abuses and those of his grandfather-in-law Don Joaquin de Pino. Accusing Baca of "having loosed the restraint on despotism," "dreaming of absolute power," and having "suppressed all manner of recourse," the

Laguna Pueblo Indians declared themselves "tired of living enslaved." Baca was "the instrument of the revenges of our persecutor Pino," who was using Baca to deprive the Laguna of the best lands and to impose tithes on the land they did farm. They accused Baca of allowing Pino to steal their animals and to permit Navajos to attack the pueblo to drive its members off their land. In making these claims, the Laguna Pueblo made a claim to its pueblo spaces that was founded in Indigenous understandings and Spanish law: "The time immemorial from which we have possessed the said lands is well in sight; no one is ignorant of the fact that we have possessed them without limitations, encumbrances, or violence."[65]

Laguna Pueblo's grievances were common among pueblos in the late 1820s and 1830s. The government at Mexico City often ignored New Mexico, Franciscan missions had been secularized, and many of the pueblos were without priests. This power vacuum left local elite families and *alcaldes* with vast discretion, and it also permitted a space in which pueblos built their own governments with real capacities, including that of political advocacy. Laguna Pueblo eventually carried its case to Mexico City, and although the link to the Laguna Pueblo petition is not clear, Baca soon resigned. In drawing up the petition of 1830, the pueblo had organized anew politically, appointing a delegate with power of attorney for conveying grievances to the governor and to the capital.[66]

Sensing a change in leadership and the decline of the Mexican liberal ideal favoring privatization, a range of pueblos began to target New Mexican governors and the territorial deputation with petitions in the 1830s. Santo Domingo Pueblo petitioned Governor Albino Perez in 1836 for adjudication of its complaints of encroachment against a Hispano settler. Perez endorsed the petition and ordered an investigation. Although the resulting administrative and legal entanglements unfolded over many years, Santo Domingo secured favorable re-measurements of its pueblo league in 1841 and 1844, and the agents and attorneys it appointed in 1836 continued to represent the pueblo in government matters into the 1840s.[67]

Further north in Taos, pueblo petitioning in the Mexican period fostered alliance building, legal representation, and protection of space. When a group of new Hispano settlers tried to reinstate a defunct land grant ("the Vigil claim") in 1836, a group calling themselves the *Indios naturales* of Taos Pueblo joined forces with Hispano *vecinos* in their midst to protest the claim. Led by Juan Manuel Lucero, the petitioners focused not on the threat to their league but on the jeopardy in which the Vigil claim would place their ecology of irrigation. Fourteen men signed the 1836 petition, and Padre Antonio José Martínez was the most notable among them. Martínez was the son of a powerful Mexican family that had entrenched itself in multiple layers of Mexican government, from territorial deputations to *alcaldes*, probate judges, and, in Padre Martínez's case, the colonial and Mexican church. In contrast to pueblo claims premised on existing legal rights, the Taos petitioners asserted that the reactivation of the Vigil claim would do them harm. Using language strikingly similar to that employed by Laguna Pueblo the same year, the Taos petition asserted that their community had held "from time immemorial" the waters of the Rio Lucero.[68] This claim lay at the nexus of Spanish law and Native custom. The demands on the *acequia* were already at full capacity, and new settlers drawing on the river would harm not only the pueblo members but their neighboring settler *vecinos*.

That the governor denied the Vigil claim, ruling in favor of Padre Martínez and the Taos Pueblo, pointed to the ambiguous, tense status of the Mexican regime, especially in the internal provinces and territories. Like the Spanish colonial regime before it, Mexican government officials served as both conquerors and protectors of Indigenous peoples. The Spanish regime had created the position of *protector de los Indios* in the early colonial period, and while its functions withered in the eighteenth century, the office had been reestablished in 1810. The weight of custom and local rule meant that Mexican officials were not in a position to dispense with longstanding precepts of Spanish law that land grants could neither infringe on nor harm pueblo communities. And as Mexican Catholic bishops were liberalizing, pueblos allied with priests such as Padre Martínez, who had ties to existing Hispano families, church parishioners and clergy, and others in government. In petitions for *acequia* protection, pueblos like Taos assembled on paper an environmental and political coalition that would outlast the document.[69]

The continuance of Indigenous communities in Spanish-governed spaces was a political outcome. That so many pueblos of New Mexico endured with much or all of their "four square leagues" intact points to the subtle power of the petition in Spanish governance. To a degree unwitnessed in the colonial regime of British Canada or the American republic of the time, Spanish law and custom specifically obligated governors and *alcaldes* to take measures to enhance and protect the welfare and survival of pueblos. The discretion with which these officials could and did ignore these obligations does not negate the reality that pueblos, by using their institutions of government and advancing legal and historical claims through repeated petitioning, achieved limited but genuine victories in the work of continuance.[70]

THE CHEROKEE SIGNATORY MACHINE: CRISES OF SOUTHERN REMOVAL

Cherokee women and men had lived in the river valleys flowing from the southern Appalachian Mountains for centuries, cultivating fertile alluvial lands, using a network of rivers for transport and diplomacy, and fostering a robust set of alliances with other tribes to establish a relatively stable regime. Alongside the Chickasaw, Choctaw, and Creek tribes, the Cherokee lived in spaces coveted from near and afar by settlers and slaveowners. Colonial, then state, governments in Georgia and North Carolina eyed Indigenous lands and facilitated the westward migration of their settlers to encroach on Cherokee spaces. The Cherokee hoped for some protection from the Treaty of Hopewell (1785) and the Treaty of Holston (1791), which aimed to define a western boundary of American settlement.[71]

The Cherokee petitioned imperial and colonial governments before 1789, but their deputation system and the use of mass signatory lists became much more common in the nineteenth century. Pressed from the East by unregulated settlers, and all too aware of the Americans' tendency to flout treaty commitments, the Cherokee from the 1790s onward turned to petitioning and lobbying. Like other tribes, they sought to restrain the imperatives of state government by involving Washington. As oppressions and misfortunes piled up in the 1810s, and as Moravian and Baptist missionaries began to descend on the tribe, Cherokee families began to split between those who steadfastly refused to cede lands and those willing to relocate. Land companies and state and federal officials sought to exploit these tensions and to deal with the pro-removal faction as the authoritative voice of the people. Representation thus became one of the central questions—and fault lines—of Cherokee politics.

Advancing this struggle over identity and land, Cherokee women began to assert themselves anew. Their power in doing so was founded on their role as clan mothers, as the rightful repositories of national membership in a matrilineal tribe. Every warrior and chief belonged to the clan of his mother, and as in other matrilineal North American societies, chiefs and warriors answered to clan mothers. Christian missionaries sought to exclude women from political processes, as part of a civilization imperative that the Cherokee would partially adopt after the war. Clan mothers began to draw on traditional women's councils to organize opposition to land cessions. These efforts were led by Nancy Ward (*Nanye'hi*) and, to a lesser degree, Ward's granddaughter Jenny McIntosh, her kin Margaret Ann Scott, and Catherine Brown. Ward brought her status of "War Woman"—a title given to women who had demonstrated bravery and skill in supporting war parties—as well as that of "Beloved Woman." She had previously performed diplomatic roles among the Cherokee, having addressed the 1785 treaty conference at Hopewell, and she had been petitioning orally for four decades. By the end of the war, she was nearly eighty years old, and her long memory of the nation's history, combined with her status as clan mother, gave her a degree of traditional authority that few if any Cherokee men could match.[72]

The women's councils approached the National Council with two petitions in 1817 and 1818. These petitions addressed the problem of land cessions as one over which the Cherokee had control. Ward pronounced herself too infirm to attend the 1817 council meeting, but twelve other women signed the petition and presented it in her stead. The first signatory was McIntosh, who moved fluidly between White and Native networks and was accustomed to petitioning.[73]

"Our beloved children and head men of the Cherokee Nation, we address you warriors in council."[74] So began the prayer of the first petition of 1817, as Ward and her compatriots reminded the warriors and chiefs of their obligations to maternal soul and soil. Recognizing the innovative, even disruptive nature of their address, they acknowledged, "We have raised all of you on the land which we now have, which God gave us to inhabit and raise provisions," and had "never thought it our duty to interfere in the disposition of it till now."[75] In argumentation that would be taken up by John Ross and later anti-removal Cherokee, the Cherokee women argued that land cession was spiritual alienation, an act against God and ancestors, that amounted to the annihilation of the nation's mothers:

> We do not wish to go to an unknown country [to] which we have understood some of our children wish to go over the Mississippi, but this act of our children would be like destroying your mothers.
>
> Your mothers, your sisters ask and beg of you not to part with any more of our land. We say ours. You are our descendants; take pity on our request.

> But keep it for our growing children, for it was the good will of our creator to place us here, and you know our father, the great president, will not allow his white children to take our country away.[76]

A second petition in June 1818 echoed these themes, hewing more closely to the ethic of civilization and refusing to remove "because it appears to us that we, by this removal, shall be brought to a savage state again."[77] The women implored their "Beloved Children"—the head men and warriors—to maintain a policy of agriculture and civilization. Echoing the mistrust that was propagating through Indigenous spaces, they expressed their own worry that White men who had married into Cherokee society and who resided on Cherokee Nation lands "ought to be our truest friends but prove to be our worst enemies. They seem to be only concerned how to increase their riches, but do not care what becomes of our Nation."[78] The solution, in these petitions, was to buy in to the Jeffersonian promise of stay and farm and Christianize, the alternative being to remove and hunt. Petitioning Cherokee women did not blindly trust Washington but recognized that the most immediate threat to national interests came from nearby—from Tennessee, Carolina, and Georgia settlers and the White men intermarrying and invading their spaces. Best to truly become an agricultural nation, a republic, they thought, and to enter treaties on equal terms with the American sovereign.[79]

Whether the women's petitions changed the minds of their audience is difficult to know, yet they clearly coincided with a shift in Cherokee policy. While some Cherokee removed to Arkansas, the steadfast refusal of other families to move became cemented, and in the Treaty of Cherokee Agency of 1817, the division between those families in the "Upper Towns," who favored removal, and those in the "Lower Towns," who refused it, was struck into parchment. The pro-removal faction, soon named the "Treaty Party," was led by war veteran Major Ridge, his son John Ridge, and Elias Boudinot. For his part, John Ross become president of the National Council, which resolved in 1819 to cede no more land.[80]

As the eastern Cherokee knew, the equilibrium of a civilized persistence in the southern Appalachian watershed depended on a national government that kept its promises. Southern governments and their Washington allies busily worked to undo them. Tennessee governor Joseph McMinn, who also served as appointed treaty commissioner with the Cherokee, wrote the National Council that removal to "a country where there is no other indian claim" was "certain to promote everlasting happiness."[81] McMinn began to explore deals with Major Ridge, the Arkansas Cherokee, and the Treaty Party for lands east of the Mississippi. Ross and his compatriots pushed back in a June 1818 epistolary memorial to McMinn, asserting "ourselves as a free and distinct nation and that the government of the United states have no police over us further than a friendly intercourse in trade."[82] Relying on the Treaty of Hopewell and the commerce clause of Article I, Section 8, of the Constitution, Ross argued that American-Cherokee relations were the relations of two sovereigns, requiring treaties signed with proper representatives of the Cherokee living east of the Mississippi, not those who had removed or who falsely claimed authority for the Nation. Like the women of his Nation, he saw and depicted treaty making in spiritual terms.[83]

Resistance to the removal coalition necessitated a thoroughly political strategy to accompany a legal defense. Anti-removal politics targeted different seats of power, tried to play settler interests against one another, and courted allies from near and far. Even as he received vital support from Cherokee women and other leading men and warriors, John Ross became the public leader of this effort. His diplomatic efforts accompanied the deployment of a legal team to press a case against Georgia in the federal courts. Ross drew on older patterns of Indigenous diplomacy, sending deputations to the treaty commissioner, state governments, and different offices in Washington. The deputation system consisted of embassies chosen by the tribe, as in 1817 when the tribe nominated six warriors to carry a petition to the secretary of war. These embassies brought petitions but also relayed speeches and other communications. Consistent with earlier diplomatic practice, Secretary Calhoun would be described not as the "Great Father" but as the "Elder Brother" of the Cherokees.[84]

In the years after the war, Ross steadily transformed this deputation system into an advocacy machine that bundled petitioning and lobbying. In some cases the Nation sent warriors and deputations to state governments, but Ross increasingly traveled to Washington himself, staying there for weeks at a time in order to meet with War Department officials, the president, senators, and members of the House. Ross and his compatriots became constant voyagers from Red Clay and the Lower Towns to Washington, so much so that in the 1830s, they would join with other frequent travelers and complain to Virginia's House of Delegates and the state's newspapers about the conditions of their travel on ferries and railroads. In part because Ross had mastered emergent forms of politics situated at the nexus of traditional

Cherokee diplomacy and bundled petitioning and lobbying, these deputations became more dependent on him as the site of business moved toward Washington. Ross's formidable intellect and his familiarity with major American political figures through his letters rendered him indispensable to Cherokee resistance.[85]

By the time Andrew Jackson had risen to the status of presidential candidate, Georgia politicians no longer hid their aspirations for the total ejection of Cherokee and other tribes from the spaces they desired. Georgia pressed for further land cessions from the Creeks and received vast new tracts in the Treaty of Indian Springs (1821). Upon ascending to the perch of Georgia governor in 1823, George Troup resolved to end the uncertainty over Indigenous presence in his state and pressured for final removal of the Creek. Troup wrote the War Department in 1824 stating his state's opposition to national Indian policy and relaying the resolution of his state's legislative delegation. Calhoun responded with his promise to do what he could to Georgians' satisfaction. The Georgia legislature then petitioned the House of Representatives stating its desire to extinguish all "Indian title" within the state's borders. Whereas Ross and his predecessors had targeted the War Department and the president for most of their memorials, he and his Nation now began to petition the U.S. Congress with new urgency.[86]

Co-signing with George Lowrey, Major Ridge (who signed with a mark), and Elijah Hicks, Ross in 1824 rendered the most forceful statement yet: that the lobbying and petitioning of Georgia officials amounted to "an attempt bordering on a hostile disposition towards the Cherokee Nation, to arrest from them, by arbitrary means, their just rights and liberties, the security of which was so solemnly guaranteed to them by these United States."[87] Ross rehearsed the abject refusal of the Cherokee Nation to remove, adding to a statement of sovereignty over their existing spaces the determination that the civilization program was now final and they would never again "return to the chase."[88] Writing at a time when the Declaration of Independence had regained popularity in national political culture, he reminded the Congress not only of its legal treaty obligations but of its commitments to equality and liberty: "We claim it from the United States by the strongest obligations which impose it upon them by treaties, and we expect it from them under that *memorable* declaration 'that all men are created equal, that they are endowed by their Creator with certain unalienable rights, that among these are life, liberty and the pursuit of happiness.'"[89]

President John Quincy Adams told Georgia to back off but agreed to move forward with another treaty of cessions in 1826. With Andrew Jackson's election in 1828, Ross and his Nation knew that no federal official would stand in the way of Georgia's project, that indeed Georgia's dreams were now Washington's aspirations. Fresh fever over small-scale gold mining in Georgia drew additional migrants and squatters. The Nation had in the preceding years continued its civilization program, adopting a constitution that emulated critical features of the U.S. Constitution of 1787, starting a newspaper (the *Cherokee Phoenix*), and propagating the use of the Cherokee syllabary that had been invented by Sequoyah.[90]

Jackson's ascendancy came in the name of democracy, and Ross and the anti-removal Cherokee adjusted their strategy accordingly. In a growing debate about whether the Cherokee wished to remain in their ancestral spaces or move west, a politics of claimed majorities emerged. Ross would contest this struggle using petitions signed by the dozens, then hundreds, then thousands.

From the Seventeenth Congress (1821–1823) to the beginning of the Twenty-First Congress in 1829, Cherokee petitions to the House of Representatives had been signed by deputation members, by chiefs and warriors, or in some cases by a single individual. Cherokee memorials to the president and secretary of war were little different. Yet beginning in 1829, Ross and his Nation began to send petitions with large signatory lists to Congress. One "Memorial of the Cherokees" appeared in both English and Cherokee, and the meaning differed subtly between the two languages. The advent of large signatory lists also came with dual signatures in signatories' English names as well as the Sequoyah syllabary. The 1829 petitions were large and signed at the top of the signatory list by prominent Cherokee, including Elias Boudinot.[91]

From 1829 to 1837, the Cherokee sent at least three petitions to the U.S. Congress with more than one thousand names affixed, while seven other petitions had more than one hundred names associated with them. In some cases, Cherokee women signed these petitions—including fourteen women of the tribe in December 1829 and hundreds upon hundreds of women in the mass petitions of the mid-1830s—making the Cherokee one of the few Indigenous communities that had women collectively signing petitions to the U.S. Congress at the time.

That Cherokee petitions had changed in tone, quantity, and potential effect was not lost on those receiving the documents or observing them.

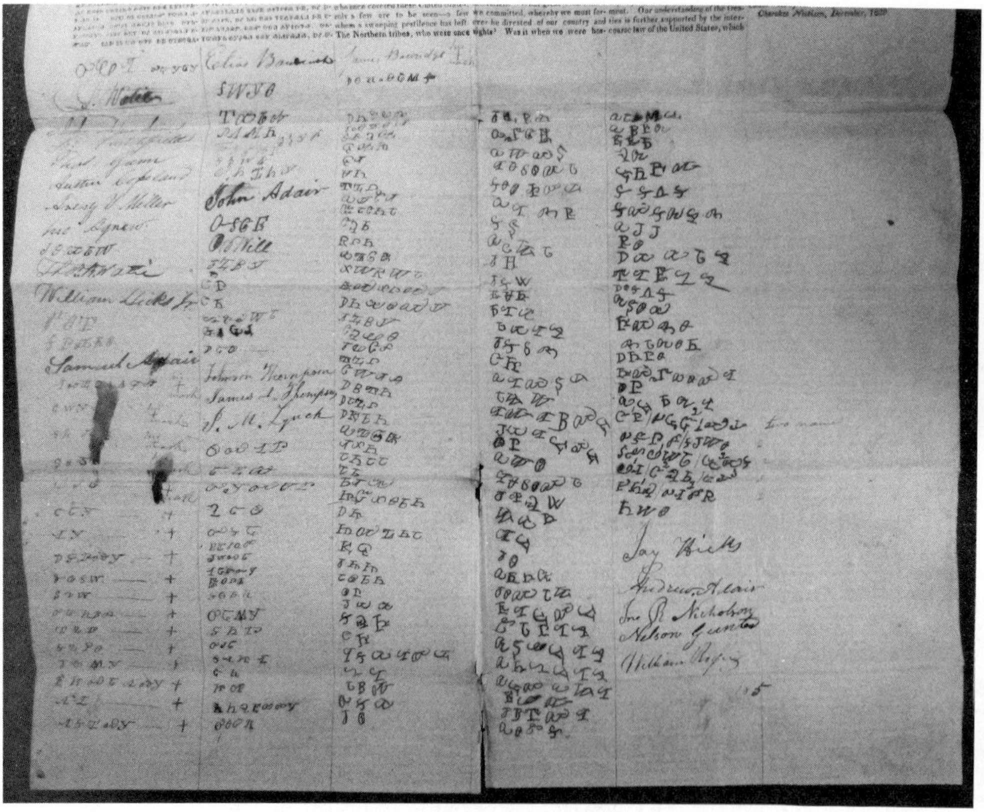

FIGURE 5.3. Signatory List from Cherokee Anti-removal Petition, 1829. *Credit:* Record Group 233, National Archives and Records Administration.

When Senator John Forsyth of Georgia tried to argue that the Cherokee petitions were inadmissible in Congress because they were from a foreign nation, Henry Clay remarked that the Supreme Court had defined the tribe as a domestic nation. He stated that the petitions were legitimate, implying that the Congress was bound to read them, refer them, and respond to them just as with any other citizen. Less visibly, both the War Department and the House Committee on Indian Affairs began asking for more resources, due in part to the administrative demands of Indian removal, but also due to the documentary weight that the treaties and protest petitions had generated.[92]

Taking cues from Native women and from surging Christian reform movements, White women and ministers joined the Cherokee anti-removal effort in droves. In the Twenty-First Congress (1829–1831), religious societies, networks of women, and citizens' groups from Maine through Pennsylvania, Ohio, and beyond were sending petitions to the House and Senate imploring Congress to leave the Cherokee as they were. Catharine Beecher, in a widely published "Circular Addressed to the Benevolent Ladies of the U. States" in December 1829, beseeched the religious women of America, indeed any who made pretense to "benevolence or humanity," for their concern and attention for the "crisis in the affairs of the Indian nations."[93] Writing pseudonymously as William Penn, Jeremiah Evarts—a Christian missionary who served as secretary of the American Board of Commissioners for Foreign Missions—argued to a broader white audience that "most certainly an indelible stigma will be fixed upon us if, in the plenitude of our power, and in the pride of our superiority, we shall be guilty of manifest injustice to our weak and defenceless neighbors."[94] In January 1830, sixty-one women in Hallowell, Maine, petitioned to caution Congress against Cherokee removal, noting their "right to speak on the subject."[95] This memorial was followed by another from sixty-three women of Steubenville, Ohio, openly wondering whether it was not apposite that the "small voice of *female* sympathy will be heard?"[96] In the ensuing two years, almost fifteen hundred additional women would sign anti-removal petitions to Congress.[97]

The anti-removal petitions of the late 1820s had emerged from a set of dispositions and alliances that extended back at least a decade. They were powerfully shaped by the Second Great Awakening and its emphasis on individual testament and expression of conscience. Ministerial petitions to the U.S. Congress had arrived in the 1810s from a diverse range of sources—including Catholic priest Gabriel Richard in Michigan, the Society for the Propagation of the Gospel, and the Friends—asking for congressional assistance and land grants for their missionary work and, in general, for a policy of support for Indigenous communities. By 1819 to 1821 (Sixteenth Congress), religious groups and citizens' networks were petitioning and asking Congress to avoid any alteration to the system of treaties and trade and, in particular, to maintain the policy of disallowing individuals to purchase land from tribes. By the Twenty-First Congress, in the midst of the Jackson administration's full-fledged support for removal, anti-removal petitions had acquired the character of a new campaign, with separate rhetorical tropes and organization. For White ministers, women, and pro-Indian activists, these petitions marked a form of benevolence and of expressive Christianity.

TABLE 5.1 Cherokee Petitions to the House of Representatives, 17th–25th Congresses, 1821–1839

Congress (year)	Title (as in original document)	Origin	Names	Syllabary Signatures	Self-Identified Women
17	John Rogers a chief of the Cherokee	Washington	2		
17	native citizens of the Cherokee nation of Indians	n/a	4		
18 (1824)	delegation from the Cherokee Nation now on a visit at the Seat of Government of the United States	Washington	4		
19	The Undersigned Memorialists under the authority and special Resolution of the General Council of the Cherokee Nation	Rossville, Cherokee Nation	3		
21	citizens of the Cherokee Nation East of the Mississippi	Washington City	4		
21	The memorial of the undersigned delegation from the Cherokee Nation, East of the Mississippi	Washington City	3		
21 (1829)	Memorial of the Cherokees	Cherokee Nation	1,308		
21 (1829)	Your Memorialists in behalf of, and under the authority of the Cherokee Nation	Washington City	6		
21 (1829)	Memorial of the Cherokees (two)	Cherokee Nation	248		
21 (1829)	Memorial of the Cherokees	Cherokee Nation	276	265	
21 (1829)	Memorial of the Cherokees	Cherokee Nation	113	73	16
21 (1829)	Memorial of the Cherokees	Cherokee Nation	84	n/a	
21 (1829)	memorialists under the Authority of the Cherokee Nation	Washington City	6		
21 (1829)	The memorial of the undersigned Chiefs	Washington	12		
21 (1829)	representatives of the Cherokee Nation	Echota	49		
21 (1829)	Memorial of the Cherokees (four)	Cherokee Nation	1,477	1,376	

Table 5.1 (continued)

22	Memorialists duly authorized and instructed by the Cherokee Nation East of the Mississippi	Washington City	3		
23 (1834)	The memorial of the undersigned in behalf of the people of the Cherokee Nation, who are in favor of emigration . . .	Running Waters, Cherokee Nation	60		
23 (1834)	Resolutions passed in Council of those Chiefs + Leading men who are opposed to State Jurisdiction, + in favor of Emigration	Running Waters	2		
24 (1836)	The undersigned Representatives of the Cherokee Nation East of the River Mississippi	Washington City	8		
25	The Memorial and petition of the undersigned a delegation appointed by the Cherokee Nation	Washington City	8		
25	The Memorial + petition of the undersigned, a deputation appointed by John Ross principal Chief of the Cherokee Nation	Washington City	5		
25	The General Council of the Cherokee Nation	Red Clay Council Ground	2,126	2,000+	n/a
25	Chiefs, Committee + Council of the Cherokee Nation West of the Mississippi	n/a	16		
25	The memorial and petition of the undersigned a delegation appointed by the Cherokee Nation in full Council	Washington City	10		
25	To the President of the United States	Washington City	10		
25	The undersigned citizens of the Cherokee Nation	Cherokee Nation	15,673	14,000+	n/a

For Ross and the Cherokee, and for many other tribes, these petitions expressed and reknit emergent diplomatic and spiritual alliances.[98]

By the time of Andrew Jackson's reelection in 1832, the Georgia government was sprinting ahead with removal. The Cherokee fragmented anew, with Elias Boudinot now resigned to the inevitability of removal, departing his editorial post at the *Phoenix* and breaking decisively with Ross. Meanwhile, Boudinot's replacement, Elijah Hicks, published the memorials and resolutions of Seneca leader Big Kettle and his anti-emigration allies, contesting any plans for removal to Wisconsin.[99] The Jackson administration commissioned treaty negotiators to advance a treaty with the pro-removal faction of the tribe for the final and complete ejection of the Cherokee from Georgia. The resulting Treaty of New Echota (1835) was bitterly contested by John Ross, who led two mass petition campaigns, one signed at the Red Clay Council Ground and containing 2,126 signatures, and the second with 15,673 names affixed.[100] These mass memorials instantly became a cultural object of vast attention and reading. White petitioners in Massachusetts and Maine referred explicitly to the signatures of "15,000" in making their arguments against the Treaty of New Echota.[101] Newspapers in northern and southern states began to reprint them, and Alexis de Tocqueville would print large sections of the petitions' prayers in *Democracy in America*.[102]

Because the Treaty of New Echota was in fact signed by Boudinot and other pro-removal Cherokee, the question of the Nation's wishes became one of representation. Boudinot contested the veracity of the signatory lists. The final petition sent to protest the New Echota "treaty" stands as one of the largest per-capita mass petitions from any community in North American history, yet it had been preceded by petitions signed by hundreds of the Nation's citizens in 1829, often signing in the Sequoyah syllabary.

The syllabary signatures of these protest petitions were as much a strike against Elias Boudinot and the Georgia state legislature as they were individual expressions in ink. The genuine wishes of the Cherokee language would be signed, John Ross felt, in an Indigenous language, in its letters, in its sovereign symbols. Ross had spent years thinking about petitions and their role in the long exhausting battle against removal. And he had thought about how the petitions of his people linked to others in the long history of struggle against oppression, not just in the nineteenth century but in the seventeenth as well.[103]

By the time he penned "The Contrast," Ross knew that his nation had been betrayed. Further petitions would flow to Washington, but by 1835 if not earlier, Ross knew that they were falling on sealed ears. His deeply spiritual condemnation of the United States in "The Contrast" echoes the prayer he had written for the 1829 mass petitions. In both writings, Ross portrayed his Nation's relationship with the White man as that of alternating supplicant and sovereign. When two centuries earlier the tables had been turned—when the White man was the "supplicant" and the Indian was "lord"—the Cherokee and other Indigenous peoples had received white settlers' laments and requests with magnanimity and justice expressed through mercy. In the Treaty of New Echota, in the repeated defiance of law and treaties, in the administrative cruelty of removal, the United States and, by extension, the White man in America had sinned against justice, against mercy between peoples. But for the Quaker and the reformer who would count herself as an Indigenous ally, American Christianity had become a hollow letter.

CODA: THE MASHPEE REVOLT

The story of Indigenous petitioning would come full circle in the 1830s. The village-based petitioning that surged in the Northeast had advanced some radical demands. In Mashpee on Cape Cod, the Wampanoag were governed by a complex of institutions involving the Commonwealth of Massachusetts and the Harvard Corporation (more formally, the President and Fellows of Harvard College). Americans have long viewed Harvard as a private institution, but in many ways it emerged as a public creation of the Massachusetts Bay Colony and of the Commonwealth of Massachusetts. Drawing in part on an endowed fund, Harvard employed a minister among the Wampanoag. Governed by a minister and a group of overseers, the Wampanoag saw their Indigenous forms of government suppressed and saw themselves at the mercy of the commonwealth and its instrument of conversion, Harvard College.

The situation was ripe for corruption in forms spiritual and material, and corruption it was that ensued. Harvard appointed the overseers for the Wampanoag, and their minister, Phineas Fish, largely kept to himself, cultivating a following. White residents of the Cape squatted on Wampanoag lands, grazed their cattle on their pastures, cut their timber, and then sold it back to the Wampanoag at inflated prices. The Wampanoag turned to the Reverend William Apess, a Pequot minister who allied with a new generation of Wampanoag to give new voice to the frustrations of the community. Apess's vision for an Indigenous future mixed Christian benevolence, racial identity, and a critique of White America. With Apess, the village petitioned the Harvard Corporation in 1833 and boldly asked for the dismissal of Fish: "We thought it very likely that you would like to know if we, as a people, respected his person and labors, and whether the money was benefiting the Indians or not. We think it our duty to let you know all about it, and we do say, as the voice of one, with but few exceptions, that we as a tribe, for a long time, have had no desire to hear Mr. Fish preach, (which is about ten years) and do say sincerely that we, as a body, wish to have him discharged."[104] The Wampanoag then listed their grievances with the reverend and the state of affairs. He had spent little time among them. The evidence had accumulated to such a point ("we think twenty years are long enough for one trial") that it was time for a decision. The tribe had never been consulted on the original selection of a minister, they complained, and their fundamental spiritual equality—"We do not believe but that we have as good a right to the table of the Lord as others"—meant that they should be equals before God and citizens with the choice in their minister. Just because "our skins are not so white as the whites'" did not mean, they continued, that they lacked spiritual citizenship or the ability to choose for themselves.[105]

Then, turning to the larger continental canvas on which indigenous politics was unfolding, they contrasted the Christian benevolence of Massachusetts elites toward the Cherokee with the relative neglect of the indigenous among them. "Perhaps you have heard of the oppression of the Cherokees and lamented over them much, and thought the Georgians were hard and cruel creatures; but did you ever hear of the poor, oppressed and degraded Marshpee Indians in Massachusetts, and lament over them? If not, you hear now, and we have made choice of the Rev. Wm. Apes to relieve us, and we hope that you will assist him."[106]

By the following year what is now known as the Mashpee Revolt had begun. Wampanoag families began occupying the meetinghouses at which Fish had preached, the village's men began confiscating stock that was grazing on trespass lands, and the Mashpee Natives announced their defiance of the status quo. Massachusetts governor Levi Lincoln called for a meeting between the village and state officials, and when his appointed diplomat Josiah Fiske arrived at Mashpee, over one hundred Wampanoag men with muskets showed. Yet perhaps the central act of the Mashpee Revolt came in a December 1833 petition to the Massachusetts General Court, a memorial far less deferential and far more forceful than any communication sent to Massachusetts authorities during the previous half century. That petition—whose prayer showed the unmistakable imprint of William Apess and was, in a demonstration of the politics of numbers, signed by 287 women and men within and outside the village—marked a turning point in the Indigenous politics of Massachusetts and the Northeast United States.[107]

The Mashpee protest petition of December 1833 was, from an initial reading, a list of grievances and requests. Yet interspersed among the items of law and policy was a larger statement about the character of Indigenous life in Massachusetts. Apess consistently underscored the centrality of the document his village had sent and the exercise of petitioning more generally. The legislature had ignored Wampanoag petitions of yesteryear, even as the laments of the Cherokee brought the sympathy of self-styled Christian philanthropists in the commonwealth.

> We wish for this honorable body to consider our oppression. While ye are filled with the fat of our fathers' land, and enjoy your liberties without molestation, will not this honorable body be as benevolent to us poor Marshpee Indians who are sighing and weeping under bondage, as ye are to the poor Cherokees.
>
> . . . We fear that our petitions have been laid aside without much notice yet [to fore] & our complaints that come before common courts as well as this honorable body have been looked at as being mere cyphers. But we hope that this indifferent spirit is dieing [*sic*] a way & that the true spirit of the Christian philanthropist is [beginning] to reign in the hearts of the people & those who compose their Legislative body.[108]

The Mashpee protest petition featured women prominently, in both its prayer and its signatory list. In ways that would have been clear to contemporaries of the time, as well as tribal elders, Apess's prayer hinted that the mode of government imposed on them erased the voices of clan mothers and women, and deprived in particular the women of choice in tribal leadership. The Mashpee complained of the system of government and hereditary leadership that had been bestowed on them since the 1790s: "We think it is time for a change—neither do we think it right for us to abide by an unconstitutional law made by our fathers forty years ago, & others meaning the whites, who had their own interest in view, we believe all together, for our sufferings by that law has been emence [immense]."[109]

Indeed, in the absence of true guardians, the Mashpee Wampanoag and those on the islands (Martha's Vineyard, Nantucket) had already become a de facto self-governing people, holding councils and electing their own officers. Women voted at these councils and in the choice of tribal officers, a pattern observed at the latest in 1827 by a Massachusetts legislative committee. As White women were just beginning to get active in the anti-Cherokee-removal debates, and at a time when suffrage rights were but a distant aspiration of the 1840s, the Wampanoag women's activity—not merely activism but regularized, legitimated patterns of citizenship—stands as an important marker of these petitions. It also explains why Phineas Fish and other Protestant traditionalists opposed the Mashpee quest for autonomy. The Mashpee saw a consistent pattern of derogatory treatment of their clan mothers and women, one in which the overseers "insulted & pushed out of doors our women & our widows neglected & our [orphan] children crying for bread."[110]

The Mashpee protest petition of December 1833 with its hundreds of signatures—most of the village signatories (ninety-two) were women—would function first and foremost as a representation of Indigenous interests. It would advance a contest over the legitimacy of claims. Phineas Fish sent his own petitions to the Massachusetts General Court and to the governor, in which he claimed that the Mashpee were under the influence of Apess or, a more common claim used to undermine Native American sovereignty in this period, alcohol. In fact, the opposite was true. Apess and other preachers had built a successful temperance movement on Cape Cod and the islands, one that like other temperance movements also brought its votaries into active political dispositions.[111]

The sweeping condemnation of a tutelary regime surely stung many readers, but Phineas Fish and his allies were more heavily focused on the particular requests of the petition. The Mashpee wanted their own government, incorporation as a new town, an abolition of the overseer position, a repeal of the existing guardianship statutes, the legislative removal of Fish, and greater liberty in managing their property and regulating their township. The Mashpee asked to "form a municipal code of Laws amongst our selves," one that used the police power of local government to regulate internal affairs and manage external relations.[112] This vision mixed Indigenous notions of sovereignty with models of republican self-government.

The Mashpee memorial was intended for audiences and soon met them. It called for alliances and boldly asked the self-styled Christian philanthropists of New England who had signed their names to anti-Cherokee-removal petitions to consider the plight of their nearby Indigenous neighbors. One William Lloyd Garrison took notice in the *Liberator*. "We are proud to see this spontaneous, earnest, upward movement of our red brethren. It is not to be stigmatized as turbulent, but applauded as meritorious. It is sedition, it is true; but only the sedition of freedom against oppression[;] of justice against fraud; of humanity against cruelty. It is the intellect opposed to darkness; the soul opposed to degradation."[113] Noting the call for self-government and a new municipal code, Garrison noted that the Wampanoag desired nothing less than to be "citizens of Massachusetts." On this front, he felt confident of the prospects for legislative success. He detected "a soul for freedom in the present Legislature. A more independent House of Representatives has never been elected by the people. The cries of the Indians have reached their ears, and we trust affected their hearts. They will abolish a needless and unjust protectorate."[114]

Garrison's end note pointed to the critical forum of the Mashpee protest petition: the legislature, or Massachusetts General Court. It is little noticed in the annals of the Mashpee Revolt that there was a brief contentious debate about whether it should be read. Representatives from Nantucket, Hingham, and Plymouth asked the petition not to be read, even as Apess and Mashpee leaders were in the chamber. The majority of legislators immediately objected, one from Boston remarking that "our native brethren the petitioners, whose agents were here on the floor . . . should be heard, and heard patiently." Jonathan Chapman went even further, arguing that the Wampanoag "have a constitutional right to be heard. I know not of what value that provision is which gives a right to petition, if the House can refuse to hear the petition. They do not ask for action, but to be heard. It can be read and laid on the table. So long as I hold a seat in this House, my hand shall be raised to give a hearing to the humblest individual who presents a petition for redress of grievances." The vote to have the petition read received only five votes against, notably from the representatives of the areas surrounding the Mashpee (Nantucket, Hingham, and Plymouth).[115]

In the long history of Native petitioning, not least of memorials and remonstrances sent in the nineteenth century, the Mashpee protest petition, presented in January 1834, seems something of a historical singularity. Exquisitely timed, it was the subject of immediate discussion in the legislature—and it was successful. On the last day of March 1834, the commonwealth's legislature passed a new statute that abolished the overseers, giving to Mashpee a district like others in the state, with the ability to elect selectmen. And at last, even Phineas Fish would be dismissed. He who ignored his flock found himself undone by its prayers.

SIX

Slavery, Skin, and Black Strategy

> That they are even treated as a race born for perpetual Bondage—for not only are manumissions taxed, whereby the glimmering of hope is forbidden to shine upon the slave, however meritorious, but even the Coloured man of free condition is made to hold his Liberty (if Liberty it can be called) by the most precarious tenure, and it frequently happens that he who cannot promptly prove his title to Freedom, by clear legal evidence, is by a presumption founded on the Colour of his Face, reduced from freedom to slavery.
>
> —**"The Humble Petition and Memorial of the Coloured Inhabitants of His Majesty's Island of Dominica," July 11, 1823**

Signing his documents as "A Free Mulatto," Jean-Baptiste Philippe spent much of the year 1823 in a labor of advocacy for his kindred population on Trinidad. In a petition and a three-hundred-page address that he delivered personally to Colonial Secretary of State Lord Bathhurst in London, Philippe argued that whatever the British Empire's policies in its other Caribbean possessions, Trinidad was governed by Spanish precedents that placed Black men in full equality with Whites. In an earlier, sweeter time, when Governor Don José María Chacón ruled the island (1784–1797), men of color moved freely and equally among Whites in military and civilian matters. Philippe reminisced over that golden age, when Chacon's "ear was open to every complaint, his arm extended for the support of every feeble petitioner." British conquest of the island never upended this arrangement, as the 1797 surrender agreement continued earlier policies. Yet as merchants and slaveholders migrated from other Caribbean islands to Trinidad, they tried to bring White supremacy with them. Philippe and his compatriots wanted none of it and sought statutory guarantees against the racists' plans. Traveling to London to present his petition to Bathhurst, Philippe asked the secretary and his government for statutory relief for Trinidad's population of "free coloured" and "mulatto" men.[1]

Philippe's appeal for complete racial equality focused on Trinidad alone, vaunting its distinctive legal history in the region. Yet as Philippe surely knew, his appeal was by no means politically unique. In 1823 and 1824 alone, the names of thousands of free Caribbean men of color appeared on memorials to island assemblies, to the Colonial Office, to King George IV, and to Parliament, calling for new statutes guaranteeing civil and legal equality between free men of color and Whites. No official was more commonly the recipient of these petitions than Bathhurst himself. Black and mixed-race memorialists heavily emulated one another's claims across island politics. Newspapers throughout the British Caribbean reprinted these petitions and followed their progress. Slaveholders in the southern United States anxiously watched these Caribbean Black petitions, warning their state legislatures of the need for countermeasures to combat free Black movements. Not unlike a tropical storm, this wave of Black memorials for legal equality swept the Gulf of Mexico, extending from Trinidad to the Virgin Islands and Jamaica to Saint Augustine, Florida, and beyond. In its path, the Black petitioning wave of the 1820s left not destruction but disrupted hierarchies and, by 1830, new protections for Black liberties.[2]

The Black Caribbean petitioning surge of the early 1820s came at a time of heavy ferment in North American politics. In the United States, where chattel slavery held over one and a half million Black women and men in bondage and was growing in scale and scope, questions of slavery and race were litigated and debated in print, in private, and in legislatures. The war for Mexican independence threw open the question of slavery as an institution. Britain ended the slave trade in 1807, and the United States followed a year later, creating precedents for restraining bondage. In all these struggles, Black women and men figured centrally as protesters, writers, litigants, and petitioners. They were joined by White allies (primarily Quakers) and among vanguard political movements in London, Paris, and American cities. Black and White antislavery petitioners were, in turn, rent asunder by factional differences in antislavery—differences over just how, to what extent, and with what resulting liberty for Black slaves the institution would end. And much of their work came in response to proslavery memorials and lobbies that organized in state and territorial legislatures, in towns, and in the U.S. Congress.

For free Black people of the Caribbean, racial equality and antislavery remained fundamentally inseparable. Transiting around the empire, shuttling back and forth from London to their home islands, a generation of free men of color possessed a modicum of civil freedom and legal equality even as White American politicians joined with a small number of Black allies to promote colonization. They owned property and in some cases held slaves themselves. Yet the vast majority had descended from slaves or had emerged from its shackles. They would resist and fight that evil institution. Freedom and equality were intertwined in their view, because freedom meant in part the enjoyment of legal protections and privileges that White men had. Abolition of slavery would offer people of color hollow hope unless liberation came with entry into a promised land of equality and freedom.

In the struggle over race and slavery, women and men turned to petitions first as an instrument of law and justice, and later as a tool of organization, advocacy, and legislative pressure. These petitions surged in the 1820s in diverse contexts—free Black communities in American cities, the Caribbean islands, the tense borderlands of northern Mexico, the spaces just west of the Mississippi River—yet evidence suggests that petitioners in one area knew about efforts elsewhere. Advancing cultural and organizational democracy, these petitions brought populations more intensely and energetically into politics than ever before. Advancing procedural democracy, the documents produced collectively and individually would occupy the agendas of state and national legislatures and the culture of print. Advancing institutional democracy, the petitions generated material progress on issues of voting rights and jury service for free Black men, especially in the British West Indies. In the United States and Mexico, the petitioning politics of slavery compelled politicians to ask fresh questions about the power of their federal governments over the far-flung jurisdictions in their extended republics.

PETITIONING AND THE ORIGINS OF NORTH AMERICAN ANTISLAVERY

The North American battle against slavery took shape, in some sense, as a petitioning endeavor. From Bartolomé de las Casas to James Otis, writers against slavery protested its sinfulness and violation of natural liberty, yet patterns of legal, judicial, or administrative action often followed the rhythms of petitioning. So did incipient organization, as when Pennsylvania's Quakers used petitions to decry "the traffick of men-body" in the 1680s, commencing agitation that would involve tracts and protests and would persist into the 1700s. The many legislative debates in the late eighteenth and nineteenth centuries often followed petitions that introduced bills. In the sweep of antislavery agitation across the colonies from 1767 to 1775, petitioning was inseparable from sermons, tracts, pamphlets, broadsides, and instructions. In claims made to governors and courts in the Province of Massachusetts Bay in the 1770s, free and enslaved Black people began to plead for slaves' liberation and to call into question the very institutions of bondage. In 1773, a slave named Felix submitted a petition to Governor Thomas Hutchison and the Massachusetts General Court (the colonial legislature) asking for selective liberation. Combining religious arguments and claims for equality, Felix wrote for "many Slaves, living in the town of Boston, and other Towns in this Province." While he saw some among his brethren as "vicious," there existed "many others of a quite different character and Who, if made free," could "bear a Part in the Public Charges." Freeing industrious Black people would, in Felix's argument, provide a supply of labor for tasks and taxes. Slavery occasioned among Black people that "intolerable Reflection" that no matter what their character, "neither they, nor their Children to all Generations, shall ever be able to do, or to possess and enjoy any Thing, no, not even Life Itself, but in a Manner as the Beasts that Perish." In a concise text, Felix pointed to slavery's dehumanization and advanced claims for equality grounded in natural right theory and in the Christianity of Jonathan Edwards. Like other slaves who asked only for their own freedom and a passageway to Africa, Felix pled for partial liberation of the Black community.[3]

Like other slaves in Massachusetts, Felix drew on currents of spiritual equality coursing through Boston churches. Whites and Blacks sat in different pews but, aware of each other's presence, heard the same sermons emphasizing Christian equality, resistance to tyranny, and natural liberty. Among the writers mixing themes of republican independence, Christianity, and equality was the Black poet Phillis Wheatley, whose writings circulated widely in the British Atlantic. Felix's claims were soon followed by more general petitions against the slave trade and the institution itself. On April 20, three months after Felix's petition, Peter Bestes and three other slaves asked for new statutes that would convert them from slaves to free men and facilitate their return to Africa. Felix and his cosigners followed their January memorial with another in April calling for the abolition of slavery.[4]

By the time that Massachusetts towns and the fledgling United States had declared independence, free Blacks in Boston began to convert petitioning to a more continual strategy, and in petitioning as well as other activities, Black and White antislavery networks formed critical alliances. Prince Hall, a former Barbados slave turned lay minister, led a petitioning drive in 1777 that advanced a sweeping rhetoric of natural right. Hall's most famous effort came in his 1777 petition, signed with seven other Black men, calling for the abolition of slavery in the new commonwealth. Speaking on behalf of the petitioners and "a great number of Negroes," the petitioners claimed that Black persons in Massachusetts "have, in common with all other Men, a natural & unalienable right to that freedom, which the great Parent of the Universe hath bestowed equally on all mankind, & which they have never forfeited by any compact or agreement whatsoever."[5] Hall's revolutionary rhetoric transcended ideological expression. It embodied a fully political endeavor aimed at assembling a coalition with the political elite of the colony-become-commonwealth.[6] Slaves in Connecticut and New Hampshire followed in 1779 with legislative petitions of their own, documents that echoed the themes woven together in Prince Hall's memorials.[7]

The 1777 petition of Prince Hall and others came before a legislature that considered itself sovereign, and the Massachusetts General Court could in theory have acted on it, but it did not. Nonetheless, Hall's petitioning efforts eventually led to changes in the language of the Massachusetts Constitution of 1780, and this new constitutional language provided a partial basis in the Quok Walker decision (1783) for the legal abolition of slavery in the commonwealth.[8]

As state constitutional reform entered a second wave in the 1780s, Black petitioners approached various state legislatures both individually and communally. Paul Cuffe, a Black marine captain from Dartmouth, Massachusetts, joined with six other of his town's "poor negroes and mulattoes" and asked for respite from a system of discriminatory poll taxes.[9] A year later they approached the town of Dartmouth itself, asking for equal political rights and privileges (not least that of voting on the taxes that burdened them). In Cuffe's grievance, free Blacks, lacking "an equal chance with white people," were not free men.[10]

When Pennsylvania's assembly proposed to weaken its 1780 gradual emancipation statute by reenslaving unregistered Blacks and exempting southern escapees from its protections, free Blacks in Philadelphia responded with two memorials and a powerful reminder that petitioning constituted their most essential voice: "The question of slavery or liberty, is too important for us to be silent. . . . If we are silent this day, we may be silent forever, returned to slavery, we are deprived even of the right of petitioning." The 1781 petitions only slightly weakened the law but marked and energized the formation of free Black political coalitions in Philadelphia. Philadelphia's free Blacks found Quaker allies who petitioned the assembly for a gradual emancipation law in December 1783, and the state responded in 1784 with just such a statute. By 1787, Philadelphia's free Blacks had formed the Pennsylvania Society for Promoting the Abolition of Slavery, and for the Relief of Free Negroes Unlawfully Held in Bondage—its very title reflecting the range of memorial claims made to Pennsylvania's assembly. Joining again with the Quakers in 1788, the Pennsylvania society petitioned for and secured the passage of a law restricting the ability of southern slaveholders to skirt the emancipation law by sending pregnant women out of state or selling slaves awaiting their imminent freedom.[11]

The Black petition of the 1780s and 1790s increasingly took on an epistolary form, a plea written as testimony. With the memoirs of Afro-British writers Olaudah Equiano and Ignatius Sancho sweeping the Atlantic, the slave narrative was emerging as a literary form in American antislavery discourse. At the same time, and decades before those narratives became popularized in the 1830s and 1840s, the petitions of slaves and free Blacks to early American state legislatures detailed the soul-breaking conditions they had endured. A 1794 petition from Cato Hanker, "an African" asking for assistance, offered numerous details on the author's life, including his enslavement, release, military service at the battles of Ticonderoga and Crown Point, reenlistment and service at West Point, and subsequent illness and poverty. Writing "in the decline of life . . . and unable to support himself," he requested compensation for his public service, which the Massachusetts General Court, like the town of Framingham before it, refused him.[12]

The most striking epistolary memorial came in "The petition of Belinda, an African," sent in 1783 to the Massachusetts General Court. Belinda Royall asked for nothing short of individual reparations drawn from the assets of her former owner. Belinda had been a slave of one Isaac Royall, now deceased, and she wrote to claim a portion of his estate. Her life of slavery under Royall had left Belinda with a face "marked with the furrows of time" and a "frame feebly bending under the oppression of years," all the while that "she, by the laws of the land, is denied the enjoyment of one morsel of that immense wealth, a part whereof hath been accumulated by her own industry, and the whole augmented by her servitude." She framed her approach in the humble and traditional terms of petitioning, even as she put forth a truly radical appeal in its statement of facts, legal implications, and political imaginary. Her testimony concluded, Belinda cast herself "at the feet of your honours, as to a body of men, formed for the extirpation of vassalage, for the reward of virtue, and the just returns of honest industry—she prays that such allowance may be made her, out of the estate of colonel Royall." In part because Royall was a Loyalist and in part because he had already left her an annual payment, the court granted Belinda's request.[13]

Less commonly but in ways that disrupted existing norms, free Blacks and their Quaker allies took their case to the national government. In 1797, four Black men—Job Albert, Jacob Nicholson, Jupiter Nicholson, and Thomas Pritchet—petitioned the U.S. Congress. Manumitted by their Quaker masters in North Carolina, they had fled to Philadelphia, where they learned of Moses Gordon, who had escaped from slavery from their state but was in jail awaiting his forcible return to his master. Persecuted themselves under the Fugitive Slave Act of 1793 and by North Carolina's refusal to recognize their manumission, the four men were "hunted day and night, like beasts of the forest, by armed men with dogs." They asked for Congress to intervene against North Carolina's efforts to reenslave them and others. The alliance of Philadelphia free Blacks and Pennsylvania Quakers fostered this pioneering effort. It forced the House to consider whether Black petitioners (slave or free) could approach Congress for redress of grievances. In that quarrel, James Madison remarked that "if they are slaves, the Constitution gives them no hopes of being heard here." Madison's argument did more than deny slaves the dignity of federal subjects; it also held that the proper forum for their concerns lay in the courts, not Congress. Whether congressmen believed that slaves had the right to petition was not clear—northern representatives argued that the right to petition applied to all, while southern legislators remained silent on that argument. Upon legal grounds, namely the inability of Congress to intrude into state jurisdiction, the House of Representatives refused to refer the petition to a committee. In the midst of the debate in Washington, Moses Gordon ended his life by drowning.[14]

Madison's argument left a hypothetical door open for free Black appeals to Congress, and in 1799, Absalom Jones and his Black compatriots in Philadelphia burst through it. With sixty other African American signatories, Jones submitted a memorial complaining of the illegal slave market trade operating openly (and with American involvement) off the coast of Guinea in stark defiance of the Slave Trade Act of 1793. In the opening lines of their prayer, Jones and his cosignatories went straight to the heart of constitutional and procedural matters. Donning the armor of petition rights, they argued that they could address the sovereign body in the name of others (namely slaves) by dint of natural right and the representative function of the U.S. Congress:

> The Petition of the People of Colour, Freemen within the City and Suburbs of Philadelphia—. . . .
>
> We are incited by a sense of Social duty and humbly conceive ourselves authorized to address and petition you in their behalf, believing them to be objects of representations in your public Councils, in common with ourselves and every other class of Citizens within the Jurisdiction of the United States, according to the declared design of the present Constitution. . . . We apprehend this solemn Compact is violated by a trade carried on in clandestine manner to the Coast of Guinea.[15]

Absalom Jones's forceful prayer advanced a new precedent. If, following Madison, slaves could not petition Congress, then free Blacks could petition for them. Slaves were rightful "objects of representations in . . . public Councils" whether or not they carried the words themselves. In its arguments about natural rights of citizenship and the expanse of its signatory list, Jones's petition leapt beyond the boundaries of previous Black memorial strategy. The Black antislavery leader James Forten of Philadelphia recognized the significance of the moment, connecting Blacks' petition rights with their wider claims to human liberty and equality. In writing in a prefatory letter to Massachusetts representative George Thatcher, Forten asserted that "though our faces are black, yet we are men and . . . as anxious to enjoy the birth-right of the human race as those who, from our ignorance, draw an argument against our petition."[16] Southern congressmen tried to bar committee referral of the petition, claiming that some of its requests (such as regulation of domestic slavery) did not concern the jurisdiction of Congress. Representative Robert Waln of Pennsylvania then edited the referral request to pertain only to those portions of the petition that dealt with the interstate or international slave trade. A mere five months after Jones's document was read on the floor, Congress passed the Slave Trade Act of 1800, which heightened the penalties for slave trading and placed new liabilities on investors and employees in slave-trading enterprises.[17]

In their turn to legislative memorials to make the case and advance their cause, Black activists and their Quaker allies were drawing deliberately on the examples of the British antislavery petition campaign. The

1788 abolition campaign delivered over one hundred petitions to Parliament, while in 1792, over five hundred petitions were sent, with the reported signature total over 400,000, a disproportionate number arriving from the working-class bastion of Manchester but flowing as well from coast towns such as Plymouth. Under the leadership of William Wilberforce, British abolitionists tied petition campaigns to consumer boycotts such as the free-produce movement, warning English households away from Caribbean sugar due to the evils of its harvest. The debate in Parliament was inconclusive, with slave trade abolition measures failing in the House of Commons in 1791 and the House of Lords in 1792. Yet Wilberforce and his movement's methods became widely noted, feared, and emulated.[18]

Harnessing the turbulence of revolutionary and founding moments in early America and calling openly for slavery's demise in local jurisdictions and in commerce, these early Black petitions both reflected and impelled new political organization, and they amplified antislavery rhetoric emerging in other theaters. More so than other forms of protest and resistance, these antislavery petitions also conveyed claims directly to legislative chambers, refocusing the statutory agenda of early American states and, briefly, the U.S. Congress. Yet they also partook of a petitioning culture that remained more individual, local, and deferential. The stark, disruptive character of the four freedmen's 1797 memorial and Absalom Jones's 1799 petition demonstrated a wider regularity. Early African American political strategy primarily targeted state legislatures, not least because Black alliances with state lawmakers were better developed and because they judged emancipation and manumission laws more likely in those venues. Black petitioners' claims concerned individual cases, state statutes, or, more generally, the slave trade. Organized petitioning activity represented few Black women as collectives; signatures of Black women numbered in the handful. While Felix and Prince Hall claimed to speak for all Blacks in Massachusetts, their petitions were signed by one or a handful of men. Free Blacks' and slaves' allies in the early petitioning cause emerged more among elites and religious minorities than among the wider White populace.[19]

These qualitative differences reflect not so much limitations of Black activism as they do variations of strategy and opportunity. Canvassing for signatures in the early republic, even in Philadelphia and Boston, also placed free Blacks in jeopardy of arrest and possible reenslavement. Transcending these limitations, free Blacks drew on the petition to build both interracial alliances and Black community institutions. Early efforts focused on educational institutions. In 1800, sixty-seven Black men signed a petition from Middleton, Massachusetts, for an African school, and as with many petitions of this period, it was sent not to the legislature but to the town meeting. In this case, the town meeting recommended that the Black men be granted a school, but the assembly said it was "reluctant to incur the additional expense" and voted its judgment that "ample provision is made for the education of all." Three petitions from 1807 to 1810 asked the Massachusetts legislature to support African schools. In asking for distinctively Black institutions through which the Gospel could be preached and education (understood as a moral and spiritual exercise) could be spread, Black leaders such as Daniel Wild were making characterizations about their communities and those communities' wishes, visions, and aspirations.[20]

As the free Black population grew in both northern and southern states, organized White opposition also emerged, and racists everywhere used legislative petitions to request surveillance and legal changes. The Pennsylvania legislature received anti-Black-immigration petitions in 1806 from Philadelphia and Chester County, and the Senate began drawing up anti-immigration bills. In southern states, White petitioners began decrying the manumissions and freedom of Black peoples. Forty white men in South Carolina worried of free Blacks "that one of the consequences of softening their condition as slaves has been forgetting that they were such and their attempting to exercise among some of the lower classes of white people freedoms and familiarities which are degrading to them and dangerous to society." For these white petitioners, privileges for free Blacks were "actuated by a false or mistaken sense of humanity" and courted social danger. White petitioners drew on these cultural complaints to limit free Blacks' economic opportunities, as in the 1817 South Carolina statute further penalizing trade with free Blacks.[21]

In the midst of these repressive efforts, the tensile web of connections among free Blacks and their White allies in the northern states continued to strengthen, fortified by shared spiritual aims, organization building, and mutual petitioning efforts. When in 1813 the Pennsylvania Senate entertained proposals for banning Black immigration and authorizing a registry documenting each of the approximately four thousand fugitive slaves in the state, free Blacks in Philadelphia petitioned aggressively along with the multiracial and Quaker-dominated Pennsylvania Abolition Society (PAS). James Forten echoed these memorials in his broadside *Letters from a Man of Colour.* The New York Manumission Society (NYMS) built legal and legislative petitioning into its routine activities, allying with supporters of free African schools in New York City, pressing for the state's general emancipation law in 1817, and supporting the freedom petitions of refugees from Haiti from 1818 to 1820. The PAS and the NYMS had coordinated on petitioning since their meetings in 1790 and after the PAS sent the New York society its pamphlet *Memorials presented to the Congress of the United States from the different Societies of the United States* (1792). In Massachusetts, petitioning campaigns to establish schools for Black Americans generated a politics that would build the Massachusetts General Colored Association in 1826, led by Thomas Dalton, James Barbadoes, William C. Nell, and David Walker. For decades, the African church and school served to educate and organize free Blacks. Yet those churches were institutions with legal bases and protections, built in part through petitions.[22]

Early American antislavery emerged as a coalition of free Blacks and their White allies. The very freedom of formerly enslaved African Americans, their political organization, and the sinews of these alliances had formed through shared spirituality and common political practices, often petitioning as much as any other mode of activism. And just as the emergence of free Blacks came in part through petitions, that emergence met with racist White reactionary petitioning in the northern and southern United States. In this countermovement of anti-Black petitioning, not just southern slaveholders but broad coalitions of Whites across the United States sought a bar on immigration and emigration, requested policing for nuisance and disruption, and generally decried the freedom of African Americans. It was in this setting that one "solution" to the problem of slavery—colonization, with gradual emancipation, followed by repatriation of Black persons to African lands or to Haiti—became markedly more popular and its advocates ever better organized. As the debate over free Blacks and the future of slavery raged in the United States, free people of color in the Caribbean were articulating an alternative vision of liberty, one that produced memorials by the dozens and signatures by the thousands.

* * *

The islands of the Caribbean Sea lay at the center of European systems of chattel slavery in the seventeenth and eighteenth centuries, with sugar, molasses, and rum economies deeply dependent on forced labor. The revolutions of the late 1700s rendered these islands ever more necessary to the imperial vision of lucrative slave economies. Britain took hold of many a French colonial possession after the Seven Years' War (1754–1761), and the loss of the North American colonies in the American Revolution (1776–1783) left Britain with a smaller space on which to turn an imperial profit. Revolutions in France and Saint-Domingue (Haiti) from 1789 to 1792 upended another European monarchy and its institutions, injected fresh nightmares into slaveholders' dreams, and induced a wave of multiracial migration. Caribbean slavery's economic trajectory had plateaued (even as it grew and became more profitable in the United States), due in part to its poor suitability for the globally exploding cotton trade, the economic and political reverberations of Britain's slave trade abolition in 1807, and a series of slave revolts that upended the region. Caribbean slavery nonetheless stayed highly profitable for slaveholders and their allies well into the nineteenth century.[23]

The Haitian revolution shook the world of Atlantic slavery like no other event of its era. The initial slave revolts raised the ire of slaveholders in Saint Domingue and the rhetoric of nationalism among Afro-Caribbean peoples practicing *vodou* and merging antislavery with bold new republican themes. Fighting off French and British armies, Toussaint L'Ouverture's military triumph in 1801 and Haitian's declaration of independence in 1804 awakened the aspirations of free and enslaved people of color in North and South America, and left slaveholders and their governments shuddering at the bloody specter of armed revolt. In the wake of that event and the British abolition of the slave trade in 1807, the racial imagination of the Atlantic world was slowly transformed. The rate of manumissions grew sharply in the Caribbean in the late eighteenth and early nineteenth centuries, just as the free Black and mixed-race population rapidly expanded.[24]

Caribbean people of color wrestled anew with the question of racial identity in the early 1800s, not least because Whites in England, the United States, and the islands governed them with growing anxiety and stringency. Interracial relationships were common in the colonial Caribbean—many slaveholders had mistresses of color, sometimes acknowledged, often erased—and the mixed-race children of White fathers suffered a variety of fates. Most of them (roughly four out of five in Jamaica) continued in bondage. White fathers failed to acknowledge their mixed-race children, and even when they did, freeing them was expensive. Manumission required the purchase of other slaves to replace the labor done by those freed. British colonies not only taxed the transaction but also put in place limits on the amount of assets that manumitted children could own. Approximately

20 percent of slaveholders' children were freed, but they encountered such extensive social and economic exclusion that they remained impoverished and marginalized their entire lives. Yet a populous minority of these children inherited large estates and monies, could travel to the metropole and obtain an English education or apprenticeship, and could draw on the combination of paler skin and White ancestry to secure favors unavailable to manumitted slaves. Traveling in intellectual and fluid currents that spanned the Atlantic, they participated in dialogues and economies from which other North American people of color, and even many Whites in the British West Indies, were excluded.[25]

As elsewhere in the Atlantic world, Caribbean slave societies distinguished among persons by ancestry and skin color, forcing racial distinctions onto more complicated histories and biologies. Children of White and Black parentage were known as "mulattoes," while "quadroons" described those with one black grandparent. The "free coloured" of the region could include any of these three identities. Yet social status often increased with whiter skin, more European ancestry, and elite parentage; in 1733, the Jamaican assembly gave the rights of Whites to any person four or more generations removed from African ancestors.[26]

People of color in the Caribbean knew that the pathways to freedom generally required individual appeals, not collective claims. Free Blacks and mulattoes recognized that their liberty had been secured through manumission and that their legal freedom was tenuous and often contested by slaveholders and governments. Even when their freedom was established, they were still governed by laws limiting their social mobility, economic freedom, and political voice. Caribbean colonies sharply limited the amount of money that free people of color could inherit, prohibited them from testifying in court against either White defendants or others of color, and restricted them from a range of occupations and investment opportunities. The possibility of non-Whites voting in island elections was, in general, far removed from the political imagination before 1820. To carve out exceptions for individuals of merit, Caribbean societies occasionally allowed individuals to advance in political and social rank by requesting legislative permission to do so. Among the starkest examples came in Jamaica's institution of privilege petitions, a kind of private bill for individualized racial equality. From 1733 onward, Jamaica's assembly permitted elite people of color to request exclusion from the burdens of racial legislation. Soul by soul, people of color petitioned to become legally White.[27]

With the turn of the century, Caribbean people of color saw doors literal and figurative being closed to them. They experienced growing discrimination in England, as the abolition debate and growing immigration led upper-class British Whites to fall back on a common racial identity. The anxious visions of Britons were evident from fiction writing of the period, including Jane Austen's unfinished novel *Sanditon* (1817), in which a "half mulatto" named Miss Lambe arrives with unnerving wealth and favor upon a White social world in upheaval. Wealthy mixed-race individuals like Miss Lambe found themselves ever less welcome, ever more surveilled, ever more excluded from economic and social circles. These sorry realities left many Caribbean people of color to look westward and, in a sense, homeward. Yet in the islands themselves, there were continued barriers to their advancement. Aside from incremental reforms in 1813 in Jamaica, restrictive statutes governing free people of color remained. Moreover, after 1802, Jamaican privilege petitions appear to have dried up, with no single petition between 1802 and 1823 being approved by the island's assembly.[28]

These limits on individual advancement, the closure of opportunities in England (inducing a return of intellectuals to the islands), and the development of a West Indian press combined with a rapid increase in the free population of color in the Caribbean to nourish free Black political advocacy. In July 1810, free men of color in Trinidad submitted a petition requesting a role in the legislative assembly debate over constitutional reforms on the island. These Trinidadians emphasized their wealth and their exemplary behavior as British subjects. Their intervention in island politics was greeted with ferocious refusal by Governor Thomas Hislop, who immediately ordered a census of the free colored population. As Hislop and other white Trinidadian elites warned one another of the specter of revolts inspired by Símon Bólivar or Haiti, the government soon rounded up dozens of free Blacks for interrogation and imprisonment. In 1811, free men of color submitted an 1811 petition with 129 signatures to the Barbados House of Assembly and sent another in 1812 to the governor, both asking for the right to testify in judicial proceedings. The petitioners included many Afro-Barbadian slaveowners, including some who had petitioned in the previous decade in support of slavery's continuance on the island.[29]

Elsewhere, these free Black petitions began to both construct and reflect budding cross-racial alliances. In 1813, free people of color in Jamaica submitted a petition to the island assembly requesting the ability to testify against Whites in court and the ability to inherit any sum of money. Reflecting and impelling new political organization that spanned free Blacks and mixed-race people, over two thousand Jamaicans signed the petition, and a White counterpetition to preserve the racial status quo quickly ensued. The Assembly of Jamaica responded by repealing an older statute limiting mulatto inheritances, setting the maximum amount heritable at 2,000 pounds sterling, then quickly passed a law permitting Blacks to testify in court, including against White defendants.[30]

In the early 1820s, Caribbean free people of color used the petition more than any other instrument to expand the arena of political struggle. Confronting in print and signature the "oppressive privations and political disabilities" of their lives, Caribbean free men of color drew up memorials by the dozens (and signed by the thousands), requesting constitutional and legal changes in island governance.[31] They targeted a number of venues in doing so—the Colonial Office, the secretary of state for the colonies, island assemblies, and governors. From July 1822 onward, free men of color found an important new venue in the Commission of Free Inquiry created by Parliament in 1822.[32] In November 1823, Fortunatus Dwarris and Henry Maddock received their royal warrant as His Majesty's Commissioners of Legal Enquiry in the West India Colonies. They began touring the West Indies in January 1824 but quickly fell ill, with Maddock dying in August and Dwarris hastily returning to England before resuming his work and being joined by Thomas Coneys and Jabez Henry. Aiming in part to render laws more uniform across the British Caribbean, the commissioners gathered documents, studied compilations of statutes, and examined the operations of courts. Yet they quickly encountered requests to meet by leading free men of color, usually bearing petitions addressed either to the commissioners themselves or to Lord Bathhurst, as well as copies of memorials sent to their island assemblies. The commissioners steadily expanded the scope of their inquiry to include the legal rights of free Black men, so much so that colonial officials later rebuked them and suspected at least one of them as showing too much favor to slaves and free people of color.[33]

With petitions flowing from Jamaica, Grenada, Barbados, Antigua, Saint Christopher, Dominica, Saint Lucia, Montserrat, Saint Vincent, and Trinidad, the years from 1823 through 1825 became an apogee of collective appeals by Caribbean people of color. The set of names attached to these petitions expanded every bit as quickly as the scope of their demands.

Gathering at the Kingston home of Alexander Sympson, mixed-race Jamaicans planned political strategy in May 1823 and launched a new petition to the island assembly. Sympson and his collaborators authorized a new lobbying representative to travel to London. The petition drawn up by mixed-race Jamaicans in May 1823 requested that people of color be eligible for officeholding, that they have the suffrage and the ability to sit on juries, that courts facilitate the provision of testimony by lightening the burden of documentation, and that funds be appropriated for schools for poor children of color. Among the petition's twenty-one signatories were Lewis Lecesne and John Escoffery, two Haitian refugees whose political activity drew the suspicion of colonial authorities. In November 1823, the men were arrested and deported to Haiti, where they sold their belongings and traveled to England to establish their identity and reclaim their liberties. Lecesne and Escoffery then petitioned the House of Commons, where their defenders alerted Parliament to the men's tribulations. In the ensuing Commons debate, the ordeal experienced by Escoffery and Lecesne became narrative evidence of the very claims made by the 1823 petitioners. The men were eventually freed and returned to Jamaica.[34]

Alexander Sympson's 1823 petition reflected free Black political organization around Kingston, but on the northern side of the island, a kindred organization had arisen at Montego Bay. A group calling itself the People of Color of the Parish of Saint James petitioned the assembly in 1821 to create a school for poor children of color, addressed the Duke of Manchester (the island's governor) in 1822, and again turned to the assembly in 1823. As the assembly held firm in its refusal to expand the legal protections awarded in 1813, the Montego Bay group approached the commissioners with a set of documents in December 1825 and expanded their claims.[35]

Changes in political climate also reignited Jamaican privilege petitions, with thirty-nine of them submitted between 1823 and 1826. Yet the cross-racial coalition seemed more focused on systematic changes that affected all men of color. In the petitions and addresses of 1823–1825, free Jamaicans of color made two logical connections between Black civil rights and the burgeoning ideology of antislavery. The first was that restrictions on free Blacks were an extension of the slave system and, to some degree, just as cruel: "There is a degradation in Slavery beyond that of the restraint of the task master. It is the absence of moral principle. The political bondage of the middle class was as abject as the bodily servitude of the field labour."[36]

Relatedly, free Jamaican men of color argued that unless liberation from slavery was accompanied by robust Black civil liberties, manumission amounted merely to a relinquishment of property claims by the slaveholder, with no conferral of rights on the freed human. While it was easier for free men of color (some of whom still owned slaves) to make this argument, the evident momentum afoot in the British Empire for gradual emancipation gave the argument additional force.

A third argument from the Jamaican petitioners of color concerned the inconsistency of racial codes with larger British values and aspirations. Free men of color, the petitioners maintained, had not demanded honors conferred by assemblies, senates, governors, or even vestries. They were simply asking for the rights of British subjects, having shown their loyalty to the Crown in many ways—through militia service, through payment of duties, and by not revolting as other colonists had. Beyond this, they claimed that genuine economic development of the colonies required the unleashing of free Black men and their capital and labor. They quickly extended this claim about economic disadvantage into a nuanced insult directed at their White audience, asserting that Europeans' relative richness flowed from their domination of opportunity: "The effort of the European monopolizes all encouragement, and receives more than a proportionate share of reward."[37] For their part, the free population of color had only the handicap of unfavorable institutions, as well as the fiction sustained by the Whites who enjoyed its advantages, as "they conceal the fact that the want of industry, enterprize [*sic*] and intelligence which seems to pervade the [Black] community is less attributable to any absence of energy in the native people, than to those political institutions, which repress their exertions or neglect to foster their capability for improvement and usefulness."[38] As the free Jamaican men of color developed a neo-republican argument that targeted monopolies and privileges, they profoundly reinterpreted British Caribbean spaces. Colonial statutes giving economic and political privileges to Whites over free Blacks stooped to the same level of Spanish depravity that Britons fancied themselves having transcended. Jamaica was suffused, the petitioners claimed, by a nomenclature and a psychology of racial privilege. White Jamaicans "have entrenched their exclusive privileges in the very prerogatives of blood, bequeathed to them by the Spanish prejudice, in perpetuating to this day the distinctive epithets of 'Negro, Mulatto, Quadroon and Mestizos.' The Mountains, Rivers and Districts of this Island retain in their names the language of their Iberian discoverers, and the laws controlling its inhabitants are still inscribed with their opinions and prejudices."[39]

The Assembly of Jamaica received but rejected these petitions in 1824 and 1825. Yet Alexander Sympson and his collaborators of color knew that the debate had started ocean-wide in earnest. From 1823 onward, Caribbean newspapers eagerly reprinted news of legislative debates and memorials being received by other island assemblies as well as by Bathhurst and other colonial officials. The *Jamaica Journal* and the *Saint Christopher Advertiser* reprinted free Black petitions from Trinidad (including those of slaveowners counterpetitioning the free Black memorialists), while the *Saint Christopher Gazette and Charibbean Courier* published legislative debates stemming from free Black petitions in Barbados. The *Grenada Free Press and Public Gazette* covered Trinidadian petitions as well as antislavery debates in Parliament and the speeches of Símon Bólivar. No island's petitions and legislative debates appear to have received more attention than Jamaica's, whose free Black petitioning politics were covered in Antigua, Barbados, Grenada, Saint Christopher's, and other islands.[40]

In Barbados, talk of possible emancipation induced by the May 1823 agreement in Parliament led a group of free mixed-race men, headed by Jacob Belgrave, to declare their loyalty to the government and their "willingness to resist, to the best of our ability, any innovations in the present form of society." A larger group of Afro-Barbadians led by Samuel Collymore—who had repeatedly organized and signed petitions from free men of color in the previous twenty-five years—quickly organized a mass meeting and counterpetition signed by 373 free men of color. The counterpetition, published by a newspaper in January 1824, clarified that the population would no longer ally with Barbadian Whites to support slavery, but also suggested a delay in any reforms until after racial tensions stoked by the recent revolt in Demerara had calmed. The counterpetitioners chose their venue carefully, going around the colonial assembly and taking their case straight to the governor. As had occurred a decade earlier in Trinidad, the counteraddress was considered sufficiently destabilizing that the Barbados assembly launched an investigation into the counteraddress in February.[41]

Further mass petitions from free men of color came from Dominica, Grenada, Saint Christopher, Antigua, Saint Vincent, Saint Lucia, and Monserrat. With larger signatory lists than had characterized petitions of the previous decade, memorialists of color targeted statutes passed in the islands that had become more oppressive from 1810 onward. In their prayers, they consistently drew attention to the "disabilities" imposed on them by discriminatory statutes. Mixed-race and Black strategists from Dominica sent a petition to Maddock and Dwarris in 1823 and transmitted another to Bathhurst; 289 of these men also signed a petition to the island's assembly. They lamented the tax on manumissions, the distinct criminal codes for Whites and "free coloured," and the lack of any opportunity to vote for those who shaped these laws. The Coloured Inhabitants of Grenada also took a memorial to Maddock and Dwarris, claiming that their ideas were "purely English, not only by Birth, but likewise from attachment to a Constitution the boast and pride of every British Subject." Emphasizing as did Jamaican petitioners their English education, their wealth, and their loyalty to the Crown, they protested the terms by which they were treated as equivalent to slaves in the criminal and civil statutes of the island. Across these islands, petitioners knew of one another's endeavors but rarely referenced other jurisdictions and their free men of color. Officially, argument and petition sought local audiences and local measures.[42]

Amid all this fury of commissions, memorials, and countermemorials, Jean-Baptiste Philippe's argument for Trinidad might have seemed indistinctive. Yet Philippe's address and memorial (the latter written with the mixed-race lawyer John Congnet) cut a remarkable and influential profile in the 1820s Caribbean. Philippe was a physician, and he rendered an extended complaint about statutory burdens that suffocated the careers of the most educated men of color. For presenting this case, Philippe selected as his audience not Trinidad's assembly (which had become increasingly hostile to free people of color) or the Commissioners of Legal Enquiry, but Lord Bathhurst himself. Bathhurst was an Oxford-educated Tory and a civil servant in a system that increasingly prized demonstrable merit and training, at least for high positions. He tilted conservative on economic issues (opposing the Reform Bill in 1832) but generally favored liberalizing colonial laws. He would have known that opportunities were closing for men like Philippe in England. Philippe's argument stood out for a number of reasons, one being his forceful rhetoric, another the plausibility of Trinidad's distinctive history as one in which free people of color had in fact experienced liberties in the late eighteenth century that their counterparts elsewhere in the Caribbean had not. After Chacon's rule (1783–1797), Sir Thomas Picton ruled Trinidad with a combination of vengeance and tyranny, while Governor Hislop's harsh reaction to the free petitioners of color in 1810 had quieted political activism. Philippe's overtures came at a low point in the experience of Trinidadian free men of color, and his petition (which preceded the published address) was followed by other petitions from free men of color.[43]

Philippe's work points to the dual political innovation among Caribbean free men of color in the 1820s. The first came in the admixture of different tools of politics into a novel democratic repertoire that included large meetings, petitions with numerous signatures, and a delegation of lobbyists visiting London or colonial officials traveling in the Caribbean. In the context of Whites' fears of Black uprisings, free people of color courted risk when they met in larger numbers, even as they visually remapped Black assembly and its implications. The fact that these meetings produced petitions left a granular record of the gatherings (with individuals who had attended) and endowed the proceedings with greater political legitimacy. Compared to earlier efforts, the "coloured petitions" of the 1820s targeted a broader set of venues, stepping outside the hierarchies and official complaint channels of the colonial Caribbean.

Second, innovation came in transformed racial organization. In these petitions of the "free coloured," men pierced the categorical divides of race that had been imposed on Caribbean people of African descent. Whether in Dominica, where free men of color argued that the transition from slavery was being clogged by manumission taxes; in Jamaica, where wealthier mixed-race petitioners of color advocated for schools for impoverished free Blacks; or in Trinidad, where petitioners appealed for a return to the regime under Governor Chacon, when officers' commissions in the colonial militia were granted to "coloured men and Blacks" who held "similar authority and received similar respect" to that of White officers, Caribbean memorialists were cementing links between slavery and racial privilege and, in so doing, crossing the artificial color lines of the colonies.[44]

As they recombined men and their ancestries into new coalitions, the Caribbean free petitioners of color sometimes observed other hierarchies in their conscious adherence to strategy. Having fled Haiti en masse, Caribbean people of color had French surnames by the thousands, yet as in other British colonies, a nervous Anglophone majority composed the audience for their memorials. Free petitioners of color often appointed educated men of English descent to head their committees and present their case. When four Frenchmen of color and an Anglophone took the petition of the free men of color of Dominica to Lord Bathhurst, they appointed the Englishman among them—Joseph Bermingham—to testify to the petition and to represent them. When men of color did put their names to documents, they judiciously concealed their French ancestry where possible. The Haitian-turned-Jamaicans Lewis Lecesne and John Escoffery who signed the 1823 Kingston petition were otherwise named Louis Celeste Lecesne and Jean Escoffery. Legal records on the island employed their French names, as did the parliamentary debates in London, where Lecesne was named "Louis Celeste" or "Lewis Celeste." Their 1823 petition signatures erased, as much as they could, these Haitian and French origins. So, too, when Jean-Baptiste Philippe signed his petition to Bathhurst in 1823, he signed his last name as "Philip." At a more aggregate level, the petitioners of 1823–1825 subjugated French surnames. They systematically placed Anglophone names higher in their signatory lists, with French surnames three places lower on average. Combined with the paucity of surname clusters in these petitions, this pattern shows that the free petitioners of color followed a mixture of political models, combining an elite petitioning approach with that of popular signatory lists.[45]

The petitioning wave of 1823 to 1826 bore little to no immediate fruit. Island assemblies generally resisted the appeals of free men of color, rejecting requests for voting rights, a lightening of tax burdens, or an easing of discriminatory codes. Yet the petitioners' targeting of metropolitan as well as island venues markedly changed the colonial governance agenda in Britain. Early nineteenth-century British parliamentary practice accorded petitions the ability to generate debate in the chamber, and considerable parliamentary debate on colonial governance ensued. The trial of Lecesne and Escoffery in London in 1827 and 1828—one that was accompanied by memorials from free men of color in Jamaica asking the government to declare them British subjects—also kept the debate in the public mind. Beginning in January 1829 with a government decree for Saint Lucia, then extending to an order covering Trinidad in March, the Colonial Office issued orders whereby restrictions and disabilities imposed on any "free persons of African birth or descent" were "repealed and forever cancelled." The orders repealed those acts that subjected free people of color to "disabilities and restrictions to which other free persons inhabiting the said island are not subject." Colonial assemblies also began to take up the initiative, with the assembly of Barbados passing laws in 1828, 1829, 1830, and 1831, and then a slew of partial emancipation bills for free Blacks and mixed-race people in Saint Vincent, Jamaica, Barbados, Grenada, Antigua, Dominica, and Tobago from December 1830 to July 1832.[46]

By 1833, a year before Parliament had abolished slavery in the British Empire, free people of color and free Blacks witnessed the erasure of most of the statutory discrimination placed on them. Other legal hurdles remained, as did cultural, religious, and other forms of political discrimination. Yet

Table 6.1 The British Caribbean Petitioning Surge of the 1820s

Island	Petitions (selected)	Signatures	Additional Signatory Ranks Downward of French Surnames and Surname Clusters
Antigua	Commissioners of Legal Enquiry, 1823	60	
Dominica	Commissioners of Legal Enquiry, 1823 (2 petitions)	• 289 • 156	French: 2.47 ($p<0.01$) Cluster: 5.53 ($p<0.05$)
Grenada	Commissioners of Legal Enquiry, 1823	128	French: 4.91 ($p<0.05$)
St. Christopher (St. Kitts)	Commissioners of Legal Enquiry, 1823	40	
Montserrat	Commissioners of Legal Enquiry, 1823	101	Cluster: –4.72 ($p<0.05$)
Saint Lucia	Commissioners of Legal Enquiry, 1823	35	Cluster: 6.07 ($p<0.01$)
Saint Vincent	Commissioners of Legal Enquiry, 1823	45	Cluster: 4.38 ($p<0.05$)
Average relationships across petitions to Commissioners of Legal Enquiry, 1823–1825 ($n=555$ signatures)		French: 2.50 ($p<0.05$)	
Jamaica	Memorial of the Free Coloured Inhabitants of Jamaica, 1825	Not available	
Barbados	• Belgrave address (1823) • Counter-address (January 1824), 323 free men of color	• n/a (Belgrave) • 323 (counter-address)	
Berbice	Commissioners of Enquiry, 1825	n/a	
Trinidad	• Memorial to Lord Bathhurst • Memorial to Commissioners • 2nd Memorial to Commissioners	n/a	
St. Augustine, Florida	To Governor and Legislative Council of Florida (May 31, 1823)	11	

Source: Commissioners of Legal Enquiry in the West Indies, CO 318/76, NAUK. UNCG, PAR 10582301. Differences reported only if statistically differentiable from zero; p-values reflect standard errors clustered on fixed effects for page and column.

voting rights, liberties for property and inheritance, and access to occupations and vestries had been greatly expanded.[47]

Men of color in the Caribbean had democratized the colonial British petition and, in so doing, had advanced electoral and economic democracy as well. They had busted the limits of imperial supplication and had courted the energies of free Blacks as well as wealthier mixed-race men. Their struggles for democracy, equality, and development would continue, but the civil rights obtained, while heavily limited by gender, would continue to shape Caribbean politics and became a model for other rights movements, including those in North America.

RESTRICTION, EXPANSION, PETITION

Two moments that collided with the global economic crisis of 1819—the debate over Missouri and the winning of Mexico's independence from Spain—combined to further unsettle the politics of North American slavery. The question of Missouri emerged in part as one of slavery and in part as an abrasion of settlement petitioning politics and the growing fear of an industrialized American North. The Missouri debate placed the U.S. Congress, more than ever before, at the center of American debates over slavery. Mexico's newly won independence and its abolition of slavery in a republican mode carried an even greater threat to the system. Suddenly the geographical and spatial threat to racial bondage came not merely from the industrializing lands of the North but also from the very places where cotton and tobacco could be cultivated. Slavery became an ever more national question, and for that reason an ever more congressional matter, as the question of its regulation in U.S. territories and its extension to states dovetailed with the crisis over which regional faction would rule the nation's political institutions. In both ways that were designed and ways that could not have been anticipated, the U.S. Senate built in a preserved advantage for slave interests, as the expansion of population in the industrializing northern states did not translate to more legislative power unless more states were created there. It was for this reason that antebellum U.S. statehood admissions had long been governed by a normative "balance rule" that prescribed one free state for every slave state. In so doing, the balance rule and the structure of geographical and nonpopular representation extended the South an effective veto over strong antislavery measures.[48]

Disputants renewed the American contest over land and slavery's imprint for several reasons. The first was the increasing rate of manumission and emancipation in the Revolution and early republic. More Virginia slaves found their freedom through manumission between the Revolution and the War of 1812 than at any time before 1865. This more gradual development threatened slavery and created larger populations of mobile, free Blacks in the United States. Second, the American victory in the war unleashed settlement pressure across the Appalachian divide, principally in southern states but also in northern states, with growing infrastructure projects, emblemized by the Erie Canal, that eased latitudinal transportation in the United States. Third, the cotton market exploded, due in part to renewed trade in the late 1810s and technological changes, especially the cotton gin, which permitted easier and more voluminous production of short-staple (or "upland") cotton. After a fungus killed off many cotton fields in the Mississippi valley in 1811, planters imported a new form of cotton from Veracruz, and these seeds and their successful hybridization with Georgian cotton assisted a sustained boom in production. With slavery ever more profitable, investors, slaveowners, and their political representatives looked westward for opportunities to expand their machinery of bondage and production.[49]

Rapid settlement of the Missouri Territory west of the Mississippi River created new opportunities and new pressures on national politics. Missouri was marked by its lack of a British past. Its lands had been Spanish ruled, then French governed before it became a U.S. territory. Long before the explicit question of slavery west of the Mississippi, the vision of settler republics took root there. Missouri was a smaller part of Jefferson's Louisiana Purchase, finalized in 1803 and with the Louisiana Territory being created in 1805. In April 1812, Louisiana became a state, and the remaining spaces became Missouri Territory in June. Settlement pressure was concentrated in the areas closest to the Mississippi, inhabited by Natives, French settlers and Creoles, and a growing number of Americans.[50]

The first petitions after the War of 1812 concerning Missouri came in not regarding statehood or slavery but regarding land title, as older landholders sought confirmation to their claims. Introduced by John Scott, a territorial delegate, several dozen Missouri residents petitioned for confirmation of Spanish land titles. Over fifty such petitions would arrive to the U.S. Congress from 1817 to 1820. Then in 1817 came the first Missouri statehood petition to Congress, not from the territorial legislature but from a group of signatories who put forth the grievances they saw in territorial status, including their lack of a "vote in your honourable body"; the "veto of the territorial executive," which was "absolute upon the acts of the territorial legislature"; the power of the territorial supreme court; and the fact that "the powers of the territorial legislature are limited in the passage of laws of a local nature, owing to the paramount authority of Congress to legislate upon the same subject."[51] American families dominated the signatory list of the 1817 statehood petition, which included a number of the land claimant petitioners from that year.[52] The coalitions for settlement and statehood drew from the same networks of families. Missouri's statehood seekers felt that the bar would be low and easily surpassed by the population numbers and the burgeoning republican industry of their state: "Your memorialists feel a firm confidence," read an 1818 petition, "founded on the wise and generous policy heretofore pursued by your honorable body . . . that they need only pray to be incorporated into the Union."[53]

As Missouri's territorial legislature lined up for statehood, two thorny questions of precedent arose and ignited national debate. The first was that no offsetting territory existed in the Northwest Territory to compensate for Missouri's admission. By the balance rule, Vermont compensated for Kentucky, Ohio for Tennessee, Indiana for Louisiana, Maine for Alabama, and later Michigan for Arkansas and Illinois for Mississippi. The second was that slavery's extension into Missouri marked a material and symbolic breach of the Mississippi River, the opening of slave state possibilities into a vast new domain. New York congressman John W. Taylor led the charge on the House floor, seeing a larger sectional plot in Missouri's statehood petition:

> Thus, on the implied power to acquire territory by treaty, you raise an implied right to erect it into states, and imply a compromise by which slavery is to be established, and its slaves represented in congress. Is this just? Is it fair? Where will it end? . . .
>
> But your list of acquiring is not yet satiated. You must have Florida. Your ambition rises. You covet Cuba and obtain it. You stretch your arms to the other islands in the Gulf of Mexico, and they become yours.[54]

Alarmed by this expansion—which they termed "diffusion"—northern activists and politicians began to call on Congress to either change the terms of Missouri's admission or to overhaul the territorial system altogether. Town meetings on the "Missouri question" were held in a range of northern and eastern states, and concerned citizens—notably the mid-Atlantic states of

TABLE 6.2 Geographic Distribution of Restriction Petitions to the U.S. Congress, 1819–1820

State	Petitions
CT	• Statewide • Hartford • New Haven
MA	• Boston • Brighton
ME (District)	• New Gloucester • North Yarmouth
NY	• Albany (city and county) • Schenectady
OH	• Steubenville
PA	• Carlisle • Columbia County • Delaware County • Northampton County • Northumberland County • Philadelphia • Union County
RI	• Newport
TN	• Manumission Society
VA	• Brooke County • Ohio County

Note: Excludes anti-slave-importation petitions in 1817 and 1818, many from New Jersey and Pennsylvania.

New York, Pennsylvania, and Virginia—began targeting Congress with petitions calling for the restriction of slavery in the territories.

When memorials poured in from northern cities and towns, including Albany, Boston, and Philadelphia, calling for Congress to explicitly regulate slavery in territories-becoming-states, southern congressmen noted the claims with fury and scorn. Federalist legislators had, during the War of 1812, called for less power of Congress over the states. Their turnabout, southern members ridiculed, seemed exquisitely timed. Southern members were also incensed at the support for restriction from mid-Atlantic Republicans and erstwhile followers of Jackson. Pennsylvania representatives like Joseph Hemphill and Samuel Moore favored restriction not least because

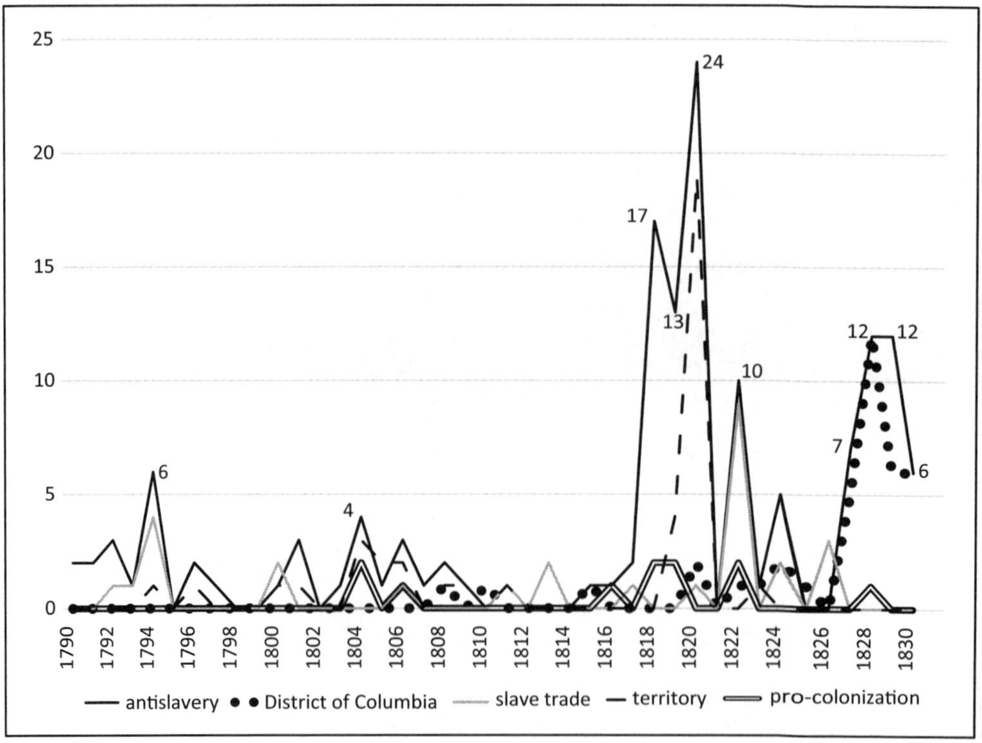

FIGURE 6.1. Antislavery Petitions Introduced to Congress, by Prayer Theme, 1789–1830.

their constituents were petitioning for it. Observing the petitioning foment, North Carolina senator Nathaniel Macon voiced the opinions of many southern legislators that antislavery petitions had become a nuisance. "Our people do not petition much," he remarked. "We plume ourselves not on pestering the General Government with our prayers. Nor do we set the woods on fire to drive the game out."[55] As the national sovereign became a chamber of debate over slavery and continental space, supplicants wanted the chamber to assert its authority, while slavery's representatives increasingly saw the petition as a tainted mechanism of politics.

The temporary settlement of this struggle emerged in the House of Representatives and through the political mastery of Henry Clay. In the Missouri Compromise of 1820—actually a bundle of two separate compromise statutes—Congress committed itself to exclude slavery from the Louisiana Territory north of the thirty-sixth and one-half degree parallel (36°30′), or a linear extension of the latitudinal boundary separating Kentucky and Tennessee west of the Tennessee River. Missouri would, in theory, comprise the sole exception to this spatial division, and Maine would accompany its admission into the Union, thus preserving the fictional balance of slave and free states and the slaveholding South's negative in the Senate.[56]

As both Black mobility and sectional antagonism rose in the United States, alarmed White citizens mobilized a new petition-based racism to lobby state legislatures to restrict or expel free Blacks and to more thoroughly police slaves. Through a range of southern states, but also in mid-Atlantic states such as Delaware and interior jurisdictions like Ohio, newly emerging White citizens' associations targeted state legislatures as their venue for anti-Black overtures. The stimuli that triggered their response came from various nodes of the Atlantic slave economy and the global debate that it engendered. In 1823, British activists formed the Anti-Slavery Society, and in March of that year, the parliamentarian William Wilberforce introduced a Quaker petition against slavery, while two months later Sir Thomas Buxton introduced a resolution into the House of Commons calling for slavery's abolition, declaring the institution "repugnant to the principles of the British Constitution and of the Christian religion." Yet nothing so stoked Americans' fear of Black liberty or mobility as the events in South Carolina the year before. In June 1822, Charleston was rocked by rumors of an imminent, massive, orchestrated Black uprising that would unite slave and free Black, a planned massacre purportedly led by the literate journeyman Denmark Vesey along with other men in the African Methodist Episcopal Church in that city. Vesey and around thirty other Black men were executed, the church was destroyed, and the fears of a Haitian-style uprising swept the state and nation. White fears vastly outran the reality of threat, but the reverberation of images and narratives of Black rampage and slave uprising created realities of its own.[57]

Defenders and representatives of slavery seized on the incident, even as they manufactured many of its publicly consumed details, to call for new restrictions on Black bodies and, especially, minds. They responded most visibly with organized coercion and violence, yet they also reacted by organizing and petitioning for legal changes to more tightly regulate free Blacks and slaves. The height of these anti-Black mobilizations occurred in South Carolina, where in 1823 hundreds of men formed the South-Carolina Association. The association was structured for the purpose of assisting the enforcement of laws encumbering free Blacks. A year after the Vesey controversy, the association took an anxious and comprehensive memorial to the South Carolina Senate. Troubled by the constant presence of free Black sailors and ship workers at Charleston, 334 officers and members of the association made themselves an enforcement posse, proudly claiming that they had arrested 154 people of color in the association's first two months. The sheer numbers of free Blacks visiting South Carolina "in defiance of its enactments" pointed to a much larger phenomenon—Black mobility and communication between North and South—that cried out for regulation: "There can scarcely exist in our southern community, an evil of greater magnitude, to the country at large, than the constant intercourse, which is maintained between the blacks of the North and the South."[58] As they expanded their list of threats to the slave order, the association's members noted with alarm the petitioning movements of the Caribbean:

> But it is not from North alone, that we are threatened with doctrines subversive of our peace. In all the British West-India Islands, with scarcely an exception, there is, at this moment, considerable inquietude, in consequence of the desire of a strong party in the British Parliament, to interfere with the regulations of their slaves. In the island of *Grenada,* a memorial was presented by the free persons of colour, setting forth, "that as loyal and dutiful subjects, they ought to be admitted into a participation, in the rights and privileges to which every Englishman is entitled, under the British Constitution." . . . In *Antigua* and *St. Christopher's,* similar petitions have been presented to their Colonial Assemblies, the fate of which is not known.[59]

The mobilization and eventual liberation of Caribbean peoples in the 1820s led to growing anxiety in the South about the political emergence of free Blacks and the possibility of abolition and liberation. The specter of Haitian revolt had never disappeared, but the mass movements of the Caribbean were newly emergent and left a documentary record that echoed through the Atlantic and American world. In the 1823 petition to the South Carolina Senate, the association converted these anxieties into an agenda of statutory action, calling for "one CONSOLIDATED NEGRO ACT, or code, for the government of this class of people."[60]

> With such proceedings in these islands, and with the known habits and sentiments of the coloured people of the North, aided and encouraged as they are, by a portion of their white population, your Memorialists cannot conceive a measure, which can give greater security to the State in general, than

to prevent ANY FREE COLOURED PERSON FROM ANY PART OF THE WORLD *ever entering again into the limits of the State of South Carolina,* BY LAND OR BY WATER.[61]

In its emphatic typescript, its rehearsal of dangers domestic and international, and its mobilization of men who served simultaneously as petition signatories and posse enforcers, the association's petition was a remarkable document. It presaged the laws, passed in South Carolina and soon extended over nearly the whole of the slave-based southern states, that sharply restricted the ability of free Blacks to visit the state.

Similar petitions, leading to similar statutes, diffused throughout the United States. In 1825, citizens of Rutherford County in Tennessee called on that state's assembly to "pass a law compelling all free persons of colour forthwith to leave the county of Rutherford and take up their abode in some State beyond the Ohio where slavery is not tolerated."[62] The Wilmington Union Colonization Society, fearful that the "free people of colour now constitute a considerable part of our population; and they are fast increasing," asked the Delaware General Assembly in 1827 for a law of expulsion for free Blacks, with quick relocation to "a place to receive these people" on the African Coast, procured for this very purpose by the society itself.[63] In 1828, the Charleston City Council called the attention of the South Carolina Senate to the impossibility of distinguishing between "the free and the slave of our coloured population," with the result that "it is extremely difficult to detect violations of the Law" prohibiting the teaching of literacy to slaves.[64] The only solution, the council concluded, lay in a blanket prohibition on institutions for teaching people of color: "We know of no remedy so effectual and at the same time so little liable to objection as the absolute prohibition of all schools for the instruction of coloured persons."[65] As the free Black population in Cincinnati, Ohio, surged in the 1820s, White residents sought municipal regulations to restrict their movement and labor. A coalition of citizens petitioned the city council in 1827 for the regulation of Black lives and property under nuisance regulations. By the end of the decade, petitioning had turned to violence. An interracial riot in 1829 led to a large-scale exodus of Cincinnati's free Blacks to Canada, where they formed a new village called Wilberforce.[66]

Slaveholder interests also targeted state legislatures for measures to shore up the slave system itself. Southern slavery depended heavily on a system of regulating the bodies and minds of Black persons in bondage.

The geography of the southern states sometimes rendered this task more complicated, as escaped slaves had much more space to which to escape than did slaves in the Caribbean, often with dense forests in proximity to farms with livestock they could poach for sustenance. Slaveholders in four North Carolina counties observed with angst that "our Slaves are become Almost Uncontroulable they go and come when and where they please and if an Attempt is made to correct them they fly to the Woods and there Continue for months and years committing grievous depredations on Our Cattle hogs and Sheep and many Other things."[67] Slave patrols, the petitioners complained, served little to help this problem, as the patrol houses were routinely sacked and burned. As slavery developed in the south after the War of 1812, slaveholders would counter these jeopardies by clearing forests and exposing the thickets and marshes in which slaves hid. The petitioners from Samson, Bladen, New Hanover, and Duplin Counties had something else altogether in mind, one that involved the assertion of government authority over White planters in order to further subdue the slave population.

The North Carolina petitioners called for nothing less than a system of surveillance militias and taxes to support them. They asked for a law "compelling Each Captain" in their four counties "to divide their companies into four equal divisions" per county, with one man "Chosen out of Each Company as a Captain or Commander of that Company the rest to be Submissive to his Orders" with statutorily defined penalties for disobedience. With these patrol companies so constituted, the requested laws would give them full ability to search "all the Suspected places, houses or thicks" where runaway slaves might lay, with the added "priviledge of Shooting and destroying all Runaway Slaves who may Refuse to Submit to Said Authority." The North Carolina assembly granted the petition, creating new rules and measures for forming slave patrol companies. The statute authorized county courts to impose taxes of ten cents per "taxable slave" to fund the program and could further appoint patrol committees of three men for each patrol captain's district, each patrol being capable of administering corporal punishment to slaves found off their master's property without the requisite pass. Slavery's continuance, its profitability, and its culture of fear depended heavily on institutions and human forces that incarcerated slaves. Slaveholders had always used the petition to construct these institutions, but in the 1820s, their anxieties led them to turn afresh to legislative memorials.[68]

These petitioning campaigns of the 1820s focused heavily on state legislatures, yet intersectional tension compelled slaveholders to target federal venues as well. Dismayed by the Woolens Bill, a tariff proposal coming from Pennsylvania in 1827 that threatened their export position, slaveholders organized gatherings and mounted petition campaigns from a rough dozen jurisdictions throughout South Carolina. The memorial from Columbia warned that "the benefit of the Union to this state is becoming more dubious and disputable," while that from St. John's Colleton wondered why "the Southern Planter [would] humbly kiss the rod which chastens him?" With these meetings and petition campaigns, state leaders intended to form a coalition of political authorities and planter interests, fusing sectional resentment against the Pennsylvania woolen lobby with a more assertive defense of slavery and its spaces. The resulting political momentum helped kick off the nullification crisis of the ensuing years.[69]

The Silence of Colonization, the Rise of the District Question. In the light of the petitioning and organizing battles over Missouri, the public force of the dominant antislavery movement at the time—colonization—remained remarkably muted in petitions. Founded in 1816, the American Colonization Society (ACS) aimed for gradual emancipation followed by settlement of freed slaves in an African colony. Its early members included Henry Clay, Andrew Jackson, Daniel Webster, and many of the United States' most prominent statesmen. The coalition included those opposed to slavery, who saw their plan as inducing slaveholders to emancipate their slaves, as well as those who feared Blacks either would not receive or did not deserve equality in the United States. Nor was the ACS the only colonization-friendly organization at this time. The American Convention for Promoting the Abolition of Slavery supported a colonization program until 1821. Neither of these organizations made much use of the congressional petition. Occasionally some state or local chapters would call on their state assembly for authorization of, or funding for, a colonization program, often as a way of advancing an argument against free Blacks. Yet these state and local petitions often emerged separately from the national colonization associations. Mass colonization would have required the administrative machinery of the general government, yet in part because the leaders of American colonization were so closely tied to political elites during the Era of Good Feelings, the colonization movement made little petitioning imprint before the U.S. Congress. Petitions favoring colonization were remarkably rare, never exceeding two in a given year from 1789 to 1830. The ACS and the colonization program remained the predominant model of antislavery before 1830.[70]

At an aggregate level, the variable flow of antislavery memorials to the U.S. Congress demonstrated the early alliance between more radical antislavery stances and petitioning. As the Missouri crisis faded from the nation's newspapers and broadsides, antislavery activists began to mount a symbolic battle for the restriction or abolition of slavery in the District of Columbia. The first congressional petition calling for this modest measure came in 1822, from the Manumission Society of Tennessee to the Seventeenth Congress. The manumission society asked for a settled date at which all District slaves would be free. In the Eighteenth Congress, the Tennessee society's petition called for abolition in the District. The District of Columbia question fell off the congressional agenda for several years, but in 1827, petitioners from northern states—from Williams College in Massachusetts, the city of Baltimore, the town of Paterson in New Jersey, Washington County in Indiana, and Columbia and Warren Counties in Ohio, with at least ten memorials from Pennsylvania—began again to raise the issue. Recognizing the consensus that Congress could not regulate the internal economies and property laws of states, antislavery petitioners focused on a jurisdiction where Congress's authority was unquestioned. The size of the slavery market in the District was not considerable, but antislavery activists knew that the battle was more than symbolic. It got to the heart of the question about the power of Congress over those lands that were not (or were not yet) states.[71]

The boldness of the District of Columbia strategy showed that the Missouri crisis had opened a new front in American slavery politics. The congressional antislavery petitions of the 1820s underscored the deep structural issue posed by slavery and race: the question of national power and congressional will.

MEXICAN ABOLITION AND THE QUESTION OF BORDERLAND SLAVERY

The fall of Spain's colonial empire after the Panic of 1819 left a shaken and unsettled world of landholders, settlers, investors, Indians, and slaves. Mexican rebels fought and won in the name of republicanism, driven by the passion and ideology of Agustín de Iturbide, whose Plan de Iguala promised independence, individual equality, and a break from centuries of Spanish oppression. In the very first years of the uprising, the assembled congress at Mexico City attempted to organize the lands under their domain. As they gathered in 1822, they were met with proposals from a variety of investors and settlers—some Mexican, most American—to create new agricultural communities in the northern borderlands according to the republican ideal. These plans ran up against antislavery views stemming from the Mexican ideal of equality championed by Iturbide and by liberals who assumed important positions in the new congress at Mexico City.[72]

Mexico's independence threw open the question of borderlands and the future of their governance. Slavery and the cotton economy rapidly expanded south and west in the United States. Crippling debt left the central government in Mexico City unable to defend its northern settlements. But because Americans desired these spaces, Tejanos and others wanted them to immigrate, and Mexico's liberal republicans wanted to preserve the vision of Iturbide and an antislavery future, an important debate unfolded over the future of the territories of Coahuila and Texas. American investors, colonizers, and slaveowners, led by the American Stephen F. Austin, saw in the Texas borderlands a chance to expand their markets west, to lands cheaper than those of the Mississippi valley, where proximity to the Caribbean offered advantages in competition and trade. For their part, Tejanos in Mexico wanted settlers to ward off the military threat from the Comanche, and other Mexican politicians desperately sought settlement and investment for the economic development they felt necessary to bring their new republic out of debt. Yet American settlers would not arrive from the places most likely to send them—the southern and western states—without security for their most prized assets: their slaves. In order to bring these various interests together, various investors and self-styled *empresarios* used colonization petitions to propose colony charters with the new Mexican government, targeting its central legislature in Mexico City.[73]

In the midst of the unfolding settlement politics, Mexico was wracked by political unrest and violence. In the summer of 1822, Iturbide's supporters commandeered the streets of Mexico City and the capitol building, demanding his installation as emperor. In July 1822, Iturbide ascended to the throne and chose a compliant congress. Austin and other petitions now had to target Iturbide himself, and they did so diligently and carefully, leading to the passage of a colonization law in 1823 that allowed the import of slaves to the northern borderlands. The 1823 law secured an opening for American settlers, and both Austin and politically active Tejanos played a role in its drafting, lobbying, and passage.[74]

The overthrow of Iturbide in 1823 further muddied the situation, and self-styled republicans led the endeavor to craft a new Mexican constitution in 1824. The primary axis of conflict concerned the degree of centralization in the new republic. Those considered conservatives favored centralization, while ever more radical liberal republicans wanted a form of federalism in which power would be devolved from Mexico City. In the wake of Iturbide's deposition (and his execution in 1824), the sentiment of Mexican elites and peoples swung decisively toward federalism. The new colonization law in 1824 gave important powers to states and their congresses.[75]

In Mexican Texas, the uncertainty was heightened by the fact that Texas would be not a territory under central government control but absorbed into the new state of Coahuila-Texas, with a new legislature at Saltillo in which Tejanos were outnumbered ten to one. The resulting uncertainty over the future of slavery in Texas—it had been permitted in the earliest constitution and colonization law but was now being threatened with abolition by the Saltillo legislature—reverberated throughout the region, into Mexico as well as the United States.[76]

Because of the Mexican republic's commitment to federalism, the venue for pressure, lobbying, and politics switched from Mexico City to Saltillo. Coahuila-Texas started writing a state constitution in 1826, and for the next three years an important battle raged in the Saltillo legislature over the governance and future of slavery and, by extension, the extent of American settlement. Article 13 of the draft 1826 Constitution, first written by Manuel Carrillo, stated unequivocally that "the state prohibits absolutely and for all time slavery in all its territory, and slaves that already reside in the state will be free from the day of the publication of the constitution in this capital." As Americans saw their existing investments about to be undone, to say nothing of their dashed aspirations for a future settler republic in Mexican Texas, Austin and his allies sprang into action to try to persuade the Saltillo legislators to rewrite their colonization law.[77]

Their first stratagem was a long petition, called for by José Antonio Saucedo, the political chief at Béxar, and written by Austin. Saucedo had long served in Spanish conciliar and legislative institutions, as a member of the *ayuntamiento* of San Fernando de Béxar from 1806 onward, and as secretary of that *ayuntamiento* from 1823 to 1827. Austin's prayer carried both laments and threats, both complaints of interference in property rights and dire warnings that implementing a strong antislavery policy would bring "the total destruction of all new colonies . . . the annihilation of all hope of emigration in the future, and the consequent abandonment of this beautiful country." In the absence of American settlement, not only would the desired agricultural communities so cherished by republicans fail to take root, but Tejanos and even Coahuilans would be subject to the whims of Comanche and other Indian hostilities. Austin used these petitions and lobbying endeavors in a strategy with two time horizons, the first one of delaying the enactment of a harsh antislavery colonization law, thereby preserving investments and inducing further immigration; the second aimed at long-term persuasion of the Saltillo legislature so that a slavery-based cotton economy could be built in Mexican Texas. Petitioning in federalist Mexico and Coahuila-Texas had become the mainstay of a settlement-slavery advocacy machine.[78]

Petitions accompanied the formal debate in the Saltillo legislature in November 1826. Article 13 was read before the Saltillo Congress on November 30, 1826, followed by the petition of Austin and another petition from Tejanos in San Antonio. The chamber then scheduled its debate, deadlocking over the precise date of emancipation for second-generation slaves born in Texas. Austin's and the Tejanos' petitions had their desired effect of delaying an antislavery ordinance, and when the Saltillo Congress reconvened, it drew up the Constitution of 1827, in which Article 13 was adopted but significantly weakened. All children born in the state were free from slavery, and all slaves had to be imported within six months of the charter's adoption. A new statute passed in May 1828 provided legal protection for Austin's colonization plan and for the near-term importation of slaves.[79]

By the early 1830s, the reality of Mexican sectional conflict over slavery had emerged clearly. Every time the republic tried to clamp down on Texas, Tejano leaders (primarily based in San Antonio) petitioned for greater autonomy for the province. And in these petitions they repeatedly reminded Mexico City that they retained the right to form a new government if their autonomy was not granted. Anglo settlers began holding conventions in 1832 and 1833 calling for the separation of Texas from Coahuila. San Antonio Tejanos sent a memorial in December 1832 complaining of national interference in their affairs from Mexico City, openly stating their desire for more immigration of Anglo "capitalists." Tejanos in Nacogdoches and Goliad drafted more extreme memorials, with declaratory prayers that vaunted “the natural right of revolutionary measures against their oppression.” Given the historical difficulties faced by the Spanish and then the Mexicans in governing these lands, these threats were anything but idle. The ensuing conflict ushered in a military confrontation, the Battle of San Antonio, and the Republic of Texas, whose proslavery constitution crushed the seeds of antislavery liberalism and, with the republic’s independence, ensured sufficient distance from the debates in Washington as to secure a legal future for slavery as solid as anywhere in North America at the time.[80]

* * *

The debates over Missouri and Texas reverberated through the Atlantic world, and they showed that just as slaves, free Blacks, and White allies could use petitions to force uncomfortable issues onto state and national agendas in the northern states and in Washington, so too could the slavery-settlement machine draw on an older world of petitioning for its own aims. In the antislavery mode of petitioning, moral and religious argumentation combined with interracial alliances for everything from freedom suits to courts and legislatures to state-by-state measures for emancipation and Black liberties. Aiming as much for small victories as for symbolic precedents, they targeted Missouri and the western territories just as they turned to the liberation of slaves in the nation’s capital. In another, proslavery mode of petitioning, planters’ memorials also attracted dozens or even hundreds of signatures but were used to legitimate and document a strategy of settler lobbying and networked political pressure, targeting key allies in state legislatures, creating a world of patrol and incarceration for free Blacks and slaves alike, and carrying threats to antislavery lawmakers in Saltillo and Mexico City. The politics of slavery became a politics of venues and of federalism, and as the debate over states’ rights crossed the Mexican-American border, its claims were defined as much by petitions as by votes.

AWAKENINGS

SEVEN

Patriotes and Rebels

Petitioning and Parliamentary Sovereignty in French Canada

Moderation and truth, essential features of any just cause, dictated this Appeal. It will bring light to all of our constituents, if indeed it has not already been viewed by all of them, and will justify our cause among other nations. Hence I have no objection to signing it.

—**Jean Dessaulles to Louis-Joseph Papineau, Sainte-Hyacinthe, 1827**

Five or six years ago the English government wished to unite the whole of Canada in one single assembly. It was the measure most fit to dissolve entirely the Canadian nation, so the whole people at once awakened, and it is from that time that it knows its strength.

—**Alexis de Tocqueville, 1831**[1]

Among the meanings that Europeans and North Americans gave to democracy by the nineteenth century, two were inseparable from the idiom: an insistence on self-rule and a strong embrace of the power of representative legislatures. The vast cultural diversity of North America rendered both concepts problematic. The United States and Mexico could establish republics and the idea of monolingual nations only by ignoring, even erasing, that heterogeneity, as John Jay had done in *Federalist* no. 2 when he wrote that "Providence has been pleased to give this one connected country to one united people—a people descended from the same ancestors, speaking the same language, professing the same religion, attached to the same principles of government, very similar in their manners and customs." In the United States, self-rule referred to English-speaking Christians (especially Protestants), and in Mexico it meant Spanish-speaking Catholics, with reduced status for mestizos and a protectorate for Indians. The growing accent on nationhood in Indigenous petitions came in part as a response to the feared erasure of Native North American sovereignty. British political models embraced parliamentary sovereignty but usually subsumed local and colonial assemblies to the will of Parliament and, beyond that, the Crown's governors and the Colonial Office. The contest between local and metropolitan assemblies fueled nothing less than the American Revolution.[2]

Nowhere did diversity and emergent democracy combine to challenge nation-building more than in British Canada, a vast realm ruled by Great Britain since the 1763 Treaty of Paris. Canada had been New France until 1763, and in the early 1800s most of its population still spoke French, while colonial administrators had decided to direct their investment and energy elsewhere. English-speaking settlers grew in number from the late eighteenth century onward, including Tories fleeing the independent United States and migrants from England and (especially) Ireland and Scotland. The contest between French Canadians' vision of their nation and their own constitution, on one side, and colonial Anglican visions for linguistic and cultural union under a British industrial model, on the other, produced vast popular agitation, a public battle over institutional form pitting parliamentary government against colonial administrative control, and—by 1837—an armed rebellion. In the Patriote Rebellion of 1837–1838, a group of francophone militiamen and habitants raised arms against British troops and were violently suppressed, resulting in 365 of them being killed. Yet in the decades before and after that bloody confrontation, French Canadians (calling themselves Canadiens) signed or marked their assent to petitions by the tens of thousands and effected a measure of change in their institutions as a result.[3]

Contemporary readers may be reluctant to associate mass petitioning or emergent democratic forms with nineteenth-century Canada, which remained officially a colony under the tutelage of the Crown. Yet the textbook differences between American "democracy" and Canadian "colonial government" can mislead. The more populous province of Lower Canada—one of two colonial provinces of British Canada, with approximately 425,000 inhabitants in 1827, and which today corresponds roughly with Québec—had many of the trappings that contemporaries and scholars associate with American democracy: highly widespread voting among men due to a low property-holding requirement, political factions that were coalescing into opposition parties, a robust press, religious diversity, and growing industry and professional work in the cities. Canada also had scattered voting among women and Indigenous populations, something the United States generally lacked. The vesting of political power in nonrepresentative bodies—the colonial governor and the executive and legislative councils—blunted popular representation, to be sure, yet these arrangements were not all that different from those prevailing in New York State (with its Council of Revision) and some New England states that stacked their upper chambers with more aristocratic protections. So too new forms of democratic idiom, incorporating a language of republicanism that stressed a more egalitarian politics, spread across the province.[4]

As much or more than any other peoples in nineteenth-century North America, Lower Canadians launched vast popular petitioning campaigns in the early nineteenth century. The historical peak of these petition mobilizations came a full decade before the Patriote Rebellion, in 1827 and 1828, when francophone Canadians circulated a pair of linked memorials compiling grievances against the colonial governor, Lord Dalhousie, and amassed eighty-seven thousand names on it. The anti-Dalhousie petition of 1827–1828 received the official assent of as much as one-quarter of Lower Canada's adult population, a feat all the more remarkable considering that the Canadian population was not concentrated in urban centers but remained spread across hamlets and farming villages, and the complications of traversing many landscapes and waterscapes to visit these populations made canvassing all the more difficult (there were no signatures from the remote Gaspé Peninsula, for example). In five counties, the names of over one-quarter of the entire population (including First Nations residents) appeared on the anti-Dalhousie petition, and in one county (Trois-Rivières), over half the total population (of whatever age) was represented. These numbers are comparable to the height of Chartist agitation in Britain, which happened ten years later and which took direct inspiration from the Patriote mobilization.

No phantom of imagination or activism, the anti-Dalhousie petition of 1827–1828 was well known to publics on both sides of the Atlantic. Large parts of it were carried to the House of Commons in 1828, and it was displayed before the provincial legislature in Québec City as well. American newspapers remarked on the agitation, and British labor activists watched the French Canadians' mobilization with a mix of affinity and desired emulation. A decade before the exposition of mass antislavery petitioning in the United States—centered on the Twenty-Fifth Congress of 1837–1839—and a decade before the peak of Chartist petitioning, the anti-Dalhousie petition stands as one of the largest mass petitions on a population-adjusted basis of the nineteenth-century Atlantic world.

The anti-Dalhousie petition was neither a one-off nor inconsequential. Five years before it was drawn up, another petition presenting over sixty-five thousand names offered a protest against a proposed union of Lower Canada and anglophone Upper Canada that would have erased much of the cultural and institutional distinctiveness of French Canada. Like that 1822 petition, which helped to derail the project of colonial fusion, the anti-Dalhousie petition of 1827–1828 was remarkably effective. A select committee of the British House of Commons in 1828 issued a report largely supporting the Canadien petitioners; armed with the report, the Crown recalled Dalhousie and replaced him. Other reforms requested by the Canadiens would take more time to come to fruition, but when they did, the Lower Canadian assembly would have new budgetary powers. The petition and the committee report it induced had set an agenda for future action and stalled other oppressive measures by Dalhousie and his allies in British colonial administration.[5]

Continued tension over questions of provincial autonomy buffeted Lower Canada in the early 1830s, and Canadiens and their allies launched new petitioning campaigns in the 1830s, particularly in support of a set of principles and demands called the Ninety-Two Resolutions. The machinery of partisan organization in the provincial assembly had begun to form, and a coalition of soldiers, French Catholic intellectuals (often allied against particular bishops), and rural farmers (called *habitants*) assembled to challenge Tory designs on Canada. Even after the failure of the Rebellion and the project of colonial union launched by Lord Durham in 1839, Canada would have greater parliamentary sovereignty than it did in the 1810s and 1820s, and while Durham called for assimilation of Lower Canada (called Canada East after the 1840 act), the prospects for anglophone hegemony had been greatly reduced by the political organization of the Canadiens. The mobilizations of the 1820s, in other words, carried legacies that would persist through and past the creation of confederated Canada in 1864.[6]

The manifold democratization wrought by mass petitioning in Canada brought greater institutional democracy in protections for provincial self-rule, especially with the preservation of cultural sovereignty and in the buttressing of parliamentary powers. The petitioning campaigns also advanced organizational democracy and forms of cultural democracy, as the campaigns led to a diffusing pattern of local meetings (often held in the parish buildings that provided a public sphere for Canadian villages), engendering the organization of a broad colonial opposition, and as the memorial campaign brought women and even children to the massive rolled signatory lists. The leaders of the francophone petitioning movement were deeply aware of the Indigenous petitioning movements in their midst and, when traveling to London to present their monster petition, carried Indigenous villagers' petitions with them.

The emergence of democracy by petition in antebellum French Canada upends the customary Anglo-American centrality of petitioning narratives. Why did early nineteenth-century mass petition-signing arguably peak first not in the English-speaking Old or New Worlds, not in a Protestant milieu, but in a largely Catholic, French-speaking British colony? The answer lies in the thoroughly political nature of the petitioning campaign: its attempt to persuade not only the House of Commons but also the far-flung publics of Lower Canada, the conscious effort to appeal to French Canadian values while recruiting anglophone allies (especially in Montréal), and the defense of parliamentary democracy. An English parliamentary tactic nonetheless reflected a deep embedment in a culture at the intersection of French history and North American experience. The mass petitions were circulated, explained, and signed in French, and their organizers were as likely to call them a *requête*, a *plainte*, and an *Appel* as a *pétition*. Canada's pre-conquest experience with French traditions of *requête* created important precedents, constraints, and opportunities for early nineteenth-century petitioners.[7]

LE RÉVEIL PATRIOTE: THE TURN AGAINST IMPERIAL ADMINISTRATION

In the wake of the Conquest of 1760 and the American Revolution, Britain's colonial project in Canada rested uneasily on the tensions of an enterprise far less attractive economically than initially hoped, a largely francophone population, and financial constraints that made investment a dubious undertaking. In ways symbolic and real, Britain quickly gave up the hope of far-reaching colonial development, having passed the Quebec Act of 1774, which returned to French Canadians much of their religious institutions and cherished civil law. After the American Revolution, Britain launched a constitutional reform process that produced the Constitution of 1791. Amending the Quebec Act, the Constitutional Act of 1791 established two provinces: Lower Canada (corresponding largely to areas of French majority) and Upper Canada. Colonial leaders understood that the idea of the 1791 law was to give Lower Canada to French Canadians and Upper Canada to English settlers. It was to Upper Canada where Tories had fled after the American Revolution, and this region was endowed with English common law. Lower Canada retained civil law (including feudal tenure) and Roman Catholic institutions.[8]

The Constitution of 1791 gave Canada its first representative assemblies. The popular house in Lower Canada was the *Chambre d'assemblée colonial* (assembly). Property requirements for the franchise were so low as to distribute voting rights more broadly than in the United States, and *habitants* (francophone rural Canadians) held a forceful majority in elections to the assembly. The assembly was accompanied by an upper chamber called the legislative council (*Conseil législatif*), which was appointed from members of the landed elite. The colonial governor (also appointed by the Crown) had an executive council at his disposal, whose membership overlapped heavily with the legislative council. The assembly had control over public expenses and control over appointments to the civil list. But the control over public expenses was limited to those revenues coming from laws passed after 1791, particularly for special projects and current expenses. In the case of deficit, moreover, the governor had the ability to dip in to the military funds without asking the assembly. These provisions deeply compromised control of government expenses by the lower assembly, which was central to parliamentary republics in Britain and the United States.[9]

In the early 1800s, economic, cultural, and international developments combined to stoke both aspirations and tensions in Lower Canadian politics. Canadiens saw revolutionary changes occurring elsewhere in the continent, including mass suffrage expansions and constitutional reform, and the Bolivarian revolutions farther south. A long decline in agricultural productivity, which started early in the new century, would reach crisis proportions in the 1830s. The economic fates of tenant farmers and rural dwellers declined while those of *seigneurs* (French and English) stabilized.

From 1805 onward, Pierre Bédard (an assembly deputy) established the philosophical and ideological foundations of a provincial movement premised on parliamentary sovereignty, aspirations of democracy, and francophone primacy. In the midst of a struggle over taxation, he founded the French language journal *Le Canadien* in 1806, calling for primacy of the *assemblée* in provincial matters. Bédard's program—one called "reformist" and not radical in light of its purported fidelity to "true" British constitutional principles—quickly became both inspiration and lightning rod. Bédard championed a strict idea of the constitutional mixed regime and specific proposals to strengthen Lower Canadian popular institutions. Theoretically, he saw in Lower Canada's institutions a parallel to those of the Crown—the colonial governor corresponding to the king, the legislative council corresponding to the aristocratic House of Lords, and the assembly corresponding to the people. In reality, Bédard and his allies understood that the king was in control, but they wanted the assembly to monitor and check the colonial government. For this reason, Bédard proposed a provincial minister, who could give to deputies the ability to keep watch over the Lower Canadian executive. These proposals were greeted with contemptuous opposition by the colonial governor of the time, James Craig. After the publication of a poem considered defamatory, Bédard and two other owners of *Le Canadien* were arrested in March 1810, and the journal was closed. Bédard would reemerge later in the decade, but his idea of a provincial minister disappeared from provincial debate.[10]

Bédard's ideas were reflected in Lower Canadian *requêtes* and other petitions to the Crown. These petitions played an ever-growing role in the development and expression of institutional theory. Petitions from Canadiens were sent to the Crown (which from 1810 to 1820 meant the prince regent, later George IV, who acted in the place of his incurably insane father George III), calling for greater power for the *assemblée* and less power for the executive council and, by extension, the legislative council. In a tract believed to have been authored by Bédard and which followed a Lower-Canadian petition—*Mémoire au soutien de la requête des habitans du Bas-Canada, à son Altesse Royale le Prince Régent* (1814)—Canadien voices called for the reform of the legislative council, making it elective. They complained that by taking up the very liberties guaranteed by the charter of 1791 and rendering *plaintes* and *requêtes,* they were being "flattened" and tarred as an illegitimate opposition. Bédardians argued further that the appointed members of the legislative council could not possibly govern with justice the very population from which it derived its taxable resources except by Canadiens themselves, at least in a consultative fashion.[11]

The man succeeding Bédard as leader of the *Parti canadien*—Louis-Joseph Papineau—became the unquestioned leader of a movement with hybrid and ambiguous identities—reformist, republican, nationalist. Papineau converted Bédard's intellectual case into potent popular symbolism and an increasingly democratic ethos. Papineau became Speaker of the *assemblée* in January 1815, and more than anyone in the history of the province, he incarnated the *nation canadienne* and articulated its aspirations and arguments for reform. In the absence of a head of government and elected ministers, the Speaker was the institutional voice of the province's people, what poet Louis Frechette called the human bullhorn who converted the forum into a public display of his own making. Papineau's ascendance also came after the War of 1812, when North American antipathies to many things British were on the rise, and when Lower Canadians viewed arrangements and personalities in the United States with increasing favor.[12]

This mixture of French Canadian, Anglo-American, and revolutionary ideals led rural French Canadians into a heightened attachment to representative institutions in the province and to newly created organizations at the local level. These institutions—the *assemblée générale* (general meeting), the *comté* (county), and even the *paroisse* (parish), with its *conseils de fabrique* (lay church ministries)—attracted growing allegiance from rural Frenchmen, and Canadiens justified them with ever greater ferocity, organizing committees at all levels. Petitions defending these institutions against threats both perceived and real grew ever more common and strident in the 1810s and 1820s, to the extent that *habitants* began to organize against the wishes of their own Catholic clergy. In the 1820s, however, lower Canadians expressed their allegiance to one institution above all others: the assembly, whose existence and functioning became especially important for the idea of popular geographic representation. The ever more fractured nature of Canadian society pitted these rural *habitant* communities against bishops, farmers against *seigneurs,* French against English, Catholic against Protestant, periphery against metropole. The Canadiens adhered to a mix of parliamentary ideals and constitutional principles. The English constitution they defended was, in its ideal type, that of the United Kingdom, but more specifically it was a variant of what they called "the Constitution of *this* province"—Lower Canada, namely—one they found superior to all others of the English colonial and postcolonial form, even those in the United States.[13]

With the appointment of Sir George Ramsay, Lord Dalhousie, as colonial governor in 1820, the stage was set for one of North America's grand confrontations of the century. Papineau refused Dalhousie's invitation to sit on the legislative council in 1820. Then, quietly in the summer of 1821, Dalhousie and his allies hatched a plan to unite the two Canadas under a system that would have privileged English models of settlement, culture, and law. Anglophone elites saw "the Union bill" as a way to circumvent the French-dominated assembly. In June 1822, Edward Ellice introduced the relevant bill to the House of Commons, and later that month the news reached Québec and Montréal, jolting French Canadians and their allies into unprecedented activism. They saw their provincial identity as under attack, so too their assembly, which would be merged with that of Upper Canada in the colonial plan.[14]

The proposed union of 1822 provoked the first monster petition of Canadian history. In Montréal, two men emerged to lead the city's committee against the Union bill: Papineau (president of the committee) and Jacque Viger (the committee's secretary). The petitioners advanced a deeply Bédardian argument, claiming allegiance to the Constitution and its provision for popular representation in the provincial assembly. Papineau and Viger quickly enlisted the help of Lower Canada's Catholic bishops, who both shared the emergent Canadien program and were gravely concerned by the Union bill's twenty-fifth clause requiring parish priests to receive the approval of the British colonial governor. The Canadian bishops—chiefly Joseph-Octave Plessis (then archbishop of Québec) and Jean-Jacques Lartigue (bishop of Montréal), the latter Denis-Benjamin Viger's cousin—opposed union even as they descended from different doctrinal camps in the early nineteenth-century church. Plessis saw himself as called to build a French-Canadian Catholic flock and had pressed the Canadian cause in the War of 1812, while Lartigue was an early adherent of ultramontane views on the primacy of papal authority in the church. The bishops brought not only new arguments about religious liberty to the campaign but also the organization of parishes, where meetings could be held and petitions signed and canvassed.[15]

The organization of the anti-unionist petition campaign drew on the many templates of politics and attachment coursing through Lower Canada in the 1820s, and it set critical precedents for the anti-Dalhousie monster petition circulated five years later. Papineau and Viger, along with the bishops, sought the alliance of anglophone Canadians (in the Lower and Upper provinces) who regarded the Union bill as heavy-handed, or who worried that French Catholic Canadians would enjoy a majoritarian hegemony in the unified legislature. To all potential allies they heralded the idea of "the constitution of this province," a constitution placed in jeopardy by the Union bill. Canadiens carried out much of the petitioning via committees formed at the county, district, and other levels, relying on gatherings they called *comités régionaux* and *assemblées régionaux*. While serving to manage the petition canvassing effort, these structures attracted loyalties of their own, as representative vessels enjoying local trust. Even as they expressed allegiance to the realm and the British constitution, these gatherings also evoked concepts that echoed institutions from Old Regime and Revolutionary France and New France—regional assemblies, estates general at the national and regional levels (and the *requêtes, plaintes,* and *cahiers* that issued from them). Popular demonstrations also partook of legislative and republican imagery. At the same time, a popular gathering called a *grande assemblée* aggregated thousands of people on Montréal's Champ de Mars on October 7, 1822.[16]

The 1822 petition marked Louis-Joseph Papineau's ascent as an organizer along with the Viger family (Jacque and Denis-Benjamin). The effort gathered 69,404 names to the petition's signatory list, including 8,762 from Upper Canada. Like the later Dalhousie petition, the anti-union petition was delivered to the Commons in October by Papineau and by the printer John Neilson, a critical anglophone ally of the Canadiens. Starkly undermining Dalhousie, Colonial Minister Lord Henry Bathhurst (who was also relaying the petitions of free Blacks in the Caribbean to Parliament) conveyed the anti-union petition to the House of Lords and later to the cabinet. Pro-fusion subjects signed and circulated a counterpetition of approximately ten thousand signatures, but the unionist project was quietly interred. As evidence that popular organization had derailed the project, the Union bill alone died in the House of Commons in 1822. Two other pieces of legislation introduced along with the Union bill—the Canada Trade Act of 1822 (supplemented in 1825) and the Canada Tenures Act of 1825—were extensively debated in the Commons and ultimately became law. Although the agitation over the union plan was short lived, the plan itself and the caustic nature of Dalhousie's administration awakened the strongest anti-imperial energies in the province since the American Revolution.[17]

Contributing as much as anything to the political efflorescence, Lower Canada witnessed a cultural transformation characterized by changes in education and print culture and a rise in provincial pride. Physicians Joseph-François Perrault and Louis Plamandon founded the Société d'éducation de Québec in 1821, and new schools for secondary education were established. (Francophone physicians would play an important role in the emergence of *patriote* organization.) A new editor of *Le Canadien,* Flavien Vallerand, would take up the Bédardian banner, and the newspaper would republish many of the important republican petitions in the decade. An 1824 law established new "*écoles de fabrique*" in numerous parishes in the province. In Montréal, two leaders of the *patriote* movement, Augustin-Norbert Morin and Denis-Benjamin Viger, created a newspaper, *La Minerve,* which enjoyed a wide readership, and sales of French-language volumes generally surged in Montréal and Québec. As testament to the impact of these journals, Dalhousie criticized their "democratic" character.[18]

Political tracts and petitions multiplied and intermingled as part of this cultural renaissance. François Blanchet—a physician and deputy in the assembly and an old friend of Bédard—published *Appel au Parlement impérial et aux habitans des colonies anglaises* (1824), which called for fundamental reform in the parliamentary institutions of Lower Canada, with full assembly control of public expenses and a reduction in the power and executive dependence of the legislative council. Petitions with similar arguments flowed into the assembly and out of it (toward Britain). Blanchet's pamphlet displayed a hemispheric imagination, expressing and invoking sympathies for Simón Bolívar and his allies. Two years later, Viger published *Analyse d'un entretien sur la conservation des établissements du Bas-Canada, des loix, des usages &c de ses habitans* (1826). As its title suggested, and in an echo of the 1822 petitions against colonial union, Viger and his allies tied together language, customs (*usages*), institutions (*établissements*), and laws (*loix*). Canada was not merely a space, or a language, or a religious persuasion; it was a complex of intertwined symbols, practices, and institutions.[19]

Dalhousie saw these developments as worrisome, and he moved aggressively to counter them. Infuriated by the Canadiens' analogy between their movement and that for Irish independence, he echoed James Craig's argument that the Parti canadien was engaged in illegitimate, "factious" opposition to the Crown. John Richardson went further, comparing the assembly's activities to those of rebels in the period of Charles I and to those of the Comité du Salut public during the Reign of Terror in revolutionary France.[20]

Far more contentious than any of Dalhousie's public arguments were his procedural initiatives before the assembly. With the plan for colonial fusion abandoned, Dalhousie attempted to press forward with a unilateral program of administrative governance unencumbered by popular resistance. He demanded that the assembly vote appropriations for the entire reign of George IV in lieu of approving spending for a single year or session.

In December 1821 he called for the summary approval of his civil appointments. The assembly passed a more limited budget in 1823, but this was rejected by the legislative council. Well beyond Papineau, prominent Canadiens such as Laurent Bédard, Flavien Vallerand, and Francois Blanchet began to defend the authority of the assembly, especially with respect to control of revenues and control over the civil list. The assembly elections of 1824 returned an even larger majority for the Parti canadien.[21]

Dalhousie returned to Britain in 1824, and his temporary replacement, Francis Burton, comported himself in a far more conciliatory manner toward the assembly. Convoking the *chambre* in January 1825, Burton struck a set of agreements with Papineau. Together, governor pro tempore and assembly quickly voted and appropriated spending and slashed the province's deficit. Dalhousie, learning of these developments from London, was furious that his principles had been undermined through compromise with the assembly. Upon his return, he declared that the Burton-Papineau compromise of 1825 was invalid and was not a precedent he would further respect.

Confronted with widespread press outrage and an unruly lower chamber, Dalhousie prorogued the assembly in March 1827. The prorogation, executed without having consulted London first, further eroded Dalhousie's legitimacy in Lower Canada and London alike. Prorogation made new elections necessary, and for the assembly elections in the spring of 1827, no question was more important than that of assembly powers, especially over revenues and appointments. The elections returned yet another large gain for the Canadiens, and Papineau and his allies felt emboldened. Yet Dalhousie was in no mood to respect the election results for the lower chamber. Blaming Papineau for most (if not all) of his problems, including the growing perception in London that the colonial governor and not the French population was responsible for the colony's disarray, Dalhousie rejected the assembly's choice of Papineau as Speaker. In the midst of these battles, the Parti canadien was renamed the Parti patriote, and a reform movement became a republican cause.[22]

THE EMERGENCE OF AN ANTICOLONIAL CAMPAIGN

The idea of a second monster petition in five years might have seemed risky to the Canadiens. Yet Dalhousie's intransigent and unilateral actions in 1826 and 1827, combined with the success of the Parti canadien in the elections of 1826, left French Canadian leaders furious and seeking drastic action. The decision to send a petition to the Commons, listing complaints against Dalhousie and the lack of separation of powers, was apparently undertaken separately in both Montréal and Québec in early 1827.[23]

French Canadians were not the only petitioners from Lower Canada in 1827. Petitions from "Townships of the Lower Province" had also been received by the Commons, asking for redress of the grievances of English inhabitants of Lower Canada, including ease of settlement, and for the union of the two provinces under English law. The demand for colonial union was quickly abandoned by the House of Commons in 1828.[24]

The more nuanced issues raised by English petitioners concerned the law of property in Lower Canada, which implemented English custom or French custom depending on whether the land was in a township or a seigneury, respectively. Of far more than legal importance, the contrast and tension between these sites of property and language acquired growing political, partisan, and electoral significance.[25]

The seigneuries where French Canadians largely lived were located on narrow tracts of land on either side of the Saint Lawrence River, ten to forty miles in width. "Behind" those seigneuries, the colony had granted townships, and these attracted English settlers. In the townships land was given by free and common socage. The seigneuries and townships represented quite different worlds, even though the former had many English speakers and French speakers had settled in the latter. In French civil law—most of it derived from the Custom of Paris—both the rights and the administration of property differed materially from the common law. The legal distinction shaped gender and family relations. In the French system, marriage established two rights, that of dower and that of *communauté*. Wives were entitled to half of the *communauté* (that is, half of the entire personal property of the husband) and half of the real property he had acquired during the marriage. This was a considerably more generous system for women compared to laws governing *couverture* in the United States, for instance. Under the Custom of Paris, the wife's property could not be alienated under any will of the husband. If an English settler died with only personal property, the property would be distributed according to French law. These partial advantages for widows plausibly led to widows' agitation for voting rights in Montréal and Québec in the late 1820s and 1830s, a movement impelled by petitioning.[26]

Seigneurial rights were another source of contention, in part because English settlers believed them to retard economic development. Those who lived on seigneurial lands did not have the right of "mutation" (under which settlers could in theory render improvements) without the consent of the seigneur. Under the *droit de moulture,* inhabitants could neither build their own mill on the seigneur's property nor take their grain to any mill other than the seigneur's. So constructed, the *droit de moulture* provided for a major portion of the seigneur's revenue.[27]

The legal and political systems governing Lower Canada remained a separate source of frustration for English settlers. In order to facilitate the efficient transfer and inheritance of property through common law, court records were required to establish land boundaries, improvements, and declension of ownership. In Lower Canada, these records were kept in the seigneuries and, for more comprehensive records, at either the seat of administration or the provincial legislature in Québec. English petitioners from the Lower Canadian townships asked for British courts to be established in the townships. Furthermore, election sites for the townships were located in the seigneuries, leading to negligible township participation in elections to the assembly.

The Canadiens were aware of these issues, and support for the seigneurial system was far from uniform. Yet in the 1820s, the primary issues animating francophone opposition had little to do with defending feudal tenure, seigneurial rights, or marriage systems. The Canadiens' main concern lay in the behavior of Dalhousie and the institutional framework that left the assembly unable to check the government.

A further issue was the growth of the legislative council. The original 1791 act gave the assembly not less than fifty members and the council not less than fifteen. By 1828, the assembly still had fifty deputies, but the size of the council had nearly doubled, to twenty-eight. As the legislative council grew, Dalhousie increasingly filled it with officers from the imperial government. The critical separation between executive and legislative—a fundamental characteristic of the mixed regime, the British constitution, and the Montesquieuvian ideal—had broken down. The 1827 petitioners complained that "the Legislative Council is nothing other than the executive under a different name, and the provincial legislature finds itself reduced to two branches, the government and the *Assemblée,* without having the advantage of any middling, mediating branch given to this province; and from this first and capital error a multitude of evils have resulted and continue daily, with no capacity for remedy."[28] These misgivings had their origins before Dalhousie's appointment, but the governor's behavior brought the Canadiens' worst fears to reality. After snubbing the people's choice of Speaker in 1827, Dalhousie dismissed a range of militia officers from their posts, largely because of their observed support for the Parti patriote (or for Papineau). Officers in the *milice* occupied a position of great status, notability, and income, and the militia dated from the pre-Conquest period of New France. Some of the officers that Dalhousie sacked had fought in the War of 1812 on the British side, and many were anglophone. In a widely distributed declaration of protest published in October 1827, Thomas Lee accused Dalhousie of trying to embarrass him before his fellow citizens—of unfairly advancing "evil, false and hurtful insinuations"—and of acting in an illegal manner. Lee's rhetoric, and that of other dismissed officers, such as Renè-Amable Boucher, articulated claims against despotism and arbitrary executive power to Canadiens. These arguments formed part of the culture of written and signed protest that exploded in the fall of 1827.[29]

Dalhousie's behavior and, beyond that, his poor reputation provided the petitioners with some of their strongest arguments. Papineau and his allies understood that an effective attack on Dalhousie would, by extension, embarrass the Colonial Office and put in doubt the Crown's colonial project. Accordingly, the petitioners of 1827 blamed Dalhousie for the economic stagnation of the colony, a situation that had stoked the ire of colonial officers in London. Behind these institutional grievances lay two more metaphysical arguments, both in keeping with the Bédardian reading of the British constitution. First, the governor was neither king nor Parliament. Unlike the king, who could do no wrong, the governor could be brought to account for his decisions, not just by the king but by Parliament. Presenting the governor as fallible and replaceable, and contrasting him with previous, more conciliatory governors such as Burton, enabled the petitioners of 1827 to align constitutional logic with political imperatives. Second, the rejection of Papineau as Speaker and the proroguing of the assembly provided the petitioners with an opening. For within the British parliamentary tradition, it was the Speaker who represented the lower chamber, and therefore the people (or electors), in communicating to the king. In the absence of an assembly with a Speaker, to what—to whom—could the governor respond? The monster petition of 1827 thus occupied a liminal space: it uniquely and powerfully represented the colony of Lower Canada in the absence of a lower chamber and its speaker.[30]

ASSEMBLÉES GÉNÉRALES AND *COMITÉS SPÉCIAUX*: THE ORGANIZATION OF A MONSTER PETITION

The monster anti-Dalhousie petition of 1827 was an amalgam of canvassing efforts and even of slightly different prayers. Two different prayers circulated, one in Montréal and Three Rivers (reflecting resolutions adopted in Montréal) and a second in Québec and the county of Warwick (reflecting resolutions adopted at Québec). John Neilson later reported that "there was no concert" between the Montréal and Québec resolutions. Yet contemporaries in London and Lower Canada understood that a centralized, committee-based structure had amassed the tens of thousands of signatures, and that although the Montréal and Québec resolutions differed slightly, they referred to the larger effort as a single petition.[31]

In their organization and their rhetoric, Canadiens drew on older political languages that incorporated metaphors and terms from the ancien régime of New France as well as the Revolutionary period. For example, organizers and signatories alike often described the monster petition as a *requête* rather than a *pétition*, which was by this time part of the French political vocabulary. Meanwhile, Englishmen described petitions as "petitions," sometimes as "memorials" or "remonstrances," but never as requests. Papineau himself described the Montréal petition as a *requête*, even when grievances composed its primary content, and lead organizers of the collection effort, summarizing their eighty-seven-thousand-plus signatures, referred alternatively to "la Requête de Montréal" and "la Requête de Québec." In county after county, organizers met by calling an *assemblée générale*, a term that had more meaning in French institutional history than in English. The *assemblée générale* was a common meeting in ancien régime France, especially at the provincial level or within estates, dating to the sixteenth century or earlier. In Lower Canada, anti-Dalhousie petitioners created *assemblées générales* at the level of the county (*comté*), sometimes in the district, and other *assemblées de la paroisse* (parish). The *assemblées générales* would then appoint a petitioning committee, specifically a *comité constitutionnel* or, at the parish level, a *comité spécial* or *comité général*. In districts of Montréal, the *comité constitutionnel* was charged with drawing up a prayer and circulating the petition for signatures, while in Québec a committee was nominated by the *assemblée générale* of the electors of the city and surrounding towns.[32]

Contemporary descriptions of the petitioning process by organizers and petitioners suggest that the mainspring of the reform and republican movements lay in the *assemblées.* After the passing of resolutions at Montréal and Québec, anti-Dalhousie petition organizers then proceeded by county. In County Richelieu, the *assemblée générale* appointed a *Comité Général,* charged with the responsibility to gather both signatures and subscriptions to assist the canvassing effort.[33] Small towns such as Saint Denis recorded *assemblées générales* of over one thousand persons, all of them free electors and property holders according to the records. Among the top signatories in these petition sheets (later aggregated into the larger petitioning effort) were many physicians. After a preliminary committee read the resolutions, special committees (*comités spéciaux*) were appointed to gather signatures by parish. Often the parish itself held another *assemblée,* such as the one held in the church of Sainte Anne de Yamachiche on New Year's Day in 1828. Every *comité spécial* operating at the level of the parish was authorized by the *assemblée générale,* and every such parish-level effort had been funded by the subscriptions gathered at the *assemblées.* A rhetoric and a material logic of legitimacy coursed through the efforts that affixed thousands upon thousands of signatures on the anti-Dalhousie memorial.[34]

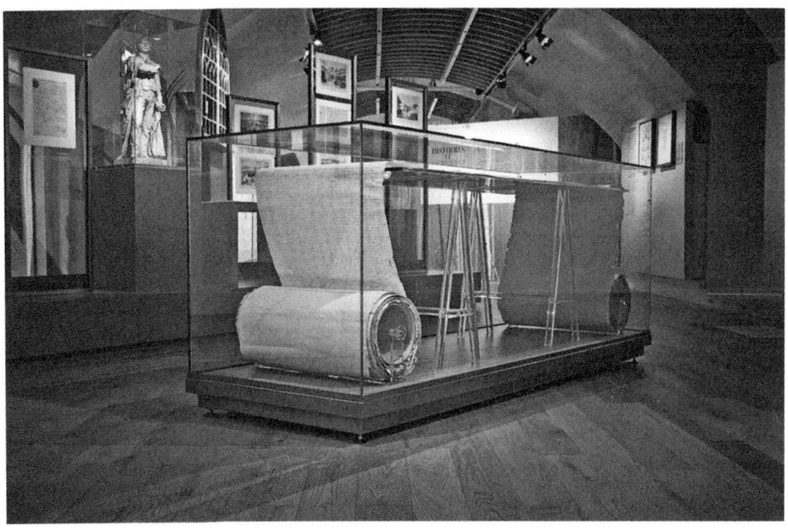

FIGURE 7.1. Rolled Portion of Anti-Dalhousie Petition, 1827–1828. *Credit:* Museé Stewart, Montréal.

FIGURE 7.2. Sample Signatory List from Anti-Dalhousie Petition, 1827–1828. *Credit:* Museé Stewart, Montréal.

The petitioners of 1827 aimed to impress the Commons with argument and with the heft of signatures. The petition when amassed and rolled became a formidable, weighty object, displaying thousands upon thousands of names in linear order, many signed, many accompanied by marks.[35]

As with many mass petitions of the nineteenth century, each page was likely the result of a distinct petitioning and canvassing effort. What remains in the archives is the glued-together composite of a number of separate (albeit orchestrated) petitioning endeavors. Signatures appear to have been entered vertically within columns, and the columns were filled from left to right, meaning that each potential signatory would have been able to view the signatures above and to the left.

The signatory lists of the anti-Dalhousie petition reveal important information lurking in the order in which the names appear. On the first and second pages of Montréal signatures, English names appeared with more frequency and appeared higher in columns, plausibly generating further inducement to sign or give a mark of assent for potential anglophone signatories. For every rank move downward in the sequence of signatures (for example, eleventh to twelfth or third to fourth) in a column on these two pages, the odds of a non-French name declined by 3 percent. These early pages of the Montréal signatory list were important for attracting anglophone elites (such as William Galt, owner of a large leather tanning business; the nail manufacturer Thomas Bigelow; Henry Ferns; or Thomas Barber, all whom signed near the top of the first full signatory page). Surname clusters appeared systematically lower in columns. This dynamic likely expresses strategic placement of individual notable names at the top of each column, allowing families to add collective signatures below. Using their commercial and marriage networks, the Canadiens recruited English merchants to forge a cross-linguistic coalition in support of their political demands.[36]

THE COUNTABILITY OF VOICE, AND POLITICAL OPPORTUNITIES FOR WOMEN

As elsewhere in the Atlantic world, protesters, lobbies, electors, officials, and petitioners pointed to their numbers as legitimating their cause. Contests between rival petitioners over the signature numbers were struggles over who could claim greater legitimacy and who could speak in the name of the people. For example, anglophone proponents of colonial fusion had assembled a signatory list with over ten thousand names, which was bettered by Canadiens by six times, which they recognized was instrumental in derailing the union project. Anglophone subjects in Lower Canada argued, of course, that their numbers represented those of the true settlers, and allied with Dalhousie, they set about disparaging Canadien signatures as coming from those who were not the true or authentic settlers in the colony, or by claiming that the total numbers for the 1827 petition were higher than that of the entire (francophone) colony at the time of British takeover (1763).[37]

The battle over numbers and legitimacy played out in the questioning of signatures and their authenticity. Rather than claiming that Francophone signatories carried less weight than English-origin or anglophone signatories, Dalhousie and his allies scoured the signatory list and sought to gather and report examples of alleged fraud to undermine his opponents. Any signature that seemed copied or sufficiently similar to others nearby, or that was accompanied by a mark, was treated by Dalhousian officials as evidence of fraud—an inappropriate injection of religious affiliation into a constitutional debate, showing that people had been unaware of the addition of their names or not fully aware of the petition's content. As with many monster petitions of the period, not all signatures were in unique manuscript, and this was more pronounced in rural areas where literacy ran lower. Yet Canadiens responded by showing that many English names had signed the petition, which was further demonstrated by Papineau's ally John Neilson in his presentation of presented signature samples to the Select Committee of Parliament in 1829.

As they scrutinized the signatures, colonial officials found that women and children were signing. George Moffatt would write to Dalhousie in 1827 that "a notorious circumstance occurred in Montréal of a whole school of females being marched in files to affix their names to the petition of grievances to the Sovereign."[38] One Thomas Porteous later testified that "he is enabled from undoubted authority to say, that he verily and firmly believes that little Girls were conducted into Dr. N's [Neilson's] house for the express purpose of signing the said Petitions, and that they did actually sign them, as if the Deponent had seen them write their names, and he has further been credibly informed that they were instructed not to sign their Christian names in full but only the initial letters thereof, in order that their sex might not thereby be known."[39]

The petition signatory list from Montréal includes women's signatures, such as those of Belonie Goyette dit Sansouci, Serapha Verge, Charlotte Magnonée, Marianne Boulagée, Angélique Lehay, Gabrielle Blais, and another Belonie Goyette. Faubourg Saint Laurent added at least two additional women—Elizabeth Troy and Marie St. Garmin—both of whose names were signed. That women would openly sign in Montréal is not entirely surprising, given that over two hundred women later showed up to the polls for the city's by-election in April and May 1832. Furthermore, because many of the signatures on the Montréal petition list included only the first initial and last name, the presence of women's names is probably larger.[40]

Dalhousie's allies were less concerned about women signing than young women signing, and they eagerly compiled evidence of young boys having signed as well. Reporting what he perceived to be the scandal of four "french Canadian boys" who boasted of having signed a petition to the king, Thomas Porteous reported that the eldest (under twelve, he confidently proclaimed) admitted he did not know how to write, but along with his classmates (numbering thirty) they had made a cross. Another testimonial reported that a father, learning of his son and classmates signing a petition, asked to have his son's name erased, but was told that the signatory list had already been sent to regional committees for delivery to the king and House of Commons in England.[41]

It is important to read these accusations of children's and women's participation in context—that is, as the complaints of officials seeking to denigrate the legitimacy of the petition. Yet the Canadiens never denied these charges, and the inclusion of women and children points to the wide range of popular participation within the anti-Dalhousie campaign. The signatures of schoolchildren also have to be situated within the context of the erection of many francophone schools as well as Canadien pressure for even more in the province. Overall, the debates of the legitimacy or illegitimacy of signatures suggests the competing frames of legitimacy used by Dalhousian officials and Canadiens in 1827 and 1828.[42]

The evidence adduced for signatures by children suggests the intricate network structures relied on for petition signing. In Montréal and Québec, Canadien merchants and booksellers played an important role in the display of the petition and the collection of signatures. Many a Montréal signature was affixed to the petition at the Librarie Édouard-Raymond Fabre of Rue Notre-Dame in Montréal, a bookstore specializing in law, literature, and Catholic theology that sat facing the colonial government's Palais de justice. Dalhousie partisans fumed that the Montréal committee appointed to draw up the petition was "anonymously called," but everyone knew that the meeting occurred at the store of one "M. Quesnel," probably Jules Quesnel, a Montréal notable, member of the assembly, and common participant on grand juries in the province.[43]

SIGNATURES AND MARKS: THE QUESTION OF AUTHENTICITY

The question of authenticity is relevant not only to understanding loyalist-*patriote* tensions in the 1820s and 1830s but also in answering the question of whether the anti-Dalhousie petition represented an awakening political consciousness in the province. William Huskisson, who became colonial secretary in September 1827, took the claims of the petition's prayer seriously but also remarked that of the eighty-seven thousand names on the petition, only nine thousand had truly been signed, an indication of the lack of intellectual development in the province. Elite Anglophones insulted those who signed with a mark by calling them "Knights of the Cross," a moniker that linked their Catholic majority to their supposed illiteracy.[44]

The presence of so many marks in place of self-inscribed signatures represents, in many thousands of cases, the signatory's lack of literacy. There remains the real possibility that Lower Canadian elites merely induced illiterate peasants, *habitants*, and other residents to sign something whose content they could not have fully understood. It is, nonetheless, important to place this dynamic in context. The question of authenticity and representation among those advancing their voice was a common problem in petitioning, and just as common a problem in voting in the nineteenth century, where studies point to drunken, poorly organized electorates in the United States, among other nations.[45]

Other patterns suggest that the signatory marks reflected a degree of volition. First, petition organizers attested on each page that the marks represented the result of a presentation process in which the language and intent of the petition was explained verbally to those whose names appeared with a mark. The repeated character of this statement, in different handwriting, suggests that organizers and canvassers were at least aware of the norm by which they were obliged to explain the petition's prayer to those whose names were affixed with a mark.[46] One biographer remarked that even literate Lower Canadians often permitted their names to be added by mark, as "a very large number of people who truly could sign didn't want to go to the trouble, and were content to allow another to affix their name."[47] Moreover, the considerable variation in many pages of inscribed marks casts doubt on the most extreme explanation that the marks were simply entered by one organizer.

Contemporaries took note, too, of the wide level of political discussion in 1827 and 1828. Jean-Marie Mondelet wrote to Denis-Benjamin Viger in April 1828 that "all of our residents now take part in public affairs, knowing them and discussing them. This unfortunate crisis in which we find ourselves will at least have the effect of opening their eyes." Mondelet had been integrally involved in the monster petitioning effort, and as he was expressing these views privately to a fellow *patriote*, it may be suggested that he had little incentive to misrepresent the state of affairs. Another contemporary remarked that Lower Canadians of all ages, most notably the young, had become much more radical and that "almost everywhere political galvanization had gained the lead." Women began voting in larger numbers in Montréal, usually for the Patriot faction. Their endeavors led to one of the first petitions for more general women's voting rights in 1828; the assembly debated claims that "the votes of women, married, unmarried, and in a state of widowhood" had been cast that year for the antiestablishment reformer Wolfred Nelson.[48]

The role of local *assemblées générales* and provincial legislators in organizing the petition also points to a more participatory process, though one in which local notables exercised some leadership, including making speeches. In Montréal, the role of the Committee of Grievances and of the *assemblées* in the petition process, led by Papineau himself, became etched into popular memory, perhaps more so than the petition itself. The *assemblée générale* at Saint Denis gathered at least one thousand persons, according to contemporary records. Another assembly at the parish of Sainte Anne de Yamachiche—held in the public meeting room of the church, implying the likely assent of the priest—appointed a committee of twelve men to gather signatures, charging them with "drawing upon all their forces to gather voluntary subscriptions and signatures to the petition."[49]

At Trois-Rivières, where the names of over half the population appeared on the anti-Dalhousie petition, the memorial harvest suggests an especially fervent reaction against the governor. Provincial deputies at Trois-Rivières (including some of the same members who would organize the anti-Dalhousie petition effort there) had canvassed for a range of petitions from *habitants* and parishioners from 1821 to 1829. The notable lawyer Charles-Elzear Mondelet represented the Trois-Rivières district in the assembly and was active in public speeches and in the city's constitutional committee for the mass petition. At the town of Nicolet in Mondelet's district, residents had become enraged at a new tribunal known as the Commissioners' Court (or Summary Court), which was advancing a process of property seizures through "execution," avoiding customary judicial process. Nicolet residents drew up a popular petition signed by about 450 Nicolet residents (more than half the town's population) to Dalhousie in 1826, calling for the Summary Court's abolition. Recognizing their political weakness and the centrality of petitions to Lower Canada's culture, Dalhousie's allies and the commissioners started a counterpetition of their own in 1827, reportedly pushing residents with business at the court to sign it. In 1829, the assembly passed a bill abolishing the Commissioners' Court, allowing re-establishment only where a township could produce petitions with more than one hundred proprietors' signatures. Animosity against Dalhousie and trust in the petition process were nowhere more intense, nowhere more widespread, than in the Trois-Rivières district.[50]

Finally, even given the presence of so many marks on the petition, there is reason to doubt Huskisson's estimate, which was not based on any thorough examination of the entire signatory list but was repeated many times over in the nineteenth century, apparently without verification. Samples presented by Neilson to the Commons in 1828 suggest a rate of names signed at about twice that of Huskisson's estimate, and when one focuses on Québec, Neilson reported a names-signed rate of 40 percent. Signatory aggregates from Montréal, Faubourg Saint Laurent, and Faubourg des Recollets suggest names-signed rates ranging from 24 to 46 percent. These estimates are of course drawn from more densely populated urban towns, with higher education and literacy rates, yet some of the locales that supplied the highest rate of names (Trois-Rivières, for instance) had similar populations.[51]

The anti-Dalhousie petition requires interpretation as a bundle of documents, each with multiple audiences. If the *patriote* organizers' sole aim was to persuade the Commons or colonial secretary of the authenticity of each name, then the marking pattern would have made little sense. Yet if the organizers' aim was manifold, and included the amplification and circulation of grievances to those who did not read the newspapers and were not hearing from the clergy, who tried to maintain a neutrality toward the colonial administration, then the marks represented not legitimacy but an understanding that tens of thousands of illiterates and those who would not bother to sign had at least heard the petitioners' argument. Since the goal of the petition was in part to inform and mobilize the Lower Canadian populace, local audiences remained as or more important than those in London.[52]

Petition organizers—especially leaders of the Parti patriote, such as Papineau, Viger, and Austin Cuvillier—also understood that the canvassing and subscription effort would generate new ties of solidarity at the local level. Coming in the wake of the prorogation of the assembly, the monster petition served not only to demonstrate the unified voice of an aggrieved people to a British sovereign but to present a case to the people themselves. As Jean Dessaulles wrote to Papineau in April 1827, the petition was necessary to present an alternative case to the very people before whom Dalhousie had tried to embarrass the assembly, and the canvassing effort would bring "light" to the Canadiens.[53]

The recruitment value of the petition provides one rationale for why organizers spent so little time circulating the petition in townships. Not only were townships dominated by anglophone interests, but they were also far removed from voting sites and consequently had poor turnout in elections. Anglophone Lower Canadians were much more likely to turn out to vote in the cities, and the Papineau network did in fact target them for petition signatures. Moreover, as in 1822, the townships sent a separate petition to the Commons. The selective nature of the canvassing effort is difficult to demonstrate with granular quantitative data, but an aggregation of the signatures by *comté* (county) provides a glimpse.

For those counties where names were affixed, township-heavy counties such as Bedford, Buckingham, and York had lower signature totals as a percentage of population, while nonmetropolitan counties with little or no township population such as Leinster and Warwick saw more than three in ten residents with their names on the signatory list.[54]

THE FRUITS OF CONTEST: DALHOUSIE AND THE ASSEMBLY AFTER 1828

With the petitioning effort of 1827 having amassed some eighty thousand signatures, an additional six to seven thousand names were added in early 1828, and a committee was appointed to deliver the petition to London. Papineau had led much of the petitioning effort but did not sit on the Comité de la pétition de 1828. Instead, three other top players in Canadien politics—Neilson, Viger, and Cuvillier—were charged with traveling to London to appear before the House of Commons.[55]

The Canadiens voyaging to London brought more than a monster petition with them. They also ferried a petition from the Huron and Wyandot Indians residing at Lorette. The Indigenous community at Lorette had long lay claim to the Jesuit lands at Sillery near Montréal—no longer occupied by the Jesuits but still retained apart from the Natives at Lorette—and this petition was the most recent in a long series of appeals to the Crown for the lands in question. Exquisitely drafted in English and with the chiefs and warriors signing their French first names followed by their Indigenous

TABLE 7.1 Aggregate Signature Patterns on the Anti-Dalhousie Petition, 1827

Comté	Population	Non-seigneurial Population (township)	Signatures (names or marks)	Percent of Population Listed
Gaspé	6,425	4,919	0	0.00%
Cornwallis	20,112	0	3,583	17.82%
Devon	11,934	0	2,139	17.92%
Hertford	14,044	0	2,394	17.05%
Dorchester	19,707	249	4,157	21.09%
Buckingham	35,522	6,450	1,538	4.33%
Richelieu	36,256	9,544	8,175	22.55%
Bedford	23,654	10,782	1,342	5.67%
Surrey	11,573	0	3,080	26.61%
Kent	10,890	0	2,163	19.86%
Huntington	39,586	5,745	5,327	13.46%
Montréal	37,085	0	7,753	20.91%
York	30,096	2,876	4,199	13.95%
Effingham	14,921	0	2,654	17.79%
Leinster	19,757	484	6,192	31.34%
Warwick	15,935	11	4,904	30.78%
Trois Rivières	21,066	0	10,660	50.60%
Hampshire	13,312	0	1,346	10.11%
Québec	28,623	0	5,870	20.51%
Northumberland	11,210	0	2,415	21.54%
Orléans	4,022	0	1,018	25.31%

Sources: Population figures and signatures from Report SCLC (1829). Signatures from "Récapitulation des Signatures en date du 6 février 1828," appendix 2, Report SCLC (1829). Total listed here is 80,909. The commonly cited total of 87,000 plus is obtained by the addition of 6,212 additional signatures collected from the districts of Montréal, Trois-Rivières, and Québec between February 6 and 17, 1828.

surnames, the petition demonstrated the work of Neilson and, beyond that, the intimate alliance that had formed between the *patriotes* and the Indigenous villages of the Saint Lawrence valley. Papineau, Viger, Cuvillier, and Neilson had long witnessed, introduced, and debated the many Indigenous petitions from their region in the Lower Canadian assembly. In Cuvillier's successful electoral run for the assembly in 1825 as a candidate for the Parti canadien, at least twenty-seven women of another Indigenous village (Kahnawá:ke) turned out to vote for him. As part of their emergent democratic rhetoric against chartered corporations, the *patriotes* would argue in the 1830s that British monopolies treated Canada's Indigenous population very poorly (a proposition with which Canada's Catholic clergy usually agreed). The *patriote* campaign allied with a range of Indigenous communities, and it is likely that the two populations learned from each other about matters of politics and petitioning.[56]

The spectacle of Papineau facing off against Dalhousie quickly drew the attention of Americans, who read it as a battle of legislatures against governors. Hezekiah Niles's *Niles' Weekly Register*, one of the most important American weeklies, began reporting on the proceedings in Canada. Both provinces, Niles wrote in April 1827, "are exceedingly disturbed." Dalhousie's actions had put a representative system of government in jeopardy: "It is about to be determined whether the representative system shall exist or be extinguished in the Canadas."[57] Niles presaged a colonial revolt similar to that of 1776. "Like proceedings lost thirteen colonies to Great Britain—and like causes may produce like effects, to bring about the loss of several more."[58] Niles wrote twice in 1827 about the opposition campaign, and reported further on the Canadian proceedings, with reference to the petitioning work. The Canadiens' leaders in the assembly "have made a decorous, but bold and manly appeal to their constituents, against the allegations of the governor," he remarked in April. In December, Niles reported that "a deputation from the assembly was to proceed to England, to prefer complaints against the Governor." Relaying the judgment of the Québec official *Gazette*, he stated that the assembly delegation's endeavors "show that there are men among them prepared to go all lengths."[59]

The monster petitions triggered a reflective debate about colonial policy in the House of Commons, especially over the question of whether military and institutional fortifications were needed to bolster the colonial project. These debates were also reprinted in the United States as well as British newspapers. MP Alexander Baring, who sat for Callington, confused memorials with signatures on them, speaking of the "more than ten thousand petitions to the king complaining of the bad government under which they lived."[60] These petitions came in "not because the people, were at all disaffected, but because they felt that they were ill governed."[61] Wondering whether Canadians would ever be satisfied, Baring and other speakers openly wondered whether it would be best to surrender the Canadas now. Others, pointing to the same mass of petitions, argued that the documents evinced the deep loyalty of the Canadians to British constitutional forms, and warned that leaving the colonies to wither would surrender them not to Papineau but to the United States. Yet whatever side of the colonial policy question they faced, members of Parliament saw the petitions as damning evidence of colonial malfeasance by Dalhousie. Baring concluded one debate by admitting as indefensible the governor's dissolution of the assembly, the dismissal of officers, and the expenditure of funds without assembly consent.[62]

The Commons appointed a Select Committee on the Civil Government of Canada in 1828 to hear the concerns and complaints alleged in the petition as well as the testimony of the men who delivered it. The petition provided an opportunity to the radical faction of the Whig opposition to attack the government. While the committee's report disparaged the actions of the assembly, it reserved far worse criticism for Dalhousie and his colonial policy. Dalhousie was recalled and retired from service in 1828, transferred to India. The select committee did not grant all of the Canadiens' wishes, but it advocated for greater power of the assembly in fiscal matters. British imperial officials never took lightly the idea of terminating colonial governors; imperial officials knew that firing and replacing governors proved disruptive to the colonial government, to its economy, and to revenues.[63]

Within a few years, the demands of the anti-Dalhousie movement had received some statutory satisfaction but had also engendered the perceived radicalization of the assembly. A key request of the petition was seeking legislative control over the various revenue streams authorized for the colony by the Crown, especially the duties imposed by the 1774 Quebec Act. In 1831, and in response to the report of the select committee, Parliament returned revenues gathered under the 1774 act to the control of the Lower Canadian legislature. Contemporaries and historians of the ensuing decades generally pointed to the 1828 committee report and to the anti-Dalhousie petition as the basis for the 1831 statute, as well as the assembly's acquiescence in funding appointments to the civil list from these revenues. As evidence that the anti-Dalhousie petitions had been effective, British MPs soon complained that the 1831 act had been *too* generous and that the *patriote* faction in Lower Canada had violated "the implied confidence, conditions and expectations on which the Parliament of Great Britain had been induced to pass the Bill which gave the Legislature of Lower Canada control over the whole revenues, always excepting the casual and territorial revenues of the province."[64]

As the *patriote* campaign acquired its own momentum and organization after 1830, it adopted many of the tactics and organizational forms that had characterized the petition-centered mobilizations of 1822 and 1827. Mass meetings of *patriote* rank and file became ever more common after 1832, not only in the cities but also in rural districts. The growing demands of the *patriote* movement included another mass petition in 1834 as well as the set of claims called the Ninety-Two Resolutions that same year. The Ninety-Two Resolutions was an odd, multiform document, a congeries of demands, threats, grievances, and proposals that reserved its principal ire for the legislative council, which had become increasingly stacked with anglophone merchants to offset the rural *habitant* representation in the assembly. The document called for an elective council. Directed toward the British colonial government and the Parliament more than the Canadian people, the Ninety-Two Resolutions nonetheless occasioned massive debate in the press and among *habitants*. Petitions supporting the document attracted more than eighty thousand signatures.[65]

The global economic crisis of 1837 would eventually combine with these tensions to feed into the Patriote Rebellion. *Habitants* organized as *patriote* militia faced off against British troops. Property was destroyed, hundreds of lives were lost, the rebellion was suppressed, and *patriote* leaders went into exile voluntarily and involuntarily. In Great Britain, the Canadian Rebellion of 1837 would carry a different legacy, as British labor organizers who soon called themselves the Chartists read of the uprising and its tactics and aspirations of emergent democracy. Leaders of the London Working Men's Association seized upon the Canadian cause: its embrace of liberty, its hatred for aristocracy, its opposition to taxation without representation, its aim to advance the rights and interests of the common man against those of oppressive government. And as important as anything else, the Chartists watched the novel modes of mass democratic politics pioneered by French Canadians. Parliament received seventy-four petitions against Whig policy in Canada during the 1837–1838 session. The twelve thousand signatures on these memorials were just four thousand fewer than the number of names appearing on petitions for universal suffrage that session and exceeded the number of signatures on British petitions for factory reform. Those twelve thousand signatures also cast in stark relief the vast scope of Canadian petitioning.[66]

The appointment of Lord Durham to report on the troubles of the Canadas, and to carry out constitutional reform, seemed for a moment to herald the end of French Canadian sovereignty. Durham aimed to unify the two Canadas under an English-friendly model, and he pursued a program of "responsible government" that aimed to weaken the Anglican stranglehold on Upper Canada. Even as Canada was formally unified in the act of 1840, the strong organization of the Lower Canadians stemming from the 1820s rendered null and infeasible any program of Anglicization. Ironically, where Durham succeeded most was in the advance of responsible government, which left Canadian legislative institutions stronger than they had been before colonial union. The strength of Canadian parliamentary institutions and the continued vigor of French Canadians shaped important debates over seigneurial tenure in the 1840s and 1850s, as well as the eventual confederation adopted in 1864.

A more democratic mode of petitioning had forcefully shaped the politics of Canada, most often in ways that advanced institutional, cultural, and organizational democracy. The democracy of agendas had reshaped the menu of the House of Commons and the Colonial Office. Mass petitions had helped to derail a unionist initiative (thereby preserving Lower Canada as a separate francophone jurisdiction), oust the colonial governor, and institute reforms that expanded the power of the assembly. In the longer run, petitioning helped cement for French Canada a modicum of provincial independence (1822, 1828), preserve a bulwark of parliamentary authority (1827–1828), and abolish a form of feudalism in the 1840s. The debate over Dalhousie provided a formative school in democracy, and while hundreds if not thousands of the conversations that went into the signing of the monster petition are irrecoverable, it seems an inescapable conclusion that the anti-Dalhousie petition of 1827–1828 served something of an educational purpose as well.[67]

Cultural and organizational democracy in Lower Canada mixed traditional idiom with new participants and strategies. Well beyond their effectiveness in British parliamentary politics, the monster petitions had played a role in galvanizing and organizing the Canadien people, through both their rhetoric and organization. As the Lower Canadian arguments championed the *Assemblée* writ large, the massive accumulation of signatures on the 1820s petitions expressed a form of popular government through *assemblées* writ small. Authorizing and funding their canvassing effort by *assemblées générales,* couching their grievances as a *requête,* canvassing by *paroisse,* and meeting in churches, Lower Canadians revived and reshaped an older language of politics, one that proclaimed ideals from the French Revolution as incorporated and celebrated institutions and practices of the Old Regime.[68]

In other ways, the Canadiens also advanced a vision of institutional democracy akin to those coursing through the United States at the time, and in ways well beyond what American democrats had imagined. Like the Jacksonian Democrats, the Patriotes opposed chartered monopolies. In Upper Canada, petitioning opponents of the colonial regime opposed British financial institutions and proposed joint-stock popular banks—in part because they saw expansive mistreatment of Indigenous peoples. Lower Canada granted Jews the right to vote in 1831, and women voted with regularity in the late 1820s and early 1830s, their right to do so also defended by *patriote* leaders in petitions. The male leaders of the *patriote* movement would abandon initiatives for women's empowerment after 1834, yet the diversity of the *Patriote* coalition (which included Indigenous voters as well as Montréal and Québec widows) pointed to uniquely multidimensional coalitions favoring greater democracy.[69]

For French and English Canadians alike, a more complete institutional democracy was a long way off in the 1820s. Yet the contest with Dalhousie had awakened aspirations to parliamentary democracy, and in the everyday organizing and political assembly that took place throughout the province in 1827 and 1828, rather different facets of incipient democratization appeared: the mobilization of popular voice, the ethic of equality in the identity of names unfolding on the pages of a mass signatory list, and later petitioning campaigns that included calls for woman suffrage roughly two decades before such a campaign would crystallize in the United States. The precise partial contribution of the petitioning effort is impossible to quantify, but the fact that Mondelet could remark in 1828 that "all of our residents take part in public affairs, know them and discuss them" marks a level of information and deliberation that simply would not have occurred without mass petitioning endeavors.[70]

EIGHT

Producers, Electors, City Democrats

> Certain people who never trouble themselves to attend town meeting,—thinking it beneath their *honorable* and *dignified* characters to meet in the same hall with mechanics and laboring men,—have presented a remonstrance against the petition. . . . It is, in short, a mere question of self-interest, in which the purse-proud landlord is arrayed against the mechanic. The remonstrance would never have existed, had not the large owners of real estates, seen in the success of the petition, a reduction of their already overgrown incomes from cruel and exorbitant rents.
>
> **—Joseph Buckingham on the Boston building code petition of 1822**

> If a petition . . . is considered and treated as an expression of public feeling, and if in deference to it any reasonable measure of the Government is abandoned, then indeed an importance will be conferred upon the few political agitators who are industrious to sow dissensions.
>
> **—Sir Peregrine Maitland, writing at York (Upper Canada), 1827, on the anti-Alien-Bill petition**

The rise of industrial cities reshaped the early nineteenth-century Atlantic world. Fueled literally and figuratively by newfound sources of energy in anthracite coal and gas; driven forward by the worldwide cotton economy; and linked to other urban centers by expanding networks of ocean shipping, roads, and canals (and, eventually, railroads), these cities produced clothing, infrastructure, homewares, and pollution on a scale never before seen. Populated by mass migration across oceans and within nations, factory-based towns and cities began to reorder the political landscape. Other cities emerged as commercial nodes that linked regional economies with ever more global trade. The arc of industrial urbanity included not just the exploding agglomerations that inspired the novelists and poets of the period—New York, London, Paris, Boston, Philadelphia, Manchester—but also Baltimore, Montréal, Charleston, Mexico City, Santa Fe, St. Louis, Buffalo and Rochester, York (now Toronto), Puebla, Cincinnati, Lexington,

Detroit, and Lynn, Massachusetts. Signified by the gas-fueled lights illumining so many of these cities, new political economies emerged in all these centers, remade by global capitalism and currents of democracy and liberal thought.[1]

As a narrative of voting, political parties, and crowds, the story of American democracy is rightly told, in large measure, as a story of cities and their transformation. As artisans and independent producers in New York, Boston, and Philadelphia confronted the burgeoning factory system, as they wrestled with the regime that challenged their livelihoods and in more traditional ways left them aside from the public sphere, they built new machines of politics to contend with the factory machines that governed their lives. They constructed alternative visions of political economy. In state after state, they fought for—and won—voting rights that were independent of property. They fought off elite initiatives and proposals, whether from Federalists seeking to limit popular voice in government or from those who sought to extend aristocratic control of financial and government institutions. Perhaps most famously, they built the first mass party of the modern democratic age, the Jacksonian Democrats, who linked legions of voters in identity and association to a set of officeholders who were committed, as part of their increasingly orchestrated campaigns, to carrying out systematic programs and distributing government office to the common man.[2]

This narrative of democracy often excludes the story of urban petitioning that gave rise to expanded suffrage rights, supported the formation of workers' associations, and often rivaled voting itself as political activity. In petitioning, city democrats articulated new identities as producers—as akin to farmers, but as distinguished from those who managed others or speculated on capital, or from those poorer souls whose lives partook too little of "work" to qualify for citizenship. These identities had older roots in the republican idiom of Thomas Jefferson. Antebellum Americans increasingly grafted these Jeffersonian ideals onto an industrial template, and they did so with petitioning. Through petitioning, city democrats found and built alliances with others they considered producers—farmers, canal diggers, turnpike workers, rural shopkeepers. In affixing their names to ever longer lists of signatories calling for tariffs, labor protections, elimination of debt imprisonment and capital punishment, and other measures, these city democrats built a common identity on paper, an identity that would outlast the memorials and the legislative or executive proceedings to which they gave rise. The producer-based petitioning campaigns of the 1820s and 1830s coevolved with massive new waves of voting. Whether in Baltimore, York, Boston, Montréal, or New York, city democrats saw petitioning as inseparable from electoral politics.[3]

The petitioning moment of North American city democrats did far more than harness an existing institution. Much as in Native American protest, in free Black memorials, and in the French-Canadian uprising of the 1820s, new industrial democrats transformed the culture and process of petitioning. They attacked a politics of deference that was most visible in New England and the mid-Atlantic but was also present in Upper Canada and newly independent Mexico, and their memorials conveyed requests that verged on ever more assertive demands. Petitions accompanied intellectual and public campaigns and relied on a deep feedback between organization and signatory-based supplication. They targeted institutions that seemed, to that time, to have the comfort of legitimacy—auctions, employers' discretion in setting working hours, municipal regulations, property.

The saga of petitioning and industrial democracy unfolded in Canada as well. Suffrage eligibility was remarkably widespread in Canada in the 1810s and 1820s due to low property-holding requirements. Statistical evidence from Toronto also suggests that more voting-eligible men petitioned than cast ballots in that city in the mid-1830s. Women and Indigenous people also voted in appreciable numbers. While Canada remained a colonial system under the tutelage of the British Crown, democratic currents gushed through its cities and hamlets alike, nowhere more in evidence than in the petitions that ran through its politics.

It is easy to read petitioning and its campaigns as an older mode of politics, something pre-democratic, a mode superseded by a more Jacksonian style. The saga of Upper Canadian politics; the reform of American city governments; the coalescence of urban artisans and middling farmers; and the American trajectories of tariff, debt, and anti-auction politics do more than undermine this assumption. They destroy it. Artisans and other self-styled producers and anti-aristocrats in the antebellum United States and Upper Canada needed allies. They desperately sought new modes of organization and collective voice. The creation of newspapers and voluntary associations provided some of these essential ingredients of a new politics, but newspaper editors dedicated themselves to printing and circulation of memorials as much as they devised electoral strategies. Many of the producer-based associations that emerged in the United States at this time were dedicated explicitly to petitioning, and the city democrats of the time saw petitioning and demonstration, memorial and strike, less as substitutes than as necessary and holy complements. In these mobilizations, there emerged networks essential to electoral organization and spacious geographic and cross-trade collaboration.

PETITIONS AND POSTWAR AMERICAN STATE CONSTITUTIONAL CONVENTIONS

The War of 1812 transformed American politics. New visions of expansionary settler republics combined with anti-aristocratic sentiment to fuel support for popular government. These forces of ambition and reaction crystallized in roughly a dozen state and territorial constitutional conventions in the two decades during and after the war.

Neither a legislature nor a court, the constitutional convention remained a relatively young creature in the early nineteenth century. Invoking memories of the English Convention Parliament of 1689 and reemerging in the 1780s in the states (especially Massachusetts, which ratified its 1780 constitution by popular vote) and then in the national convention at Philadelphia in 1787, the constitutional convention claimed authority above that of a legislature yet lacked the permanence of a lawmaking body.[4]

The postwar constitutional conventions of the American states became a site of democratic action and an object of democratic aspiration. They recast governmental forms, extending suffrage to those without landed property. State after state opened its polls to all white men or to those who had paid taxes regardless of landholding. These apertures came with pressures for racial exclusion. States defined electoral citizenship racially even as they unmoored the concept from property. Nor did the political imagination of the time favor the idea of women electors. The resulting expansion of electorates nonetheless furthered democracy in its institutional, procedural, and cultural forms—by extending the vote, tethering governments more to electoral forces, reducing the privileges of larger landholders and freeholders, and doing so in ways that reinforced a particular model of citizenship.[5]

The American state conventions of the 1810s and 1820s were often initiated and heavily influenced by petitions. Petitions became the dominant mode of expression and organization for exerting popular pressure for new constitutions. Once called and gathered, the postwar conventions were often flooded by petitions and puzzled over what to do with them. The model of the French Estates General of 1789—where petition-like compilations of complaints deluged the deliberative bodies of clergy, nobility, and bourgeoisie, which rethought the entire structure of a regime and toppled its aristocracy—remained prominent both in the minds of American democrats and their opponents.[6]

Some of the earliest and most transformative moves came in Connecticut. The state's Federalists had been badly weakened by their opposition to the war (a stance congealed publicly at the ill-fated Hartford Convention of 1814–1815) and their alliance with the dominant Congregationalist Church. The aristocracy founded in that alliance had entrenched itself in the state's upper chamber, the Council, a small body of elites whose membership changed slowly due to local electoral practices that favored incumbent councilors and fidelity to the Congregationalists. The Council had vocally supported the Hartford Convention. Armed with an absolute veto over legislation and conducting its operations in secret, the Council only received petitions, institutionalizing the culture of deference that characterized Connecticut petitioning before the war. In the autumn of 1817, however, Cheshire town meeting officials prepared a memorial calling for a new constitution consistent with the principles of "republican government." Town after town followed: New Haven, Wallingford, Danbury, and at least a dozen more through April 1818. Harnessing the language of republicanism spread anew by the former Federalist but now Republican George Richardson, these town meeting officials called for a written constitution and equality of citizenship. A separate petition campaign targeted the state legislature in Hartford.[7]

Even before the General Assembly and then a convention took up constitutional reform, the twin energies of petitioning and town meeting memorials had begun to change the culture of Connecticut politics. The Connecticut town meeting drew on popular energies in ways that Alexis de Tocqueville would marvel at two decades later in his volume *Democracy in America* (1835). And in ways that eluded Tocqueville, those same town meetings harnessed the memorial to raise their voices to state legislatures. By stepping outside the customary legislative process at the state level, using petitions not merely to express but to mobilize reform advocates, and reshaping political processes within the towns themselves that weakened the hegemony of Congregationalist ministers, Connecticut's reformers empowered new voices.[8]

The memorials of the fall of 1817 and the spring of 1818 emboldened Republicans and convinced Federalists that they would need to compromise, first and foremost by giving way to a convention. The constitutional convention of August 1818 opened suffrage for white men who met a brief residency criterion and who had a small freehold, had performed militia service, or were taxpayers. The convention strictly and consciously excluded Black voting, disenfranchising a small but burgeoning African American community in the state. In other ways, the convention proved more radical. Connecticut's new constitution established strict equality among Christian denominations, toppling the Congregationalist hierarchy in the first article of the new charter. And in a move as democratic as any other, the new constitution replaced the Council with an annually elected Senate that deliberated openly. A ratification vote in October cemented the new changes, the last new constitution that the state would adopt until 1965.[9]

Legislators in early national New York noted a steady flow of memorials to Albany calling for new political arrangements. Like Connecticut's charter, the state's 1777 constitution retained a heavily aristocratic element. Voting was elaborately regulated, dominated by freehold suffrage and with debt provisions that excluded the growing ranks of small farmers in the state's central and western reaches. New York's Council of Revision was weaker than Connecticut's, yet it sat above the assembly and the senate and functioned to protect large freeholders. It also strengthened the hand of postwar governor DeWitt Clinton, who sat on the council along with the state's supreme court justices and its chancellor.[10]

The energy for reform was evident before the outbreak of war with Britain, as in March 1811, townships from Ontario County and, separately, citizens of Rensselaer submitted petitions calling for a constitutional convention and for "general suffrage" accorded to all men regardless of their property. In the aftermath of the war, township memorials and resolutions combined with petitions signed by the thousands to stoke popular pressure. Frustration with Governor Clinton crystallized in a new political party in New York City, the City Democrats, who allied with breakaway upstate Republicans who named themselves the Bucktails, including the talented moderate Martin Van Buren. Clinton and his allies succeeded in stalling but not killing the convention project, and the assembly passed a strong convention bill in 1820.[11]

When the convention assembled in August 1821 and began debating the question of general suffrage, New York's democrats advanced arguments about equality, voting rights earned through military service, and the mass of petitions that supported the people's call for expanded electoral citizenship. Peter Robert Livingston, then a state senator and delegate from Dutchess County, openly mocked the antidemocratic forces who doubted the people's voice, pointing first to petitions in doing so: "But we are asked," Livingston held forth, "what evidence we have that the people want this extension of suffrage? Sir, 74,000 witnesses testified, last spring, that they wanted it. Meetings and resolutions, public prints, and conversation have united to require it."[12] Former New York mayor Jacob Radcliff also pointed to the popular pressure for suffrage extension and to the exemplar of French republicanism. Responding to Clintonians' dismissal of public support for general suffrage, John Z. Ross from petition-happy Genesee County reminded the convention that they were assembled together for no reason more powerful than that they had been asked by repeated memorial to gather. The "supporters of this amendment [retaining propertied suffrage]," Ross noted, had argued "that the people of this state have expressed no wish in favour of its abolition," that "they [are] incapable of manifesting their wishes."[13] Petitions gave the lie to this claim. "In fact [by] every channel through which public opinion could be conveyed, not by one party alone, this anti-republican distinction has been for years the theme of complaint. The executive of this state, we are informed, has been petitioned to recommend it to the legislature to call a Convention."[14]

Confirmation of the weight of these petitions and the arguments invoking them came in the vehemence with which Clintonians, including the Council, denounced them. Elisha Williams and others who rejected open suffrage focused their rebuttal heavily on the petition-based character of suffrage claims, insulting in one breath the preposterous fact that "the people demand it" while in the next pointing to the specter of France's abolition of landed aristocracy. Convention delegates should not blindly accept but need actively question, Williams insisted, the deliberative assemblies in western New York and other locales.[15]

New York also witnessed the most far-ranging debate on race and voting rights among the American state conventions, as it had the largest African American population among the northern states. Around thirty thousand free Blacks lived in New York in 1820 (fully a third of them in Manhattan), and another ten thousand slaves would be due for emancipation under state law in 1827. Free Black men who met the property requirements of the 1777 constitution already voted in significant numbers, so much so as to form what state elites identified as a bloc, one successfully courted by the Federalists. The idea of suffrage for those without land bespoke not only the surging ethos of equality and the changing nature of wealth and income but also the idea of whiteness. In addition to Connecticut's full disenfranchisement, the New York convention entertained amendments for a White-only electorate in New York.[16]

So it was that Thomas Sipkins and other "free people of colour" sent their own memorial to the convention in September 1821, asking not only for the maintenance of existing voting rights but for a "declarative article" protecting their suffrage.[17] Foregrounding many of the antislavery arguments to emerge in the ensuing three decades, Sipkins's argument invoked the Declaration of Independence and its ideals of equality. Sipkins was no chance author of the 1821 suffrage petition; he had organized the new Asbury Methodist Episcopal Church in 1813, departing from the Zion Methodist Church and further breaking from alliances with the city's White Methodists. His son Henry would emerge in the 1830s as an important leader of the city's antebellum Black community.[18]

Thomas Sipkins's memorial was one of only a handful entertained by New York's 1821 meeting. It was referred to the convention's committee of the whole, meaning that the entirety of the assembly would debate it. That it changed the terms of the debate is evident from the denunciations of delegates who tried to undermine the legitimacy of Sipkins and his fellow Black citizens. The racist arguments against Black voting invoked the claimed inferiority of African American intelligence, independence, and loyalty to the state. And pro-restriction delegates explicitly targeted the Sipkins petition. Pointing to the memorial as it lay on the table at the front of the assembly, Peter Livingston insisted that twenty or more of the signatories had not truly signed their own names. Denying the very agency of the Black petitioners, John Z. Ross claimed (without evidence) that the memorial "in all probability has been instigated by gentlemen of a different colour, who expect to control their votes."[19] Livingston and Ross vaunted petitions that served their vision of White democracy but delegitimized them when claiming Black democracy.[20]

Nonetheless, Sipkins's petition and in turn Martin Van Buren would remind New York's conventioneers that free Black men were already voting in their state. In a compromise among these views, and wanting to avoid the odious example in Connecticut, the New York convention granted limited suffrage to African American men, according voting rights to all whose freeholds were valued at $250 or higher. New York thus maintained a property requirement for Black men even as their heralded democratic reform abolished property qualifications for Whites.[21]

New York's democrats thus avoided what they saw as Connecticut's distasteful full Black disenfranchisement, consigning Black men to a status slightly less inferior than that of their neighbors. The persistence of a Black electorate in the Empire State owed not merely to factional compromise but to petitions that reminded convention goers of the existing rights and practices at stake in their deliberations. In the end, New York's electorate for governor and the state senate expanded by 150,000 voters, from one-third of white males to four-fifths.[22]

Petitions also launched and shaped the debates over the shape of the electorate in postwar Virginia. The state still operated under the Constitution of 1776, whose defects motivated widespread lament. Petitioners from Henry County in 1805 declared the revolutionary constitution "Unequal, Inadequate, Oppressive, and Aristocrattical."[23] With evident ire did Thomas Jefferson coldly analyze the document in query 13 of *Notes on the State of Virginia* (1782), where he listed its defects, starting first with malapportionment: "The majority of men in the state, who pay and fight for its support, are unrepresented in the legislature," while "among those who share the representation, the shares are very unequal."[24] The "100 fighting men" of the county of Warwick had as much delegated presence in the legislature as the 1,746 men of the county of Loudoun. The apportionment of districts generally favored the tidewater region—what Jefferson termed that land "between the sea coast and the falls of rivers"—with its landed gentry and slaveholders, to the detriment of piedmont residents to the west.[25]

Petition campaigns that echoed Jefferson's concerns about the 1776 Constitution and that called for expended suffrage began trickling into the House of Delegates in the 1790s. Yet from 1807 to 1816, the petitions became more numerous and more declarative. Ninety-one petitioners from Accomack County in 1810 decried the creeping "aristocracy" and "corruption" in the state, called for reapportionment and general suffrage, and maintained that a constitutional convention—stepping outside legislative politics itself—was the only evident solution to the state's ills.[26] The petition became a bill but was voted down by the assembly on the grounds that the assembly was the ultimate caretaker of the constitution, and no single county should be able to induce a convention by petition. Only a qualified "majority" would be able to bend the will of the assembly.[27] James Madison remarked that having himself seen "democracy run wild in France," the democratic project of the Accomack County petitioners was unsuitable for Virginia.[28]

The petition-based movement for a convention reached a new crescendo in the 1815–1816 session. Men without freeholds in the piedmont region began organizing assemblies in 1815, first in Rockingham County and then elsewhere, and launching a statewide petition campaign. Their complaints ranged from "inhibitions to the elective franchise"—any male taxpayer as well as anyone recently conscripted in the war should enjoy the vote, they argued—to malapportionment in the Virginia House of Delegates and Senate. Echoing Jefferson's argument from three decades earlier, they noted that tidewater regions enjoyed half again to almost double the numerical representation of the piedmont regions in these chambers. A self-styled reform convention of piedmont leaders was held in Staunton in August 1816, issuing in further memorials to the delegates.[29]

Both their proponents and their detractors saw these petitions not merely as "republican" but as "democratic." Pro-reform petitioners targeted the very structure of the legislature that provided a venue for the receipt and hearing of their complaints. And they proposed an alternative venue—a constitutional convention—that they knew had gained traction in other states. For this reason, and for a time, Virginia's democratic thrust foundered on opposition from landed gentry and slaveholders based in the tidewater region. Despite the support of Jefferson, the Virginia Senate killed momentum for a convention in 1816.[30]

Pro-democracy reformers developed new tactics in the late 1810s and 1820s, combining petitions with a call for polls in different counties that would give the weight of numbers to their claims as well as instructions to legislators. Combining polls, newspaper prints, and pamphlets with petitions, the reformers succeeded in stoking energy for a convention in 1825. Jefferson wrote an open letter calling for a reform convention, and pro-convention petitions again surged in the legislature. Reformers held a second convention at Staunton in July 1825, and from that meeting came a petition and a draft bill for the legislature, as well as a template for the petitions that would circulate around the west and north of the state later that year. Sensing the threat of reform mobilization by petition, eastern interests started a counter-memorial campaign of their own. The next session of the assembly received fifty petitions supporting a convention and thirty opposed. The House of Delegates appointed a committee to examine these memorials, which found that over twenty thousand Virginians had signed them. Impelled by instructions and by these petitions, the assembly in December 1827 session voted to submit the question of a new convention to the state's freeholders, and the pro-convention tally of the following spring was solidly in the majority. The resulting convention, held in 1829, would trim the size of the House of Delegates and reduce but not eliminate the malapportionment problem. Virginia would not take up the question of universal White male suffrage for another two decades.[31]

Pro-suffrage petitioning activity figured differently but substantially in the western territories, where suffrage was limited by the fifty-acre freeholding requirement of the Northwest Ordinance of 1787, leaving a small fraction of the White male population eligible to cast ballots. Western settlers eagerly challenged these restrictions in petitions before and after the war, and these calls for electoral reform set the tone and terms of constitutional debates, flowing into Congress as the relevant venue. Often the memorials came from conventions of settlers assembled in a given town or county. In many cases the constitutional conventions arose as territories decided to mount campaigns for statehood, which itself required a petition process. Voting rights were expanded in Alabama, Illinois, Indiana, and Missouri in this way, though petitions appear to have played less of a role in the southern states.[32]

Petitioning advanced a more robust procedural democracy that was critical to a more egalitarian electoral sphere. Memorial campaigns both prompted and fashioned the age of suffrage expansion after the War of 1812, and they triggered state constitutional conventions. Petitions introduced agenda items for consideration, and their arguments and sheer mass pressured delegates. These patterns call for a different understanding of the electoral democratization of White American men. Before but especially during and after the war, claims for equal citizenship independent of property coursed through the United States. Popular pressure for electoral reform was not merely inseparable from petition movements. Only through memorials did that pressure become politically tangible and procedurally real for state legislatures. And just as petitions impelled electoral democracy for White men, Black petitioners reminded state conventioneers of their limits, skillfully preserving select rights in an adverse environment. Claims that suffrage extension proceeded largely from elite calculations miss the sources, the agendas, and the most important instrument of antebellum electoral democratization: memorials for conventions and petitions to them.[33]

CONTESTING THE AMERICAN CITY—NEW YORK, BOSTON, BALTIMORE

The burgeoning cities of the early American republic owed their legal existence to their state legislatures. Their charters placed power in a mixture of municipal councils, mayors, and courts. The aggrieved and the aggressive took their complaints and requests to all these venues. And in the midst of the War of 1812 and its aftermath, they sought to reform the very institutions they approached. Resentful at what they considered an aristocratic control of city politics, worker-petitioners targeted both parchment and practice, bringing institutional and organizational democracy with them.

In the northeast United States, Federalists and elite allies retained a significant power hold in the very areas of the new Republic where industrial capitalism was most rapidly growing. And a culture of deference that had characterized politics even during the Revolution—marked by the sway of established Protestant churches and their ministers, the presumption of governance by those with long-held landed wealth, and the added privileges of a still-living aristocracy—remained in place. The battle for urban democracy would have to be waged against Federalists and city fathers.[34]

New York City's transforming economy spawned both differentiation and cohesion. A scattered population of orphans and widows, itinerant laborers, free Blacks, and immigrants constituted the city's working poor. Fully one in seven city residents (fifteen thousand persons) needed some form of poor relief, while roughly eighteen hundred of them lived in the city's almshouse. Far above the fray lived the city's aristocratic elite—the Knickerbocker families that derived their wealth from Dutch and late-colonial New York, aristocratic families descended from New England, and nouveau riche men such as John Jacob Astor. Just one in twenty-five New Yorkers owned over half of the city's noncorporate assets in 1817. These families controlled New York politics but were riven by faction throughout the early national and Jeffersonian periods. The battle for supremacy between Jeffersonian and Hamiltonian factions shot through nearly every institution.[35]

It was in the rough middle of this economic hierarchy that a more unified craft-based assemblage of men emerged, one that began to form a distinct interest in city politics and to speak an artisan republicanism. Generally defined as those who directly produced their commodities, artisans included coopers, cabinetmakers, carpenters, mechanics, shoemakers, metalworkers, and tanners and other leather workers in the Swamp District. At the peak of the artisanal hierarchy were master craftsmen, whose reputation and position in the craft economy gave them easier credit through social networks and advantages in sales. They were, in a sense, entrepreneurs who prized their autonomy as much as or more than their wealth. Just below them were journeymen who had completed an apprenticeship and who were legitimated practitioners of their craft, while apprentices had not yet acquired the legitimacy and social position to stand with them socially. The organization of economic production in these domains was dominated by small firms with a handful of workers. In the early national period, artisans showed a decided preference for Federalists, yet they began to drift toward Jeffersonian ideas in 1800 and afterward. The "middling republicanism" they adopted stood in opposition to the interests and plans of the city's aristocracy but also differentiated them as producers from the dependent poor.[36]

City artisans had long benefited from organization, with the General Society of Mechanics and Tradesmen representing many of them since its founding in 1785. The society incorporated petition-based lobbying and complaint making into its very fabric, launching memorial campaigns in 1787 and 1789 in concert with associations from other states. In 1810, the society petitioned the state assembly for renewal of its charter and embarked on a new, more coordinated endeavor of organization building, alliance formation, and petitioning. That year, the society also sent a delegation of members to Albany with a petition to the assembly for a bank charter in 1810 and soon founded the Mechanics' National Bank. It then joined with the city's Society of Cabinetmakers to create a grievance committee for their members. By 1820, the General Society of Mechanics and Tradesmen had also created the Mechanics' School and the Apprentices' Library. The growing number of petition campaigns served both to advocate interests and to build alliances with other trades and crafts.[37]

With the end of the war, new economic forces buffeted the city's artisans, and in voicing their grievances, those artisans responded with new alliances, new tactics, and new modes of petitioning. British manufacturers dumped surplus products on city markets using a socially closed system of auctions to undercut artisans' sales and prices. Impersonal systems of credit increasingly suffused the urban economy, disrupting the socially networked, reputation-based lending on which artisans had long depended. The Panic of 1819—during which a wave of bank failures and mortgage foreclosures brought mass unemployment and declining prices—created something of an organizing moment for New York artisans, in which they refocused their energies on common enemies. They targeted the auction system, the city's established religious authorities, and what many considered a culture of decadence among American workers.

Auctions had become commonplace in American cities up and down the Atlantic coast, but they grew dramatically in New York during and after the war, from $4.7 million in auction sales annually in 1812 to $13.5 million in 1818, with another surge to $24.2 million in 1825. The ownership of the auction houses gradually shifted to British merchants, and these houses tightly controlled the ability to sell one's goods at auction in the postwar period. New York State imposed a slight duty on auction sales in 1817, but relative to Boston and Philadelphia, the city lightly regulated the houses. As a result, New York (and, to a lesser extent, Baltimore) attracted both an ever-greater volume of auction business and swelling anti-auction resentment. Repeatedly after the war—in 1817, 1818, 1819, 1820, 1821, and 1824—New-York based alliances of mechanics and merchants petitioned Congress for taxation or regulation of auction sales. The petitioners decried the "frauds of British agents" who hawked "goods of inferior quality, of cheap and temporary dye, of specious appearance, and slight fabric." Characterizing the auction business as a monopoly, they excoriated its closed nature. Speaking on the House floor in May 1820, New Jersey republican Charles Kinsey gestured to "the numerous petitions . . . from various classes of society" as "the strongest evidence" in favor of an auction taxation bill. Relaying the laments of these memorials, he noted the "demoralizing effect" that auctions had exercised on the "sinking American manufacturer." Auctioneer interests mounted a counterpetitioning campaign, arguing that their work served to lower prices for consumers and that the Panic, not their operations, was hurting mechanics and artisans' business. The auction duty bill would die that year and repeatedly through the 1820s, but Kinsey spoke correctly in noting that auction protest and reform efforts had in fact brought a diverse range of interests together. Anti-auction committees organized from the late 1810s through the 1820s. They held meetings primarily for the purposes of petitioning, and in these efforts there formed alliances among small manufacturers, artisans, mechanics, and petty merchants that would not have readily emerged otherwise.[38]

What started in New York soon spread to other coastal cities and around the Empire State. An anti-auction coalition of small merchants, manufacturers, and artisans in Baltimore began petitioning Congress in 1824. Yet the center of the anti-auction forces remained in New York. In 1828, city anti-auction groups formed a Committee of Fifty to circulate memorials and gather signatures. Petition prayers varied but generally asked for a 10 percent duty on auction sales. The auction system, their prayers maintained, "encourages fraud on the revenue, depresses domestic manufacture, . . . destroys the mercantile character," and had especially "ruinous" consequences for "the agricultural and laboring part of the population." The volume of signatures quickly exploded. An auction tax memorial with ten thousand New Yorkers' names affixed was presented to Congress on December 10, 1828, to be followed five days later with another seventy-six hundred names. The *New York Evening Post* would report, right before Christmas Day 1828, that the signatures of twenty-two thousand New York citizens had appeared on anti-auction petitions just sent to Congress. The memorials flowed from Baltimore as well. Anti-auction forces mounted electoral candidacies in 1828, but these were swept aside in the Jacksonian surge in city and state elections. Undeterred, the anti-auction forces regrouped in 1829 and kept up a frenzied memorial campaign until 1832, this time directed at the New York State legislature. The volume and intensity of the petitions gave rise to select committees in the assembly, which did not change the tax but tightened criminal penalties from the 1817 statute.[39]

Even as artisans failed to win new statutes, they advanced organizationally. Anti-auction forces never succeeded in obtaining their broad tax in Albany or in Washington, but their work complemented the pro-tariff campaign of manufacturers and enlivened other measures aimed at ameliorating the conditions of the American producer. Auction and tariff politics brought together "the agricultural and laboring part of the population" in ways that existing associations had not yet done. In the collective prayers of "farmers, manufacturers, mechanics and merchants"—from places like Rensselaer County in New York, Somerset County in Maine, the state of Ohio, central and western Pennsylvania, and numerous city associations—there emerged in the early 1820s a coalition that would persist and grow.[40]

Emanating from Philadelphia more than New York, the post-1819 tariff campaign buffeted the U.S. Congress like no other question. In the fifteen years following the war with Britain, not even slavery drew more petitions to Congress. At the time, no party sufficed to adequately represent American workers whose interests and representatives favored the tariff. Benefiting from southern support and postwar nationalism, the tariff bill of 1816 had imposed duties on woolens and leather goods, but these were sunset in 1820. A vote on the duty-hiking measure of Pennsylvania Republican Henry Baldwin in March 1820—which failed to pass the Senate—showed that tariff politics cut across sections and parties, with neither a free state–slave state nor a Federalist–Republican divide accounting for the distinctive voting patterns in the House. In the absence of party organization and sectional alignment, the tariff petition became the central tool of advocacy and political coalition-building in state capitals and in Washington.[41]

Tariff politics generated new groups, such as the Philadelphia-based National Institution for the Promotion of Industry and the American Society of the City of New York. Still others, like the Society of Paper Makers of the States of Pennsylvania and Delaware, seemed to form just for the purpose of petitioning. The papermakers argued that foreign paper products entering the U.S. market after the war had decimated an economic landscape. Manufacturing had declined from "seventy Paper Mills . . . which were in full operation" with "ninety-five paper vats . . . employing nine hundred and fifty persons" to a depressive state of "but seventeen vats at work . . . leaving unemployed 775 persons." New York City petitions lamented that "a great portion of our mechanics and artists are unemployed," pointing to the "embarrassment, depression and distress which is so universally felt." Memorialists also complained that the tariff could be undercut by auction sales, linking the two issues together. The apparent impermanence of these groups masked their ability to coalesce otherwise diverse interests, whether across states (as with the papermakers) or across industries and trades (as with New York City memorials).[42]

Unlike the auction movement, producers' aggregate push for tariffs saw several legislative triumphs, most notably the tariff bills of 1824 and 1828. By the mid-1820s, American tariff politics had changed appreciably. Southern representatives—ever less trusting of Henry Clay's American System of infrastructure, which would be funded at their expense, and ever more anxious to guard their exploding cotton economy—resisted further tariffs at every turn. In 1824, the woolen goods tariffs were hiked appreciably, and duties on iron and cotton goods were added; other duties from the 1816 tariff were increased. In 1828, Congress passed and President John Quincy Adams signed what southern politicians would call the "Tariff of Abominations." That law imposed a tax of 38 percent on over nine-tenths of imports to the United States.[43]

The twin political enigmas of the 1820s tariffs were that protective measures emerged for incumbent producers that were so small and scattered, and that coastal states with urbanizing factory cities (New York and Pennsylvania) allied with western agricultural states. It is tempting to see well-organized business behind these efforts, yet the vast majority of firms were small and relied heavily on worker pressure for petitioning and for their arguments. In the absence of partisan glue, the coalescence of tariff coalition came from elsewhere. Much as in Rensselaer County, New York—where the merchants, mechanics, farmers, and manufacturers petitioned together in 1824—tariff politics linked the producers of the field and the producers of the shop. Petitioning allowed broad populations in Ohio and Kentucky as well as the mechanics and manufacturers of New York and Philadelphia to pressure Congress simultaneously on the same issue without the bonds of partisan harmonization, in-person coordination, or a lobbying association. An industry like leatherworking, where production sites in New York's Swamp District were joined politically to rural tanning shops with nearby hemlock forests, required what was literally and functionally a spacious coalition for its protection. Organized pressure for tariffs came not from established firm or industry associations but from petitioning collectives and the producer consciousness they both represented and spawned.[44]

Throughout the tariff and auction debates, city democrats in New York, Boston, and Philadelphia found and targeted other enemies, and they increasingly looked within. During the Panic, workshop owners began to demand wage reductions and extensions of working hours. Cabinetmakers drew on their new organizational forms and their alliance with the General Society of Mechanics and Tradesmen and staged a mass walkout in May 1819. New York City bakers petitioned against onerous working hours. Yet in the aftermath of the Second Great Awakening and its challenges to established religion and to masculinity and household mores, workingmen's groups also advocated moral reform. The General Society of Mechanics and Tradesmen evinced the starkest transformation, endorsing a program of "piety" among its members and introducing reform energies to city politics.

In these endeavors, the society and its allies repeatedly petitioned the city's common council and the mayor's office, not least for regulation of taverns and for preservation of the Sabbath. The flow of tavern complaints was sufficiently large as to standardize the form and processing of temperance grievances. The larger Sabbatarian movement saw hundreds of petitions sent to Congress to restrict mail distribution on Sundays, fully 467 memorials arriving during the campaign of May 1829. While most of the Sabbatarian petitions had twenty to fifty signatures, the city-based efforts were far larger. In 1828, one Boston Sabbatarian petition garnered two thousand names, while one from New York City displayed seven thousand signatures. Lewis Tappan confided to his diary in December 1828 that he had personally collected fifty-six hundred names, at least four in ten of them artisans.[45]

The combination of worker energies and religious revival opened spaces for new personalities in city life. A wave of itinerant preachers—Lorenzo Dow, John Summerfield, Amos Broad—began to tour northern cities, or to move there and establish new churches. The Welsh immigrant and master craftsman Johnny Edwards held forth from a wagon and castigated Wall Street's moneylenders with a trumpet. As they converted artisans in their midst, these new preachers also petitioned city venues, tightening the links of the new politics to the new spirituality. To Edwards and other reformers, city leaders took sides in the emerging debates among Protestants, openly subsidizing missionary efforts of established clergy. Edwards took his mocking, disdainful grievance—one that buried any pretense of the deference that had long governed city politics but was giving way to a democratization of rhetoric—in a petition to the common council: "I firmly believe it would be far more acceptable to God and all good and wise men had you laid out 300 dollars in fat geese and turkeys and given them to the poor who have seen better days and they would prefer it at any time to 300 dollars worth of wind."[46]

Political and labor reform showcased new politicians practicing new forms of mass politics, including Stephen Allen of New York and Josiah Quincy of Boston. Allen personified a rags-to-artisan-riches story. Orphaned during the Revolution, he was steeped in reading the American radicals (including Thomas Paine) and in his early adulthood joined the Democratic-Republicans against the Federalists. Allen built his wealth in sail making, progressing from apprentice to journeyman to master craftsman, and was elected president of the General Society of Mechanics and Tradesmen in 1802, and elected to the common council in 1812, where he served for nearly a decade. He was elected mayor in December 1821 and twice thereafter in the city's annual mayoral contest, his career cementing the presence of craftsmen in city Republican politics in the 1820s. By 1825, he had moved to the state assembly, then to the state senate from 1829 to 1832.[47]

Allen's career combined organizing in political and labor spheres, and his innovations in city politics had much to do with his management of petitioning in the common council and the mayor's office. His years on the common council positioned him to read, respond to, and advocate for the memorials of the city's artisans at a time when their organization was changing rapidly, and when he became mayor, he carefully shepherded many a memorial of the common council to Albany. Allen devoted much of his mayoral work to coordinating his endeavors with the city's various petitioners, whether on matters of Sabbath observance, the poor laws, the formation of school societies, or the Mechanics' National Bank. When in 1824 the General Society of Mechanics and Tradesmen appealed to the common council, the mayor, and aldermen for a home for juvenile correction and instruction—presenting themselves as "men who in their youths have been deprived of the advantages of education" and who wished to assist "the rising generation"—Allen repeatedly brought the petition before his allies in Albany. It was Allen who presided over the introduction of new public health and public morals statutes that marked an era of municipal regulation, and these endeavors meant managing memorials and complaints from the city's population.[48]

In Boston, a still-formidable Federalist establishment controlled much of city politics through its hold on the state's legislature (general court) and judicial department (the court of sessions), and an elite grip on the Boston town meeting. Following a series of failed attempts to create a city government in 1784, 1792, 1804, and 1815, Boston had no mayor at the time of the Panic. As Joseph Buckingham, the editor of the *New England Galaxy* and a prominent spokesperson for Boston's laboring orders, put it in 1820, the town meeting amounted to a local oligarchy, in which as few as "fifteen or twenty, seldom more . . . do all the business of a town that contains near seven thousand voters."[49] Quincy mounted a campaign to reform the city's charter, reducing executive power in the town by giving the people direct choice of the mayor and limiting mayoral terms to one year at a time. Such proposals had been repeatedly shot down by Federalist forces in the party's Central Committee.[50]

In the wake of the Panic, Boston's middling and lower-class interests newly coalesced in a series of petition campaigns that focused on the dominant sources of workers' anxiety: their debt and their imprisonment on account of it, the arbitrary weight of their militia obligations, and their housing. As with artisans and the poor in other American cities, the Panic and the resulting depression had left many women, men, and households unable to pay debtors. Tensions between creditors and debtors had remained a staple feature of American politics since the Revolution, but the conflict now took on a more localized flavor. As hundreds of unemployed mechanics and small merchants faced time in Boston's almshouse and debtor prisons, political pressure to reform the state's debtor laws mounted. An "Association of Gentlemen" founded the *Debtor's Journal* in 1820, aiming to "subdue aristocracy and promote our freedom and happiness, as Americans." The *Debtor's Journal* devoted much of its work to petitioning the general court. Debt prisoners were permitted furloughs to labor and potentially repay their debt, and petitioners called for an extension of the domain of labor to include the whole of the city rather than just the blocks around the prison. The petition amassed four thousand names, a level unwitnessed in Boston politics since the war. The general court refused to act, and debtor advocates filed a lawsuit, ultimately unsuccessful, in the court of sessions. The failed petition drive nonetheless stirred a new form of class consciousness in Boston, focusing the resentments of the city's middling and lower orders on an "aristocracy."[51]

A broader partnership soon emerged to attack other institutions that burdened the city's working and poorer peoples. Like other early American states, Massachusetts relied heavily on a militia system for defense. Middle and lower orders of society were under compulsory militia service, while clergy, doctors, schoolmasters, and elected as well as appointed public officers received an exemption. Militia service wrested men from their families and jobs at important times of the economic calendar and further indebted them. Buckingham's *Galaxy* took up the aegis against the militia law, calling for its abolition and assisting in another mass petition drive in the spring of 1820. Once again, the general court refused the petition.[52]

Boston's housing code provided the target for what was perhaps the most sustained and invigorating petition drive. In the midst of Quincy's charter revision strategy, the city's workers and poor began to voice their frustration with an 1803 building ordinance that limited the construction of wooden buildings to no more than ten feet in height within the city. The 1803 code inflated housing prices just as it limited economic opportunities for master carpenters and journeymen, yet it enriched Boston's landlords by restricting residential supply. After some 1821 petitions that concerned the neighborhood of South Boston, Josiah Jones and then John Wheeler petitioned for a total repeal of the ten-foot restriction. Wheeler's petition boldly challenged Boston's representatives in the general court to "use their influence" to advance a wooden-buildings bill, a not-so-subtle message to city delegates that the city's working population was not being adequately represented in the state's legislature. Federalist leaders in Boston not only rejected the wooden-buildings petition, but they undermined its very validity in a breathtaking manipulation of power. The Federalist Harrison Gray Otis, then in Washington serving as a U.S. senator, directed his Federalist ally William Sullivan to bury the workers' initiative. Sullivan stacked the town meeting with landlord interests, and the meeting quickly passed a formal grievance against the Wheeler petition, arguing that the initiative was illegitimate. Sullivan's maneuver meant that the Federalist Central Committee could bury the petition's project procedurally in the general court, which would have to contend with the grievance before dealing with the petition. No bill came up for a vote.[53]

Otis's parry of the housing petition would prove to be his near-term undoing, and it hastened the Federalists' demise as well. To the resentment of housing law, Federalists had now stoked Bostonians' added fury at the sight of a legitimate petitioning effort sidelined by elite machinations. Buckingham expressed the wrath of city democrats in a savage editorial: "Certain people who never trouble themselves to attend town meeting,—thinking it beneath their *honorable* and *dignified* characters to meet in the same hall with mechanics and laboring men,—have presented a remonstrance against the petition. . . . It is, in short, a mere question of self-interest, in which the purse-proud landlord is arrayed against the mechanic. The remonstrance would never have existed, had not the large owners or real estates, seen in the success of the petition, a reduction of their already overgrown incomes from cruel and exorbitant rents."[54]

Far from walking away from their initiative, housing reform advocates doubled down on the petitioning effort. A new petition signed by more than 4,500 of Boston's residents came before the town meeting. Fully 3,411 men voted with written ballots at the Boston town meeting of March 6, 1822, with 2,263 of them declaring for the housing measure, providing a near two-to-one margin for the abolition of the 1803 code. The town meeting measure not only instructed Boston representatives to press for the bill in general court but also held that "the petitioners [themselves] be empowered to appear . . . on behalf of the Town or City, to advocate, and defend the petition before the Hon. Legislature."[55]

Federalists now ran scared, and their opponents among municipal reformers detected new opportunities. One Boston representative whose name had graced the antipetition remonstrance now had his name affixed prominently at the head of the housing reform petition. Wondering aloud as to what explained the switch, the paper surmised that "the fear of losing his seat in the legislature in the approaching election" had operated with severe effect on the representative's mind. Reformers and mechanics turned on their common enemy in the Federalist Central Committee, which came to personify the "aristocracy" not only as a body of political men but also as an antidemocratic suppressor of the petition. An alternative city party emerged, Josiah Quincy's "Middling Interest." Federalist politicians and religious elites hammered their insistence that no such thing as a middling interest set against the interests of the city's wealthy could exist, yet the massive memorials that had descended on the general court from 1820 to 1822, often signed by two thousand to four thousand Bostonians, gave the lie to these denials.[56]

Petition democracy and electoral democracy grew in mutual local feedback. In March 1822, Josiah Quincy's reform efforts—to overhaul city government and to toss out the older city charter in favor of a more democratic mayoral system—came before voters, and Quincy won. With new campaigns against city taxation added to the élan of the housing petition scandal and the energies of the militia and debtor law reform efforts, Quincy's push could not have come at a more propitious time. Like New York, Boston would now have annual elections for mayor with ward-based voting, a city government, and a symbolic blow against the older culture of deference. Quincy's cousin John Phillips ran for the mayoralty, upsetting Otis, who had retired from Washington in the assumption that he would take the mayor's office as a sort of career capstone. Quincy himself would wait until 1823 to campaign for mayor, and when he did, he campaigned on the abolition of debt imprisonment. Quincy's rise spelled the death of the Federalist Party in Massachusetts. Yet Quincy himself ruled Boston with an iron fist, displaying tendencies that belied his democratizing reforms of previous years, and so in 1828 a chastened Otis returned to the city's political scene. His mayoralty was governed under a new, more egalitarian age in city politics. Tellingly, reform momentum came not only from Quincy but also from the general court, which began in the early 1820s to consider, and occasionally to grant, debtors' petitions for personal and financial "discharge." When the debtor and militia movements united around the cause of ward voting, they found an ally in the general court, which advanced ward voting from 1822 onward and enacted other reforms to advance workers' interests. The rise of an artisan and working-class political coalition in the form of a Middling Interest had begun and had accelerated with the petition campaign.[57]

City reform in New York and Boston took different paths but also took common inspiration from the developments of the war and the Panic of 1819. Artisans, mechanics, and the poor had found a common enemy—"aristocracy" and "nabobs"—one to whom they would no longer defer. This anti-aristocratic moment was fueled by an anti-British sentiment as well and, occasionally, an embrace of French and even medieval ideals, as when New York City hatters carried a portrait of Clement, the patron saint of felters and hat makers, with the title "St. Clement—Hats Invented in Paris in 1404." It was in the late 1820s that worker celebration of the Erie Canal displayed a new form of organizational consciousness, Lafayette made his fabulous tour of the United States to massive and adoring anti-British crowds, and Jackson unseated John Quincy Adams and pronounced his administration in favor of the common man in areas ranging from government appointments to national finance to settlement policy. The attack on aristocracy had taken an electoral turn in the 1820s, but city democrats had started that attack in local organizations and in persistent, sometimes massive local petitions that envisioned bold egalitarian reforms of basic American institutions ranging from the militia, to markets for capital and sales, to prisons, and to housing itself.[58]

* * *

The late 1820s and early 1830s saw a revitalization of urban reform and a turn to more radical postures among American workers. Pressure for tariffs continued, as did work against auction houses. To these measures were added fresh pressure for the abolition of imprisonment for debt and prison reform, and restrictions on working hours. In New York City, a more radical popular movement, led by a committee composed primarily of journeymen mechanics, emerged in December 1829. With a recommitment to petitioning campaigns, to anti-auction agitation, and to organization building, this movement saw new alliances among the General Society of Mechanics and Tradesmen, the new American Institute of the City of New York (founded in 1827), and lien-law and auction reformers.[59]

The repertoire of action evolved considerably, and workers in the United States mounted strikes and boycott campaigns with much greater frequency. Despite their distaste for the British aristocracy and its seeming American allies, working-class reformers in the United States admired ideas and emulated tactics being promoted in England. Sir Robert Peel sponsored a parliamentary inquiry into child labor practices that issued in the Cotton Mills and Factories Act (1819). In the mid-1820s, British cotton spinner millworkers—inspired by a Christian radicalism that bore important connections and similarities to the American Second Great Awakening—organized and began pressing for broad labor reforms. The British campaign accelerated in 1829 and resulted in the passage of the 1833 Factory Act, which limited working hours for those under eighteen years of age. The aim of a ten-hour workday remained unattained, but these laborers had altered the British parliamentary agenda in ways that were unimaginable in the early 1820s.[60]

As these currents of reform spread to the United States, concerted working activity became a complement, not a substitute, to laborers' petitions. In the early 1830s, the cross-trade and cross-state coalitions that had emerged in the tariff debates began to reorganize and to press for changes in working conditions. A New York State Workingmen's Convention was held in Salina in 1830, while the New England Association of Farmers, Mechanics, and Other Workingmen was founded in Boston in 1832. In petition and newsprint, the association took the lead in decrying the evils of the factory system. The association published *New England Artisan and Laboring Man's Repository* (whose publishers called it the *Artisan*) and, following its convention plea for petitions in October 1832, approached several legislatures in the region and Congress itself. Connecting the factory system with monopoly and aristocracy, a Massachusetts petition maintained that "numerous bodies of monopolists in New England . . . triumph over the salutary prescriptions of the constitution, [and] have erected themselves into a self-created aristocracy." Articulating an expansive identity of the free workingman, the *Artisan* expressed the emergent coupling of anti-aristocratic causes that united rural and city interests, publishing editorials such as "The Freedom of Labor Depends upon the Freedom of the Soil" (1833). The *Artisan*'s essay was an attack not on slavery but on the institution of rural mortgages, but it nonetheless struck a notable early link between notions of "free soil" and "free labor" long before the emergence of either the Liberty or Free-Soil parties. Other petitions from the association and its allies targeted the Rhode Island legislature in Providence, and some ended up in Congress.[61]

Workers' agitation arose up and down the Atlantic coast, most notably in the exploding urban center at Baltimore. Increasingly, this activity involved women, who had been entering the factory system by the thousands. New York seamstresses went on strike in 1831, and three hundred female shoe binders in Reading, Massachusetts, organized to publish their wages the same year. Yet in considering new strike activity, the New England Association had its eye on developments in Baltimore and the more orchestrated unrest among seamstresses there. Baltimore lacked the older political structure against which artisans and the poor had rebelled in the 1820s. A new agglomeration by the terms of the early Republic, its population and economy had exploded during and after the war. Baltimore became the third largest city in the United States, and with slavery still legal in Maryland, it had more people of color (many free, many slaves) than any other American city. In the autumn of 1833, women in Fells Point and Baltimore had coordinated a price list and began planning to circulate minimum pay rates to the town's employers. The strike began on the first of October 1833, followed by publication of a price list. Baltimore women's working conditions, if anything, deteriorated in the years to follow.[62]

As tenuous as their political status remained, laborers of all sorts in Baltimore tied individual and collective petitioning to their labor turnouts and strikes, their publication of wage rates, and their support of a print discourse. Unskilled laborers began to petition to lament their pay and working conditions, including one group of four "scrapers of the streets," who approached the city council in 1829 to complain of their wages. City life in Baltimore had become prohibitively expensive over the previous decade, with exploding rents and rising prices for foodstuffs and wood for heating. The street scrapers shoveled and cleaned Baltimore's streets of manure, and they were, in more than one sense, at the symbolic bottom of the working order. Yet they still had the status of petitioners, they had enjoyed suffrage rights in Maryland since 1818, and they were not alone. Petitions from free Black workers and White journeymen surged in the early 1830s. White city workers assembled in 1834 a petition—whose signatory list, encompassing twelve hundred names, extended twenty-four feet—calling for a minimum pay of one dollar per night for watchmen. The ability of White workers to petition collectively stood in sharp contrast with that of free Black workers, who petitioned for privileges that could be awarded only on a case-by-case basis, requesting exemptions from their curfew, a passport, or permission to engage in moneymaking activities.[63]

Beyond the divergence in Black and White petitioners on matters of work, gender marked the overwhelming silence of American workers' memorials before 1840. Early labor agitation and petitioning reflected the divided gender spheres of the United States, and while women often petitioned individually and occasionally in small groups, they did not—before the revolution in women's petitioning that shook the United States in 1837—collectively petition with any regularity on wages or working hours. When New York City needlewomen expressed their grievances about "the inequality of our wages with that of the men's" in 1831, they did it to their employers, and not collectively to the common council or the State Assembly. The restricted sphere of women's petitioning likely gave rise to quicker strike activity than it would have otherwise—which seemed to make little if any dent in prevailing wages—but also may have delayed the construction of more formal organizations.

As the Jackson administration took power in Washington and as city democrats set their sights anew on unjust laws and institutions, the question of debt and in general of imprisonment arose again. In response to numerous petitions of the previous decade, the New York assembly created an investigative committee to examine the state's prison system. An 1828 memorial from an agent of the Prison Discipline Society stated that women's imprisonment amounted to "a blot upon the fair character of the State." An 1831 report to the New York Common Council—occasioned by a petition of Thomas Stokes for the reform of women's penitentiary institutions—expressed the emerging consensus in northeastern American cities: "It cannot be denied that our Prison confinement does not improve the Prisoners"; rather, prisons "do demoralize, rather than improve their inmates." Petitioners in New Jersey and Pennsylvania agreed, their memorials conveying not only the weight of argument but often statistics that appeared nowhere else in public debate. From 1829 to 1831, petitioners across New York began to assail the wisdom and propriety of debt imprisonment, the conditions of women in penitentiary institutions, and the concept of life imprisonment. The state abolished imprisonment for debt in 1831. Petitions flooded state legislatures in Massachusetts, Pennsylvania, and other states calling for the abolition of debt imprisonment. Prison reform became one of the durable legal changes effected in Jacksonian America. Its triumph owed not only to new forms of working-class organization but also to the democratization of the state and municipal petition.[64]

ELECTORAL MOBILIZATION VIA PETITION: COLONIAL POLITICS IN YORK

Anglo-American settlers long coveted Upper Canada, so named by virtue of its position upstream of its largely francophone counterpart Lower Canada on the Saint Lawrence. In their belief that French Catholic culture retarded economic and social progress, and in their comfort with the property systems and legal regimes that resembled the English model, colonial officials regarded the province (created under the Constitution of 1791) as the best of hopes for a territorially massive settlement project. With proximity to the Great Lakes and their abundant natural resources and trading routes, with rich agricultural possibilities in the southern Canadian littoral above Lake Erie and Lake Ontario, Upper Canada became the desired site of settlement for English, Irish, Scottish, and American families who came by the tens of thousands.

The political center of Upper Canada lay squarely in its provincial capital at York. York housed the main colonial institutions under the 1791 Constitution—the province's elective legislative assembly, its appointed legislative council (the upper chamber to the assembly) and executive council, and its lieutenant governor. The governor appointed the councils and courts of general sessions, which functioned as the main instrument of civil administration in the province. Colonial officers converted the patronage available to them into a form of patrimonial rule. These men—Lieutenant Governor John Graves Simcoe, Chief Justice John Beverley Robinson, the Tory French Canadian James Baby, Richard Cartwright, and William Osgoode—had been the earliest Loyalists in the American Revolution, and they moved to York from the province's original capital at Niagara-on-the-Lake. The network of families hewed to the line of the Anglican Church and the elitist vision of Anglican Bishop John Strachan, and they coalesced socially and politically in a unit known (derisively) as the Family Compact.[65]

York was nowhere near as large as the urban agglomerations that had sprouted in the United States or even Montréal, but it was at York that British imperial designs and alternative settlement visions collided. The town's population exploded from one thousand to around nine thousand residents by 1834, when it was renamed Toronto. This expansion—fueled by immigration from England and the United States—cast in ever starker relief the tensions between "pioneer" settlers and newcomers. The British vision emphasized deference to those appointed by the Crown, those whose position as colonial officers gave them political and social advantages from which economic returns followed in abundance. Among newer settlers, an alternative vision of settler republicanism arose. They desired the same rights and privileges, especially landholding, that pioneer families enjoyed. And these reformers wanted more expansive immigration policy, especially from the United States.[66]

As in Lower Canada, the question of whether critics of government could organize as a separate force remained ambiguous. Upper Canadian reformers wished to congeal not as a party but as a loyal opposition. Wary of American invasion and even of French designs on its project, the provincial government had passed the Sedition Act of 1804 (which remained in effect until 1829) and the Seditious Meetings Act (operative from 1818 to 1820). These statutes and other practices cemented the Loyalist understanding that an imperial project could not tolerate dissent, especially in a subject colony. After the jurist Robert Thorpe won election to the assembly and took office in January 1807, he argued for greater responsiveness of the executive council to the assembly. Thorpe used provincial juries as an audience for his reformist theories, openly lecturing the captive audiences in his courtroom. Lieutenant Governor Francis Gore dismissed him from office in 1807. Thorpe's former constituents in the York District petitioned the British Parliament to alert them to the practices of corruption in the colony. As they did so, they knew they risked arrest, one of them fearing that "any man should be sent to prison who signed any petition or address whatsoever."[67]

It was the Scottish immigrant Robert Gourlay who launched the transformation of Upper Canadian politics upon his arrival in 1817. Gourlay settled on land owned by his family in Dereham Township but found his land grant application in York refused soon after his arrival. Familiar with modes of organization among British radicals and having himself published several radical pamphlets before 1810, he then campaigned for the more equitable distribution of land in the province. Arguing that Upper Canada needed settlement for its political as well as economic development, he called for an open immigration policy. He directly excoriated the Family Compact and was twice prosecuted for libel, but was acquitted both times.[68]

Gourlay adopted more radical tactics in 1818. In February of that year, he called for the impeachment of Governor Gore for his refusal to open immigration to Americans. He also openly excoriated the government for its corruption, for running "a system of paltry patronage and ruinous favouritism."[69] And perhaps most notably, Gourlay openly turned to the petition as a fundamental right of every British subject and, beyond that, as a tool of organization. He called on his fellow settlers to address petitions "from every quarter . . . it should appear, if possible to be the unanimous desire of the whole population."[70] In April 1818, after Gore prorogued the provincial assembly, Gourlay called for constitutional reform and a Parliamentary inquiry.[71]

Gourlay set about to coalesce the unprivileged White settlers whose social positions excluded them from land distribution and economic advantages. A meeting in Niagara district in April 1818 set the stage for an organized petitioning campaign and a blanketing of the province with published circulars and tracts. Gourlay began with a moderate grievance: the "system of patronage and favouritism, in the disposal of the Crown lands."[72] Signatures and financial contributions poured in by the hundreds. Gourlay and his associates drew on newspapers to spread their gospel and grievance, and for those areas in Upper Canada where newspaper circulation was feeble, the campaign personally carried circulars and published tracts. Gourlay's next meeting came in York in June 1818, where the burgeoning reform movement held a provincial convention. The convention produced a petition to Lieutenant Governor Sir Peregrine Maitland, who refused it on the grounds that the meeting producing it was unconstitutional.[73]

The Family Compact took square aim at Gourlay and his fledgling organization. In addition to derisive sermons from Strachan and charges of seditious libel in the summer of 1818 (for which he would be acquitted), the reformer was targeted by personal violence. In an echo of the Tumultuous Petitioning Act of 1662 (whose legal status remained ambiguous in Britain), the Upper Canadian assembly passed a law against township meetings, alleging that these gatherings would "encourage riot, tumult, [and] disorder."[74] A Niagara newspaper publisher was jailed for seditious libel and then Gourlay himself was arrested for violating the Sedition Act of 1804. At the head of the coalition targeting Gourlay lay Strachan himself—archdeacon and members of both the legislative and executive councils—who warned that Gourlay's public meetings and petitioning campaigns risked "the horrors of a revolution" and "struck . . . completely at the root of all civil government."[75] Robert Gourlay was banished from the province and was forcibly exiled to London in January 1819.

Far from weakening his coalition, Gourlay's ouster stoked his supporters to new action. Eight candidates allied with his cause won election to the assembly in the 1820 elections, and Gourlay's *Statistical Account of Upper Canada* (1822)—part scholastic endeavor, part pro-settlement publicity compendium—gained him wide fame and sincere admiration among many who traditionally allied with the Family Compact. His exile strengthened momentum for the repeal of the Seditious Meetings Act, which was accomplished in 1820, and Gourlayite reformers quickly set their sights on striking from law the Sedition Act of 1804 itself. And perhaps most influentially, Gourlay had identified a set of enemies against whom opposition could be organized, not merely the Family Compact and civil and ecclesiastical officials but the land distribution and patronage system and, beyond that, the colony's very constitution and institutions of government.[76]

The fissures over settlement policy and favoritism opened anew in 1827 when the provincial government passed the Alien Bill, limiting the rights of those born in the United States. Family Compact allies and established settlers wanted to restrict the political power of newcomers, and the Alien Bill would have stripped American-born settlers (known as "Late Loyalists") of their citizenship. Assembly representative Robert Randal organized a public meeting in February 1827 to protest the Alien Bill, and he was joined there by assembly member Jesse Ketchum of York. Ketchum, an Anglican dissenter and a fierce critic of Strachan, reserved his greatest vitriol for the Clergy Corporation, one of the province's chartered monopolies and the body governing the clergy reserves, which amounted to one-seventh of the public lands that were reserved under the 1791 Constitution for the maintenance of a "Protestant clergy," which early governors read as Anglican alone.[77]

Jesse Ketchum intended the February 1827 gathering at York to inaugurate a petitioning campaign, and the meeting would leave a spacious organizational legacy. Ketchum allied with other reformers to build a remarkably wide-ranging coalition of workers, farmers, mill and forge owners, lawyers, and other professionals against the Alien Bill. Ketchum had made a fortune in the tanning business and continued a career in philanthropy directed toward laborers and the poor. The reform movement included some who had supported Robert Thorpe's electoral and petition campaigns more than a decade earlier, and Ketchum used some of the tactics from that effort, including the appointment of a "Central Committee" (chaired by Ketchum himself), to coordinate the petitioning effort.[78]

It was at the York meeting of February 1827 that William Lyon Mackenzie took an unambiguous leadership role in the anti–Alien Bill initiative. Mackenzie was already well known in York, in part for the vituperative criticism of the Family Compact that he published in his paper, the *Colonial Advocate*. The 1826 destruction of his press by a young mob and the resulting jury award of significant damages only augmented his fame. Mackenzie joined forces with Ketchum at the 1827 York meeting, read the petition aloud before the assembled, and worked to diffuse the prayer throughout the province, where it would be canvassed to obtain a large number of signatures.[79]

Robert Randal carried an anti–Alien Bill petition to London in mid-April 1827 with fourteen thousand names affixed. The sheer number of signatures—the province's total population was about 186,000 at the time—evinced the broad antigovernment energy that the campaign had organized. The written records of the York meeting of February 1827 and those of other Upper Canadian towns highlight the leadership of prominent businessmen, many of whom started their careers in the trades. Yet the vast number of signatures virtually guarantees that thousands of affirmations came from American settlers and those without property-based suffrage. The April 1827 signatory list demonstrated to Upper Canadian readers, to the astonished provincial government, and to the worried colonial office in London that a wide and rapidly expanding alliance outside the Family Compact wanted provincial reform. As government forces mocked the meager education and social status of the petitioners, they unwittingly testified to their economic breadth and character as producer republicans. The provincial administration's fears came true when Robert Randal traveled to London, met with a generous and official reception, and succeeded in persuading the British government to renounce the Alien Bill in 1827. In frantic missives to the Colonial Office, Governor Peregrine Maitland tried to dissuade Crown officials from giving to the petitioners any form of reception, warning that "if a petition . . . is considered and treated as an expression of public feeling, and if in deference to it any reasonable measure of the Government is abandoned, then indeed an importance will be conferred upon the few political agitators who are industrious to sow dissensions."[80] The

British government instructed its appointees at York to draft a new Alien Bill that satisfied the objections raised in the Randal memorial.

The imperial metropole was reading anxieties that had eluded the gaze of the colonial periphery. As with the massive petitions that had come in to protest the Union Bill of 1822 and as would happen in 1827, when French-Canadian *patriotes* would convey a mass petition to the Colonial Office, London's response undercut colonial governors like Dalhousie and Maitland, prompting charges of capitulation. Maitland was in the wrong on matters of policy and justice, yet his prediction of further petitioning and opposition proved rather sage. The threat to York administrators and the Family Compact carried by Upper Canadian petitioning lay precisely in its democratizing energy: its undermining of deference norms and its steadfast antagonism to venality.[81]

Temporarily defeated but undeterred, John Strachan and the Family Compact turned their efforts to other imperial ventures. In response to immigration and the rise of Methodism among Upper Canadians, Strachan launched an aggressive rhetorical assault on non-Anglican faiths and on those "voluntarists" who wished the colonial regime to dissociate itself from matters of official religion. These dissenting voices betrayed the fundamental ethic of "loyalty," Strachan argued. He secured support in a lobbying trip to London in 1826, after which the Imperial Parliament passed the Sales and Improvement Acts (1827) and Strachan secured a charter for a new university—King's College—to be governed by Anglican persons and precepts. Strachan also inflamed non-Anglicans with a statistical map called the "ecclesiastical chart" that greatly overstated Anglicans' numbers and cast other faiths as a small minority of the province. Opponents collaborated to counter these initiatives, and they did so in meetings at Methodist churches that generated fresh petition drives.[82]

At first glance, the new politics of religion concerned matters of church and state. At another level, it was about matters of monopoly, corruption, and immigration all over again. Most of the early Methodist ministers in Upper Canada had come from the United States. To these men and thousands of their followers—the Methodist population had increased from 9,678 to 14,999 between 1828 and 1832—the new religious debate bore a symbolic relationship to the alien question. Reformers also targeted the clergy reserves and the King's College charter. They combined proposals for a more liberal King's College charter with an argument that proceeds from the clergy reserves be used for secular ends. The new petitioning campaign brought Jesse Ketchum to the fore, as he had been elected to the assembly from the York district in the 1828 elections. Amassing about three thousand signatures, the petition did not result in the kind of legislative or administrative success that the anti–Alien Bill campaign had won. A religiously polarized status quo combined with inertia in the Colonial Office to stymie further action on the reformers' demands from 1828 to 1831. Yet what the petitions had not moved in statute and decree they had shifted in organization. The ties among Methodists, American immigrants, newer settlers and investors, and politicians and families outside the Family Compact had begun to congeal into an antiestablishment movement.[83]

William Lyon Mackenzie reemerged in 1831 to transform that movement into a political coalition united by common ideology and knit together by networks formed in massive petitioning campaigns. Mackenzie's coalition transformed Upper Canadian politics. Mackenzie drew on his visible experience as a critic (and target) of the Family Compact, to become both a focal personality for organization and a target for colonial government suppression tactics. Every time that the government assailed his credibility or tossed him from the assembly, his stature and popularity grew, and with them, wider energies for provincial reform.[84]

Mackenzie and Jesse Ketchum found their tool of organizational democracy not in extraparliamentary elections but in massive signed memorials. Both men had been elected to the assembly from the York district in 1828, but both found that petitioning campaigns were more effective than electoral organization. Their allies recalled with satisfaction the campaign against the Alien Bill in 1827. The combination of cogent argumentation and sheer signatory aggregates had given "strong and convincing proofs that the British ministry would willingly redress our grievances if made known to them."[85] Mackenzie and Ketchum detected in the Colonial Office a willingness to avoid colonial tumult and a growing wariness of the rash actions being taken by Canadian provincial elites. A new petitioning campaign amounted to a wager upon the receptivity of the empire's administrative venues.[86]

The program championed by Mackenzie and Ketchum consisted of the basic elements of provincial reformers allied against the Family Compact, plus a number of proposals of voluntarists and Anglican dissenters. Yet it also included proposals for constitutional reform that were informed by the Patriotes' petitioning campaign against Dalhousie in 1827 and 1828. Upper Canada's legislative council had spurned too many bills passed by the assembly, Mackenzie felt, while both the executive and legislative councils were staffed by a narrow and well-connected list of Family Compact supporters who enriched themselves through provincial government. Mackenzie called for a redistribution of power away from the councils and toward the assembly, especially with respect to provincial government expenditures, which, he believed, should require the approval of the lower chamber. Mackenzie published and distributed a list of thirty-one resolutions and introduced it to the assembly. The list proved popular with his York constituents, but when he also began publishing the proceedings of the legislative council in 1831, he was targeted for proposed censure and expulsion from the assembly.[87]

As government forces arrayed themselves against him and diverse reformers flocked to his side, Mackenzie had many organizational options at his discretion. He chose petitioning in part because he was familiar with Gourlay's career and the controversy over Thorpe's dismissal. He had petitioned and organized petitioning campaigns repeatedly in the late 1820s and early 1830s. He joined the campaign against the Alien Bill in 1827, supported Methodist memorials in 1828, added his name to memorials for constitutional reform in 1829, and served in 1831 on the central committee of the Friends of Civil and Religious Liberty, which had petitioned the House of Commons. From publishing the *Colonial Advocate,* he had reported on many a petitioning campaign and was sufficiently conversant with printed prayers for distribution. To this experience with print politics he added his fluency with organizing committees that were structured locally as well as provincially.[88]

Mackenzie drew inspiration, advice, and formal support from the Patriotes in Lower Canada. He consulted extensively with Denis Benjamin Viger of the Lower Canadian assembly, now the London agent of that body, and Viger agreed to support Mackenzie's program. The principal petition Mackenzie began to circulate in 1831 was drafted by none other than John Neilson, who had helped to draft and organize the anti-Dalhousie petition of 1827–1828, and who had helped present the petition (along with Viger) to the Crown in 1828. The Upper Canadian petition of 1831 would include some of the same requests that had characterized the Lower Canadian petition of three years before: assembly control of the civil list and of all provincial government revenues, plus reform of judicial and penal institutions. To these were added some items that reflected the separate issues that buffeted Upper Canada—abolition of the clergy reserves and of the banking monopoly of the Bank of Upper Canada, plus elimination of special privileges for any particular religious group.[89]

Mackenzie published a new manifesto in the summer of 1831, and its central message lay not in substance but in tactics. "*Petition the King:* . . . from every town, township, village and hamlet in the colony; humbly yet firmly recapitulate your grievances, and patiently but perseveringly seek redress."[90] Accordingly, Mackenzie and his allies set out by publishing a prayer with sixteen resolutions communicating suggested reforms (likely written by Neilson), then by arranging first a signature-gathering effort in York. Another twenty town meetings occurred in the summer of 1831. Mackenzie later estimated that between two and three thousand persons attended these meetings, which exhibited neither pomp nor parades nor customary deference to imperial administration.[91]

The combination of meeting and signature, when married to the assertive calls for provincial reform, antagonized the government to the point of suppression. The assembly majority—which had grown in a pro-government direction during the elections of 1830—expelled Mackenzie in December 1831. A week after his expulsion, Mackenzie won election to his open seat, only to be expelled again. Four more times in the ensuing two years would Mackenzie be expelled, each time to be returned to office by his York constituents. The government saw in expulsion a way of undermining Mackenzie's legitimacy, but their tactic backfired by bringing sympathy to Mackenzie, by casting the Family Compact and the provincial government as oligarchic, and by giving yet another grievance to the editor and his followers. Publishing in the *Colonial Advocate* a general address "To the People of Upper Canada" in January 1832, Mackenzie shrewdly connected his expulsion to other narratives of repression in British history, especially that of John Wilkes, expelled from the Commons following his arrest for seditious libel in 1763. In his rhetoric and his symbolic connection to Wilkes, Mackenzie was reinvigorating and harnessing the republican tradition in British political ideology, one that arrayed the country against the court and the people against the administrators of the Crown.[92]

Mackenzie's expulsions led to new memorial campaigns, to new pro-reform demonstrations, and finally to the emergence of alternative electoral organization. In three large meetings in York in December 1831 and January 1832, citizens of York rallied behind and agreed to form a new electoral coalition. These meetings now took on a tone characteristic of the Jacksonian political displays of the same period in the United States, fea-

TABLE 8.1 Signatures on Opposition and Pro-Government Petitioning Campaigns in Upper Canada, 1831–1832

District	Opposition Signatures	Pro-Government Signatures
Home district (York)	10,318	3,273
Gore	2,490	2,340
Midland	2,094	5,562
Niagara	1,809	1,172
Johnstown	2,332	5,147
Eastern	1,454	100
London	260	2,400
Newcastle	211	5,400
Bathurst	1,615	1,178
Total	22,573	26,572

Source: Wilton, *Popular Politics,* appendices B and C.

turing parades of hundreds of reformers through York, with a seated Mackenzie being carried on the shoulders of his supporters through York at one meeting and ferried by a sleigh in another, and banners proclaiming "King William IV and Reform," "Mackenzie and the People," "The Liberty of the Press," and "A Free Press Is the Terror of Sycophants," among others. Government forces—encouraged by Lieutenant Governor Sir John Colborne—quickly targeted these meetings for repression, including beatings, arrests, and the burning of Mackenzie in effigy. Mackenzie himself was nearly beaten to death in Hamilton in 1832.[93]

The combined petitioning of 1831 and the post-expulsion petitioning of 1832 left a weighty mass of signatures attached to the cause of provincial reform. Mackenzie's organizational work led to approximately ten thousand signatures on pro-reform petitions to Parliament in 1831. Another twelve thousand signatures (undoubtedly including some who had signed from 1831) were added in 1832. Even accounting for duplicate signatures, these 22,573 names composed the largest outpouring of opposition voice in the province's history to that date, and they well outnumbered the population voting in provincial elections at the time. Moreover, the center of reform forces lay squarely in the province's urban and political center at York. There the petitioning campaigns amassed over ten thousand signatures on pro-reform petitions—approximately half of the signatures collected—whereas the pro-government canvassing effort produced only 3,273. York was a settler nexus rapidly becoming a frontier city, but its combination of professional networks, artisans turned businessmen, and dissident settler communities nourished a new urban politics of opposition.[94]

Pro-government forces soon mounted their own petitioning campaign, and their tally of signatures was not inconsequential. Rehearsing an older ethic of loyalty, these pro-government memorials claimed that Upper Canada flourished under existing leadership and that the reformers' grievances were in fact ephemeral. Administration loyalists canvassed these documents by creating their own petitioning organization, first the General Constitutional Committee of York, which soon led to the British Constitutional Society. The Sturm und Drang of competing canvasses lay bare the geographic basis of two rival constituencies (see Table 8.1). Whereas opposition forces were best organized in York and Niagara, pro-government forces garnered far more signatures from districts like Midland, Johnstown, and Newcastle—that is, on the north-central and northeastern shores of Lake Ontario, where the more traditional forces of Loyalist populations remained. Pro-government organizers also held public meetings, and as the winter of 1832 gave way to spring, Tory forces dominated public meetings numerically. De-energized and rendered ever warier by government suppression, reformers began to meet less frequently.[95]

In the years after 1832, as Canadian provinces lurched toward colonial crisis, these petitioning campaigns formed the basis for the emergence of rival political unions premised on the British model. After the depressing spring and summer of 1832, reformers used the petitioning movement to build more formal organizations. They began in York in the autumn of 1832 with the Upper Canada Central Political Union. The question of whether opposition could form legitimately continued to dog Mackenzie and reformers, even after his reenergized reform forces—once again rebuilt through a petitioning campaign but now harnessing the language of British political unionists—won a resounding victory and a majority in the assembly in the 1834 elections. Mackenzie and the Upper Canadian Union lay claim both to a more radical agenda and to an expression of pacific intent, disavowing any form of radicalism. The rebellions to come would severely test that posture. Yet in the petitioning movements led by Gourlay, and later by Ketchum and Mackenzie, reformers in Upper Canada had shaped an opposition politics that at least looked like that of Lower Canada, minus the linguistic conflict. They had advanced organizational and cultural democracy, forming the template for a larger, more durable apparatus.[96]

NINE

The Coalescence of Opposition

From the Bank War to Canadian Reform

Few institutions stand as reliably associated with contemporary democracy as the political party. As the organizations linking citizens to politicians under a common label, providing structures for disciplining politicians across space and levels of government, all the while generating vast resources deployable in electoral campaigns, parties powerfully map voters' and politicians' often inchoate wishes into concrete agendas and shepherd legal and administrative proposals into platforms—and, often enough, into statute itself. In American national memory, too, the identification of democracy with party formation runs deep. Americans' everyday association of the Jacksonian era with American democracy stems not only from the title of Jackson's new organization, "the Democracy," but also from the truly broad mobilization of interests that the Jacksonian Democrats achieved. Whether or not citizens belong to any party, their political and civic lives are ineluctably shaped by parties. While models of nonpartisan democracy exist—ranging from Athens to the plebiscite—no mature democratic regime operates without some constellation of political parties.[1]

Without competition, however, political parties bring not democracy but authoritarian rule. Scholars and observers alike identify in party competition a bellwether indicator of democracy's health. Yet the emergence of electoral mass parties does not translate immediately or mechanically into a world of stable rivalry. The system of two dominant parties that has characterized the United States since the late 1830s was by no means either natural or foreordained. After the Democrats' victory in 1828, it took a rough decade for their opponents (eventually organized as the American Whig Party that launched in 1834) to assemble anything like the vast apparatus—replete with local and national networks and patronage funding—that the party of Jackson and Van Buren had built. Nor did the multiparty world of Canadian politics follow directly from battles over colonial policy. Broad suffrage in Canada developed at first with political networks tightly harnessed to the British colonial enterprise. Dominant political factions in Upper Canadian politics benefited from direct and open assistance from imperial administration and its preferred settlers. Those who imagined themselves as the opposition faced immense tactical and coalitional challenges.

The emergence of opposition requires, in some sense, the legitimated organization of grievance. In the Anglo-American world of North American parliamentary government, the question of an opposition's legitimate existence remained unsettled in the eighteenth and early nineteenth centuries. Traditional petitioning systems had allowed for claimants to express their grievance without forming an opposition that could contest elections and present an alternative platform for governance to the legislature. A more democratic petitioning, with its mass emergence in concatenating vectors of signatures, ran alongside new political repertoires to facilitate the development of opposition parties that could reliably and broadly contest the dominant electoral and governing forces of the early nineteenth century. In what is known as the American Bank War of the 1830s, an anti-Jacksonian petitioning coalition—never reducible to the rotting National Republican corpse that decomposed as memorials surged into Congress—emerged four to six months before the formal organization of Whig Party meetings, and the contours of that petitioning coalition would characterize Whig organization for two decades to follow. Whereas in Lower Canada the Patriotes fashioned a colonial opposition through mass petitioning, in Upper Canada, the Durhamites built an organized opposition within the confines of a linguistically more unified province.[2]

Party rivalry does not necessarily engender egalitarian parties. To say that the rise of the American Whig Party rendered the United States more democratic is not to assert that the Whigs were somehow more egalitarian than the Democrats (they were not). The Whigs themselves would be undone by their inability to incorporate antislavery forces—forces impelled by democratized petitioning and new associational forms—that best coalesced in a series of third parties that crystallized in the new Republican Party in 1854. Nor does the centrality of party competition to democratization imply that opposition coalitions in Canada provided anything like a true egalitarian politics. The democratizing nature of party competition does, however, imply that a regime with genuine two-party competition provided for greater institutional and procedural democracy than did the preceding world of one dominant electoral and administrative apparatus. The Whigs (sometimes furtively) brought issues to the table—including the question of capacious executive action and the tangle of ministerial and political corruption under Democratic rule—that would not have otherwise received such a hearing. Whig stances on issues of Indian removal were more progressive than their hesitancy on slavery, and important protections for Indigenous rights (especially among the Seneca in New York) came from their governance. So, too, did Durhamite opposition in Canada raise a number of political and constitutional questions that the Tories had ignored (or had wished to), such as the question of Anglican clergy reserves, the banking system and its monopolies, and the land department. Just as important, the rise of Whigs and Durhamites brought about changes in Democratic and Tory party politics, especially in those states and jurisdictions (like New York State and the York district) where tense electoral competition ensued.[3]

Two troubling challenges dogged those who wished to build new parties: the legitimacy and feasibility of opposition. Whether in a time of new national instability and imperial threat (1796–1816), at a time when a hulking new political force (Jacksonian Democracy) was claiming the mantle of "the People" and its will, at a time when activists challenged the partisan and constitutional compromises over slavery in the 1830s, or throughout British Canada when the threat of sedition was ever invoked (especially after the Patriote Rebellion), those who arrayed themselves against the assumptions and organizations of the established regime risked body and life, property, and status. The question of legitimate opposition expressed an older quandary, the republican antireality that the popular will was not unified. It also spoke to what was lawful in a republic, whether democratic or colonial, and to what those popular wishes really were. When politicians and citizens alike referred to "public opinion," as they did ever more in the antebellum period, they both restated the nonidentity of government and people, and admitted that elections never uttered the last word on the meaning of popular will.[4]

For Americans, the legitimacy of opposition had been partially settled by the Jeffersonian revolution and, later, by the demise of the Federalists in the wake of the War of 1812. Still, from the ashes of Jackson's broad electoral college victories in 1828 and 1832 and the Democrats' new cross-class coalition of voters and workers came a different question: Could any formation other than Jacksonian Democracy lay claim to the will of the people and the equalizing spirit of the age? And could any alternative vessel bring its adherents to the ballot box with the steadiness and breadth of the Democrats? Whig leaders would declare their own membership "the *true* Democrats, if there be any such in the land," yet Clay and others knew that an effective response required eliciting state-by-state engagement, the ability to conduct a campaign.[5]

In colonial Canada, the terms of legitimacy were somewhat different, though not so different as to impede useful comparison. The question confronting opponents of the government, especially in Upper Canada but also in Lower Canada, was whether opposition could be organized constitutionally. The Patriotes had answered this question with their tens of thousands of signatures—judged sufficiently legitimate by the House of Commons and the Crown as to justify Dalhousie's removal—and the creation of a party in the assembly. In Upper Canada the stakes would be less clear, the terrain more fluid.

Popular petitioning figured centrally in the origins of competitive party politics in the United States and later Canada. In ways both intended and never fully conceptualized, petition campaigns served as organizing devices. They identified and brought into popular politics a set of people whose views on issues had seemed to matter less, having been left aside by electoral recruitment. Petitions also formed the basis of association-building and the politics of counting voices, whether in anti-Jackson (and later Whig) assemblies or in the sixteen Durham meetings that sprouted in Upper Canada in 1839. And in ways that the shrewdest of political minds—Henry Clay, William Lyon Mackenzie, and William Lloyd Garrison—understood at the time, memorial campaigns also served to support claims of legitimacy, either the constitutional legitimacy desired by Canadian reformers or the statistical legitimacy desired by opponents of Jackson and, in a different vein, by antislavery reformers. Petitioning gave to Clay and his opposition forces a means of arguing that the people were not with Jackson, at least not all of them for all time. Petitions gave to Upper Canadian reformers a more plausibly constitutional method of opposition, one that was being tried in Britain and that they saw in the United States as well. Finally, petitions and battles over them also refocused citizens' and elites' attention on representative venues. At a time when Jackson and his administration were redefining the power of the American national executive, popular petitions refocused attention on Congress. At a time when, in the wake of the Rebellion, developments of the 1840s left little doubt that Parliament had backed out of Canadian politics for a time, campaigning petitioners learned to approach not London but Ottawa.

BANK POLITICS AND THE EMERGENCE OF OPPOSITION

The American Bank War of the 1830s was both a moment of crisis for an industrializing economy and a moment of reconfiguration in national and state politics. The emergence of the Democrats as a mass party apparatus, united under Andrew Jackson but clearly capable of carrying their force beyond the general, meant that until the late 1830s, one party was hegemonic in American politics. The Democrats in 1828 marshaled an unprecedented network of newspapers spanning the nation's sections, enjoyed an associated group of brilliant publicists—Duff Green, Amos Kendall, and Isaac Hill chief among them—and, more than any party before, deployed a cadre of campaign workers embedded in state committees. It was the most expensive presidential campaign, by far, in American history to that date, and it foreshadowed a new era of politics to come. Once Jackson was elected, Duff Green's strategy of tethering party operatives to federal positions by dismissing postal workers and replacing them with Democrats, thus harnessing the simultaneous expansion of the American electorate and the postal system, gave the Democrats a source of campaign funds and loyal workers that no existing party could match. These organizational advantages, all united under Jackson's democratic and nationalist symbolism, rendered previous forms of opposition futile. The Democrats were particularly effective in organizing in the one true prize of nineteenth-century national electoral politics: New York. In the absence of city political organizations in New York and Albany, the Democrats would not have enjoyed the dominance they displayed until the 1840 national elections.[6]

The Bank of the United States was one of the preeminent administrative institutions of the early American nation, and probably the most controversial by a wide scale. The brainchild of Alexander Hamilton, the bank was created in 1791 and then suffered its first demise in 1811 after a rechartering bill failed in Congress. In part because of the disruptions to state banking incurred during the War of 1812, national legislators reasoned that the bank served a previously underappreciated regulatory function. President James

Madison premised his advocacy for a second bank on the need for uniform national currency, the need to efficiently finance national government operations, and the specter of "embarrassments" in the international arena in the absence of a unified monetary system. In the pivotal Fourteenth Congress (1815–1817), led by Speaker Henry Clay and with one John C. Calhoun chairing the House Committee on the National Currency, legislators voted to reauthorize the institution in 1816. By the 1830s, as state banks continued to proliferate, the regulatory role of the Bank of the United States gained in importance.[7] The institution, headquartered in Philadelphia, also continued to serve as a depository home for vast wealth held both domestically and abroad. Its organizational development in the 1820s was marked by relative stability, not least because of the *McCulloch v. Maryland* (1819) decision legitimating the institution and because the disruptions of the early Madisonian period were behind it.

Andrew Jackson's plan to remove the deposits had both constitutional and partisan logics. Jackson invoked Jeffersonian principles in rejecting the bank's constitutionality, and in his famous bank veto message of 1832, he invoked his authority as president to weigh in on the issue separately from, and coequally with, the Supreme Court. Politically, the deposits removed from the national bank branches would, according to Jackson's plan, be placed in state banks that were known to be loyal to the Jacksonian cause. Principles of small-*f* federalism thus dovetailed with electoral considerations to give Jackson rationale and incentive to remove the deposits. Treasury Secretary Roger Taney, exploiting the fact that the bank held the revenues of the U.S. Treasury upon deposit, played a key role in the removal of the deposits, outlining the Jackson administration's logic in a government circular and using his power as treasury secretary to effectuate removal of assets from the bank.

Bank president Nicholas Biddle had other ideas, and he was not about to let his institution disappear without fierce combat. He began systematically curtailing new loans and calling in old ones, and a minor panic set in. Biddle's plan massively backfired, generating resentment in the business community and all but proving President Jackson's point that the powers of finance were not to be entrusted to a single incorporated institution. By early 1835, Biddle had made a quiet and stunning volte-face, recapitalizing the bank to its pre-1832 levels. With the American economy in full swing in 1835 and 1836, the bank expired quietly. Yet the forces given life by the bank-related petitioning campaign of 1832–34 would live on.[8]

The petitioning campaign coincided with a new solidity among Jackson's opponents in Congress in 1833. National Republicans, Nullifiers, and southern states' rights supporters all opposed Jackson's move against the bank, even if for a disparate set of reasons. Henry Clay took the lead in orchestrating a response. He sought passage of two motions of censure, one rejecting Secretary Taney's report outlining the logic for removal of the deposits, the other rebuking Jackson for executive usurpation.[9]

Even one year earlier, this level of cohesion would have been hard to foresee. In 1832, Clay expressed a mix of pessimism and concern about the lack of organized opposition to the "tyrant of the White House." The advancement of the Jacksonian agenda, culminating in the first bank rechartering veto of July 10, 1832, left a wide range of politicians dismayed. Many of these turned to Clay for advice and support. Erastus Montague of Waltham, Virginia, told Clay that the "wealth and prosperity of our people" and nothing less than the "very existence of republican institutions" rested on Clay's shoulders. Clay had tried to organize an anti-Jacksonian opposition to help support the recharter bill and to prepare for the upcoming general election. Yet as he took a survey of the country, he noted the profound challenges facing opposition forces. Clay understood that the National Republicans were simply too weak on their own to combat the administration in New York, and he hoped for "the progress of measures to produce cooperation between the anti-Masons and the National Republicans" in the state. If such a coalition could be forged, "the Jackson party could be defeated in New York, there is only wanting a perfect persuasion of that result, throughout the Union, to insure a signal overthrow of Jackson at the approaching election." Nor was the need of alliance confined to the particular politics of New York. Clay and his allies were actively trying to facilitate cooperation between anti-Masons, Clay loyalists, and Calhoun loyalists in Kentucky and Ohio.[10]

The 1832 election demonstrated the futility of these attempts. As the adverse election results rolled in from state after state in November 1832, Clay displayed a mix of despondency and resignation. With palpable distress, he confided to friends and allies that American liberty, indeed the very foundations of the young republic, were at risk.[11] Yet as the sorry weeks of November and December 1832 unfolded, Clay and his allies took political lessons from the election results. One of the most painful but obvious of these lessons concerned the weakness of the National Republican position, both its own organization and its alliances with the anti-Masons. In state after state—New York, Pennsylvania, Ohio—National Republican hopes based on alliances with anti-Masons were dashed as anti-Masonic voters went to Jackson. Anti-Masons could not be trusted to deliver votes.[12] As Charles Shaler of Pittsburgh wrote to Clay, the 1832 election was a defeat for the entire National Republican Party, and "its coalition with Anti-Masonry was its death warrant."[13] A new political coalition was needed, and Clay earnestly sought the bases on which to build one.

The National Republican defeat of 1832 left but a congeries of anti-Jackson forces in the early 1830s, and individually and collectively, they faced the challenges of building new organizations and new alliances. Petitioning on the bank deposits gathered steam for many reasons, but key among these was that its practice facilitated the identification and recruitment of a new coalition. Earlier modes of National Republican politics weakly engaged non-elite publics. Coalition building was all the more important to anti-Jackson forces than to Jacksonian Democrats for three reasons. First, older lines of cleavage and organization were not reliable in the wake of the defeat of 1832. The National Republican coalition was falling apart, and in forging campaigns at the state level, anti-Jackson leaders often found it necessary to assemble coalitions with states' rights parties and anti-Masonic movements. After November 1832, however, Clay and his allies knew that states' rights and anti-Masonry alliances were stopgap measures insufficient to defeat Jackson's organization. Alliances based on new principles and on opposition to the administration would be needed. Second, and relatedly, the anti-Jacksonian opposition was weakly organized at the state level save for southern states like Virginia, where many states' rights enthusiasts organized against what they perceived as the administration's aggressive executive imperative, and South Carolina, where nullification energies were surfacing. Third and perhaps most important, the anti-Jacksonians lacked the partisan organization—and the opportunities to build such an organization at least partially through policy and patronage—that had been enjoyed and exploited by the Jackson administration for four years.[14]

In short, the emergence of an anti-Jackson party would require the development of a new kind of party organization, one that responded to but did not mirror patterns of Democratic mobilization. In the new world of American politics after the expansion of suffrage, such a party had to engage in the countability of voice, identifying salient "units" of public sentiment and locating and enumerating them. Those who led the bank petitioning campaigns in the early 1830s also swam in broader currents of publicity and organized public sentiment. Beyond mass petitioning itself, the transformation of the press into a more polarized partisan tool meant print-based technologies of politics were increasingly serving partisan ends. The competing journals of legislative affairs—the Jacksonian *Congressional Globe,* which began in December 1833, and the anti-Jacksonian *Register of Debates*—which began in 1825 but would die out in 1837—exemplified the partisan production and refraction of political news. Many speeches and reports from the administration were, simultaneously or afterward, published and distributed as pamphlets. Hence, bank war petitioning emerged in the midst of a print-based publicity war over the deposit removal issue and over the terms and stakes of the Jackson administration more generally.[15]

Composed of hundreds of memorials for and against the removal of bank deposits, bank petitioning in 1833 and 1834 bore similarities to and distinctions from other forms of petitioning in the antebellum United States. The issuance of petitions from meetings of interested citizens—whether those opposed to or in support of deposit removal—distinguished bank petitioning from the mass circulation and canvassing that characterized the temperance, anti-Cherokee-removal, or antislavery movements. Moreover, when the meetings called by Jacksonians or partisans of Clay and the bank came together, they assembled not under the auspices of an existing moral reform society or an antislavery organization but on an issue that united newer and more issue-specific interests and passions and that was part of a concerted effort to influence the votes cast by members of Congress.

Indeed, while Clay and his allies controlled the Senate—holding roughly an eight-person advantage over the Jacksonians—they found themselves outnumbered substantially in the House. The shortfall in votes in the House prevented passage of the proposed censures as well as any attempt to address removal of the deposits. Clay conceived an idea to pressure undecided House members and Jackson himself. He would encourage supporters to petition Congress, outlining their distress at the removal of the deposits. A forceful show of public opinion might break the gridlock preventing a meaningful response to Jackson's removal.[16]

Clay had an early hand in the organization of public meetings and the submission of resolutions and memorials. In a December 1833 letter to bank president Nicholas Biddle, Clay hinted that "it would be well to have a general meeting of the people to memorialize Congress in favor of a restoration of the deposites. Such an example might be followed elsewhere; and it would be more influential as it might be more general."[17] Biddle responded affirmatively to Clay's request and immediately set to work organizing meetings in Philadelphia. Several weeks later, in a letter to his son, Clay remarked that "popular meetings are taking place everywhere, and our success in [the House] will depend upon the extent of the re-action among the people. Do you intend at Lexington to have a meeting? It might do good."[18] Clay also engaged in an ongoing correspondence with Littleton W. Tazewell in Virginia. Critical to Clay's strategy was the fact that Tazewell was not a National Republican but represented the emergent states' rights faction in the Virginia legislature (he would be elected governor by that faction and begin service in March 1834).[19]

The timing of these appeals to friends and allies coincided with a subtle but powerful change in rhetorical strategy, one that emphasized directing attention away from the bank issue and toward the "usurpations" and purportedly tyrannical behavior of Jackson himself. Five days after writing to Biddle, Clay took to the Senate floor and delivered a celebrated address. The address spanned two days (December 26 and December 30), between which the Senate adjourned. Southard would rise and give a similar address focused more directly on the bank deposits issue on January 8, 1834, but Clay's address was a clear shift in tone and subject.[20]

While some other Jackson opponents and partisans of the bank focused on financial questions, Clay began in December 1833 to connect a number of issues—the conduct of Indian wars, rotation in office, the behavior of Taney, and, more generally, the purported lawlessness and constitutional disrespect demonstrated by President Jackson. "We are in the midst of a revolution," he began, "hitherto bloodless, but rapidly tending towards a total change of the republican character of the Government, and to the concentration of power in the hands of one man."[21] Consistently deploying the old republican term "civil liberty" and vaunting a Montesquieuvian vision of separated and shared powers, Clay argued that nothing less than the achievement of the Revolution of 1776–77 and the founding was at stake. He interpreted Treasury Secretary Roger Taney's initiative to remove deposits as a larger pattern of executive liquidation of contracts, tantamount to the creation of an executive-centered partisan state: "Let this doctrine be once established, and there is an end to all regulated government, to all civil liberty. It will become a machine, simple enough. There will be but one will in the State; but one bed, and that will be the bed of Procrustes! Sir, such an enormous and extravagant pretension cannot be sanctioned."[22] In Clay's accounting, there was scarcely an aspect or actor in the American polity that was not victim to Jacksonian aggression. The aggrieved included not merely those who suffered directly from the president's decisions but also the judiciary (with its power reduced and its legitimacy disregarded), Congress (whose authorities were, Clay claimed, violated by Taney's initiative in removing the bank deposits), the press (Clay made allusion to the Sedition Act of 1798), and American voters who would be subject, he claimed, to Jackson's wish to regulate the franchise from the federal level.

Concluding his remarks on Thursday the 26th of December, Clay poetically cast the issue as one of law and fidelity to the country's essential institutions. Bemoaning the "bleeding constitution of my country," he voiced his hope for popular rejection of a presidency gone mad:

> If a bountiful Providence would allow an unworthy sinner to approach the throne of grace, I would beseech Him, as the greatest favor He could grant to me here below, to spare me until I live to behold the people rising in their majesty, with a peaceful and constitutional exercise of their power, to expel the Goths from Rome; to rescue the public treasury from pillage; to preserve the Constitution of the United States; to uphold the Union against the danger of the concentration and consolidation of all power in the hands of the Executive; and to sustain the liberties of the people of this country against the imminent perils to which they now stand exposed.[23]

In the early months of 1834, Clay came to see public outcry expressed through petitions as an increasingly important lever for swaying members of Congress sympathetic to Jackson. After the state legislatures in New Jersey and Ohio passed resolutions instructing their representatives to oppose restoration of the deposits, Clay remarked that "unless the popular demonstration should be very powerful and general the Administration will maintain its majority in the House."[24] While Clay and his allies clearly encouraged and orchestrated the early public meetings, the wave of petitioning also quickly gained a momentum of its own, giving an outlet to citizen concerns about the crisis.

The volume of meetings and petitions submitted to Congress quickly expanded beyond Clay's immediate network of contacts. In fact, the leaders of public meetings—often a committee whose members' names were published—had few formal links to state or national politics. Rather, most meeting organizers appear to have been local notables, leaders of guilds or unions, and occasionally even military officers.[25]

Memorialists sent in a variety of different resolutions, though most shared some version of the common themes of decrying executive tyranny and deploring the "pecuniary embarrassment" following removal of the deposits. A sample petition from Philadelphia appears in Figure 9.1 (which displays the petition's prayer and part of its signatory list). The prayer calls attention both to the "distress . . . everywhere prevailing" (caused by the threat of deposit removal) and to a set of themes anchored in republican political discourse. Most of the petition's prayer is devoted not to currency and financial issues but to the actions of the Jackson administration. "There is no warrant in the Constitution and Laws for the act of the Executive," the memorialists complain, and they pray that Congress remove the deposits from "the arbitrary and uncontrollable disposition" of Taney.[26] The signatories described themselves as laborers—painters and glazers, hardware merchants, piano makers, bricklayers, smiths. Clay would seize on this point to note that the petitions were coming from a wide range of social interests and that it was not merely the deposits issue but the inflammatory actions of "Jackson men" that were sowing such broad discontent.

Petitions of this sort both reflected and attracted the action of a broad range of antebellum elites. Key allies such as Virginia's Tazewell joined in the action. As the *Spectator* of Norfolk reported in January 1834, Tazewell's leadership at a Norfolk meeting was centered on the issue of executive usurpation: "Mr. Tazewell's gigantic mind was elicited on this important occasion—the flood of light which he shed upon all the topics connected with it, and the strong illustration which his facts and his arguments afforded of a dangerous assumption of power by the Executive—carried conviction to every mind present."[27] Some petitions went further and expressed a lack of confidence in the state banks (now holding the deposits removed from the Bank of the United States), defended borrowing practices, warned against the risks of a metallic currency, thanked members of Congress for their actions against removal of the deposits, or even asked for a recharter of the Bank of the United States. Resolutions asking for a recharter provide additional evidence that the petitioning campaign expanded beyond the hands of members of Congress.[28] Communicating with allies and taking stock of the situation in Congress and state electorates, Clay came to realize early on that a recharter would be impracticable and a strategic misstep. In early February, he wrote to Biddle that "the Bank ought to be kept in the rear; the usurpation in front. If we take up the Bank, we play into

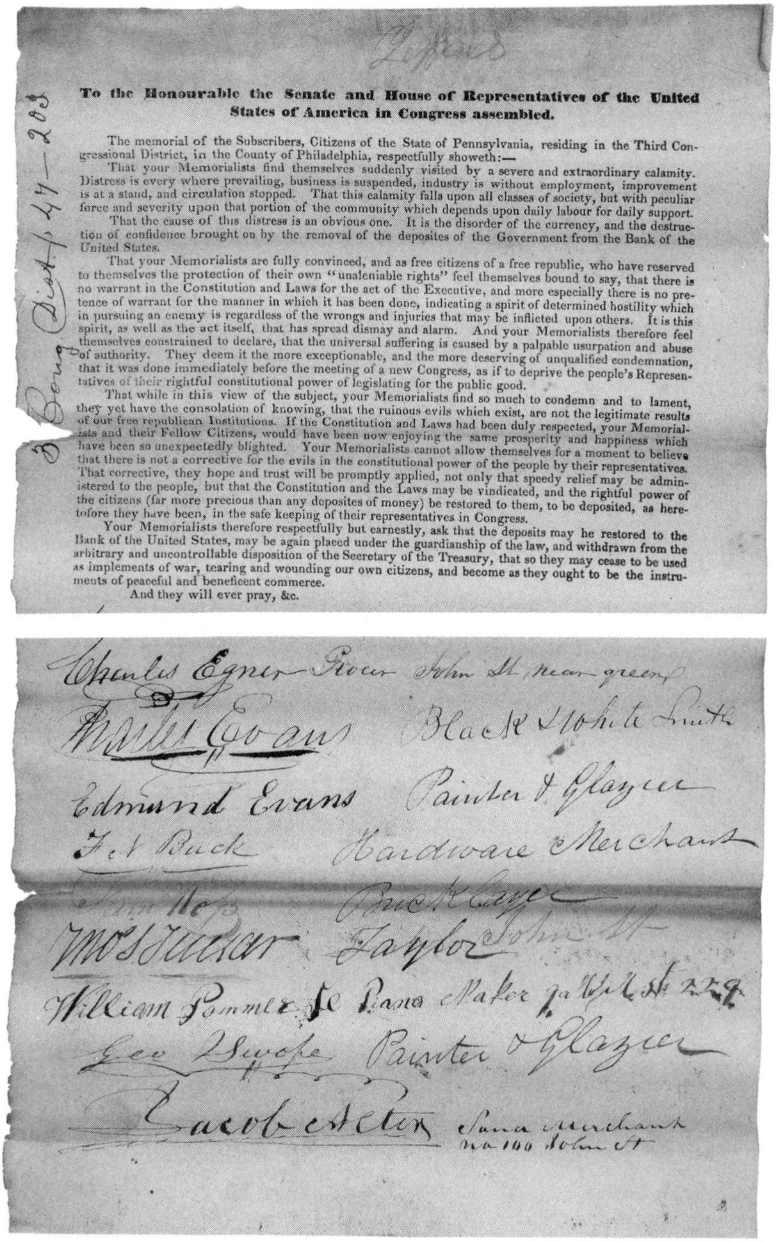

To the Honourable the Senate and House of Representatives of the United States of America in Congress assembled.

The memorial of the Subscribers, Citizens of the State of Pennsylvania, residing in the Third Congressional District, in the County of Philadelphia, respectfully showeth:—

That your Memorialists find themselves suddenly visited by a severe and extraordinary calamity. Distress is every where prevailing, business is suspended, industry is without employment, improvement is at a stand, and circulation stopped. That this calamity falls upon all classes of society, but with peculiar force and severity upon that portion of the community which depends upon daily labour for daily support.

That the cause of this distress is an obvious one. It is the disorder of the currency, and the destruction of confidence brought on by the removal of the deposites of the Government from the Bank of the United States.

That your Memorialists are fully convinced, and as free citizens of a free republic, who have reserved to themselves the protection of their own "unaleniable rights" feel themselves bound to say, that there is no warrant in the Constitution and Laws for the act of the Executive, and more especially there is no pretence of warrant for the manner in which it has been done, indicating a spirit of determined hostility which in pursuing an enemy is regardless of the wrongs and injuries that may be inflicted upon others. It is this spirit, as well as the act itself, that has spread dismay and alarm. And your Memorialists therefore feel themselves constrained to declare, that the universal suffering is caused by a palpable usurpation and abuse of authority. They deem it the more exceptionable, and the more deserving of unqualified condemnation, that it was done immediately before the meeting of a new Congress, as if to deprive the people's Representatives of their rightful constitutional power of legislating for the public good.

That while in this view of the subject, your Memorialists find so much to condemn and to lament, they yet have the consolation of knowing, that the ruinous evils which exist, are not the legitimate results of our free republican Institutions. If the Constitution and Laws had been duly respected, your Memorialists and their Fellow Citizens, would have been now enjoying the same prosperity and happiness which have been so unexpectedly blighted. Your Memorialists cannot allow themselves for a moment to believe that there is not a corrective for the evils in the constitutional power of the people by their representatives. That corrective, they hope and trust will be promptly applied, not only that speedy relief may be administered to the people, but that the Constitution and the Laws may be vindicated, and the rightful power of the citizens (far more precious than any deposites of money) be restored to them, to be deposited, as heretofore they have been, in the safe keeping of their representatives in Congress.

Your Memorialists therefore respectfully but earnestly, ask that the deposits may be restored to the Bank of the United States, may be again placed under the guardianship of the law, and withdrawn from the arbitrary and uncontrollable disposition of the Secretary of the Treasury, that so they may cease to be used as implements of war, tearing and wounding our own citizens, and become as they ought to be the instruments of peaceful and beneficent commerce.

And they will ever pray, &c.

FIGURE 9.1A, B. Prayer and Sample from Signatory List of Anti-deposit-removal Petition, 1833. *Credit:* Record Group 233, National Archives and Records Administration.

the adversarys [*sic*] hands. . . . We may and probably would divide about the terms of the charter, and finally do nothing leaving things as they are."[29]

Although comforted and energized by the wave of petitions, Clay began to express doubts over the prospect of success for the petitioning campaign in Congress by the end of March 1834. In a letter to his son, he noted that while no direct vote in either the House or the Senate had occurred, it was "well understood that a majority in the H. of R. still exists in favor of the measure of the Executive." Furthermore, he began mentioning upcoming elections in Kentucky, New York, and Virginia as alternative demonstrations of public opinion that might influence members of Congress. That is, it appeared to Clay that the petitions had not done enough, at least in the House. On March 27, Clay gave a closing speech on the removal of the deposits and his resolutions for censure. His measure for censure against Jackson passed in the Senate by a vote of 26–20. But with no movement in the House, he confided to Tazewell that there was "no prospect of Congress regaining its lawful custody of the Treasury, unless the President shall voluntarily loosen his grasp of it." Even as Clay had expressed reservations, petitions continued to stream into Congress through April, May, and June. Considering that prospects for restoration of the deposits had likely dimmed at this point, the fact that petitions continued to come in suggests a degree of mobilization that went beyond anti-Jacksonian congressional leaders.[30]

Yet throughout the spring of 1834, Clay and his allies began to detect that the petitioning campaign was helpful in shaping and measuring public opinion even as the House was a lost cause. At the dawn of a new year, New York ally Peter B. Porter wrote to Clay that the state of public opinion looked hopeless: "The people of this country appear to be perfectly spellbound. Lulling at their ease, in wealth and luxury, they seem to be entirely unconscious of the causes of their prosperity, and insensible to the dangers which threaten it; and if they are not awakened to a sense of their true situation by the bold and prophetic expostulations of yourself and copatriots, nothing short of the actual adversity which must soon follow (and which, if not the best, is always the most infallible instructor) can teach them practical wisdom."[31] Yet just six weeks later, Porter wrote of his sense that the tide was turning against Jackson, and that the debate had exposed weaknesses in the administration.[32] Clay himself began to focus less on restoration of deposits and more on the immediate aim of shaping the "will" of the public, an entity that could be shaped, expressed, produced, displayed, and even enumerated. As he wrote to his ally James Brown of Philadelphia, restoration of the bank's deposits "depends upon the People, and demonstrations of their will. They can produce it." And to Littleton Tazewell, now on his way to taking office as governor of Virginia, Clay would write, "We are gaining ground, and I am not without hopes of final success in the H. of R. It will depend on the amount of public opinion brought to act upon it. And in that respect the movements in Virginia have been of inestimable service."[33]

While expressing mixed opinions of his prospects for restoration in the House, Clay expressed his growing sense that the petitioning momentum was expanding, that anti-Jackson energies were appearing in several states, and that support for the petitioning campaign extended well beyond the anti-Jackson vote of 1832. In March, April, and May, Clay took repeatedly to the Senate floor to draw attention to the size of the individual petitions, the diversity of towns and states that were producing them, and the breadth of support.[34] Even "Jackson men" and committed "Administration men" were petitioning and remonstrating Congress against deposit removal, and many of the petitions mentioned the theme of executive usurpation.[35] In late March and early April, Clay's focus turned more numerical, even statistical. After being alerted to an Erie county petition with between four thousand and five thousand signatures, Clay formally proposed that the Senate collect and summarize all the petitions that had been received on the deposits issue.[36] In April and again in June, he took the Senate floor to draw attention to the Senate's tally (150,000) of signers of petitions and memorials critical of Jackson's fiscal policies and praying Congress for economic relief. He even chided the opposition for not seeing this as "one of the best tests of public opinion, next to the evidence which the ballot-boxes afford."[37]

The character of the petitioning campaign suggests that two complementary conditions contributed to its wide reach. First, its origins came from above (from members of Congress), which resulted in some distinct organizational advantages. While no party infrastructure existed to aid in collecting signatures, existing networks between members of Congress in Washington and local elites (especially state legislators and other elites) made a coordinated response possible. Furthermore, memorialists situated themselves within a broader anti-Jackson coalition and would at times even refer in their own petitions to text produced in neighboring towns or counties. Second, there was sufficient public opinion against Jackson and his move against the bank to facilitate a petitioning campaign. The campaign could not have occurred if Jackson had held strong, relatively homogeneous support among citizens.[38]

THE CONTOURS OF ANTI-JACKSON MEMORIALS

Closely watched by Clay and tethered to the rhythms of the House, the anti-Jackson petitioning campaign essentially ran from December 1833 to June 1834. The petitioning for restoration of the deposits followed a heterogeneous geographical pattern that neither Clay nor anyone else could entirely predict, much less control (see Figure 9.2). Clay directed his clerks to record the totals arriving in the House and Senate, and at least 715 petitions on the issue of bank restoration arrived. There was at least one petition from a total of twenty-three states or territories, ranging from a single petition from Illinois to fully 244 from Pennsylvania. Among states whose residents submitted more than thirty petitions, Clay's home state of Kentucky had the greatest share favoring restoration of the deposits. Meanwhile, New York, which recognized its financial rivalry with Philadelphia and which stood to benefit greatly from the removal of the deposits, had the lowest share (at 55 percent) of petitions expressing a desire for restoration.[39]

The majority of petitions submitted to Congress favored the restoration of the deposits. In all, 70 percent of the 715 petitions supported restoration. To be sure, invited as these petitions were by Clay and his allies, the petition aggregates cannot be interpreted as an unbiased measure of exogenous public sentiment on the matter. For one, citizens immediately outraged by the removal of the deposits appear to have been more likely to notify Congress of their displeasure than were their counterparts who approved of Jackson's action against the bank. Figure 9.3, which displays the geographic distribution of petitions over the course of the crisis, bears this story out. In the first several months after removal of the deposits, the counties that had sent petitions to Congress primarily urged restoration of the deposits. At one level, the uncertainty over bank chapters' future reverberated in local economies. Not surprisingly, Philadelphia County (home of the bank's main branch) submitted three times more petitions than the next most prolific county, in part because the bank's allies and staff lay behind that local petitioning campaign and in part because the Philadelphia economy was being battered by the deposit removal campaign. Only by March 1834 did House clerks begin to observe appreciable numbers—

in some cases responding to earlier memorials from the same county—supporting Jackson in his quarrel with the bank.[40]

Among the heterogeneous set of petitions calling for deposit restoration or excoriating Jackson and Taney, higher rates of petitioning reflected a set of local conditions favorable to future Whig party organization, despite the fact that no developed party organizations existed at the time of the crisis over the bank. Chief among the instruments of recruitment were anti-Jackson meetings at which the memorials were discussed, distributed, signed, and prepared for transmission to Congress. Anti-Jackson meetings demonstrated the relative strength of the links between national party leaders such as Clay and operatives at home, who could be called on to organize citizens. Clay and key organizers of the meetings corresponded, but local leaders of anti-removal meetings often traveled to Washington and hand-delivered their petitions. In other cases, local anti-Jackson meetings were followed by attempts to organize for local elections and to develop the beginnings of a state party infrastructure. The resolutions from one meeting in Ohio explicitly stated that they would be appointing delegates to travel to an upcoming convention where a candidate would be chosen to run in the upcoming race for governor.[41]

The anti-Jackson petitioning campaign left templates, networks, and resources for later Whig party organization at the state and local levels. The meetings provided an outlet through which to develop additional organizational expertise. Invariably, newspaper accounts of such meetings described the appointment of a committee or board to lead the event. The *Alexandria Gazette* recounted a January meeting in that city that "on motion of R. H. Henderson, Esq. Col. William Ellsey was called to the chair and F. Hixon, Esq. appointed Secretary. Cuthbert Powell, Esq. addressed the Meeting, going into a general examination of the subject; and moved that a committee . . . be appointed to report resolutions."[42] These committees drafted points of order, resolutions, and were also responsible for the submission of the agreed-upon memorial to Congress. Some committees traveled to Washington, where they would deliver a petition directly to a representative and attempt to meet in person with those sympathetic to their position. The committees also sought coverage of their activities in local newspapers, which represented a concerted effort to gain publicity and spread their message. Resolutions drafted at the meetings often contained explicit instructions to distribute the meeting minutes for publication to nearby newspapers.

In a number of prominent and pivotal cases, petition meeting attendees later had careers as Whig Party politicians. The *Alexandria Gazette* reported that one Cuthbert Powell, Esq., served on the leadership committee at a January 13, 1834, public meeting in Loudoun County, Virginia. Powell later served as a Whig in the Twenty-Seventh Congress. David Crooker Magoun led a March 8, 1834, meeting in Bath, Maine; he later served as the town's Whig mayor. That said, attending such a meeting by no means ensured a life of service to the Whigs. Nathan Beverley Tucker helped lead a January 9, 1834, meeting at New Kent County, Virginia. But throughout the 1830s and later, he remained a states' rights proponent and never fully embraced the Whig Party.[43]

The anti-Jackson opposition would never break from more elite patterns of National Republicanism if it could not systematically recruit those who identified themselves as republican producers. A critical feature of the pro-restoration campaign is that it began to facilitate this recruitment. Guilds, boards of trade, and other occupational associations provided an important organizational structure through which petitioners gathered signatures before submitting a memorial to Congress. Petitions from Pennsylvania in February and March 1834 suggested an extremely wide variety of occupation-based groups who referred to themselves directly in the prayers.[44]

The bank petitioning campaign displayed patterns that demonstrated its growing separation from anti-Masonic and National Republican campaigns, especially after March and into May and June, when the petitioning campaign was no longer being actively encouraged by Clay. Especially in its spread to the Ohio valley (well outside Clay's strongholds in Kentucky) and to western New York, Ohio, Virginia, and North Carolina, the petitions pointed to an emerging, if inchoate, voice arrayed against Jackson and Taney that had not simply reproduced earlier patterns of support for President John Quincy Adams.[45]

The geography of anti-Jackson petitioning from December 1833 to May 1834 anticipated with considerable precision the performance of American Whig candidates in 1836, 1838, and 1840, and indeed for another decade after. Normalized by population, every additional standardized movement in favor of deposit restoration was associated with a nearly 4 percent increase in vote share for the Whigs in the corresponding county in 1836. The Whigs' organization was remarkably weak that year, and the party did not even hold a national convention. The fact that the petition aggregates precede the development of state party chapters and candidacies, much

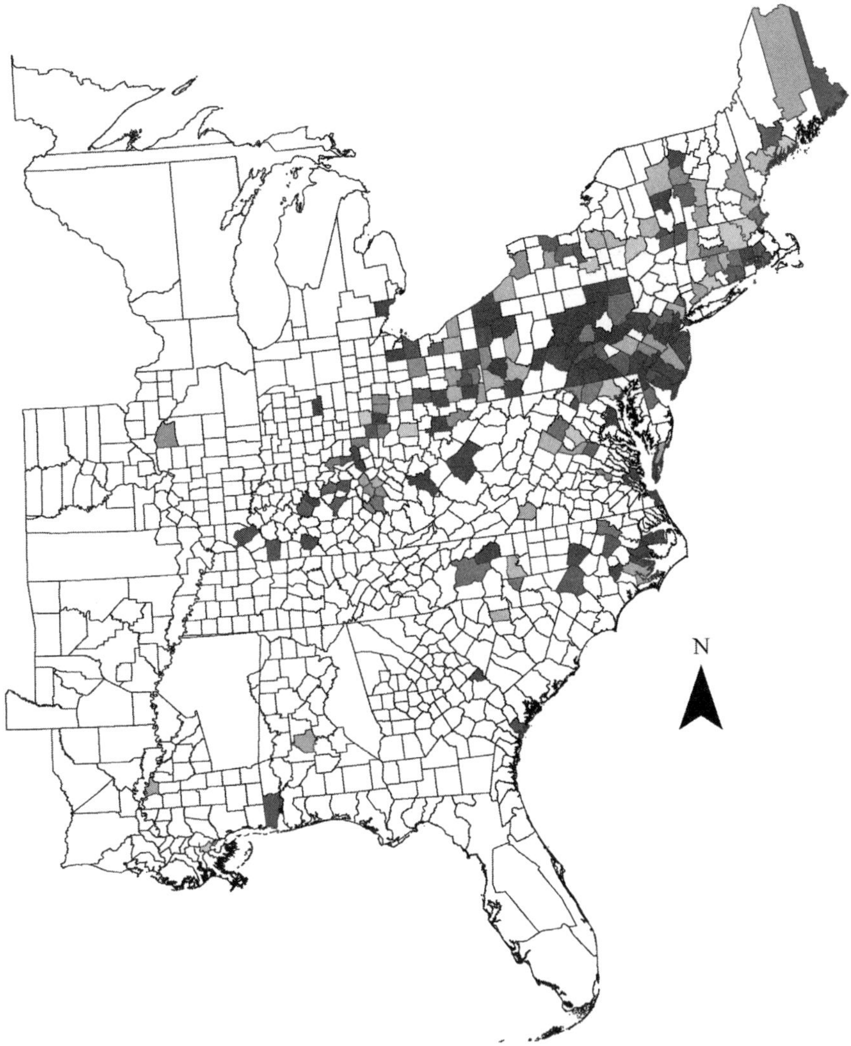

FIGURE 9.2. Geographic Distribution of Petitions Per Capita after Removal of the Deposits, 1833–1834. *Credit:* Daniel Carpenter and Benjamin Schneer, "Party Formation through Petitions: The Whigs and the Bank War of 1832–1834," *Studies in American Political Development* 29 (October 2015): 2013–2234. Used by permission of Cambridge University Press.

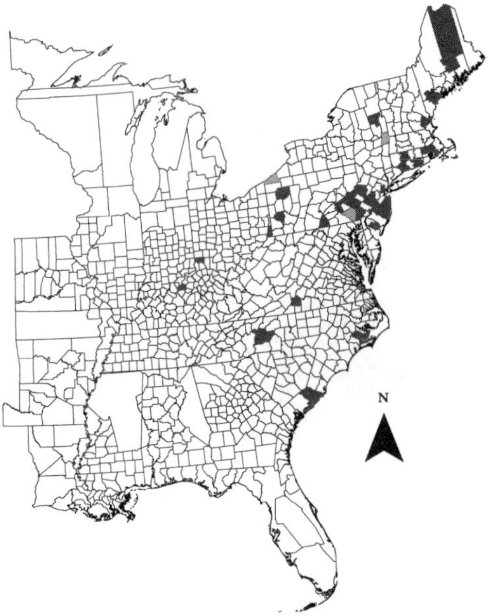

Dec. 1833 – Feb. 1834

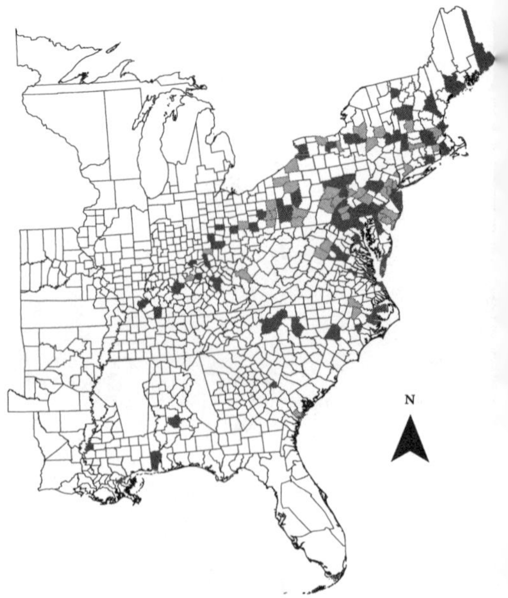

March 1834 – April 1834

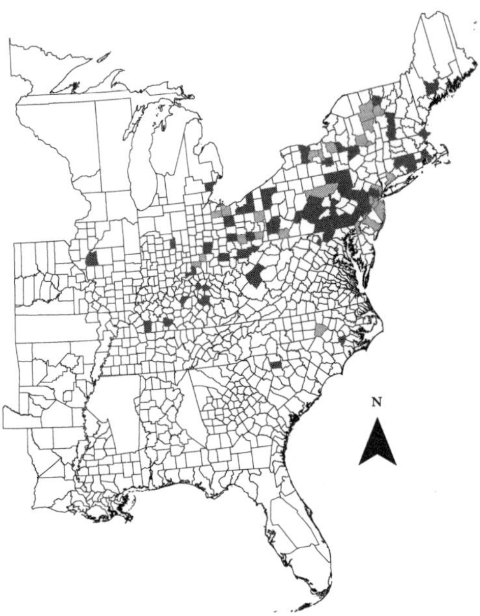

May 1834 – June 1834

FIGURE 9.3. Time Lapse of Bank War Petitions by Stance. Darker counties had a majority of petitions favoring restoration of the deposits. Lighter counties had a majority of petitions supporting President Jackson in the removal of the deposits. *Credit:* Daniel Carpenter and Benjamin Schneer, "Party Formation through Petitions: The Whigs and the Bank War of 1832–1834," *Studies in American Political Development* 29 (October 2015): 213–234. Used by permission of Cambridge University Press.

TABLE 9.1 The Electoral Legacy of the 1834 Anti-Jackson Petitioning Campaign

Additional Whig vote share in later presidential elections for every standard deviation increase in pro-restoration petitioning in 1834 (5.7 petitions/100,000)				
1836	1840	1844	1848	1852
3.80%	2.76%	2.50%	2.10%	1.95%
$p<0.001$	$p<0.001$	$p<0.001$	$p<0.001$	$p<0.001$
Implied additional Whig vote share in later presidential elections for every movement from 10th to 90th percentile in pro-restoration petitioning in 1834 (17.75 petitions / 100,000)				
1836	1840	1844	1848	1852
11.83%	8.59%	7.79%	6.53%	6.06%

Note: Regressions include control for population (logged), petitions against restoration, distance from county centroid to nearest bank branch, nonwhite population, female population, urban population, previous anti-Jackson voting, and fixed effects for each state.

less anything like a national machinery, points to the pre-partisan nature of the petition mobilization, and the weak association of these patterns with National Republican voting patterns in 1828 suggests that something new was afoot. Anti-restoration petitions did not predict new votes for Van Buren in 1836 or 1840, nor for Democratic congressional candidates, suggesting that the petitioning struggle left its organizational imprint precisely where preexisting party organization was weakest. Nor do socioeconomic or ethnic political factors appear to account for the geographical patterns. The association appears to have been stronger in smaller-population counties where the Whigs, at least outside New England, struggled to assemble the accoutrements of party strength. While the predictive association would diminish by the 1852 elections, the geographic legacy of the petitioning campaign would remain.[46]

High levels of petitioning gestured to an emergent Whig political culture, especially in places where cleavages had formed in response to Jackson and Taney's policy, where there were emerging linkages between local notables and anti-Jacksonian representatives, and where citizens had begun developing organizational capacity by holding meetings on deposit removal. Those counties with a large number of petitions expressing outrage and calling for restoration were on their way to developing a party structure designed to transmit grievances and sentiments on policy—opposing Jackson's perceived "executive tyranny" and decrying periodic financial downturns—to political representatives of their choosing. The crisis over the removal of the deposits created the necessary conditions for the formation of a cleavage that Whig politicians could exploit.[47]

The differential configuration of state party organization followed these more granular geographic patterns. Kentucky's higher level of Whig voting and anti-Jackson petitioning undoubtedly followed from preexisting patterns of National Republican organization. Yet New York and especially Ohio were far less likely places for stronger state Whig organizations to emerge, and Clay and his allies felt as much in 1832. The imprint of bank war petitioning emerged not so much across these states as within them, especially in New York, where anti-Jackson memorials surged and Whig votes thereafter materialized along the Erie Canal and in Buffalo, and in Ohio, in the villages and counties near and west of the state capital, Columbus (Franklin, Clark, Clinton, and Champaign Counties), and near the Lake Erie littoral (Huron and Medina Counties). In line with the anti-Jackson petitions in the winter and spring of 1834, Whigs performed better at the polls in these states, as New York and Ohio Whigs controlled the state's lower chamber for a majority of the years between 1836 and 1848. It was in Pennsylvania, partially because its pro-restoration petitions reflected the bank's embeddedness there, that the depth of early anti-Jackson mobilization translated so weakly into state party strength.[48]

All told, petitioning brought organizational democracy and served a variety of purposes as a political tool after Jackson's removal of the deposits. It linked meeting attendees in states such as Maine and Ohio to the political maneuverings of Henry Clay back in Washington; it allowed members of Congress to formally register the opinions of constituents at home while giving voice to newly mobilized groups roused by the economic downturn and suspicion of Andrew Jackson; it even played a role in the evolution of Clay's thinking as he tested different angles for his anti-Jackson appeal. The congealing of written grievances served as connective tissue linking citizens and government before a party organization was in place. In this manner, petitioning played a key role in the development of the newly emergent American Whigs.

In ways that reflected political consciousness and the social forces they could not entirely dominate, the Whigs changed considerably after the Panic, but retained many of the organizational patterns and geography that had emerged in the petitioning campaign. As the party's formal organization developed, the role of petitioning in its development declined accordingly. The Whigs probably gained additional adherents from the growing opposition to the Mexican War and annexation in the 1840s, though by 1844 antislavery parties had eagerly joined the battle.[49]

The legacy of the restoration battle suggests that petition campaigns in antebellum America could carry visible legacies long after the immediate issue had fallen from the national agenda. Henry Clay and other Jackson opponents knew as they entered the 1836 campaign that their prospects were not good, but they recognized, if only dimly, that something with structure and momentum was afoot. The coalescence of a true organizational rival to the Democrats had begun not in a conscious act of party building but in an older mode of grievance carried to assemblies, newly transformed in diffusive patterns of meetings and signatures.

DURHAMITES AND CANADIENS: THE CRYSTALLIZATION OF OPPOSITION IN UNIFIED CANADA

The Patriote Rebellions of 1837 and 1838 brought new uncertainty and freshly opened cleavages to Upper Canada. The Crown's appointment of the Whig John Lambton, 1st Earl of Durham, to investigate the causes of the rebellion set all sorts of possibilities and processes in motion, including the possibility that French Canada would be truly converted to English language and customs, and that in both colonies (whether united or not), new forms of representation and administration would be created. Durham's *Report on the Affairs of British North America* (1839) presented a liberal and colonial outlook, calling for the union of Upper and Lower Canada into a single colonial province, the assimilation of the French Canadian population—"a people with no literature and no history," as he characterized them—in a model of British cultural domination that would favor anglophone immigration and school reform, and a program of "responsible government." It was not without justification that Louis-Joseph Papineau, writing from exile in Paris in his essay *Histoire de la résistance du Canada au gouvernement anglais* (May 1839), lamented that Durham had ignored the considerable anglophone support of the rebellions, and that for "sixteen years" Papineau and his compatriots had been pressing the issue of responsible government, especially equal representation in a strong legislative assembly. With many Patriote leaders in disarray or overseas, much of the French Canadian resistance to assimilation devolved on the Catholic Church. Only later in the 1840s would a new generation of French Canadians, led by Louis-Hippolyte Lafontaine and deeply conscious of the power of signed memorials, leverage popular petitions into political blocs and proto-partisan formations.[50]

Yet even as French Canadian opponents seized on the assimilation program, Durham's other suggestions for a model of "responsible government" threatened to undermine Anglican-Tory governance in Upper Canada. Even as Durham favored British cultural models, he distrusted the political system and constitution of Upper Canada, which had become what one of his advisers called "a petty, corrupt, insolent Tory clique."[51] Responsible government meant, for Durham, the freeing of governmental machinery from political factions and elite networks, provisions for religious plurality and liberty, and the openness of political and economic systems to contestation.[52]

The only fully adopted recommendation of Durham's *Report* came in provincial union, as Parliament passed the Union Act in July 1840 and the colonial administration created the Province of Canada the following year, with Canada East now the name of Lower Canada and Canada West the name of the upper province. French assimilation would depend on a capacity of state that neither the British nor the Upper Canadians possessed, and French Canadian resistance to that program generated a cultural and geographic stalemate, leading in part to the creation of a confederation in 1867.

It was in Upper Canada where the *Report*'s mark on politics would be most acutely and durably felt. Lieutenant Governor Sir George Arthur remarked in 1839 that Durham had "thrown a firebrand amongst the People."[53] Whereas French Canadians seized on the assimilation program to trash the report, Upper Canadian Tories expressed their outrage that their daring settler project had been undermined, first by revolt and now (more legitimately) by the Whig document. With rebellion leaders in exile and little political machinery to produce headway in the Tory-dominated colonial assembly, Robert Gourlay (who had briefly returned to the colony) once again seized on petitioning, calling for township-by-township drafting and signing of memorials in favor of the *Report*'s responsible government program. Yet it was a new generation of activists that took up the aegis of reform and that coordinated a petitioning campaign designed to legitimate opposition to the Tory government and to demonstrate an alternative public will to Parliament. Clothing themselves in the language and symbolism of Durham's *Report*, the emergent opposition combined petitions and public meetings that issued in resolutions.[54]

The sixteen Durham meetings in Upper Canada in 1839 proceeded under the shadow of tension, legitimacy, and potential violence. The legitimacy of government opposition remained a serious issue in light of the rebellions. Following Gourlay's vision, the leaders of these meetings almost always came from the milieu where they were held, and the organizers strained to prevent violence of any sort from unfolding. They even invited prominent local Tories to testify at the meetings, often against Durham's *Report*. Yet local reformers dominated the Durham meetings in numbers and in words, giving memorable speeches that were quickly printed and distributed. The speeches that ensued raised a host of issues, with speakers focusing their ire less on the metropole than on the local elite. In Beaverton, Eldon, Hamilton, Niagara—everywhere but Toronto—the meetings passed resolutions that called for provincial government reform, for an overhaul of the privileges of clergy reserves, and for open and less partisan banking institutions.[55] The arguments and program of the Durham meetings echoed the earlier Mackenzie-led petitioning of 1831 as well as the "Objects and Rules" of the Canadian Alliance Society in 1834, the latter of which aimed to "strengthen the hands of a liberal [Upper Canadian] parliament."[56]

A network of liberal reformers—democrats, in many ways, who aspired to an American model of government—emerged in Upper Canada in the wake of these meetings. In contrast to the Tory model of "loyalty," with its fierce rejection of compromise with French Canadians, its embrace of Anglican supremacy and tradition, and its rejection of American ideas—these "reform party" activists sought a democratic republicanism that would organize in a sovereign provincial parliament. They confined their agenda largely to issues that dominated Canada West, leaving to Canada East the thorny question of linguistic separatism. The leaders of the reform party that emerged in Canada West in the 1840s—including the men known as "Old Reformers" from the Mackenzie days (such as Caleb Hopkins and Richard Woodruff) and a host of newcomers, like Niagara's William Hamilton Merritt, Hamilton's George Tiffany, and Israel Wood Powell—descended heavily from the Durhamite petitioning and the Durham meetings. The coalescence of opposition depended heavily on local organization and relied less on newspapers than would party emergence in the United States, in part because colonial officials restricted press freedoms in the wake of the Rebellion of 1837.[57]

So heady was the Durhamites' momentum in Upper Canada that Tories launched new petitioning campaigns of their own in 1839 and 1840, directing their appeals to the Crown. The Tories knew that Durham's *Report* had considerable legitimacy, so they sought to weaken its provisions for Upper Canadian responsible government more than they sought outright rejection. The Durhamites, for their part, had drafted and collected names on their own petitions to Britain, but decided against transmitting them "under the impression that Your Excellency has in view the promotion of the objects to which the prayer of said Petition is mainly directed."[58] Selected Durhamites opted instead to send their pro-*Report* petitions to the newly appointed governor general, Charles Poulett Thomson, who arrived with considerable reputation and discretion. Soon the Canadian Tories had figured out that Thomson was the proper audience for their appeals, and Thomson had, by this point, received some of his largest signed appeals from Tory committees that had organized locally on a Durhamite model, in Brockville and Toronto. These Tory documents straddled the boundary between signed addresses and petitions, and their abundance demonstrated the spatial thinness and precarity of the network's coalition.

Combined with the emergence of petition-based opposition, affairs in the assembly of unified Canada began to take on a more polarized tone. Lower Canadians tended to vote together as a bloc, all the more so after a combined petitioning and rhetorical campaign targeting seigneurial rights gave them a new leader—Louis-Hippolyte Lafontaine—and extra adhesion. General elections in January 1848 returned to the Canadian House of Assembly a positively reformist majority, headed by Lafontaine in the East and Robert Baldwin in the West. Baldwin's and Lafontaine's partisan formations reflected their origins as petitioning coalitions, even as each leader departed from the politics of their predecessors. The power of Baldwin and Lafontaine came in part from the fact that assembly politics required dual sectional majorities, among representatives from East and West, in order to advance legislation. Among representatives in Canada West, strong divisions between Tories and Durhamites remained through the 1840s, with the Tories wishing for greater British involvement in the unified colony, while Durhamites, for reasons both similar to and different from those animating the Québécois, wanted local self-rule. Besides the thorny debate over seigneurial tenure, the important break with colonial pasts came in the Rebellion Losses Bill, passed by the provincial assembly in 1849 to compensate those who had fought in the Rebellions of 1837–1838, especially in Lower Canada, for property damaged or destroyed during the conflict. Tories now pressed the Crown, through the Colonial Office, to intervene and block the bill, which merely rewarded the tumultuous and factious behavior of the Patriotes. Their petition accumulated thirteen thousand signatures from Tory strongholds, including Toronto and Kingston.[59]

The Tories had miscalculated. Their error was to misconstrue the venue of politics. Parliament decided not to intervene, leaving unified Canada to govern itself on the most pressing and divisive issues confronting its people. The partisan groupings in unified Canadian politics emerged from the political unions and petitioning movements of the 1820s and 1830s. Petitioning for and against the Rebellion Losses Bill in 1849 newly catalyzed organization but taught unified Canadians that the politics of distribution and justice would forever be more of a domestic matter than one whose terms were hashed out at the metropole.[60]

The memorial campaigns of William Lyon Mackenzie—best known for his later role in the Upper Canadian rebellions—had produced a legacy far beyond his personal reputation. Petitioning bestowed legitimacy on the Tories' opponents, gave them a vehicle for organizing locally and for the Durham meetings, and provided a crucial technology of organization at a time when newspapers had become less salient and less powerful in performing that function. The Tories' own petitioning failure in 1849 merely confirmed the fact that the organizational work of Mackenzie and Durhamite petitioning had been completed, so much so that the truly sovereign venue for rebellion losses and land reform had crossed an ocean, from Parliament to the assembly in Montréal and Toronto. The party formations that ruled the new assembly reflected their origins in the named grievances of the previous two decades.[61]

TEN

Abolition and the Transformation of U.S. Politics

> Let every man of color throughout the United States, who possesses the spirit and principles of a man, sign a petition to Congress to abolish slavery in the District of Columbia, and grant you the rights and privileges of common free citizens; for if you had had faith as a grain of mustard seed, long before this the mountains of prejudice might have been removed.
>
> **—Maria W. Stewart, Address delivered at the African Masonic Hall, Boston, 1833**

> Especially, let me urge you to petition. Men may settle these and other questions at the ballot box, but you have no such right. It is only through our petitions that you can reach the Legislature. It is, therefore, peculiarly your duty to petition.
>
> **—Angelina Grimké, 1838**

> Our Government is a democracy. We, the farmers and mechanics, are the rulers. We are the governors—you, our servants.
>
> **—an abolitionist letter writer, defending the right to petition, 1841**

The global quest to free slaves—often inspired and led by free and enslaved Blacks themselves—shook the nineteenth-century Atlantic like no other development. In no setting were the politics more ferocious than in the United States, where the debate over slavery and race split the faithful, rent asunder the family, emboldened Blacks free and in bondage, enraged Whites defensive of tranquility and privilege, and set region against region and state against state in a swelling sectional crisis. The rise of immediatism (a commitment to instant uncompensated emancipation of slaves, accompanied by full legal and political rights for those freed) radicalized the opponents and defenders of slavery. Robert Wedderburn of Jamaica, Boston's David Walker, Maria Stewart and William Lloyd Garrison, sisters Angelina and Sarah Grimké, Quaker Benjamin Lundy—these and dozens of other leaders formed a cross-racial alliance in defense of the full liberation and equality of Black people. Slavery's enemies assailed the institution ever more zealously, attacking it with new modes of prayer, text, song, and association. They also excoriated defenders of colonization, equating that program to a racist compromise with slavery. Immediatists relied heavily on memorials even as they transformed their content and numbers.

Abolition changed the mass petition, and mass petitioning changed American abolitionism. The intercourse of argument and tactic, of ideology and strategy, issued in new forms of consciousness that recruited the young, the Black, the female, and the radical into everyday politics. Women had been drafting, signing, and presenting petitions in growing numbers in the early nineteenth century, but in immediatist abolition, they found a cause in which they expanded this activity to a mass continental scale. Following the clarion call of prophets like Maria Stewart, Black women and men authored memorials and affixed their names to them at rates never before seen in the United States. Children surged collectively into politics as "minor's petitions" signed by girls and boys ranging from eight to nineteen years of age consumed pages of ink. All these developments had precedents before the 1830s, but the battles of that decade exploded the scale of activity and brought millions of North Americans into a new mode of politics. The congressional suppression of antislavery memorials led to new debates about what the right to petition meant, and it kindled a conflagration of petitioning as diffuse and intensive as at any other time in U.S. history.[1]

Abolition was more than a petitioning movement, but its advance was inseparable from the use of signed memorials. The rapid growth in new associations and their chapters in the 1830s came along with and often after (but not before) vast petitioning campaigns. The surge of women's activity in the movement came with petitions more than with any other form of activity. Interracial associations were the lifeblood of the campaign, but as Black and White signed the same pages, as they collaborated to draw up and canvass signed memorials, racial alliance become more intimate, more tangible. Black men and women joined legal action and petitioning campaigns, taking appeals to courts and legislatures. A surging, more individualized Protestant Christianity fueled tens of thousands of moments of testimonial conversion that issued in fervent commitments to abolition, yet the drawing up of prayers and the work of signing and canvassing brought abolitionists into prayerful appeal, concrete evangelism, and signed testimony. Chapter-based associations populated the American North in rural hamlets and industrializing cities, yet the most transformative new organizations embedded petitioning in their constitutional and in their most fundamental routines. The petition surge following the gag rule in 1836 and the crises of 1837 anticipated, as no other force quite could, the growth and diffusion of antislavery chapters; the transformation of sentiment and organization toward third parties, such as the Liberty and Free-Soil parties; the revolution of women's political organizing; and the emergence of civil egalitarian ideas regarding the vote and property. The indignation that burst forth after Congress passed the Fugitive Slave Act of 1850 and the Kansas-Nebraska Act of 1854 engendered a new flood of petitioning that again brought hundreds of thousands of signatures and reenergized abolition organizations and energies in ways that would prove crucial during the Civil War.

THE URGENCY OF THE IMMEDIATE

The clash over slavery in the United States unfolded not only as a battle between slavery's enemies and its defenders but also as a spirited conflict among alternative antislavery visions. In the late 1820s, even as the American Colonization Society solidified its status as the predominant antislavery organization, skepticism for colonization among free Blacks and their White allies grew louder. An interracial coalition behind immediatism formed and grew in numbers, diversity, and strength. Free Black ministers and speakers, especially in the northern states, began to advance the case for racial solidarity and for the uncompromising rejection of slavery. Benjamin Lundy founded the paper *Genius of Universal Emancipation* in 1821, and the free Black minister Samuel Cornish founded *Freedom's Journal* in 1827, creating a printed bullhorn for the rejection of American colonization. With New York State's abolition of slavery in 1827, Albany Baptist minister Nathaniel Paul called openly for universal emancipation and attacked colonization.[2] Boston merchant David Walker wrote for and circulated *Freedom's Journal*, and his *Appeal . . . to the Coloured Citizens of the World* (1829) marked a radical shift, abjectly criticizing the rhetoric of slavery and of American culture for its dehumanization of Blacks, pointing to slavery's very existence as incompatible with Christianity and with America's self-styled "Republican Land of Liberty," calling Black "men of sense" to "enlighten their brethren" and to take up the cause against oppression, false religion, and colonization.[3]

This second wave of American antislavery drew inspiration from the British world, not only the parliamentary debates in the metropole but also the unrest and advocacy buffeting the West Indies. The 1823 Demerara rebellion in what is now Guyana provoked, along with the Commission of Free Enquiry in the West Indies and the Caribbean Black petitioning campaign of 1823–1825, a searching period of debate, introspection, and, perhaps most importantly, activism among people of color in the British Atlantic and their allies. A wave of petitioning and pamphleteering crested in the late 1820s, along with consumer movements to boycott commodities produced by slave labor (known as the "free produce" initiative). The abolition petition campaign from 1828 to 1830 flooded Parliament with over five thousand petitions.[4]

Two women of the British Atlantic, the philanthropist Elizabeth Heyrick and the slave Mary Prince, led a dramatic change in authorship and activism. Heyrick's pamphlet *Immediate, Not Gradual Abolition* (1824) marked a clarion call for British women turning away from half steps and toward a radical antislavery program.[5] In passages reprinted in Benjamin Lundy's *Genius of Universal Emancipation* in 1825, Heyrick denigrated legislative campaigns for gradual abolition as a form of dishonesty and false consciousness: "Why then, in the name of humanity, of common sense, and common honesty, do we petition Parliament, year after year, for a gradual abolition of this horrid system?"[6]

Mary Prince was both the first known Black woman to publish a slave narrative and, before that, the first woman to present an antislavery petition to Parliament. Prince was born into slavery in Bermuda in 1788, married a free Black man in 1826 (for which she was cruelly beaten by her master), and was transported to England in 1828. That November, she visited the Aldermanbury Anti-Slavery Society and asked for a means by which she could get manumitted. Recognizing the legal powers of her master, the society's members decided that Parliament, and not a British court, was the proper venue. Together with the society she drew up a petition. The prospect of a petition greatly agitated Mary's master, John A. Wood, as he knew it would occasion a debate in Parliament and then the newspapers. Still, he steadfastly refused to grant Mary's freedom. She then expressed her desire to publish her memoirs, and *The History of Mary Prince, A West-Indian Slave* appeared in 1831. Three editions of Prince's narrative came out that year, and the third edition included the history of her petition, a supplemental story that underscored her appeal to English people to follow her lead and take the cause of total abolition to the nation's sovereign: "This is slavery. I tell it, to let English people know the truth; and I hope they will never leave off to pray God, and call loud to the great king of England, till all the poor blacks be given free, and slavery done up for evermore."[7] In a marker of how North American dialogue shaped British politics, the first known female slave narrative and the first woman's antislavery petition to Parliament had been authored by the same Bermudan woman.[8]

The year of Mary Prince's narrative also saw two slave revolts that heightened White anxieties and left slaveholders fuming at abolitionists. Nat Turner's uprising in Southampton County, Virginia, left fifty-seven White men, women, and children dead, after which a far greater proportion of violence was visited on Virginia Blacks. December 1831 saw the revolt known as the Baptist War (or Christmas Rebellion) in Jamaica, in which fourteen White persons died. The retaliation of colonial authorities, in which over five hundred slaves were killed and Baptist missionaries to the island summarily imprisoned, tilted the debate in Britain further toward abolitionists. In 1832, one week after the leader of the Christmas Rebellion was executed, Parliament appointed a select committee to investigate the eventual "Extinction of Slavery throughout the British Dominion."[9]

Inspired by these events and angered by the reactionary posture of slaveholders and their representatives, American immediatists started a more public campaign aimed at venues national, state, and local. In contrast to organized colonization, which made little petitioning imprint, Black and White immediatists turned to the signed memorial as an instrument of testimony, justice, and organization. Boston free Blacks who founded the General Colored Association (GCA) in 1826 were regular petitioners in city and commonwealth politics, especially Frederick Brinsley, Thomas Dalton, John Telemachus Hilton, the Reverend Thomas Paul, and Samuel Snowden. Reverend Paul headed the 1819 association petition for the African Humane Society, signed by Dalton and his father, Scipio. Hilton led the 1829 petition for the commutation of Washington Goode's capital sentence, which amassed one of the largest Black signatory lists seen from Boston to that time, with 118 signatures, including Snowden and the names of 55 Black women. In Albany, Nathaniel Paul joined with other free Blacks to petition for the formation of the Albany African Clarkson Society.[10]

The familiarity with which early Black antislavery leaders petitioned their governments for various causes before 1833 manifested their fluency with an older mode of petitioning—for licenses (Frederick Brinsley), for school and associational formation (Revs. Nathaniel Paul and Thomas Paul, Abel and James Barbadoes), and for individual pardons (Hilton). All of these petitions evinced racial consciousness. Among the arguments that Hilton and others advanced for Goode's commutation was that "he belongs to a race whom a cruel prejudice robs some of the best influences which contribute to the elevation of man."[11]

Two international examples—the free Black Caribbean movement that had resulted in important advances toward civic equality and the British abolitionist campaign—now stood as paradigms that the deep feedbacks between petitions and associations could be harnessed further. Benjamin Lundy's *Genius of Universal Emancipation* had been reprinting and covering antislavery petitions consistently since 1821, but Lundy's paper gave fresh attention to the "great anti-slavery meetings" in the spring of 1830 in England, attended by thousands, that resolved to bring full abolition before Parliament. In the January 1831 issue, just before he directed his readers' attention to the first issue of William Lloyd Garrison's *The Liberator,* Lundy exclaimed the new energy emanating from England in a column titled "PETITIONS, PETITIONS!": "Late English papers state, that at no former period were the tables of Parliament so loaded with petitions, as they now are, from various parts of the kingdom, for the abolition of slavery in the colonies. This has been found an efficacious mode of proceeding, at other times, and they are resolved to give it full latitude now."[12]

It was likely from working with Lundy that the young William Lloyd Garrison began to set his sights on petitioning as critical antislavery work. Garrison served as Lundy's apprentice for six months in 1829 and 1830, and Lundy let the earnest young man take over much of the content of his paper. In Garrison's first issue of the *Genius* (published September 2, 1829), Lundy featured the petitioning campaign against slavery in the District of Columbia, proclaiming, "The ice is broken!—The important work has commenced."[13] In the November 6, 1829, issue, Garrison went further, proclaiming that petitioning for abolition in the District was among the most important labors committed abolitionists could perform. "Petitions should be thickened until the halls of Congress are filled to repletion," he argued. "The friends of the measure must be up and active. A little moral effort can perform a great moral achievement."[14]

As he worked in Baltimore with Lundy and observed that city's dynamic free Black population, Garrison saw troubling currents in national affairs. Viewing the Jackson administration's alliance with Georgia settlers and their government's eviction of the Cherokee and Choctaw as a way to extend the geographic reach of slavery, he expressed his frustration that the president could ally with slaveholders all the while that antislavery petitions piled up unanswered and tabled in the national legislature. "Our politics are rotten," Garrison fumed. Slavery's enemies could count on "no cheering reliance on 'the powers that be.'"[15] At the age of twenty-five, Garrison moved to Boston to found a new paper, one that would be launched in January 1831 as the *Liberator.* Garrison explicitly disavowed moderation and declared war—political, spiritual, rhetorical, total—on slavery and any who compromised with it. "I am in earnest—I will not equivocate—I will not excuse—I will not retreat a single inch—AND I WILL BE HEARD."[16]

William Lloyd Garrison and the *Liberator* refashioned the agendas of American politics, and they did so through petitioning. Twice in its first issue and twice more in the ensuing month, Garrison devoted columns to the promotion of petitioning. As he and Lundy had done in Baltimore, he vaunted the significance of the petitioning campaign for abolition in the District, both as a mode of political pressure that focused on the attainable and as an advance of spiritual testimony against the profane representation of slavery in the capital of the Republic. On the first page of his very first issue, Garrison made petitioning the first call to political action:

> That District is rotten with the plague, and stinks in the nostrils of the world. Though it is the Seat of our National Government . . . yet a fouler spot scarcely exists on earth. In it the worst features of slavery are exhibited; and as a mart for slave traders, it is unequalled. . . .
>
> Hitherto, a few straggling petitions, relative to this subject, have gone into Congress; but they have been too few to denote much public anxiety, or to commend a deferential notice. It is certainly time that a vigorous and systematic effort should be made, from one end of the county to the other, to pull down that national monument of oppression which towers up in the District. We do hope that the "earthquake voice" of the people will this session shake the black fabric to its foundation.[17]

In Garrison's metaphor of "the 'earthquake voice' of the people" lay a new vision of American democracy, a radical disruption of agendas, and an emergent mobilization accomplished by petitioning. His clarion call for District abolition offered an expansive vision of antislavery and of everyday politics. No issue related to slavery—even if it might seem symbolic—would go uncontested, and every part of the American population (by geography, sex, and race) would receive an appeal to petition. In early February 1831, he published an open call for free Blacks to petition for equal rights: "Take the Constitution of your country in your hands, go to the proper tribunal, and break those odious fetters with which you are now bound. Pour your petitions into the Legislature of each State, and ask in a respectful but firm tone to be restored to that great family of freemen, of which you are legitimate members. If you are defeated once—twice—thrice—do not give up the cause."[18] Given that the Black community—at first in Boston, then in other northeastern Atlantic cities—constituted an important fraction of the *Liberator's* early readership, and given that Garrison was imploring his Black readers to target state legislatures, his February 1831 overture marked an important stratagem of interracial political alliance through petitioning. Beyond this, Garrison saw more than any other activist of the time that antislavery required, at least in part, a politics of numbers—of countable masses of prayers and signatures attached to them.

Garrison aimed his appeals at elites as well as the masses. He devoted two columns in the January 21, 1832, edition of the *Liberator* to John Quincy Adams. President from March 1825 to March 1829, Adams became the first former president to hold a seat in the House, serving from 1831 to 1835 as a U.S. representative from Plymouth. When on December 12, 1831, he presented petitions for abolition in the District of Columbia on the House floor, Adams pronounced himself unable to give "countenance or support" to their prayers. The *Liberator's* first page of January 21, 1832, relayed a complaint from the Philadelphia Society of Friends, expressing the discouragement of abolitionists that Adams had, from all appearances, chosen to "desert the cause": "His example will be doubly injurious to the cause of abolition—by disheartening its friends, and by adding strength of the opposition of its enemies." Then on the third page of the edition, Garrison himself implored Adams to join his countrymen in the immediatist endeavor and to do so on the floor of Congress. Remarking on his election to Congress as a "proud commentary upon our republican institutions," Garrison reminded Adams that "the ex-president of the United States ought to be the least affected by popular clamor, and the best qualified to behave independently." Garrison started tactfully, avoiding what he called "political disparagement," moving to "simply recapitulate facts, and leave others to make an application." By the end of his letter, however, a stentorian rebuke had emerged: "It is evidently your desire to conciliate all parties. Beware, Sir, lest this pliant disposition lead you astray from the path of duty. An error of judgment is easily forgiven; but a sacrifice of principle is an offense without mitigation." Adams would remain on the sidelines of the district petitioning battle for another four years.[19]

Garrison's model of petitioning emphasized national debates as a critical part of the process. He never limited his vision to that of drafting prayers, canvassing and signing, and citizen mobilization. However corrupt the institution had become, Congress needed to hear the voice of slaves and their defenders reverberate through its sandstone chambers. Petitions for abolition in the District focused on the singular shame the slave market brought on the United States by being at the seat of Congress—several markets and slave prisons lay mere blocks away from the Capitol and in full view of its occupants. As the former congressman Abraham Lincoln, campaigning anew in 1854, would observe at a speech in Peoria, "The North clamored for the abolition of a peculiar species of slave trade in the District of Columbia, in connection with which, in view from the windows of the capitol, a sort of negro-livery stable, where droves of negroes were collected, temporarily kept, and finally taken to Southern markets, precisely like droves of horses, had been openly maintained for fifty years."[20]

Garrison next set out to build antislavery organizations, and he did so in a deepening alliance with Boston's Black community, including the orator Maria Stewart. He founded the New England Anti-Slavery Society in 1832, one year after launching the *Liberator*. The society held its first meeting in the basement of the Belknap Street Baptist Church, a Black community church, and leaders of the General Colored Association signed the society's charter alongside the society's leadership. The two groups quickly set about to draft and circulate memorials. Maria Stewart's bold addresses to mixed-race audiences of women and men called on Black men to petition, and Garrison published her speeches in the *Liberator*. Thomas Dalton and James Barbadoes served notice in the *Liberator* of November 24, 1832, that the Massachusetts General Colored Association would meet that month to "consider the expediency of petitioning Congress" to abolish slavery in the District.[21] Two months later, at the first annual meeting of the New England Anti-Slavery Society, its leaders and members opened their meeting by decrying the slave markets operating openly in the nation's capital. The society's first resolution excoriated District slavery and declared any man obliged "to use the same exertions to put an end to [slavery] in that District, which he would be if it existed in his own State."[22] From 1832 to 1834, membership in Garrison's fledgling and biracial alliance surged to almost two thousand members. Using a petition by its president Jonathan Dalton in January 1833, the General Colored Association requested entry into the New England Anti-Slavery Society, and the merger was complete that year. Meanwhile, local antislavery societies began to sprout up all over the northern states and territories—in Maine, the Western Reserve District of Ohio, and the "burned over" districts of upstate and western New York. By late 1833, Garrison's vision of a national antislavery organization had begun to take shape, with a meeting of sixty-three delegates from far-flung locales assembling in a Black benevolent society's building in Boston. The American Anti-Slavery Society was founded in December 1833.[23]

Garrison and his compatriots wove petitioning into the very fabric of the American Anti-Slavery Society's constitution. In the society's Declaration of Sentiments, adopted in December 1833 in Philadelphia, the organization rehearsed the logic and rhetoric of the Declaration of Independence struck fifty-seven years before in the same city. In what would become a common American trope, the society melded the fervor of the Second Great Awakening to the egalitarianism of the American Revolution: "With entire confidence in the overruling justice of God, we plant ourselves upon the Declaration of our Independence and the truths of Divine Revelation, as upon the Everlasting Rock."[24] The complaints that had led men in Philadelphia to break from their empire were real, but the immediatists considered them trifling next to the grievances of the slave. The society then advanced its "views and principles—these our designs and measures." First to "organize antislavery societies if possible, in every city, town, and village in our land," then to "send forth agents to lift up the voice of remonstrance, of warning, of entreaty, and rebuke," and then to "circulate, unsparingly and extensively, anti-slavery tracts and periodicals." At the end of this list the society declared that it would "spare no exertions nor means to bring the whole nation to speedy repentance."[25] Petitioning had audiences far beyond Congress. The circulation of memorials and pamphlets delivered remonstrance to the American public, following New Testament prescriptions of using scripture "for teaching, for reproof, for correction" (2 Timothy 3:16–17).

Among the many sins inherent to American slavery, none attracted so much attention in the society's petitioning designs as did the profitable and busy slave markets of the nation's capital. Three months before the Declaration of Sentiments was adopted, the poet John Greenleaf Whittier, a longtime Garrison friend and collaborator in publishing, issued his pamphlet *Justice and Expediency.* Whittier told his New England readers that they, too, shared in the sin of slavery: "Palliating the Evil—hiding the Evil—voting for the Evil, do we not participate in it?" As his example of "voting for the Evil," he presented the votes of Vermont and Rhode Island congressmen against an 1829 District abolition bill. For Whittier, nothing lay more visible or centrally on the abolitionist's agenda than District and territorial abolition, to be undertaken now. "The friends of abolition would urge in the first instance the immediate Abolition of Slavery in the District of Columbia, and in the Territories of Florida and Arkansas." The persistence of slavery in these spaces meant that "*twenty-six thousand human beings*, fashioned in the image of God, the fitted temples of His Holy Spirit," were "held by the Government in the abhorrent chains of Slavery." "The power to emancipate them is clear," he asserted. "It is indisputable." District and territorial slavery implied not merely the national government's tolerance of slavery but its active participation in "the Evil." The jurisdictional arguments of congressmen against petitions for District abolition had evinced "the veriest sophistry which ever supplied the place of argument."[26]

The Declaration of Sentiments recognized "the sovereignty of each State to legislate exclusively on the subject of the slavery which is tolerated within its limits," yet also declared that "Congress has a right, and is solemnly bound, to suppress the domestic slave-trade between the several States, and to abolish slavery in those portions of our territory which the Constitution has placed under its exclusive jurisdiction."[27] Whittier helped to draft the Declaration, an act he considered among the most important of his life.[28] The society launched a new petition drive in December 1834, aimed at ousting slavery from Washington, D.C. Dozens of these petitions arrived to the Twenty-Third Congress in 1834 and 1835, from Tennessee, Ohio, Pennsylvania, Massachusetts, Maine, Vermont, and Rhode Island. The Twenty-Fourth Congress would continue the pattern, the clerk of the committee receiving the memorials reporting of the first session that 176 petitions had come in, "a little rising 34,000 nearly 15,000 of whom were females."[29] The society saw in these numbers a gross underestimate, with "not less than 75,000 or 100,000 signatures" in the mix.[30]

The District abolition campaign of the Twenty-Third Congress built on earlier patterns but infused antislavery petitioning with new energies and rhetorical innovations. A young orator named Theodore Dwight Weld had just left Lane Theological Seminary near Cincinnati in the autumn of 1834 and quickly took a post as American Anti-Slavery Society agent for the State of Ohio. Weld lectured dozens of times in the southeastern reaches of the state—fourteen times near the town of Circleville alone, where he was injured by anti-abolitionist mobs. After starting new antislavery societies in Pennsylvania, Weld returned to tour the state's Western Reserve, which included Cleveland, Elyria, and Oberlin. In what was no happenstance, Ohio sent more District abolition petitions to the Twenty-Third Congress (at least thirteen) than any other state. Beyond linking antislavery petitioning to lecture tours, Weld also helped launch petition campaigns directed toward women. Either Weld himself or one of the women in his group drew up a new petition form for the use of women's auxiliary antislavery societies, a ready-made text called the "Fathers and Rulers Petition." "*Fathers & Rulers of our Country,*" its prayer began, "Suffer us, we pray you, with the sympathies which we are constrained to feel as wives, as mothers, and as daughters, to plead with you in behalf of a long oppressed and deeply injured class of native Americans, residing in that portion of our country which is under your exclusive control."[31]

The Fathers and Rulers Petition linked the ideals of the Second Great Awakening and the aspirations of the American Revolution, and it reimagined women's roles in politics by recasting traditional narratives. Focusing squarely on the District and on the responsibilities of congressmen as "the legislators and guardians of a Christian people," the women's prayer invoked "the patriot Jefferson," who had remarked that "we tremble for our country when we remember that God is just, and that his justice cannot sleep forever." For their part, the women presented themselves as engaged foremost in a form of prayerful supplication, their aim being "to importune high Heaven with prayer, and our national Legislature with appeals, until this Christian people abjure forever a traffic in the souls of men." The prayer of women had, they noted—pointing to the book of Esther, chapter 5, and to Roman precedents—swayed the choices of monarchs and tyrants. All the more so, they would expect, would it be heard with favor in the proceedings of a representative legislature on a subject so proximate to its chambers:

> In the name of humanity, justice, equal rights and impartial law, our country's weal, her honor and her cherished hopes we earnestly implore for this our humble petition, your favorable regard. If both in Christian and in Heathen lands, Kings have revoked their edicts, at the intercession of woman, and Tyrants have relented when she appeared a suppliant for mercy, surely we may hope that the Legislators of a free, enlightened and Christian people will lend their ear to our appeals.[32]

To these petitions, southern members of Congress began to react with indignation that bled into rage. The House of Representatives remained under the control of the Jacksonian Democrats and Speaker James K. Polk of Tennessee. James Henry Hammond of South Carolina remarked that he "could not sit here, and see the rights of the southern people assaulted day after day, by the ignorant fanatics from whom these memorials preceded." To abolish slavery in the District, he further claimed, would be to abolish it in the states. Senator William Campbell Preston continued, asserting that "the concerted movement" for District abolition was nothing less than "an attempt to storm the gates of the citadel—as throwing the bridge over the moat. The South must resist the danger in its inception, or it would soon become irresistible." Abolitionists took comfort and cue in the fact that, as the society put it, "A Senator from South Carolina discloses the fact, that the District of Columbia, is the 'CITADEL' of American slavery; and that, unless its assailants are speedily defeated, THEY WILL CONQUER IT."[33]

The antislavery petitions of the Twenty-Fourth and Twenty-Fifth Congresses transformed the career of South Carolina Senator John Calhoun. Calhoun would become known for his "positive good" theory of slavery, articulated in a speech on the Senate floor on February 6, 1837. A year before he gave that oration, Calhoun laid out what might be called the positive good theory of petition repudiation. Calhoun and Hammond shared a residence at what was known as Mrs. Lindenberger's boardinghouse, where other members of their state's congressional delegation also stayed. These boardinghouses were the basic unit of social life in antebellum Washington, and at Mrs. Lindenberger's, Hammond and Calhoun shared meals and regularly communicated. Their shared tactics quickly converged on a strategy of defending regional honor. After Ohio's Thomas Morris introduced antislavery petitions on January 7, 1836, Calhoun rose to propose that his chamber rebuff them. Under this proposal, the petitions would not even be read on the floor or into the record, or officially tabled. North Carolina senator Bedford Brown quickly objected that to refuse receipt would "cause excitement and agitation," stating his preference for tabling the petitions. Calhoun responded that rather than "receive and quietly pocket the insult," the Senate should act by "repelling it promptly and decisively." The petition was no mere act of supplication but had pronounced him (and his region) "a robber, kidnapper, pirate, with all the other abusive terms used in these petitions." In response to any such insult, the proper response was not to "quietly take the petition and put it in his pocket" but to "knock the scoundrel down." In the Calhoun-Hammond theory of legislative procedure, petitions that lay an affront on one state or region were not even to be given the dignity of formal receipt. No insult disguised as supplication should pierce "the threshold" of the chamber.[34]

The Senate voted down Calhoun's proposal, rendering his argument moot for a historical moment. Yet in the House, South Carolina representatives harnessed their wider coalition and acted on the petitions again in the spring of 1836. Congressman Henry Laurens Pinckney, elected as a Nullifier from Charleston, proposed a select committee to receive the petitions and discuss how to act on them. Speaker Polk stacked the committee with eight Jacksonian Democrats and a single Whig. After meeting from February to May, the Pinckney committee proposed a rule of disposition for all petitions relating to slavery, which was not finalized until May 1836. Declaring it "extremely important and desirable, that the agitation of this subject should be arrested, for the purpose of restoring tranquility to the public mind," the Pinckney committee's resolution declared that "all petitions, memorials, resolutions, propositions, or papers, relating in any way, or to any extent whatsoever, to the subject of slavery or the abolition of slavery, shall, without being either printed or referred, be laid on the table and that no further action whatever shall be had thereon." The Twenty-Fourth House voted to approve the restriction by a large margin in both its first and its second sessions. As Adams rose to present another set of petitions on May 25, 1836, he found himself blocked and asked whether he had been "gagged." He had been.[35]

The radical nature of the Pinckney resolution lay in its summary and prospective nature. Well over a thousand times before 1836 had the House tabled, decided not to print, or refused to act on a petition. Pinckney's rule, once adopted, amounted to a repudiation of all slavery-related petitions from that point forward. Approximating Senate practice at the time, the House had altered the very time and space of legislative supplication and hence of representative debate in a republic. Since legislative proceedings had to be adopted session by session, members of the House debated the gag policy in various forms about once per year from 1836 to 1844. Enforcement of the rule relied not only on elected officeholders but on zealous clerks, such as Benjamin Brown French. The gag rule went hand in hand with southern politicians' other restrictions on speech, press, and communications. In 1834, thieves broke into the Charleston post office and stole antislavery periodicals, setting them afire in a burning that attracted around two thousand people (roughly one in seven of the town's residents). Soon thereafter, Jacksonian postal officials implemented a policy by which antislavery materials would not be circulated in the South. In the South itself, states legislated the death penalty for circulating abolitionist tracts or publicly criticizing slaveholding. Back in the House, meanwhile, matters became vitriolic. As John Quincy Adams continued to present antislavery petitions, including those from slaves themselves, South Carolina Representative Waddy Thompson introduced a resolution censuring him. The resolution failed, but the House quickly agreed to refuse Adams's memorials and to forthrightly deny slaves' right to petition the chamber.[36]

It was antislavery petitioning, as much as anything else, that triggered Calhoun to launch his now infamous defense of slavery as the South's "peculiar institution" and wholly "a positive good." Late in the second session of the Twenty-Fourth Congress, on February 6, 1837, Calhoun rose to present his rebuttal to antislavery petitions in all respects. The petitions directed to the Senate advanced a "systematic design of rendering us hateful in the eyes of the world—with a view to a general crusade against us and our institutions." In a speech that quickly entered the annals of history as a vindication of racial bondage, Calhoun spent as much time denying the obligation of the Senate to receive these petitions as he did defending slavery. The Senate had no more obligation to receive antislavery petitions, he intoned, than it had the right to abolish slavery itself. In the petitions he rose to block, he saw the seeds of war. "They who imagine that the spirit now abroad in the North, will die of itself without a shock or convulsion, have formed a very inadequate conception of its real character; it will continue to rise and spread, unless prompt and efficient measures to stay its progress be adopted." So vitriolic was their dislike for antislavery petitions that Calhoun and his extremist allies seized on Pinckney's gag as too permissive and ran him out of the Nullifier Party. Yet Calhoun still retained great hopes for gagging petitions. Beyond its defense of southern honor and its work in keeping slavery off the national political agenda, the rule would, Calhoun predicted, fully dishearten antislavery petitioners. More so than their newspapers, abolitionists' memorials set Calhoun on his amateur path of racist philosophy and led him to proclaim that "abolition and the Union cannot co-exist."[37]

The petitions blocked in the winter of 1837, late in the second session of the Twenty-Fourth Congress, came disproportionately from women. They came from Ohio; from Bucks County, Pennsylvania; from Plymouth and

Rockingham, New Hampshire; from "Evalina Reed, and 18 other minors of Taunton," Massachusetts; and from Rachael Sterns and the "ladies of Fredericksburg," Virginia.[38] All these petitions were tabled. Representative John Patton of Virginia arose to announce that the nine ladies of Fredericksburg were not White and did not deserve the appellation of "ladies." Patton's attack on the Black women petitioners of Fredericksburg presaged a larger attack of petitions from women and from people of color, whether slave or free.[39]

Women in the northern states had already amplified their outcry, but as they saw their petitions blocked from discussion or action, their resolve became steeled and fueled by new indignation. The Antislavery Convention of American Women assembled in New York City on May 9, 1837, and on the minds of the seventy-one Black and White women delegates gathered there was the gag rule, newly reenacted by the Twenty-Fifth Congress, which had started two months before. Angelina Grimké introduced her resolution "that the right of petition is natural and inalienable, derived immediately from God, and guaranteed by the Constitution of the United States." Any attempt to abridge that right was "a high-handed usurpation of power, and an attempt to strike a death-blow at the freedom of the people." Grimké's resolution then turned to her primary audience, stating unequivocally that "it is the duty of every woman in the United States, whether northerner or southerner, annually to petition Congress with the faith of an Esther, and the untiring persistence of the importunate widow," for abolition in the District and Florida and for the "extermination" of the interstate slave trade. Grimké then offered a more general resolution calling on "woman to move in that sphere which Providence has assigned her, and no longer remain satisfied in the circumscribed limits with which corrupt custom and a perverted application of Scripture has encircled her."[40]

Angelina Grimké's argument carried dual implications. First, women were wrongly excluded from debates such as those over slavery. Second, women could not shirk from their responsibilities in the name of either comfort or tradition. The first claim faulted men and American society itself, the second laid blame at the feet of American women, assumed White in Grimké's vernacular. Grimké chaired a committee that called for an appeal to American women, and the convention also called for an "Address to Free Colored Americans." Grimké's committee then issued a convention circular, which became the pamphlet *An Appeal to the Women of the Nominally Free States.* The pamphlet combined extended arguments from scripture while also marshaling Roman history and the medieval example of Joan of Arc.[41] At the center of the argument, the committee called on readers to transcend the joining of associations and engage in petitioning as an act of spreading knowledge:

> But be not satisfied by merely setting your names to a constitution—this is a very little thing. . . .
>
> The seeds of knowledge must be sown broad-cast over our land—light must be increased a thousand-fold—and woman ought to be in this field: it is *her duty, her privilege* to labor in it, "as woman never yet has labored."
>
> By spreading correct information on the subject of slavery, you will prepare the way for the circulation of numerous petitions, both to the ecclesiastical and civil authorities of the nation.[42]

In what amounted to a vast battle over northern public sentiment and the future of women in politics, John Calhoun and South Carolina politicians placed a massive bet, Angelina Grimké and her sisterhood countered, and women's conquest changed American political history. Calhoun expected that the petition gag would dishearten abolitionists; instead, it triggered the largest and most transformative petitioning campaign in American political history. The response of tens of thousands of northern women and men to the gag rule, a response unfolding in the Twenty-Fifth Congress (the first full Congress under the gag rule), greatly expanded the theater of the antislavery debate; portrayed southern defenders of slavery as fundamentally antirepublican and tyrannical; and mobilized American women, free Blacks, and slavery's skeptics as never before.

Northern antislavery societies insisted on petitioning more, not less, in view of the gag. The American Anti-Slavery Society issued *An Appeal to the People of the United States* (1836), stoking outrage over the violation of a cherished republican principle and a First Amendment right.[43] The *Liberator* of June 23, 1837, republished another society appeal, which claimed that "the right of petition is one of the most sacred ever enjoyed by man. When that is lost, there is little left in civil government which is valuable. In this country, that right is now jeopardized,—yea, well nigh destroyed. The time to exercise it the most effectually is when it is endangered."[44] The former Kentucky slaveowner James Birney, now converted to abolition and soon to take an ever more instrumental role in its political expansion, argued that the gag rule should be met with "every effort" to continue the memorial campaign for District abolition. As the North saw the "rabid contempt" with which petitioning was being treated by the people's House, he presaged, public sentiment would change. Both by appealing to political indignation and by means of proselytizing soul by soul, Birney thought, petitioning "would give us a great means of moving people."[45]

From 1836 onward, antislavery petitioning exploded in the United States. At least 5,437 antislavery petitions were sent to the Twenty-Fifth House (March 1837 to February 1839), with another 1,600 sent to the Twenty-Sixth House (March 1839 to February 1841).

The frenzy of antislavery petitioning swept the North from 1837 to 1839 (see Figure 10.1). Almost the entirety of Massachusetts witnessed high per capita signature rates, as did southern New Hampshire and northern Vermont as well as Rhode Island and eastern Connecticut. Populations in Boston, New York, and Philadelphia were also active in petitioning and signing. Yet the spatial diffusion of antislavery petitioning points to ongoing transformations in central and western New York State as well as western Pennsylvania, wide swaths of Ohio and Indiana, southern Michigan, and northern and western Illinois.

Due mainly to antislavery memorials, the Twenty-Fifth Congress, which ran from March 1837 to March 1839, became the nominal high point of petitioning (the number of petitions sent to a given Congress) to that point in American history (see Figure 2.2). The Twenty-Fifth Congress still remains the historical peak of American per capita petitioning activity. Over half of the petitions sent to that Congress that were mentioned in legislative journals concerned slavery. The Panic of 1837 and the widening economic dislocation of women's and men's lives also helped to account for the surge.

The numbers both bespoke and concealed a deeper transformation in petitioning politics, one that had commenced before but that attained new heights in 1837. The Twenty-Fifth Congress witnessed the most dramatic expansion of women's political activity in American political history to that date. The indignation of the gag rule and the clarion call from Grimké and her collaborators at the 1837 convention, combined with the Grimké sisters' speaking tour through the northern states, lifted women's political activity to new numerical heights and to unprecedented geographic and socioeconomic breadth.[46]

The response to the gag rule issued in a change in petitioning tactics that emphasized short prayers that could be read aloud on the House floor before Adams, Slade, or another sponsor was shouted down or procedurally

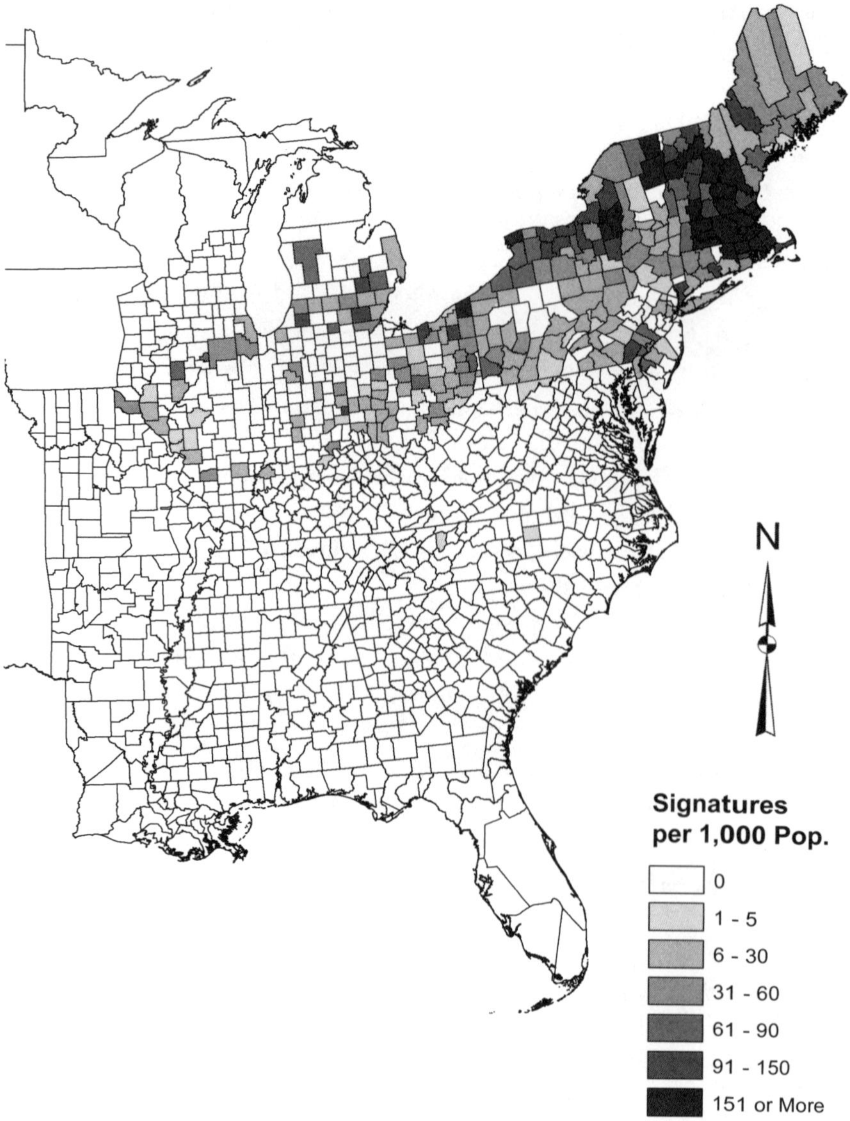

FIGURE 10.1. Geographic Distribution of Antislavery Petition Signatures to U.S. House, 25th Congress (1837–1839). *Credit:* Daniel Carpenter and Colin D. Moore, "When Canvassers Became Activists: Antislavery Petitioning and the Political Mobilization of American Women," *American Political Science Review* 108, no. 3 (August 2014): 479–498. Used by permission of Cambridge University Press.

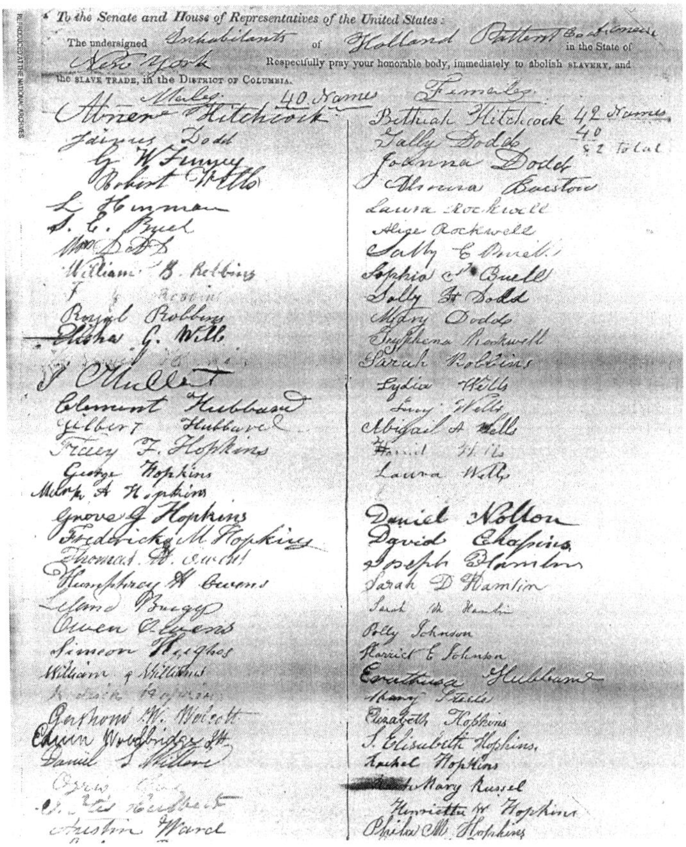

To the Senate and House of Representatives of the United States:

The undersigned Inhabitants of Holland Patent in the State of New York Respectfully pray your honorable body, immediately to abolish SLAVERY, and the SLAVE TRADE, in the DISTRICT OF COLUMBIA.

Males 40 Names | Females 42 Names

FIGURE 10.2. Antislavery Petition, New York, 25th Congress, with Short-Form Prayer and Sex-Separated Columns. *Credit:* Record Group 233, National Archives and Records Administration.

braked by southern Democrats (see Figure 10.2). The short prayer forms were issued in a circular, reprinted in the *Liberator,* and available by request from the American Anti-Slavery Society's headquarters. The circular offered six ready-to-cut prayers to Congress, each of a sentence or two, to be pasted onto blank sheets of paper for signature collection. Another five prayers—calling for state declarations as to Congress's constitutional power over slavery, restriction of fugitive slave law enforcement, and repeal of all state statutes "which make any distinction among its inhabitants, on account of color"—were to be sent to state legislatures.[47]

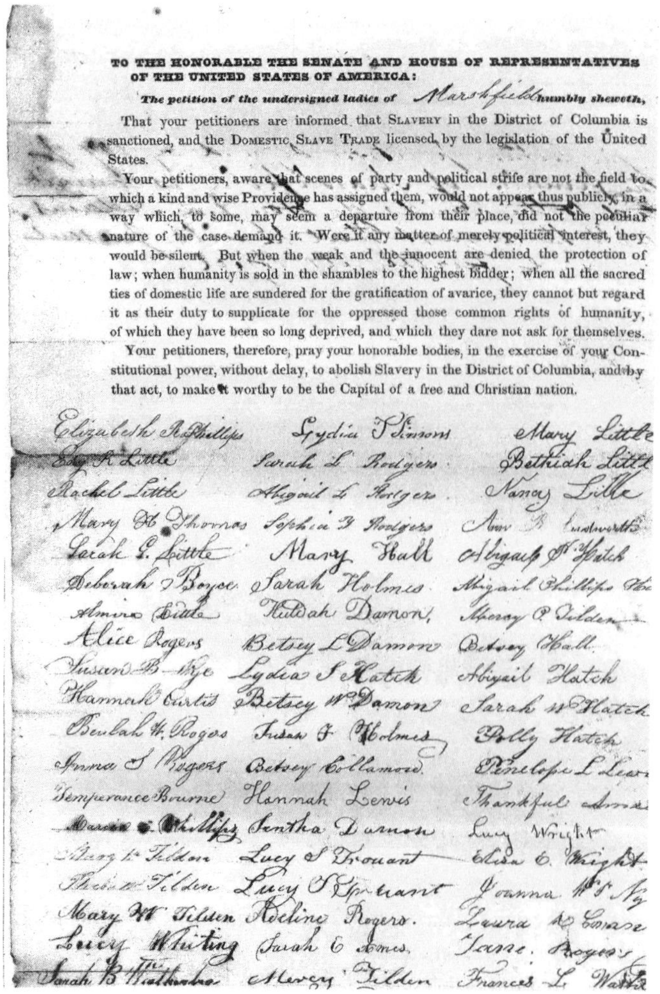

TO THE HONORABLE THE SENATE AND HOUSE OF REPRESENTATIVES OF THE UNITED STATES OF AMERICA:

The petition of the undersigned ladies of Marshfield *humbly sheweth,*

That your petitioners are informed that SLAVERY in the District of Columbia is sanctioned, and the DOMESTIC SLAVE TRADE licensed, by the legislation of the United States.

Your petitioners, aware that scenes of party and political strife are not the field to which a kind and wise Providence has assigned them, would not appear thus publicly, in a way which, to some, may seem a departure from their place, did not the peculiar nature of the case demand it. Were it any matter of merely political interest, they would be silent. But when the weak and the innocent are denied the protection of law; when humanity is sold in the shambles to the highest bidder; when all the sacred ties of domestic life are sundered for the gratification of avarice, they cannot but regard it as their duty to supplicate for the oppressed those common rights of humanity, of which they have been so long deprived, and which they dare not ask for themselves.

Your petitioners, therefore, pray your honorable bodies, in the exercise of your Constitutional power, without delay, to abolish Slavery in the District of Columbia, and by that act, to make it worthy to be the Capital of a free and Christian nation.

FIGURE 10.3. Women's Antislavery Petition, Massachusetts, 25th Congress. *Credit:* Record Group 233, National Archives and Records Administration.

The society's 1837 circular expressed the petition as a form of political experiment. The question of District abolition was the first petition prayer presented. "That is now a test question," the circular asserted. "As it shall be decided, so will be the fate of liberty in this nation."[48] District abolition was considered to be the most moderate of antislavery prayers and the one most likely to gain signatures (see Figure 10.3 for an example). Along with

District abolition were prayers for ending the internal slave trade (between the states) and memorials against the admission of Florida and Texas. The circular advised agents to circulate the prayers separately so as to permit those who wished to sign one prayer but not another to exercise their discretion in doing so. As agents learned of the wishes of their community, they could proceed to further requests.

The circular also advanced new petitioning tactics. It echoed Grimké's appeal for women's entrance into petitioning, saying that "every man and woman should be an agent."[49] Each agent so enrolled should "commence obtaining names 'immediately,' and to canvass your town thoroughly." Even as the circular emphasized the maximization of numbers—Congress "is more powerfully moved by large numbers, than by strong arguments"—it also counseled canvassers to march exhaustively through their environs in search of signatures and converts. "Leave not a person uninvited," the society counseled, even those deemed "incorrigible." Canvassers were warned to have each signatory sign his or her own name, so as to reduce opportunities for slavery's defenders to claim fraud or misrepresentation. Each blank page signed to a given prayer would then be glued to another, and the resulting concatenation of paper would produce a list of names hundreds, even thousands, of souls long.[50]

Evidence from narratives and from aggregate statistics suggests that the society's counsel was followed, with transformative effects witnessed in registers both micro- and macroscopic. As women sprinted into canvassing in particular, they often worked by lining up signatures from their relatives—mothers inducing daughters to sign and canvass with them, going to other women in their neighborhood. Mary Avery White of Boylston, Massachusetts, wrote that, on June 30, 1837, her own daughter "Mary took a circuit round the Neighbourhood with petition for the Abolition of Slavery in the district of Columbia & a remonstrance against the annexation of Texas to the United States as a Slaveholding territory." Two weeks later, on July 14, daughter Mary again carried an antislavery petition, this time to "to Miss Lucy Goodenow to circulate for subscribers."[51] Before and after these canvassing activities, the elder Mary attended antislavery lectures and concerts, including the lecture tour by the Grimké sisters in October 1837. The various events of antislavery life, including church services themselves, became opportunities for the extension of the canvas, and once a woman's friend had signed, she became a potential canvasser herself.[52]

The Weston sisters of Boston also detailed their endeavors in 1837. They recounted how they often went canvassing after church, getting a handful of names at a time, and that on any number of days the solemn performance of duty nonetheless brought "fatigue and embarrassment." Embarrassment came in part because many households were not ready to sign antislavery petitions, Lucia Weston reporting in March 1837 that one woman "of the elite" had "almost turned her out of the house" during a solicitation. The social tension involved in canvassing, the argumentation with friends and neighbors or with those unknown, added to the sheer physicality of the endeavor. "Thursday forenoon I wore myself out petitioning," wrote Anne Weston to her sister Deborah in September. Deborah could sympathize. Two years later she would recount that the numerical successes of the antislavery canvass felt, in some respects, like debilitating failures. In a deeply evangelical mode, every signature was like a soul to be saved, and Deborah Weston always yearned for more:

> I could only get 25 names to the women's petition & I could have got no more I think if I had had ever so much time. William Coffin got a good many more to the men's petition—many signing it were not abolitionists. I am very busy now with the "gag" petition. There are about 250 names I suppose on the men's, scarcely anyone refusing—I have got 82 to the women's & every one of them I got with my own feet and hands. . . . I have calculated that I walk at the rate of 21 miles a week.[53]

Deborah Weston's twenty-one miles per week, a sheer length that she repeated for month after month, were trodden in a world without sidewalks, without pavement, and with wooden shoes, and often through mud and unplowed snow.

The work of canvassing entailed a kind of social surveillance. In a world shot through with familial, neighborhood, and economic connections, canvassers and others noticed when a citizen's name was on a petition and when it was not. "Tell Mrs. Emerson that I did not see her name on the petition," wrote Anne Weston to Deborah in September 1837, "tho' I found sundry ones that I know."[54] Once completed, a canvassed petition was often displayed in a public setting (a church, perhaps) before or even after being sent to Congress. William Duvall of Port Bryon sent a petition to Vermont representative William Slade in January 1839, but the petition's signatures were written entirely in his hand. The reason, for Duvall, was simple. He had kept the original in his possession as an antislavery society officer. The impera-

TABLE 10.1 Signature Averages by Sex for Petitions Sent to 25th and 26th U.S. House, 1837–1841

Prayer Theme	Average Signatures	Average Women's Signatures	Average Men's Signatures
District Abolition (2,531 petitions)	110.8	66.3	44.7
Territories (890)	120.6	72.4	48.3
New States (1,093)	103.7	45.8	57.5
Texas (2,131)	106.4	59.8	46.6
Florida (611)	103.4	48.6	55.1
Slave Trade (1,341)	94.6	42.5	52.2
Gag Rule (1,626)	90.4	35.2	55.6

Note: Men's and women's rows do not add up perfectly because of rounding and because some petitions (less than 3 percent for each theme) do not tabulate by sex. Some petitions have more than one theme in prayer. *Source:* Congressional Antislavery Petitions Database, Harvard University; RG 233, NA.

tives of local organization could outweigh the legitimacy of showing a petition to Congress with individualized signatures.[55]

All told, the antislavery petitions sent to the House during the Twenty-Fifth and Twenty-Sixth Congresses (March 1837 to March 1841) totaled at least 745,000 signatures (just over 598,000 in the Twenty-Fifth Congress alone), with at least 367,000 women's signatures and 364,000 men's signatures. These aggregates exclude the vast petitioning activity directed at the Senate and at state legislatures, for which comprehensive data on signatures do not yet exist. Because many people signed more than one petition, the number of signatories is considerably lower than that for signatures but likely entails hundreds of thousands of men and women.

Women did tend to sign some kinds of petitions more than others and more so than men (Table 10.1). For petitions calling for District abolition, women's signatures outnumbered men's by about twenty per petition, while for petitions calling for the exclusion of slavery from the territories, the difference was twenty-four. Men's names were more numerous on the signatory lists of petitions against new slave states and against the interstate slave trade.

The surge in petitioning activity was about slavery and its victims but also petitioning itself. Petitions concerning the gag rule grew from the late Fourteenth Congress but swelled in the middle of the Twenty-Fifth, and prayers against the gag rule found special popularity among men. Deborah Weston had remarked in 1840 that the gag rule petition had made her "very busy," and her experience—with 250 men signing and 82 women signing—was not unusual. Town by town, county by county, men in the Twenty-Fifth and Twenty-Sixth Congresses added twenty more signatures, on average, to a petition whose prayer protested, or called for a repeal of, the gag rule. It is not so much that women refused to sign gag rule petitions—the Grimké sisters added their own signatures to them in 1837—than that women's activities were more heavily focused on other causes. Antipathy toward the gag rule brought heretofore little-mobilized men into the antislavery fold.[56]

The aggregate patterns suggest a story not only of women signing in greater numbers but also of women canvassing with particular zeal and efficacy. Women-only petitions and petitions with sex-separated columns are brute indicators of women's canvassing activity, and township by township and county by county, these petitions systematically displayed higher signature totals. Petitions that did not involve women circulating to other women averaged 84.9 names per petition. To this baseline, petitions circulated by women among women garnered 76 additional names on average, compared to other petitions circulating through the same geographic location at the same time, a 90 percent increase over the baseline. Yet it was during the Twenty-Fifth Congress (1837–1839) that these effects became apparent, not before. Compared to petitions in the Twenty-Third and Twenty-Fourth Congresses, women's-only petitions circulated in the Twenty-Fifth Congress averaged nearly one hundred more signatories than did male-only petitions circulated through the same localities. An examination of signature aggregates by county (which permits a control for population) suggests a similar boost in women's canvassing efficiency. From the Twenty-Third to the Twenty-Eighth Congress, the level of antislavery petition signatures per 1,000 county residents averaged 13.7 per Congress. A standard-deviation increase in the percentage of women's-only petitions was associated with 9.7 to 10.6 additional signatures per 1,000 county residents, an increase of 70 to 77 percent from the baseline. Whether measured petition by petition or county by county and controlling for population, women's canvassing nearly doubled the harvest of signatures.[57]

Canvassing represented an important part, but hardly the whole, of women's work. After the signatures were harvested, women did most of the hard work of making a backup copy of the petition, gluing different pages of signatures together, and sending the petition to elected officials. In town after town throughout the northern states, men's antislavery activity had declined in the early 1830s, but 1836 and 1837 witnessed a frenzy led by women. As Sarah and Angelina Grimké toured New England in 1836 and 1837, antislavery petitioning exploded. A statewide petition drive launched in Providence, Rhode Island, in 1838 garnered six thousand signatures and launched an initiative to organize a women's auxiliary in every town in the state. Rhode Island women thought consciously and at length about the canvassing strategies they employed. Their circulars urged women to rely on their informal connections as well as their family networks. Whereas they had previously laid out petitions at church and society meetings, Rhode Island women began walking petitions door to door. Women's initiative in the work of canvassing rendered Rhode Island antislavery work an act and a process of evangelical labor with local targets and aspirations.[58]

The transformation of petition canvassing led by women emerged more starkly in New York than anywhere else, though less in the Empire State's sprawling city than in its central and western reaches. From Albany to Buffalo and especially along the Erie Canal, where petition forms as well as new consciousness transited rapidly, women's activity in petitioning erupted. New York women focused explicitly on numbers, one of them maintaining that "if the prayers of five hundred inhabitants will turn the scale in favor of liberty, the slave's Jubilee is at hand." Led by the antislavery periodical the *Friend of Man,* central New York citizens followed closely the debate over the gag rule in Congress. The gag rule led central and western New Yorkers to consider the formation of antislavery candidacies and organizations separate from the Democratic or Whig parties as early as the fall of 1837. The *Friend of Man* published three petition forms for widespread use in the fall of 1838, and the newspaper also distributed speeches of Adams and Slade defending the right to petition. Even as their aims encompassed political and ecclesiastical organization, rural New Yorkers agreed with the sentiment that "petitioning stands among the first of anti-slavery instrumentalities."[59]

The New York experience suggests that the petitioning campaigns of the late Twenty-Fourth and Twenty-Fifth Congresses facilitated the development of antislavery societies. As a matter of precedent (though not necessarily of causality), petitioning anticipated the formation of new antislavery organization chapters and auxiliaries, more so than the other way around. Those counties where more petitioning occurred also saw the highest growth of antislavery organization until 1840, even when previous antislavery organization is taken into account. In other areas, too, ranging from Rhode

Island to Salem, New Jersey, petitioning campaigns preceded the formation of antislavery associations or coincided with them. Consistent with this dynamic, antislavery candidates who ran for office in 1838 did not fare well in central and western New York; only after the cementing and growth of associations during the petitioning surge of the Twenty-Fifth Congress and the organization of indignation over the gag rule did antislavery political organizations begin to emerge in 1839.[60]

Compared to newspaper subscriptions and group building, petitioning had several advantages as a recruitment and mobilization strategy. The petitions calling for District abolition, for territorial restriction, or for reversal of the gag rule were not considered radical at a time when the word "abolitionist" was out of favor in much of the northern states. At a time when Garrison—known more than anything else for his editorship of the *Liberator* and his alliance with other newspaper editors—was considered a quack or a seditious rebel by many citizens, contemporaries remarked that newspapers were not effective tools with which to attract people to the cause. Antislavery petitions asked the citizen to sign a more moderate prayer, which did not, in and of itself, commit the signatory to more radical positions but which did convey information about likely supporters to local associations.[61]

Angelina Grimké's leading role in the organization and appeal for petitioning soon led to another democratizing moment. A petitioning campaign aimed at the Massachusetts General Court deposited memorials with the signatures of twenty thousand women, Black and White. The memorials asked the Massachusetts government to formally endorse District abolition, among other measures. The sisters Grimké had lectured widely in the northern states in the summer and fall of 1837, a tour spanning twenty-three weeks, with at least eighty-eight meetings in sixty-seven different towns. Arriving in Boston in February 1838, Angelina was asked to present the petitions to the general court. Her speech on February 21, 1838, was scheduled before the senate but attracted such interest and crowds that it was moved to the house. It was the first invited address by a woman before a state or national legislative body in the United States. Grimké marked the moment by noting its historicity, but the central move of her address was to present petitions:

> I stand before you as a citizen, on behalf of the 20,000 women of Massachusetts, whose names are enrolled on petitions which have been submitted to the Legislature of which you are the organ. These petitions relate to the great

> and solemn subject of American slavery,—a subject fraught with the deepest interest to this republic, whether we regard it in its political, moral, or religious aspects. And because it is a *political* subject, it has often been tauntingly said, that woman has nothing to do with it. Are we aliens, because we are *women*? Are we bereft of citizenship, because we are the mothers, wives, and daughters of a mighty people? Have women *no* country—*no* interests staked in public weal—no liabilities in common peril—no partnership in a nation's guilt and shame?[62]

Grimké understood well the private, religious spheres of activity to which women were relegated at the time. In recasting the petitions and the twenty thousand signatures of women as citizen acts, she redefined what was political. With her address and, before that, the mass of signed petitions, American women had already made an entrance into politics. The question was whether American men would recognize it as such. "I hold, Mr. Chairman, that American women have to do with this subject, not only because it is moral and religious, but because it is *political*, inasmuch as we are citizens of this republic, and as such, *our* honor, happiness, and well being, are bound up in its politics, government, and laws."[63]

When two weeks later the *Liberator* took note of Grimké's address, it published her remarks and noted her argumentation about the merits of the petitions. The presentation of petitions acknowledged as women's memorials remained, to Angelina Grimké and to Garrison, inseparable from her chamber speech and her lecture circuit with her sister Sarah.[64]

Grimke's address in February 1838 brought condemnation, just as her lecture tour had done when she addressed audiences of men and women alike. Yet for one letter writer to the *Liberator* (probably Maria Weston Chapman), the most striking thing about the day was the decorum with which Grimké was received. The orator addressed a large crowd, but under the auspices of a committee hearing (the Legislative Committee on Slavery). Her allies present that day feared disruptions and interference, but "their fears were not realized. Well might her heart and her voice grow strong as she went on, to feel herself sustained by their unuttered prayer."[65] Indeed, the audience listened respectfully, and the only violation of decorum (which occasioned the chairman's gavel and a verbal warning) came in the form of applause: "With the best possible disposition to obey the genius of the place, the audience was more than once impelled, by the force of sympathy, to rise out of its cloak of invisibility."[66]

Angelina Grimké's February 1838 address demonstrated not merely a politics of audacity but a legitimacy of venues and their solemn receipt of petitions. Far from interjecting her voice in an unwilling chamber, Angelina Grimké spoke by invitation. Those who objected composed a distinct minority and lay silent. Just as the *Liberator* had noted the dignity and listening posture with which the Massachusetts legislature had received the Wampanoag five years before in the midst of the Mashpee Revolt, so too Maria Weston Chapman observed the willing ears of the legislature as a woman addressed a committee hearing by invitation, conveying in a rhetorical and visual swoop the voices of twenty thousand other women.

As abolitionist women unsettled and reordered American citizenship, their work brought fierce criticism, not least from other women. The rift that opened about and among women would prove to be enduring and diffusive. Condemning the "disorganization and anarchy" witnessed in the emergence of women's petitioning and speaking, Protestant ministers and seminarians throughout the northern states denounced the memorials to Congress and state legislatures, the Grimké lecture tour, and the arguments about women's citizenship carried in these endeavors. The renowned educator and social reformer Catherine Beecher composed her *Essay on Slavery and Abolitionism, with Reference to the Duty of American Females* (1837) as a targeted affront to Angelina Grimké's appeal for women's petitioning. "Petitions to congress, in reference to the official duties of legislators, seem IN ALL CASES," Beecher intoned, "to fall entirely without the sphere of female duty."[67] Women should exercise influence on men, Beecher agreed, but only in the venue of the home, not in the venue of the legislature. Grimké's response to Beecher, published in 1838, emphasized a larger ethic of equality. "The right of petition is the only political right that women have," she wrote. "Why not let them exercise it whenever they are aggrieved?"[68] Women had at least the permission to petition given the lessons of the American Revolution, wherein those who lived under the weight of taxation and property laws in which they had no say "ought to be permitted at least to remonstrate against every political measure that may tend to injure and oppress our sex."[69] Grimké converted a constraint into a felt duty. Speaking at Philadelphia's Pennsylvania Hall in May 1838, she again insisted that women had not merely permission but an obligation to petition Congress: "Especially, let me urge you to petition. Men may settle these and other questions at the ballot box, but you have no such right. It is only through our petitions that you can reach the Legislature. It is, therefore, peculiarly your duty to petition." As Grimké delivered these words, an angry mob of anti-abolitionist men assembled outside and began shattering the windows with rocks. The decorum she had experienced at the Massachusetts General Court would not be accorded at the Second Anti-Slavery Convention of American Women. Pennsylvania Hall would be torched the following night.[70]

The aspirational and physical presence of women—first in petitioning, then in lecturing and as voting members of antislavery societies—soon split the abolitionist movement itself. Debate erupted within the councils of the American Anti-Slavery Society over whether women's role was a distraction from what male leaders considered the higher goal of immediate abolition, or whether (as Garrison and his followers believed) women's liberation came of a piece with that of the slave. Garrison's advocacy for women's rights brought him condemnation from ministers who saw the editor advancing decidedly anti-Christian doctrine. When at the 1840 meeting of the American Anti-Slavery Society Garrison and his allies nominated Abby Kelley to the society's business committee and she won the initial vote, forces opposed to Garrison led a mass walkout. The society had "blown up," "exploded," on the Kelley issue, remarked the society's stunned members. Other antislavery associations in Boston and New England also split, though others (as in Pennsylvania) remained largely intact. In critical respects, these fissures of gender arose because of the petitioning transformation. Kelley's initial antislavery work in Lynn—petitioning—had come in response to the Grimké sisters' lecture tour. She, like other petitioning women, now wanted a role in governance.[71]

The schism of antislavery associations ran alongside a partial withdrawal of women from petitioning activity and toward a more private and local realm of activity. Antislavery fairs became a crucial site of ongoing activity, where an alternative vision of economic production, social gathering, and even consumption took root. While the volume of petitioning declined, it did not stop, and the petitioning to state legislatures grew, even as the volume of documents conveyed to Washington declined to a level still above that witnessed in the Twenty-Third Congress. Taking stock of the movement in 1847, William Lloyd Garrison credited women with the success of the antislavery enterprise.[72]

By the time the society had ruptured in 1840, its patterns of growth had reflected the rhythms and patterns of congressional petitioning. Both in time and space, chapter growth was tightly coupled with petitioning campaigns. From 1832 to 1838, monthly chapter foundings more than doubled when Congress was in session and petitions were being introduced or, after

TABLE 10.2 The Organizational Legacy of America's Antislavery Petitioning Surge

a. Antislavery parties in northern states, 1844 and 1848 general elections[1]

Northern states only	County-level per-capita antislavery petition signatures for selected Congress				
	24th Congress (1835–37)	**25th Congress (1837–39)**	26th Congress (1839–41)	27th Congress (1841–43)	28th Congress (1843–45)
Pairwise correlation with 1844 Liberty Party (Birney) presidential vote (county %)	0.08 $p=0.076$	**0.16 p = 0.003**	−0.09 $p=0.04$	0.003 $p=0.95$	−0.08 $p=0.08$
Pairwise correlation with 1848 Free-Soil (Van Buren) presidential vote (county %)	−0.03 $p=0.52$	**−0.01 p = 0.82**	0.03 $p=0.48$	0.03 $p<0.53$	−0.03 $p=0.48$
Pairwise correlation with 1848 Free-Soil congressional vote (county %)	0.13 $p=0.004$	**0.32 p < 0.001**	−0.02 $p=0.66$	−0.01 $p=0.88$	−0.06 $p=0.15$

Additional percentage point in Birney 1844 county vote for every additional 25th Congress antislavery signatory per 1,000 county population, multivariate regression	1.41 $p<0.001$
Additional percentage point in Free-Soil 1848 county vote for every additional 25th Congress antislavery signatory per 1,000 county population, multivariate regression	1.12 $p=0.01$

b. American Anti-Slavery Society (AASS) chapters and members[2]

	Congress out of session	Congress in session	Difference
AASS chapter creation, June 1832—May 1838	6.87 chapters / month	14.72 chapters / month	7.85 $p<0.01$

TABLE 10.2 (continued)

Seasonally adjusted difference			5.34 $p=0.07$
AASS chapter memberships, 1838	Founded out of session 424.7	Founded during session 1,104.9	649.2 $p<0.001$
Seasonally adjusted difference			518.2 $p=0.02$
Pairwise correlation between county-level AASS chapters (1840) and county-level petitioning (1837–1839), New York State			0.38 $p=0.001$

1. Northern states (all eventual Confederate states and Kentucky, Maryland, and Tennessee are excluded). Counties are defined by 1840 census; $n=480$. Multivariate regressions include controls for county population, capital, labor and agriculture aggregates, and sex and age composition. For multivariate regressions demonstrating robustness of associations, see Carpenter, "Recruitment by Petition: American Antislavery, French Protestantism, English Suppression," *Perspectives on Politics* 14 (3) (September 2016), 700–723, Table 1.

2. $n=71$ months; seasonally adjusted difference is coefficient from regression of chapter creation or memberships upon in-session indicator, with 12 monthly controls.

the gag rule, blocked (see Table 10.2). Indeed, it was the first few petition-heavy months of the congressional calendar (December and January) that brought peaks of chapter foundings from 1832 through 1838. Accordingly, after the gag rule was adopted in May 1836, the establishment of American Anti-Slavery Society chapters did not explode until the rule was adopted and enforced in the second session of the Twenty-Fourth Congress in December 1836 and January 1837. Calendar year 1837 was the single strongest year of antislavery chapter founding and membership growth in the society's history. Beyond these temporal patterns, antislavery petitioning to the Twenty-Fifth Congress also anticipated the geographical spread of American Anti-Slavery Society chapters. Even once previous chapter aggregates are accounted for, petitioning in the Twenty-Fifth Congress strongly anticipated chapter growth in New York counties.[73]

The 1840s brought new forms of organized antislavery, including the first national political parties to espouse antislavery platforms. Former Kentucky slaveholder James Birney ran on the presidential ticket for the Liberty Party in 1840 and amassed 6,797 votes nationwide, but when Birney led a better organized campaign in 1844, the Liberty ticket garnered 62,103 votes (over

2 percent of the national popular vote). Many Whigs thought Birney's campaign had plausibly tipped New York's electoral votes—and thus the general contest—from Henry Clay to James K. Polk. (In fact other factors had also intervened, including tariff politics and Whig troubles with immigrant voters in the mid-Atlantic states.) The Liberty Party's 1844 campaign had leveraged new organization, new activist energy, and a network of abolitionist newspapers. Party leaders like Alvan Stewart saw petitioning as meek and proclaimed the need to coalesce the so-called nonpolitical wing of abolitionism (led by Garrison and many radicals) with those interested in formal politics. To accomplish this, Liberty Party activists used petitioning campaigns in the 1840s as a way to build their organization, to such an extent that Garrison accused Liberty men of exploiting for "partisan gain" an important Massachusetts mobilization (in defense of the free Black man George Latimer) in 1842. While the 1844 results were sobering for many—and not entirely surprising given Garrison's avowed distaste for the party—Liberty leaders noted that of the 501 counties in free states in 1844, the Liberty ticket had picked up votes in all but a hundred of them.[74]

That county-level harvest in 1844 reflected the seeds of antislavery petitioning labor that had swelled seven years before in the Twenty-Fifth Congress. Accounting for a range of social and economic factors, including patterns of Liberty Party congressional voting in 1842, those counties where petitioning grew more between the Twenty-Fourth and Twenty-Fifth Congresses in the 1830s were counties that witnessed a systematic upswing of Liberty Party voting in 1844. This pattern evinced a deep mutual embedding of petitioning and electoral politics. The 1844 campaign rested on an emerging set of local alliances between political and Garrisonian antislavery men, and in part because antislavery newspapers (which had printed abolition petition prayer forms) figured so vitally in 1844, petitions had literally brought political men disgusted with the gag rule and Garrisonian radicals onto the same page.

Until the demise of the Whigs in 1856 and the cementing of the Republican Party's status as the Democrats' primary opposition that year, antislavery party campaigns would confront the limits of the Liberty Party's mobilization in 1844. Like the Liberty Party's peak, the Free-Soil Party's peak in 1848 would demonstrate a remarkable association with the surge of petition signing a decade before. Presidential candidate Martin Van Buren received no electoral votes, but the party did elect candidates to Congress—two senators and fourteen House members. The party's congressional vote at the county level was strikingly anticipated by the petition mobilizations of the Twenty-Fifth Congress (see Table 10.2). The very locales where Van Buren did the most damage to the Democratic ticket of Lewis Cass—such as northern-central New York's Oneida, Lewis, and Jefferson Counties—had witnessed abundant antislavery petitioning ten years before. Critically, important Free-Soil converts like Joshua Giddings had steeled their antislavery commitments during the gag rule crisis; Giddings's own efforts brought the gag rule to an end in the Twenty-Eighth Congress, and his campaigning in Ohio assisted Salmon Chase's Senate victory there in 1848. Ohio women had also extensively petitioned churches for adoption of more rigid antislavery stances, and the new ecclesiastical periodicals that arose, such as the *True Wesleyan*, actively supported women's petitioning.[75]

What emerges from these geographic patterns is the historical legacy of congressional petitioning for antislavery party formation (see Table 10.2). At the county level, the petitioning intensity of the Twenty-Fifth Congress antislavery effort anticipates Liberty and Free-Soil voting substantially better than do the petitioning efforts of the early 1840s, which were temporally closer to the 1844 and 1848 elections. That antislavery petitioning reinforced ongoing and later political organization would have surprised few at the time. Those who fought for District abolition and against the gag rule saw their combat as being every bit as political as Angelina Grimké said it was. Even as they turned more to petitioning state legislatures in the early 1840s, abolitionists who began to consider political organization drew on the networks that had emerged in the Twenty-Fifth Congress. And among political elites, subtle tides began to turn, as "political abolitionists" could agree on opposition to the gag rule as much as anything else, constituency pressure against the gag rule mounted, and John Quincy Adams became the leader of the "conscience Whigs."[76]

The language of democracy was everywhere. The battle over the gag rule would continue through the early 1840s, and those who championed the abolitionist cause increasingly adopted the terms of equality, citizenship, and popular sovereignty. An abolitionist defending the right to petition wrote, "Our Government is a democracy. We, the farmers and mechanics, are the rulers. We are the governors—you, our servants."[77] In the signatures of women and men, and in the growing attachment of petition signers to associations (and of association joiners to petitioning), towns throughout the northern states saw working families enter into a new form of politics, with an emboldened public voice. Whether in Lynn, Massachusetts; Utica, New York; or Rochester and New York City, the congressional petitioning campaign saw masses of signatures from artisans and factory workers.[78]

THE MASS MOBILIZATION OF BLACK AMERICA

The narratives that accompanied this upwelling of antislavery petitioning—then and now—emphasized the labors of White women. Yet just as free Blacks had pioneered critical petitioning efforts for liberation and equality in the northern states and the British West Indies before 1830, so too did free Blacks' pioneering efforts continue during and after the gag rule controversy. Maria Stewart's open call for Black men to petition for District abolition and civic equality had come four years before Angelina Grimké's more famous missive. The 1840s saw an unprecedented level of mass petitioning among free Blacks in the northern states, and in this development, the logic of venues again played a critical role.[79]

What differed in most respects were the venues to which free Blacks petitioned. While leading midwestern Black abolitionists like Indiana's George DeBaptiste and William and Elijah Anderson had petitioned the Twenty-Fifth Congress, Black abolitionists were more likely to target state legislatures and municipal councils, as well as courts, in their efforts. In some ways, this differential targeting reflected the stakes of the matter. The Black abolitionist struggle had centered on issues—such as manumission, local emancipation, countering fugitive slave measures, laws for racial equality—that affected Black lives more directly and for which state legislatures were in the best position to deliver victories in law and right. In other ways, the relative predilection of White abolitionists to petition Congress while Black petitioners targeted state legislatures reflected a division of labor that unfolded both consciously and perhaps implicitly as well. Black and White allies joined together in many cities and towns, and in larger cities their signatures appear on the same petitions to state legislatures, yet rarely do they appear together on petitions to Congress. Still, the ideal of genuine and lasting interracial alliance remained elusive and came to fruition only locally.[80]

In several areas where free Blacks lived in large numbers, free Black antislavery petitioning surged in 1836 and 1837. Black activists in the southern and northern states had been active in antislavery petitioning, but the gag rule crisis brought a wave of mass signatures that appears far larger than any witnessed before. As before, free Blacks targeted more of their petitioning to state legislatures.

In Cincinnati, known as the "Queen of the West," a burgeoning Black community was targeted in the early 1800s by legislative regulation and, repeatedly from 1829 to 1841, racial violence. A set of coordinated attacks on Black households and businesses in 1829 was rightly termed a race war, and it led to a mass exodus of hundreds of families to Canada, where the emigrants founded a town named Wilberforce, after the British antislavery leader. Yet thousands of other free Blacks stayed, and especially after 1836 they composed, signed, and delivered many a petition to the Ohio General Assembly. Their chief target was the set of laws imposing "disabilities" on Blacks, especially the denial of work in trades and exclusion from schools. The volume produced by Black and White petitioning allies was sufficiently large that the House Judiciary Committee felt compelled to issue a report defending state apartheid, and on two occasions—in 1837 and again in 1839—the house voted to uphold Ohio's "Black Laws." Yet in the political battles of the 1830s, free Blacks in Ohio had begun to organize in ways that would facilitate their work in the underground railroad, bolster formal alliances with Quakers and other religious faiths, and pressure organized officials for new equality statutes. Legal discrimination (denial of voting rights and jury service, for example) would continue until well after the Civil War, but through repeated memorials, Blacks and their allies placed Black Law repeal on the legislative agenda from 1836 to 1848, and Ohio partially repealed its Black Laws in 1849.[81]

Black petitioning also surged in New York City in 1836, led by an activist clergy that sought to transcend the limits of Black association politics and to shape political agendas among White politicians. Black clergy had played important roles at the national Black conventions from 1831 to 1835, but New York City Black leaders, such as Samuel Cornish and Theodore Wright, felt these meetings to be insufficiently effective. Taking note of British abolition and following from the American Anti-Slavery Society's petition work—Cornish and Wright served on the society's executive committee—they launched a statewide petition campaign in late 1836. They founded the Black newspaper the *Weekly Advocate* (soon renamed the *Colored American*) in part to facilitate the petition campaign. A new series of mass meetings of free city Blacks began in 1837, and they initiated petitioning drives that would continue until the Civil War. Cornish took note of the petitioning endeavors in Ohio and, with Wright and others, established committees in each ward in the city to canvass for signatures. The 1837 petitions were signed by hundreds—620 men for Black male suffrage, along with over 400 Black women and men from Brooklyn, Albany, Troy, and other towns. Petitioners also aimed to repeal a law allowing slave owners to retain ownership of slaves after they entered New York, and asked for a guarantee of jury trial for those claimed to be fugitive slaves. The campaign leaders then formed a new group in 1838—the Association for Political Improvement of People of Color—which sought more durable ties with White abolitionists. The interracial harvest of Cornish, Wright, and their collaborators was plentiful; petitions signed by ninety-three hundred persons reached Albany in 1838. While these petition campaigns at first met with tabling by the New York legislature, their political transformations proved lasting. As the petitions gagged in Washington mobilized White women, the memorials of 1837–1838 brought hundreds of free Black men and women into politics.[82]

In Pennsylvania, efforts to insert the word "white" into the constitution's sections defining voting rights brought a mass mobilization of free Blacks and their allies in 1838. Robert Purvis authored his *Appeal of Forty Thousand Citizens, Threatened with Disfranchisement, to the People of Pennsylvania.* Purvis rendered his argument for Black citizenship not in the context of the United States but in the long republican tradition of the Pennsylvania Constitution. Racializing citizenship would, Purvis argued, invoke the specter of "dominion" by another class, which would rival the tyranny of an autocrat. "When a distinct class of the community, already sufficiently the objects of prejudice," he remonstrated, "are wholly, and for ever, disfranchised and excluded, to the remotest posterity, from the possibility of a voice in regard to the laws under which they live—it is the same thing as if their abode were transferred to the dominions of the Russian Autocrat, or of the Grand Turk. They have lost their check upon oppression, their wherewith to buy friends, their panoply of manhood; in short, they are thrown upon the mercy of a despotic majority."[83] On this occasion, though, the forces of despotism won. Voters ratified the Pennsylvania Constitution of 1838 by a narrow margin (113,971 in favor, 112,759 against). Petitioning to reverse the racial restrictions of the Pennsylvania Constitution would continue, led by Philadelphia's free Black community, but the community also became the target of anti-abolitionist and racist violence. African Americans in Pennsylvania would not gain voting rights until the ratification of the Fifteenth Amendment in 1870.[84]

In Massachusetts, Black women and men began signing petitions in greater numbers in the 1830s as well. Whereas lists of several to a few dozen Black signatories marked some of the petitions before 1836, the decades after the gag rule controversy correspond with signatory lists regularly

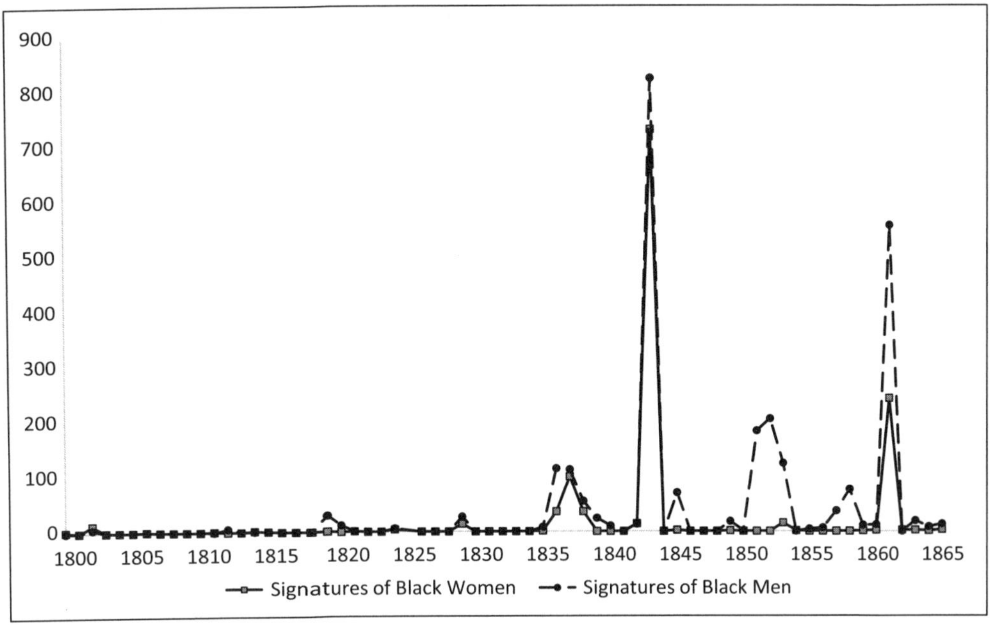

FIGURE 10.4. Signatures of Identified Black Women and Men on Civil Rights Petitions to Massachusetts Legislature, 1800–1865.

reaching into the hundreds (see Figure 10.4). As the Black organizational landscape changed in the 1830s, petitions from Black Americans began to reflect the organizational bases in which Black lives were lived, structured, and identified. The Boston Black leader William Cooper Nell led a petition from "Colored Citizens & Seamen of Boston" in 1837, which asked the legislature to allow for the free travel of Black sailors in slave states. The petition extended an earlier language of "color" as opposed to African-based identity, but it also connected the language of color with the language of citizen. At a time when major Black leaders (later Frederick Douglass himself) were calling for a demonstration of "respectability," petitions like Nell's connecting work to citizenship continued an earlier discourse of respectability but tied it to new anxieties, as southern states and slaveholders began pressing for new, nationalizing, and more oppressive measures designed to restrict the freedom of northern Blacks.[85]

Black women also petitioned in new modes and numbers, targeting not only antislavery politics but also church patriarchy. The controversy they triggered—among both White and Black men—testifies to the energy of their commitments. New Black women's antislavery organizations had emerged in the 1830s—created in Salem in 1832 and followed by others in Providence, Middletown, Nantucket, and Rochester—often preceding those of White women. With the upswing in abolitionist petitioning in 1837, Black women's petitions took aim at national slavery issues and exhibited ever larger signatory lists—for instance, the "Petition of Ruth C. Johnson and 106 Other Colored Ladies of Massachusetts on the Subject of Slavery and the Slave Laws" from 1837. This petition was sent to the legislature along with a similar petition from Black men, led by the prominent Black abolitionist Ezra R. Johnson, who later published *Emancipation Oration* and held a festival for the famed Fifty-Fourth Regiment of Massachusetts Union soldiers. Black women inspired by the itinerant preacher Julia A. J. Foote also petitioned for preaching licenses in the African Methodist Church in 1843, and while their prayers were denied, they stoked important debates about women's voices within churches that would be later echoed by advocates for woman suffrage.[86]

One of the largest petitioning mobilizations in any American state during the nineteenth century occurred when the agents of slave master James Gray seized the fugitive slave George Latimer in October 1842. The interracial abolition community in Boston had already created a Vigilance Committee to protect the city's free Black population. Led by William Cooper Nell, Latimer's allies surrounded the jail in which he was being held, secured a writ of habeas corpus for his transfer to a public jail, and, by November 18, won Latimer's release from jail. Eagerly seeking White signatories, Nell and his coalition then formed a Latimer Committee, which drafted and circulated what was known as the Latimer and Great Massachusetts Petition. The resulting petitions were rolled together into a large instrument of weight, totaling more than sixty-five thousand signatures. On March 24, 1843, the Massachusetts legislature passed the Latimer Law, a personal liberty statute that prohibited judges from hearing cases under the Fugitive Slave Act of 1791 and forbade state law officers from taking part in arrests of anyone suspected of being a fugitive. Northern states quickly adopted the Latimer Law as their model statute for personal liberty regimes.[87]

Yet as transformative as anything else was the sheer number of Black women and men who, in 1843, signed petitions, whether the Latimer prayer or others. That year also saw a battle within Black communities over laws banning interracial marriage. The antebellum period in Massachusetts was characterized by a "surplus" of Black men relative to Black women, leading to many Native women marrying Black men and, in 1843, a petition by Black men asking for marriage rights to White women. Black men's petitions for unlimited marriage rights were, of course, in part a strike against the racism of marriage laws, but Black women saw this initiative as a threat, and they responded with a petition of 114 signatories, led by Lucia Weston. Weston and her cosignatories argued that the measure would give more liberty to Black men than to Black women and would "exert a most pernicious influence on the condition of colored women." Lucia Weston's petition marked an early example of counterpetitioning in Black politics as well as a critical case of gender-based division within the Black Massachusetts public. The state legislature repealed the anti-miscegenation law. In all, Black women signed their names at least seven hundred times to petitions on civil rights in Massachusetts in 1843, while Black men's names appeared more than eight hundred times. Because many signatories affixed their names to petitions with self-identified racial categories, these figures likely understate substantially the breadth of Black petitioning. The unfolding numbers show not only that Black women and men were petitioning more but that they felt more comfortable in declaring themselves as Black signatories.[88]

Black counterpetitioning would continue, particularly against the initiatives of White racists. In the late 1850s, White Massachusetts citizens began to lobby the legislature for the repeal of personal liberty laws, passed in response to the Dred Scott decision. Arguing that they brought South Carolina–like shame on Massachusetts as a potential "nullifier" of the United States Constitution, these claimants called for compliance with the Fugitive Slave Act and the terms of the Scott decision. This brought forth some of the largest and most quickly drawn up petitions from Black Americans in the history of the commonwealth, including a series of three petitions signed by 169, 150, and 414 Black citizens, who explicitly identified themselves as "citizens." Unlike earlier Black petitions, these anti-repeal petitions were written entirely in manuscript and repeatedly invoked the citizenship status of Black Americans.[89]

The Dred Scott decision resulted from doctrinal and sectional collisions that were prompted in part by activism stemming from a distinctive Black legal culture. Slaves who petitioned and sued for freedom thrust slave law on the national agenda and reinforced the swelling sectional crisis. Black men and women, both slave and free, combined a variety of instruments—many of which were called "petitions," but they were legally distinct and targeted different venues—in the early Republic and antebellum period. Advocates like the free Black New Yorker Louis Napoleon often alternated among petitions for a writ of habeas corpus to courts, petitions to governors, and memorials to legislatures. In a different way and in a different legal system, Harriet Scott's appeal for liberty harnessed her networks at the Second African Baptist Church, where her minister, Reverend John Anderson, was accustomed to petitioning and legal action and where, through Anderson, she probably met Francis B. Murdoch, who from 1844 to 1846 launched more freedom petitions in St. Louis than any other attorney. Thousands of such freedom suits flowed to courts in the antebellum South.[90]

The possibilities of Black petitioning and political organization came starkly into view in the contrasting trajectories of Maryland and Virginia. In Virginia, White citizens began in the late 1840s to petition for a colonization plan that entailed "the removal of free negroes"—continuing a long campaign to legislate out of existence free Blacks that had taken off after the Nat Turner revolt—and the Virginia project soon received its own select committee and then a joint committee between the house and the senate. The committee, in turn, quickly met with more White petitions for Black removal. Momentum for free Black removal grew across the South. The Kentucky preacher W. S. Brown, in his *Plan of National Colonization* (1853), pointed to the rationale and scale of Indian removal in justifying a national plan of free Black expulsion. In February 1856, Virginia passed the nation's first so-called voluntary enslavement law. Six other states followed Virginia in the ensuing years. More than one hundred free Black women and men in Virginia, some only recently manumitted by deceased owners, applied for slavery under new masters from 1854 to 1864.[91]

In Maryland, where by 1850 over seventy-three thousand free people of color lived, the surge of people and of Black discretion disquieted Whites and the politicians who shared and exploited their fright. Grievances and proposals flowed in small but influential numbers from the 1840s onward to the state legislature, where a slaveholder-dominated Committee on the Colored Population passed laws defining and regulating the status of free Blacks. Both Maryland's constitutional convention of 1850–1851 and its state legislature in 1852 considered but repeatedly rejected a range of bills to tax, impose compulsory labor on, require bond from, otherwise regulate, and even expel free Blacks. An especially odious threat resurfaced in the February 1860 bill of Curtis Jacobs, chair of the Committee on the Colored Population, who proclaimed the right to reenslave free Blacks. The bill would outlaw manumission, require free Blacks to register with the state, and develop an expulsion and colonization program. A vigorous petitioning campaign with hundreds of Black signatories ensued, and the petitions were carried to Annapolis by George Alexander Hackett. In a partial victory, the Jacobs bill was jettisoned, and weakened measures were passed in its place. Stung by his failure, Jacobs threatened to leave the legislature. The ability of Maryland's free Black population to target a consequential venue—one in which they had no representation—with a concerted and multifaceted campaign bespoke a partial democratization of agendas and organization.[92]

Black counterpetitioning campaigns demonstrated that new forms of procedural and organizational democracy were emerging. This profound transformation of Black politics in Massachusetts and Maryland was echoed in Pennsylvania, New York, and Ohio. The evolution of counterpetitioning expressed new forms of consciousness and identity, but well beyond that, it reflected a set of highly efficacious political associations and networks. In order to follow developments in lawmaking and in White petitioning (and even other developments in Black petitioning), counterpetitioners had to take advantage of structures attuned to the nuances of legislative politics, structures with connections to White legislators, the very kinds of connections that Prince Hall had wished to foster in the Revolutionary and early national period. Then they had to mount an organizing drive of their own in order to demonstrate to the commonwealth legislature that an opposition existed, and that consciousness, strategy, and, indeed, organization lay behind that opposition.

DEMOCRACIES AND CLOSURES

ELEVEN

Women Contesting Collectively

Work, War, *Iglesia,* and the Ballot

Resolved, That the Female Labor Reform Association deeply deplore the lack of independence, honesty, and humanity in the committee to whom were referred sundry petitions relative to the hours of labor—especially in the chairman of that committee; and as he is merely a corporation machine, or tool, we will use our best endeavors and influence to keep him in the "city of spindles," where he belongs, and not trouble Boston folks with him.

—Eliza K. Hemmingway, resolution offered at the Lowell Female Labor Reform Association meeting, April 1, 1845, adopted unanimously

Long live religion and death to its enemies!

—Señoras of Mexico City, 1856

These petitions should be firm and uncompromising in tone; and a hearing should be demanded before Committees, specially empowered to consider and report upon them. In my judgment, the time is not distant, when such petitions will be granted, and when justice, the simple justice they ask, will be cordially, joyfully rendered

—William Channing (letter read by Antoinette Brown) on petitions for women's equality, at the 1853 Women's Rights Convention in Cleveland, Ohio

In spite of its renown as a democratizing moment, the early nineteenth century witnessed the ever more formal subjugation of millions of North American women. Women in the United States had scattered voting rights after the Revolution, a pattern ended when New Jersey amputated its "Petticoat Electorate" in 1807. For a generation thereafter, the exclusion of females from the electoral realm became more a matter of assumption than of argument. The 1840 transformation of dower in Lower Canada extended husbands' power over marital property. In the United States, a series of court decisions and state laws in the 1830s and 1840s confirmed and cemented the common-law doctrine of coverture by which married women relinquished property and income to their husbands. The extension of common-law principles to American jurisprudence reinforced women's dependent status within the household. Even as the independence campaign in Mexico courted women's energies, the state in postindependence Mexico consigned women to the domestic sphere.[1]

From the 1820s through the 1850s, North American women began to more systematically contest these institutions. They did so heterogeneously in time and national space, raising in Canada arguments different from those in the United States, and mobilizing far more in the northern and western American states than in slavery-based jurisdictions. In Mexico, the sphere of debate was much more heavily restricted, but women began signing mass memorials in ways that brought astonishment, affirmation, or ridicule (or all three), depending on the audience. The Seneca Falls Convention of 1848 became the focal event of American feminism. The Convention's Declaration of Sentiments outlined broad principles of gender equality and women's grievances. Echoing the catalog of grievances listed in the Declaration of Independence, the women of Seneca Falls declared that "mankind," acting with the singularity of George III, "has not ever permitted her to exercise her inalienable right to the elective franchise," that "He has compelled her to submit to laws, in the formation of which she had no voice," that "He has made her, if married, in the eye of the law, civilly dead," and that "He has taken from her all right in property, even to the wages she earns."[2]

Women petitioned in ways normal and radical throughout nineteenth-century North America. They had been petitioning for a century or more beforehand, often about their own condition. Yet in a moment of cultural and procedural democracy, a more individualized practice of supplication, occasionally rising to collective claims about the welfare of others, gave way from the 1820s to the 1850s to more assertive prayers contending for legal and constitutional equality. These prayers attracted the signatures of many thousands of women, and many men as well. In aggregate and in miniature, women's petitioning activity on issues of gender complicates the story of national and continental feminism. For one, the earliest North American petitions for woman suffrage came not from New York State before and after Seneca Falls, nor from the United States itself, but from Québec City in 1828. Canadian widows and their allies advanced republican principles in contrast to the more explicitly democratic logic that animated American women two decades later, but Québécoises and their male allies nonetheless put forth a remarkable argument, and their work ran alongside women's widespread participation in provincial elections for a time.[3]

The organizational democracy of American feminism also arrived through petitioning. Women's activism emerged and reproduced itself through associations; through writings, both published and private; through practices such as prayer and sewing circles, fairs, and concerts; and through political campaigns and concerted pressure in which women focused much of their effort on signed memorials. Petitions for women's citizenship followed from petitions over the slavery debate but also from petitions for penal reform, petitions for changes in labor practices, and steadfast opposition to wars of aggression. Especially in Massachusetts, New York, Pennsylvania, and Ohio, but extending throughout the northern and western states as well, women bundled together a range of issues that might otherwise have seemed separate.

Antagonism between Mexico and the United States—and the resulting war of 1846–1848—reshaped women's political participation on both sides of the border. In the United States, women led the petitions against the Mexican war much as they had impelled the mass antislavery drives of the previous decade, but with newfound argumentation. They built the broadest popular antiwar movement in American history to that time. In Mexico, the American invasion galvanized women's nationalism and a stronger alliance with, and role in, the Catholic Church. These seemingly conservative postures actually strengthened women's position in local and ecclesiastical politics, especially in the central *estados* of Guadalajara, Oaxaca, Puebla, and Veracruz. While no democratizing feminist movement emerged in Mexico at the time, the scale of women's petitioning was greatly expanded as women entered at once into debates over immigration and religious tolerance. In American culture, images of activist Mexican women spread widely, compelling a reexamination of femininity that reinforced the push for women's rights.[4]

Why did North American women turn so massively and radically to the petition to advance claims specifically about gender? The answer depends on the context, but in part, the emergence of intellectual feminism came from the very distinct sphere to which women had been systematically and ideologically confined. In the United States, the binary governing public life that relegated women to domesticity—often observed in the breach—gave them a consciousness of their plight and their capacity. Women's growing reliance on petitioning for explicit advancement of their rights came not only from their formal exclusion from the electoral realm but from the ways they newly used petitioning campaigns to organize and pressure both politicians and publics. Mexico's relegation of women to domesticity during the early decades of independence gave thousands of them space and status to make claims about Catholicism; immigration; and the deep connections of family, faith, and nationhood.[5]

The politics of venues also impelled women's petitioning on issues that more directly or officially affected them as women. Perhaps more than any other institution of American public life, county and state courts cemented the subservience of women—in North and South, in city and hamlet. The steady erosion of women's rights in the court system left early feminists and their allies with few better alternatives than to attempt to change state statutes and, beyond this, to shape legislative agendas. This turn to the legislature explains, along with the global antislavery campaign, why women's petitioning turned so heavily from the individual and supplicative to the collective and radical during the 1830s and 1840s, especially in the United States.

Beyond the court, the church—in so many incarnations—became a site of blockage and mobilization for millions of North American women. The reactionary posture of so many American, Canadian, and Mexican churches on issues of sexual equality, labor, political reform, and slavery created a target for women's activism. Women increasingly sought and carved out spaces in ecclesiastical institutions for devotional groups, charity associations, and networks of mobilization that verged on the explicitly and openly political. As the industrial and commercial economy both mobilized and demobilized men, so too did Protestant and Catholic churches begin to depend more heavily on women's energy and labor.

Women found in petitioning an instrument of politics with which they built alliances and networks. The associations that sprouted in the 1840s and 1850s had their roots in earlier organizations, yet as a consciousness of sex began to crystallize, these associations turned ever more to political pressure, to a diffusive and infectious form of campaigning that both mimicked and mocked the Jacksonian political style.[6] Their target was the legislature and the constitutional convention, and beyond those, the pastors of the faithful. "Inasmuch as man, while claiming for himself intellectual superiority," resolved the gathered at Seneca Falls, "does accord to woman moral superiority, it is pre-eminently his duty to encourage her to speak, and teach, as she has an opportunity, in all religious assemblies."[7] As women reimagined their place as North America's guardians, pacifists, and educators—and with it the call for women's role in selecting lawmakers—they perfected new modes of instruction by memorial.

A WOMEN'S ELECTORATE IN TIME—QUÉBEC CITY AND MONTRÉAL

On August 14, 1827, as the debate over the future of Lower Canada reached a fever pitch and petitioners scoured the cities and villages for signatures and new meetings, one Madame Laperrière, a widow, approached the polling station near Bishop's Palace and announced her vote in the district election. The returning officer for the election—William Fisher Scott, appointed by the Dalhousie administration—refused to record her selection. Madame Laperrière immediately registered her protest and the election ensued, with two representatives (Joseph-Rémi Vallières de Saint-Réal and Andrew Stuart) chosen from the contest of four men. In December 1828, with Dalhousie having left Lower Canada and the authority of the colony's assembly having been newly asserted, a petition contesting the election of Stuart arrived. It advanced two simple legal claims, "1. That Mr. Scott acted contrary to law; 2. That the election of Mr. Stuart is void."[8] Although Mme. Laperrière's preferred candidates were not made public in the petition, she probably announced her vote for Amable Berthelot, who, like the victorious Saint-Réal, was a Patriote candidate. The memorialists took Scott's refusal to record Laperrière's vote as "a most dangerous precedent, contrary to law, and tending to subvert their rights and constitutional privileges." And because "the free choice of all the electors was not made known," the election of Mr. Stuart (but somehow not the victory of Saint-Réal) was void.[9]

In their insistence that matters of constitutional right were at stake, the petitioners advanced an expansive argument about the right to vote as inseparable from the right to property. At a time when Patriote petitioners vaunted "the constitution of this Province," the widow suffrage advocates here emphasized its English and Whig aspects. "Neither in men nor women can the right to vote be a natural right; it is given by enactment." If women had property, as French Canadian widows did, then they had all that was necessary, as "property and not persons is the basis of representation in the English government." The "Widow," as a general class of citizen, "duly qualified by our Election Laws, is in every essential respect similarly situated with the man: her property is taxed alike with that of the man." Women could not serve in militias, but neither could voting men above the age of forty-five years. Women could not serve on juries, but neither could voting physicians. Women could not be elected to the assembly, but neither could "a Judge or a Minister of the Gospel." The fundamental basis of voting was the holding of property, and extending a well-known argument of Montesquieu in *Spirit of the Laws*, the possession of property functioned as evidence of a person's independence of will, and of reason.[10]

In case the assembly entertained the argument that property somehow enabled the will and judgment of men but not that of women, the Upper Town Québec petitioners had a different argument ready. "It may be alleged that nature has only fitted her for domestic life," they admitted, "yet the English Constitution allows a woman to sit on the throne, and one of its brightest ornaments has been a woman."[11] This presumptive reference to Elizabeth I and the memory of her excellence as a martial leader and lawgiver was followed by a recitation of those benefits that women especially brought to the public as well as the private sphere: "It is she who breathes into man with eloquent tenderness his earliest lessons of religion and of morals; and it shall be said that his country shall be forgotten, or that she shall mould his feelings while smarting under hateful laws."[12] Returning again to their insistence that widows, and not all women, "exercise, generally, all the rights of men" and were "liable to most of the same duties toward the State," they concluded their argument with a reference to ongoing practice in Lower Canada: They had "not learned that there exist any imperfections in the minds of women which place them lower than men in intellectual power, or which would make it more dangerous to entrust them with the exercise of the elective franchise than with the exercise of the numerous other rights which the law has already given them. That, in point of fact, women duly qualified have hitherto been allowed to exercise the right in question."[13] Guilty of "malversation in office," William Fisher Scott had broken the law not merely as the petitioners aspired to read and apply it but as it had in fact been applied. Widows and other married women were actively voting in assembly elections. The question was not whether the assembly should change the statutes and permit these women to vote but whether they should punish Scott for failing to recognize that they already did. The Constitutional Act of 1791 establishing Lower Canada used male descriptors only in referring to political candidates. Otherwise, a prospective voter had only to demonstrate minimal qualifications—twenty-one years on the earth, status as "a natural citizen or subject" of the Crown, and sufficient interest in land (by ownership or rent)—to surpass a rather low bar for property holding. Property-based suffrage was widely distributed in Canada. Catholics could vote, so too Jews after 1831, and so could Indigenous women and men.[14]

Between 1824 and 1844, at least 950 women tried to vote in Lower Canadian assembly elections, around half of them from Montréal, where they constituted 2 percent of the electorate. Whether their votes were registered is not always clear, but between 1791 and 1800, women successfully registered their votes at least fourteen times in Montréal, while as late as 1844, nine women voted in the new district of Montréal Centre. Lower Canadian women surged to the polling station in unprecedented numbers in the 1820s, with 102 women showing up in the Montréal East district in 1820, while in the Montréal West district, 111 appeared in 1827, the same year that Mme. Laperrière announced her choice in Québec's Upper Town district. The high point of women's voting attempts came in 1832, with 297 women showing up at Montréal East and West polling stations. As early as 1820, an article in the *Montreal Gazette* warned of the "absurd and unconstitutional" vortex of women's influence in Lower Canadian politics, creating the specter of a "petticoat polity."[15]

The connections of these women voters to the Canadien reform network meant that the female electorate tended, for a time at least, to tilt aggregate voting outcomes away from the interests of Tories and administration loyalists. In the 1825 assembly district elections in Huntingdon County, twenty-seven Kahnawá:ke women voted, and their votes helped swing the contest to Austin Cuvillier, who ran with the Parti canadien (soon the Parti patriote). The ties between Patriote reformers and Kahnawá:ke and other Native villages were strengthened by the nexus between petitioning and voting. The 1827 petitioners for widows' suffrage felt that William Scott's refusal to record Mme. Laperrière's vote stemmed from Scott's opposition to her preferred candidate. That preference could only be known when the act of voting was, in Lower Canadian elections, viva voce. Endowed with considerable discretion, election administrators regularly scrutinized the credentials of electors and inscribed their selections in the "poll book."[16]

Along with the flood of women to the polls, violence scarred the 1832 election in Montréal. Aided by viva voce elections, partisans of a candidate could contest the eligibility of prospective voters, and women (often impoverished widows) confronted not only the gaze of male partisans but also the fear of physical and emotional intimidation. Sixty percent of the women who attempted to vote in Montréal in 1832 had their eligibility contested, and roughly one in six of these women (more than 10 percent overall) either were rejected at the polls or decided not to try further. The 1832 elections and a momentum of radicalization led prominent Patriote leaders to call for an end to female voting. Their principal argument, one undermined by the abundance of widows at the polls, was that women were being manipulated by men and were voting against their will.[17] Louis-Joseph Papineau, for one, declared, "It is silly, nay odious to see women dragged to the hustings by their husband, girls by their father, often enough against their will."[18] Patriotes dropped their advocacy for woman suffrage and passed a law prohibiting it in 1834 (rejected on other grounds by the Colonial Office). Only in 1849 did the prohibition on female voting take root in statute.[19]

The very network of reformers that had petitioned for Lower Canadian parliamentary sovereignty had turned on the women of the province and their participation. The Patriotes vaunted a masculine notion of citizenship. Concomitant with this irony came an abiding reality. Aside from their possible involvement in the 1827 Montréal memorial, Lower Canadian women did not petition for the continuance or return of their suffrage rights. The petitioning initiative of the 1820s came at a time when they already voted in substantial numbers, and after 1832, the turbulence of the 1830s quieted both their activity and discussion of the issue. Canadian women would not gain the right to vote until the twentieth century.[20]

* * *

No moment of nineteenth-century activism left a larger imprint on American gender politics than the mass antislavery petitioning campaigns of 1831 to 1845—especially the female-led burst of 1837–1839—yet those canvasses were quickly followed by others in which women took prominent roles that caught the attention and ire of men. Outside the slavery debate and the church, women's activism also emerged in the workplace. The vagaries of industrial capitalism had already fueled labor organizing and agitation on the Atlantic coast of the United States. In response to the painful combination of wage reductions and increased workload in 1834, women mill operators in Lowell, Massachusetts, organized a strike and began calling for a reduction in the workday to ten hours. In Great Britain, a labor campaign had already won reductions in children's working hours in the Factory Act of 1833, which created the Factory Inspectorate, a professional cadre appointed by King William IV for monitoring and enforcement. Yet these reforms had not touched the United States. By the early 1840s, Lowell millworkers were laboring from twelve to thirteen hours per day, exclusive of the time spent commuting—long walks that added an hour or two more to their toil. The agitation of the 1830s was unsuccessful. When in 1840 Martin Van Buren ordered all federal projects to observe a ten-hour workday, emergent leaders of labor associations and workers themselves saw a precedent and an opportunity.[21]

Labor activity declined during the Panic of 1837 and for some time thereafter, perhaps displaced by the antislavery cause, perhaps reduced by the decline in external labor demand occasioned by the depression. The upwelling of women's and men's labor activity came after the economic recovery that began in 1842. The men of Fall River and Lynn had organized the New England Workingmen's Association in October 1844. Three months later, in January 1845, Lowell women would organize again, this time with a more direct focus on the Massachusetts General Court. Sarah Bagley and her fellow laborers in the new Lowell Female Labor Reform Association began a petitioning campaign for a ten-hour workday. Wedding petitioning to publishing as initiatives for Indigenous rights, artisan advancement, francophone representation, and antislavery had done, Lowell women hitched their work to a new journal, the *Voice of Industry*, also launched in 1845.[22]

The centerpiece of the Lowell women's 1845 campaign lay in a petition for a ten-hour workday, a document whose nuanced prayer attracted over two thousand signatures. Men and women vouched their joint authorship of the prayer, presenting themselves as "the undersigned peaceable, industrious and hardworking men and women of Lowell." They combined the short-form prayer of the antislavery surge with a more testimonial rhetoric about their conditions. They decried "the evils come upon us, by toiling from 13 to 14 hours per day, confined in unhealthy apartments, exposed to the poisonous contagion of air . . . debarred from proper Physical Exercise, Mental discipline, and Mastication cruelly limited, and thereby hastening us on through pain, disease and privation, down to a premature grave." The statutory change they sought was a ten-hour limit on the workday in all factories of the commonwealth. The Lowell workers mounted a signature-gathering campaign based on townships. The aim was to assemble signatures in townships and then to have the completed rolls returned to the offices of the *Voice of Industry*. Over half the signatures came from Lowell, where the vast majority of names were women's. Fall River also contributed several hundred signatures, all of them from men. The Lowell Female Labor Reform Association presented the petition to the General Court in January 1845.[23]

In the wake of Angelina Grimké's address of 1837, the possibility of women presenting this memorial in legislative or committee session could not be ruled out. When William Schouler, chair of the Committee on Manufactures, replied to the ten-hour petition on February 6, he noted that "as the greater part of the petitioners are females, it will be necessary for them to make the defence, or we shall be under the necessity of laying it aside." Sarah Bagley replied immediately, writing for "the Operatives of Lowell," affirming that "we hold ourselves in readiness to defend the petitions referred to at any time when you will grant us a hearing." One week later, on the 13th of February, the committee summoned a range of witnesses, including Bagley herself and the lead male petitioner, John Q. A. Thayer. Whereas some of the male testimony was from mill overseers, all the women's testimony came from factory workers themselves—Bagley, Olive Clark, Eliza Hemmingway, Judith Payne, Cecilia Philips, and Elizabeth Rowe. Schouler's committee invited a number of women who were not petition signers to speak, some of whom testified, like Rowe, of having heard few complaints about long working hours. The committee also took a well-publicized tour of the Lowell factories.[24]

With Schouler facing off against Sarah Bagley, the hearings showcased a collision of partisan, industrial, and petitioning politics. Schouler was the Whig state representative from Lowell and the editor of the *Lowell Courier*. He also owned the magazine *Lowell Offering*, which situated itself at the intersection of the town's growing class of literature, industrial, and female readers. Schouler's committee issued its report on March 12, 1845, extensively rejecting the petitioners' requests. The committee deferred to the mix of hours and wages as a "a matter which experience has taught can be much better regulated by the parties themselves than by the Legislature." Rejecting the British precedent that capped working hours at sixty-nine per week, Schouler's report proclaimed that in Lowell, and generally in America, "labor is on an equality with capital, and indeed controls it." Nor was "the factory system," as they hesitated to call it, "more injurious to health than other kinds of labor."[25]

Bagley and her group pounced on the report, passing resolutions denouncing the inhumanity of the report and openly calling for Schouler's ouster at the impending autumn elections. Eliza Hemmingway's resolution deplored "the lack of independence, honesty and humanity in the committee to whom were referred sundry petitions relative to the hours of labor—especially in the chairman of that committee." Her second resolution pronounced the group "highly indignant at the cringing servility to corporate monopolies manifested by said committee." Bagley next introduced a resolution for another petition, to ask the general court to "extend to the operatives the same protection they have given to animals," and asserting openly that the committee members "are guilty of the grossest dishonesty" in withholding facts from the larger body. Miss A. Skinner brought the matter to a head: "If the Representatives of the State of Massachusetts have no higher aim than that of competing with the pauper labor of Europe, and for that reason refuse to grant the prayer of the petitioners," her resolution stated, "they are unworthy of a seat in the halls of legislation."[26]

American politics had never quite seen something like the Lowell women's response to the Schouler committee's report. A group of laboring women openly accused a committee chairman of dishonesty, not only with respect to the petitioners but also with respect to the rest of his chamber. They publicly called for his electoral ouster, not on the basis of party but on the basis of having acted as a servile instrument of aristocracy and having refused a just petition. The Lowell women did not claim that they themselves would cast the ballots that would return Schouler to Lowell, but they boldly asserted that they would influence those who could vote. Sarah Bagley, Eliza Hemmingway, and their fellow operatives had seized on a petition rejection to make an intrepid entrance by factory women into the American electoral sphere.[27]

Bagley and her associates now set about to unseat Schouler. The Massachusetts state elections would occur that fall, and Bagley appeared before the New England Workingmen's Association. "For the last half a century," she intoned, "it has been deemed a violation of woman's sphere to appear before the public as a speaker; but when our rights are trampled upon and we appeal in vain to legislators, what shall we do but appeal to the people? . . . It is for the workingmen of this country to answer these questions—what shall we expect at your hands in future?"[28] As articles from anti-Schouler advocates poured into Democratic newspapers like the *Lowell Advertiser,* they centered their complaints on the committee's dismissal of the ten-hour petitions. One week before the election, an *Advertiser* column appealed boldly to men to exact revenge on the candidate who had rejected the memorials of factory women and men.

> WORKINGMEN, do you remember the fate of YOUR PETITIONS!!
> MEN in favor of railroads, independent of existing corporations,
> DO YOU REMEMBER THE FATE OF YOUR PETITIONS!!
> Choose Democrats, and your interests and wishes will be respected.[29]

The marriage of labor petitioning and partisanship bore remarkable fruit. In the multimember district system employed by Massachusetts at the time, Lowell could have sent as many as nine candidates to the house, but only five candidates received sufficient votes. The *Voice of Industry* reported mockingly that "our neighbor Schouler . . . received a very *polite* invitation by the voters of Lowell, to stay at home this winter, or at least not go to Boston on their expense."[30] In the wake of the election, he also folded up the *Lowell Offering.* In tying a committee's response to a petitioning campaign directly into the subsequent election, the Lowell Female Labor Reform Association had rapidly expanded its membership as well, from fifteen members in January to five hundred by June. The Lowell women's extraparliamentary agitation and direct targeting—not of partisan opponents but of a petition's opponents—mark an important moment of antebellum democratization. Schouler had been not just any representative in the Massachusetts House but the chair of the primary venue for matters of labor and industry: the Committee on Manufactures.[31]

A democracy of organizations newly reinforced the Lowell women's aspired democracy of agendas. Convinced that the petitioning campaign had given them momentum and that they enjoyed changes of legislative success, the working women and men of Lowell redoubled their efforts. In April 1846, the *Voice of Industry* reported that a spring petitioning campaign had delivered over five thousand signatures from Lowell and ten thousand from other towns in Massachusetts on petitions in favor of ten-hour workdays. Now the Lowell operatives learned that the opposition to their plans was not limited to Schouler and his committee but ran statewide among Whig officeholders. Reformers created a new organization—the Labor Reform League of New England—which focused more on land reform and consumer cooperatives in addition to ten-hour-day measures. The Lowell Female Labor Reform Association's secretary, Huldah Stone, now took a more expansive leadership role in these efforts. Lowell factories did reduce working hours by fifteen to thirty minutes per day in 1847, and their examples were followed elsewhere in Massachusetts. As the bargaining position of Lowell workers was undercut by Irish immigration, the heady activism of the mid-1840s began to wane.[32]

Women also dominated petition-based mobilizations in New Hampshire, where in December 1845 Lowell factory operatives presided over a meeting of one thousand workers, roughly two-thirds of them women. The Manchester meeting passed resolutions calling for the ten-hour workday, and women and men set up parallel associations, with sixty women operatives joining the Manchester Female Labor Reform Association. Within weeks, Manchester operatives had harvested more than four thousand signatures on petitions supporting ten-hour workdays. New Hampshire passed the nation's first ten-hour law in 1847, though it was essentially unenforced and undercut by aggressive employer contracting. Similar dynamics unfolded in Maine and Pennsylvania, which passed their own laws in 1848, while New Jersey's legislature responded to a series of strikes by passing a ten-hour workday in 1851, Rhode Island following in 1853. The terrain of the factory economy remained remarkably tilted in favor of employers, although an aggregate reduction in working hours appears to have spread among firms in New England and the mid-Atlantic states from 1847 to 1853.[33]

The surge of activism in Lowell, Manchester, and other industrial towns is rightly seen as a pivotal moment in American labor organization. For a time, there arose collective claims for the power of workers, a fledgling and aspirational democracy that tied workplace to legislature. These democratizing moments would not last, but the organization and precedents they left were tied inseparably to factory women's mobilization by petitioning. The ten-hour-workday idea remained on the agenda of many a state, and by 1853, five states had such laws on their books. The idea of systematically using statutes—and with them, petitioning campaigns directed at state legislatures—to publicly regulate working conditions became a central strategy of the American labor movement.

* * *

As factory protest fluctuated in the northern United States, an international struggle unfolded two thousand miles to the South, where pro-slavery Texas landowners pushed for independence from Mexico and sought American allies. A congeries of colliding dynamics brought the battle to a head. The continued development of cotton cultivation and of slavery in Texas brought more American settlers, and when Mexican president Antonio Lopez de Santa Anna discarded his country's 1824 constitution and began to recentralize power, "Texians" organized their own military force under Stephen Austin and declared Texas an independent republic in 1836. The fledgling Republic of Texas encountered its most formidable enemy not in Santa Anna's forces at Mexico City but in the Comanche. The weakness of Mexico's central state and the bold expansionist dreams of slaveholders and cotton cultivators led many to regard Texas as a new promised land of cultivation. The surprise and narrow victory of Democrat James K. Polk over Whig Henry Clay in the 1844 general election left the United States governed by a leader committed to slavery's expansion. Though some wished to remain independent, Texas politicians called for annexation by the United States, and southern politicians began to imagine a much more expansive space where a slaveholding, cotton-harvesting republic could unfold, as far south as Nicaragua and as far west as California.[34]

The mass campaigns for and against American annexation of Texas and concomitant war with Mexico issued from the slavery debate. Abolitionists had shrewdly made petitions against annexation of Texas an important centerpiece of their 1830s campaign, focusing the attention of potential signatories and legislators on the expansionist tactics of slaveholders and their representatives. From 1836 to 1844, fully 2,657 petitions arrived at the House with prayers opposing Texas annexation, carrying over 250,000 signatures. Most of these were received by the Twenty-Fifth Congress (1837–1839), but after a slight drop-off, the issue resurfaced in the Twenty-Eighth Congress (1843–1845), where of 387 slavery-related petitions sent to the House, fully six in ten addressed annexation.[35]

Mexico refused to recognize the Republic of Texas and threatened war if Polk went ahead with annexation. Polk and the Democrats did so anyway. The compromise passed by one vote in the Senate; the House followed, and a supermajority of Texas voters also approved of annexation. Texas became the twenty-eighth American state on December 29, 1845. Polk had already proposed buying territories of Alta California and Santa Fe de Nuevo México from the Mexican government, and upon Mexico's refusal, Polk sent troops into the disputed Nueces Strip, in part to provoke the Mexicans into action that would make a war declaration more palatable in Washington. A set of delicate negotiations ensued, whose failure left the fate of matters in the hands of opposed troops. After a series of battles and other skirmishes, Mexico's president Mariano Paredes issued a declaration of defensive war in

April 1846, the U.S. Congress declared war in May, and the Mexican Congress ratified a declaration in July.[36]

The Mexican-American War reshaped politics on both sides of the border. By 1846, the tide of American prayers had shifted decisively to pacifist requests to pull troops out of Mexico. One memorial from Salem, Massachusetts, called on Congress to "adopt the Christian policy of terminating the war, by sending a minister of peace to Mexico, and declaring on our part a cessation of hostilities."[37] From 1846 to 1848, at least 254 antiwar petitions flooded Congress. A widely copied prayer called on Congress to exercise "all constitutional measures" (including war powers under Article I, Section 8, Clause 12 of the Constitution of 1787) to bring a "speedy termination" to the war, "without further effusion of blood."[38] These petitions were then referred to the House Foreign Affairs Committee and the Senate Foreign Relations Committee. When in 1848 the House began to print the antiwar petitions of Quakers, Democrats objected, leading Whigs to publish and diffuse a cleverly titled eight-page pamphlet—*Quakers Grossly Insulted: The Great Constitutional Right of Petition Violated by the "War" Party in Congress.* In one fell swoop, the Whigs had courted religious voters and rebranded their opposition as the party of aggression against humanity and the Constitution.[39]

War with Mexico also reshaped women's activism in the United States. Prominent figures in the antislavery campaign now began to reflect more commonly on the question of peace, the institutions of war, and the responsibilities of women and mothers to combat the culture and institutions of American war-making. These developments unfolded in the transatlantic culture of petitioning. In 1846, the women of Exeter, England, wrote an open petition, signed by 1,623 of their fledgling peace association's membership, to "the women of Philadelphia."[40] Philadelphia women met in a convention that June organized by Lucretia Mott, Sarah Pugh, Anne D. Morrison, and others. The convention drafted a response to the Exeter women, read aloud and into the convention records by Mott, and reportedly signed by over three thousand Philadelphia women. Other English and American towns exchanged similar addresses and petitions—Worcester, Massachusetts, with Worcester, England; New-Castle-upon-Tyne with Knox College in Illinois; Edinburg and Washington, D.C., among others. The immediate aim of these exchanges was to extend peace agreements between England and the United States given a quarrel over the Canadian-American border, but the timing of the events was hitched to Mexican war declaration and developments in Europe, and the English and American women's addresses emphasized general matters of peace.[41] "We hold it the duty of women," Mott intoned, "to look with an attentive eye upon the great events which are transpiring around them; in order that . . . they may direct the force of their moral influence against the iniquitous spirit of war." Launching a critique of American domestic and consumer culture, Mott decried the "false love of glory, the cruel spirit of revenge, the blood-thirsty ambition, swelling the breast of the soldier in the battlefield; these are often ripened harvest from the seed sown by his mother's hand, which in his childish hours she gave him tiny weapons, and taught him to mimic war's murderous game." Mott's address was converted into a signatory petition, which itself attracted the names of 3,525 names, a document "about 10 yards long," consuming "24 sheets of foolscap," as *Niles' Weekly Register* put it.[42]

Women in Philadelphia had been entering into a new and more assertive public stance for months. In response to newspaper attacks on the New York doctor Frederick Hollick, whose liberal doctrines on birth control and sexuality brought widespread condemnation from the press, approximately three hundred women gathered to defend the doctor and excoriate the "unmanly and slanderous" anonymous assaults on his character. By June 1846, the women who mainly belonged to the Philadelphia Female Anti-Slavery Society petitioned and wrote as the "Women of Philadelphia, U.S.A." A new associational identity had surfaced.[43]

American antiwar petitioning had roots in earlier decades but now became a national endeavor and a congressional issue as never before. The American Peace Society had been organized in 1828 in New York (moving to Boston in 1834)—almost two decades before Mott's address in Philadelphia—and regional and state peace societies dated to the early 1820s. An international movement also grew rapidly in the 1840s, with International Peace Congresses being held in London (1843), Brussels (1848), Paris (1849), Frankfurt (1850), and London (1851). Yet the war with Mexico deepened the contemporary imprint of the American peace movement, in part by magnifying the outrage among abolitionists and in part by reenergizing the peace organizations. When Philadelphia antislavery leader Mary Grew attended both the New England Antislavery Convention of May 1846 and that month's coordinated meetings with the American Peace Society, she observed a new level of outrage among the assembled (including William Lloyd Garrison, Abby K. Foster, Theodore Parker, and Wendell Philipps). The cause of emancipation had become "the banner of liberty and peace."

Reflecting on the English-American exchange of petitions in 1846, *Niles' Weekly Register* noted the "remarkable incident" of the "organization of a Peace Society, embracing philanthropists of many nations and Christian members of many denominations."[44]

As antiwar memorials poured in to Congress, the scope of the possible greatly expanded, and citizens countenanced ever more drastic action. The most radical prayers were coming from Ohio, where Jane Elizabeth Jones and Abby Kelley had begun editing the *Anti-Slavery Bugle* in 1845, where women took leadership roles in the Ohio American Anti-Slavery Society and Western Anti-Slavery Society, and where women often voted in school elections.[45] A striking petition from citizens of Belmont County called for the impeachment of President Polk "for having, as they allege, involved the United States unconstitutionally in a war, and given 'aid and comfort to the enemy,' by permitting Santa Anna to pass into Mexico."[46] This was the third petition for impeachment of a President published in the legislative journals of Congress to that time, the first from 1844 by citizens of Niagara County, New York, on account of Tyler annexation policy. Polk had been targeted with an impeachment petition once before, from one Edward Chase of Lockport, New York, on tariffs and the Mexico question. But the prayer was not as directly connected to the launch of the war, and the memorial was from a single individual. The Belmont County impeachment petition was accompanied by other prayers equally as strident. As Senator John Parker Hale presented a petition from Lock's Village in Massachusetts calling for war termination and District abolition, he introduced two more far-reaching petitions from Ohio. The first, from "citizens of Erie county," prayed "the enactment of a law organizing a volunteer force, for the suppression of insurrections in the southern States." The second called for "the adoption of measures for releasing the citizens of the non-slaveholding States from all constitutional obligations to countenance the institution of slavery."[47]

The surge of radicalism from Ohio was a reminder that annexation and war had fundamentally altered the contest for many in the northern states. While much of the activity followed along lines and contours established following the gag-rule surge of 1837, those patterns did not always serve to forecast antiwar petitioning. In several states—especially Ohio, Indiana, and Illinois—antiwar petitioning was higher than would be expected were it just an extension of pre-1844 antislavery trends (see Table 11.1). By 1846–1848, while the overall rate of petitioning declined from the heady summit of the Twenty-Fifth Congress, the geographic distribution of petitions concerning

TABLE 11.1 Percentage of Texas-Mexico Petitions from Selected Northern States, 1833–1848

	Anti-Annexation, 25th Congress (1837–1839) (House)	Anti-Annexation, 28th Congress (1843–1845) (House)	Antiwar, 1846–1848
Illinois	0.6%	8.8%	2.7% (1.0 per 100,000)
Indiana	1.7%	2.3%	3.5% (1.1 per 100,000)
New York	26.4%	19.1%	9.8% (0.9 per 100,000)
Ohio	6.9%	16.5%	20.1% (2.9 per 100,000)
Pennsylvania	18.7%	9.8%	10.2% (1.3 per 100,000)
Total petitions	1,851	376	254

Texas and Mexico had shifted westward. Over one-fifth of the antiwar petitions of 1846–1848 came from Ohio, which had a population-adjusted petitioning rate three times that of New York and double that of Pennsylvania.[48]

These geographical shifts were accompanied by more public and forceful actions by women of the northern states, and anti–Mexican War energies began to differentiate themselves from the antislavery movement. Women called on one another to create specifically female national petitioning campaigns against the war with Mexico. They circulated calls for antiwar pledges in Salem, Ohio, and Worcester, Massachusetts, in the summer of 1846.[49] In the ensuing year, women jointly signed the calls for peace conventions, most prominently in Ohio. One Lydia Chevalier of McKean County, Pennsylvania, addressed her call for "Petitions for Peace" in September 1847 to "all the Women of these States, and especially of the Free States, who love the Human Race." Praying Congress for a withdrawal of troops, Chevalier wrote, was necessary in "consideration of the untold horrors of all war, and the atrocity of the Mexican war in particular."[50] The "Women of the United States" petition conveyed by Chevalier advanced a humanistic prayer to Congress: "We, the undersigned Women of the United

States, regarding with unmixed sorrow and disapprobation the act of this nation in engaging in aggressive war against any nation, especially one much weaker than herself, and as wives, mothers, sisters and daughters, sympathizing in human suffering, do implore your body, as you love all that is holy and honorable, to withdraw your armies from Mexico, and to offer that country peace on terms that this nation would think just were the relative positions to the two nations reversed."[51]

Chevalier's petition was one of many distinctive antiwar petitions drawn up, published, circulated, signed, and conveyed to Congress by American women. Its prayer mentioned neither God nor any other stated precept of Christianity. Like hundreds of other antiwar petitions flooding Congress, it mentioned slavery not once. Perhaps most striking, it asked Congress to consider not just the fate of those on the battlefield but also the welfare of the Mexican nation, the "position" of those souls facing down American artillery. This appeal to consider the view of the Mexican, the other, came not from fate but from reimagination. American women's rethinking of their rights came at a moment when their society was rereading Mexico and what little it knew of women there. And at that very moment, Mexican women, in ways impelled by and expressed in new mass memorials, were rethinking their nation, their sex, and the mutual constitution of the two.

REPRESENTACIONES, VELAS, Y GUERRAS—GENDER AND THE PETITION IN WAR AND POSTWAR MEXICO

Beyond its confrontation of armies, war between Mexico and the United States forced a reckoning of cultures. The conflict extended the gaze of each society on the other. Americans read and heard many narratives of Mexican women, usually cast as a homogeneous lot. These stories were at times conveyed with mockery, often received in genuine but sheltered curiosity. They nonetheless shot through American print culture of the late 1840s, contrasting different stylized versions of womanhood. Mexican women's experience of the war remains far less documented than in the United States, yet the role that women could and did play in supporting the Mexican war effort, and in helping to articulate an anti-American ethic of Mexican nationalism, changed the tenor of Catholic and local politics.

The war of 1846–1848 brought several issues in Mexico to a head. The most obvious was the jeopardy of American incursion, not merely the ultimate surrender of Texas but also the threatened loss of Alta California, Nuevo México, and, if some Americans would have their filibustering way in the 1850s, Sonora and other states. The war came at a time when earlier republican visions were falling apart—and with them the aspirations of an imagined nation. Mexico had suffered an embarrassing defeat in the Pastry War (1838–1839) with the France of King Louis-Philippe. The war furthered a number of centralizing tendencies begun in the 1830s, and from 1841 to 1843, a provisional dictatorship governed the nation under the Bases de Tacubaya. The government reformed its basic constitution (the Bases Orgánicas) again in 1843, buttressing both executive power and religious intolerance. By 1846, the same year that the Constitution of 1824 was restored and Pius IX ascended to the papacy, the evanescent strongman Antonio López de Santa Anna was exiled to Cuba but retained a solid base of support in Mexico. Annexation of Texas and defeat in war resulted in Mexico losing over half its claimed territory. Without its modern Caesar and reeling from military humiliation, Mexico entered an open political crisis.[52]

War also led women and men in Mexico to reckon with the new others in their midst, including American settlers in borderland spaces as well as thousands of European immigrants who had arrived in the previous three decades, many bringing Protestantism with them. Debates over religious tolerance had occupied Mexican society since the 1820s. In the midst of war, the threat posed by these *extranjeros* grew in appearance and myth. After the war, as Mexico's leaders—never with a steady hand on power—wrestled with what kinds of laws and institutions to craft in the wake of defeat, the intertwined questions of immigration and religious tolerance became the crux of debate. The liberals pushing for greater toleration included many Catholics, not least the priest José María Luis Mora. Mora, a leading voice of reform after independence, was forced to leave the country in 1834 but kept an eye on (and a hand in) Mexican affairs into the 1840s from his abode in Paris. Mora favored a weakening of the church and religious pluralism. Immigration could enhance economic development, Mexican liberals believed, pointing to the United States. Yet the new status of America—not as liberal paragon but as imperial aggressor—changed the debate in important ways. In the eyes of many Mexicans, the Americans were taking Mexican lands and projecting an alternative vision of society nowhere more so than in matters of religion.[53]

In the context of national humiliation, the question of Protestant presence suddenly rendered the issue of toleration more tangible than before. The government created the Colonization Directorate in 1846 for promoting foreign immigration, and minister of internal and external relations Mariano Otero called for new policies to attract foreigners, among them statutes permitting greater religious tolerance. These initiatives were quickly met by calls from Catholic clerics to resist further liberal reforms. The appeal of the clerics was met by a new wave of popular petitioning the likes of which Mexico had not seen in decades. Over two thousand men of Puebla signed an anti-tolerance petition to the national congress. These memorials or "representations" (*representaciones*) were somewhat unlike other petitions in that their sponsors had them printed, including the entire signatory list. They were mass signed documents that combined longer prayers than were commonly included in petitions to governors, *ayuntamientos*, and other bodies. They were intended for several audiences, not only for the Constituent Congress but also for the literate public.[54]

Among these memorials, two from women stood out in public reading, one from the *señoras* of Oaxaca and another from the *damas principales* of Orizaba. The Oaxaca women's petition of February 1849 asked the *congreso* not to tolerate Protestant faiths (*cultos*). The transmission of a memorial directly to the national congress represented an end-run around the state authorities to whom Oaxacans would usually have petitioned. It is possible that Oaxacan *señoras* knew that in the wake of military defeat, the national congress would assume a more important role in matters of ecclesiastical policy and constitutionalism, or that Oaxacan governments would have been particularly unreceptive to their appeal. Both possibilities receive support from the fact that Oaxacan newspapers soon began to mock the women, one publishing a poem titled "Womanly Rebellion," whose verses postulated that Mexican women now aspired to "govern the universe." What piqued the mockery of Oaxacan men was not so much women's collective petitioning as their apparition in a national political debate. The church and Mexican federalism had previously limited Oaxacan women's sphere to that of ecclesiastical matters and, only occasionally, local and state councils.[55]

In January 1849, Orizaba's leading *señoras* asked the Congress not to surrender Mexico's religious unity and to protect the institution of marriage. Describing themselves as "the fairer sex," Orizaban women made a direct appeal countering liberal proposals for the tolerance of faiths, positioning themselves opposite Mexican reformers.[56] The Orizaba petition came at a delicate moment in the town's postwar experience. In 1847, a citizen militia called the Batallón Orizaba mobilized to counter American forces, and after Mexican declaration of defeat, American brigades still occupied the town. The articles of capitulation signed at Veracruz in March 1847 by Batallón leader Colonel José Gutierrez de Villanueva guaranteed religious liberty. Several months before the petition, a citizen uprising was put down by the Mexican *guardia nacional.* As in Oaxaca, the petitioning women of Orizaba appear to have represented a wealthier, more established stratum of the towns' class structures. In Orizaba, however, questions of religious tolerance were more closely tied to American imperialism.[57]

The independence of these women's memorials from local clergy remains unclear, but it is doubtful that their role was one of either nonparticipation or false consciousness. For one, the ridicule directed at women petitioners—whether from journals in Oaxaca or later, in the 1850s, from liberals like Francisco Zarco—suggests that many Mexican audiences, including prominent politicians and newspaper editors, saw women as largely responsible for the memorials.[58]

In other ways, the *representaciones* reflected the changing role of women in Mexican Catholicism. Beginning in 1840, Mexican women had begun creating Vela Perpetua (continuous vigil) groups throughout the country, especially in Bajío (lowlands) regions northwest of Mexico City. When they did so, they used petitions that raised fresh questions of venue precisely because they were largely unprecedented. The women of San Miguel de Allende (in the state of Guanajuato) petitioned their parish priest to create just such a model in April 1840. An organization for the perpetual adoration of the Blessed Sacrament (the communion host) would, it was hoped, extend popular involvement in Catholic ceremony and also bring women more vocally into parish and community governance. The San Miguel women proposed to elect female officers to their Vela Perpetua, including a senior sister (*hermana mayor*) and a treasurer. The priest looked favorably on the petition but did not know how to respond to it, so he quickly consulted episcopal officials in the diocese of Michoacán. The bishop himself confessed ignorance as to what to do with the document, and he consulted the governor of the Department of Guanajuato, judging that according to Spanish legal precedent, any new social organization (*cofradía*) required approval by the civil authorities. The governor punted the matter further, creating a departmental junta, which finally, in June 1840, reported favorably on the petition.[59]

Once approved, the San Miguel Vela Perpetua functioned as a model for others. A rough dozen such groups emerged in the diocese of Michoacán, and by 1843, the organizational form had spread to Guadalajara. Episcopal and civil sanction of the Vela Perpetua in Michoacán served as precedent for its approval by the bishop of Guadalajara. By 1848, Señora Salvadora García de Vara proposed the first Vela Perpetua in Mexico City. Its approval brought an institution that was initially peripheral into the nation's capital. Across Mexico, in a pattern of local assembly that would endure into the twentieth century and beyond, new devotional organizations emerged with both male and female members, though women alone would serve as officers. Where some Velas emerged from the action of priests, others emerged primarily from women's activity, and Vela organization almost invariably came from ecclesiastical petitioning.[60]

Beyond the Vela Perpetua, women in Mexico had amplified their voices during the war, vouching nationalism and resistance to American invasion. Mexican women wrote poems calling on Mexican men to defend their honor and their virginity. Only "Vile and Cowardly men/abandon the muskets" went one verse written by women in San Luis Potosí in 1846. If Mexican men, many who had deserted their posts and their cause, would not take up the muskets or "The mortars and the Cannons," then "We will take them/Let's see if we can use them/and if by chance we do not triumph/At least we won't run away."[61]

Whether from women or from men, the anti-toleration Mexican memorials of the late 1840s emphasized the dignity and responsibility of representative venues and vaunted the unity of family and nation. The *vecinos* of Teocuitlatán wrote that to tolerate all faiths would be to wound and divide "the grand Mexican family," Etzatlán memorialists warned the Congress that tolerance ran against "national will," and Autlán petitioners called on lawmakers to remember their obligations as Catholic men. "Mexican legislators! Catholic legislators! You stand at the edge of precipice where you soon plummet if, for lack of foresight or by caving to demands, you decree religious tolerance in our homeland."[62] Especially in Guadalajara, men's memorials were published at a common print shop, and many of these memorials (Córdova, Etzatlán, Guachinango, Tala, Teocuitlatán) came not only from self-styled communities of *vecinos* but from the town *ayuntamiento* itself. Anti-tolerance campaigners embedded their organization and their rhetoric in the larger debate over localism versus centralization.[63]

The source of this aspired national unity, according to the petitioners, came from the "horrific and humiliating lesson" of the recent war, and the continued threat posed by the "greedy neighbors to the North." A surging anti-American rhetoric—endowed with suspicion of immigrants, liberals, Protestants, and imperious settlers—shot through the *representaciones,* especially in the Guadalajara region. To admit Protestants' practices and beliefs on a legal equality with those of Catholics would be to undermine national unity at the very time it had been shattered by Protestant imperialism. Cementing the legal privileges of Mexican Catholicism would be, according to the *ayuntamiento* of Etzatlán, to "weld the already broken bonds of our national fraternity."[64] After a war in which Mexico had lost half of its claimed national territory, the petitioners plausibly claimed that Mexico's sinews of nationhood were weaker than at any time since independence, though they also referred to the Pastry War's losses against France as a memorable wound. Yet no threat stoked more anxiety than the United States. Standing against those bonds of fraternity, and all too ready to undermine them, as the *ayuntamiento* of Autlán feared, were the "ruthless Americans of the North."[65]

The Mexican congress and the ministry continued debating the colonization projects, but legal progress toward religious tolerance stalled, not least due to a random succession of presidents and the inability of the government to commit to a durable policy. Burdened by debt and central government corruption, and weakened by repeated Comanche raids in the North, Mexico was soon beset by Indigenous revolts in the Sierra Gorda and Yucatán regions in the late 1840s and early 1850s. A retrograde movement—many of whose principles and metaphors were expressed in the memorials of 1848 and 1849—arose and aspired to centralize Mexico under Catholic rule, with Santa Anna as the lever of power. Organizing as the Santanista party, it toppled the moderate president Mariano Arista. Santa Anna would return to the presidency in April 1853 and begin trying to patch up the country's finances and rebuild its army. His feeble remilitarization, his domineering and autocratic style, his tax hikes, and his hasty sale of more lands in the Gadsden Purchase weakened his popularity and enraged opponents. Liberals organized in the southern state of Guerrero and offered a new vision in the Plan of Ayutla (1854), which called for an end to the Santanista dictatorship and a new constituent assembly that would draft a constitution.

Santa Anna was deposed in August 1855 and returned once again to exile. The era of reform (La Reforma) had begun, and chief among the liberals' aims stood the limitation of ecclesiastical powers. The Ley Juárez, passed in 1855, removed clerical exemptions from the civil jurisdiction of the Republic, while the Ley Lerdo of 1856 forced the church to part with holdings that were not directly related to religious functions.[66]

Beyond these statutes, liberals vested their hopes for the reform project in a Constituent Congress announced for 1856, which was charged with drafting a new constitution. The idea of an extraordinary popular assembly, positioned above the nation's historical Congress, served as aspiration (from the Plan of Ayutla), as legitimation of reform, and not least as instrument of cohesion for the tense coalition of radicals and moderates governing under President Ignacio Comonfort. When the Constituent Congress took up the draft constitution, it debated it article by article, and in late July 1856 it turned to the question of religious tolerance. Article 15 of the proposed constitution held that the Republic should issue "no law or decree of authority that prohibits or impedes the exercise of any religious faith." Anticipating the opposition yet to come, the article continued that Catholicism, "having been the sole religion of the Mexican people, . . . the Congress of the Union will take care, by way of just and prudent statutes, to protect it so long as neither the interests of the people nor the rights of national sovereignty are impaired."[67]

However diversely organized, conservative Catholics remained unassuaged by Article 15's textual reassurance and mobilized to combat it. In 1856 and 1857, dozens of memorials descended on the Constituent Congress, many carrying thousands of names represented as signatories arguing against "the tolerance of faiths," by which the petitioners understood the legal equality of Protestantism with Catholicism. The Catholic journal *La Cruz* functioned as a central node of the opposition network, yet its concerns were much more clerical and doctrinal, and less anti-American and immigration wary, than were the mass petitions—especially those signed by women.[68]

Memorials poured in from nearly every corner of the Republic, but especially from the central states. Men representing themselves as citizens (*vecinos*) sent in mass petitions from Guadalajara, Pihuamo (the state of Jalisco), La Barca (Jalisco), Tlalnepantla (Edo de México), and Mexico City. An Indigenous petition from villages in Jalisco also rejected tolerance of faiths, while a men's memorial from Veracruz supported religious liberty.

Six *representaciones* opposing Article 15 came from women—from Guadalajara, León (Guanajuato), Mexico City, Morelia (Michoacán), Patzcuaro (Michoacán), and San Luis Potosí. They carried the names of hundreds, sometimes over a thousand, persons, with the women of Mexico City adding more than one thousand names to their prayer.[69]

Among the threats triggering resistance to Article 15, the trauma and continued menace of American Protestant incursion most tangibly piqued fear and resentment. The prominent villages in petitioning—Guadalajara, Leon, San Luis Potosí, and others in the nearby state of Jalisco—were just south of Zacatecas, where the Presbyterian doctor Grayson (Julio) Mallet Prevost arrived in 1856 and added missionary work to his medical endeavors. Prevost had served in the U.S. Army in 1847, at a time when the Reverend William Norris, a colporteur of the American Biblical Society, engaged in door-to-door missionary work along with the invading army. Prevost's arrival in Zacatecas was well known in the region, and he soon married the daughter of a prominent Zacatecas liberal, Severo Cosío. Zacatecas had served as an important outpost for anti-American leaders and radical federalists (including the Cosío family) during the war.[70]

"Long live religion and death to its enemies!"[71] So intoned the ladies of Mexico City in the midst of a long prayer to the Constituent Congress in 1856. The memorials from Mexican *señoras* in 1856 echoed many of the themes from *representaciones* eight years earlier, yet they also advanced some radical, even violent claims against Protestants and Americans. The women of San Luis Potosí represented themselves according to the domesticity still governing national imaginaries, but they linked religious and family unity to national unity: "As mothers, as sisters, as wives and as daughters we cannot remain indifferent to . . . the baneful seed of domestic disunity" that religious tolerance would bring. What would break apart the family and the church would soon dissolve the nation, they warned. "Our soul trembles just when countenancing that, with all religions introduced, we will have yet another factor of division in our Republic, already so poor and enfeebled by the power of the disharmony that shreds us."[72]

The *señoras* of Guadalajara typified many of the arguments made about the American threat, anti-Americanism, and the links between domestic and national unity, reminding the Constituent Congress of the "multitude of memorials in shocking numbers" that had arrived in 1848 and 1849. A constitutional policy of toleration, which would "heighten the incentives for disharmony" and offend "the vast majority of the Nation," would bring the demise of "that unconquerable barrier that separates we Mexicans from our greedy neighbors."[73] That reference to the avaricious enemy to the north (*codiciosos vecinos*) had appeared in the memorials of 1848 and 1849. If it was science, commerce, and agriculture that the congress wanted, then it should heed the example of Spain under Carlos V, the ladies of Guadalajara argued, where all had flourished without religious toleration. If it was more immigration that the government wanted, then better to encourage it among the Irish (a "martyr people under the oppression of England") and the French, who had already supplied a loyal Catholic population to the country.[74] Even as they engaged in these arguments about immigration and progress, the women of Guadalajara ended their prayer with a forceful appeal to the cult of Mary.

Amid variable insulting references to Jews, Muslims, and Confucians, the women of Guadalajara directed their primary anger at Protestantism. What would happen to Mexican women if Protestantism was openly allowed in Mexico? "Could they bear a faith, like the Protestant one, which deprecates and insults the Most Blessed Virgin . . . who with her motherhood of Jesus Christ and her precious virginity elevates and ennobles the female sex?" Could they suffer a religion that "horribly attacked the veneration of the Virgin Mary," especially as that veneration formed the identity of Mexican womanhood, providing "the poetry of infancy, the sweet dreams of childhood, the exemplar of modesty and all virtues in the days of youth"?[75] Read in light of the increasing activity of women in Velas Perpetuas, in ecclesiastical petitioning, and in charity organizations from the 1840s onward, the 1856 memorial of Guadalajara *señoras* depicts Article 15 as jeopardizing not only their religion but their persons and life pathways.

As in 1848 and 1849, women's activity brought ridicule. Liberal reform leader Francisco Zarco mocked the women and expressed his disdain for their entry into a national constitutional debate. "Poor ladies!" he intoned on the floor of the Constituent Congress. Clearly if Article 15 advanced, then "we are going to build temples to Venus in the square, bring back human sacrifices at Huitzilopochtli, establish polygamy and dissolve marriage." As laughter filled the chamber, he turned his mockery into a more sober argument for women's exclusion from the public sphere of national debates. "Of what importance to women are matters of religious freedom? Living in the domestic space, serving as the ornaments of their families, . . . what have they to do with the issues that agitate society?"[76]

These arguments suggest that while local clerics and bishops were acting in concert with the women, the women were likely adding their own voice. Women's voices were all the more important at this time because men's membership in many church functions, especially voluntary associations, was flagging. In contrast to the thousands of names on anti-tolerance memorials, membership aggregates in the Society of Saint Vincent de Paul fluctuated around 500; only in the late 1860s did they reach into the thousands, with a peak of 2,824 in 1875, at which point they were massively outnumbered by women, whose numbers had already attained 2,251 in 1866. The number of names on women's memorials vastly outstripped either men's or women's membership in these societies at the time. Voluntary associations like the Society of Saint Vincent de Paul and the Ladies of Charity would, by the 1890s, attract ten to fifteen thousand of the Mexican faithful and leave a vast imprint on society. In the 1840s and 1850s, however, petitioning and Vela Perpetua organizations composed the principal lay voices of Mexican Catholics, and both were led in important ways by newly assertive Mexican women.[77]

The mass petitioning women of Mexico won a momentary victory in law and left a more durable legacy in organization and culture. Article 15 was weakened in the new Constitution of 1857. That constitution was soon jettisoned in the midst of a combined military and ecclesiastical revolt, but the larger reform would implement important changes from 1860 to 1862. The more enduring imprint of Mexican women's petitioning in the 1840s and 1850s was not any sort of feminist movement but a renewed posture in the Mexican Catholic Church. Historians increasingly date the resurgence of women's Catholicism in Mexico to the mid-nineteenth century. The Vela Perpetua would endure deep into the twentieth century, and women's augmented role in Catholic charity (especially in the Archdiocese of Guadalajara, where women had been so active in both ecclesiastical and national petitioning in the 1840s and 1850s) resulted in the creation of important schools, asylums, and health services. Women situated these endeavors in the very central states that would form what historians have called "the Catholic axis" of the Porfirian period—Guanajuato, Michoacán, Puebla, and Jalisco (which included Guadalajara). This organizational legacy would, in turn, facilitate women's mass participation in the long Mexican Revolution (including the expansive Damas Católicas founded in 1912 and the mass petitions women signed during the 1910s). Petitioning was one part of this larger counteroffensive against liberal reform and the threat of American imperialism. Yet given the paucity of tools available to Mexican women at the time, it was a pivotal instrument of expanded voice. Lacking control over print or episcopal office, Catholic women mobilized locally, with perpetual adoration and durable prayer.[78]

* * *

It was of little coincidence that the war with Mexico coevolved with women's reconceptualization of the right to vote in the late 1840s. War and peace were fundamentally matters of elected authority—congressional authorization, presidential direction, and, at the state level, senatorial elections and governors' control over the state militias that were mobilized to wage battle. Many a peace petition from 1846 to 1848 from men reminded Congress that the "undersigned" were "entitled to vote."[79] If white American women were going to weigh in on matters of war and peace, then the older claim that they had departed from the "woman's sphere" only in defense of the Indian and slave would not suffice. The role of Mexican women in the war also attracted the attention of American news editors. And the newly witnessed aggression of the slaveholding South—no longer content merely to restrict press distribution and to sully the right to petition but instead to launch an international war in quest of new lands for subjugation—raised the stakes of all elections.

The war of 1846–1848 forced a reckoning among American society about what femininity meant. The *National Intelligencer* and other outlets reported on women serving in the Mexican armed forces, some in positions of leadership. Many men favored the recruitment of women into the war effort. Meanwhile, antiwar writers castigated American women for their support of warmongering male politicians, and when they did so, they pointed to a different portrait of bravery. William Burleigh faulted the women of Newburyport for their celebration of Colonel Cushing's military triumph, pointing instead to a truer model of women's valor and bravery, that of Mexican women who ventured into the midst of battle carnage to aid the injured and dying. The *Louisville Courier* in 1847 republished the letter of an American soldier—published again in 1850 by the American Peace Society—who witnessed "a Mexican woman busily engaged in carrying bread and water to the wounded men of both armies. I saw the ministering angel raise the head of a wounded man, give him water and food, and then bind up his ghastly wound with a handkerchief she took from her own head." The woman departed for a while, but as "she was returning on her mission of mercy . . . I heard the report of a gun, and saw the poor innocent creature fall dead!" The soldier and his fellow men buried the woman.[80]

Among these tales of Mexican women's activity, reports occasionally surfaced of their writing and petitioning. In October 1847, the *American Star* remarked on a women's petition to the Americans and published in *El Aguila Mexicana* (The Mexican Eagle). The petition was signed by "Varias Mexicanas." "It came almost as unexpectedly upon us as did the earthquake of the same day, but thanks to our iron frame, we have survived them both. The note solicits us not to flatter them, for flattery from an enemy is an insult to their dear patriotism! . . . We admire you, ladies, and will continue to do so, despite all the effusions you can send us through the columns of the *Eagle*."[81] Fancying themselves as having captured affection and of having triggered the jealousy of Mexican men, the *American Star* writers and many American soldiers regarded Mexican women with an imperial gaze that mixed objectification, curiosity, and admiration.[82]

Without doubt selected and curated, these tales of Mexican women exercising their patriotism and valor in the domains of battle and of print were nonetheless widely distributed and read. Whether in the *Louisville Courier*'s 1847 portrait or in the American Peace Society's war reminiscences of 1850 (published at the same time, and among the same networks, that women's rights conferences were emerging), the symbolism of Mexican femininity offered an implicit and explicit contrast to the life of the northern American white Protestant woman.[83]

A more conscious affirmation of women's rights came from the intertwined activity of antiviolence and petitioning. The "Public Meeting of Women" that unfolded in Philadelphia in 1847 had in mind a memorial campaign that would call on the state legislature to abolish the death penalty. Its leader was none other than Paulina Wright, who had been active in the fugitive slave mobilization. Quite rapidly the resulting canvass harvested 11,777 signatures on petitions for the abolition of capital punishment in the state. No less than 792 names were gathered by the Quaker agitator Marie W. Horton—"house to house," as she recalled it—who also served as one of the "commission" of twenty-five women to gather signatures for the anti-death-penalty memorials.[84] Women took leadership roles in the formal and informal proceedings of antiwar conventions in Philadelphia in June 1847 and in Randolph, Ohio, in September of that year.[85]

The currents of antislavery, international women's exchanges, and especially the experience of the Mexican War combined to infuse American women's activism with new, contestatory energy. The electoral sphere of the 1840s had witnessed the growing participation of women, not least in the Whig Party's use of women in propaganda and party campaigns. Especially in Virginia, Whigs vaunted the decorum and dignity bestowed by women's presence in their campaigns, trying to distinguish themselves from the Democrats.[86] Yet a more egalitarian and authentic emergence of women in the United States came from the Liberty Party. Even as the party lost ground electorally after the 1844 election, it took up an important presence in linking pacifism and antislavery. Women were allowed to vote at the 1847 Liberty League convention in Macedon, New York, and in August 1846, the Liberty League sent a memorial to Congress praying that "women may be represented in the State and National Councils, it being their right."[87]

Perhaps the first pro-suffrage petitions from American women also came in August 1846, to the New York State Constitutional Convention. The first and most noted came from six women of Jefferson County. Two years before the better-known Seneca Falls Convention and its Declaration of Rights, the Jefferson County women voiced an explicitly democratic argument for women's equality. The "present government of this state," they argued, "has widely departed from the true democratic principles upon which all just governments must be based by denying to the female portion of community the right of suffrage and any participation in forming the government and laws under which they live.[88]

The Jefferson County petitioners used an argument not of republican motherhood, not of inherent corruption in the male-dominated party system of the republic and how women could serve as a force countervailing it, but of government legitimacy. Citing Madison's *Federalist* no. 39, they argued that the legitimacy of rule rested on full elective consultation of all parts of society. At least two other petitions favoring woman suffrage entered the record that summer, though neither received the reading or attention experienced by the Jefferson County memorial of Eleanor Vincent and five other women. None of these petitions occasioned concrete action by the convention.[89]

The call for suffrage rights accompanied a new contestatory posture by American women, one that elided the boundary between the literary sphere and the political sphere of American politics. That divide—already rendered paraffin by women's leading role in 1830s petitioning to national and state legislatures—nonetheless sanctioned women gathering under the banner of antislavery societies or reform associations, and not on the subject of women's rights generally. The women's meetings organized in Philadelphia in 1846 (against the war) and 1847 (against capital punishment, led by Paulina Wright) quickly became female meetings called independently of any other reform cause. Women governed the Seneca Falls Convention procedurally, and by 1849 in Philadelphia and Salem (Ohio), and in Worcester in 1850, women presided over the meetings.[90]

In important ways, these convention efforts incorporated and harnessed the energies of earlier activity, especially petitioning campaigns in combination with temperance activity. Important signers of the Seneca Falls Declaration of Sentiments had not only signed antislavery petitions during the late 1830s but also canvassed those petitions and organized signature-gathering efforts. More than half of the signers were from a small Hicksite Quaker network in New York, but it appears that critically active members of this network rounded up the signatures of others. Prominent among these was Mary Ann McClintock, one of the five women who planned the Seneca Falls Convention. McClintock had just arrived in western New York in 1837, and although she and her husband had founded antislavery societies in the early 1830s, she does not appear on congressional petitions until 1837 and later (notably, her husband appears not to have canvassed antislavery petitions). Another Seneca Falls signer who had previously canvassed for antislavery signatures was Charlotte Woodward, whose petitioning likely represented her very first political work, inasmuch as she was ten or eleven years old when she canvassed an antislavery petition in western New York (1839), later signing the Seneca Falls declaration when she was eighteen.[91]

When women called for a women's rights convention in Salem, Ohio, in 1850, the signatories of the call—including Elizabeth Stedman, Rebecca Thomas, Eliza Holmes, Esther Richmond, and Cordelia and Sophronia Smalley—had also signed the appeal for the 1847 Peace Convention in Randolph. These peace convention signatories, in turn, had led a number of Ohio antislavery and anti-annexation petitions in the preceding years, including K. G. Thomas and Rebecca Thomas, Joseph Dugdale, Lyman Peek, and George Garretson. Some of these male names appeared on Ohio antislavery petitions in the early 1840s only as the token male signatory on a petition signed otherwise by women, in order to legitimize a woman's petition at a time when the American Anti-Slavery Society had split over the issue of women's participation. The Salem Women's Rights Convention of 1850 came the same year as Ohio's constitutional convention, and the petitions for suffrage reform to that convention included not only gender but also racial equality.[92]

Alongside and after these women's assemblies, ever more radical and weighty petitions for suffrage flowed to state legislatures and constitutional conventions. While the Jefferson County petition of 1846 was an originary document, the first pro-suffrage petition campaign—involving multiple documents and multiple venues—appears to have emerged in Massachusetts under the leadership of Lucy Stone. Stone began her work in 1849, carrying women's rights petitions with her during antislavery travels. "Let every person have an opportunity to sign the petition or to refuse to do so," she wrote. "It is the commencement of our agitation. Let it have a good beginning."[93] Stone saw suffrage petitioning as a means not only of persuading legislators but of forcing the public to confront the possibility of woman suffrage, whether or not they were initially disposed to agree with the idea. In a particular reading of the norm of petition and response, Stone decided not to tour Ohio and assist with the petitioning drive there. Legislatures should be petitioned by their own constituents, she thought, and Ohio reformers should proceed on their own.[94]

Beyond their more expansive prayers, women also transformed the performance of signature. Forty-one men and women of Feltonville, Massachusetts, petitioned the Massachusetts General Court in 1850 for women's voting rights and, beyond that, eligibility to hold government office (see Figure 11.1).[95] It was common in nineteenth-century petitions for women and men to sign in separate columns, in part as a representation of the separate spheres inhabited by the sexes but also as a way to permit the recipients of petitions to distinguish between those who could vote and those who could not. Many petitioners titled these two columns of signatories as "Voters" and "Women," but the Feltonville petitioners upended this binary by describing men as "Legal voters" and women as "Should be voters." That same year, women of Plymouth headed their signatory column with "Those that should be voters." Unlike so many movements where women had drawn on gender stereotypes and failed, the early suffragists in Massachusetts and New York upended conventional rhetoric and representations. Beginning in 1850, women began to regularly outnumber men in the signatory list of these petitions (see Table 11.2), with an average across the 1849 to 1851 petitions of roughly three female to every two male signatories.[96]

The Feltonville and Plymouth petitions were but two examples of a surge of woman suffrage petitions sent to the Massachusetts legislature from 1849 to 1851. Suffrage radicals sent at least twenty-three petitions to the general court during these years (see Table 11.2). Some of these were probably

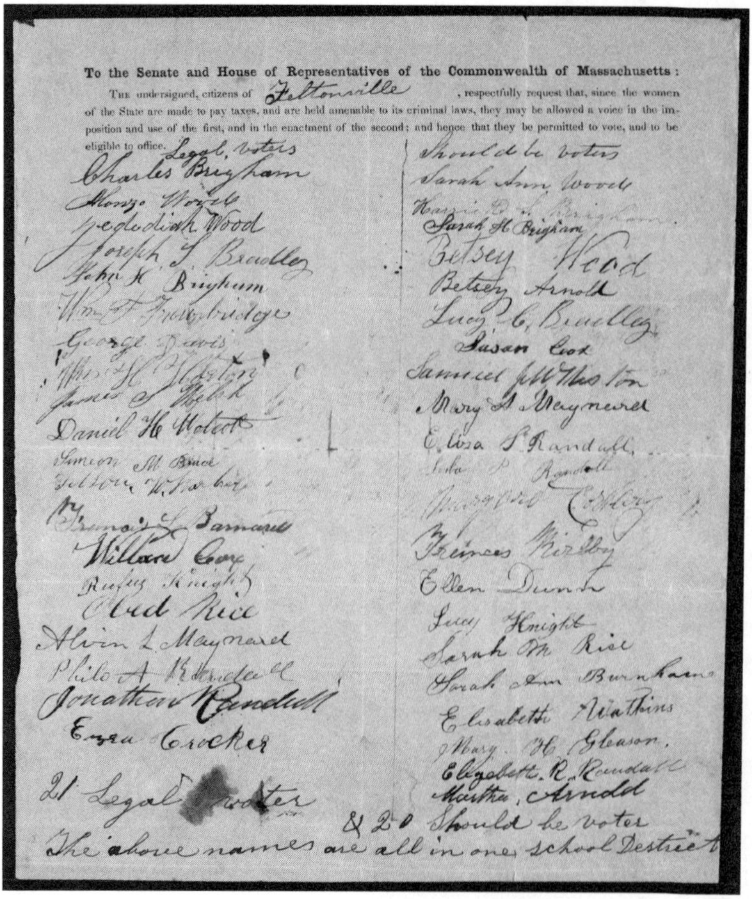

To the Senate and House of Representatives of the Commonwealth of Massachusetts:

The undersigned, citizens of Feltonville, respectfully request that, since the women of the State are made to pay taxes, and are held amenable to its criminal laws, they may be allowed a voice in the imposition and use of the first, and in the enactment of the second; and hence that they be permitted to vote, and to be eligible to office.

Legal voters	Should be voters
Charles Brigham	Sarah Ann Wood
Jedediah Wood	Sarah H. Brigham
Joseph S. Bradley	Betsey Wood
John H. Brigham	Betsey Arnold
Daniel H. Wolcott	Lucy C. Bradley
Willard Cox	Susan Cox
Rufus Knight	Mary A. Maynard
Obed Rice	Ellen Dunn
Alvin L. Maynard	Lucy Knight
Jonathan Randall	Sarah M. Rice
Ezra Crocker	Elisabeth Watkins
	Mary H. Gleason
	Elizabeth R. Randall
	Martha Arnold

21 Legal voter & 20 Should be voter

The above names are all in one school District

FIGURE 11.1. Suffrage Petitioners Representing Themselves as "Should be Voters" (Feltonville, Massachusetts, 1850). *Credit:* Massachusetts Archives of the Commonwealth.

coordinated at the National Woman's Rights Convention in Worcester in October 1850, but others were not, having arrived before that convention and having been separately coordinated depending on their town of origin. Lucy Stone and Paulina Wright Davis together issued the Worcester convention appeal and recruited conventioneers. Having fallen ill just before the convention, Stone was unable to play the role she had wished, but she gave a short address on the last night of the convention and urged the assembled to petition their state legislatures.[97]

Table 11.2 The Massachusetts Suffrage Petitioning Campaign, 1849–1851

Year	Location	Men	Women	Selected Signatories
1849	Boston	5	6	William Lloyd Garrison, Robert F. Wallcut, Samuel May, Wendell Phillips, Ann Greene Phillips, Eliza Garnant
1849	Danvers	35	18	Henry Elwell Jr., Lucy Thurston, Eunice H. Merrill, Mary P. Clough, Charlotte Roberts, Sarah N. Bancroft, Martha M. Cutler, Lydia W. Endicott, Elizabeth H. Reed
1850	Lexington	6	19	G. W. Simonds, Hannah S. Robbins, Caroline Wellington
1850	Lancaster	3	11	Francis F. Hussey, Olive W. Hastings, Caroline A. Bell
1850	Dennis	13	14	Prince Crowell, Polly D. Crowell, Minerva C. Hall
1850	Abington	64	24	Josiah D. Emery, Anna Ford, Clarissa Wales
1850	Westminster	7	16	Alfred Wyman, Abby W. Wyman, Mary A. Morrill
1850	Pembroke	2	2	Lewis McLauthlin, Polly McLauthlin, Judith W. Smith
1850	Gardner	17	14	William B. Stone, Samantha Robinson, Sarah W. Lawrence
1850	Brewster	3	8	Barnard Freeman, Melinda D. Freeman, Mary Clark
1850	Salem	25	27	Eliza J. Kenny, Hannah Kenny, Eliza P. Austin
1850	Lawrence	5	5	Charles Hanson, Benjamin Stevens, Harriet Stevens
1850	Raynham	5	12	Samuel Gilmore, Abby Gilmore, Charlotte Gilmore
1850	Feltonville	20	21	Charles Brigham, Sarah Ann Wood, Harriet Brigham
1850	Plymouth	28	16	Edwin Lewis, Phebe P. Blackmar, Betsey Morton
1851	Worcester	35	73	Martin Stowell, Eliza A. Stowell, Sarah H. Earle
1851	Gloucester	6	14	Thomas Haskell, Jonathan H. Riggs, Sarah E. Haskell

(*continued*)

TABLE 11.2 (continued)

Year	Location	Men	Women	Selected Signatories
1851	Worcester	4	9	Caleb A. Wall, Effingham L. Capron, Sarah E. Wall, Sarah Wall, Abigail Graton, Anne H. Southwick
1851	Hanson	13	18	Mary Perry, Joshua Perry, John S. Pratt
1851	Leominster	13	17	Jonathan Drake, Frances H. Drake, Mariana Durant
1851	Westminster	11	27	Sarah W. Hoar, Ira Hoar, Abby W. Wyman
1851	Abington	51	59	Dana Smith, Abigail S. Turner, David Pool
1851	W. Brookfield	12	12	Francis Stone Jr., Phebe Stone, Mary Arthur, Melinda Fry

Source: House Unpassed Legislation, 1849, 1850, 1851 (SC1-230), MAC.

The American initiative for sex equality soon developed the kind of full steam that hotly powered the nation's railroad locomotives. Noting the commonwealth's call for a constitutional reform convention in the spring of 1853, Stone started a new petition drive in December 1852. Among the petitions she carried was one asking the convention to strike out the word "male" wherever it appeared in the state constitution.[98] When it convened in May 1853, the convention met with memorials signed by hundreds, in some cases a thousand or more. On May 12, the "petition of Francis Jackson, and fourteen hundred and seven others," and another "petition of Harriet Randall, and two hundred and three others," were introduced. Nine days later, the "petition of Wendell Phillips and nine hundred and thirty others" came. The convention rejected these petitions. Such a constitutional amendment would have changed not only voting eligibility but also property laws, jury eligibility, and other domains of women's lives.[99]

By 1853 and 1854, petitioners for the rights of woman labored to publicize their endeavors in the nation's exploding newspaper network. The expansion of the penny press in the 1830s meant that newspapers enjoyed larger circulation than ever before, and by 1856, three of them—the *New York Herald*, the *New York Times*, and the *New York Daily Tribune*—had a combined printing of roughly 397,000 copies daily.[100] Advocates for the rights of women did launch their own presses, and they relied heavily on the antislavery press, but the size and scale of the large papers placed a premium on getting content into them. From June to September 1853, Lucy

Stone's efforts in Massachusetts—the constitutional convention and the two hearings granted women at that gathering—were covered in the *New York Daily Tribune*, in the *Anti-Slavery Bugle*, in the *Pennsylvania Freeman*, and in the recently launched *Una*.[101]

Just as newspapers spread information about memorial campaigns for women's rights, Lucy Stone and her allies began a new push for multistate petitioning operations in 1853 and 1854. At the 1853 National Women's Rights Convention in Cleveland, Antoinette Brown opened the second day of proceedings by reading aloud a letter from Rochester's William Henry Channing, calling for a Declaration of Woman's Rights. His second proposal called for "Forms of Petition [to] be drawn up and distributed for signatures, to be offered to the state Legislatures at their next sessions." Channing's envisioned campaign would launch memorials for suffrage as an egalitarian project: "That the right of suffrage be granted to THE PEOPLE, universally, without distinction of sex." Well beyond the ballot, Channing's proposed campaign aimed at a broad range of democratizing reforms, including equality in "all laws relative to the inheritance and ownership of property," trial by jury for female defendants, equal parenting and guardian rights, and the right of divorce for wives of alcoholic husbands as well as tax exemptions for women until they received the ballot. Channing called for a politics of venue and a careful advance beyond mere supplication. "These petitions should be firm and uncompromising in tone," he wrote, "and a hearing should be demanded before Committees, specially empowered to consider and report upon them. In my judgment, the time is not distant, when such petitions will be granted, and when justice, the simple justice they ask, will be cordially, joyfully rendered."[102]

The advocacy of Lucy Stone and Paula Wright at Worcester, the example of Stone's endeavor in Massachusetts, and William Channing's open call in Cleveland anticipated a range of campaigns in state legislatures across the northern states. After consulting with Antoinette Brown and William Channing in late 1853, Susan B. Anthony launched a new suffrage petitioning operation, recruiting Lucy Stone into the work. Her 1854 memorial made several requests: control by women of their own earnings, guardianship of their children in case of divorce, and the vote. In an innovative organizational method, Anthony appointed sixty women in 1854, one from each county in New York, and designated them as "captains." Anthony's designation of county captains mirrored the organization of precinct "captains" in nineteenth-century party organization, developed nowhere more vividly than in New York State. Again, habits of petition organizing mimicked and presaged habits of electoral organizing. Within ten weeks, Anthony and her captains had collected six thousand signatures, and Anthony coordinated the presentation of the petitions with a state legislative session in Albany. When the hearings that Channing envisioned were called, Stone tried to attend, and when her illness prevented her from traveling, Anthony, Channing, and Ernestine Rose appeared at the March 1854 proceedings. Ohio petitioners succeeded in getting a Senate hearing in March 1854 as well.[103]

Woman suffrage petitioners mastered the politics of venue. Even petitioners to the state legislature prayed for constitutional reform as much as calling for new statutes. Often their petitions proposed a constitutional convention, where a more expansive reimagining of higher law was possible, often by a body composed separately from the legislature itself. Following the state Woman's Rights Convention in Rochester in December 1853, two mass petitions were authorized and approved for presentation to the state legislature, one (with 5,930 names) for legal equality between men and women of the state, the second (with 4,164 signatories) proposing a constitutional amendment guaranteeing woman suffrage. Elizabeth Cady Stanton took to the floor of the New York legislature and delivered an address with the petitions. February 14, 1854, became Stanton's (and New York's) Angelina Grimké moment, an appearance of woman as proposer and petition presenter in the lawmaking councils of the state. In Massachusetts, Sarah Earle and 137 other citizens from Worcester petitioned the Massachusetts legislature in 1855 to strike the word "male" from the state's constitution. By 1858, pro-woman-suffrage petitioners could expect to regularly send a petition like that delivered from Nantucket, which produced 277 signatures on a suffrage petition, 191 of them from women of the island, proportionally larger than any city-based petition at that time. The petition for the Ohio woman suffrage bill in 1857 presented more than ten thousand names to the state senate. Following Channing's advice, women's rights petitioners knew the venue, not only the legislative chamber but the committee (on "Electors" or "voter qualifications"), to which they would be referred. From 1854 to 1860, petition campaigns for the rights of women met with distinct legislative hearings in twelve cases across seven states and one territory, and women testified in at least nine of these twelve proceedings (see Table 11.3). In some cases, as when Mary Frame Myers Thomas testified before the Indiana legislature, it was the first time a woman had appeared before the state's sovereign body. Appearances like Angelina Grimké's before the Massachusetts General Court in 1839, itself occasioned by the petitioning surge, were becoming the established norm.[104]

TABLE 11.3 State Legislative Hearings or Reports Induced by Petitions for Women's Equality, 1854–1860

State	Time	Women Appearing at Hearing
New York	March 1854	Susan B. Anthony, Ernestine Rose
Ohio	March 1854	Caroline Severance
New York	1855	Susan B. Anthony, Ernestine Rose, Antoinette Brown
Wisconsin	1855	none
Nebraska Territory	1856	Amelia Bloomer
Maine	1857	Lucy Stone
Massachusetts	1857	Lucy Stone
Ohio	1857 (Senate)	Anthony
Wisconsin	1857	n/a
Kansas	1858	Clarina I. H. Nichols
Indiana	1859	Mary Frame Myers Thomas, Mary B. Birdsall, Agnes Cook
New York	1860	Elizabeth Cady Stanton

Note: Million, "Seeking Simple Justice," 26–27; adjusted by my survey of other state legislative sessions. *Report of the select committee of the Ohio Senate, on giving the rights of suffrage to females* (Columbus, 1858). Pat Creech Scholten, "A Public 'Jollification': The 1859 Women's Rights Petition Before the Indiana Legislature," *Indiana Magazine of History* 72, no. 4 (1976): 357–359.

As petitioning women were getting heard in state legislative chambers, they encountered both promise and obstacles. The promise came from favorable committee reports in two state legislatures on suffrage proposals, in Wisconsin in 1857 and Ohio in 1858. The larger chambers did not amend the constitution in line with the committee proposals, but the placement of suffrage on state agendas had never been so far advanced. The Civil War arrested this state-level momentum.

The state legislature became both refuge and obstacle for American women for others outside the electoral sphere. The institution of marriage in common law left the husband in complete control of the wife's earnings. Ohio's Caroline Severance remarked that the husband was "absolutely the master of the profit of his wife's hands during coverture." Married women had begun to petition for changes in property law during the 1830s. Ernestine Rose petitioned for married women's property rights soon after emigrating from Poland in 1836, and in 1837, the freethinker jurist Thomas Herttel proposed a statutory measure "restoring" the "Right to Property" among married women. Rose, Paulina Wright Davis, Lydia Mott, and Elizabeth Cady Stanton lobbied for the measure, but the idea fell off the agenda until the Mexican War reawakened women's protest. By the 1840s, state legislatures had begun to rectify some of the most egregious lapses in statute, especially with bankruptcy reforms. The New York Married Women's Property Act of 1848 protected the wife's assets from the bankruptcy of her husband and served as an exemplar for other states. In most other respects, New York and other states left wives in the position of legal abjection, with all the "disabilities" attendant to coverture.[105]

Only in Massachusetts did a state pass a married woman's earnings act before the war. That 1855 law enabled Massachusetts women to enter willfully into contracts, to make wills, and to retain ownership and control of property held before the marriage. The statute also allowed women to bring suit, to be sued themselves, but to evade liability for their husband's debts. The petitions and legislative testimony of Salem's Mary Upton Ferrin played a significant role in the placement of this statute on the general court's agenda from 1848 to 1853. Ferrin was married to a husband considered upright in the community but who, she testified in 1850, habitually abused her to the point that she could no longer live with him. The arrival of the Know-Nothings to a general court majority in 1855—a much younger and less wealthy cohort of lawmakers, with no ties to the established Brahmin leadership of previous generations—was the final step needed. Ferrin's advocacy and the experience of New York in the 1850s demonstrates that women petitioned state legislatures in part because the statutes passed there would govern the courts in which their liberties and lives were ever more circumscribed.[106]

CONTESTATION AND AGENDA DEMOCRACY ACROSS BORDERS

Democratization in North America cannot be understood apart from the emergence of women's contestation in defining matters of the public sphere, constitutional rights, property, and electoral democracy. Our narratives of that advance, especially its nineteenth-century origin, usually emphasize its distinctively American achievements, perhaps with some discussion of British correspondence. The history of petitioning offers a cautionary note, a chance to reinterpret American women's interaction with legislatures and constitutional conventions while also urging us to look elsewhere for critical action.

In some ways, women's contestation in North America long predated the 1830s, whether in the divorce insurgency of the American Revolution; the changing character of women's property claims, which linked French-Canadian widows to Mexican women making ranching claims after independence to the emancipated slave Belinda Sutton; the surging practice of American war widows sending "Petitions without Number" to Congress for family support; or the reassertion of clan matron authority in dozens (if not hundreds) of Indigenous communities.[107]

Women in antebellum North America converted these earlier moments of supplication, largely individual, into collective petitioning campaigns. Campaigns not only repeated and organized the petitions across geographic and political spaces but applied a form of political pressure to venues. And in these campaigns, women willfully intruded into new spaces—the debates of Lower Canadian assemblies over fundamental matters of political right; the reelection of a Whig representative in Lowell, Massachusetts; the ecclesiastical offices of the Mexican Catholic Church; matters of war and peace, which American saw as the weightiest obligations of their legislature; Mexico's Constituent Congress and its debates over national religious policy; state constitutional conventions across the northern states in the 1850s and 1860s.

The vast differences across these spaces usually command our attention and respect, and justly so. Yet when Francisco Zarco mocked the thousands of Mexican women petitioning against religious tolerance in 1856, characterizing their place as "the ornament of their families, forming the hearts of their children" and asking "what have they to do with the issues that agitate our society?" he proved that "woman's sphere" was the construction of liberal reformers as well as Christian traditionalists.

In the United States, collective petitioning campaigns enabled women's consistent access to crucial venues of lawmaking, especially to legislative hearings. This new ability to shape agendas did not translate into immediate legal changes, but it represented a fundamental change in American politics and a different form of democratic advance. The ability of organized lobbies to gain access to legislative committees has long been considered a hallmark of their success. While not yet having the kinds of established lobbying associations that would come after the Civil War, collectively petitioning women had developed and repurposed a technology with which they simultaneously organized, lobbied, and prayed.[108]

TWELVE

The Eclipse of Lordship

Petitioning and Land Tenure in the United States and Canada

Many and legendary are the thinkers who, in reckoning with North America and especially the United States, locate its political distinctiveness in an emancipation from feudalism. Interpreters of American democracy from Jefferson to Tocqueville to Louis Hartz have, for over two centuries, connected its vitality to its system of free property, its limits on inherited privileges, and its absence of lordship. Republican ideas of citizenship like those in query nineteen of Thomas Jefferson's *Notes on the State of Virginia*—where he vaunted the "immensity of land courting the industry of the husbandman" and located in those men "the manners and spirit of a people which preserve a republic in vigor"—could gain little traction in a world where small landholders could not purchase their lots, "improve" them, and build their necessary "independence."[1] John Locke's idea that "property" results from the fusion of nature and human labor—and, beyond that, the labor theory of value that fueled republicanism and later socialist writings—required the assumption that labor remain, as Locke put it, "the unquestionable property of the labourer."[2] In these liberal and republican readings, North America's feudal virginity made it a freer place. It had never been touched by medieval *dominatio,* where lands lay in a structure of lords entitled not merely to fealty but to a separate tier in the order of government, and where those who worked those lands owned neither their plot of earth nor the fruits of their endeavor.[3]

Thinkers grappling with the new regimes on the continent understood clearly that colonial systems had created their own forms of privilege by vesting rights in chartered corporations, clergy, and family networks. Early

Americans also believed that important vestiges of this privilege were, in the United States, swept away in the Revolution. Beginning with Georgia in 1777, revolutionary state legislatures abolished primogeniture and entail and thereby weakened the massive advantages of firstborn sons as well as the concentrated inheritance patterns that had characterized British colonial gentry families. Clergy privileges remained an important source of contestation in Lower Canada, Upper Canada, and the United States (not least the Congregationalist network in Connecticut and Massachusetts). Yet by the 1830s, these advantages had withered. Jesuit seigneuries in Lower Canada had long since passed into British hands, while Anglican clergy reserves in Upper Canada were under attack, and American Congregational strongholds, having allied with the Federalist Party in New England, were badly weakened in the 1820s. Lower Canada had a system of seigneuries remaining from the French colonial system, but even Canadians were reluctant to call it a feudal system on the order of the ancien régime. One reason that Tocqueville, writing about Canada in 1831, focused on administrative centralization as its essential difference with the United States is that he believed what John Neilson and a Montréal seminarian had told him: that feudalism prevailed in French Lower Canada more as "a name than anything else."[4]

For those hundreds of tenant farming families in New York's Hudson valley and Canada's Saint Lawrence valley who, along with their allies, petitioned by the tens of thousands from the 1830s to the 1850s, any assumptions of a nonfeudal past would have come as a surprise, if not an affront. Hemmed in by manorial contracts that their ancestors had signed, unable to sell their lands or to reap the income from improvements upon them, compelled (in Lower Canada by the *droit de banalité*) to bring their grain only to the mill of the seigneur, forced (in New York) to pay annual rents in the form of fowl or grain to their landlord—weighted by all these legal burdens and more, they turned to strategically timed and framed petitioning campaigns and association building. Especially as industrial economies exploded in worlds they read and heard about, and as far-flung settlement and small family landholding spread in their midst, they urged legislative sovereigns to release them from an inefficient, antimodern servitude. Antitenure politicians and writers noted not just the irony but the "shame" that it was in New York—the jewel of America's commercial republic, the proud home of its working class Democracy and its Whiggish system of internal improvements, an important locus of its booming free-soil movement that excoriated the slave system of the south, a capitalist society whose investors mocked the backward society of French Canada to the north—that a form of feudalism had survived and entrenched itself. Nor did the institution prevail in some far-off corner of the state. The most heavily tenured lands surrounded the state capitol at Albany.[5]

By 1861 and the initiation of hostilities in the U.S. Civil War, both forms of land tenure had essentially vanished. Yet the demise of land tenure played out differently in the United States and Canada, and not in ways either contemporaries or later theorists would expect. Manorial tenure in antebellum New York was plausibly more burdensome to its farmers than Canadian seigneurial tenure was. Canada, and not New York, eliminated tenure by legislative enactment. On one New York manor, Rensselaerwyck, manorial tenure persisted long after the Civil War. In those New York counties and patents (descended from Crown land grants) where landlords bargained with tenants and left the system by contract, they did so not under the incentives given them by law or electoral politics but under popular pressure that expressed itself through local organization, petitions, and occasional but orchestrated violence. Legislative momentum in Canada followed neither economic exigency (coming more than fifteen years after the crash of 1837) nor the long train of complaints calling for seigneurial reform that dated from the early 1800s.

The nineteenth-century battle over North America's feudal institutions came in the midst of the continent's petitioning explosion, and it was petitioning more than electoral politics that shaped the demise of land tenure. Despite New York's status as the largest, wealthiest, and most politically pivotal state in the Union, petitioning coalitions for and against tenure reform were only lightly associated with the parties, as anti-rent organization split both the Democrats and the Whigs. Tenant agitation emerged and harnessed the power of violence, but it was well after violence had peaked that landlords began to alienate their manors. Canada eliminated seigneurial tenure in 1854, after more than a decade of anti-tenure agitation on the part of socagers in Lower Canada, whose petitions were weakly linked to the party formations of the period.[6]

The history of the United States and Canada offer a stark corrective to the understanding that the post-Jacksonian United States had become an electoral democracy while unified Canada remained under the harness of colonialism. Here the formal institutions could mislead. Neither electoral competition nor judicial review nor legislative enactment gave the tenant farmers of the Hudson valley the relief they sought. Queen Victoria assented to the 1854 act for the abolition of feudal rights and duties in Lower Canada, but Victoria and her Colonial Office were passive witnesses to the statute and the legislative process. A regional surge in petitioning that plausibly shaped assembly elections but that certainty altered the legislative agenda had changed the contours of the possible and the costs of remaining with the seigneurial status quo. Canada's colonial institutions gave its legislators more leeway than that faced in New York for dismantling the vestiges of feudalism. In both places, mass petitioning and its democratization of agendas provided the crucial momentum for political and legal change.[7]

* * *

Had Stephen Van Rensselaer III somehow timed his death on January 28, 1839, he would not in retrospect have chosen more poorly. The "patroon" of Rensselaerwyck descended from the upper Hudson valley's first land baron, Kiliaen Van Rensselaer (1595–1644), and tenant farmers on his manor expected that their considerable accumulated debts—mainly from annual rents in arrears—would be forgiven upon his passing. During decades of declining agricultural prices and rising competition from farmers accessing markets by the Empire State's canal system, tenant farmers at Rensselaerwyck had enjoyed the forbearance of their patroon and his manorial office. Stephen Van Rensselaer's death came in the wake of the continent's most shocking economic depression, when misery surrounded him, and as the Whigs, with wind in their sails like a sloop on the Hudson, were mobilizing for the upcoming general election in 1840 and hoping to end twelve years of Democratic presidents in the White House. With New York ever the prize of the U.S. Electoral College, any economic issue that shook the state in 1839 would soon become a legislative and even a partisan issue.[8]

In the midst of a nationwide economic slump, Rensselaerwyck's tenants could perhaps have been forgiven for thinking that their unpaid rents—debts amassing to over $400,000 by the date of the patroon's death—would be absolved. Yet the same economic depression that had sunk their fortunes had also dwindled the assets of the patroon's descendants, and the landlord's son, Stephen Van Rensselaer IV, quickly charged his trustees with collecting the back rents. In May 1839, the trustees and their attorneys drew up writs of fieri facias (orders of execution by a sheriff and levied on the assets of the debtor) and sent them around to the farmers. The young Van Rensselaer wanted not only settlement of debts in arrears but immediate and complete payment, with failure to remit resulting in the seizure of stock, capital, and existing crops. Spontaneous assemblies of tenant farmers sprang up all over Albany County, and by July 4, 1839, the tenants had issued their own declaration of independence.

The tenants of Rensselaerwyck lived on the most well-known of a set of manorial holdings in Albany and Rensselaer Counties bordering the upper Hudson. Their legal position was unlike that of other tenants under common law, where a lease implied the landlord's continued ownership of the plot but conveyed a right of possession to the tenant for a fixed term. Such common-law leases, along with the system of fee simple ownership and allodial tenure, essentially characterized the United States at the time. Yet the leases on New York manors qualified as what lawyers called "leases in fee" and were perpetual. The tenant's interest was not alienable. If a tenant wanted out of the contract, he had to pay a substantial fraction of the original purchase price (usually one-quarter) to the landlord. In addition, all "taxes, charges and assessments" imposed by New York or local governments would need to be paid by the tenant, not the manorial lord. These terms carried the immediate and implied meaning that tenant families were trapped by lease-in-fee contracts, especially at a time of declining margins. All the interest, and the totality of the value of the farmer's investments and improvements to the land, reverted to the lord.[9]

Few if any in New York politics seemed inclined to defend the lease-in-fee institution. Those inclined toward the Democrats and their Jeffersonian heritage saw independent land ownership and cultivation as a political ideal. The very dispossession and removal agenda of the post–War of 1812 period that had turned countless Indigenous peoples off their lands was motivated in part by the assumption that the resulting White settlement would take the allodial form. The Whigs and, before them, the Federalists wanted national infrastructure and a system of credit for the very reason that geographical mobility of the kind so hindered by manorial tenure could facilitate development and, with it, a harmony between agriculture and industry.[10] In his 1840 message to the legislature, Whig governor William Seward—who, along with his party, was caught between the tides of law, politics, and protest—summarized a broad consensus. The "tenures, introduced before the revolution, are regarded as inconsistent with the existing institutions, and have become odious to those who hold them. They are unfavorable to agricultural improvement, inconsistent with the prosperity of the districts where they exist, and opposed to the sound policy and the genius of our institutions."[11]

These arguments notwithstanding, the lease-in-fee contracts stubbornly withstood amendment and legal challenge. A New York statute in 1787 prohibited leases in fee on any land granted by the state, but the contracts on the New York manors long predated the Revolution. The U.S. Constitution's clause held all such prior contracts inviolable by subsequent governments. Tenure critics pointed to the older doctrine of Quia Emptores—from a 1290 statute passed during the reign of Edward I that prohibited subinfeudation and opened the terms of land alienation—and its apparent voidance of rentier arrangements without the possibility of alienation. Yet much as reformers thought Quia Emptores applied through the common law, the New York Supreme Court in a crucial 1820 decision agreed with a Rhinebeck manor's lawyer that it did not. Not only did lease-in-fee arrangements defy the common law and the principles of republicanism and liberal jurisprudence, they were impermeable to judicial remedy. New York's tenant farmers were ensnared in a Dutch institution in which their forebears had trapped them.[12]

When the tenant farmers saw their hopes for forbearance dashed by their deceased patroon's son, their first steps were to form temporary assemblies, draw up grievances, and insist on their redress. The first venue they chose was that of the Van Rensselaer family itself, situated at the manorial offices. They asked Van Rensselaer to lower their aggregate debt and for the conversion of each lease in fee to what would essentially be a mortgage. If the patroon sold his interest in the farms and invested the cash value with sufficient interest (which they set at 7 percent per annum) to substitute for the lost rent payments, the tenants would gain their freedom and, in principle, the patroon could be made whole. Van Rensselaer was unconvinced and flatly rejected the tenant demands. He was open to converting lease-in-fee arrangements to allodial plots, but any release of tenant obligations could come only after the full payment of accrued rents. Farmers assembling at Bern on July 4, 1839, denounced the patroon's response, and they did so using the terms of the Revolution and the new democratic age. They would refuse any "unconditional submission to the will of one man, elevated by an aristocratic law, emanating from a foreign monarchy."[13]

The tenants' Independence Day 1839 assembly crystallized a network linked in organization, united by an egalitarian and producer-based ideology, and skillfully mixing new technologies of influence. Farmers recomposed themselves as a signatory community, and their declaration became a mutual avowal of commitment, with the ominous warning that they tendered "each unto the other our fortunes and our sacred honor even to the last extremity in protesting our rights and property from being wantonly and unjustly forced from us." When in August and September 1839 Albany County sheriffs began making visits to tenant farmers and delivering fieri facias writs, they were greeted with warnings to leave, assembled crowds, and thinly veiled physical threats. When one sheriff hired a supposedly "fearless" young contractor to serve the writs in his stead, the anti-rent farmers chased the young agent from their lands and villages, then formed a mob in a nearby town, captured him, and threatened to tar and feather him. They burned the writs in his possession and finally released their "prisoner" after humiliating him. Albany County sheriffs backed down, and while Governor Seward sent militia into Albany County and later proclaimed a "cheerful and patriotic submission to the law," the tenant farmers had given up nothing in the exchange.[14]

The September 1839 warning letter sent by a New Scotland farmer to Albany County sheriff Michael Artcher displayed both the intimidation and the changed thinking of the anti-renters in their expression of demands. Trashing Artcher as acting "in favor of the tenants' monarch," the farmer warned him that his writ-submitting journey would be a "perilous tour" for which he "could not pledge for your safe return." The tenants were acting as they did, the farmer maintained, because their first supplication to Van Rensselaer had met with flat rejection. No longer would the tenant producers "pray to their landlord like children to a parent." Now, in the wake of Van Rensselaer's elevation of stakes, "The tenants have organized themselves into a body, and resolved not to pay any more rents until they can be redressed of their grievances."[15]

The New Scotland farmer's letter made the tenants' strategy clear. Not only did farmers intend their violence to dissuade sheriff-enforced eviction, but they also hoped to change the court of proceedings. The farmers' first set of grievances were submitted to the venue they knew best: the patroon and his office. Van Rensselaer's rejection of their initial demands and his serving of writs was, in part, an attempt to reinforce the immediacy of the venue, and the farmers' response was, in turn, a refusal to deal with the sheriff on the terms of county-level enforcement of state property statutes. The Independence Day declaration of 1839, the rent strike, and its violence, when combined with a subsequent petitioning campaign to the New York legislature, reveal the transformation that became clear in the New Scotland farmer's missive: the abrupt transition from a language of supplicatory requests to one of collective, demand-conveying petitions. Their consistent repetition of the language of "redress of grievances" conjured legacies of the Revolution, its own Declaration of Independence (with Jefferson's reminder that the colonists had "Petitioned for Redress in the most Humble Terms" to be "answered only by repeated injury"), and the U.S. Constitution's First Amendment. The tenant farmers' grievances bespoke a larger ethic of equality, and they announced that the stage on which they would be heard would be Albany, not Van Rensselaer's office or the county courts. In turn, Van Rensselaer's attempt to involve the governor and the militia can be read as an attempt to locate the dispute at higher levels of authority.

Governor Seward's discussion of the rent strikes in his January 1840 address led to the appointment of a select committee chaired by the Whig lawyer William Duer. Duer's committee soon became the target for "numerous petitions, signed by a very large number of persons," all decrying the tenure laws. Duer was new to the assembly in 1840, but the chamber was composed of experienced legislators who had seen thousands of petitions in their years. To describe the signatory aggregates as "very large" was a remarkable note for a committee report, especially one that had been occasioned by a governor's address. The assembly clerks did not customarily report the number of signatures on every petition, but when they did, the totals for anti-rent petitions (which they described uniformly, as they did not for most petitions in the 1840 session, as praying "for redress of grievances") were usually over one hundred, as with the memorial from 142 inhabitants of the East Manor of Rensselaerwyck, and that of Knox and Bern with 151 signatures. Yet Duer was likely referring, at least in part, to the petition of 744 Albany County residents and tenants introduced on January 31. In the 1840s, petitions of such size on issues other than slavery and temperance came from New York City or possibly Buffalo, not from farmers, much less tenants in the Hudson valley.[16]

The early 1840 petitions advanced not only surprising signatory numbers but also novel arguments and legal strategies. Anti-rent farmers demanded an investigation of the Van Rensselaer titles and whether any were "defective" or endowed the patroon with "more land than he is entitled to," such that the "grant may be abrogated."[17] These demands jeopardized not only Van Rensselaer's manors but also the holdings of any other lord to a lease-in-fee arrangement in the Hudson-Mohawk region. Beyond this call for inspection, the petitioners also claimed that many of the tenants were, "being poor and illiterate," long ago "induced to enter upon and cultivate the land by promises which have not been fulfilled, and by misrepresentations as to the nature of the leases which would be granted."[18] Backing these claims were a range of affidavits from the petitioners, who now mixed their testimony with their signatures. With this mixture of fraud claims and legal challenges, the petitioners were placing before the assembly a complex portfolio of grievances, evidence, legal questions, and signatures.

Duer's committee had a difficult task facing it, a jointly legal and political problem whose solution would, they knew, please no one fully. Duer's committee eventually proposed an altogether different idea, one inspired by Whig ideology of internal improvements, by which the state would claim the manorial lands under eminent domain. This idea had legal plausibility, for a time, but it would require immediate payment of equivalent value under the Takings Clause, and New York, like other depression-era states, was seriously in debt. Duer's committee eventually punted the issue before it, calling for the establishment of a Manor Commission that would examine the problem. In the shadow of the impending election campaign, the Duer committee's handoff left no one satisfied, but as the chairman had probably surmised, statewide attention on the issue would quickly be diverted to the national partisan contest.[19]

The Whigs triumphed broadly in the autumn of 1840, bringing William Henry Harrison to the presidency and claiming a House majority. (Control of the Senate would not come until early 1841, after the Whig state legislatures had made their elections for the upper chamber.) Even as it raised aspirations for a favorable settlement of their debts, Whig victory at the national level complicated the tenants' program. States hoped for a generous distribution of funds from federal land sales, but federal land revenues plummeted in the wake of the depression, and the Harrison administration did not convey them to the states. Harrison's unexpected death in April 1841 and his succession by the more fiscally conservative and irascible John Tyler, who refused to continue revenue distribution, dashed whatever hopes Seward and the New York Whigs had for funds to assist with infrastructure and an eminent domain settlement of the manorial tenure problem. The 1841 legislative session in New York ended in a stalemate for Van Rensselaer and the tenant farmers. The Manor Commission report arrived too late in the session to be acted on. Seward lacked the votes in the assembly to pass the commission's bill, and the New York Treasury lacked the funds for immediate payment of lands taken by eminent domain.

The inaction of the legislature, combined with continued grievances, brought a new stage of tenant organization and petitioning. For the second time, on April 28, 1841, anti-rent farmers held a broad demonstration in the township of Bern, and the assembled adopted a set of resolutions soon known as the Bern Manifesto. The manifesto's three resolutions announced an ideology married to political strategy. The first declared that "the holding of so large a territory by one man" violated the Declaration of Independence and the Guaranty Clause of Article IV of the U.S. Constitution, which assured to each state a form of "republican government." The second resolution set forth a change of venue, namely that "we petition the next Congress for a redress of grievances." It was the first time that organized anti-renters had publicly vowed to petition the national government about their cause. Finally, the Bern assembly declared that they would enter a "contest" with their patroon for up to ten years, or "until a redress of grievances be obtained." The "contest" was not defined further, but it clearly implied the continuation of rent strikes and whatever means were necessary to maintain them.[20]

New confrontations between sheriffs and tenant farmers clarified the stakes, the technology, and the alternative venues of this new approach. With action foreclosed by Albany, anti-renters took their petitions to Washington, while creating a new theater of resistance on the manorial domains. From April through September, sheriffs who arrived to enforce land sales met crowds of anti-rent protesters presenting themselves as "Indians." Organizing into performative (but nonetheless armed) "tribes" who declared their independence from the landlord and any legal system enforcing his decrees, these disruptors were greeted with praise and large local crowds and succeeded in nullifying the land sales, as no one would show up to buy. After one tense standoff in 1841, it was clear that sheriffs could no longer compel tenant foreclosures and that the sympathies of the New York militiamen lay with the tenants. There followed a nearly three-year pause in attempts to collect rent on Rensselaerwyck.[21]

The Democrats took back the statehouse in a rout in the state elections that autumn. The election returns showed that the anti-renters were loyal neither to the Whigs nor to the Democrats. Tense electoral competition in New York might have propelled partisan maneuvering on the tenants' demands, but it did not. Politically and legally, the Whigs were unable to advance a legislative agenda to help the tenants. Democrats, ever more rent asunder by slavery politics, offered sympathy for the anti-renters but abided by their unwillingness to help with government projects of the sort that would invoke eminent domain or commit the Empire State to new debt. The new Democratic governor, William C. Bouck, went so far as to side with the manorial landlords in his 1843 address.[22]

Amid electoral maneuvering and seeming gridlock, the legislative pressure of 1841 had kindled momentum for a different change in law, one constraining the ability of creditors to force the sale of any and all personal items for rent repayment. Petitions for "property exemption" asked that the state exempt from forced sale all "necessary" property up to $250. New York had long exempted certain articles of personal property—only those "articles of prime necessity for a small family" and "altogether inadequate for the absolute wants of a large one"—from compulsory sale.[23] The statutes solidifying this exemption had come at around the same moment in state politics when debt imprisonment was being abolished. The idea was to find "the amount of property that an honest policy may leave inviolable—so that while the debtor is required to be just to his creditors, he shall not be left without essential and reasonable comforts for himself and his family."[24] The petitions coming to the 66th Senate were referred to the Committee on the Judiciary, led by Whig Mark Sibley. The *Albany Evening Journal,* led by Whig reformer Thurlow Weed, favored "immediate action on the petitions" that asked for a furniture exemption of between $200 and $300: "We know of no law in existence in our state, the repeal of which would give so universal satisfaction, and which justice and humanity so strongly demands, as the 'six spoons and six knives and forks' statute. Its existence is disgracing the age in which we live. Next to the abolishment of imprisonment for debt in the scale of humane legislation stands the object prayed for, and our only surprise is, that its passage was not effected years ago."[25]

Sibley introduced a bill extending the property exemption to $150, three-fifths of the amount the petitions had requested.[26] Yet internal divisions among Whigs, whose more conservative members decried impositions on creditors, stymied the measure. Even as more humane Whigs followed Weed's *Evening Journal* in connecting property exemptions to abolition of debt imprisonment, conservatives like Erastus Root decried the trend toward "protecting property from its rightful owners by legislation," and warned that "the law to abolish imprisonment for debt is sufficiently mischievous in its operation, without trying another experiment, vastly to increase the evils that already exist."[27]

Sibley's committee and the legislative and print debate over the exemption bill both responded to previous memorials and encouraged petitioning over the ensuing year. Even as conservative Whigs were scuttling his $150 exemption measure, Sibley and his allies presented petition after petition in its support, including several calling for more general exemptions to property seizure and sale on behalf of the "honest insolvent." At the beginning of the 1842 session in January, as more petitions arrived on the exemption proposal and manorial rent generally, Senator Henry W. Strong introduced a new exemption bill, partially styled after the Sibley measure from the previous legislative session. To the rationale for the Sibley bill, Strong's bill and the accompanying committee report added the lessons garnered from a review of other states' legislation. "Among all the States and Territories of the Union," Strong's judiciary committee stated, "it is a remarkable fact that in no two of them are the provisions of the exemption law alike." Delaware made no property exemption, while many states protected minimal livestock ("six sheep" appearing commonly in the various statutes), and Arkansas typified a range of states in protecting "all arms and military equipments required by law." Even dispossessed debtors were expected to show for muster roll. Maine, Michigan, and North Carolina, among other states, protected Bibles and schoolbooks from forced sale. Alabama, Arkansas, Connecticut, Rhode Island, South Carolina, and Virginia did not.[28]

Strong's committee seized on this heterogeneity of statutes to assume wide discretion in framing its own law. It argued that the forced sales exemptions ought not to be targeted toward specific forms of real property ("furniture") but should instead be set at a dollar amount of equivalent value, for which he suggested the $150 initially proposed by Sibley. Such an "exemption in value only, without an enumeration of articles, would be an innovation" without precedent in the United States. Value-based exemptions would rationalize the arbitrariness of legislative protections so randomly scattered across the American states and territories, prevent extraordinary abuses where particular items were cherished or necessary to a tenant family, and leave to farmers themselves the discretion as to how to allot their property between the fraction put up for sale and what was exempted. The measure passed a close vote in the legislature and became law on April 11, 1842. Far more than a bone tossed to the tenants, the exemption law in fact changed the terms of debtor-creditor relations in the Empire State—a fact borne out in the hundreds of petitions calling for its repeal that soon flooded the assembly. At $150, the statutory level of exempted value lay at or above what most tenant families held in real property. Over a decade later, in 1856, Josiah Marshall's *Farmers and Emigrants Complete Guide* would estimate that the necessary property required for a "new settler" who, unlike the Hudson-Mohawk region's existing tenant farmers, had to clear lands before farming them amounted to $254.50. Sample items in the *Guide*'s calculation included a double wagon ($50), a span of horses ($100), a yoke of oxen ($50), a single cow ($15), and a "superior plough" ($10). Most New York tenant families needed much less than what the *Guide* deemed essential. Prices for many consumer goods in 1842 and 1843 had, moreover, fallen in the late 1830s, and were well below the values used in the *Guide*'s 1855 calculations. Hence, for many rent-distressed tenants, the 1842 exemption act had the effect of doing legally what the anti-renters' resistance had been doing in practice: ending forced sales.[29]

Petitions also came in on the rent issue, and they raised a new dimension of the conflict. Tenants now claimed that whatever fealty their ancestors owed to the manor, those ancestors were long since gone from the earth and the current occupants of the land were trapped in a contract to which they had never consented. These petitions came not only from the Helderberg towns but also from the fifty-thousand-acre Scott Patent in Schoharie County. The descendants of the original signers were trapped in the old contracts, with the reversionary interest of the land held by the manorial landlord as long as they occupied it, and unable to sell their stake without a quarter of the value being turned over to the same lord. Hence, returns on tenant investment ("improvements") were captured by the landlord almost entirely. Coming amidst the debt and bankruptcy crisis of the late 1830s and early 1840s, this generational and historical claim was a powerful argument.[30]

In the ensuing year's 1843 session, the exemption debate took the place of the rent debate as the central economic issue confronting the state legislature. Erastus Root and other Whig conservatives targeted the exemption law for repeal, and Whigs circulated exemption-law repeal petitions at party meetings throughout the state. After the Democrats shot down several repeal attempts on party-line votes, conservative Whigs and merchants launched another memorial campaign. The petitioning battle gave rise to another report by Strong's judiciary committee. Writing for his committee in February 1843, Strong focused on the petitions and asked why the exemption law's opponents had remained silent for so long. "The act in question," the committee wrote, "was passed after a full and ample discussion of its merits and effects. For two successive sessions it was agitated in the Legislature and canvassed by the public. Petition after petition was presented for the enactment of a law exempting necessary property to a greater amount than is even now allowed, and no remonstrance was heard from the people against it, until the law now on the statute book was ordered to third reading" in the assembly. Strong reported that petitions with 7,127 signatures came in support of a repeal of the exemption law, while a counterpetitioning drive produced petitions with 9,416 names. The exemption bill and the petitioning clash of 1843 touched on the encompassing issue of the age: the terms of repayment for debtors and any and all renters. Merchants now joined landlords on the creditor side, while farmers and small debtors far and wide joined forces with the tenant farmers. The rent war had given way to a statewide conflict between debtors and creditors.[31]

Henry Strong's committee report had tallied over sixteen thousand signatures in the petition and counterpetition campaign of the early 1843 session, but the legislative clerks for the assembly would continue recording petitions for the remainder of the session. While the clerks did not aggregate signature totals, their efforts would produce still different numbers, numbers far exceeding those of the Strong report. The assembly alone recorded 539 petitions on the exemption law in the 1843 session, and for those 287 documents for which it recorded the signatory aggregates, there were 27,853 names affixed (the others were described by the clerk as "sundry" inhabitants or citizens signing). The signature aggregates, especially those for and against exemption law repeal or modification, showed that whereas more pro-repeal petitions came into the 1843 session, the anti-repeal forces had more signatures petition-by-petition. Petitions favoring repeal averaged 83 names per document, whereas petitions against averaged 127 signatures (see Table 12.1). These differences remained consistent over the term of the 1843 session (see Figure 12.1) and held across petitions coming from the same county. It is highly likely that legislators noticed them, and that these patterns contributed to the reluctance of the legislature, following Strong's report, to alter the law.

These aggregate patterns showed popular support for the exemption statute even at a time of intense mobilization against it by conservative Whigs. The state's rural landlords were disproportionately concentrated in

TABLE 12.1 Petitions for and against Repeal of the Property Exemption Law, New York Assembly, 1843

	For Repeal of Exemption Law	Against Repeal of Exemption Law
Petitions introduced	379	160
Petitions with recorded signature totals	194	93
Signatures	16,026	11,827
Signature totals in Strong report (February 1843)	7,127	9,416
Average signatories per petition [95% confidence interval]	82.6 [72.1, 93.1]	127.2 [112.1, 142.3]
Difference[1]	Unadjusted difference: 44.5 signatories ($p < 0.001$) Difference constrained to within-county comparisons: 39.2 ($p = 0.04$)	

Source: JASNY (1843).

1. Unadjusted comparison derived from pairwise means comparison (replicated in linear regression); within-county comparisons derived from county fixed-effects regression model with standard errors clustered on county.

New York City. Yet of the petitions recorded from the city, there were 1,067 signatures on petitions favoring exemption repeal and 1,263 on those that came in against repeal. Pro-repeal petitions included one led by former mayor Stephen Allen (whose name led a memorial with 263 signatures), but an anti-repeal remonstrance came in from the Democratic-Republican Committee of the city's Eighth Ward, the city's largest and most rapidly growing by 1840 and home to many laborers and unionists active in the General Trades' Union. From Buffalo, all the petitions with recorded signatures came in against exemption law repeal, with a total of 1,168 men signing memorials supporting the status quo of exemption. Similar anti-repeal majorities came from towns like Canandaigua, Utica, and Williamsburg. The aggregation practices of assembly clerks reflected the fact that legislators were watching the thousands of names (and voters) behind these memorials. The weak correlation of these signatory patterns with known Empire State voting patterns implies that the exemption coalition was not captured by either the Whigs or the Democrats. Democrats like Strong and Governor

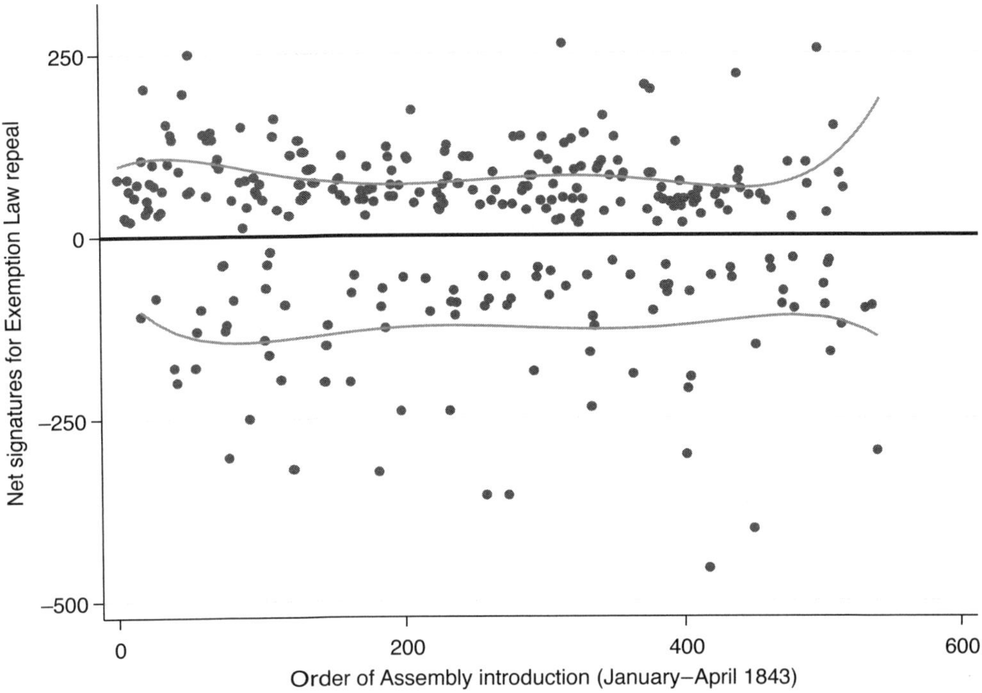

FIGURE 12.1. Signature Aggregates for Pro- and Anti-Repeal Petitions, by Order of Assembly Introduction, New York (1843).

Bouck undoubtedly saw popular forces arraying themselves behind the exemption statute. The petitioning battle instigated by Erastus Root and conservative Whigs had, if anything, demonstrated the strength of support for protections for tenants and other renters.[32]

The passage of the debtor-exemption law and its stabilization in the midst of the petitioning campaign shifted the debate on several fronts. First, the law certainly coincided with the decline in violence on the manors and may have aided the peace. Second, the legal arguments and strategies of the anti-renters changed, as they now contested the title of Van Rensselaer and coordinated with legislative allies to introduce the Act concerning Tenures by Lease. Petitions in support of this bill poured into the 1844 session, not only from the tenants of Rensselaerwyck but also from Schoharie County. Third, and reflecting these patterns, the contest of mobilization also coincided with the emergence of stronger tenant organization; by the end of

1843, the Anti-Rent Association of Rensselaer County had four thousand members, and various county and town associations had assembled war chests for mutual support and legal counsel. The surge of these associations outside Rensselaerwyck had come during the exemption petitioning campaign.[33]

In the 1844 general election, New York Whigs focused heavily on state offices in addition to their support of Henry Clay. They sought to redouble their efforts on land tenure issues. New petitions from anti-rent organizations made their way to the 1844 assembly, one signed by four thousand members of the Anti-Rent Association of Rensselaer County, another by roughly two thousand members of the Albany County Association. These petitions called on the legislature not merely to redress grievances or to tinker with exemptions and land sale conditions, but to abolish the lease-in-fee arrangement altogether, constitutional structures notwithstanding. The petitions induced the assembly to appoint a select committee, chaired by Whipple, to respond. Whipple's committee report rehearsed older arguments about the stain that manorial tenure left on the Empire State, pointing to its "direct tendency to suppress that spirit of enterprise and improvement so essential to the prosperity of this county." The institution also undid the promise of Jeffersonian republicanism. The leases "had their origin in Europe in the age of feudalism," as the Whipple committee soberly noted, and "still preserve those restrictions which were engrafted upon them at that barbarous period, and which are so unjustly odious to every friend of free institutions of government."[34] As long as the leases remained, New York would undermine "that spirit of independence which is not humbled by the payment of an annual tribute, acknowledges no superior, and which raises the American farmer of more favored districts to a rank in the social scale never attained by the working man of any country but our own."[35] Yet the Whipple select committee's sympathetic rhetoric led to nothing in the way of proposed changes. The committee punted the proposal, claiming insufficient legal expertise to tackle the issue.

As the sixty-eighth session of the New York legislature convened in January 1845, anti-rent reformers sought to bust the stalemate. The Anti-Rent Associations had formed a "party" and, at the organization's convention in January, two hundred delegates from across the state assembled in the symbolic town of Bern, where the network's Independence Day manifesto had been issued in 1839. Taking inspiration from an earlier meeting in West Sandlake in Rensselaer County, the convention united behind a threefold platform: pass the Act concerning Tenures by Lease (which would permit tenants to challenge the title of their manorial lords), abolish distress sales, and impose state taxes on rent charges. The last of these measures changed the game. Rent-charge taxation threatened the revenue streams of manorial landlords, which had been excluded from taxation under statutes of 1828, and rather accidentally. The Bern convention vowed to gather a petition for the sixty-ninth session of the legislature at Albany, and quickly created a committee on petitions to coordinate the effort. One convention attendee surmised that the group could, by the first of March, gather as many as fifteen thousand signatures on a petition behind the three measures.[36]

The popular weight of those petitions would, according to the assembly's own report, amass to more than twenty-five thousand signatures. As the memorials "praying for an alteration of the law of landlord and tenant" rolled in to the assembly, legislators saw that the rent issue had been transformed and a new coalition awakened. On forty different session days were petitions for tenancy reform read into the record, while not one memorial from any sort of counterpetition campaign entered the record that year. Geographically broader than the earlier Rensselaerwyck petitions but far more concentrated and radical than the exemption memorials that arrived from nearly every county in the state, the "alteration" petitions exhibited a geographic concentration among those counties with manorial lands (see Table 12.2). Assembly clerks described the petitions by county origin only, but even the county-level distribution highlighted the shifting nature of the debate. After Albany County (which includes Rensselaerwyck), the heaviest petitioning counties appeared to be Rensselaer and Schoharie. Rensselaer County had produced the four-thousand-signature anti-rent petition of January 1844, while Schoharie County tenants had already begun contesting the validity of manorial titles. Schoharie County housed the fifty- thousand-acre Scott Patent and the Blenheim Patent. On the former, the descendants of the late John Livingston held the tenancy contracts. The wheat rent on Scott Patent was appreciably higher than at Rensselaerwyck, and the land contracts limited tenants to two lifetimes, after which the farmers could be dispossessed entirely, all interest on the land (including the value of any improvements) reverting to the Livingston family. Many of the farmers on that estate were approaching the end of the second tenant's life span and anxiously feared the disposition of their family holdings. The Blenheim Patent was also large, and partly owned by the prominent Whig John A. King.[37]

TABLE 12.2 Tenancy Alteration Petitions, New York State Assembly, 1845

Total Sample, 1845 Assembly	Session Days with Alteration Petitions Introduced	Total Petitions
	40	288
By County	**Session Days by County**	**Petitions by County (estimate)**
Albany	19	63
Columbia	10	32
Delaware	11	31
Dutchess	2	7
Fulton	2	2
Greene	3	12
Montgomery	6	15
Niagara	1	1
Oneida	2	2
Otsego	2	3
Rensselaer	8	49
Schenectady	1	4
Schoharie	18	57
Sullivan	2	5
Ulster	1	1

Note: Assembly journals list number of petitions introduced by day, from a list of counties bundled together (petitions not disaggregated across counties). Estimates assume uniform distribution across counties per day of introduction; estimates do not add up to total because of rounding. *Source: JASNY*, 68th Sess. (1845).

By April 1845, the terrain of the rent debate had changed subtly but durably. Full legislative abolition of lease-in-fee contracts remained unlikely, as lawmakers continued to doubt its constitutionality. Yet the abolition of distress sales and the taxation of rent charges remained very much alive. Governor Silas Wright surprised many an observer with an endorsement of the mass petitioners' rent-charge taxation request, and the state comptroller Azariah Flagg unsettled manorial lords by calling for rent-charge taxation on the principle of equality of fiscal burdens. As the governor and comptroller acted on the new agenda laid out by petitions to the legislature, conservative lawmakers tried to blunt the anti-renters' momentum. A scuttle quickly ensued in the assembly over the legislative report from the select committee appointed to deal with the "numerous petitions from manor tenants." The majority of the committee, led by lawyer and conservative Democrat Anthony J. Constant, issued an opinion without consulting the minority, deciding against action on any of the demands. As if to counter the publicity of the petitions with the distributed reasoning of the committee, the assembly printed ten times the usual number of copies of the majority report. Angry and undeterred, minority members Ira Harris and Seymour Boughton issued a minority report, but they agreed to do so only after Flagg had initiated momentum for rent-charge taxation.[38]

Tenants, landlords, and politicians alike understood that the tax measure would induce landlords to negotiate with tenants on the terms of a buyout. The fact that the rent strikes principally affected Rensselaerwyck and the Helderberg towns in Albany County, while the taxation would fall on other manors as well, especially those in Rensselaer and Schoharie Counties, implied that the geography as well as the stakes of the tenancy battle had shifted. In August 1845, seventeen prominent New York City landlords—including Frederick De Peyster, the Verplanck family, and the Livingston descendants—published and circulated a remarkable proposal offering to sell their contracts and create "grants in fee." These manorial proprietors held titles in the very "downriver" and west-of-Albany counties that had sent alteration petitions to the assembly earlier that year—Columbia, Delaware, Greene, Schoharie, Sullivan, and Ulster. In some sense, the negotiated conversion of lease-in-fee contracts to allodial holdings was the very thing wished for by jurists, conservatives, and any politician wanting to minimize violence. The momentum for buyouts soon reached Schoharie County. On January 6, 1847, after a lengthy set of negotiations, the tenants on the Blenheim Patent, led by the anti-rent farmer John Mayham, offered the King family a purchase of terms.[39]

The momentum for buyouts preceded the ultimate legislative decisions at Albany, but those statutes soon came, and they did so with overwhelming bipartisan support. The Act to Equalize Taxation passed the assembly with 84 votes in favor and 9 against, while distress sale abolition passed 94 to 7. The senate soon followed suit, with 23 senators favoring the distress bill and 3 against, while senators divided 15–11 in favor of the tax bill. Governor Silas Wright signed both measures into law on May 13, 1846. The wide majority in favor of rent-charge taxation and distress sale abolition suggests that partisan divisions had little to do with the adoption of these measures. To be sure, Wright was angling for Anti-Rent Party votes, but the program of rent taxation had been established not by his party but by petitioning anti-renters at manors all over the Hudson-Mohawk region. (Crucially, these proposals arrived heavily from the manors where rent strikes were not capturing the news.) To conclude that the measures were foregone conclusions in 1845 or 1846 would be erroneous. Only when the distress sale abolition and, more pivotally, the taxation of rent charges had been proposed by the Anti-Rent Party petition campaign did the agenda for such overwhelmingly popular measures materialize. When Governor Wright endorsed the taxation plan in that crucial month of April 1845, he did so with specific reference to the anti-renters' convention meeting and their petitions.[40]

By 1860, manorial tenure remained in New York State, but its imprint had withered. The lease-in-fee arrangements survived in Albany County (especially Rensselaerwyck), but almost six in ten had been bought out (from 1,397 manorial contracts in 1839 to 580 in 1859). Roughly 250 farmers still had lease-in-fee holdings in Rensselaer County. A battle over statutory abolition waxed and waned in the 1850s, largely focused on Rensselaerwyck, where anti-rent organization held most fervently. Courts upheld the lease-in-fee arrangement, and many anti-rent holdouts were removed from their lands in the 1860s.

In a series of reforms that appear misleadingly incremental, however, a politics of petitioning had accomplished de facto what party politics and jurisprudence could not achieve de jure. Rent strikes and violence had for a time halted the distress sales in the Hudson-Mohawk region, but the exemption law—brought into being and protected by systematic petition mobilizations that were closely followed by legislators in Albany—had already dented proprietors' ability to collect rent by distress sales. The statutes of 1846 further codified this regime, but they left manorial landlords without redress for rent collection and facing a new tax that ate away at their revenue. It was in 1845, in the midst of a dramatically altered agenda, that landlords began to buy out their tenants in Schoharie and Rensselaer Counties and to convert tenancy into allodial holdings. More than a movement of public sentiment, the tenants' petitions of 1843 to 1845 had changed the menu of options before the legislature and had conveyed an anti-rent politics that stood astride, but separably, from the rent strikes. For the real, material terms of thousands of farmers in Schoharie, Rensselaer, Columbia, Greene, Sullivan, and Ulster Counties who saw the specter of distress sales vanish—first by exemption, then by legislation—and who witnessed with amazement the fresh willingness of their manorial landlords to bargain in

1845 and 1846, nonpartisan organization and petitioning had delivered a painful but real liberation. Neither ballots nor violence presaged the movement of buyouts. The mutual construction of petitioning and nonpartisan political organization had altered the legislative agenda, forcing manorial landlords to the table.[41]

* * *

As petitioning campaigns, rent strikes, and occasional violence washed over the Hudson-Mohawk region in the early 1840s, Lower Canada (known as Canada East) was still recovering from the Rebellions of 1837 and 1838. Durham's *Report* had charted a course to reconciliation and renewal with the fusion of colonial government, and in 1841 the Legislative Assembly of the Province of United Canada met for the first time. Important patterns of law and politics still differentiated Lower Canada and Upper Canada (Canada West and later Ontario), and in addition to land laws and linguistic differences, partisan configurations mattered heavily. The Parti patriote remained an important force in Lower Canadian politics.

Seigneurial tenure in Canada had never taken quite the form it had in France. French settlers in ancien régime Canada were few, and land was far more plentiful in Canada than in France. The owners of seigneuries were not always lords proper, with many proprietors gaining their lands through public service to the colony or the Company of One Hundred Associates. The royal charters dating from the seventeenth century had relied heavily on subinfeudation, giving more power to longer-dwelling tenants. The concentration of seigneuries in the Saint Lawrence valley and the presence of alternative markets and lands left seigneurs and tenant farmers more vulnerable to export competition and price instability. The weak presence of state authority and the mass of settlement provided arbitrage opportunities to colonists old and new, and the Crown spent much of its time and energy trying to contain speculation. Still, the seigneurial fees (*cens*) and rents payable in money or "nature" (grain or animals) imposed an ever-increasing burden on the tenants (*censitaires*). The Canadian seigneurial system severely constrained free alienation and property mutation through the system of *lods et ventes*.[42]

The Conquest of 1763 left seigneurs at the theoretical mercy of Parliament and the Colonial Office. Yet the early British governors knew that they faced a population management problem, and they saw in the continuation of feudal hierarchy a means for containing a potentially hostile mass of

French-speaking Catholic farmers. Both the Quebec Act of 1774 and the Constitutional Act of 1791 gave Lower Canada considerable space for seigneurial tenure, even as France itself proceeded to abolish feudal tenure from 1789 to 1793.[43]

The predominant economic shift in pre-Rebellion Lower Canada saw a growing number of anglophone proprietors take up the seigneuries. Many of them bought titles in the first decade after the Conquest of 1763, during which British proprietors purchased twenty-four seigneuries outright, another four in part, and held lands granted by principal tenants (known as *arrière-fiefs*) in ten others. By 1831, proprietors of British origin fully held eighty-four seigneuries, owned another thirty-five partially, and had *arrière-fiefs* in another thirty-five. Most of these had been purchased before the War of 1812.[44]

In two related ways, contestation over seigneurial tenure in Canada surfaced but remained muted in the 1820s and 1830s. The Commerce Act of Canada (1822) permitted proprietors in the towns of Québec and Trois-Rivières to convert vacant seigneurial holdings to free and common socage, while the Canada Tenures Act of 1825 extended an allodial conversion option to tenants. Coming as they did during the emergence of the Canadien movement and its debates over provincial autonomy, these very statutes brought the condemnation of Papineau and allied reformers. Francophone republicans believed that the provincial assembly only, and not Parliament, should regulate internal land title. Second, selected anglophone proprietors, principally Edward Ellice, began to push for abolition of feudal tenure so that the value of improvements could be captured and competition over agricultural productivity could be sharpened. Recognizing the feudal tenure still existing in the United States, Ellice wanted abolition for the purpose of national progress and competition with the Americans. Ellice succeeded in ceding his holding at the seigneury at Beauharnois to the Crown in 1833, but his commutation remained the exception, demonstrating the rule of seigneurial stability. Ellice's allies would recall that no further demands for commutation arose in the three years following his concession. The imperial and colonial crises running from 1827 to 1838—as Canada lurched between legislative prorogation, the mass anti-Dalhousie petitioning campaign, Dalhousie's demise, the Patriote Party, and the Rebellions—sidelined the tenure issue for a time, as provincial reformers focused on other issues, and the Colonial Office showed itself reluctant to intervene.[45]

To the campaign for feudal abolition, the Union of 1840 brought not momentum but a venue. The economic crisis of 1837 had not only triggered a francophone rebellion but also cemented hostility toward the seigneurs as never before in Canada. Many rebellion leaders, including Robert Nelson, promised to eliminate both the rents and the alienation constraints. Lord Durham addressed the issue of feudal tenures in his 1839 report, and drafted a plan for commutation of tenure, yet Durham's piecemeal solution confined its vision to Montréal, where support from the city's anglophone notables and its seminaries conveyed sufficient political influence to broker an agreement that would indemnify the proprietors. The very partiality of the 1840 Montréal plan, combined with Ellice's 1833 cessions at Beauharnois, left other tenant farmers incensed. Why, they wondered, were well-connected Anglophones and city residents getting relief while their feudal plight was ignored? Petitions flowed to the assembly in 1840 and 1841, most with English language prayers and signed by a majority of anglophone tenants—two from La Prairie, two from Beauharnois, two from La Colle, two from Noyan-Foucault. In 1841, acting on an early petition from his district that openly called for abolition of the seigneurial system, the new deputy from Beauharnois called for an inquiry into the possibility of tenure reform. The assembly appointed a committee of inquiry to report later in the term.[46]

When the commission of inquiry reported in late July, the assembly formed as a Committee of the Whole to hear the report (which was common) and scheduled a vote on the resolutions proposed by the commissioners (which was not). The commission's report later that session outlined three broad conclusions. First, the assembly noted the progress that had been made in commutations but concluded that the burdens of tenure still weighed too heavily on the province. Second, lawmakers recognized both that the province had a broad desire to do away with feudal tenure and replace it with "free holding" (*tenure libre*), and that the acts of Parliament passed in the previous two decades had been quite insufficient to advance these aims. In the finer details of the report, the commission estimated that about half of the population wanted commutation of tenure, while the other half wanted reform and amelioration of "abuses," such as rent and alienation conditions. Finally, the assembly argued that any solution to the problem had to include a fair indemnity to seigneurs. The resolutions passed the chamber—45 votes in favor to 3 against—but the dissenters were notable: Amable Berthelot, John Neilson, and Denis-Benjamin Viger.

Viger's opposition demonstrated the politics at work in the early unified assembly. Still a social conservative, Viger would become proprietor of the Ile Bizard seigneury from 1842 to 1861, constructing a manor on the lands in 1843. The early legislative action on the tenure issue highlighted the tension prevailing between linguistically defined political coalitions, as the older Patriotes avoided working with anglophone politicians and embraced an agrarian, anticommercial ideal.[47]

In the late 1840s, two political transformations shifted the politics of land tenure in Lower Canada. The first was the emergence of a new francophone leadership less tethered to the rural idealism of the earlier generation of Patriotes. Led by the jurists Louis-Hippolyte Lafontaine, Augustin-Norbert Morin, and Joseph-Amable Berthelot, these reformers expressed loyalty to French traditions and rejected colonial fusion along with any other anglophone initiatives to dominate the province, yet they also spurned what they saw as the overly bucolic vision of the Papineau-Viger cohort. They aspired to a mixed republican model with a provincial economy that would rival that of the United States—noting the abundance of water power available to Lower Canada—while also preserving French language and other noneconomic institutions.[48]

The second transformation came in the formation of anti-seigneurial organizations and petitioning. The Association for the Reform of Seigneurial Rights formed in 1848 and launched a broad, province-wide petitioning campaign. *La Minerve* would report in 1849 that in the previous two years alone, fully 32,700 persons had signed anti-seigneurial memorials (*requêtes*) to the government, 4,700 from the counties of Rouville, Chambly, and Laprairie. Viewing the previous nine years of unified assembly history, the paper reported, "It's the largest number of petitioners who have addressed the assembly asking for the redress of a single grievance."[49] Twenty-six of those petitions came to the assembly in 1849 (Figure 12.2), with fully thirteen demanding commutation of tenures into allodial holdings. Few petitions were demanding full abolition of seigneurial tenure. Assembly lawmakers responding to the memorials told the petitioners that justice was on the way and that Lafontaine had in fact outlined a plan for redress in a series of resolutions.

As these petitions and their signatory lists deluged the assembly, legislators noted something else. Increasingly the prayers were being written in French, not English, as had been the case in the early 1840s (Figure 12.3). This linguistic transformation, accompanied by signatory lists that were now

FIGURE 12.2. Anti-Seigneurial *Requêtes,* with Number of Commutation versus Abolition Prayers, 1840–1854.

majority francophone, heightened the importance of having respected French Canadian politicians respond to the documents. The physician Pierre Davignon, who represented Rouville in the assembly from 1848 to 1851, wrote the response to the forty-seven-signature Rouville-Chambly-Laprairie petition in *La Minerve,* and he tried to reassure the petitioners that Lafontaine was on their case. Davignon also invited tenant farmers from the province to send delegates to a meeting at Montréal in the fall of 1849. In November, 120 representatives from the districts of Montréal and Trois-Rivières descended on the city, resolving there for regulation of seigneurial rights and the abolition of tenure.[50]

With the rise of anglophone seigneurs and the emergence of francophone petitioners, the possibility of renewed linguistic strife seemed evident. The earlier petitions attacked the onerous rents and taxes that, in the view of French Canadians, violated the ancient Custom of Paris and pre-

FIGURE 12.3. Number of *Requêtes* drafted in English and French, 1840–1854.

Conquest royal decrees. These prayers called for the restoration of the rights of tenants under the ancien régime. Yet now petitioners were calling for these measures and more, moving (especially from 1848 to 1851) from prayers for commutation to open calls for full abolition, indemnities be damned. These demands—summarized in the wish for summary and declaratory abolition legislation (*loi déclaratoire*)—raised at least two thorny issues. Full abolition with indemnification would not only violate seigneurs' property rights but would leave many dispossessed almost entirely. Yet if the colonial government stepped in with indemnities for the proprietors, the provincial budget would explode at the very time when revenues were starting to return to Lower Canada after the crash of 1837 and the Rebellions.[51]

The issue was taken up in the assembly in 1850, and legislators were fiercely opposed on the issue. Lafontaine (representing the Montréal District) and Saguenay representative Marc Pascal De Sales Laperrière openly worried that the "incessant agitation" against seigneurs as a class had become so forceful as to reduce the value of their property. Seigneurs now feared that the swell of abolition petitions would lead to quick, total, and uncompensated abolition of seigneurial rights. Pivotal legislators such as Lafontaine, for their part, wanted to avoid the explosion of class and linguistic conflict that threatened to plunge the province into another rebellion. Moderate legislators could take some solace in the fact that while petitions with abolition-favorable prayers outnumbered those favoring commutation, those calling for commutation carried many more signatures. Among anti-seigneurial petitions received by the assembly from 1849 to 1854, those with abolition prayers averaged 161 signatures, while those calling for commutation averaged 401 names. Petitioners from the Montréal District (Chambly, Rouville, and Huntington Counties) and the Québec District (Dorchester and Saint Maurice) had each peppered the chamber with memorials bearing over one thousand signatures. Because Attorney General George-Étienne Cartier surmised that many tenants wanted reform and alleviation of seigneurial impositions rather than outright abolition, he counseled the abolition petitioners' representatives to accept a moderate course outlined by Lafontaine.[52]

Lafontaine took the lead in fashioning a proposal. Positioning himself between the defenders of seigneurial tenure and those who wanted immediate abolition without indemnity, he called for a plenary session in June 1850 to debate the issue. Noting the swell of organization and petitioning, he warned his chamber colleagues of two contending jeopardies. To those who wanted minimal or no reform, he warned that further deferral of land reform would allow the development of more radical energies that would "undermine society; there comes a time when the people say, 'It is too late.'" On the other hand, he warned that "one can get a certain degree of popularity in attaching oneself to public opinion," and tenant agitation made real the possibility of abolition without indemnity. The specter of uncompensated tenure abolition, in turn, had the dual effect of reducing the value of seigneurial holdings and of leading seigneurs to dig in their heels and avoid the subject of reform altogether. The time was now, Lafontaine argued, to strike a deal. His plan avoided any declaratory statute and contained an indemnity plan. The tenure abolitionist Pierre Davignon, previously having told his constituents to trust Lafontaine, found himself incensed by Lafontaine's bill (and the momentum behind it) and exchanged terse and bitter words with Cartier on the chamber floor. Along with other tenure abolitionists, Davignon believed that the Lafontaine plan left his petitioning constituents with no concrete remedy and saw the moderates' solutions as too conciliatory toward anglophone seigneurs. Davignon's constituents in Rouville County were soon petitioning for the abolition of the legislative council itself and an elective governor.[53]

The 1851 session saw a new flood of memorials, and the weight of anti-seigneurial petitioning was the highest in the history of the province (see Figure 12.3). The tenor and content of the prayers had changed, becoming overwhelmingly francophone and calling largely for an abolition statute. More petitions came in the 1852–1853 session, and some of the bills introduced by assembly leaders began to propose phased abolition within five years of legislative enactment. Others allowed tenure to remain, but nearly all permitted tenants to exit their tenure if they wished, whether individually or when voting as a bloc (with a two-thirds majority) to free themselves as a seigneury. The assembly passed a bill in 1852 with alienation mechanisms, but the legislative council (the province's unified upper chamber) rejected it quickly. After a new attempt in the beginning of the 1854 session, the prime minister was reversed by his own majority, and Lord Elgin dissolved the assembly.[54]

Tenure questions came to dominate the 1854 assembly elections—in which Morin found himself deposed over the tenure issue—but the message of the ballots was not entirely clear. Those who stood in the way of any reform found themselves, like the Speaker, tossed from office. Yet the dominant faction among those elected from Lower Canada in 1854 favored not total abolition but the restoration of ancien régime rights and constraints on the seigneurs. The new assembly met in September 1854, and its first bill was inspired by tenant farmers' petitions and the resolutions of their representatives. It bundled together a number of the proposals that had floated in petitions and the assembly in the previous five years. It greatly restricted seigneurial rights, abolishing all claims over navigable waters as well as the *droit de banalité* and *retrait conventionnel.* It limited the rent and taxes to a level that prevailed in the ancien régime, and it permitted individual purchases of lands as well as tenants' collective purchases. The legislative council converted the possibility of commutation into a set of obligations that accompanied any tenant attempt to purchase land rights, and it combined all seigneurial charges into a single rent; in the case of commutation, indemnities would be applied to the single rent. The law of 1854 then created a special court for administering and adjudicating the issues that arose from determining the rights of proprietors.[55]

The decisive shift in the battle over land tenure in Lower Canada came when tenants found a new enemy. Legislative reform came when the memorials of tenant farmers grew in number and in hostility toward the abusive practices of anglophone proprietors. In petitioning and in subsequent electoral campaigns, the *censitaires* applied unprecedented force on the assembly, and their petitions changed the menu of options from which the assembly and the legislative council would create a bill. As Louis-Hippolyte Lafontaine warned their representatives in 1850 and afterward, the specter of uncompensated tenure abolition forced proprietors to the table.

* * *

Land reform in nineteenth-century Canada and the United States carried two related enigmas. The first was that in neither New York nor Lower Canada was manorial tenure fully abolished in the nineteenth century, and to the extent that feudal institutions came to an end, it was the colonial government of Canada, led by its French Canadian petitioners, that interred feudal tenure more deeply than in New York, at least to the time of the Civil War. Legal debates and even forced evictions would continue in New York through the 1860s, and rents on lands at Rensselaerwyck would continue into the twentieth century. While twentieth-century debates raged in Québec about whether the 1850s had witnessed a reform or an abolition of the seigneurial regime, the lawbooks of 1861 evinced little about the point: the province's statutes had, seven years earlier, abolished "all feudal rights and duties." The links and burdens tying tenants and seigneurs would continue to tie up courts, not least due to the liberal character of the 1854 law and its preservation of the lands of the older seigneurs, but the regime of feudal privileges had come to an end.[56]

The second enigma is that during a democratizing age, elections and party competition had considerably less influence than petitioning on the process by which North American feudalism perished. Where electoral strategies mattered, it was often in concert with nonpartisan associations and petitioning. Repeated contests of Democrats and Whigs in New York brought little relief to the lamenting tenant farmers in the Hudson-Mohawk valley. The true reforms occurred in the exclusion of real property from distress sales in 1843, which gave tenants real time and material wealth, as well as in the 1845 reforms by which rent charges were taxed and distress sales formally abolished. These seemingly incremental reforms followed from concentrated, specific petitioning campaigns. The proprietor-initiated movement to buy out tenants happened once these legislative changes ate away at renters' revenue streams and diminished the likelihood of near-term eviction. In Lower Canada, the legislative elections of 1854 were crucial to the passage of the final bill, but the agenda for these elections had already been set by previous mobilizations and by the assembly and legislative council's response to them.

The democracy of agendas and organizations had generated a democratization of institutions. Tenant farmers, whether they spoke French in Lower Canada or English in New York, used petition campaigns to change the menu of the possible and the likely. Beyond this, tenant farmers coordinated and built networks through these campaigns. The mutual construction of farmer association and petition campaign played out in the anti-rent organizations in New York and the Association for the Reform of Seigneurial Rights in Lower Canada. With the tumult of 1837–1838 in Canada and the armed conflict in 1840s New York, violence had shaped the visibility of the conflict and the reluctance of conservatives to push too hard on tenants. Yet violence and organized revolt did far less to fashion the schedule of the legislatures where North American manorial tenure would perish. Democratization of a sort had indeed come in the decline of seigneurial institutions, but it was a democracy of petitioning more than electoral democracy or partisan democracy. The quieter revolution against feudalism in North America happened prayer by prayer, signature by signature.

THIRTEEN

Native Continuance, Native Governance

To Alexis de Tocqueville and millions of other observers, the erasure of Native America seemed imminent with the Treaty of New Echota and the Trail of Tears. Indeed, far-reaching acts and policies of dispossession of Indigenous communities continued east, west, and south of the Mississippi valley, as did raw campaigns of violence. Yet another story, far less documented, also unfolded in the wake of New Echota. Native Americans continued petitioning, and often inspired by the model of the Cherokee against Jackson and Georgia, these tribes, bands, and nations changed legislative and administrative agendas and recruited allies in their quest to fend off removal. In the partial reversal of the Buffalo Creek Treaty of 1838, in the resistance of removal efforts in Michigan, and in the successful campaign for reserves in eastern Canada, Indigenous North Americans used the petition to build new political formations, change their models of governance, and carve out lasting spaces of continuance. These partial victories testified to the procedural democracy of petitions, as Natives, without evident electoral power in New York, French Canada, or Michigan, combined with their allies to reshape legislative and diplomatic agendas.

The Native victories in the mid-nineteenth century were won not by forbearance on the part of sovereigns but by agenda setting and coalition building. It was the democratizing petition rather than an older supplicatory mode that, by reshaping agendas and courting allies, gave Native North Americans some select but lasting political triumphs.

COMPROMISE AND CONTINUANCE: THE SENECA

Cherokee removal gave comfort and incentive to dispossession forces elsewhere. When in 1837 Martin Van Buren succeeded Andrew Jackson as president, Empire State removal interests saw renewed chances for a final ejection of the Haudenosaunee. As New York's most powerful Democrat, Van Buren was building the Albany Regency and envisioned a post-Jackson alliance with Democrats in the South. Indian removal in New York State would forge a latitudinal link between northern settler and southern slaveholding interests. Using a combination of fraud, bribery, and booze, they saw a short-term triumph in 1838. In that year's Treaty of Buffalo Creek, the Seneca supposedly ceded all their lands in New York State to the Ogden Land Company, save for the one-square-mile reserve at Oil Spring. The Seneca would move to Kansas and would receive a pittance from the federal government. The Ogdens' major prize was Buffalo Creek, yet they also coveted the land bases at Allegany, Cattaraugus, and Tonawanda. Now, it appeared, they had them all.[1]

In an earlier time, or perhaps a later one, the Ogden Land Company's ploy would have succeeded entirely. Yet the Seneca themselves had, with their allies, subtly changed the terms and space of political contest. While Seneca political organization appeared to weaken after Sagoyewatha's death in 1830, the legacy of alliance building in the 1810s and 1820s lived on. Anti-removal Senecas had cultivated friends, built organizations, and developed the elements of a petitioning and lobbying conduit to Washington. New leadership emerged in the communities at Buffalo Creek, Allegany, Cattaraugus, and Tonawanda. The sinews connecting opposition to Indian removal and antislavery had grown stronger in argument and in collaboration. The Panic of 1837 had unleashed forceful anti-Jacksonian sentiment, vast spiritual energies, and economic grievance. The off-year elections of 1838 brought a Whig surge in the House and Senate, and in 1840, Democratic presidential hegemony was broken with the victory of Whig presidential candidate William Henry Harrison, accompanied by a clear Whig House majority and then a Senate majority by 1841.

Even before the Treaty of Buffalo Creek's conclusion, many anti-removal Seneca composed oral and written protests against its form and content. The anti-removal chief Big Kettle joined Oneida and Onondaga chiefs in a signed protest in the fall of 1837 contesting the early procedures of consultation and treaty negotiation. Big Kettle had been active with Sagoyewatha but was now chief and head of the anti-removal party. On February 28, 1838, he and fifteen other Seneca leaders wrote Vermont senator Samuel Prentiss, warning that the Seneca were being threatened by New York and the United States with eviction if they did not agree to the removal plan to Green Bay. Big Kettle, William Kronse, and John Kennedy wrote Prentiss again three days later, alerting the Whig senator to the ongoing fraud and bribery involved in obtaining Seneca individuals' support for a removal treaty. Besides these issues, anti-removal Seneca lamented that the required assent of the governor of Massachusetts to approve any treaty was lacking, and that the required majority of Seneca chiefs had not signed the final document. Some pro-removal chiefs had signed the purported agreement at treaty commissioner Ransom Gillet's office, still others at Gillet's tavern room, where they were bribed and plied with alcohol. The gathering of these treaty signatures violated Seneca treaty-making protocol. Land sales required first consultation with clans (which included, for the Haudenosaunee, clan mothers), and any final agreement required a majority of chiefs assembled together, in council, for proper representation. As Big Kettle and his fellow chiefs put it, "The council house, and not a tavern, is the place for making treaties."[2]

Ransom Gillet knew that his gambit was politically risky, and he knew that the contest would play out partially in petitioning. He had already, in May 1836, joined with other prominent Democrats in petitioning the Office of Indian Affairs to request the accelerated removal of all Indians from the Empire State. Having assembled a coalition that united Washington, the Albany Regency, and the Ogden Land Company behind the treaty of 1838, he anticipated the countermovement to come. He would be pleased to parry "any remonstrance aimed to impinge on this transaction," he boasted. And those protests came, first from the Seneca and then from the hundreds of Quaker allies they had recruited. The Senate voted in June 1838 that the treaty needed redoing, requiring the president to obtain a majority of Seneca chiefs. Gillet went back to work with methods largely unchanged from the previous year's and falsely claimed, by January 1839, to have procured the required majority of chiefs' assent.[3]

Having secured alliances in the Senate and among Hicksite Quakers, Seneca leaders turned in 1838 to repeated petitioning. They combined appeals to traditional Haudenosaunee law, to U.S. statutes, and to ethical precepts. The fraudulent treaty proceedings in August 1838 were premised on Gillet's claim that sixteen chiefs had signed the treaty, and even among these sixteen many later testified that they had been bribed or misled. Yet among eighty-one Seneca chiefs and warriors, sixty-three (including forty-eight acknowledged chiefs) quickly came forward in September 1838 with a remonstrance decrying the proceedings and asserting their lack of assent. Gillet ignored the document, but General Henry Dearborn, Massachusetts Superintendent for Indian Affairs, witnessed the protest and relayed it to the Senate. Seneca leaders produced a range of signed documents, affidavits, and memorials in January 1839, including another petition against the Treaty of 1838, led by Big Kettle, to Van Buren, as well as affidavits authorizing four of the nation's leaders—Seneca White, Israel Jemison, Maris B. Pierce, and John Kennedy Jr.—to represent the Nation as a delegation.[4]

Beyond the protestations of chiefs, Seneca warriors and residents also organized their own petitions. Petitions of warriors and residents—explicitly excluding chiefs—from Buffalo Creek, Cattaraugus, and Tonawanda reservations were separately organized in September 1838 and signed by the hundreds (see Table 13.1). The names of 81 warriors and residents appeared on the Buffalo Creek petition, while 87 names appeared on the Cattaraugus petition, and fully 125 names appeared on the Tonawanda petition. Seneca leaders themselves appear to have organized the "warriors and residents" petitions from Buffalo Creek and Tonawanda—Maris Pierce and Thomas Jemison, respectively, testified to the authenticity of names attached—while Quaker John Hillman likely organized the Cattaraugus petition of residents and warriors.[5]

In December 1839, Seneca chiefs and warriors shifted the venue from individual legislators and the president to the U.S. Senate, asking it to postpone ratification of the fraudulent 1838 treaty and requesting a hearing on the matter (see Figure 13.1). The Seneca had been and would again be divided along generational and clan lines—the Wolf, Bear, Beaver, and Turtle clans belonging to the first "animal clans" moiety, the Snipe, Hawk, Heron, and Deer clans belonging to the second "bird clans" moiety. Yet the principal signers and organizers of these petitions—Big Kettle, Seneca White, Maris Pierce, Israel Jemison, John Kennedy—spanned generations and moieties. The primary differences would emerge among parties and, in part, across reservations.[6]

Known in Seneca as *Ha-dya-no-doh* (Swift Runner), Maris Bryant Pierce emerged as perhaps the single most important organizer of the Seneca petitioning machine. Born on the Allegany reservation, Pierce was educated at Quaker schools and attended Dartmouth College, taking time from the

Table 13.1 Petition Signatures and Anti-removal Census figures, by Seneca Village, 1839–1840

Reservation/Village	Allegany	Buffalo Creek	Buffalo Creek (Cayuga)	Cattaraugus	Cattaraugus (Cayuga)	Tonawanda
Warriors and residents signing anti-removal petitions (September 1838)		81		87		125
Anti-removal census aggregates (August 1839)						
Chiefs	19	37	3	20	1	No petition census available
Warriors	177	146	17	115	4	
Women	218	455 (women & children combined)	19	126	5	
Male children	133				8	
Female children	129					
Children (undifferentiated)			15	168		
Total Census (August 1839)	676	720	54	429	17	
Chief voting patterns, Treaty of 1838						
Chiefs opposed	14	19		10		13
Chiefs favorable	1	14		11		0
Chiefs neutral	1	9		0		0
Percent of chiefs opposed	93.3%	57.6%		47.6%		100%

Source: SEN26A-G7, RG 46, NARA; *The Case of the Seneca in the State of New York* (1840), 113–164.

academic year in 1840 to represent the Seneca Nation in Washington. He corresponded regularly with allied members of Congress and tried to detect changes in legislative sentiment through correspondence and visits to Washington. Throughout the Seneca Nation and especially at Buffalo Creek, he organized a number of protests and petitions, signing and delivering many of these documents personally, including the earliest appeals to the president and the War Department. His essay *Address on the Present Condition and Prospects of the Aboriginal Inhabitants of North America, with Particular Reference to the Seneca Nation* (1839)—written in the midst of the upheaval over the fraudulent 1838 agreement—was published and widely read as a pamphlet and marked an important entry into the intellectual and spiritual discourse of the time.[7]

Yet Pierce did not labor alone, and the collective effort of the Seneca called on the tactics and memory of its ancestors. Roughly a decade after his death, Sagoyewatha's imprint on these proceedings remained visible through the signatures of his stepsons, Daniel Two Guns and Henry Two Guns. The names of both sons appeared on the October 1837 petition to Van Buren, and among the signatories, only Daniel Two Guns and Maris Pierce signed their names without making a mark. A similar pattern emerged in the petition for a delay in proceedings in the Senate in December 1839 (Figure 13.1), where among the seventy-five names appearing, Daniel and Henry Two Guns were among the eleven Seneca signing their own names on the first page.[8]

By advancing and adapting the petition form, the Seneca newly amplified and quantified their voice. By August 1839, the chiefs at each Seneca reservation—Allegany, Buffalo Creek, Cattaraugus, and Tonawanda—had collaborated with Quakers and Erie County allies to produce a series of "census" documents. These documents require cautious interpretation, as censuses were in part undertaken and subsidized by Quakers with their own material and spiritual aims. Yet they generally characterized the differences across villages and chiefs on the issue of removal. In each of these documents, the Seneca and the Quakers laid out the numbers of men, women, and children opposed to removal on their site. According to U.S. laws and the 1795 Canandaigua Treaty, such citizen-level listings would not have been necessary, as a majority of chiefs assembled at council could speak for the nation. Yet in 1839, anti-removal chiefs and others felt another statement was needed.

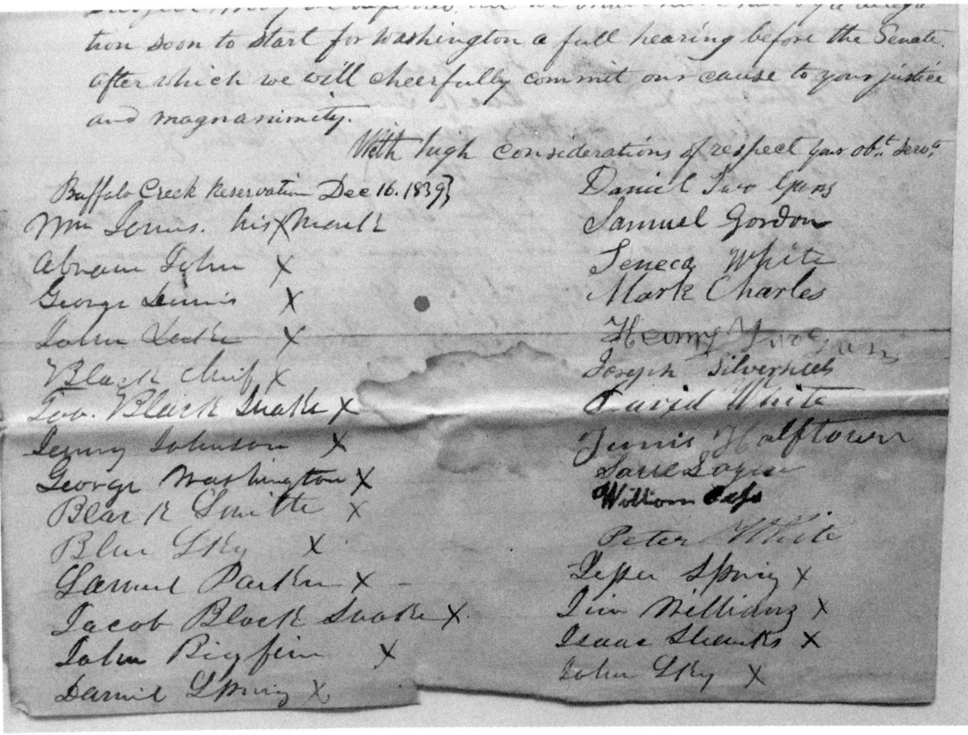
tion soon to start for Washington a full hearing before the Senate. after which we will cheerfully commit our cause to your justice and magnanimity.

With high consideration of respect your obt. servts

Buffalo Creek Reservation Dec 16. 1839

Wm Jones his X mark
Abram John X
George Jones X
Black Chief X
Gov. Black Snake X
Henry Johnson X
George Washington X
Black Smith X
Blue Sky X
Samuel Parker X
Jacob Black Snake X
John Bigfire X
Daniel Spring X

Daniel Two Guns
Samuel Gordon
Seneca White
Mark Charles
Henry Two Guns
Joseph Silverheels
David White
Peter White
Isaac Shanks X
John Sky X

FIGURE 13.1. Signatory List from Seneca Petition to Senate (December 1839). Daniel and Henry Two Guns (stepsons of Sagoyewatha) are first and fifth signatories in right-hand column. *Credit:* Record Group 46, National Archives and Records Administration.

Anthropologists and historians then and now relied on these August 1839 censuses as an exercise in demography, as a way of characterizing the tribe's population. Yet in two ways—as majoritarian statements and as a reappropriation of the Indigenous census instrument—the census documents were works of petition politics and of rhetoric. The August 1839 censuses took on an explicitly political form. The idea was less to describe the population than to characterize the majority sentiment of a nation. None of the villages needed to calculate the political division of their populations, for only a few dozen individuals, at most, in any village declared themselves in favor of removal. Second, the Seneca Nation censuses of 1839 functioned as a powerful rebuttal of the administrative apparatus of Indian removal, in which the federal government had conducted censuses of the Cherokee and other tribes to document the person-by-person ejection of Natives from their lands and to calculate treaty and removal annuities. Knowing of the federal censuses of the Cherokee that had been carried out as a means of removal and relocation, Seneca leaders and the Quaker allies re-politicized the census document and redirected the counting of Indigenous souls toward anti-removal ends. Accordingly, a new generation of Indigenous leaders helped to organize these censuses and memorials, and they could count on the help of Quakers in doing so. John Kennedy Jr. and John Hudson helped conduct the census at Buffalo Creek, while Pierce had collected the signatures of warriors and residents there.[9]

In 1840, Hicksite Quakers organized as the Joint Committee on Indian Affairs of the Four Yearly Meetings of Genesee, New York, Philadelphia, and Baltimore collected many of these documents together and published a 256-page pamphlet called *The Case of the Seneca Indians in the State of New York.* They regarded the censuses as sufficiently akin to the petitions that they combined them for purposes of presentation in an Appendix titled "Memorials, Remonstrances, Censuses, Etc." The Quakers widely distributed *The Case of the Seneca Indians* in New York, Boston, Philadelphia, and other cities. As the pamphlet with its abundant evidence circulated, the Ogden Land Company tried in vain to counter the movement in White public sentiment.[10]

Seneca women also appeared regularly in the August 1839 political censuses, reflecting and presaging their participation in petition campaigns. Their phoneticized Haudenosaunee names appear repeatedly in the censuses and suggest that, especially at Buffalo Creek, many women served as the operative heads of families. They included Betsey Bennett, Mary Crow, Widow Fishhook, Squaw Fishhook, Da-gr-a-o-dr-ga, Gr-yr-sont-hoh, Sally Sky Carrier (Cayuga), Sally Two Guns (Cayuga), and Old Peggy from Buffalo Creek, and Nancy Big Chief and Ann York (Cayuga) from Cattaraugus.

Seneca women petitioned separately, too, and the March 1841 petition of Minerva Blacksmith and seven other clan mothers at Tonawanda to the president marks one of the earliest Indigenous women's petitions sent directly to a U.S. president. Whereas the reservations would soon split over the course of the amended treaty, Blacksmith and her fellow clan mothers—signing as Widow Little Beard, Susan Black Smith, Lo-no-que-no, Gar-near-no-wit, O-no dy, Dor-wa loes, and Gao-e war ha dus—offered a heartfelt lament that echoed antislavery warnings of bondage and oppression: "Father: We write to you, and desire you to hear our words. . . . We, the women of our race, feel troubled[.] We feel deep anxiety for our children. We feel as though we were bound up with our children in our arms—We pray our great father, the President, to loosen our bondage, for we are in great trouble." While Blacksmith and her fellow women petitioners were likely assisted by Quaker Amy Kirby Post, the Tonawanda clan mothers' petition of 1841 reflects long-standing Seneca understandings. It premised claims to sovereignty on the Treaty of Canandaigua of 1794, lamented that "all our women of the other reservations are of the same mind, and all are in trouble," and echoed many of the protests being made by the Tonawanda chiefs, who had voted with unanimity against the 1838 Treaty.[11]

The subtle inversion of traditional hierarchy in these documents—warriors and residents petitioning separately from chiefs, and women adding their voices to petitions separately from men—stemmed not only from traditional forms of governance such as clan mothers' consultative roles but also from tensions opened by removal between chiefs and their peoples. If the numbers in the Seneca "petition censuses" of 1839 are anywhere close to accurate, then anti-removal sentiment among Seneca chiefs, while still characterizing a solid majority of the chiefs, was dwarfed by opposition to removal among warriors and residents. Whereas roughly half of the chiefs at Buffalo Creek and Cattaraugus had signed the 1838 Treaty, none had done so at Tonawanda, and just one of fifteen had signed at Allegany. Even before the petition-censuses, the remonstrances of "warriors and residents" had flowed in to the president and the Senate in the early winter of 1839, and the August censuses suggested that at Buffalo Creek and Cattaraugus, pro-emigration Seneca were outnumbered by a ten-to-one to even fifteen-to-one factor. The petitions and censuses revealed, albeit strategically, the underpinnings of tension between chiefs of rival factions and between chiefs and the warriors and women in their communities. Many pro-emigration chiefs appear to have received regular payments from the Ogden Land Company. The chiefs, too, split among themselves, with Sagoyewatha's stepsons Daniel and Henry Two Guns heading an October 1841 petition against the pro-emigration chiefs and asking that the New York State annuity not be paid to them but only to the chiefs who properly represented the Seneca: Daniel and Henry, Seneca White, Maris Pierce, William Krouse, Adam Doxtator, and others. The issue of annuity payments would soon divide the Seneca anew.[12]

In 1838 and for at least a decade afterward, the long-standing Seneca-Quaker alliance began to bear political fruit, though of a sort that nourished some Indigenous communities more than others. The Yearly Meetings at Genesee, where a number of women held leadership roles, began to work alongside Seneca women and men to assist with outreach and petition censuses and to organize Quaker petitions that came in alongside Seneca memorials. Many of these meetings occurred at the Farmington meetinghouse in Ontario County, where several generations of Seneca leaders, ranging from Big Kettle to Seneca White, met with Friends to collaborate politically. The Yearly Meetings at Genesee, New York, Philadelphia, and Baltimore united to create a Committee on Indian Affairs to thwart the Ogden Land Company's assault on Seneca spaces. Quaker memorials poured into the Twenty-Sixth Congress, and Presbyterians and other mainline Protestant churches sent memorials as well. These signed documents of White Protestant indignation descended on Congress and Albany, and under Whig leadership in the U.S. Congress, these remonstrances had a more favorable reception than they would have under the Democrats.[13]

Combining petitioning and in-person lobbying with political intelligence, the Seneca sensed an opening in early 1841. Maris Pierce detected in February of that year a growing hesitancy among Whigs to carry the 1838 fraudulent treaty into execution, whether through appropriations or in assisting the Whig administration of William Henry Harrison. Harrison's death in April 1841 brought John Tyler to the White House, and while Tyler cleaved to the Jeffersonian vision of westward expansion, he also expressed a willingness to see the 1838 treaty renegotiated. Maris Pierce attended meetings of Quakers from April 1841 through the summer of 1842, encouraging the Friends' repeated petitions and outreach to Whig politicians (especially Secretary of State Daniel Webster, New York governor William H. Seward, and Massachusetts governor John Davis) for a new treaty. Negotiations began afresh, and in 1842 a new Compromise Treaty was struck and signed, which returned the Allegany and Cattaraugus reservations to the Seneca but surrendered those of Buffalo Creek and Tonawanda.[14]

Historians and the Tonawanda Seneca have fairly questioned the view of many contemporary Seneca that the Hicksite Quakers were largely benevolent. The Quakers allied with Whig politicians and administrators in the 1842 negotiations, including treaty commissioner Ambrose Spencer and Secretary of War John Spencer. The Spencers and the Quakers pushed the Seneca to accept a surrender of Buffalo Creek and Tonawanda, arguing that it was the best attainable settlement. Tonawanda Seneca leaders protested vigilantly in the summer of 1842 about the fact that the agenda for treaty negotiations had already been set in meetings between Quakers and Whigs, and that other Seneca chiefs, such as Maris Pierce, Seneca White, and the Two Guns brothers, had traded in Tonawanda for the rough certainty of Allegany and Cattaraugus. For his part, Pierce maintained that the Compromise Treaty was "the best bargain they can make now."[15] Tonawanda chiefs, led by John Blacksmith, felt differently, and sent bitter petitions of protest and remonstrance to the president, the Senate, and other officials for years to come.[16]

The political fissures in Seneca space would reopen and unfold in ways that Sagoyewatha, Big Kettle, and their coalition could not have anticipated in the 1820s. By 1848, the center of Seneca politics had moved to Cattaraugus, and a movement of warriors and women set against the older generation of chiefs had taken root, assisted by the Hicksite Friends. The chief complaints of the protesters concerned the legacy of the 1838 and 1842 treaties, corruption in the use and administration of the treaty annuities from 1842, and the harrowing tales of death and starvation from Seneca who had chosen to emigrate after 1842. In 1848, Cattaraugus Seneca women led by Betsey Snow petitioned the Quaker Philip Thomas to intervene in the distribution of annuities, stating that the annuities should be distributed in a spirit of equality that befitted the traditions of the nation: "We have taken the same view of the subject which was taken by the old men long since dead, who first entered into these arrangements. They declared that every individual, man, woman and child, had an equal right to our moneys and to our lands, in short, to all our national property; that it was so from the beginning, and that it always should be so."[17] Decrying the "avarice and pride" of the chiefs, they asked Thomas to intervene with the secretary of war. The pattern of independent women's and warriors' petitioning had now matured to the point that Seneca memorials openly undermined political patriarchy.[18]

The Seneca anti-chief movement took on momentum, and a convention of the people formed in December 1848. As the Hicksite Quakers sided with the anti-chief factions developing at Cattaraugus, the more traditional Orthodox Quakers sided with the chiefs, who were badly outnumbered and had lost legitimacy. The resulting Seneca Constitution of 1848 abolished all chieftainships and created a three-branch government, with a legislative council, three-man judiciaries at Allegany and Cattaraugus, and an elected president. The new government bore complicated legacies for gender and Indigenous governance. Despite Seneca women's newly asserted voice in petitioning, the new government undermined clan mothers' consultative role even as it eliminated the chiefs. The Seneca Constitution was nonetheless remarkable, taken in part from emulation of the 1827 Cherokee Nation Constitution, Hicksite Quaker advice, and a factional dispute dividing the nation at Cattaraugus. And its institutions would persist, as the constitution would survive in amended form until the present day. Seneca democracy disenfranchised some, but democracy of a form it was. In an 1849 petition to President Zachary Taylor, Maris Pierce vaunted the new constitution as a tool of sovereignty wielded by a nation newly reconstructed.[19]

The politics of 1838 to 1842 had left a deep fissure in the Iroquois world, as the Seneca Nation organized its own government and left the Confederacy, while the Tonawanda remained in it. The Tonawanda Seneca launched their own political and petitioning struggle, one independent of the Allegany and Cattaraugus Seneca. Drawing again on the Quaker alliance, Tonawanda Senecas petitioned and lobbied for the preservation of their spaces. In 1857, the Tonawanda Seneca struck an agreement with the U.S. government to surrender all land claims in Kansas (the removal machine's intended destination for them) and to purchase with federal funds their lands from the Ogden Land Company.[20]

The Compromise Treaty of 1842 remains in many ways a historic loss for Haudenosaunee peoples, having split the Confederacy and representing a capitulation to the divide et impera strategy of colonizing governments and imposed rubrics of civilization. At a time of vast, orchestrated removal, however, another puzzle confronts us. That the Haudenosaunee generally and the Seneca in particular remained in western New York at all by 1860, and that they remain at all today, represents something of a political miracle and a stunning victory for Indigenous rights. That victory may seem marred by the loss of vital spaces at Buffalo Creek and Tonawanda, yet the tension confronts readers now, as it confronted the Seneca then, with a troubling counterfactual. How did the Seneca reverse lands grabbed by Albany and Washington in 1842, during the national heyday of Indian removal? The return of Buffalo Creek was unlikely for a number of reasons, not least that since 1838, settlers had already encroached on and occupied those spaces. It is far from coincidental that the Seneca reservations that remained in 1860 were located south and west of Buffalo and its canal terminus.

Through the nineteenth century and beyond, the lands returned to the Seneca by the Compromise Treaty of 1842—especially the Allegany and Cattaraugus reservations—combined to form the largest land base for any federally recognized tribe in the United States residing east of Detroit and north of the Mason-Dixon line.[21] Those boundaries encompassed the massive industrialization and settlement—all advanced by canal, turnpike, and railroad building—of the antebellum period that did so much to oust Native Americans from their ancestral spaces.

Electoral politics—the customary designation that summarizes America's democratizing at this time—explains little of the return to Seneca peoples of reservations at Allegany and Cattaraugus. The Whig Party did not count the small-numbered Seneca among its constituencies. The moral arguments for reversal of the 1838 treaty fell upon awakened Christian ears, it is true, but those moral arguments were echoing anti-removal leaders' claims from a decade earlier, and while the unpopularity of the Seminole War in the early 1840s may have dulled appetites for further Indigenous removal, it could hardly have sufficed as a rationale for returning to Native Nations lands already surrendered to Whites. The shift in White public opinion, so pivotal to Senecas' partial reversal of the 1838 debacle, came not from passive observation of events but from political engagement.

So, too, a narrative of spiritual indignation reflects but a bare tendril of the process of dispossession's partial reversal. In the centuries-long history of Indigenous dispossession, outrage did not merely appear when beckoned by injustice. Outrage over the Treaty of 1838 was instead awakened by the oppressed and echoed by their allies, summoned by association, and organized into something anew. Not alone but as much as any other tool of Seneca politics, petitioning had stitched together a human coalition that carried a moon in the long history of Haudenosaunee continuance.

THE DEMISE OF REMOVAL IN MICHIGAN

To the west of New York, where settler states were newly forming and where the federal government's administrative apparatus figured more prominently in day-to-day Native politics, Indigenous communities adjusted their venue strategies accordingly. Administrative petitions figured prominently in resistance and reshaping efforts in the western Great Lakes. In the midst of an orchestrated effort by Lewis Cass, then secretary of war, to remove Odawa and Ojibwe peoples from present-day Michigan—which harbored one of the largest remaining populations of Native Americans east of the Mississippi River in the United States—Native American peoples united to shape the terms of debate and negotiation. Odawa and Ojibwe officials joined to send a petition to Cass in December 1835 expressing their willingness to cede some lands but not to remove entirely, as "it is a heartrending thought to our simple feelings to think of leaving our native country forever, the land where our forefathers lay thick in the earth."[22]

Less than two months later, the Odawa again sent a petition, this time to President Jackson himself, remarking, "You know we obtained our land from the Great Spirit. He made it for us who are Indians. When we die, we expect to rest on this land. . . . We have not a mind to remove to a distant land."[23] While the Odawa and Ojibwe ceded significant lands from the Grand River (near present-day Grand Rapids, Michigan) to the Chocolate River in the Upper Peninsula, they did not remove and remained on small reservations scattered through the present-day Lower and Upper Peninsula. Sensing the threat of removal, they started buying lands in fee simple and petitioning for American citizenship. Among the greatest burdens of the removal initiative was the uncertainty that it visited on the Odawa and Ojibwe.[24]

The Odawa and Ojibwe faced a thorny problem in representation, as there was no single spokesperson for the tribes, which were essentially band confederations organized by villages. Their leaders (*ogemaag*) claimed political authority among kin. Beyond these networks, claims to authority were tenuous. Odawa and Ojibwe petitions served functions of representation and alliance building, extending earlier patterns of *requête* making and coalescence with regional Catholic churches and missionaries. Administrative petitions to Indian agents, the secretary of war, or the president himself were sent from assembled Odawa chiefs and often carried by priests or Catholic laity—by Father Gabriel Richard in 1816, by Augustin Hamelin in the 1830s, and by Father Francis Pierz in the 1840s and 1850s. It was Hamelin, a Catholic Odawa man educated in Rome who knew Anishinaabe, English, French, and Latin fluently, who led the Michigan Native advocacy effort, sending dozens of letters and petitions. In the 1830s, these petitions permitted the Odawa to end-run Indian agent Henry Rowe Schoolcraft by taking their concerns both directly to the president and through the Diocese of Detroit. Schoolcraft wanted the flow of information to run through him alone. Hamelin became Schoolcraft's principal Native adversary. The Catholic officials' stake in the matter was, at least in part, their claim to one of the most thriving missions in North America, with thousands of reported converts. Schoolcraft favored Protestant missionaries. Missionaries' petitions thus positioned the Odawa and Ojibwe between two bureaucratic organizations—the Catholic Church of the Great Lakes and the Indian Affairs administration (with its Protestant and Democratic Party leanings).[25]

As the Jackson administration and subsequent administrations began to press for additional cessions, the Odawa and Ojibwe recruited additional White allies to assist in their petitioning campaigns. Congregationalist minister Alvan Coe circulated a petition among the Odawa and Ojibwe at Mackinac and sent the document to the War Department in 1841. Further petitions were sent to the Michigan legislature, which rather cryptically expressed its opposition to removal but did little to combat the administrative processes emanating from Washington. The petitioning battle against removal continued throughout the 1840s, and by the end of the decade, the state of Michigan had become an Indigenous ally. Important reservation villages and lands were established at the Cheboygan River, Grand Traverse Bay (Peshawbestown), Wing River, and Grand River.[26]

The victories of Odawa and Ojibwe peoples in Michigan were, to be sure, limited. White settlers took almost all the Lower and Upper Peninsulas, and rank subjugation and informal dispossession continued. Exploitation of Native Americans who received their annuity payments only to see their value disappear in price discrimination persisted. Yet the petitioning campaigns established important traditions of legal contestation, and it is plausible that the most important petitions were not those directed to Congress or even to presidents but to the bureau, the motive force of the removal machine. It was the Bureau of Indian Affairs that, in 1851, decided that the Odawa and Ojibwe would remain. In the Treaty of July 31, 1855, the Odawa and Ojibwe were assured that they would not be removed, and the amended treaty also incorporated enduring hunting and fishing rights.[27]

FIRST NATIONS IN A UNIFIED CANADA

After the Act of Union (1840), London officials sought more settlement, industrial development, and a fargoing change in managing their relations with Canada's Indigenous populations. Wherever they lived, Natives saw growing encroachments on their lands and a loss of hunting and fishing spaces. The politics differed in terms of whether the Indigenous population inhabited a village near one of the major cities or whether the tribe claimed lands and spaces in the vast, sparsely settled King's Domain. The *villages domiciliés* in French-speaking Canada like Odanak and Kahnawá:ke still considered it essential to exclude, as much they could, Whites from their lands. This meant limiting the rights of Whites who had married into Native society. The villagers' anxieties concerned not merely the specter of White spouses obtaining land rights but also the threat of village governance. The concerns of other Indigenous communities in Canada—the Innu (Montagnais), the Têtes-de-Boules, the allied Algonquin-Nipissings, and others—differed both subtly and markedly. These populations lived more nomadically for generations, and their subsistence patterns depended on alternating hunts of game animals in the fall and winter, salmon and seal harvests in the late spring through the summer, hunting migratory birds in the spring, and summer fishing. The development of settler logging and mining interests north and west of Montréal, coupled with the growing incidence of Canadian and American fishing on the Saint Lawrence and its many tributaries, combined with population growth—these all served to hamper Native economies.[28]

The claims made by the Indigenous peoples of eastern Lower Canada posed a number of thorny problems for British Canada's customary models of "Indian affairs." The first was that the agreement struck in the Proclamation of 1763 surely applied to them, but provincial governors had never had to wrestle quite so much with what its terms meant. As petition after petition flowed in from these communities, one colonial officer anxiously acknowledged that the communities could argue for the entirety of unclaimed Crown lands. A second problem was that the British had designed their colonial system of Indian affairs around those Indigenous peoples living closest to White settlement, especially the Saint Lawrence valley. For generations, the more nomadic communities in eastern Canada had not regularly participated in diplomatic affairs. Who would represent them, and how? Whereas Saint Lawrence valley tribes showed up at councils, many important bands of these communities lived too far away from Kahnawá:ke to attend. Petitioning became an important means of representation for these distant villages. They also drew on missionaries for political alliance and the transportation and legitimation of memorials. Chief among these priests was Flavien Durocher, who began in the late 1830s to convey petitions from the Algonquins and Nipissings in their request for missionaries, church buildings, and, later, lands on the Ottawa River.[29]

It was in this context of alliance with Catholic officials that the Innu, adopting a French colonial term for their tribe (the *Montagnais*, or Mountaineers) that belied their fishing practices, began approaching the colonial government. The Hudson's Bay Company signed a new contract with the Crown in 1842 and planned to cede large portions of the King's Domain, thereby inviting settlers and foresters into lands occupied by the Innu. In February 1843, five Innu men of Escoumins village sent a petition to the governor general, asking for a land grant in Escoumins Bay—a free grant of lands from the King's Domain, a total of 1,300 arpents (roughly 1,100 acres) of land. Another petition came from Tadoussac (Ile Jérémie) in 1844 asking for a larger grant of land; it was signed by over two hundred tribal members. The governor general did not act on these petitions, but observers (including the Hudson's Bay Company) took notice of the claims.[30]

Innu memorials soon came from villages farther downstream, to the north and east, and they reflected a change in self-presentation. The bilingual petition of April 1847 (see Figure 13.2) was written northeast of Escoumins, and its authors were different from those of the 1843 petition. The approach to colonial government in 1847 marked three significant changes: Indigenous expression, longer signatory lists, and the multiplying of petitions sent to plural venues.

Among the near-dozen petitions that Innu villages sent to the Canadian government during the 1840s, the document of April 8, 1847, alone displayed the Innu language. Scholars have long debated the authorship of this petition, but certain telltale characteristics suggest heavy contributions from Innu elders. The handwriting of the left-hand column (Innu) differs materially from that of the right-hand column (French), such that the person who wrote the Innu text was not the one who wrote the French. The consistency of the Innu handwriting also suggests that the author was accustomed to writing the Innu language. The Innu prayer's expressions, moreover, use the kind of emphatic negation—such as *mauats,* or "not even" ("soon we will not even have a river in which to cast our nets")—that would have been very difficult for any recently arrived interpreter to understand, much less master and write. And subtle cues in the text suggest that the Innu were prioritizing exclusive fishing and hunting rights on rivers and the Baie des Outardes (Goose Bay) in their requests. As hunting grounds were surrendered to settler agriculture, the Innu saw their best shot for material

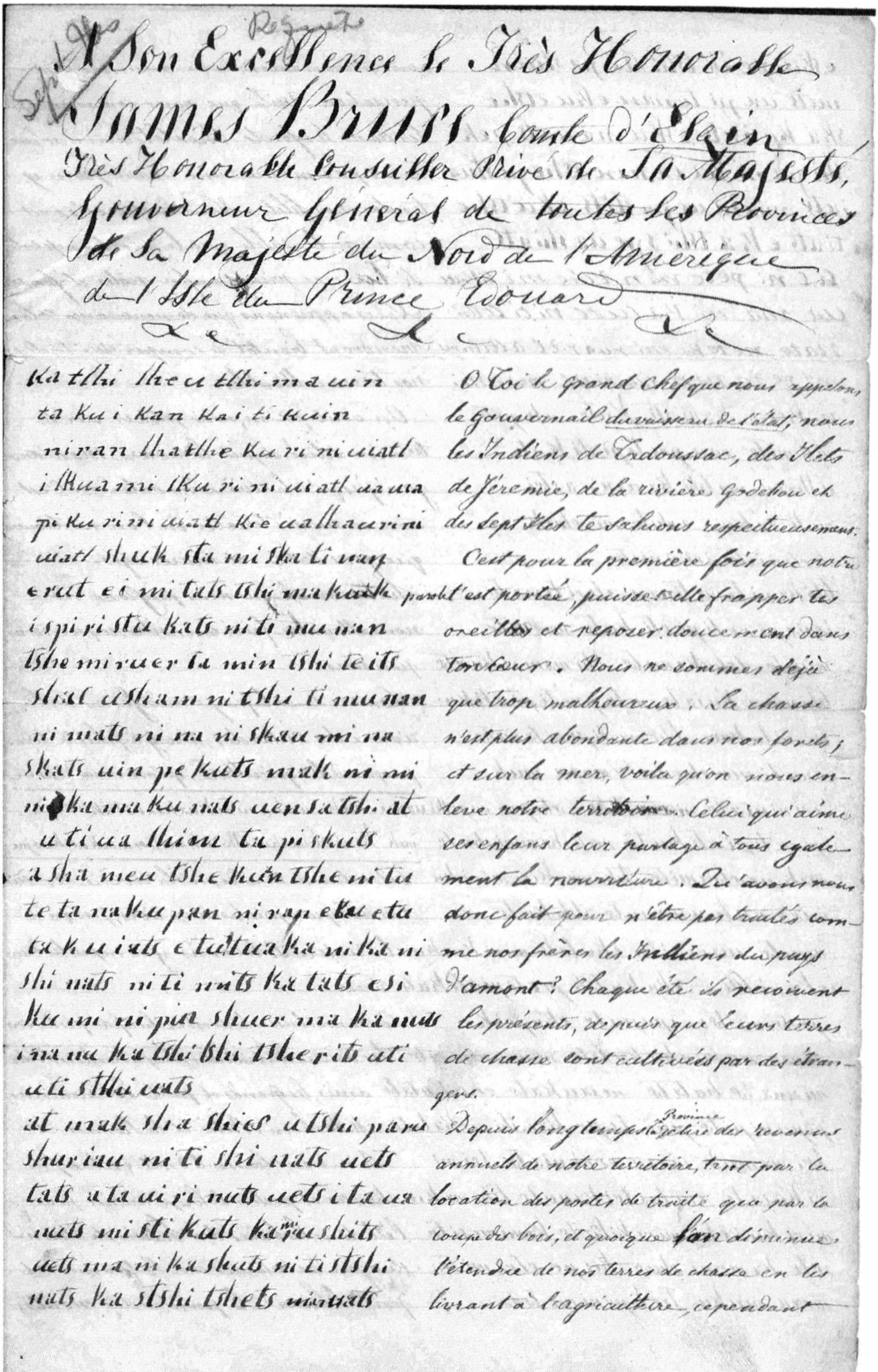

A Son Excellence le Très Honorable
James Bruce Comte d'Elgin
Très Honorable Conseiller Privé de Sa Majesté,
Gouverneur Général de toutes les Provinces
de Sa Majesté du Nord de l'Amérique
de l'Isle du Prince Edouard
&c &c &c

O Toi le grand Chef que nous appelons, le Gouvernail du vaisseau de l'état, nous les Indiens de Tadoussac, des Ilets de Jérémie, de la rivière Godebou et des Sept Iles te saluons respectueusement.

C'est pour la première fois que notre parole est portée, puisse-t-elle frapper tes oreilles et reposer doucement dans ton cœur. Nous ne sommes déjà que trop malheureux. La chasse n'est plus abondante dans nos forêts, et sur la mer, voilà qu'on nous enlève notre territoire. Celui qui aime ses enfans leur partage à tous également la nourriture. Qu'avons-nous donc fait pour n'être pas traités comme nos frères les Indiens du pays d'amont? Chaque été ils reçoivent les présents, depuis que leurs terres de chasse sont cultivées par des étrangers.

Depuis longtemps la Province retire des revenus annuels de notre territoire, tant par la location des postes de traite que par la coupe des bois, et quoique l'on diminue l'étendue de nos terres de chasse en les livrant à l'agriculture, cependant

FIGURE 13.2. Bilingual Petition of Innu (1847) to Canadian Governor General. *Credit:* Quebec Ministry of Energy and Natural Resources.

survival in salmon and seals as well as the migratory birds that visited these waters.[31]

Unlike other Innu petitions of the time, the bilingual petition of 1847 is accompanied by 125 signatures. All these signatures came from men, and the list started with the chiefs. The signature of Chief *rui paku* (Louis Bacon) closely resembles the handwriting of the Innu prayer, implying that *paku* or whichever elder signed his name was also responsible for writing down much of the Indigenous expression. (Bacon would soon emerge to higher positions of leadership, including the first chief under tribal government at Pessamit in 1856.) Some of the signatures reflect a similar handwriting, yet the signatory list contains a remarkable diversity of handwriting styles, with variable spacing between letters and names, and different formations of letters, suggesting that the many men signed for themselves. While the intentions of the signatories remain invisible in the archives, the unfolding of individual Innu men's names points to the need for representing the community beyond just the signatures of the chiefs. The audiences for that representation were themselves manifold, not merely the governor general but also Catholic priests and missionaries who would have seen the petition as it made its way to colonial officials, as well as those who read the petition in colonial offices and assemblies.

The Innu sent not one but three petitions in the spring of 1847. They addressed the bilingual petition of April 8, 1847, not merely to the governor general as an office but to its named occupant, James Bruce, Earl of Elgin. Bruce had been appointed just three months earlier, and the placement of his name at the head of the petition suggests a familiarity with Canadian colonial appointments. Two other petitions reflecting essentially the same prayer were sent to the colonial state: one to the executive council and one to the assembly. These were accompanied by endorsements from Catholic clergy. Joseph Signay, the archbishop of Québec, supported the petition in a note to the governor general. Priests Flavien Durocher and Pierre Boucher also sent supportive notes to the assembly in May. In interpreting the petition, Boucher argued that the Innu wanted a "Reserve" more than a system of presents. Pointing to other tribes that had reserved lands—the Abenaki, the Micmac, the Hurons—and to the more generous policy of presents in Upper Canada, Boucher called for a large reserved territory that would encompass a large portion of the Innu's desired claims over fluid and solid spaces. With the French Canadian reformers resurgent in the assembly, these notes helped legitimize the Innu's appeal. They offered assurances that the laments of the Innu were genuine and that the petitioners were true Christians and had embraced the temperance movement spread in the early 1840s by French priests.[32]

The assembly was sufficiently taken with the Innu petition of 1847 that it was printed by consent of the chamber, along with the supportive note from Father Boucher. This was an uncommon response to any petition of the period; no other Indigenous petition was consensually printed by the assembly. Another petition came to the assembly in 1849, sent by the tribe through Father Durocher, asking for an annuity and an additional grant of hunting lands on the north shore of the Saint Laurence. The land and water rights requested in the 1849 petition were sufficiently worrisome to Canadian shipping and trade interests that a counterpetition quickly arrived from Québec, taking no issue with the requested annuity but asking that the Innu land request be rejected. The Québec merchants and shippers were right to be concerned. As Lord Elgin and the land office signaled their willingness to go along, the assembly advanced a series of bills granting Lower Canadian tribes a set of lands and exclusivities on them. While the 1848 assembly adjourned without passing legislation on the Innu's requests, the work of that assembly would be taken up in 1851.[33]

The Innu's appeals came at a propitious time, during a swell of pressure for land reform in the province. A surge in petitions from tenant farmers from 1849 to 1851 shifted the debate over feudal tenure in the assembly and in the regional presses. As proposals flourished, thinkers and jurists tried to balance the imperatives of colonial progress and the need to protect proprietors' vested and stranded interest in the seigneuries. In this context, Clément Dumesnil electrified the debate with his pamphlet *De L'Abolition des Droits Féodaux et Seigneuriaux au Canada* (1849). Dumesnil proposed a commutation plan that would, he believed, indemnify existing seigneurial proprietors. After nearly fifty pages of argumentation and program, Dumesnil took a different tack in his last three pages. He added a short essay on the "Montagnais of Saguenay," namely the Innu. "Their distress is already well-known to the government," he wrote, remarking on the Innu deputation of 1848 to the provincial parliament of Montréal and the attention it had received. Dumesnil argued for "aid and missionaries" to the Innu, not for any sort of autonomy but for the purposes of "civilization," so that, possessed of their own lands and manners of progress, "the trees of the forests will fall, houses will be built, a school be founded and frequented, fields be planted, and the children of the earth will leave their misery and sufferings."[34] Dumesnil's plan of paternalism and evangelism, centered on Catholic missionaries, pointed toward Canada's long and torturous civilization enterprise in the late nineteenth and early twentieth centuries. Yet in 1849, his addendum on the Innu also demonstrated how the petitions of 1847 and 1848 had caught the attention of liberal reformers, whose support would be essential for any comprehensive program of Indigenous reserves.

Indigenous communities in Lower Canada received their first set of protections in the 1850 Act for the Better Protection of the Lands and Property of the Indians in Lower Canada. The act created a new post in colonial administration: commissioner of Indian lands. The system was explicitly paternalistic, endowing the commissioner with the right to act "for and in the name of" Natives, regarding them as minors of a sort. The commissioner and not the tribes administered rents and profits off their lands, and exercised rights over lands in the name of the tribes. The commissioner also held "full power and authority" to cede lands exercised right of rents.[35] The fictional protection for Indian lands came in the fact that now only the government could sign off on their alienation. The reality of the matter was that cessions required the assent of only one individual.

Lower Canadian Natives rightly saw the 1850 act as creating a tutelage system and immediately sent protest memorials demanding statutory changes. At a meeting at Kahnawá:ke on September 18, 1850, Natives from Kahnawá:ke, Kanesetake, Akwesasne, and Odanak gathered to draft and jointly sign a petition to the governor. The rarity with which these villages had petitioned together in the previous half century demonstrated the immense stakes that Natives saw in the 1850 act. Those who had made the statute, they decried, "never consulted us, nor any other Indians of Canada." Had such consultation occurred, the drafters would have heard that "what they have done and everything it contains is contrary to our own Laws, our norms, our customs and our rights." Specifically, the 1850 statute defined as an "Indian" those who had married an Indigenous person. Yet in patterns established by the village in the 1820s, no such right was accorded to Whites intermarrying with Native villagers, and "no white who situates himself among us thereby enjoys our rights."[36] In a dual summary of their laments, the Native villages objected to the new governance of their affairs (and their lack of representation) as well as the way the act enabled further cessions of lands. In a council held at Kahnawá:ke, the allied villages decided to send a delegation to Toronto to lobby the governor. Napier dissuaded them from doing so, telling the villagers that the 1850 act was now "the law of the land."[37] Yet Native villagers had also taken their case to the provincial assembly, making Napier's statement less factual than he had presented it to be.

The provincial assembly had new powers under the governorship of Lord Elgin (James Bruce), and these powers created new opportunities for Native petitioners. After the Reform Party claimed a broad victory in 1847, Lord Elgin invited French reform leader Louis-Hippolyte Lafontaine to form a new government, which meant that the elected premier of the assembly and not the governor would be the head of the government and would control patronage. The assembly had already become more powerful in Canadian affairs after 1840, and now it would be more so. The Native villages of Canada East also had historic alliances with French Canadian reformers—Patriote scion Denis-Benjamin Papineau served as commissioner of Crown lands from 1844 to 1847—and saw the chance to draw on these relationships. Meanwhile, the 1850 statute had not really addressed the problem of those Indigenous communities who lived apart from Canadian settlements on the Saint Lawrence.

From 1847 to 1851, Indigenous communities in Lower Canada sent eight petitions to the legislative assembly. More so than memorials before 1840, these petitions concerned general matters of law and right. Most of them involved claims that had been made before to governors or administrators; what had changed was the venue. Beyond the Innu petitions of 1847 and 1849, Algonquins living on the Gatineau River asked the assembly for grants of land on the Rivière Désert. This request was only in part a particular claim; it also advanced the Algonquins' advocacy (along with the Nipissings) for protection of their lands and a solution to the northward push of settlement from Montréal and Québec. The Abenaki had asked for a trustee (*syndic*) to manage and protect their funds and spaces in 1849. And the Algonquins and Nipissings asked for a new statute not only to protect their own lands but also to address indemnifications and land protection for all of Lower Canada. The combined petition of villages asking for reform of the 1850 statute was the penultimate of a series of Indigenous memorials that thrust general issues of law before the Canadian legislature.[38]

The villagers' alliance assembled at Kahnawá:ke soon witnessed a partial victory. In 1851, the Provincial Parliament debated and passed a statute titled To Repeal in Part, and Amend, the Act for the Better Protection of the Lands and Property of the Indians in Lower Canada. The new statute

TABLE 13.2 Reserves in Former Lower Canada Created by 1851 Indian Act

Site	Acreage	Indigenous Nations and Communities Granted
Lac Temiscamingue	38,400 acres	Algonquins, Nipissings, Odawa
Rivière Désert	45,750 acres	Algonquins, Iroquois, Têtes-de-Boule
Doncaster	16,000 acres	Kahnawá:ke, St. Regis Iroquois
La Tuque	16,000 acres	Abenakis, Algonquins, Têtes-de-Boules
Rocmont	9,600 acres	Hurons
Viger	3,650 acres	Maliseets
Rivière Peribonca	16,000 acres	Montagnais de lac Saint-Jean (Innu)
Rivière Metabetchouan	4,000 acres	Montagnais de lac Saint-Jean (Innu)
Manicouagan	70,000 acres	Montagnais de Tadoussac (Innu), Papinachois, other nomadic communities
Restigouche	9,600 acres	Micmacs

Source: Alain Beaulieu, *La question des terres autochtones au Québec, 1760–1860* (Varennes, 2002), 503–504.

significantly restricted the definition of "Indian" and prevented those Whites adopted into Native communities from claiming land rights. Contemporary elders in the First Nations acknowledge that the 1851 revisions to the Indian Act created a preserve of Native autonomy, securing to villages in Lower Canada local governance of their membership, citizenship, and spaces. Court cases more than a century later would cite the approaches of Kahnawá:ke.[39]

The legislative energy for regulation of Indigenous affairs included a separate act in 1851, this one creating a set of reserves in Lower Canada. The act created reserves totaling 230,000 acres in Lower Canada (Table 13.2). The largest grant of 70,000 acres in this act, a territory of about 20 miles along the north shore of the Saint Lawrence, "between the River Betsiamite and the River *des Outardes*" and extending 10 miles inland, was to the "Indians of Tadoussac, Isle Jeremie, River Godbout and *Des Sept Isles*."[40] The Innu would cede large portions of this land in the decades to follow, and contests over use and governance of these spaces would persist for decades. Yet the reserve established a beachhead for the tribe that would survive.

An appreciation of the power of Native petitioning neither can nor should distract our memories from the vast machineries of Indigenous disempowerment, dispossession, and removal that marked nineteenth-century North America. The clawing back of reservations at Cattaraugus and Allegany, the creation of reserves and rights throughout Lower Canada, and the political persistence of Michigan villages might seem, in the midst of so much carnage, negligible. Yet at a time of massive European settlement and migration and the supremacy of settler governments, none of these outcomes were either foreordained or, for that matter, probable. Whether in western New York or in Québec or in Michigan, Native Americans secured a hold on spaces—a political and legal grip that would last for a century or more afterward and that provided the basis for reconsolidation.

Revisiting these narratives also permits another reading of the tortured but innovative history of Cherokee petitioning. The Cherokee petitioning campaigns of the 1820s and 1830s have often been viewed as a heroic effort in the face of overwhelming force, a noble attempt but one whose victories lay in historical commemoration rather than spatial defense. Viewing the history of Indigenous petitioning on a larger, more continental scale opens a view toward a fuller legacy of the Cherokee struggle. Much of the fruit of Cherokee petitioning came in the continuance of other tribes who learned directly from their example: the Seneca, bands of Ottawa and Ojibwe in the Great Lakes, and other Indigenous nations.

Threats to autonomy and sovereignty would persist and further dispossession would ensue, to be sure, and in the construction of new governments on their reserved lands, Native communities encountered bitter fights over corruption, factional splits, and legal tangles. Yet for Indigenous North American communities, survivance by petition meant not only the persistence of cultures but new possibilities of reorganization and new alliance formation, with fresh opportunities and tools to contest settlers and their governments.

FOURTEEN

The Closure of Petition Democracy in the U.S. South, 1839–1860

> Our people do not petition much, we plume ourselves on not pestering the General Government with our prayers. Nor do we set the woods on fire to drive the game out.
>
> —**Senator Nathaniel Macon (North Carolina), 1819**

> The numerous examples of hasty and inconsiderate legislation, which we so often witness, are becoming a source of great detriment to the State, and should be discouraged by all prudent legislators. One of the great evils of the present age is, that we legislate too much.
>
> —**Georgia Governor Joseph E. Brown, annual message, 1859**

> Our citizens are sick of petitions in favor of guilty negroes.
>
> —***The Richmond Republican*, May 1852**[1]

Nathaniel Macon was both wrong and prescient when he characterized his region's folk as petition wary. He erred in missing the fact that, in the 1810s, the people of his region petitioned far more than he thought, not only to their state legislatures but also to Congress, not only on matters of slavery but on matters of labor, church, agriculture, and education. Yet his claim reflected an elite consensus that would converge on a popular reality. Like other southern political leaders, Macon saw petitioning—with its traditions of vocal grievance and its emerging patterns of citizen challenge to law and administration—as undignified of loyal republican subjects. In the two decades following the antislavery convulsions of 1837–1839, a stifling opprobrium would weigh on southern petitioning and on the agendas of southern legislative legislatures. Neither the level nor the transformations of petitioning witnessed in the northern states would materialize in the region.

In the poverty of its petitioning, the antebellum American South furnishes not merely a national but a continental contrast. As the voices of women arose in Mexico and across the northern United States, southern

White women in the 1840s launched no such mass popular petition campaigns voicing the consciousness of sex. As tenant farmers' and debtors' campaigns surged in New York and Canada, as anti-tax campaigns arose in the Plains and California in the 1850s, and as petition-based agitation targeted the growing power of corporations (including railroad companies) across northern legislatures, similar campaigns were largely absent from the southern states. As Indigenous peoples mounted new initiatives in the Great Lakes, New Mexico, and the Saint Lawrence valley, tribes in the southern states were removed or, where they remained, were confined to political action at the margins. And while free Blacks in Pennsylvania, Massachusetts, Ohio, and New York contested their states' structures of apartheid, free Blacks in Virginia, Kentucky, and other southern jurisdictions were the subject of White petitioning campaigns and legislative initiatives that were writing their lives out of existence in the law. An induced silence settled in on the state legislatures of the U.S. South in the 1840s and 1850s.

The trajectory of the American slave states in the decades before the Civil War resists a simple explanation. Contemporaries then and historians ever since have documented the southern states' restriction of political liberties in the 1840s and 1850s—the crackdown on antislavery advocacy, the monitoring of mails. In other ways, however, southern society functioned and even flourished much as elsewhere in the United States. While southern schools were not as well-funded by taxes as in the North, southern states saw the proliferation of schools, universities, professions, and a burgeoning White middle class in the antebellum period. Southern newspapers and periodicals also flourished, many of them led by women. Perhaps most tellingly, compared to White male voting patterns in the North, electoral turnout in the southern states did not differ significantly, and contemporaries then and later historians interpreted a flourishing of electoral democracy. Important currents of intellectual, cultural, and religious dialogue suffused both the antebellum North and South, and the regions were less disparate than Alexis de Tocqueville's narrative descent down the Ohio River in *Democracy in America*—with slavery-choked Kentucky on the left, freedom-breathing Ohio on the right—might suggest. It was in civil and political liberties and in the practice of petitioning, far more than in the electoral sphere, that southern democratic closure became evident.[2]

* * *

In the late autumn of 1859, in a session extending roughly six weeks (November 2 to December 16), whose journals consumed 516 pages of print, the Georgia House of Representatives recorded a total of ten petitions or memorials. Clerk James J. Diamond dutifully chronicled the proceedings of the chamber and its 180 members assembled at Milledgeville, yet of the handful of petitions he noted, two were from societies (the Cass County Agricultural Fair and the Cherokee Baptist College), while three accompanied bills and were possibly written by legislators themselves. The agenda items they raised were of the most mundane sort—changing the line separating Glasscock and Warren Counties, poor relief for selected citizens and families, incorporation of societies and colleges. Even accounting for the brief nature of state legislative sessions at the time, 1859 marked a low point for the Georgia House, which had recorded at least 56 petitions in 1843. And the same year that the Georgia House recorded 10 petitions in its proceedings, the Michigan House of Representatives recorded 287 petitions to its lower chamber. Michigan's legislators represented a population of just over seven hundred thousand souls in 1859, while Georgia's total population that year was over one million. The two states' sessions had met for about the same time: six weeks (Michigan's House gathered in Lansing from January 5 to February 16).[3]

Legislative sessions vary by their length and their workload, but something about Georgia's 1859 experience gestured to more general patterns. Adjusting for population, petitioning to state legislatures and to the U.S. Congress had already been considerably lower in southern states than in northern states, yet the late 1850s saw a plummeting across the Deep South, where records from the lower chamber are available (Alabama, Florida, Georgia, South Carolina). While the numbers of petitions were also declining in the northeastern states from the heady peak of activity in the late 1840s, the drop in southern petitioning was much more pronounced (Table 14.1). Florida's lower chamber marked seven petitions in 1859, while the number of petitions recorded and retained archivally by Virginia's House of Delegates also plummeted in 1859 to an all-time low (119) for the entire national period (1789–1860). Of the five House of Delegates sessions since 1789 until secession registering less than 150 petitions—the 1808 session (139), the 1814 session (147), and the sessions of 1855 (134), 1857 (120), and 1859 (119)—three came in the decade following the supposedly democratizing constitutional reforms of 1851, during which suffrage was extended widely and after which the commonwealth elected its governor by

TABLE 14.1 Petition Aggregates across Lower Legislative Chambers by U.S. Region, 1851–1859

	Census Region—Northeast (excluding Maryland)	Upper Midwest (Illinois, Indiana Iowa, Michigan, Minnesota, Ohio, Wisconsin)	"Deep South" (Alabama, Florida, Georgia, Louisiana, Mississippi, South Carolina)
Petitions per session, 1851–1855	465.4	189.4	144
Petitions per session, 1856–1859	432.8	140.2	116.5
Sessions with fewer than twenty petitions, 1851–1855	0	0	1
Sessions with fewer than twenty petitions, 1856–1859	0	1	3
Petitions per 10,000 population, 1851–1855	4.9	3.7	2.4
Petitions per 10,000 population, 1856–1859	3.4	2.8	1.5
General Election Turnout [% of eligible], 1852	58.9	68.0	53.2
General Election Turnout [% of eligible], 1856	66.5	80.3	71.2

Note: South Carolina chose its electors in the state legislature until 1868 and is thus excluded from the general election turnout averages. *Source:* Harvard State Legislative Petitions Data, from lower chamber legislative journals for selected years; Jerrold G. Rusk, *A Statistical History of the American Electorate* (Washington: CQ Press, 2001), Tables 3–23, 3–24.

popular vote. While other southern states like Kentucky registered healthier numbers, even their totals were off by half from their value of ten years earlier. When compared on the basis of population, petitioning in southern states had been less than in the northern states for quite some time, since roughly 1800 or 1805. Yet from a statistical viewpoint alone, the additional decline witnessed in southern (especially Deep South) state legislatures in the late 1850s was notable. In the early 1850s, the rate of southern state legislative petitioning in lower chambers lay at half the level in the northeastern states and nearly the level in the Great Lakes midwestern states. From 1856 to 1859 the rate in the Deep South plummeted to less than one-half that witnessed in the midwestern states and less than one-third that seen in the northeastern legislatures. If available records on signature aggregates are any guide, the participation of southern citizens and inhabitants on these petitions was even lower than would be suggested by documentary counts alone.[4]

Far more than in the aggregate documentary counts, the antebellum constriction of southern democracy becomes visible in the identity of the petitioners themselves and the issues they raised (or could not). As collective petitions by women inundated legislative chambers in Albany, Augusta, Boston, Columbus, Harrisburg, and Lansing, southern states in the 1850s saw but a handful of petitions from women. In 1853 alone, the Michigan House of Representatives recorded fifty-nine petitions from various "ladies," "women," or "females" in the state, more so than were recorded in the state legislative journals during the entire decade of the 1850s across a range of southern states (see Table 14.2). Existing archival collections in Virginia and Tennessee suggest that the legislative clerks of lower chambers across the South were neither misled nor undercounting. For the entire two decades from 1839 to 1860, Virginia archivists recorded but four petitions presented consciously and collectively by women as women.

The juxtaposition of these southern silences with legislative agendas of the period exposes the political weakness of anyone who was not a White male slaveowner. South Carolina's House debated a measure establishing protections for married women's estates in 1850 and 1852, while Virginia's House of Delegates authorized its Committee on Courts to investigate married women's property law in 1856. The only thing missing from these debates were any petitions from women themselves, such as the dozens of petitions that had animated the debate for such a statute in New York and Massachusetts in the 1840s and 1850s. So, too, debates about temperance raged in the southern and northern states in the 1850s, most often on the idea of the Maine law (originally introduced in 1846 by Portland mayor Neal Dow), which prohibited all purchases of liquors and spirits except for "medicinal, mechanical or manufacturing purposes." These were the petitions that attracted thousands of names to women-only memorials in Michigan

TABLE 14.2 Collective Petitioning, Select Venues, North America, 1850s

	Number of Women's Petitions	Number of Signatures on Women's Petitions
Florida (House Journals, 1851, 1853, 1854, 1855, 1858, 1859)	0	0
Virginia (House Journals, 1852, 1855–1856, 1857–1858, 1859–1860)	0	0
Virginia (Archives, 1850–1859)	4	175
Kentucky (House Journals, 1851, 1852, 1853, 1855, 1857)	0	0
South Carolina (House Journals, 1850, 1851, 1852, 1853, 1854, 1857, 1859)	2	n/a
Missouri (House Journals, 1850, 1852, 1856, 1857, 1858, 1859)	6	n/a
Michigan, 1853 Session alone	59	3,408
México, Convención Constituyente, 1856	At least 6 (Guadalajara, León, Mexico City, Morelia, Patzcuaro, San Luis Potosí)	Guadalajara: 550 Mexico City: > 1,000

in 1853 alone—many thousands of other women in Michigan and elsewhere in the northern states signed along with men as "not voters" or "not legal voters"—and that attracted tens of thousands of men's signatures in the 1850s. The Maine law agitation in 1850s Virginia did bring more women's signatures, but rarely apart from the men who had led the petitioning effort. Of the 217 temperance petitions sent to the Virginia legislature from 1850 to 1859 and later archived, only 15 had women's signatures alongside men's (totaling 466 women's signatures), and only 3 were women's-only petitions. Restricting the comparison to women advocating for religious conservatism, even Mexico's Constituent Congress in 1855 received more signatures from women.[5]

Starting with Angelina Grimké in Massachusetts in 1839, "ladies' petitions" had induced officially recognized appearances of women before state legislatures throughout the northern states, whether in plenary session or before a select or standing committee hearing (see Table 11.3). Such appearances were unheard of in the southern states, including outside the Deep South. Instead, southern legislatures occasionally offered women a role as passive observers. In its 1856–1857 session, the North Carolina House of Representatives entertained a resolution that "the ladies of this city [Raleigh] and vicinity be invited to take seats in the gallery, and suitable accommodations there be provided for them." During the entire 1850s, the House of Representatives entertained one petition from women: for incorporation of a ladies' benevolent society.[6]

As southern states finalized the ejection of their Indigenous populations and suppressed, eliminated, and enslaved their free Black populations, they starved off a civil society. Indigenous communities petitioned far and wide in North America in the 1840s and 1850s—including the Seneca in New York, the Ojibwe and allied bands in the western Great Lakes (including communities removed from the East), the Mashpee in Massachusetts, the Penobscot in Maine, dozens of pueblo communities in New Mexico, and tribes in the Saint Lawrence valley of Canada. These voices remained muted in the halls of southern state legislatures. The Pamunkey families that composed the Virginia remnants of the tribe at Pamunkey Indian Town launched a counterpetitioning campaign in 1843 against White petitions for sale of their lands in King William County. After that episode, Virginia's House of Delegates and Senate would not record another Indigenous petition before the end of the Civil War.[7]

So, too, free Black petitioning in the northern states surged in the 1840s and 1850s with agitation over personal liberty laws and protests against the Fugitive Slave Act and the Dred Scott decision. In the southern states—not only the Deep South but also Virginia—slaveholders and allied politicians had begun imposing new penalties on free Blacks after the Nat Turner revolt in 1833. (An earlier 1806 statute required manumitted slaves to leave the state within a year.) Free Blacks petitioned county courts for the freedom to remain "at the pleasure of the Court," while White petitioners (including slaveowners) in turn petitioned county courts to refuse these "leave to remain" judgments and also pressured the legislature at Richmond to further enforce the Black removal statutes. Commonwealth elites continued a broad push for the regulation and, beyond that, the elimination of the free Black population of the state, echoing the argument of Governor William Smith in 1847 that "the free negro seriously affects the value of our slaves, awakens in the slave new appetites and wants, teaches to the road to crime, makes him restless and dissatisfied, [and] increases the spirit of insubordination."[8] In the 1850s, these sentiments acquired the commonality and organization of a movement, with petitions and newspaper editorials calling for greater "regulation" of Virginia's free Black population, including county hiring of free Blacks and new legal mechanisms of enslavement. The Virginia General Assembly passed a voluntary reenslavement law in 1856, and petitions for free Blacks for voluntary reenslavement had become common.[9] As Virginia and other southern states legislated free Blacks out of existence, the complaints and appeals of those few that remained came to county courts.[10]

In other matters, Virginia's politics exposed the growing asymmetry between slave owners and factory owners who employed slaves on the one hand, and White industrial laborers and western residents on the other. In an attempt to shore up their waning bargaining power, White Virginia laborers pushed to exclude slaves from more remunerative industrial sites. In 1847, ironworkers at the Tredegar plant in Richmond petitioned their manager for removal of slaves from the ironworks, then launched a strike that year to back up their demands. The failure of the Tredegar strike lay bare the harsh stakes of the new industrial economy, as slave industrial labor would undercut the pay of White workers with the support of Virginia's planter and tidewater elite. To the west, Panhandle residents (especially those residing in Brooke, Hancock, and Ohio Counties) griped that their concerns were being routinely ignored and dismissed by the general assembly and began discussing secession in the 1850s. The promise of the 1851 constitutional reform had been dashed, these men felt, as the reforms had done nothing to contest the political hegemony of the tidewater region and the eastern powers of the state. The Panhandle counties had been "reduced to the condition of a mere tributary province, and our claims and petitions have alike been treated with contumely, neglect and contempt."[11]

If there was a partial standout in the southern states, it came in the Commonwealth of Kentucky, where the house of the general assembly continued receiving hundreds of petitions in the 1850s and where even the senate debated petitions and other resolutions encompassing a wide range of issues. Under Democratic governor Lazarus Powell (1851–1855) and Know-Nothing governor Charles Morehead (1855–1859), the commonwealth embarked on agricultural improvement policies, new schools and universities (reorganization of the state's idle Bacon College into the Kentucky University in 1857, as well as a range of reforms to the state's Transylvania University in 1856), and reform of the state's burdensome militia system. In other ways, however, Kentucky reproduced the limited nature of political debate in the 1850s slave states. Despite a robust debate over importation of slaves in the 1840s, the assembly in 1849 repealed an 1833 law on the re-importation of slaves, and the pro-slavery majority at the state's constitutional convention that same year prevented any further change on the issue. Unlike New York's constitutional convention of 1846, Kentucky's in 1849 entertained but a handful of petitions (most having to do with delegates elected to the meeting), the convention's agenda having been established from among its members. Antislavery advocate the Reverend John Gregg Fee found that even the question of colonization—long championed by a number of leading men of the state's political elite, including Henry Clay—could not be openly debated in the state in the late 1850s. Fee's sermons were mobbed by anti-abolitionist men, and his coworkers were stripped and beaten. From 1857 onward, Fee appealed to Henry Clay himself, whose support and counsel against anti-abolitionist violence he hoped would give his movement some legitimacy, but the Great Compromiser declined to lift a finger in the reverend's defense. In the spring of 1859, Fee's fledgling Berea College was persecuted, its students run out of the commonwealth. In contrast to the 1840s, slavery disappeared from the state's petitions and its legislative agenda.[12]

In the Deep South, where slavery was more deeply embedded in the economy and where state politicians—like South Carolina's John Calhoun—had begun to premise their worldviews on defense of the institution, the political closure of legislative agendas and popular debate was particularly evident. In South Carolina, slaveholder representatives were entrenched in state government from the 1830s onward, with little threat of political competition from alternative interests. South Carolina's politicians had already intercepted abolitionist mailings in the 1830s, but by the 1850s, discussion of slavery was being formally and informally proscribed, vigilance committees had organized in different towns, and, in the most notable incident, an Irish stonecutter suspected of abolitionist sympathies had been lynched and then tarred and feathered in Columbia. In the late 1850s, vigilance committees and informal mobs were regularly expelling anyone, woman or man, suspected of being an abolitionist. Preachers and state legislators openly supported the work of the vigilance committees and called for statutes that would regularize and legitimize their practices.[13]

Memorials continued flowing into South Carolina's lower chamber in the 1850s—fully 251 in the 1859 session—yet these documents expressed the settlement agenda that had characterized American states since before the War of 1812. South Carolina's House examined petitions for incorporation, for new county or township governments, for roads, for railroad lines, for claims of indemnity and pay in arrears, and others. Counterpetitioning campaigns were limited to roads and were decidedly absent from the state's discussion of railroads (where all of the petitioning was by companies or for new lines). Women's petitions in South Carolina were, as in other southern states, limited to requests for local society incorporation. In debates over temperance, South Carolina's legislators recorded but a handful of petitions in which the state's women were silent. Temperance politics in the South had seemed to peak in the late 1830s, with a broad petitioning campaign in Georgia and the organization of the Sons of Temperance. Yet in the 1840s, temperance petitioning fell in Georgia and other southern states, and following the decline of petitioning, Georgia's Sons of Temperance membership fell, too—from over thirteen thousand members in 1851 to about fifteen hundred by 1860.[14]

As every American student and scholar knows, the differences between these northern and southern states before and after the Civil War are so vast as to defy a simple categorical attribution of difference. Petitioning and its agendas reflected one of the many differences in political culture and institutions at the time. Still, such stark regional differences—not merely in aggregate levels of activity but also in trajectories—do not emerge in a host of other indices on which contemporaries compared the northern and southern states. As the region's promoters and defenders of slavery vouched repeatedly, Southern economic and cultural activity surged during the 1850s. Southern manufacturing exploded and became better capitalized. There were increases in state expenditures for public schools, banks, and railroads, and associated infrastructure. Land distribution also became more equal among White men during the period. Although they were poorly funded and more often private, Southern schools grew rapidly in the 1850s, both in their numbers and in their enrollment. Alabama had 1,323 schools in 1850 and fully 2,126 in 1860, and its student population surged from 62,846 to 98,204 in the same ten-year period. Across the slaveholding states, newspapers exploded in number and circulation in the 1850s, Georgia's number doubling from 50 in 1850 to 105 in 1860, while circulation almost tripled from 64,155 to 180,972. And it appeared that women's silence in petitioning was not a function of their exclusion from the world of the press, as women in a range of southern states took up editorial positions and worked as journalists.[15]

Finally, as observers of the South have noted for almost a century, the 1850s witnessed a heady rise in electoral participation, including among less literate men. Across the nation, the highly competitive contest of 1840—in which in the midst of the Panic and the resulting depression the Whigs first rallied to a degree of organizational competitiveness with the Democrats—marked a high point from which most states saw a decline in turnout. But in the 1850s, southern states generally saw voting in general elections that, when measured as a fraction of eligible population, rivaled if not exceeded that of northern states. Nor did the 1850s see any falloff in electoral participation in the Deep South (Table 14.1).[16]

In the northern states and as far west as California, petitioners were newly taking up economic issues in the 1850s. Lawmakers assembled at Lansing, Michigan, in the 1850s witnessed one petition campaign after another followed by counterpetitioning campaigns on the rights of corporations. These included petitions for a general statute regulating railroads, along with a campaign against such a law; for regulating the crossing of farmland by railroads and the draining of marshes; and for and against amendments to railroad charters. In California, petitions flowed to the governor and the assembly upon statehood, and while many of the early petitions were for appointments and privileges, soon antimonopoly and anti-speculator campaigns emerged in these memorials. Petitioners in Butte County started a campaign against taxes imposed for the contraction of a road near Oroville, while Sacramento residents started a campaign against a toll bridge law and accompanying speculator interests. The Sacramento petition included a systemic canvass of the city's street grid. California petitioners also appeared regularly against emerging rail interests.[17]

In the southern states, by contrast, the petitioning decline restricted the agenda on a range of questions related to debt, labor, and political economy. Railroad politics differed from state to state in the South, and in Virginia, the monopoly rights of the Baltimore and Ohio Railroad became a sore point among those burdened by the restrictive character of its 1847 and 1851 charters. Yet the vast majority of railroad-related petitioning in 1850s Virginia came from western and southwestern residents asking for new roads with a terminus on the Ohio, Potomac, or Shenandoah Rivers. And farther south, the abundance of railroad company memorials successfully asking for state grants in aid—as in South Carolina from 1852 to 1854, where many a railroad company petitioned successfully for charter amendments and subsidies and where little opposition was encountered—pointed to a different political regime, one that blunted procedural democracy by greatly restricting the agenda and one that suffocated cultural democracy by sharply limiting contestation.[18]

The oft-narrated kernel of the region's trajectory—the power of planters—obscures as much as it reveals. Southern state legal culture had changed profoundly in the early nineteenth century. A system that, in the wake of the Revolution, left to local judges and clerks discretion over all kinds of questions of property had, by the late 1830s, increasingly leaned on the idea of rights established in state statute. It was the nullifiers, more than other factions, who successfully organized as a political force to defend the sovereignty of state laws, and their work was aided by a cohort of legal minds that sought to compile state statutes so as to give regularity and consistency to southern law.

Southern politicians and jurists had always located their sovereignty in a combination of local justice and state legislatures. These lay in tension, but the primacy of state legislation grew in the late antebellum period as southern legislatures and jurists began to restrain county courts.[19]

By the 1850s, though, southern elites began to offer a different defense of state law, one accompanied by an abiding skepticism about lawmaking and legislative activity. When Governor Joseph E. Brown addressed the Georgia legislature in 1859, he argued that the chambers had been too busy processing "hasty and inconsiderate legislation." "One of the great evils of the age," he intoned, was that "we legislate too much." "Wholesome rules of law with which the people have become familiar," he scolded his lawmakers, "should not be changed, unless for good cause, after very mature deliberation." Better to let the status quo govern itself, he thought, than to consider a constant renewal of statutes. Brown extended arguments elsewhere about the perils of particular legislation such as private bills. Categorizing these as "trivial, local, private and class legislation," a nefarious species of bills that were "introduced into almost every General Assembly" and ranged from the "useless because it benefits no one" to the "unjust and mischievous, because it benefits a few individuals at the expense of many." Every such bill inflated the size of the legislative journals, which were printed at public expense. Not merely the passage of such trivial laws, then, but the consideration of bills of the sort lay beneath the proper functioning of a republican legislature. "It would, in my opinion, be much better for the Legislature, with few exceptions, to lay down general rules of law, and let all alike regulate their conduct by them."[20]

Like other southern political leaders at the time of secession, Governor Joseph Brown set Georgia on a path of self-determination that limited the involvement of popular voices, especially from his upcountry jurisdictions in which slaveholding was less widespread. Like other southern states, Georgia seceded through a state convention that ran around the potential dilatory actions of its legislatures. And in Georgia, Brown beat even his state conventioneers to the punch, seizing the defenseless federal Fort Pulaski in January 1861 before the state convention voted to secede.[21]

The dormancy of petitioning both weak and thin in the late antebellum South—feeble in its numbers and heavily constrained in the breadth of the issues raised before legislative sovereigns—reveals something about democracy and civil society. With a thriving middle class, a bounty of associations, expansive and growing common schools, a flourishing print culture, and electoral participation that rivaled that of the northern states, late antebellum southern politics had many of the hallmarks of democracy. Yet along with their restrictions on civil liberties, the southern states in the 1850s lacked a democracy of agendas. The endeavor of ideological rigidity was both symptom and cause of the feeble petitioning culture witnessed in the South's state capitols, and that endeavor reverberated in the feedback between legislatures, governors, and citizens. What these state institutions and cultures subdued was not a print public sphere among journals and newspapers, or the class-based institutions restricted to Whites, or even women's involvement in crucial features of society. The closure of political space to a range of issues that would have challenged White supremacy both relied on and reinforced a broader constriction of political claims-making in the states' institutions. The ties that withered in the antebellum South were not the bonds of cooperation and trust but the lines of communication that brought dissent and unexpected voices and questions to the halls of lawmaking. Whether construed as "civil society," as "civic engagement," or as "social capital," the networks of communication that compose contestatory democracy must include the agenda-setting, complaint-registering and request-making institutions and practices that link society to sovereign. The submission of late antebellum southern democracy lay in the asthmatic space relating subject to sovereign.

FIFTEEN

Freedom and the Petitioner's Democracy

> We complain of our Chief Executive of causing, by his agents, and Indulgence of Outlaws, much of the Outrages and Murders that have been committed on Loyal Subjects and Citizens of the Union in ten Rebel States since May 29th, 1865.
>
> We charge President Johnson, with giving aid and comfort to Outlaws . . .
>
> We charge him with Usurping Legislative and Judicial power . . .
>
> We charge him with wickedly, & boldly, striving to Reproduce Rebellion, by making Rebel Outlaws Governors, Judges, Sheriffs, Mayors, Clerks and the Police of the Ten Rebel States.
>
> —"Petition of the Colored Free & Freed Citizens of Savannah, Ga.," 1865

A document mixing humility with audacity, at once meticulous yet coursing with rage, the petition of Asa Cotton, James Hewett, Aaron Bradley, William Brown, Ishmael Palmer, and dozens of other men of color from Savannah arrived at the U.S. House of Representatives in the autumn of 1865. Walking their readers through a list of offenses, interspersing newspaper cuttings freely among their handwritten arguments to provide ready evidence for their claims, referring abundantly to constitutional clauses and to statutes, they laid out the case for President Andrew Johnson's impeachment. The offenses alleged against Johnson by Savannah's Black men were comparable in some sense, and yet far worse in other ways, to those launched by Thomas Jefferson at King George III in 1776. Having usurped powers not his, having failed to enforce laws passed by Congress, having aided an enemy (and in doing do plausibly committing treason), having encouraged a rebellion, having acted in ways murderous and wicked, Johnson deserved removal at minimum. The Savannah freedmen's prayer reads as part memorial, part indictment list for a capital trial. It was possibly the first, and certainly the most radical, in a slew of petitions for Johnson's impeachment that would arrive to Congress between 1865 and 1867.[1]

Americans have told and retold their story of freedom by reference to the pivotal era of Civil War and Reconstruction—to President Abraham Lincoln's proclaimed emancipation of slaves; to congressional and state passage of three constitutional amendments that reshaped the meaning of liberty, law, and citizenship; to the military conquest of Union over Confederacy; and to the efforts of the U.S. government to remake Southern society. The partial and incomplete fruition of these efforts, especially that of Reconstruction, demonstrate the incomplete, inchoate character of American freedom. In memory and in political economy, in constitutional and statutory text, in bodily freedom and intertwined sectional and racial violence, the legacies of the 1860s were tangible, transformative, and, for millions, lasting.

In ways that have yet to be fully acknowledged, petitioning—especially petitioning by Black Americans and their allies—figured centrally in these developments. Nearly every dimension of democracy and its emergence was involved, from formal rights to mobilization to the assumptions and vocabularies that defined a new culture. Abolitionists Black and White shaped the agenda for emancipation by aggressively petitioning president and Congress soon after southern states seceded. They used memorials to press Congress for African American voting rights and constitutional and legal reform. These efforts, in turn, brought White women into massive petitioning again, their signatures roughly doubling those of men on weighty scrolls of prayer, their names flooding Congress. Enhancing organizational democracy, these petitions evolved alongside new Black assemblies and associations, ranging from the Colored and Freedmen's Conventions to various civil rights leagues at the state and national levels. And as African Americans and women openly called for emancipation, as Savannah's men of color helped launch the drive for impeachment of Johnson, and as Sojourner Truth toured the northern states and started a campaign for land distribution, American petitioners advanced a new vision of cultural democracy in which arguments and aspirations for equality took root.

The contours of American freedom's saga in the 1860s—encompassing emancipation, constitutional amendment, civil rights laws, and Reconstruction—entail other, better known developments. These include the evolution of slavery itself, the centuries' long struggle against slavery, swelling sectional antagonism between an imagined South and a North defined in part by opposition to it, the rise of the Republican Party and the election of

1860, southern secession and the great war of 1861–1865, the election of 1864 that returned Lincoln to the presidency, and the election of 1866 that gave Republicans massive majorities arrayed against President Andrew Johnson. Democratizing petitions interacted with all these patterns. The mass mobilization over the gag rule and, later, the Kansas-Nebraska Act reshaped northern public opinion and gave important antislavery constituencies momentum, information, and the accoutrements of new organization. In some cases, petitions provided additional impetus to officeholders where electoral signals were unclear. Abolitionists seized on southern secession as an opportunity for Lincoln to do what Congress could not, using his authority over enemy lands to free slaves in a military jurisdiction. The countermobilization against Andrew Johnson relied heavily on petitions long before as well as after the 1866 midterms.[2]

PRAYERS, PROCLAMATIONS, AND THE ABOLITION OF SLAVERY

Falling like axe blows on the body politic, the serial announcements of secession by southern states shook and enraged citizens of the northern United States. For many steeled abolitionists, however, the Slave Power's departure from government, combined with the onset of war, presented a remarkable opportunity. The Republican Party had won control of elective branches of government in part from the popularity of free labor and free soil ideology; in part from the identification of the South as not merely a region but a "Slave Power" dedicated to undoing free labor, free soil, and true republican values; and in part from the Republicans' slavery containment platform. Yet the predominant model of antislavery among Republican political leaders remained Lincoln's—a program of compensated emancipation and colonization (forced exportation) for freed slaves, and of a post-slavery world that flatly and categorically restricted civil and legal rights to White men. With Lincoln's decision to prosecute a war for national reintegration, with the mass deployment of the Union and its Army, and with the northern and Republican-dominated rump Congress that remained after secession, abolitionists who rejected the colonization saw the radical possibility of state action.

The freeing of American slaves in the Emancipation Proclamation of January 1863 has been read, rightly, as an administrative decision by President Lincoln, a war measure that he took for reasons that reflected strategy and a changing personal reflection on slavery and race. Yet more than a year before Lincoln arrived at his final decision, bold activists and petitioners from all across the northern (and some southern) states fashioned the agenda for a massive wartime liberation of southern slaves. The first battles of the secession crisis came in the question of whether compromise should be attempted, either by a convention or by legislative measures. Once the firing on Fort Sumter commenced the war in earnest, the debate shifted, as did the radicalism of proposals.

The earliest petitioning battles after secession occurred during the first months of 1861, in the waning days of the Thirty-Sixth Congress. Kentucky senator John J. Crittenden's compromise, offered December 18, 1860, in the Senate, would permit slavery in territories below the 36°30'N latitude, excluding it above. Proposals to adopt the Crittenden plan, to hold a national convention where it would be considered, or to put the matter to national referendum were sent to Congress. For many, this seemed the basis of a sectional compromise that would avoid war, but for strong abolitionists and those incensed by what they described as a "rebellion" committed by "traitors," it compromised with the Slave Power and, beyond that, extended slavery into the West. There is also reason to doubt that it would have brought the Deep South states back into the Union. Yet border state representatives, many Democrats, and conservative Republicans pressed for congressional adoption of the Crittenden plan, and they enlisted petitions to do so. In January, Crittenden and his pro-compromise allies in Congress began introducing petitions supportive of compromise—either directly supporting Crittenden's proposal or calling for measures that would "embrace substantially" the proposals of "the representatives of the border states." Memorials of support for the compromise began to fill the legislative journals.[3]

By early February, the tide of petitioning in Congress had begun to turn. Petitions calling for Congress to "hold firm" on the Union, demanding a preservation of "the Constitution as it is," and warning legislators against any embrace of compromise came in greater numbers, with larger and larger signatory lists, and soon outnumbered the pro-Crittenden memorials. These petitions came disproportionately from Pennsylvania, especially the Philadelphia area. Some of the countermobilization appears to have been arranged by abolitionist Republicans, including William Seward and Thaddeus Stevens. Yet the increasing involvement of women petitioners is undeniable. On days where women's antislavery petitions were read into the record (a practice occasionally coordinated by sponsoring legislators), the anti-Crittenden forces presented an average of two additional petition introductions. By the end of the Thirty-Sixth Congress in early March, anti-compromise petitions regularly outnumbered pro-Crittenden memorials. When the Thirty-Seventh Congress met in July, the war was underway and the flow of memorial support for Crittenden was reduced to a trickle.[4]

The April 12, 1861, attack on Fort Sumter changed the stakes and the possibilities. Occurring between legislative sessions, it quickened Northerners' anger, confirming the warnings of the radical abolitionists who foretold the aggression of the South as "Slave Power." Antislavery became, more than ever, tied to the war effort. As and even before prominent abolitionists like Frederick Douglass and Thaddeus Stevens spoke in favor of emancipation measures, petitioners calling for various means to end slavery directed their appeals to Washington. Near the end of the Thirty-Sixth Congress, on February 6, 1861, Senator Simon Cameron introduced two Philadelphia petitions proposing appropriations for slavery's "extinguishment" where states wished to apply for it. Petitions far more radical rolled into the following Congress, the first legislative session of Lincoln's presidency, which assembled on July 4, 1861. The first memorial for wartime liberation came in the sixteenth petition introduced to the Thirty-Seventh House, on July 9, wherein Williams County, Ohio, citizens called for the "immediate and unconditional emancipation of the slave." Five days later came the first abolition petition of the Senate session, from Connecticut memorialists who identified slavery as "the cause of the present war," praying "it may be removed." Other petitions praying the "abolition of slavery" came later that month, again from Ohio. Ohio's move to the vanguard of the abolitionist movement had begun in the gag rule crisis and materialized in the antiwar agitation of the 1840s. By the time that Thaddeus Stevens introduced his first bill for total emancipation in November 1861, legislators in the Senate and House had introduced eight petitions for the measure in the preceding four months, not one from Stevens's home state of Pennsylvania.[5]

With war underway, activists eagerly wedded pro-emancipation arguments to anti-rebellion invective. The earliest emancipation petitions arrived before military hostilities, coming to the House at the close of the Thirty-Sixth Congress in February 1861, calling for emancipation by purchase. By the summer, with attacks and deaths mounting, petitioners changed their focus to target both abolition and the Confederacy. The most common form of emancipation prayer in 1861 and 1862 pressed Congress to abolish slavery, "compensating loyal masters." This prayer reflected compromise only in part; its true aim lay in sapping the Confederacy's cohesion, energy, and unity. The second most common prayer was one of emancipating slaves "under the war power," prayers that became far more common by the ensuing summer. As the second session of the Thirty-Seventh Congress commenced in December 1861, the intertwined logics of emancipation and rebel suppression unfolded on memorial parchment, with abundant proposals for the total confiscation of all property of "rebels," while many an abolition or emancipation petition called for the freeing of "slaves of rebels." One canvasser remarked that of the twenty-five names he had gathered, "not four of these men would have signed this petition previous to the bombardment of Sumpter [*sic*]." Emancipation and property confiscation ran hand in hand in these anti-Confederate petitions, which grew in number and vitriol as the early military campaigns unfolded. Of the fifty-eight petitions introduced to the Thirty-Seventh Congress before 1863 that prayed for confiscation, well over half (at least thirty-five) came from Ohio, those arriving to the Senate being referred to the select committee established for that purpose in 1862. Meanwhile, over one hundred petitions coming before 1863 excoriated "rebels," "traitors," or "rebellion."[6]

President Lincoln and the Thirty-Seventh Congress appear to have paid close attention to these petitions. Lincoln had presented a gradual, compensated emancipation plan for the border states in March 1862, but the press of immediate emancipation and confiscation petitions as well as the developing atrocity of war appears to have weighed on him. The pro-emancipation drive of early 1862 was, based on signatures, the largest antislavery petition mobilization since the 1830s. The seven emancipation bills that Republican legislators introduced to Congress in the summer of 1862 came after these petitions, not before. William Goodell, who personally pressured Lincoln at this time, believed that these emancipation petitions shaped debate and sentiment in both chambers of Congress. While a late May vote for confiscation measures failed in the House, the agenda had already been established, and Congress mustered the votes to pass the Second Confiscation Act on July 17, 1862.[7]

Recognizing Lincoln's concern for "public opinion," preachers, religious radicals, and politicians brought petitions with them when meeting Lincoln to press him on presidential emancipation. Evangelical and Quaker visitors were especially common in the summer of 1862, and Quakers brought with them a petition started by Garrison himself. By August, writers like Benjamin West could refer to the petitions as conveying "public sentiment" and "the wish of the Father" for abolition. In early September, after he had already drafted the proclamation but ten days before issuing it, a delegation arrived from Chicago presenting emancipation petitions. One of the visiting ministers reportedly told Lincoln that the petitions were a message not merely from his home state but "from our Divine Master, through me, commanding you, sir, to open the doors of bondage." Lincoln reportedly joked of the oddity that the Lord would direct divine will through "that roundabout route" of the "awfully wicked city." Whatever Chicago's role had been in this supplication, the summer's visitors and writers had repeatedly impressed on Lincoln the identification of "public opinion" with the will of God. Prayers massively signed worked hand in hand with personal lobbying to demonstrate both propositions to the reluctant president.[8]

Lincoln's September 22, 1862, proclamation was both radical and incomplete. In its all-at-once thrust, avoidance of gradual liberation, and refusal to compensate slaveowners for false property, it partially advanced an immediatist, Garrisonian vision of abolition. Slaveowners and Democrats felt that any hope of compromise with any Southern states had been dashed by the drastic measure. In other ways, because the action as a military order pertained only to those areas of the United States under Union Army control, it left aside slaves held in non-occupied states, Maryland foremost among them. For abolitionists and radical Republicans, the proclamation's materialization on January 1, 1863, merely shifted to the agenda the quest for a wider and more permanent abolition of slavery in the Union. The Democrats' gains in the 1862 elections provided little electoral force to the push. Renewed legislative momentum would derive from other sources, other voices.[9]

Neither entirely grassroots nor manipulated by legislators, emancipation petitions unfolded in a deep interplay of activism and congressional strategy. Popular organization provided critical fuel to the campaign, especially among women. When Elizabeth Cady Stanton and Susan B. Anthony together created the Women's National Loyal League in the spring of 1863, they held as the primary aim of their new organization a petitioning campaign that would gather one million signatures to persuade Congress to pass a national emancipation law. Their efforts built on an ongoing abolitionist mobilization that was particularly energetic in the northwestern states, especially Illinois, Iowa, Michigan, and Ohio. In Washington, meanwhile, Owen Lovejoy, Justin Morrill, Thaddeus Stevens, and other legislators invited petitions from their own districts as well as others. In April 1862, in the midst of the emancipation debate, the House created its Select Committee on Emancipation. Initially charged with emancipation in the border states and possible colonization plans, this body would soon receive and discuss the most radical petitions on slavery in 1863 and 1864, including the earliest bills to create a Bureau of Emancipation (which later evolved into the Freedmen's Bureau). On December 14, 1863, another Select Committee on Emancipation was appointed. In the Senate, Charles Sumner called for the creation of a new committee to discuss the many abolitionist petitions descending on that chamber, and he would chair the Select Committee on Slavery and Freedmen.[10]

In the waning days of the Thirty-Seventh Congress in the early months of 1863, a set of debates unfolded in Washington on two intersecting themes: pay and status for Black soldiers, and broader emancipation and civil liberties for African Americans. The question of whether liberated slaves could be employed in the Union Army had arisen from the first battles of the war, and the question became especially pointed after the First Confiscation Act freed slaves used in the rebellion. Union officials were recruiting Black troops in Kansas in the fall of 1861, and while in May 1862 Lincoln rescinded General Henry Halleck's General Order No. 3 expelling fugitive slaves from army lines, the president repeatedly refused Black activists' requests for open military enrollment of Black men. By 1863, with the proclamation opening the path toward Black soldiers in the Union Army, Lincoln tasked the War Department with recruiting, training, and deploying Black regiments. By the end of the year, the pay and status of Black soldiers had become not merely an administrative question but a political question, and thus a petitioning question. In some cases, Black soldiers themselves did the petitioning, while in other cases their White comrades petitioned on their behalf. Massachusetts senator Henry Wilson presented the petition of the Fourth and Sixth regiments of "colored troops" in December 1863, praying "that colored soldiers may be placed on an equal footing with white solders in the United States service." That day, Maine senator Justin Morrill also presented a petition of his state's citizens, calling for Black soldiers to "be placed on the same footing, as to pay and privileges, as white soldiers." Maine's petitioners combined racial equality in military service with a prayer for a universal emancipation law, as did Michigan citizens a month later. Brigadier General William Birney joined Union volunteers and a number of Black noncommissioned officers in praying for a boost in Black soldiers' pay from seven to thirteen dollars per month, to equal the rate of White soldiers' pay.[11]

Black soldiers' appeals gestured to the political centrality of petitioning during the Civil War. Wartime memorials placed issues of military administration on the public agenda. Questions of who could serve, what their status and pay might be, and all manner of subjects usually regarded as "administrative" were debated not only in War Department offices but in Congress, the press, and petitions. From 1861 onward, American Jews started enduring debates on issues of religious discrimination and military identity. A chaplaincy law passed in July 1861 specified that only Christian ministers were permitted in military service, leaving thousands of Jewish Union soldiers bereft of acknowledgment and spiritual support. Critics noted the irony that rabbis could deliver invocations and congressional prayer but not minister to troops. Rabbis, Jewish community leaders in the northwestern Union states, and Jewish newspapers—the *Jewish Messenger* of New York and the Cincinnati-based *Israelite*—took the lead in launching and publicizing a petitioning campaign in 1861. "Wherever Israelites live," declared Reform congregation rabbi and *Israelite* publisher Isaac Mayer Wise, "draw up a petition to abolish that unconstitutional law, have it signed by every neighbor you find disposed to do so, and send it" to Congress.[12] On December 14, Lincoln wrote Rabbi Arnold Fischel (whose appointment had been denied months earlier) that the subject would be taken up in Congress the next month, and petitioners quickly pressed the case on the chambers. Memorials came from Jews and allied Christians, including thirty-seven members of the Maryland House of Delegates and a petition of seven thousand names from Baltimore. Congress passed a law authorizing non-Protestant chaplains on March 12, 1862, and in September, Lincoln appointed the first Jewish chaplain, Rabbi Jacob Frankel, to service in Philadelphia.[13]

Jewish congregations and their allies used a slightly different strategy in response to Major General Ulysses Grant's General Order No. 11 of December 1862—expelling Jews from his military district on the stereotypical argument that as a class of traders, they exploited and destabilized cotton markets near army lines. Largely eschewing petitions to Congress, Jewish activists took their campaign to the White House, using petitions and telegrams with signatory lists. Their efforts became more urgent when Jewish families near Paducah, Kentucky, were forcibly removed on December 28, 1862. Jews in Kentucky and elsewhere—including the B'nai B'rith Missouri Lodge in St. Louis—quickly petitioned Lincoln and sent what newspapers called "deputations" to appeal to him on the matter. The president, who did not learn of the order or the attacks until several days after the Emancipation Proclamation became effective on January 1, 1863, quickly declared that he knew of "no distinction between Jew and Gentile," and reversed the order. The order and its rescission also made the congressional agenda that January. In these and other affairs, Lincoln appeared to read the petitions of American Jews with particular interest and compassion.[14]

Petitions for increase in military and civilian pay were quite common during the war, reflecting not merely the inflationary environment but also the expectation of a gracious hearing by a Congress determined to support all aspects of the Union effort. Yet the petitions for "colored soldiers" and "colored troops" aspired to broader equality, and they were coming from Black soldiers themselves—Black soldiers allied with their commanders and comrades—and from interracial and White abolitionist constituencies. By the summer of 1863 through early 1865, these petitions came in regularly to Congress—from the Black troops posted at Helena, Arkansas, or Camp Casey, Virginia; from abolitionists in Wisconsin, Indiana, Ohio, and Massachusetts; from "1,065 citizens of the United States"; from Colonel Thomas Wentworth Higginson, who had led the First South Carolina Volunteers, the first Black regiment authorized in the war. Petitioners from Greene County, Indiana, exemplified the mixture of argument in calling for "a vigorous prosecution of the war; that colored soldiers be placed upon a footing equal with the white soldiers; and that emancipation be decreed to all slaves in the United States." They amplified arguments being made to the president and Congress by Frederick Douglass, among others, that the reality and heroism of black military service created powerful claims for citizenship and legal equality. What many of these petitions added was a vociferous call for full military conquest of the South.[15]

As supplicants military and civilian called on Congress to boost the pay and status of Black Union soldiers, emancipation petitions also began to present prayers with more explicit racial consciousness and a full embrace of military onslaught against the rebellion. Whereas the memorials of 1861 and 1862 had sought emancipation of "slaves," emancipation petitions in 1863 and 1864 increasingly prayed for the liberation of "all persons of African descent" or the abolition of "African slavery." Joining other Black petitioners of the time, roughly one thousand Black signatories from Louisiana affixed their name to a petition calling for suffrage rights for "all of the natives of Louisiana of African descent." Reflecting the mass printing of the "Woman's Emancipation Petition" by Stanton and Anthony in 1863 and 1864, antislavery petitioners who self-identified as women were systematically more likely to pray for those of "African descent" and deploy the language of "universal emancipation." The change in language partially reflected the sponsorship of Massachusetts senator Charles Sumner, as Sumner had used the phrase "African descent" for a number of years, particularly when defending Blacks' right to petition. Yet the language of race and slavery was diffusing throughout the North, including on many a petition that Sumner did not introduce. And as the debates over the universality of emancipation raged, children and their schoolteachers entered the arena, as with the "Little People's Petition" from Concord, Massachusetts, in April 1864, to which Lincoln responded personally with his endorsement. In the aspiration of prayer and the audacity of persons, the antislavery memorial verged on the radical.[16]

Garrison approached Elizabeth Stanton and Susan B. Anthony later in 1863 and urged them to shift their petitioning prayer to the request for a constitutional amendment, one that in its fixity and symbolism would be less reversible. By February 1864, antislavery societies were circulating emancipation petitions that prayed for constitutional amendment, and over two thousand women and men were at work in the canvassing endeavor. The initial fruits of their harvest were sent to Congress on February 1864, when Anthony and Stanton presented petitions reportedly carrying 100,000 names (65,601 women and 34,399 men) to Massachusetts senator Charles Sumner. Sumner's committee kept records of a petitioning campaign that aggregated 90,062 signatures, and the committee's records show especially heavy signatures from women in Ohio, Illinois, Iowa, and Wisconsin (see Table 15.1). In an act of enduring symbolism, the day after introducing his bill for emancipation by constitutional amendment, Sumner asked two Black men to transport the petitions to his desk in the Senate on February 9, at which point he rose to proclaim that the signatories composed "a mighty army, one hundred thousand strong, without arms or banners, the advanced guard of a yet larger army." In Charles Sumner's view, the primary carriers of the slave's cause to Congress formed a battalion neither military nor partisan but prayerful.[17]

Table 15.1 The Congressional Petitioning Campaign for Wartime Abolition by State

State	Petitions for "Abolition of slavery": Total, 36th–38th Congresses	36th Congress (1859–1861)	37th Congress (1861–1863)	38th Congress (1863–1865)	Petitions per 100,000 population, 36th–38th Congresses	Sumner Committee Petition Signatories (women)
NY	60	0	45	15	1.55	13,349 (6,857)
OH	47	3	26	18	2.01	8,636 (5,432)
PA	47	0	33	14	1.62	1,754 (687)
MA	36	4	26	6	2.92	3,438 (1,626)
IL	33	5	20	8	1.93	14,766 (7,778)
MI	22	1	13	8	2.94	5,892 (2,532)
VT	16	1	12	3	5.08	4,392 (2,200)
ME	12	0	6	6	1.91	7,089 (3,675)
NH	12	0	2	10	3.68	3,537 (1,589)
CT	10	0	7	3	2.18	4,138 (2,618)
WI	9	0	8	1	1.160	8,314 (3,867)
IN	7	0	3	4	0.52	2,945 (1,378)
KS	5	0	3	2	4.66	500 (300)
RI	3	0	2	1	1.72	314 (135)
NJ	2	0	2	0	0.30	1,110 (780)
MN	2	0	2	0	1.16	1,396 (713)
DE	1	0	0	1	0.89	n/a
Total (incl. unassigned)	324	14	231	128		

Source: CPD. Total includes petitions not identified from a single state. Only fifteen petitions are recorded for abolition of slavery in the District of Columbia, all before 1863. Sumner committee aggregations on clerk's written note in SEN 38A-H20, RG 46, NARA; Iowa had 6,638 signatories on the Sumner petition, 3,053 of them women.

Abolition petitions provided both a rationale for a new agenda and an opportunity for innovative legislative maneuver. Congress was clearly groaning under their weight and rate of arrival. Congressional clerks could not store them quickly enough, one noting that "these were so numerous that they have been removed to the Store Room." Their geography reflected the shift of Republican radicalism to the west, with Illinois, Michigan, Ohio, and Wisconsin contributing many petitions and thousands of women signers (see Table 15.1). The emancipation law petitions of the winter of 1864 mattered more than usual because passage of the amendment was proving difficult going into a general election year. Pro-amendment legislators stood to introduce emancipation law petitions to the floor no less than fifty-two times from December 1, 1863, through the end of April 1864. After delivering their petitions to Sumner, Stanton and Anthony redoubled their efforts, issuing a general call "To the Women of the Republic" in January 1864. The petition campaign allowed Senator Charles Sumner of Massachusetts to jump-start the legislative process though his control of the Committee on Slavery, which received the petitions. Sumner's preferred language of emancipation—declaring "all persons equal before the law, so that no person can hold another as a slave"—lost out to Senator Lyman Trumbull's preferred alternative based on the Northwest Ordinance of 1787. On April 8, 1864, under the watchful gaze of female petitioners who had packed the women's gallery, the Senate voted thirty-eight to six to adopt the Judiciary Committee's reported amendment. The House bill failed to achieve the required two-thirds majority. After Lincoln's reelection in November 1864, the president seized on the opportunity to press the lame-duck second session of the Thirty-Eighth House to pass the amendment, cajoling eight members to change their votes.[18]

The road from secession to military emancipation to abolition by constitutional amendment had taken many turns. No single factor alone explains this wartime triumph over American slavery. Yet electoral and partisan democracy provide some of the weakest explanations for the shift. Emancipation was buried deep in the agenda of the abolitionist faction in December 1860, while Lincoln, modal among his fellow Republicans, remained committed to Union first and colonization second. Secession provided the catalyst for a general petition campaign invoking the war power, and military combat combined with the general emancipation drive transformed the congressional and presidential agenda, even while combat raged. So, too, the Republicans' weak showing in the 1862 midterm elections and the tepid legislative approach the party took in 1864 blunted whatever force electoral calculations may have brought to bear. The Republicans' 1864 success certainly provided energy and legitimacy to Lincoln's final push, but by December 1864, he was working with what the Senate had already passed under the instigation of Sumner, Stanton, and Anthony and their Prayer of One Hundred Thousand and more. The very people who figured most centrally as political strategists in the story of constitutional abolition either exercised leadership in the petition campaigns themselves (like Sumner in Congress and, from outside, Stanton, Anthony and Douglass) or were, like Lincoln, subject to massive personal and collective appeals from Black men and women and their abolitionist allies. The advance of American freedom relied on the democratization of agendas and the cultural democracy enacted through signed prayers. And the organizational legacy of the movement would live on, as many of the postwar civil rights and reform organizations would be led by those who had canvassed and organized the memorial campaigns of the 1830s through the 1860s.[19]

FROM GRIEVANCE TO IMPEACHMENT: THE PROSECUTIONS OF ANDREW JOHNSON

The slaying of President Lincoln by John Wilkes Booth in April 1865 shook the continent. In Frederick Douglass's timeless words, the murder established Lincoln as "the first martyr President of the United States." Celebrated by southern whites, who saw an opportunity for newly reestablishing racial supremacy and even slavery itself, the event troubled and enraged freedmen and their abolitionist allies alike in the North. Andrew Johnson's ascension to the American presidency was as accidental as the rise of any preceding executive. The rupture of his administration with Lincoln's policies and temperament would be felt in Mexico and Canada as well as in the American South.[20]

Johnson's behavior intertwined with White supremacist violence in the South, so much so that Black women and men, along with White abolitionists, rightly connected the two patterns. Johnson started provisionally readmitting southern states to the Union, acting on a theory that they had never truly left it (he could not, however, unilaterally admit them to representation in Congress). Harnessing Article II authorities in new and sweeping ways, he pardoned thousands of former Confederates in the summer and fall of 1865 (at a rate of approximately one hundred per day), quickly installing many of these men at the helm of reconstructed southern state governments. Pardoned and paroled Confederate soldiers, in turn, led the wave of violence on Black bodies and souls across the South. A former Treasury agent related the story of a pardoned former Confederate soldier who murdered a Black child, shooting him fifty-seven times. White southern men terrorized Black families, declaring them no longer free because Lincoln had died, attacking households and their property in ways wanton and systematic. Because Johnson's actions were undertaken in the context of ongoing use of post-surrender war powers and because they undermined military occupation of the South, his presidency became especially odious to soldiers, veterans, and others well informed of the war effort.[21]

The Savannah freedmen's petition in the summer of 1865 conveyed precisely these kinds of stories, persuasively linking Johnson's pardoning behavior with the wave of White-on-Black violence coursing through the South. The newspaper clippings attached to the prayer relayed the "disgraceful scenes" of violence and required Confederate attestations that had unfolded at Norfolk municipal elections, the new daily reality of freedmen being "hunted down like dogs and dispatched without ceremony" wherever there were "no National troops," and the "Horrible Condition of the Freedmen in Alabama," as a *Boston Journal* headline put it. To these newspaper reports the Black petitioners added other atrocities, primarily from Alabama, where Johnson's "agents burn at will Negro houses and churches." Those agents were Johnson's responsibility under Article II, Section 4 of the Constitution. Beyond this, the unfolding list of brutalities was, in the petitioner's charge, a willful violation of Black people's Fourth Amendment rights. "They arrest and imprison at will men, women and children. . . . One hundred and thirty-three dead bodies were counted in the woods. Five bodies were seen floating in the water. Two white men were seen to pull a Negro down across a log, and cut his head off with an ax."[22]

Savannah was a logical font of Black organization and testimony. The city had become a center of Reconstruction Black community. Earlier that year, in January 1865, twenty of Savannah's Black men, many of them Baptist and Methodist ministers in the city's emerging independent churches, had met Union Army officers at General William Sherman's request. The meeting resulted in a frank exchange of views that would come to be known as the "Savannah Colloquy." The twenty congregants at Savannah espoused lucid conceptions of slavery and the freedom that they had won, and they reasoned strategically about how Black men free and enslaved could assist the Union effort. Some of the men who met with Sherman and Stanton appear on the Savannah impeachment petition's signatory list, including William Campbell, yet the autumn 1865 petition appears to have been led less by ministers than by veterans, including several who had fought in Massachusetts' famed Fifty-Fourth Regiment, which had served in Savannah in March 1865, staying in Charleston and elsewhere in South Carolina for much of the summer (at least five of the signatories noted they were from Charleston). The drawing up of the petition coincides with the mustering and retirement of the Fifty-Fourth Regiment in August and September, and the regiment's signatories—Asa Cotton, William H. Brown, Ishmael Palmer, Henry A. James, James C. Hewett, most from the Fifty-Fourth Regiment's K Company—would have been in good position to receive news of the atrocities and lawlessness throughout the South.[23]

The radical nature of the Savannah freedman's petition lay not just in its text but in its targeted venue. For a half century or more, free people of color had rarely petitioned the U.S. Congress, especially when compared to the steady flow of their memorials to American state legislatures. Yet in 1865, the freedmen of Savannah launched their radical claim directly at Johnson and directly to the body that alone could impeach him. Ironically, Senator Charles Sumner's response to the petition may have undermined the venue strategy of its Black signatories. Sumner's aide Moorfield Storey reported that Senator Sumner himself received such a petition and took it directly to the president.[24]

The assassination and Johnson's early policies induced a renewed push for voting rights for Black men, and the petitioners who led this effort most vocally were Black men themselves—Black men from Washington, D.C.; Bern, North Carolina; Richmond, Virginia; Vicksburg, Mississippi; and Natchez, Tennessee. Directing many of their petitions directly to President Johnson himself, the early post-assassination memorials approached the new President with caution and respect. A petition displaying almost fifteen hundred names from South Carolina, men who said they "glory in the name of American Citizens," prayed Johnson to grant them the "protective rights of the elective franchise, which privilege we regard as the only means by which our class . . . will have the power of protecting ourselves and our interests, against oppression and unjust legislation." Whenever possible, Johnson redirected most of these petitions to the War Department, a pattern he did not repeat with White petitioners. Save for his curt dialogue with a delegation of Black ministers in June 1865, Johnson was generally unwilling to grant Black souls a hearing. He was, however, ready to tour his White constituencies in the North and South and deliver demagogic addresses with impromptu remarks insulting Black Americans.[25]

The role of Black networks at the intersection of military and ministry resulted in other petitions in the fall of 1865, including the earnest appeals from Black farmers on South Carolina's Edisto Island. Approaching Freedmen's Bureau director Oliver O. Howard in October, in the midst of Whites' fresh appeal to reclaim the lands they had just lost in the rebellion, the Edisto petitioners announced their refusal to leave. "This is our home," they intoned, reminding Howard, "We have made these lands what they are." Echoing the logic of the Savannah freedmen's impeachment memorial, the Edisto petitioners employed the rhetoric and fact of "Loyalty"—Black petitioners systematically capitalized the word—to the Union cause, along with a Lockean logic of possession. Being "the only true and Loyal people that were found in possession of these Lands," they argued that their rights as "A free people and good citizens of these United States [are] To be considered before the rights of those who were Found in rebellion against this good and just Goverment." Johnson countermanded General Howard's Circular No. 13 that, had it been enforced, would have redistributed just short of a million acres of slave plantation land to free Blacks. In January 1866, he dismissed Brigadier General Rufus Saxton, the Union commander in charge of land distribution, putting an effective end to the project.[26]

Black petitioners were busy contesting Johnson's agenda elsewhere. The Freedmen's Bureau established a petitioning system for grievances that lay somewhere between a judicial system, administrative routine, and more traditional grievance petitioning. The bureau often set up offices in county courthouses or in the former properties of slaveholders whose assets had been confiscated by the Union. These places had conflicting meanings for Black petitioners. On the one hand, they were venues where freedwomen and freedmen could appear as citizen petitioners, with Black women having access to these spaces theoretically and symbolically equal to that of Black men. On the other hand, when freed Blacks brought their complaints to these places, they saw the sites of their recent bondage and they risked White aggression. In part for this reason, Freedmen's Bureau visits often took the form of kinship-based petitioning collectives.[27]

Black Americans also recommitted immense time and energy to the "Colored Convention" in 1865. National, regional, state, and local conventions of free Blacks had been meeting from 1830 onward. The purposes and settings varied widely, from the earliest gatherings of the National Convention of Free People of Colour in Philadelphia to a burst of activity in the 1840s around temperance and civil liberties. Yet emancipation, Union military victory, and Lincoln's assassination brought an unprecedented wave of conventions, first a widely attended National Convention of Colored Men at Syracuse in October 1864, then fully twenty different Black conventions in 1865 alone. The reasons and the proceedings varied with political geography. In places like Michigan, Black conventioneers were repairing internal rifts and founding a new association: the Equal Rights League of Michigan. In Mississippi at Vicksburg, Black conventioneers let out a warning about White efforts to nullify the Emancipation Proclamation in their amended state constitution as they sought reentry to the Union. North Carolina Black men assembled in Raleigh to salute recent developments and declare their refusal to cooperate with any colonization plan that would have them leave the state. Black men assembled at Xenia, Ohio—long a nexus of abolition and free Black organization—for launching several initiatives, including a resolution supporting a vigorous prosecution of the war effort, another calling on emancipated men and women to marry, and a petition for equal rights to the Ohio legislature.[28]

It was in South Carolina—with its ties to the Massachusetts Black regiments and to the Savannah petitioners—where the Black conventioneers engaged in the most prolific and radical action. Meeting in Charleston in November, the Colored People's Convention issued a stout portfolio of new assertive texts, including "The Declaration of Rights and Wrongs," an "Address to the People," and petitions to both the South Carolina legislature and the U.S. Congress. Delegates emphasized the importance of suffrage rights for men; in many such gatherings, women were invited to sit in a separate observing gallery but were not invited to take part in the official proceedings. Allen Coffin, editor of the *Leader,* invoked the human equality championed in the Declaration of Independence and also the Guarantee Clause of the U.S. Constitution, which secured a "republican form of government" for the American states. The meetings ended with the adoption of a prayer for the South Carolina legislature petition that asked for rights of voting and jury testimony in the state, and a simultaneous memorial to Congress praying for equal suffrage, jury service and testimony, and protected rights to bear arms, combined with a protest over emerging "black laws" in the southern states. The dual petitions evinced the considered strategy of venue that South Carolina's Black conventioneers had developed; southern observers White and Black knew that the conventioneers were taking their case directly and simultaneously to Washington and Charleston, as well as to wider Black and White publics.[29]

Johnson further enraged freedmen and their allies with his veto of the Freedmen's Bureau bill in February 1866 and his veto of the civil rights bill the next month. The Congress acted quickly to override these vetoes. Amid the struggle in Washington, White violence exploded in the South. White rioters massacred forty-six Black people in February 1866, while over one hundred African Americans perished in July riots in New Orleans. A perceptible swing toward Republicans in the autumn elections of 1866 (when the Republicans gained eight House seats while the Democrats lost a total of three, including three Pennsylvania districts surrendered to the Republicans) left the president facing his most radical legislative opposition yet.[30]

Impeachment was not at the top of the Fortieth Congress's agenda. Yet by the time the House had convened in March 1867, the previous Congress had, in its waning days, received and read thirty-eight petitions for Johnson's impeachment into the record. Impeachment petitions came disproportionately from the northwest—Illinois, Michigan, Ohio, and Wisconsin—as well as from the usual strongholds in Massachusetts, New York, and Pennsylvania. Two came from Georgia and one from Louisiana, two jurisdictions that still lay outside the Union but whose freedmen the Thirty-Ninth Congress recognized as petitioners; another came from the Black community at Paducah, Kentucky, and was read into the record in November. In the Senate, Charles Sumner read the "petition of colored citizens of the State of Georgia" first among impeachment petitions in his chamber's record that calendar year; it asked for the protection of their "lives and property" and, in a radicalism that echoed that of the 1865 Savannah freedmen's petition, called for payment of the war debt "from the proceeds of confiscated rebel property." Eight times in January and February 1867 did Sumner introduce Black petitions to the Senate floor, not only from Massachusetts but also from Virginia and North Carolina. The only petitions read into the record against impeachment in the late Thirty-Ninth Congress came from New York, marked by two from the city and its "business men."[31]

In a sign of the interplay between congressional strategy and mass petitioning, virtually every leader of the impeachment effort had received and introduced petitions calling for Johnson's trial and removal. James Mitchell Ashley's impassioned, thunderous speech on the House floor in January 1867—in which he proclaimed that "I do impeach Andrew Johnson, Vice President and sitting President of the United States, of high crimes and misdemeanors"—followed petitions for impeachment introduced in the preceding days, and Ashley himself soon delivered impeachment petitions from Georgia and Indiana. Thaddeus Stevens teamed with John Bingham to introduce the impeachment resolutions in the House on February 21, 1868, and it was Stevens who had both invited and introduced petitions against the Crittenden Compromise, for emancipation, for an abolition amendment, and for Johnson's impeachment. James F. Wilson of Iowa chaired the House Judiciary Committee that considered Ashley's original resolution and the Stevens-Bingham articles, and Wilson's state provided a disproportionate share of pro-impeachment memorials, including the first such memorial introduced to the House floor in 1867. The February 1868 impeachment articles were focused on Johnson's dismissal of Edwin Stanton as Secretary of War and his unauthorized appointment of Lorenzo Thomas in Stanton's place, but the spirited call for Johnson's "punishment" had been much wider, detailing the manifold "lawlessness" and omnipresent "corruption" of his administration that had been laid out so eloquently by Savannah's freedmen and by Ashley. The House presented the articles of impeachment to the Senate on March 4, 1868. As much as anything, the candidacy of Ulysses Grant for the presidency stopped the momentum of conviction in the Senate. Removal of Johnson would have placed Wade in the presidency, thereby blunting Grant's momentum toward the Republican nomination. Johnson's narrow escape from Senate conviction ensured a different form of demise.[32]

SOJOURNER TRUTH'S PETITION

Emancipation, constitutional abolition, and military victory created new realities and possibilities. The freedmen of Savannah could believe that Johnson was impeachable, not only in the sense that sound legal grounds existed for a House indictment but also because national political institutions offered as never before a hearing for Black claimants. Those claimants could express not merely their humility but their fury and robust claims of vast lawlessness by the president. Impeachment would ensue but conviction would not. It was only in 1868 that Republican voters, and not Senators, removed Andrew Johnson from office. Ulysses Grant's victory in the

1868 general election meant many things, but by ending Johnson's presidency, it quickened faith in the possibility of Reconstruction and a range of political and legal reforms. Alas, that same year fiscal pressures and political opposition began to converge on Reconstruction, Freedmen's Bureau camps and programs began closing, and thousands of freed people faced growing difficulty finding work and shelter.[33]

It was this space of new political aspirations and free Black anxiety that Sojourner Truth entered boldly in 1869 and 1870. Truth is best known as the former slave turned itinerant preacher who challenged American political culture and abolitionists alike over a lecturing campaign that spanned three decades. But the Washington experience of the 1860s and the hardship she both witnessed and presaged there led her to fashion an alternative vision for Black Americans. Her fierce Protestant spirituality led her to criticize what she saw as fellow freed Blacks' reliance on government assistance. (This stance was not a popular one among freed people and led to her split with many Black abolitionists, including, in part, Frederick Douglass.) Drawing on experiences with Reconstruction and the Homestead Act, she conceived of a plan to relocate Black refugees to the West (preferably Kansas), where they could construct a farming-based economy and citizenship. "The freed colored people in and about Washington," she wrote, "dependent upon government for support, would be greatly benefited and might become useful citizens by being placed in a position to support themselves." Her memorial prayed the creation of "a portion of the public land in the West," with "buildings thereon for the aged and infirm." She then traveled to New England, then back through New Jersey and Philadelphia, then through Syracuse and Rochester, and then to Ohio, Michigan, Indiana, Illinois, Wisconsin, Iowa, Missouri, and Kansas. Truth collected names on these petitions until at least 1874, when she left her home in Battle Creek, Michigan, and traveled to Washington to present them to Congress.[34]

Sojourner Truth's vision expressed a Jeffersonian logic in more ways than one. It wedded citizenship to land ownership, just as Jefferson had done throughout his political and intellectual career, most notably in query nineteen in *Notes on the State of Virginia*, and as Reconstruction policy had aspired to do in the South. Like Jefferson, and like most Americans in Washington in the late 1860s, Truth's plan saw vast Indigenous spaces west of the Mississippi as open and ready for occupation and development. The primary difference came in Truth's decision to use a petitioning campaign and not a published essay or pamphlet to develop and popularize her idea.

(Her illiteracy forms an insufficient explanation for this decision, as it did not prevent her from dictating and committing her memoirs to print later on, and she had many collaborators and observers who published her speeches.) In her justification for a petitioning endeavor, Truth embraced cultural and procedural democracy, expressing hope that agendas closed in Washington would be opened up by an appeal to the American populace. She recognized with disappointment that women's rights were limited in the electoral arena but proclaimed that she could always "stand on praying ground" and petition. Disappointed with the pace of change in postwar Washington, she voiced her intention to take the question of the land distribution "before the people."[35]

Truth's connection to a democratic petitioning culture had been a long time in the making. Sojourner Truth was, until June 1, 1843, Isabella Baumfree, and within the year after changing her name upon instruction from the Holy Spirit, she began signing civil rights petitions from Northampton, Massachusetts, including a winter 1844 petition calling for the abolition of capital punishment. In 1855, she joined more than seventy other women, including many women of color, in Florence, Massachusetts, calling for the removal of judge Edward Greeley Loring over his odious decision in a Fugitive Slave Act case. She had participated in the abolitionist campaigns of the 1840s and 1850s and then in the woman suffrage petitioning campaigns in the 1860s. In her 1870s campaign for land grants, she approached canvassing as inseparable from lecturing and from the work of radical change. Even as she split with Frederick Douglass over questions of policy and strategy, she formed new interracial alliances across the northern states, adding allies and raising funds for her quest.[36]

* * *

Reflecting on his deep study in *Black Reconstruction* (1935), W. E. B. DuBois remarked that of the Civil War and its immediate aftermath, "the meetings and petitions of Southern Negroes were significant and cannot be discounted."[37] The radicalism of language, proposal, and campaign that DuBois saw in the Black conventions and petitions, and that Americans witnessed in freedmen's impeachment petitions and in Sojourner Truth's land campaign, gestured to a newly crystallized reality—one several decades in the making. Those who did not yet have suffrage rights or who had just won them, those who dared not ask before, felt an opening from 1865 to 1870.

Only in a narrow reading of politics as the immediate procurement of material results would a philosophical democrat regard the Savannah freedmen's and Sojourner Truth's memorials as failures. Black Americans and their abolitionist and radical allies saw new openings in the national agenda, and their efforts had brought about the first impeachment of a president in American history. Their memorials of grievance, and Congress's response to these appeals, framed the debates in Congress and set forth a range of issues far more expansive than that advanced in the narrow articles of impeachment. While some of the impeachment speeches and petitions resulted from coordination between constituent and legislator, the Savannah freedmen's impeachment petition seems to have arrived, like many Black impeachment petitions, unalloyed and uninduced.

The petition campaigns that blunted the Crittenden Compromise, that pressed Lincoln and the Congress on emancipation and a constitutional amendment for abolition, and that engendered the prosecution of a U.S. president fashioned the war and Reconstruction agenda in ways that neither wartime elections nor Republican party machinations alone can account for. It was in light of petitioners' real contribution to the agenda of abolition that Black men in Savannah and an itinerant Black woman in Massachusetts could believe that signed memorials from the electorally weakest of American citizens could refashion the set of questions on which a nation's highest body would deliberate and later vote. If newly freed men and women of color, still electorally negligible, could plausibly believe that their grievances and proposals would be heard by the highest organs of the land, then the United States had briefly achieved a kind of equality that eluded notions of contractual government. It was in that space of aspiration and strategy—in the confidence that the agenda of government was open to anyone, a belief that the signatures of hundreds and thousands could advance an appeal, a faith that memorial campaigns could generate fledgling organizations dedicated later to other, still noble purposes—that the petitioner's democracy came into view.

Afterword

Agendas, Organization, and the Democracy of Petitions

> New Claims will arise. Women will demand a Vote. Lads from 12 to 21 will think their Rights not enough attended to, and every Man, who has not a farthing, will demand an Equal Voice with any other in all Acts of State. It tends to confound and destroy all distinctions, and prostrate all Ranks, to one common Levell.
>
> —**John Adams to James Sullivan, May 26, 1776**

Democracy and its arrival are hard things to define, but in part their meaning emerges in answering the question of what so frightened John Adams in 1776. Americans have long remembered Adams as the brilliant architect of republican institutions and the country's second president. Far less frequently do they recall his career as an anxious and remarkably shrewd opponent of democracy. He shuddered at the rush of incipient "New Claims": from women, from adolescents and teenagers, from those without enough property. As he wrote in the 1770s, other "New Claims" would come from Black petitioners who, in 1773 and 1774 and again in January 1777, led by Prince Hall, appealed to Massachusetts officials for freedom and equality. Adams would soon oppose an emancipation bill in his home state, hoping the matter would "sleep for a time." The "New Claims" that Adams feared primarily took the form of petitions. What scared Adams most about democracy was the specter of "Equal Voice" in "all acts of state." In Adams's vision of a nondemocratic republic, administrators, executives, judges, and many legislators would be insulated from the pressing "New Claims" of the whole people.[1]

The people from whom "New Claims" arose must be understood both as petitioners and as authors of democracy. A focus on petitions in North American democratization centers the labor of people of color and the Indigenous: the dispossessed, the enslaved, the dominated. It centers the work of women across a hemisphere—Indigenous women at Kahnawá:ke, Buffalo Creek and Cattaraugus, Red Clay, Michigan, and Taos; Black women ranging from Mary Prince of Bermuda and Mary Venus of Trinidad to Maria Stewart of Boston and Sojourner Truth; Québécoise widows and Mexican *señoras católicas* along with Angelina Grimké and Protestant women in the United States. Democratization by petition also points to the authorship of those who wrote in languages other than English, whether the chiefs at Odanak and Uashat and Red Clay, the women demanding a voice in the public sphere of mid-century Mexico, or the Canadiens whose petitioning intensity rivaled that of any other population on the continent.

The democracy of petitions that emerged in the century following John Adams's letter to Sullivan never created a fully "Equal Voice" in American affairs. Petition democracy was always partial, and it arose in a profoundly brutal and unequal world, a world that would remain so for decades to come. The democracy of petitions deserves no Panglossian shine, no romantic retelling of accumulated triumphs. Black and Native women and men petitioned from their pain, anguish, and unfreedom; women from their deprivation and subjugation; farmers, producers, and French Canadians from their entrenched disadvantages. Aristocratic and settler interests had used petitions to monopolize, enslave, and dispossess, and racists and anti-immigrant leaders continued using them to great effect.

Still, vital advances in institutional democracy—the basic rules and conventions that support democracy, which include the absence of aristocracy, feudalism, and slavery—came from popular petitioning. Canadians and Americans harnessed a more democratized supplication process to end the last vestiges of feudal and manorial lands in their nations. Caribbean men of color gained rights to vote and to jury service, while American White men divorced the right to vote from property in part through petitioning. American opponents of Jackson and Canadian opponents of the Family Compact used petitions to create the rudiments of opposition parties. French Canadians preserved parliamentary authority in their province while fending off attempts at cultural erasure. Important progress in the abolition of slavery came from Caribbean and American petitions, as did crucial moments of Indigenous continuance. If we measure democratization by "success" and equality in law, surely the nineteenth century stands out for its limitations. But petitions reshaped the agenda of politics (procedural democracy), the terrain of politics (organizational democracy), and the assumptions of politics (cultural democracy).

A democracy of agendas took root in North America through petitions in ways that elections and party competition could not alone push forward. Women used mass petitions to transform the antislavery campaign, to assemble and advance labor organization, to build the first broad-based American antiwar movement, to normalize their appearance before legislative committees and chambers, to advance and make public their role in church governance, and to put the possibility of partial or full voting rights in the national imagination. Petitioners established and advanced congressional and presidential agendas for emancipation and for constitutional abolition of slavery.

The petition-based transformation of agendas was itself significant. Representation is not merely a matter of what is struck into law but a matter of what and who is at the "table" of discourse, where that discourse is understood to occur between those in office and those affected by their decisions. Agendas, too, are far more than the mere static collections of the choices available to ultimate decision-makers. Agendas include the matters debated in both government organizations and localities. Other non-electoral dimensions of democracy, such as assemblies and crowd action, figured critically in nineteenth-century political change, but these endeavors changed government agendas less regularly than petitions did.[2]

Beyond agendas, waves of popular petitioning built new, more energetic, and more egalitarian organizations. "New Claims" came not just individually but collectively in the marriage of prayer and testimony, supplication and signature. From local assemblies of Canadian Patriotes and Mexican Velas Perpetuas to meetings and conventions of men of color in Caribbean islands and American cities, from antislavery organizations whose emergence followed more than anticipated the rhythms of petitioning to new political formations in Canada and the United States, and from worker associations combating debt-based imprisonment and auction monopolies to new Indigenous governments and alliances, these achievements of civil society depended heavily on the recruitment technology of the petition and its ever expanding signatory lists. The petitioning authors of North American democracy did their work not merely as writers of prayers and signatures but as orchestrators of a common voice.

Organizational democracy entails not just the founding of individual groups but the building of alliances—Black and White abolitionists, Native Americans and White religious allies, Patriotes and rural *habitants*, farmers and artisans uniting under a producer label. The democratizing petition rendered the antislavery movement more egalitarian, courting the energy of Black Americans, children, and women and placing their thousands of names alongside those of electorally endowed White men. Those who defended slavery most absolutely, like Calhoun and the Fire-Eaters, derided and obstructed popular petitioning, while those who took the mildest approaches to antislavery, like colonization, made little use of it. Little about the logic of electoral democracy gave incentives for those with votes to strike up alliances with those who lacked them. Everything about petition democracy pointed in the direction of these alliances.

Even electoral democracy depended heavily on petition democracy. In the slew of suffrage extensions in the early United States, the awakening of woman suffrage energies, and the development of opposition parties in the United States and Canada, petitioning campaigns advanced electoral institutions. And the narratives of this study—the Lowell Female Labor Reform Association, the anticolonial networks emergent in Montréal and Québec, the mobilizations of tenant farmers in New York and the Saint Lawrence valley, or the pressure applied to the Thirty-Seventh, Thirty-Eighth, and Thirty-Ninth Congresses—make clear that petitioning campaigns often carried their influence through their implicit and explicit electoral pressure. In a world before systematized public opinion polls emerged, anxious politicians and party elites saw in petitions a distinctive indicator of emerging public sentiment. Petition democracy worked with and alongside the democracy of elections, and indeed challenged that democracy.

The emergence of cultural democracy—the ideals of equality, the practice of citizenship, the assertiveness of voices neither endowed with votes nor courted by parties—both transformed petitioning and relied on petitioning for its diffusion. When Indigenous women could approach tribal councils and national congresses with their grievances, when African American women could collectively approach state legislatures on matters of marriage law, when Mexican women could enter publicly into debates on constitutional reform, or when individuals like Sojourner Truth or the women of Jefferson County could place radical ideas before the highest chambers of the land, the audacious imagination prerequisite to democratic culture had taken root.

No founder or design architect created the democracy of petitions. Instead, petition democracy flowed from a collective but little coordinated refashioning of an ancient institution into a transformative new technology that organized peoples, spread the language and assumptions of equality, and channeled visions and aspirations in ways that partisan elections could not alone accomplish. The culture of democracy was wider than petition democracy alone, and it transformed petitioning. The transformation of petitioning was a necessary step in petitioning's contributions to democratization. The older world of more individualized supplication and a culture of deference would not have sufficed. In democratized petitioning, the orderly and disorderly were more often complements than substitutes. In the face of turbulence, North Americans embraced, and then remade, what they knew. Buffeted by international war, explosive industry and expanding settlement, revolution and violence, they refashioned the petition as an instrument more egalitarian than ever before, their democratic aspirations glowing through their endeavors.

A skeptic might fairly pose counterfactuals about the mechanics of causation. Did petitioning really change agendas, laws, and decisions, or was the ultimate effect of these petitions to enact just what the legislators, governors, and administrators who received them would already have done at the outset, and in their absence? Quantitative and narrative evidence points to the granular timing of changes in institutions, agendas, and organizations that followed petitioning campaigns. Organizational change often followed the rhythms and geography of petitioning, including the burst of petitioning activity that accompanied the beginning of legislative sessions. When legal changes favored those who could not vote—such as personal liberty laws in the Caribbean and the northeastern United States, or the many mobilizations of Native Americans for their continuance—the resulting changes remain difficult to explain by reference to electoral or partisan politics, at least without including petitioning as central within those politics. In other cases, petition campaigns predicted the form and timing of change where electoral politics could not. In New York and French Canada, the demise of feudal tenure had eluded partisans and legal minds until mass petition campaigns changed the stakes and agendas of the contest. Electoral democracy privileges not just citizens but what Madison called the republican principle, namely majoritarian rule. Petition democracy offered another model of aggregation, where numerical minorities could still make a case for quantitative relevance. Causal claims are always difficult to make in the messy world of political history. Yet if petitioning energies did not mechanistically cause the transformations of North American democratization, they always served as necessary conditions and usually as remarkably capable predictors of the transformation.

The democracy of petitions would both endure and fade. The U.S. Civil War ushered in novel forms of corporate lobbying, perfected nowhere more than in the new transcontinental railroads, and the demise of Reconstruction left the hegemonic Republican Party in a tight lock with industrial interests. Industrial corporations began to establish lobbies in national and state capitals, as more and more claims were diverted to tort and administrative systems. The alliance of farmers, workers, and women that would contest that industrial hegemony in Populist and Progressive movements would use petitions among other repertoires of action to do so, but petitioning became one among many tools in national politics, less procedurally and culturally central than before. Precisely as the Populist and Progressive movements tethered the power of the petition to the power of the vote, they left aside Indigenous people and people of color. The rise of cultural and institutional apartheid in the Jim Crow South came (and did not merely coincide) with a steep drop in popular petitioning, and democracy in all its dimensions suffered. Canadian politics would enter a more conservative and expansionary age, though campaigns for general health insurance in the early twentieth century would again rely heavily on petitioning. War and autocracy would dash republican hopes in Mexico for a half century, while women's voice (often amplified in petitions) in ecclesiastical matters would endure, and popular petitions would lubricate much of the revolutionary energy of the early twentieth century. After the 1860s, American and Canadian governments pursued a more aggressive campaign to erase Indigenous peoples—their languages, spaces, and cultures. Natives continued to use petitions and new legal tools to contest this apparatus, yet they found themselves facing far more comprehensive and rationalized machineries. The petition-fueled continuance of Native communities in the early nineteenth century established important bulwarks in Canada and the United States, many of which endure to this day.

The elaboration of tort and claims systems redirected millions of grievances to more individual, local settings, while the rise of initiative-and-referendum institutions gave rise to the plebiscitary petition, one that did not seek a response but instead mechanically placed a candidate or proposition on a ballot. The emergence of regular and cheaper communications to governments—letters, telegrams, and electronic forms of mail and petitioning—made grievance cheaper to express, but none of these vessels requires or regularly meets with an official response. The norm of petition-and-response has migrated from the realm of elective office, of legislative and executive organs, to the venue of individualized courts and anonymous administrators.

No anachronistic resurrection of the petitioning culture of nineteenth-century North America is possible or, imagined simplistically, desirable. Universal voting rights; more efficient party machinery; the development of administrative organs and judicial systems to handle claims and complaints; the rise of interest groups, policy institutes, and vast machineries of campaign finance—these and other transformations are partially or wholly irreversible. Only a fool would surrender the right to vote for the right to petition. Somewhat less a fool would regard the petition and the ballot as substitutes as opposed to the complements that they have remained for centuries. The wisest of citizens have long insisted that democracy remains incomplete unless peoples are regularly, collectively, publicly, and responsively heard.

Archives and Manuscript Collections Consulted

ABC—Archives of British Columbia, Victoria, British Columbia
- Commissioner's Correspondence (GR 0868)
- Crease family fonds
- Executive Council Records (GR 0444)
- Great Britain, Colonial Office; Correspondence with the Hudson's Bay Company
- Gertrude Ann Rhodes fonds

ACAM—Archives de la Chancellerie de l'Archidiocèse de Montréal
- Registres de lettres de Mgr Bourget
- Registres de lettres de Mgr Lartigue
- Registres de cahiers divers (RCD) 95—H. Moreau, prêtre: Cahier de notes et de correspondance

ACASC—Amherst College Archives and Special Collections, Amherst, Massachusetts
- Emma Willard Family Papers

AGN—Archivo General de la Nación, Mexico City
- Ayuntamientos
- Californias
- Provincias Internas
- Tierras

AOManitoba—Archives of Manitoba, Winnipeg, Manitoba
- E. E. Rich fonds
- Fort Victoria and Western Department miscellaneous records
- Ile Jerémie miscellaneous records
- Red River District miscellaneous records

Tadoussac miscellaneous records
Three Rivers miscellaneous records
APS—American Philosophical Society, Philadelphia, Pennsylvania
Ely Samuel Parker Papers (digital materials)
BANC—Bancroft Library, University of California, Berkeley
California legislature miscellany, 1850–1870
Documentos para la Historia de California
Documents from the Spanish and Mexican periods in California, 1780–1849
John McDougal correspondence, 1851–1860
Official documents relating to early San Francisco
Peter H. Burnett Papers
San Francisco Committee of Vigilance Collection
San Francisco de Asis Mission, San Francisco, petition
BAnQ-Montréal—Bibliothèque and Archives nationales du Québec—Archives de Vieux-Montréal, Montréal, Québec
Fonds Jobin
Fonds Comité de Pétition de 1828
BAnQ-Quebec—Bibliothèque and Archives nationales du Québec—Archives de Québec, Québec City, Québec
Archives du Ministère de Terres et de Forêts (E21)
Benson-UT—Nettie Lee Benson Latin American Collection, University of Texas, Austin
Catholic Church in Mexico Collection
Documentos Relativas a la Reforma y a la Intervención Francesa en México
Carlos García y Arriaga Papers
Jesús González y Ortega Collection
Vicente Guerrero Collection
José María Luis Mora Papers
Mariano Riva Palacio Collection
BHC-DPL—Burton Historical Collection, Detroit Public Library
Lewis Cass Papers
Millard Fillmore Papers
Gen. William Hull Papers and Manuscripts
Mary R. Lacey Papers
Sidney Trowbridge Miller Papers
Gabriel Richard Papers
Solomon Sibley Papers
Charles C. Trowbridge Papers
William Woodbridge Papers
BHM—Buffalo Historical Museum, Buffalo, New York
Erastus Granger Papers

Peter B. Porter Papers
Maris B. Pierce Papers
Seneca Indian Collection
Transactions between the Ogden Land Company and the Seneca Indians, 1826–1871 (Mss. A2016–35)

BPL—Boston Public Library, Boston, Massachusetts
Antislavery Collection
Chapman-Weston Papers

CHM—Chicago Historical Museum, Chicago, Illinois
Illinois and Michigan Canal Records
Zebina Eastman Papers

CSA—California State Archives, Sacramento, California
Military Department. Adjutant General. Indian War Papers, 1850–1880 (F3753)
Office of the Governor, Petitions to the Governor, 1850–1890

CSL—California State Library, Sacramento, California
George McKinstry Papers

DBC—Dolph Briscoe Center for American History, University of Texas
Archivo General de la Nación (México), Provincias Internas, Transcripts
Béxar Archives (microfilm and online)
James F. Perry Records, Records of Antebellum Southern Plantations (microfilm)

DMR-Duke—David M. Rubenstein Rare Book & Manuscript Library, Perkins Library

Duke University, Durham, North Carolina
Confederate States of America Collection, 1850–1867 and miscellaneous
Confederate States of America Congressional Records
Marie W. Horton Letter, 1847 February 21
Andrew Johnson Papers
James Knox Polk Papers
Richard Singleton Papers

FACHL—Fray Angélico Chávez History Library, Palace of the Governors, Santa Fe, New Mexico
Bureau of Indian Affairs Collection
Manuel Montoya Collection

GLC—Gilder Lehrman Collection [digital], NYHS

GSA—Georgia State Archives, Atlanta, Georgia
Governor's Subject Files—Joseph Emerson Brown
Governor's Subject Files—Wilson Lumpkin

HL-UGA—Hargrett Rare Book and Manuscript Library, University of Georgia, Athens, Georgia

E. Moulton Coulter Collection
Telamon Cuyler Collection (MS 1170)
Gazaway Bugg Lamar Papers
Wilson Lumpkin reminiscences
William Holland Thomas Papers
C. Mildred Thompson Papers (MS 606)
James Wilson Yazoo land documents

HSP—Historical Society of Pennsylvania, Philadelphia, Pennsylvania
James Buchanan Papers
Edward Carey Gardiner Collection
Miscellaneous Papers of the Northern, Interior, and Western Counties of Pennsylvania
North American Land Company Records
Philadelphia City Council petitions to the Select and Common Councils, 1783–1868
George Wolf Papers

IHS—Indiana Historical Society, Indianapolis, Indiana
Alphonso Albert Cole Papers (M 586)
William Henry Harrison Papers (M 364)
Indiana lands and Civil War documents, 1833–1893
John Nilson Papers

ISA—Illinois State Archives, Springfield, Illinois
Abraham Lincoln Papers

LAC—Library and Archives Canada, Ottawa, Ontario
Record Group 10—Indian Affairs
Fonds Dalhousie
Fonds Neilson
Fonds Papineau

LOC—Library of Congress, presidential and congressional papers
Susan B. Anthony Papers
Nathaniel P. Banks Papers
Salmon P. Chase Papers
Joshua R. Giddings and George Washington Julian Papers
Andrew Jackson Papers
Joshua Leavitt Family Papers
Amasa J. Parker Papers
Elizabeth Cady Stanton Papers
Charles Sumner Correspondence
Martin Van Buren Papers

LOV—Library of Virginia, Richmond, Virginia
Board of Public Works, Turnpike Companies (#30030)

John Goode, Jr. Papers, 1854–1878 (#23830k)
Francis Walker Gilmer Letters, 1818–1827 (#18764)
Madison County Free Negro and Slave Records, 1859 (#23219)
Roanoke County Free Negro Register, 1838–1864 (#23219)
Smyth County Free Negro and Slave Records, 1859–1861 (#23219)
Edgar Snowden Papers (#27156)
Executive Papers of Governor Littleton W. Tazewell, 1834–1836 (#42998)
Virginia Auditor of Public Accounts, Free Black Records, 1833–1863 (APA 757)
Virginia General Assembly (RG 78), House of Delegates, Speaker, Executive Communications (#36912)
Virginia Legislative Petitions, 1776–1865 [online]
Warren County Free Negro and Slave Records, 1836–1861

LTP-BYU—L. Tom Perry Special Collections, Harold B. Lee Library, Brigham Young University, Provo, Utah
Hyrum Smith Papers
Daniel Spencer Papers
Fisher Family correspondence

MAC—Massachusetts Archives of the Commonwealth, Boston, Massachusetts
Council legislative records, 1689–1837 (GC3-1701x)
Files of Inactive Pardons and Pardons Not Granted (GC3-771)
House unpassed legislation, 1775–1996 (SC1-230)
Massachusetts Archives Collection, 1629–1799 (SC1-45x)
Passed acts, 1775–1997 (SC1-229)
Senate unpassed legislation, 1780–1996 (SC1-231)

McCord—McCord Museum of Canadian History, Montréal, Québec
Badgley Family Papers
George Etienne Cartier Papers

McGill—McGill University Rare Books and Special Collections, Montréal, Québec
Thomas Storrow Brown Papers
Special Collection: Seminary of Saint-Sulpice
Special Collection: Records of the Executive Council, Legislative Council and Governor

MCHS—Monterey County Historical Society, Salinas, California
Mexican Archives of the County of Monterey
Thomas Larkin Journal
Archives of the American Period, Monterey County

MERN—Ministère de l'Énergie et des Ressources Naturelles, Québec City, Québec
Archives des Arpentages, Réserves indiennes (Correspondance)

MHS—Massachusetts Historical Society, Boston, Massachusetts
 Adams Family Papers
 Leverett Saltonstall Family Correspondence
 Lewis Cass—Leverett Saltonstall Correspondence
MLUU—Marriott Library, University of Utah, Salt Lake City, Utah
 Heber C. Kimball Papers
 H. Michael Marquardt Collection
 Madeleine R. McQuown Papers
 Mormon Petition Records
MSA—Missouri State Archives, Jefferson City, Missouri
 Records of the Second Board of Land Commissioners [digital]
NARA—National Archives and Records Administration, Washington, D.C.
 Records of the U.S. House of Representatives (RG 233)
 Records of the U.S. Senate (RG 46)
 Records of the War Department (RG 107)
 Records of the Bureau of Indian Affairs (RG 75)
NAUK—National Archives of the United Kingdom
 Commissioners of Legal Enquiry in the West Indies, 1822–1828 [CO 318/76]
 Commissioners of Legal Enquiry in the West Indies, 1825, volume 2 [CO 318/58]
 Despatches from Governor William Lumley [CO 37/81]
 Petitions of grievances; reports of committee [CO 42/218]
 Records of the Office of Registry of Colonial Slaves and Slave Compensation Commission
Newberry—Newberry Library, Chicago, Illinois
 Edward E. Ayer Manuscript Collection
 John Norton Papers
 Oneida Indian Documents, 1787–1833
 Stockbridge and Munsee Indians Documents
NMSRCA—New Mexico State Records Center and Archives, Santa Fe, New Mexico
 Arthur Bibo Collection of Acoma and Laguna Pueblo Documents
 Bergere Family Papers
 Blazer's Mill Records
 Donaciano Vigil Collection
 Felipe Chaves Family Papers
 Manuel Alvarez Papers
 Maria G. Duran Collection
 Mexican Archives of New Mexico (MANM)
 New Mexico acequias and water rights collection

Ortiz Family Papers
Spanish Archives of New Mexico I (SANM I)
Spanish Archives of New Mexico II (SANM II)
Ted Otero Collection of Historical Documents
Territorial Archives of New Mexico, 1846–1912

NYHS—New York Historical Society, New York, New York
Stephen Allen Papers
Bankruptcy bill letters, 1840–1842
John W. Cady letters to Richard Dodge, 1822–1825
DeWitt Clinton Papers
Edward Curtis letters
Robert Fulton Papers
Addison Gardiner Letters
Rufus King Papers
Benjamin Watkins Leigh Papers, 1835–1848
Robert R. Livingston Papers
Herman Melville Letters
Samuel J. May Collection
Thurlow Weed Papers

NYPL—New York Public Library, New York, New York
Bancker family papers
Perry G. Childs Papers
DeWitt Clinton Papers
Fairchild Collection
New York Custom House Records
Philip Schuyler Papers
Society of Tammany, or Columbian Order Records

NYSL—New York State Library, Albany, New York
New York County, Wills and Probate Records
Petitions and Appeals to the Canal Board, 1828–1926, Comptroller's Office Records, Series A1140

OCHS—Oneida County Historical Society, Utica, New York.
Oneida County Historical Pamphlet Collection

Rauner-Dartmouth—Rauner Special Collections Library, Dartmouth College, Hanover, New Hampshire
1854 Petition on Kansas-Nebraska to John C. Rives
Amos Kendall Collection
Letters of Abraham Lincoln
Papers of John Otis
Papers of Samuel Kirkland
Maris Bryant Pierce Book of Memorandum, 1840

Schlesinger—Arthur and Elizabeth Schlesinger Library on the History of Women in America, Radcliffe Institute for Advanced Study, Harvard University, Cambridge, Massachusetts
- Susan B. Anthony Papers
- Beecher-Stowe Family Papers
- Blackwell Family Papers

SHSMO—State Historical Society of Missouri, Columbia, Missouri
- Missouri Collection [digital]

Stewart—Musée Stewart, Montréal, Québec, Canada
- Pétition des comtés des districts de Montréal et des Trois Rivières (numéro d'inventaire 1957.6)

SUNY-Oswego, Oswego, New York
- Erastus Granger Papers [Erastus Granger Digital Library Collection]

TLSA—Tennessee Library and State Archives, Nashville, Tennessee
- Acts of the General Assembly
- General Assembly Original Bills, Petitions, Report, 1790-
- Legislative Petitions Collection
- John Ross Collection
- Tennessee Constitutional Convention Records, 1834–1977

UH—University of Houston, Archives and Special Collections, Houston, Texas
- Mexico Documents Collection, 1570–1913 (digitized)

UNM—University of New Mexico, University Libraries, Center for Southwest Research, Albuquerque, New Mexico
- D'Armand Collection of Spanish Language Documents, 1792–1871
- Indian Affairs Collection, 1684–1903
- New Mexico Documents Collection, 1758–1876
- Sandoval County, New Mexico, Land Documents, 1790–1872

UWGB—University of Wisconsin, Green Bay, Archives and Area Research Center
- Eleazar Williams Papers

Vassar—Vassar College Digital Library, Poughkeepsie, New York
- Jasper Parrish Papers

WCL—William Clements Library, University of Michigan, Ann Arbor, Michigan
- Lewis Cass Papers
- Daniel Coxe Collection
- Great Britain Indian Department Collection, 1753–1795
- Native American History Collection
- Thomas Flournoy Papers

WHC-OU—Western History Collection, Oklahoma University Libraries, Norman, Oklahoma

Cherokee Nation Collection
Paul Niebell Collection

WHS—Wisconsin Historical Society, Madison, Wisconsin
Thomas Dean Papers
Draper Manuscripts: Daniel Boone Papers
Draper Manuscripts: Thomas Spottswood Hinde Papers
Eleazar Williams Papers
Nathaniel P. Tallmadge Papers
Henry Hastings Sibley Papers
Florantha Thompson Sproat letters, 1838–1845
Wisconsin Legislature, Assembly—Standing and Special Committee Reports (Series 171)
Wisconsin Legislature, Senate—Standing and Special Committee Reports (Series 170)
Wisconsin Legislature—Miscellaneous Correspondence, 1836–1941

Abbreviations

AC	*Annals of Congress*
APMD	*Antislavery Petitions of Massachusetts Dataverse*
ASP	*American State Papers*
CPD	Congressional Petitions Database, Harvard University and University of Pennsylvania
DCB	*Dictionary of Canadian Biography*
JAPC	*Journal of the Assembly of the Province of Canada*
JCABC	*Journal de la Chambre d'Assemblée du Bas-Canada*
JHDV	*Journal of the House of Delegates of Virginia*
JHRUS	*Journal of the House of Representatives of the United States*
JSUS	*Journal of the Senate of the United States*
NWR	*Niles' Weekly Register*
PAR	Petition Analysis Record, in Race and Slavery Petitions Project, University of North Carolina–Greensboro, ed. Loren Schweninger
TP	*Territorial Papers*

Notes

1. SIGNATURE MOMENTS, 1846–1849

1. Pétition No. 213 (marked "Requête, Sept-Îles"), Archives des arpentages, Réserves indiennes (Correspondance), Filière 23, MERN-Québec; see also *Copie authentique d'une requête que les Indiens de Tadoussac et des Iles de Jérémie, de la rivière Godebou et de Sept Iles doivent présenter aux trois branches de la législature de la province du Canada dans le cour de l'année 1847,* ACAM. The Innu transcription reported here is from an older dialect of the language and follows the MERN-Québec document. My English translation follows the original version and is based on consultations with Institut Tshakapesh (especially Innu linguists Jérémie Ambroisie and Marjolaine Tshernish) of Innu Takuaikan Uashat mak Mani-Utenam of the Innu First Nations, and with anthropologist José Mailhot and the linguist Lynn Drapeau. See also Jacques Frenette, "L'original de la pétition montagnaise du 8 avril 1847: Un document inédit," *Recherches amérindiennes au Québec* 43, no. 2–3 (2013): 77–91.

   The French expression for the month was *la lune des outardes,* and *outarde* can signify a range of birds, but by *nishk* the Innu would refer to Canadian geese.
2. I have taken the notion of waterscapes here from consultations with Innu cultural specialists at the Institut Tshakapesh and from the writings of Lisa Brooks (Missisquoi Abenaki), especially *The Common Pot: The Recovery of Native Space in the Northeast* (Minneapolis: University of Minnesota Press, 2008), and Micah Pawling, *Wabanaki Homeland and*

the New State of Maine: The 1820 Journal and Plan of Survey of Joseph Treat (Amherst: University of Massachusetts Press, 2014).

3. Innu transhumance patterns depended on caribou migration and salmon runs. Traveling the Great River (*mishta shipu,* or Rivière Moisie), the downriver migration took one week, whereas autumn's upriver migration consumed three. The arrival of the geese in April and May signaled the end of winter's famine and the migration. Consultation with Innu elders and Institut Tshakapesh, July 2019; Henry Youle Hind, *Explorations in the Interior of the Labrador Peninsula: The Country of the Montagnais and Nasquapee Indians* (London: Longman, Green, Longman, Roberts & Green, 1863), 170–171, 201.
4. "The memorial of six ladies in Jefferson county," August 15, 1846; in William G. Bishop and William H. Attree, *Report of the Debates and Proceedings of the Convention for the Revision of the Constitution of the State of New York, 1846* (Albany: Evening Atlas, 1846), 646; Lori D. Ginzberg, *Untidy Origins: A Story of Woman's Rights in Antebellum New York* (Chapel Hill: University of North Carolina Press, 2005), 2–3 (reprinted petition). James Madison, *Federalist,* no. 39, in Alexander Hamilton, John Jay and James Madison, *The Federalist*, ed. Robert Scigliano (New York: Random House, 2000), 240.
5. "The memorial of six ladies in Jefferson county."
6. Elizabeth Cady Stanton, Susan B. Anthony, and Matilda Joslyn Gage, eds., *A History of Woman Suffrage*, vol. 1 (Rochester, N.Y.: Fowler and Wells, 1889), 71–72.
7. Petition of undersigned, inhabitants of Gettysburg Adams County, to the Senate and House of Representatives of the State of Pennsylvania. The petition is discussed and reprinted in David G. Smith, *On the Edge of Freedom: The Fugitive Slave Issue in South Central Pennsylvania, 1820–1870* (New York: Fordham University Press, 2014), 227. Constant was born in 1810, and since the petition was dated January 1847, my estimate of his age is a probabilistic guess; 1850 census.
8. Smith, *On the Edge of Freedom,* 227–228.
9. The classic treatment of the varied antislavery positions taken in the 1840s and 1850s is Eric Foner, *Free Soil, Free Labor, Free Men: The Ideology of the Republican Party before the Civil War* (Oxford: Oxford University Press, 1970). For a recent study that positions Black abolitionists at the center of the antislavery movement, consult Manisha Sinha, *The Slave's Cause: A History of Abolition* (New Haven, CT: Yale University Press, 2016). See also Patrick Rael, *Black Identity and Black Protest in the Antebellum North* (Chapel Hill: University of North Carolina Press, 2002).
10. Smith, *On the Edge of Freedom,* 81–82.

11. Massachusetts Petition, Stat. 1843, c. 69, passed April 26, 1843, House Unpassed Collection, Docket 1891, MAC. These petitions have been published electronically by Harvard University in the Digital Archive of Massachusetts Antislavery and Anti-Segregation Petitions, https://dataverse.harvard.edu/dataverse/antislaverypetitionsma.
12. The Petition of the Undersigned Laborers to Honourable Col. Oakley, July 12, 1847, Illinois and Michigan Canal Archives, box 2, folder 4, CHM. To my knowledge, the petition was first discussed in Ryan Dearinger, *The Filth of Progress: Immigrants, Americans, and the Building of Canals and Railroads in the West* (Berkeley: University of California Press, 2015), 95–96. Dearinger does not quote the passage presented here, however.
13. Dearinger, *Filth of Progress*, 23.
14. The Petition of the Undersigned Laborers to Honourable Col. Oakley, July 12, 1847.
15. The Petition of the Undersigned Laborers to Honourable Col. Oakley, July 12, 1847. On canal workers and their political participation, consult Peter A. Wallner, "Politics and Public Works: A Study of the Pennsylvania Canal System, 1825–1857" (PhD diss., Pennsylvania State University, 1973).
16. An exhaustive study of racial citizenship in labor appears in David Roediger, *The Wages of Whiteness: Race and the Making of the American Working Class* (New York: Verso, 1999); Noel Ignatiev, *How the Irish Became White* (New York: Routledge, 1995). On republican Whiteness as identified with freedom and Blackness as identified with slavery, see Edmund Morgan, *American Slavery, American Freedom: The Ordeal of Colonial Virginia* (New York: Norton, 1975).
17. Lea VanderVelde, *Mrs. Dred Scott: A Life on Slavery's Frontier* (Oxford: Oxford University Press, 2009), esp. chaps. 26–30 (on the erasure of Harriet as petitioner, see chap. 32). For digital versions, consult The Revised Dred Scott Case Collection at Washington University in St. Louis, http://digital.wustl.edu/d/dre. For more on the process of discovering and curating these documents, see VanderVelde, *Mrs. Dred Scott*, xxiii–xxv.
18. David Thomas Konig, "The Long Road to *Dred Scott:* Personhood and the Rule of Law in the Trial Court Records of St. Louis Slave Freedom Suits," *UMKC Law Review* 75, no. 1 (Fall 2006): 54–79; Don E. Fehrenbacher, *Slavery, Law, and Politics: The Dred Scott Case in Historical Perspective* (Oxford: Oxford University Press, 1981).
19. On suits, consult Lea VanderVelde, *Redemption Songs: Suing for Freedom before Dred Scott* (Oxford: Oxford University Press, 2014); Loren Schweninger, *Appealing for Liberty: Freedom Suits in the South*

(Oxford: Oxford University Press, 2018). On legislative petitions, consult Loren Schweninger, ed., *The Southern Debate over Slavery*, vol. 1, *Petitions to Southern Legislatures, 1778–1864* (Urbana: University of Illinois Press, 2001), and the remarkable databases of Schweninger and his collaborators in the Race and Slavery Petitions Project (https://library.uncg.edu/slavery/petitions). *Laws of the State of Missouri, Passed at the First Session of the Fourteenth General Assembly* [. . .] (Jefferson, MO: James Lusk, 1847), 103–104 ("An Act respecting slaves, free negroes and mulattoes"), 301 ("An Act to authorize James H. Hanson [. . .] to bring certain negroes into the State"); Schweninger, *Southern Debate*, 1:195–196.

20. Mark Graber, *Dred Scott and the Problem of Constitutional Evil* (Cambridge: Cambridge University Press, 2007).
21. *Petition of the People of New Mexico, Assembled in Convention, Praying the Organization of a Territorial Government*, U.S. Senate, 30th Cong., 2nd Sess., Miscellaneous Document No. 5 (Washington: Tippin & Streeter, 1848). The petition was widely reprinted around the West in newspapers, such as *Weekly Alta California*, February 8, 1849.
22. James Brooks, *Captives and Cousins: Slavery, Kinship and Community in the Southwest Borderlands* (Chapel Hill: University of North Carolina Press, 2001); Ned Blackhawk, *Violence Over the Land: Indians and Empires in the Early American West* (Cambridge, MA: Harvard University Press, 2006). On Martínez's probable children, consult Fray Angelico Chavez, *But Time and Chance: The Story of Padre Martínez of Taos, 1793–1867* (Santa Fe: Sunstone, 1981).
23. Robert W. Larson, *New Mexico's Quest for Statehood, 1846–1912* (Albuquerque: University of New Mexico Press, 2000), 11–12; "According to its signers, the petition was drawn up to correct an erroneous impression that they were involved in certain acts of rebellion, including the killing of the late governor" (11).
24. See Chapters 2 and 3 for discussions of the difference between petitions, memorials, and remonstrances, among other documents.
25. Juan Manuel Lucero and others, Petition against Vigil's Claim to Land along Río Lucero, August 13, 1836, SANM I, no. 628, reel 4, frames 142–145; reel 5, frame 310 (English translation), NMSRCA. Quoted and discussed in Denise Damico, "'*El agua es la vida*' (Water Is Life): Water Conflict and Conquest in Nineteenth-Century New Mexico" (PhD diss., Brandeis University, 2008), 35n72, 50–53. On Padre Martínez's later attempts to gain land for colonization purposes and for profit, consult Howard Roberts Lamar, *The Far Southwest, 1846–1912: A Territorial History* (Albuquerque: University of New Mexico Press, 2000), 35, 44.

26. Ray John de Aragon, *Padre Martínez and Bishop Lamy* (Santa Fe: Sunstone, 2006), 64.
27. The distinction between Black and Indigenous slavery qualifies the New Mexicans' achievement considerably. As James Brooks has revealed, Indigenous slavery persisted deep into nineteenth-century New Mexico, and the territorial legislature was soon pressed by calls to introduce southern slavery. Brooks, *Captives and Cousins*, 295–300.
28. *Representación de los vecinos de Guadalajara al Supremo Gobierno Federal, contra la introducción de falsas religiones en el país* (Guadalajara: Imprenta de Rodríguez, 1848). Author's translation from Spanish.
29. Dieter George Berninger, *La inmigración en México, 1821–1857* (México: Secretaria de Educación Publica, 1974).
30. Charles A. Hale, *Mexican Liberalism in the Age of Mora* (New Haven, CT: Yale University Press, 1968), 39.
31. *Representación que los habitantes de Puebla eleven al soberano congreso de la Unión, contrariando los conatos, que para establecer la tolerancia religiosa en nuestro país, aparecen hoy desgraciadamente* (Puebla: Imprenta de Juan Nepomuceno del Valle, 1848). On the Orizaba women's *representación* of 1849, see Berninger, *La inmigración en México*, 131; on the American brigade's occupation of Orizaba and the Batallón Orizaba, consult Benjamín Maciel Gómez, *Síntesis cronológica de los principales hechos históricos de Orizaba: Historia de cinco siglos, del año 1051 al 2000* (Orizaba: Archivo Municipal, Orizaba, Veracruz, 2003), 49–69, esp. 53–54.
32. Susana Sosenski, "Asomándose a la política: Representaciones femeninas contra la tolerancia de cultos en México, 1856," *Tzintzun. Revista de Estudios Históricos* 40 (July–December 2004): 51–76; Silvia Marina Arrom, *The Women of Mexico City, 1790–1857* (Stanford, Calif.: Stanford University Press, 1985), 42–43.
33. Sosenski, "Asomándose a la política."
34. William A. Green, *British Slave Emancipation: The Sugar Colonies and the Great Experiment, 1830–1865* (New York: Oxford University Press, 1976), 233, 233nn14–16. On petitions against the Mexico War, see Chapter 11 (this volume). On the original proposal for a corporate charter governing Vancouver Island, consult B. Hawes to J. H. Pelly, 14 December 1846, Great Britain, Colonial Office, Correspondence with the Hudson's Bay Company, 1822–1851, microfilm GR-0332, vol. 1, fol. 89, ABC.
35. Stephen Kantrowitz, *More Than Freedom: Fighting for Black Citizenship in a White Republic, 1829–1889* (New York: Penguin, 2012).

2. ERUPTIONS AND DEMOCRACIES

1. Comparative indices of democracy center free and competitive elections in their measurements; see the Freedom House Index (*Freedom in the World*, 2019); the Democracy Index of the *Economist*; Heather K. Gerken, *The Democracy Index: Why Our Election System Is Failing and How to Fix It* (Princeton, N.J.: Princeton University Press, 2009).
2. The petition performs a dual transformation: first, the conversion of individual and communal pain into textual grievance and signed testimony; second, the conveyance of this document to an office and its apparition and disposition there (including its reading and possible conversion into law). This transformative rendering of technology coheres with many of the approaches taken in philosophy and social science; see Giovanni Dosi and Marco Grazzi, "Technologies as Problem-Solving Procedures and Technologies as Input–Output Relations: Some Perspectives on the Theory of Production," *Industrial and Corporate Change* 15, no. 1 (February 2006): 173–202. In philosophy, consult Friedrich Rapp, *Analytical Philosophy of Technology* (Berlin: Springer, 2012), chap. 3. Even Ernst Kapp's classic *Elements of a Philosophy of Technology* (1877) draws on this representation (chap. 7, "Steam Engines and Rail Lines"). I discuss aspects of this technological notion of petitioning in "Recruitment by Petition: American Antislavery, French Protestantism, English Suppression," *Perspectives on Politics* 14, no. 3 (September 2016): 700–723.

   The petition as technology adapts a common mechanism—prayer and signatory vector—across many forms. As such, petitions incorporate but transcend basic notions of "institution" and of "practice," in part because they *wed* formal institutions with a set of accreted social practices. What moderns call "the petition" combines rhetorical practices (the prayer, often evolving from the medieval *ars dictaminis*, see Chapter 3), systems of aggregation (the signatory list), institutional rules of presentation to office, and representational norms of response. Neither the rules-based notion of institutions advanced in political economy (e.g., Douglass North, *Institutions, Institutional Change and Economic Performance* [New York: Cambridge University Press, 1990]) nor the systems-based or organization-based notions in anthropology and sociology (e.g., Mary Douglas, *How Institutions Think* [Syracuse: Syracuse University Press, 1986]) suffices to describe this complex, at least not without some notion of technological conversion of anguish into text and testimony. Similar technologies include torts and suits (including class-action litigation), harangues, acts of vengeance, perhaps even the kinds of technologies of rule and of self that Foucault studied at length (*Le gouvernement de soi et des autres* [Paris: Seuil, 2008]). My purposes in examining the technological features of petitions differ from those guiding these regnant approaches.

On the people "without doors" and their representatives "within doors," consult Alison G. Olson, "Eighteenth-Century Colonial Legislatures and Their Constituents," *Journal of American History* 79, no. 2 (September 1992): 543–567; Barbara Clark Smith, *The Freedoms We Lost: Consent and Resistance in Revolutionary America* (New York: New Press, 2010), chap. 1, esp. 12–13; Peverill Squire, *The Rise of the Representative: Lawmakers and Constituents in Colonial America* (Ann Arbor: University of Michigan Press, 2017), chap. 7. The notion of the people "without doors" and representatives "within doors" figures centrally in Thomas Jefferson's thinking about petitions in his 1801 *Manual of Parliamentary Procedure* (section 19.2).

3. On the idea of institutional conversion, consult Kathleen Thelen, *How Institutions Evolve: The Political Economy of Skills in Germany, Britain, the United States, and Japan* (Cambridge: Cambridge University Press, 2004), 23–37, 292–296; Jacob S. Hacker, Paul Pierson, and Thelen, "Drift and Conversion: Hidden Faces of Institutional Change," in *Advances in Comparative-Historical Analysis*, ed. James Mahoney and Thelen (Cambridge: Cambridge University Press, 2015), 196–224. On the linkage between courts and petition venues, see Maggie McKinley, "Lobbying and the Petition Clause," *Stanford Law Review* 68, no. 5 (June 2016): 1131–1205.
4. On retrospective judgments, consult James Fearon, "Electoral Accountability and the Control of Politicians: Selecting Good Types versus Sanctioning Poor Performance," in *Democracy, Accountability and Representation*, ed. Adam Przeworski, Susan Stokes, and Bernard Manin (Cambridge: Cambridge University Press, 1999), 55–97. For skepticism about elections' ability to perform these functions, see Christopher Achen and Larry Bartels, *Democracy for Realists: Why Elections Do Not Produce Responsive Government* (Princeton, N.J.: Princeton University Press, 2016). On the stable coexistence of elections and authoritarianism, see Stephen Levitsky and Lucan Way, "Elections without Democracy: The Rise of Competitive Authoritarianism," *Journal of Democracy* 13, no. 2 (April 2002): 51–65.
5. Philip Pettit, *On the People's Terms: A Republican Theory and Model of Democracy* (Cambridge: Cambridge University Press, 2012); Pierre Rosenvallon, *La contre-démocratie: La politique à l'âge de défiance* (Paris: Seuil, 2006), 9–32; Amy Gutmann and Dennis Thompson, *Why Deliberative Democracy?* (Princeton, N.J.: Princeton University Press,

2009); Hannah Pitkin, *The Concept of Representation* (Berkeley: University of California Press, 1967). My thinking most closely aligns with that of Nadia Urbinati, *Representative Democracy: Principles and Genealogy* (Chicago: University of Chicago Press, 2006), introduction and chap. 1, and with Jane Mansbridge, "Recursive Representation," in Dario Castiglione and Johannes Pollak, eds., *Creating Political Presence: The New Politics of Democratic Representation* (Chicago: University of Chicago Press, 2019), 298–338.

6. On children signing petitions in 1820s French Canada, consult Chapter 7. On girls and girls aged eight to twelve signing and canvassing petitions in western New York and other northern U.S. states, see Chapter 10.
7. For the purposes of this study, I generally equate "petition" and "memorial." Although the latter term retained some of its original meaning as an institution's official statement of position before a legislature (such as the memorial of a state legislature to Congress), their meaning and usage had been converging for some time (see the remarks of Candidus in *Gazette of the United States* on "petitions and memorials," introduction to *Documentary History of the First Federal Congress, 1789–1791*, vol. 8, *Petition Histories and Nonlegislative Official Documents*, ed. Kenneth R. Bowling, William Charles DiGiacomantonio, and Charlene Bangs Bickford [Baltimore and London: Johns Hopkins University Press, 1998], xii). On a functional and procedural basis, late eighteenth-century legislatures regarded "petition" and "memorial" as functional equivalents even before the American Revolution, sending them to the same committees with identical instructions. See the treatment of "petitions" and "memorials" from individuals by the late colonial House of Burgesses, November 10, 1766; *Journal of the House of Burgesses of Virginia, 1666–1669*, ed. John Pendleton Kennedy (Richmond, Va.: The Colonial Press, 1906), 21. Memorials were, moreover, increasingly applied to documents sent from a single person, and the term also began to subsume "propositions" from governmental entities. My analyses often include "remonstrances" as petitions quantitatively, but these account for a very small fraction (well less than one percent) of the documents analyzed here.
8. Laura Edwards, *The People and Their Peace: Legal Culture and the Transformation of Inequality in the Post-Revolutionary South* (Chapel Hill: University of North Carolina Press, 2009).
9. Calculations taken from *JHRUS* and *JSUS*.
10. Population aggregates come from the *Historical Statistics of the United States*. I use the general population because it is highly correlated over time with the available subset of nonslave adults and also because many children and slaves did in fact petition or have others petition on their

behalf. Territorial and foreign petitions were of a sufficiently small scale as to not affect the calculations presented here.

11. Virginia totals from analysis of LOV data, checked against *JHODV;* calculations from petition summaries in TLSA.
12. As Carol Wilton summarizes, "a much higher percentage of the population signed petitions than voted in provincial elections." Wilton, *Popular Politics and Political Culture in Upper Canada, 1800–1850* (Montréal: McGill-Queen's University Press, 2000), 6.
13. Juan A. Mateos, *Historia parlamentaria de los Congresos mexicanos de 1821 a 1857* (México, 1877), two volumes; author summaries from SANMI, SANM II, and MANM.
14. But see Chapter 3, which describes some of these venues for certain municipalities.
15. For efforts in this direction, see the monumental scholarship of Loren Schweninger and collaborators, *The Southern Debate over Slavery, Volume I: Petitions to Southern Legislatures, 1776–1861* (Urbana and Chicago: University of Illinois Press, 2001), as well as the accompanying microfilm collection. The Library of Virginia has exhaustively cataloged its legislative petitions archives. Another database of over eight thousand (largely northern) antislavery petitions sent to Congress is described in Daniel Carpenter and Colin D. Moore, "When Canvassers Became Activists," Antislavery Petitioning and the Political Mobilization of American Women," *American Political Science Review* 108, no. 3 (August 2014): 479–498. On digital petition databases completed for Massachusetts, consult the Digital Archive of Massachusetts Antislavery and Anti-Segregation Petitions and the Digital Archive of Native American Petitions in Massachusetts, available at https://dataverse.harvard.edu /dataverse/antislaverypetitionsma.
16. Susan Zaeske, *Signatures of Citizenship: Petitioning, Antislavery, and Women's Political Identity* (Chapel Hill, University of North Carolina Press, 2003). In the Progressive era emergence of initiative and referendum institutions, state statutes against signature fraud began to proliferate.
17. On the nineteenth-century American ballot box as a place of endemic corruption, see Mark W. Summers, *The Plundering Generation: Corruption and the Crisis of the Union, 1849–1861* (Oxford: Oxford University Press, 1987), esp. 23–36; Michael Holt, *The Rise and Fall of the American Whig Party* (Oxford: Oxford University Press, 1999), 113; Richard Franklin Bensel, *The American Ballot Box in the Mid-Nineteenth-Century* (Cambridge: Cambridge University Press, 2004), esp. 9–10, 20–21.

18. "Introduction into Politics," in *The Promise of Politics*, ed. and with an introduction by Jerome Kohn (New York: Penguin, 2005), 97.
19. The literature on nineteenth-century democratization in North America is vast. On democratization at the regime level as well among subcultures in the United States, consult Sean Wilentz, *The Rise of American Democracy: Jefferson to Lincoln* (Oxford: Oxford University Press, 2005); Sean Wilentz, *Chants Democratic: New York City and the Rise of the American Working Class, 1788–1850* (Oxford: Oxford University Press, 1984); Nathan O. Hatch, *The Democratization of American Christianity* (New Haven, Conn.: Yale University Press, 1989); Paul Starr, *The Social Transformation of American Medicine* (New York: Basic Books, 1982), esp. chap. 2; John Aldrich, *Why Parties? The Origin and Transformation of Political Parties in the United States* (Chicago: University of Chicago Press, 1995), chaps. 3–5; Mary Ryan, *Civic Wars: Democracy and Public Life in the American City during the Nineteenth Century* (Berkeley: University of California Press, 1997); Richard R. John, *Spreading the News: The American Postal System from Franklin to Morse* (Cambridge, Mass.: Harvard University Press, 1995). On nineteenth-century democratization in Canada, see Allan Greer, "Historical Roots of Canadian Democracy," *Journal of Canadian Studies* 34, no. 1 (Spring 1999): 7–26; Gilles Gallichan, "Le crise parlementaire de 1827 au Bas-Canada," *Les Cahiers des dix* 66 (2012): 95–166; Wilton, *Popular Politics*; Albert Schrauwers, *"Union Is Strength": William Lyon Mackenzie, The Children of Peace and the Emergence of Joint Stock Democracy in Upper Canada* (Toronto: University of Toronto Press, 2009), esp 14–17. On democratizing tendencies in nineteenth-century Mexico, consult Carlos A. Forment, *Democracy in Latin America, 1760–1900*, vol. 1, *Civic Selfhood and Public Life in Mexico and Peru* (Chicago: University of Chicago Press, 2003); Jaime O. Rodriguez, ed., *Mexico in the Age of Democratic Revolutions, 1750–1850* (Boulder: Rienner, 1994); Peter Guardino, *The Time of Liberty: Popular Political Culture in Oaxaca, 1750–1850* (Durham, N.C.: Duke University Press, 2005).
20. John Adams, "Marchamont Nedham: The Right Constitution of a Commonwealth Examined," in *Defence of the Constitutions of the Governments of the United States of America*, in *The Works of John Adams*, vol. 6 (Boston: Little and Brown, 1851), 109; "Thomas Jefferson to Peter H. Wendover (Draft), 13 March 1815," *Founders Online*, National Archives, https://founders.archives.gov/documents/Jefferson/03-08-02-0270-0002.
21. James Madison, *Federalist*, no. 39, in Alexander Hamilton, John Jay and James Madison, *The Federalist*, ed. Robert Scigliano (New York: Random House, 2000), 240, emphasis in original.

22. Robert A. Dahl, *A Preface to Democratic Theory* (New Haven, Conn.: Yale University Press, 1956), 10. "A republic was used to refer to what we would call a representative democracy." Larry Diamond and Leonardo Morlino, "The Quality of Democracy: An Overview," *Journal of Democracy* 15, no. 4 (October 2004): 20–31.
23. Wilentz, *Rise of American Democracy;* E. E. Schattschneider, *Party Government* (New York: Holt, Rinehart and Winston, 1942), 1. On suffrage, see Chapters 8 and 11. On the Bank War petitioning campaign and the Whigs, see Chapter 9. For related evidence on the Liberty Party and radical antislavery, consult Bruce Laurie, *Beyond Garrison: Antislavery and Social Reform* (Cambridge: Cambridge University Press, 2005), 110–149, esp. 148; Carpenter, "Recruitment by Petition: American Antislavery, French Protestantism, English Suppression," *Perspectives on Politics* 14, no. 3 (September 2016); Chapter 10 this volume.
24. Consult Robert A. Dahl's reading of Madison, *Federalist,* no. 39, in Dahl, *Preface to Democratic Theory,* 10. Tom Downey, *Planting a Capitalist South: Masters, Merchants and Manufacturers in the Southern Interior, 1790–1860* (Baton Rouge: Louisiana State University Press, 2006), chaps. 2, 3, esp. 42–98, 167; Thomas B. Stockwell, *A History of Public Education in Rhode Island, from 1636 to 1876* (Providence: Providence Press Company, 1876), 39, 42; W. A. Maddox, *The Free School Idea in Virginia before the Civil War* (New York: Columbia University, 1918).
25. Theda Skocpol, *Protecting Soldiers and Mothers: The Political Origins of Social Policy in the United States* (Cambridge, Mass.: Harvard University Press, 1993); Laura Jensen, *Patriots, Settlers, and the Origins of American Social Policy* (Cambridge: Cambridge University Press, 2003); Kristin A. Collins, "Petitions without Number: Widows' Petitions and the Early Nineteenth-Century Origins of Marriage-Based Entitlements," *Law and History Review* 31, no. 1 (February 2013): 1–60; Michele Landis Dauber, *The Sympathetic State* (Chicago: University of Chicago Press, 2013), 17–45.
26. Urbinati, *Representative Democracy,* 2, 4, and generally chap. 1; Maria Paula Saffon and Nadia Urbinati, "Procedural Democracy, the Bulwark of Equal Liberty," *Political Theory* 41, no. 3 (2013): 443–445; Deva R. Woodly, *The Politics of Common Sense: How Social Movements Use Public Discourse to Change Politics and Win Acceptance* (Oxford: Oxford University Press, 2015), chap. 5; John Dryzek, "Democratization as Deliberative Capacity Building," *Comparative Political Studies,* 42, no. 11 (2009): 1379–1402.
27. On "democratic influence" and "contestatory democracy," consult Pettit, *On the People's Terms,* chap. 4, 208 (insufficiency of elections), 215 (institutional contestability), 226–227 (contestatory citizenry). See also Rosenvallon, *La contre-démocratie,* 35–121; Frank Baumgartner and

Bryan A. Jones, *Agendas and Instability in American Politics* (Chicago: University of Chicago Press, 1993).

28. Rosenvallon, *La contre-démocratie,* pt. 1; Jean Cohen and Andrew Arato, *Civil Society and Political Theory* (Cambridge: Cambridge University Press, 1994); Jurgen Habermas, *The Structural Transformation of the Public Sphere: An Inquiry into a Category of Bourgeois Society* (Cambridge: MIT Press, 1991); Juan J. Linz, *Totalitarian and Authoritarian Regimes* (Boulder: Rienner, 1975), 165–167; Robert D. Putnam, *Making Democracy Work: Civic Traditions in Modern Italy* (Princeton, N.J.: Princeton University Press, 1994), esp. chap. 6; Theda Skocpol, *Diminished Democracy: From Membership to Management in American Civic Life* (Norman: Oklahoma University Press, 2003), esp. chaps. 2–3.
29. Danielle Allen, *Education and Equality* (Chicago: University of Chicago Press, 2016), 14–18, 34–37, 38–49 ("participatory readiness"); Johann Neem, "Two Concepts of Democratization," in Daniel Peart and Adam I. P. Smith, *Practicing Democracy: Popular Politics in the United States from the Constitution to the Civil War* (Charlottesville: University of Virginia Press, 2014), 247–279; Martha Nussbaum, "Aristotelian Social Democracy," in *Liberalism and the Good,* ed. R. Bruce Douglass, Gerald M. Mara, and Henry S. Richardson (London: Routledge, 1991), 203–252.
30. Diamond and Morlino, "The Quality of Democracy"; Gutmann and Thompson, *Why Deliberative Democracy?*
31. This notion of minimizing majoritarian losses is one I take both from Pettit's understanding of republican freedom as nondomination and from political scientist Melissa Harris-Perry, "Who's Choosin' Who? Race, Gender and the New American Politics" (Dean's lecture, Radcliffe Institute for Advanced Study, October 23, 2014).
32. See the searching examination of Reeve Huston in "Democratic Discontent: Remaking American Politics, 1815–1840" (unpublished manuscript, Duke University, 2019); David Waldstreicher, *In the Midst of Perpetual Fetes* (Chapel Hill: University of North Carolina Press, 1997); Jason Frank, *Constituent Moments,* 24–27, 44–45; Dana Nelson, *Commons Democracy: Reading the Politics of Participation in the Early United States* (New York: Fordham University Press, 2016), 1–52;
33. See David Cannadine, *The Decline and Fall of the British Aristocracy* (New Haven, Conn.: Yale University Press, 1990), who concludes that in the 1870s, the British aristocracy still held most of its powers enjoyed before the American Revolution; Daniel Ziblatt, *Conservative Parties and the Birth of Democracy* (Cambridge: Cambridge University Press, 2018), chap. 3. See also Hatch, *Democratization of American Christianity,* on

the conservatism of British Methodists compared to Americans. On parliamentary hostility to Chartist national petitions and the decline of Chartism after the 1840s, consult Malcolm Chase, "What Did Chartism Petition For? Mass Petitions in the British Movement for Democracy," *Social Science History* 43, no. 3 (Fall 2019): 531–551; Benoit Agnès, *L'appel au pouvoir: Les pétitions aux Parlements en France et au Royaume-Uni (1814–1848)* (Rennes: Presses Universitaires de Rennes, 2018).

34. On the breadth of electoral participation in Canada, see Allan Greer, *The Patriots and the People: The Rebellion of 1837 in Rural Lower Canada* (Toronto: University of Toronto Press, 1993), 113–115. See also Allan Greer, "Historical Roots of Canadian Democracy," *Journal of Canadian Studies* 34, no. 1 (1999): esp. 7–8; Carol Wilton, *Popular Politics and Political Culture in Upper Canada, 1800–1850* (Montréal: McGill-Queen's University Press, 2000).

35. On Indigenous persistence in Mexico, consult John Tutino, *The Mexican Heartland: How Communities Shaped Capitalism, a Nation, and World History, 1500–2000* (Princeton, N.J.: Princeton University Press, 2018); Michael Thomas Ducey, *A Nation of Villages: Riot and Rebellion in the Mexican Huasteca, 1750–1850* (Tucson: University of Arizona Press, 2004); Brian R. Hammett, *Roots of Insurgency: Mexican Regions, 1750–1824* (Cambridge: Cambridge University Press, 2002). On republican features in independent Mexico, see Peter Guardino, *Peasants, Politics and the Formation of the Mexican National State* (Stanford: Stanford University Press, 2002); Jaime Rodriguez, ed., *The Origins of Mexican National Politics, 1808–1847* (Berkeley: University of California Press, 1997); Timothy E. Anna, *Forging Mexico: 1821–1835* (Lincoln: University of Nebraska Press, 1998).

3. PETITIONS, PRAYERS, AND THEIR VENUES

1. Petition of Mary Venus to the Government House, July 22, 1835, reprinted in Studholme Hodgson, *Truths from the West Indies, Including a Sketch of Madeira in 1833* (London: W. Ball, 1838), 355 (see also 149).
2. Petition of Mary Venus to the Government House, July 22, 1835.
3. Petition of Mary Venus to the Government House, July 22, 1835. The outcome of Mary Venus's ordeal is unknown, but her husband may have been Auguste Victorine, whose owner in 1834 was Sophia Massey (Hodgson reports that Mary's owner was a "Mr. Massey, junior" [355]).
4. Records of the Office of Registry of Colonial Slaves and Slave Compensation Commission, Microfilm T71, NAUK. On the more general strategy of Afro-Caribbean peoples petitioning multiple venues, consult Chapter 6.

5. On the Grimké address, see Chapter 10. The key distinction in 1838 is that the Massachusetts General Court gave Grimké parliamentary recognition.
6. Daniel Walker Howe, *What Hath God Wrought: The Transformation of America, 1815–1848* (Oxford: Oxford University Press, 2007), esp. chaps. 5, 6.
7. Calculations from Daniel Carpenter et al., Digital Archive of Massachusetts Antislavery Petitions, Harvard University.
8. Memorial of the Legislature of the Indiana Territory to the Senate and House of Representatives, September 10, 1814, William Henry Harrison Papers, box 2, folder 13, IHS.
9. Christine A. Desan, "The Constitutional Commitment to Legislative Adjudication in the Early American Tradition," *Harvard Law Review* 111 (1998): 1381–1503, esp. 1463; Kenneth R. Bowling and Donald R. Kennon, eds., *The House and Senate in the 1790s: Petitioning, Lobbying and Institutional Development* (Athens: Ohio University Press, 2002), including chapters by Desan ("Contesting the Character of the Political Economy: Rights and Remedies in the Early Republic") and diGiacomantonio ("Petitioners and their Grievances: A View from the First Federal Congress"); Olson, "Eighteenth-Century Legislatures and Their Constituents," 543, 556–57; Hannah Weiss Muller, "From *Requête* to Petition: Petitioning the Monarch between Empires," *Historical Journal* 60, no. 3 (September 2017): 659–686; Colin G. Calloway, *Pen and Ink Witchcraft: Treaties and Treaty Making in American Indian History* (Oxford: Oxford University Press, 2013), esp. chaps. 1, 3.
10. Richard Witt, "Medieval 'Ars Dictaminis' and the Beginnings of Humanism: A New Construction of the Problem," *Renaissance Quarterly* 35, no. 1 (Spring 1982): 1–35; Malcolm Richardson, "The *Ars Dictaminis*, the Formulary, and Medieval Epistolary Practice," in Carol Poster and Linda C. Mitchell, ed., *Letter-Writing Manuals and Instructions from Antiquity to the Present: Historical and Bibliographical Studies* (Columbia: University of South Carolina Press, 2007); Quentin Verreycken, *L'État de grâce? Guerre et usage du pardon en Angleterre, France et anciens Pays-Bas au XVe siècle* (PhD diss., Université catholique de Louvain et Université Saint-Louis–Bruxelles, 2018).
11. Thomas Bisson, *The Crisis of the Twelfth Century: Power, Lordship and the Origins of European Government* (Princeton, N.J.: Princeton University Press, 2009); Gwylim Dodd, *Justice and Grace: Private Petitioning and the English Parliament in the Late Middle Ages* (Oxford: Oxford University Press, 2007); Sophie Petit-Renaud, *"Faire Loy" Au Royaume de France: De Philippe VI à Charles V (1328–1380)* (Paris: De Boccard,

2001); Elizabeth Read Foster, "Petitions and the Petition of Right," *Journal of British Studies* 14, no. 1 (1977): 21–45; David Zaret, *Origins of Democratic Culture: Printing, Petitions and the Public Sphere in Early Modern England* (Princeton, N.J.: Princeton University Press, 2000); Steven Pincus, *1688: The First Modern Revolution* (New Haven: Yale University Press, 2009); Joanna Innes, "People and Power in British Politics to 1850," in *Re-Imagining Democracy in the Age of Revolution*, ed. Innes and Mark Philp (Cambridge: Cambridge University Press, 2013); Leah Whittington, *Renaissance Suppliants: Poetry, Antiquity, Reconciliation* (Oxford: Oxford University Press, 2016), esp. chaps. 4–5.

12. The evolution of petition signatory lists requires further research. French Protestants were using the technique no later than 1561. Allan Tulchin, *That Men Would Praise the Lord: The Triumph of Protestantism in Nîmes, 1530–1570* (Oxford: Oxford University Press, 2010), esp. chap. 3. On Stuart England, see Zaret, *Origins of Democratic Culture;* Mark Knights, "London's Monster Petition of 1680," *Historical Journal* 36, no. 1 (1993): 39–67. On the 1661 act, consult Daniel Carpenter, "Recruitment by Petition: American Antislavery, French Protestantism, English Suppression," *Perspectives on Politics* 14, no. 93 (September 2016): 714–715.

13. Lois Schwoerer, *The Declaration of Rights, 1689* (Baltimore: Johns Hopkins University Press, 1981), 15; Pennsylvania Constitution of 1776, "A Declaration of the Rights of the Inhabitants of the Commonwealth or State of Pennsylvania," art. XVI; Massachusetts Constitution of 1780, Part the First, art. XIX; Constitution of the United States, First Amendment (1791); McKinley, "Lobbying and the Petition Clause."

14. R. C. Bailey, *Popular Influence upon Public Policy: Petitioning in Eighteenth-Century Virginia* (Greenwich: Greenwood, 1979), 64; introduction to *Documentary History of the First Federal Congress, 1789–1791*, vol. 8, *Petition Histories and Nonlegislative Official Documents*, ed. Kenneth R. Bowling, William Charles DiGiacomantonio, and Charlene Bangs Bickford (Baltimore and London: Johns Hopkins University Press, 1998), xi–xxvi; Maggie McKinley, "Petitioning and the Making of Administrative State," *Yale Law Journal* 127, no. 6 (April 2018): 1551–1569; William Lee Miller, *Arguing over Slavery: John Quincy Adams and the Great Battle in the United States Congress* (New York: Random House, 1995), 199; *JCABC, 1793* (Quebec, 1793) (starting January 16, 1793), 126–135.

15. Brian P. Owensby, "Pacto entre rey lejano y súbditos indígenas: Justicia, legalidad y política en Nueva España, siglo XVII," *Historia Mexicana* 61, no. 1 (2011): 59–106; Alfredo Gallego Anabitarte, *Poder y derecho: Del antiguo régimen al estado constitucional en España: Siglos XVIII a XIX*

(Madrid: Marcial Pons Ediciones, 2009); Adrian Masters, "A Thousand Invisible Architects: Vassals, the Petition and Response System, and the Creation of Spanish Imperial Caste Legislation," *Hispanic American Historical Review* 98, no. 3 (2018): 377–406; Tamar Herzog, "Colonial Law and 'Native Customs': Indigenous Land Rights in Colonial Spanish America," *Americas* 69, no. 3 (January 2013): 318.

16. Wood, *Creation,* esp. chap. 2; James T. Kloppenberg, *Toward Democracy: The Struggle for Self-Rule in European and American Thought* (New York: Oxford University Press, 2016), chaps. 6–9; Jill Lepore, *These Truths: A History of the United States* (New York: Norton, 2019), chaps. 3–6; Joyce Appleby, *Capitalism and a New Social Order: The Republican Vision of the 1790s* (New York: New York University Press, 1984), esp. chaps. 2–3; *Liberalism and Republicanism in the Historical Imagination* (Cambridge, Mass.: Harvard University Press, 1992).
17. Linda K. Kerber, *Women of the Republic: Intellect and Ideology in Revolutionary America* (Chapel Hill: University of North Carolina Press, 1980), 41, 85–104, 167–174; Christopher Leslie Brown, *Moral Capital: Foundations of British Abolitionism* (Chapel Hill: University of North Carolina Press, 2006), 25–30, 455–457; Wood, *Creation,* chap. 2.
18. "Ten-thousand name" petition, October 16, 1776 (digital copy at the American Memory webpage, LOC); William Lee Miller, *The First Liberty: Religion and the American Republic* (New York: Knopf, 1986), 31–53. The correspondence between the petitions and subsequent legislation has been noted before; see Carl H. Esbeck, "Protestant Dissent and the Virginia Disestablishment, 1776–1786," *Georgetown Journal of Law and Public Policy* 7 (2009): 51–103. Virginia data for 1776 session compiled by author from Legislative Petitions Digital Collection, LOV, and checked against *JHDV.* On the creation of the new Committee of Religion, the first not revived from the colonial House of Burgesses, see *JHDV,* October 11, 1776, 9 (compare delegates' committee revivals from Burgesses on October 8, pp. 4–5).
19. Dana Nelson, *Commons Democracy: Reading the Politics of Participation in the Early United States* (New York: Fordham University Press, 2016), 175–178; James Morone, *The Democratic Wish: Popular Participation and the Limits of American Government* (New Haven, Conn.: Yale University Press, 1992); David Waldstreicher, *In the Midst of Perpetual Fetes: The Making of American Nationalism, 1776–1820* (Chapel Hill: University of North Carolina Press, 1997); Jason Frank, *Constituent Moments: Enacting the People in Postrevolutionary America* (Ithaca: Cornell University Press, 2009), 130–151; Sandra Gustafson, *Imagining Deliberative Democracy in the Early American Republic* (Chicago:

University of Chicago Press, 2011); Michele Orihel, "'Mississippi Mad': The Democratic Society of Kentucky and the Sectional Politics of Navigation Rights," *Register of the Kentucky Historical Society* 114, no. 3–4 (2016): 399–430.

20. David Waldstreicher, *Runaway America: Benjamin Franklin, Slavery, and the American Revolution* (New York: Hill and Wang, 2004), 235–237; Sean Wilentz, *The Rise of American Democracy: Jefferson to Lincoln* (Oxford: Oxford University Press, 2005), 38; see also Nicholas Guyatt, "The Complexion of My Country: Benjamin Franklin and the Problem of Racial Diversity," in *A Companion to Benjamin Franklin*, ed. David Waldstreicher (New York: Wiley-Blackwell, 2011), 183–210. "Petition to the Mayor, Aldermen, and Commonalty of the City of New York, [24 April 1797]," in *The Papers of Alexander Hamilton*, vol. 21, *April 1797–July 1798*, ed. Harold C. Syrett (New York, 1974), 57–58.
21. Nancy F. Cott, "Divorce and the Changing Status of Women in Eighteenth-Century Massachusetts," *William & Mary Quarterly* 33, no. 4 (October 1976): 586–614; Cynthia Kierner, *Beyond the Household: Women's Place in the Early South, 1700–1835* (Ithaca: Cornell University Press, 2018 [reprint]), 100–101; Rosemarie Zagarri, *Revolutionary Backlash: Women and Politics in the Early Republic* (Philadelphia: University of Pennsylvania Press, 2011), 39, 80; Kristin A. Collins, "'Petitions without Number': Widows' Petitions and the Early Nineteenth-Century Origins of Marriage-Based Entitlements," *Law and History Review* 31, no. 1 (February 2013): 1–60; Steven Watt, "'Duty Bound and Ever Praying': Collective Petitioning to Governors and Legislatures in Selected Regions of Lower Canada and Maine, 1820–1838" (PhD thesis, University of Québec at Montréal, 2006), 121–125.
22. *Pétition Nouvelle des Citoyens de Couleur des Îles Françoises, à L'Assemblée Nationale, précédé d'un Avertissement sur les manœuvres employées pour faire échouer cette Pétition* (Paris: L'Imprimerie National, 1791); Sinha, *Slave's Cause*, 53–54. Petitions of Sarah Greene, Fairfax County, to Virginia House of Delegates, 1784; of James, New Kent County, to Virginia Assembly, 1786; of Thomas Cole, Peter Bassnett Mathewes, and Matthew Webb to South Carolina Senate, 1791; of John Carruthers Stanly, Craven County, to North Carolina Assembly, 1798; all in Schweninger, ed., *The Southern Debate Over Slavery*, 7–17. On Prince Hall and "Belinda's petition," see Chapter 5.
23. Melville to Julius Rockwell, March 20, 1861; Melville to Abraham Lincoln [1861], Melville Letters, Rauner-Dartmouth. Mark Twain petition discussed in Sinha, *Slave's* Cause, 230–31; "Moses Seixas on behalf of Congregation Yeshuat Israel, to George Washington, 17 August 1790," in

The Papers of George Washington: Presidential Series, ed. Dorothy Twohig et al. (Charlottesville: University of Virginia Press, 1986), v. 6, 286 (note 1); Washington, "Letter to the Jews of Newport," 18 August 1790, 6: 284–85. Mormon "scroll petition": "Memorial," November 28, 1843, RG 46, NARA. The appeals are reproduced, with affidavits, in Clark V. Johnson, *Mormon Redress Petitions: Documents of the 1833–1838 Conflict* (Provo: BYU Press, 1992), yet Johnson's publication of the signatory list does not exactly match the ordering on the 1843 memorial signatory list. See also Brent M. Rogers, "To the 'Honest and Patriotic Sons of Liberty': Mormon Appeals for Redress and Social Justice, 1843–44," *Journal of Mormon History* 39, no. 1 (Winter 2013): 36–67; Benjamin E. Park, *Kingdom of Nauvoo: The Rise and Fall of the Religious Empire on the American Frontier* (New York: Norton, 2020), chap. 5.

24. Washington to Robert Dinwiddie, April 22, 1756, *The Papers of George Washington,* Colonial Series, vol. 3, *16 April 1756–9 November 1756,* ed. W. W. Abbot (Charlottesville: University of Virginia Press, 1984), 33–35.
25. "Petition to the King for the Virginia Regiment, 11 March–10 July 1762," *Papers,* Colonial Series, vol. 7, *1 January 1761–15 June 1767,* ed. W. W. Abbot and Dorothy Twohig (Charlottesville: University of Virginia Press, 1990), 117–119. Adams, "[The Stamp Act, 1765]," *The Adams Papers,* Diary and Autobiography of John Adams, vol. 3, *Diary, 1782–1804; Autobiography, Part One to October 1776,* ed. L. H. Butterfield (Cambridge, Mass.: Harvard University Press, 1961), 282–284 (also at Founders Online). "Petition from Inhabitants of TN, Miro District," 1796, cited in Gregory Ablavsky, *The Adjudicatory State: Sovereignty, Property and Law in the U.S. Territories, 1783–1802* (PhD thesis, University of Pennsylvania, 2016), 74; Wilentz, *Rise of American Democracy,* 244 (Jackson anti-paper-money memorial); Charles Sellers, "Banking and Politics in Jackson's Tennessee, 1817–1827," *Mississippi Valley Historical Review* 41 (1954): 79–81; Harrison, Will[ia]m Henry, Vincennes, petition to legislature of New Jersey, October 10, 1810, box 1, folder 17, Harrison Papers, IHS; Robert M. Owens, *Mr. Jefferson's Hammer: William Henry Harrison and the Origins of American Indian Policy* (Norman: University of Oklahoma Press, 2012), 46; Abraham Lincoln, "Report of Select Committee regarding Division of Sangamon County," February 13, 1857, General Assembly Session Records 10th Assembly, 1st sess., Lincoln Papers, ISA.
26. Carole Sue Humphrey, *The Press of the Young Republic, 1783–1833* (Westport, Conn.: Greenwood, 1996); John L. Brooke, "To Be 'Read by the Whole People': Press, Party, and Public Sphere in the United States, 1789–1840," *Proceedings of the American Antiquarian Society* 110 (2002):

41–118; William A. Dill, *Growth of Newspapers in the United States* (master's thesis, University of Kansas, 1928), 12–13; James L. Crouthamel, *Bennett's New York Herald and the Rise of the Popular Press* (Syracuse: Syracuse University Press, 1989); Nicholas Marshall, "The Rural Newspaper and the Circulation of Information and Culture in New York and the Antebellum North," *New York History* 88, no. 2 (Spring 2007): 133–151. On Canada, see Chapters 7 and 8. See also Adán Benavides and Agnes L. McAlester, "Independent Mexico in Newspapers in the 19th-Century: Guide to the Microfilm Set," Benton-UT; *Cherokee Phoenix* (New Echota), 1828–1834; Asher Wright, *Ne jaguhn̄igoǎgesǵwathah* (*The Mental Elevator*) (Buffalo Creek, Cattaraugus Reservation), 1841–1850.

27. Henry Mayer, *All on Fire: William Lloyd Garrison and the Abolition of Slavery* (New York: Norton, 1998); Samuel Kernell, "The Early Nationalization of Political News in America," *Studies in American Political Development* 1 (1986): 255–278.
28. Richard R. John, *Spreading the News: The American Postal System from Franklin to Morse* (Cambridge, Mass.: Harvard University Press, 1995); Otto Yag and John K. Bash, *The Pre-Stamp Postal Markings of Mexico* (Elmhurst, Ill.: Elmhurst Philatelic Society, 1965); Canadian Museum of History, "A Chronology of Canadian Postal History," accessed June 27, 2019, www.historymuseum.ca/cmc/exhibitions/cpm/chrono/chs1760e.html.
29. On linked fate, consult Michael C. Dawson, *Behind the Mule: Race and Class in American Politics* (Princeton, N.J.: Princeton University Press, 1995); Claudine Gay and Katherine Tate, "Doubly Bound: The Impact of Gender and Race on the Politics of Black Women," *Political Psychology* 19 (1998): 169–184. On capitalism, consult Sven Beckert, *Empire of Cotton: A Global History* (New York: Random House, 2014); Charles Sellers, *The Market Revolution: Jacksonian America, 1815–1846* (Oxford: Oxford University Press, 1991); Douglass C. North, *Economic Growth of the United States, 1790–1860* (Englewood Cliffs, N.J.: Prentice-Hall, 1960).
30. On feudal tenure, see Chapter 12. On slavery, see Walter Johnson, *River of Dark Dreams: Slavery and Empire in the Cotton Kingdom* (Cambridge, Mass.: Harvard University Press, 2013); Beckert, *Empire of Cotton*.
31. Sarah Vowell, *Lafayette in the Somewhat United States* (New York: Penguin, 2015), 3; Nicole Eustace, *1812: War and the Passions of Patriotism* (Philadelphia: University of Pennsylvania Press, 2012); Steve Inskeep, *Jacksonland: President Andrew Jackson, Cherokee Chief John Ross, and a Great American Land Grab* (New York: Penguin, 2015), 133–139. For a few among the many examples of Americans trying to secure a glimpse of

or a meeting with Lafayette, see John W. Cady letters to Richard Dodge, 1822–1825, NYHS Mss Collection; Letter of "Mary" to Snowden, 1824, Snowden Family Papers (Accession #27156), LOV; Sean Wilentz, *Chants Democratic: New York City and the Rise of the American Working Class, 1788–1850* (Oxford: Oxford University Press, 1984), 92 (independence, in 1825 as in 1788, signified "in the first place, independence from Britain"); Wilentz, *Rise of American Democracy*, 344 (Richmond Convention); Marcel Ducharme, *Le concept de liberté au Canada à l'époque des révolutions atlantiques 1776–1838* (Montréal: McGill-Queen's University Press, 2010), 89.

32. Adams in Miller, *Arguing over Slavery*, 266, 262; A. M. Hills, *Life of Charles G. Finney* (Cincinnati: Mrs. M. W. Knapp, 1902); Finney, *Memoirs of Rev. Charles G. Finney, Written by Himself* (New York: A. S. Barnes, 1876), 309 and "Revival in Buffalo."
33. Margaret Chowning, "Gender, Politics and the Church," *Berkeley Review of Latin American Studies*, Fall 2010, https://clas.berkeley.edu/research/mexico-gender-politics-and-church.
34. Nathan O. Hatch, *The Democratization of American Christianity* (New Haven, Conn.: Yale University Press, 1989); John H. Wigger, *Taking Heaven by Storm: Methodism and the Rise of Popular Christianity in America* (Oxford: Oxford University Press, 1998).
35. Catherine A. Brekus, *Strangers and Pilgrims: Female Preaching in America* (Chapel Hill: University of North Carolina Press, 1998), 139; Whitney R. Cross, *The Burned-Over District: The Social and Intellectual History of Enthusiastic Religion in Western New York, 1800–1850* (Ithaca: Cornell University Press, 1950); Nancy A. Hewitt, *Women's Activism and Social Change: Rochester, New York, 1822–1872* (Ithaca: Cornell University Press, 2001); Nancy F. Cott, "Young Women and the Second Great Awakening in New England," *Feminist Studies* 3, no. 1 (Autumn 1975): 15–29; Wilentz, *Rise of American Democracy*, 265–272, 279–280, 322–327, 349–352, 427–429; Howe, *What Hath God Wrought*, 164–202, 446–482.
36. Neil Mayer, "Falling for the Lord: Shame, Revivalism, and the Origins of the Second Great Awakening," *Early American Studies* 9, no. 1 (Winter 2011): 142–166.
37. Margaret Chowning, *Rebellious Nuns: The Troubled History of a Mexican Convent, 1752–1863* (Oxford: Oxford University Press, 2006); Jessica Delgado, *Laywomen and the Making of Colonial Catholicism in New Spain, 1630–1790* (Cambridge: Cambridge University Press, 2018), introduction, esp. 8–14. As Chowning writes of nineteenth-century Mexican Catholicism, "The modern image of the Christian woman, then,

was an activist: she was either a mother and community leader, or a nun who lived in and served her society. In either case, she was not the cloistered nun of the colonial period" ("Convents and Nuns," 1291).

38. Gordon S. Wood, *The Creation of the American Republic, 1776–1787* (Chapel Hill: University of North Carolina Press, 1998), chaps. 4, 5, 137–138. On the divergence of colonial legislative models from Parliamentary frameworks, see L. W. Labaree, *Royal Government in America: A Study of the British Colonial System before 1783* (New Haven, Conn.: Yale University Press, 1930); Sean Gailmard, "Building a New Imperial State: The Strategic Foundations of Separation of Powers in America," *American Political Science Review* 111, no. 4 (2017): 668–685.
39. Peverill Squire, *The Evolution of American Legislatures: Colonies, Territories and States, 1619–2009* (Ann Arbor: University of Michigan Press, 2012).
40. Squire, *Evolution;* Laura Edwards, *The People and Their Peace: Legal Culture and the Transformation of Inequality in the Post-Revolutionary South* (Chapel Hill: University of North Carolina Press, 2009). See the voluminous collection at Petitions and Appeals to the Canal Board, Series A1140 (partial index in Series A1434), NYSL.
41. Gerald Gamm and Kenneth Shepsle, "Emergence of Legislative Institutions: Standing Committees in the House and Senate, 1810–1825," *Legislative Studies Quarterly* 14, no. 1 (1989): 39–66; Jeffrey A. Jenkins, "Property Rights and the Emergence of Standing Committee Dominance in the Nineteenth-Century House," *Legislative Studies Quarterly* 23, no. 4 (1998): 493–519; Jenkins and Charles Stewart III, *Fighting for the Speakership: The House and the Rise of Party Government* (Princeton, N.J.: Princeton University Press, 2012).
42. *JHRUS*, October 27, 1793, 439; October 18, 1803, 408; December 4, 1817, 19–23. Bowling, DiGiacomantonio, and Bickford, *Documentary History*, xii (Candidus).
43. Benjamin Schneer, Tobias Resch, Maggie Blackhawk, and Daniel Carpenter, "The Popular Origins of Legislative Jurisdictions: Petitions and Standing Committee Formation in Colonial Virginia and the Early U.S. House," working paper, Harvard University (2020).
44. *JHDV* (1781–1786) (Richmond, 1823); aggregates for early national Virginia from Legislative Petitions Digital Collection, LOV; Maggie Blackhawk, Daniel Carpenter, Tobias Resch, and Benjamin Schneer, "Congressional Representation by Petition: Assessing the Voices of the Voteless in a Comprehensive New Database, 1789–1949," *Legislative Studies Quarterly* (2020), https://doi.org/10.1111/lsq.12305; *JCABC* (Québec, 1793); John Hare, "L'Assemblée législative du Bas-Canada,

1792–1814: députation et polarisation politique," *Revue d'histoire de l'Amérique française* 27, no. 3 (December 1973): 361–394; *Supplique et Pétition des Citoyens de Couleur des Îles & Colonies Françoises à l'Assemblée Nationale* (Paris: L'Imprimerie Nationale, 1789); *Pétition Nouvelle des Citoyens de Couleur des Îles Françoises* (Paris: Chez Desenne, 1791).

45. As one of hundreds of examples, consult Petition of Laurel Court subscribers (including Sarah Rhoads) to Common and Select Councils of Philadelphia, January 19, 1807, F "Petitions, Jan-Feb 1807," B1, Petitions of the Common Council, Collection 1002, HSP. New York's Common Council dated from the colonial period; see, for example, Jill Lepore, *New York Burning: Liberty, Slavery and Conspiracy in Eighteenth-Century Manhattan* (New York: Random House, 2006); "Memorial to the Supervisors of the City of New York" (1847), B1, F11 (Misc. Papers No. 1), Allen Papers, NYHS; Alan I. Marcus, "The Strange Career of Municipal Health Initiatives: Cincinnati and City Government in the Early Nineteenth Century," *Journal of Urban History* 7, no. 1 (November 1980): 3–29.

46. *Journal of Proceedings of the Right Worthy Grand Lodge of the Independent Order of Odd Fellows . . . from the Formation in 1821 . . .* (New York, 1844).

47. Robert J. Kaczorowski, "From Petitions for Gratuities to Claims for Damages: Personal Injuries and Railroads during the Industrialization of the United States," *American Journal of Legal History* 57 (2017): 261–315.

48. My treatment of Mexican institutions from 1808 to the 1830s depends heavily on the classic study of Nettie Lee Benson, *The Provincial Deputation in Mexico: Harbinger of Provincial Autonomy, Independence and Federalism* (Austin: University of Texas Press, 1992), 12–13, 79–83.

49. Jaime O. Rodríguez, "La Constitución de 1824 y la formación del Estado mexicano," *Historia Mexicana* 40, no. 3 (1991): 507–535; Timothy E. Anna, *Forging Mexico: 1821–1835* (Lincoln: University of Nebraska Press, 1998), 105–106.

50. Charles W. Macune Jr., "The Impact of Federalism on Mexican Church-State Relations, 1824–1835: The Case of the State of Mexico," *Americas* 40, no. 4 (April 1984): 505–529; Guy C. P. Thompson and David G. LaFrance, *Patriotism, Politics and Popular Liberalism in Nineteenth-Century Mexico: Juan Francisco Lucas and the Puebla Sierra* (Austin: University of Texas Press, 1999), 215–221; Frederick J. Shaw Jr., *Poverty and Politics in Mexico City, 1824–1854* (PhD thesis, University of Florida, 1975), 36; Petition of the town of Puebla to Deputy Pedraza, March 2, 1845, calling for restitution of the *Ley orgánica* of August 6, 1824 and the

State Constitution of February 14, 1827, Mariano Riva Palacio Collection, Benson-UT.

51. Manifiesto del estado de San Luis Potosí, July 10, 1834 (pronunciamiento de adhesión); Pronunciamiento federalista de San Luis Potosí, April 14, 1837 (armed pronunciamiento in opposition to centralizing reforms of 1833–1834); Representación del ejército y empleados de hacienda en Tehuacán (non-armed petition), August 20, 1842; all in Will Fowler et al., *The Pronunciamiento in Independent Mexico, 1821–1876*, digital archive, University of St. Andrews, accessed August 22, 2019, https://arts.st-andrews.ac.uk/pronunciamientos/index.php. On the petition-like character of pronunciamientos and the caution to be observed in comparing them to other documents, consult Will Fowler, "The Nineteenth-Century Practice of the Pronunciamiento and its Origins," in *Forceful Negotiations: The Origins of the Pronunciamiento in Nineteenth-Century Mexico,* ed. Fowler (Lincoln: University of Nebraska Press, 2010). See also Anna, *Forging Mexico,* 201, 217–218, who regards pronunciamientos generally as "armed petitions," and the careful study of Kerry McDonald, "The Experience of the Pronunciamiento in San Luis Potosí, 1821–1849" (PhD thesis, University of Saint Andrews, 2011). On Indigenous pronunciamientos, consult Michael T. Ducey, "Municipalities, Prefects and Pronunciamientos: Power and Mobilization in the Huasteca during the First Federal Republic," in Fowler, *Forceful Negotiations,* 97–101.

52. *Dictámen de la Comisión Especial de la Cámara de Diputados Encargada del Proyecto presentado por el señor Ramírez en la parte que arregla el derecho de petición* (México: Ignacio Cumplido, 1833).

4. PETITIONING IN THE SETTLER REPUBLIC: SPACE, CAPITAL, SOLDIERS

1. Sidney Aronson, *Status and Kinship Ties in the Higher Civil Service: Standards of Selection in the Administrations of John Adams, Thomas Jefferson and Andrew Jackson* (Cambridge, Mass.: Harvard University Press, 1964). On the limited nature of women's petitioning before the 1820s, consult Linda K. Kerber, *Women of the Republic: Intellect and Ideology in Revolutionary America* (Chapel Hill: University of North Carolina Press, 1980). From analyses of the Congressional Petitions Database at Harvard and the University of Pennsylvania, petitioners' self-references as "laborers" and "workmen" tripled in the decades during and after the War of 1812, compared to the years covering the founding to 1811. Even terms such as "carpenter," "chairmaker," and "apprentice"

greatly increased after the War of 1812; the term "mechanic" was used at about the same rate.

2. While settlement and colonial models suffused nineteenth-century political and economic development. I avoid the now-popular term "settler colonialism" here, mainly out of its origins in Australian scholarship. See Patrick Wolfe, "Settler Colonialism and the Elimination of the Native," *Journal of Genocide Research* 8, no. 4 (2006): 387–409. Saliha Belmessous's scholarship offers a nuanced alternative portrait: "D'un préjugé culturel à un préjugé racial: la politique indigène de la France au Canada" (PhD thesis, Lille, 1999); *Empire by Treaty: Negotiating European Expansion, 1600–1900* (Oxford: Oxford University Press, 2015). On the differences between Australian models and North American understandings, consult Lisa Ford, *Settler Sovereignty: Jurisdiction and Indigenous People in America and Australia, 1788–1836* (Cambridge, Mass.: Harvard University Press, 2010). On "settler republic" models, consult Bethel Saler, *The Settler's Empire: Colonialism and State Formation in America's Old Northwest* (Philadelphia: University of Pennsylvania Press, 2015).
3. Mary Johnson, "A Nineteenth-Century Mill Village: Virginius Island, 1800–1860," *West Virginia History* 54 (1995): 1–27; Alan I. Marcus, "The Strange Career of Municipal Health Initiatives: Cincinnati and City Government in the Early Nineteenth Century," *Journal of Urban History* 7, no. 1 (November 1980): 3–29.
4. Hendrik Hartog, *Public Property and Private Power: The Corporation of the City of New York in American Law, 1730–1870* (Chapel Hill: University of North Carolina Press, 1983), chaps. 1, 3, 7; Daniel Joseph Hulsebosch, *Constituting Empire: New York and the Transfomation of Constitutionalism in the Atlantic World, 1664–1830* (Chapel Hill: University of North Carolina Press, 2006); Laurence M. Hauptman, *Conspiracy of Interests: Iroquois Dispossession and the Rise of New York State* (Syracuse: Syracuse University Press, 1999); Brian Murphy, *Building the Empire State: Political Economy in the Early Republic* (Philadelphia: University of Pennsylvania Press, 2015).
5. On refugees, consult Richard White, the *Middle Ground: Indians, Empires and Republics in the Great Lakes Region, 1650–1815* (Cambridge: Cambridge University Press), chaps. 1–2; Alan Taylor, *Divided Ground: Indians, Settlers, and the Northern Borderland of the American Revolution* (New York: Vintage, 2006); Hauptman, *Conspiracy of Interests,* 251 (Oneida holdings); Karim M. Tiro, *The People of the Standing Stone: The Oneida Nation from the Revolution through the Era of Removal* (Amherst: University of Massachusetts Press, 2011); Francis Jennings, *The Ambiguous Iroquois Empire* (New York: Norton, 1984);

Daniel K. Richter, *The Ordeal of the Longhouse: The People of the Iroquois League in the Era of European Colonization* (Chapel Hill: University of North Carolina Press, 1992); Jon Parmenter, *The Edge of the Woods: Iroquoia, 1534–1701* (East Lansing: Michigan State University Press, 2010).

6. Hauptman, *Conspiracy of Interests,* chap. 2; Tiro, *People of the Standing Stone,* 66.
7. Hauptman, *Conspiracy of Interests,* 29–31, 63, 67, 79–81; Tiro, *People of the Standing Stone,* 68–69, 96.
8. Hauptman, *Conspiracy of Interests,* 61–64, 114–115; Tiro, *People of the Standing Stone,* 129; Ogden to Monroe, February 17, 1818, and September 15, 1819, Letters Received by the War Department, RG 107, NARA; draft memorial is reprinted in Papers of David A. Ogden, Ogden Family Papers, WCL.
9. Murphy, *Building the Empire State,* chap. 1, esp. 29–41, 43.
10. Hamilton, "Outline of a Charter for the Bank of New-York" (February 23 to March 15, 1784) and "Constitution of the Bank of New-York," *The Papers of Alexander Hamilton Digital Edition,* ed. Harold C. Syrett (Charlottesville: University of Virginia Press, 2011) (hereafter *PAH-DE*); Murphy, *Building the Empire State,* 44 (Hamilton's probable contributions to the BNY constitution); *JSSNY* 7th Session (1784), 63; Hamilton, "Petition to the New York Legislature," February 4, 1784; Hamilton to John B. Church, March 10, 1784; *PAH-DE.*
11. Gregory S. Hunter, "The Manhattan Company: Managing a Multi-Unit Corporation in New York, 1799–1842" (PhD diss., New York University, 1989), 8–9; Hartog, *Public Property and Private Power,* pt. 2; Murphy, *Building the Empire State,* 27.
12. *JASNY* 7th Session, March 12, 1784, 69 (Van Zandt petition). BNY backers sent another petition for incorporation on February 10, 1785. Staughton Lynd, "The Revolution and the Common Man: Farm Tenants and Artisans in New York Politics" (PhD diss., Columbia University, 1962), 209–210; Robert Eric Wright, *Origins of Commercial Banking in America, 1750–1800* (New York: Rowman & Littlefield, 2001), 108n156; Murphy, *Building the Empire State,* 45.
13. Hamilton would draw on New York's thriving newspaper sector to advance his argument against a national bill of rights; *Federalist,* no. 84, in Hamilton, John Jay, and James Madison, *The Federalist,* ed. Robert Scigliano (New York: Random House, 2000), 546–556; Henry W. Domett, *A History of the Bank of New York, 1784–1884* (New York: G. P. Putnam's Sons, 1884), 33–36 (petitions of 1789 and 1970).
14. Murphy, *Building the Empire State,* 28.

15. Robert E. Wright, "Artisans, Banks, Credit and the Election of 1800," *Pennsylvania Magazine of History and Biography* 122, no. 3 (July 1998): 211–239; Hunter, "Manhattan Company"; Beatrice G. Rubens, "Burr, Hamilton and the Manhattan Company. Part I: Launching a Bank," *Political Science Quarterly* 73, no. 1 (March 1958): 100–125; Murphy, *Building the Empire State,* 77–79.
16. On the overlap of the company's subscribers and petitioners, see Rubens, "Burr, Hamilton and the Manhattan Company," 104–105n15), 108–110; Murphy, *Building the Empire State,* 87, 101–102, 252n97.
17. *JASNY,* 23rd Session (1800), 108 (petition introduction), 211 (committee rejection); Rubens, "Burr, Hamilton and the Manhattan Company," 115–117; Murphy, *Building the Empire State,* 92–102, 104, 108–109.
18. Albert Gallatin, *Report of the Secretary of the Treasury; on the Subject of Public Roads and Canals made in pursuance of a Resolution of the Senate, of March 2, 1807* (Washington, D.C., 1808), 5–6, 18–19; Murphy, *Building the Empire State,* 104.
19. *JASNY* 34th Session (February 8, 1811), 27 (Dox petition), 32 (Company remonstrance), 53–55 (committee report and details on the Bridge history); Walt Gable, "Cayuga bridges eased movement west," *Finger Lakes Times,* July 27, 2014. Dox was a director of the proposed Western District Bank, whose directors would also include Augustus Seymour Porter and for which the assembly would vote a charter in the same session (*JASNY,* March 11, 1811, 238), but which the Senate would kill (*JSSNY,* 34th Session, March 12, 1811). Murphy, *Building the Empire State,* 103.
20. *JASNY* 35th Session (June 5, 1812), 168–69; *JSSNY* (June 15, 1812), 274; John W. Wells, *Cayuga Bridge* (Ithaca: DeWitt Historical Society of Tompkins County, 1966), 7–8.
21. Murphy, *Building the Empire State,* Figure 5, 138.
22. George Rogers Taylor, *The Transportation Revolution, 1815–1860* (New York: Rinehart, 1951); Noble W. Whitford, *History of the Canal System of the State of New York: Together with Brief Histories of the Canals of the United States and Canada* (Albany: State Engineer and Surveyor, 1906).
23. Thomas H. Cox, Gibbons v. Ogden, *Law, and Society in the Early Republic* (Athens: Ohio University Press, 2009), chaps. 3–4, esp. 44–46; Murphy, *Building the Empire State,* 110–113, 131–33, 142 (Ogden petition), 146–147, 153–154, 199n20; Johnson, *River of Dark Dreams,* chap. 3; John D. Ward, "Steamboat Controversy between New York and New Jersey, 1811 to 1824," *Proceedings of the New Jersey Historical Society* (1864), 117–134, esp. 121–123, 124; *Memorial & Petition of Robert Fulton and Edward P. Livingston in Behalf of Themselves and the Heirs of the late Robert R. Livingston* (Albany, 1814); *Report of the*

Committee to Whom was Referred the Memorial of Aaron Ogden, A Citizen of the State of New Jersey (Trenton, 1814).

24. Cox, Gibbons v. Ogden, chap. 7, esp. 131–132; Murphy, *Building the Empire State,* 149–154.
25. Gibbons v. Ogden, 22 U.S. 1 (March 2, 1824), 11.
26. *Gibbons,* 22 U.S. 1 at 185.
27. Cox, Gibbons v. Ogden, chaps. 6 and 7, esp. 112–126; Murphy, *Building the Empire State,* 150–152; *Gibbons,* 22 U.S. 1 at 55 (petitioning and state sovereignty over prohibition of economic acts).
28. Ronald E. Shaw, *Erie Water West: A History of the Erie Canal, 1792–1854* (Lexington: University Press of Kentucky, 1966), chaps. 1, 2, esp. 10–11, 32–33; Francois Furstenburg, "The Significance of the Trans-Appalachian Frontier in Atlantic History," *American Historical Review* 113, no. 3 (June 2008): 647–677; John Lauritz Larson, *Internal Improvement: National Public Works and the Promise of Popular Government in the Early United States* (Chapel Hill: University of North Carolina Press, 2001); John Wallis and Barry R. Weingast, "Equilibrium Impotence: Why the States and Not the American National Government Financed Economic Development in the Antebellum Era" (NBER Working Paper No, 11397, June 2005); Shaw, *Erie Water West,* 14–17, 27 (canal's God-furnished advantages).
29. Gallatin, *Report of the Secretary of the Treasury; on the Subject of Public Roads and Canals* (Washington, 1808); Shaw, *Erie Water West,* 35; Murphy, *Building the Empire State,* 163–170.
30. Shaw, *Erie Water West,* chap. 3, esp. 38–41, 53–54; Murphy, *Building the Empire State,* 170–182.
31. DeWitt Clinton, "Memorial from Inhabitants of New York on Canal between the Hudson River and Lake Erie," Series A4682–99, box 20, folder A; New York (State), Legislature, Assembly, "Files related to Revolutionary War claims and other subjects, ca. 1777–1830," NYSA. The petition has now been digitally imaged. The printed petition appears in *Laws of the State of New York, in relation to the Erie and Champlain Canals* (Albany, 1825), 122–141; DeWitt Clinton, *Memoir of DeWitt Clinton* (New York: New Library Press, 1829), 103–104.
32. *Laws of the State of New York, in relation to the Erie and Champlain Canals,* 119–122 (summary of townships presenting petitions); Charles Z. Lincoln, *The Constitutional History of the State of New York,* vol. 1, *1609–1822* (Rochester: Lawyers Co-operative, 1905), 705–706; Murphy, *Building the Empire State,* 184 (canal memorial as "a petition intended to identify, recruit, and mobilize constituents for the canal); also 183–186, 192n59.

33. Murphy, *Building the Empire State,* 192–194, 202–206.
34. William M. Holland, *The Life and Political Opinions of Martin Van Buren, Vice President of the United States* (Hartford: Belknap and Hamersley, 1836), 115.
35. Holland, *Life and Political Opinions,* 115.
36. Murphy, *Building the Empire State,* 202–206.
37. Shaw, *Erie Water West,* 58–60, citing *Memoir of DeWitt Clinton,* 426–427.
38. *Report of the Canal Commissioners to whom was referred the petition of William Brayton and others, praying for a re-appraisal [of] damages done to their lands, by the construction of the Champlain canal,* in assembly, March 12, 1829.
39. Gregory Ablavsky, *Federal Ground: Sovereignty, Property, and Law in the U.S. Territories, 1783–1802* (Oxford: Oxford University Press, forthcoming); Saler, *Settler's Empire,* chaps. 1–3; Paul Frymer, *Building an American Empire: The Era of Political and Territorial Expansion* (Princeton, N.J.: Princeton University Press, 2017).
40. Charles H. Haskins, *The Yazoo Land Companies* (New York: Knickerbocker Press, 1891), 4–5, 13–14, 18–19, 31–32; Charles F. Hobson, *The Great Yazoo Lands Sale: The Case of* Fletcher v. Peck (Lawrence: University Press of Kansas, 2016), 26–27.
41. Abraham Bishop, *Georgia Speculation Unveiled: In Two Numbers* (Hartford: Elisha Babcock, 1797), 3–4; "Petition of the Tennessee Company to the General Assembly of the State of Georgia" (1791) and "Memorial of Alexander Moultrie, etc., to the . . . senate of Georgia" (1791), box 83, folder 31, Telamon Cuyler Papers, HL-UGA; Hobson, *Great Yazoo Lands Sale,* 27–29.
42. Bishop, *Georgia Speculation Unveiled,* 5; Hobson, *Great Yazoo Lands Sale,* 29–35, 37. The actual size of the lands included in the sale was 35 million acres.
43. Haskins, *Yazoo Land Companies,* 26; George R. Lamplugh, *Politics on the Periphery: Factions and Parties in Georgia, 1783–1806* (Wilmington: University of Delaware Press, 1986), 152; Hobson, *Great Yazoo Lands Sale,* 43–46.
44. See, for example, "Petition of Citizens of the County of Chatman to the honorable the President and the Honorable the Members of the Convention of the State of Georgia," 1796; Yazoo Land Petitions, box 83 (Oversize Collection), Telamon Cuyler Collection (MS 1170), HL-UGA.
45. County-level totals tabulated by an unnamed clerk for the sample retained at the Yazoo Land Petitions group, Telamon Cuyler Collection, HL-UGA: Burke, 715 subscribers; Chatham, 196; Effingham, 123; Elbert, 101;

Oglethorpe, 371; Washington, 201. *Historical Collections of the Joseph Habersham Chapter, Daughters of the American Revolution*, vol. 2 (Atlanta: Blosser printing, 1902), 27 (Burke County veterans). Similar patterns emerge in signatures from Washington County; Robert Scott Davis, "Georgians Protest the Yazoo Land Fraud, 1795," *Georgia Genealogical Magazine* 22, no. 2–3 (1993): 95. The large numbers from Burke County, the Emanuel family's presence on these petitions, and David Emanuel's role in the rescission process seem to suggest a westward shift in the locus of anti-aristocratic republicanism in the 1790s (compare Lamplugh, *Politics on the Periphery*, 69–71, and his emphasis on other lowcountry counties).

46. Bishop, *Georgia Speculation Unveiled*, 18; *Sundry Papers, in Relation to Claims, Commonly Called the Yazoo Claims* (Washington, 1809), 22–23 (petitions). End quote from rescinding statute, February 13, 1796; *Sundry Papers*, 14, 22. Hobson, *Great Yazoo Lands Sale*, 41–42, 49–50, 65, 75–76.
47. Denison's claims on Georgia were considerable; see Georgia land deeds, vol. 9, North American Land Company Records, HSP. See also "Memorandum of James Wilson, Esq.," September 24, 1803, James Wilson Yazoo land records, MS 1402, HL-UGA. Hobson, *Great Yazoo Lands Sale*, 56–61.
48. On the cession of 1802, see "Articles of Agreement, &c," in *Sundry Documents*, 58–62; *Report of the Committee to Whom were Referred . . . the Memorials of Alexander Moultrie . . . in Behalf of Himself and Others, and of the Virginia Yazoo Company* (Washington, 1804); *Remarks, Occasioned by the View Taken of the Claims of 1789, in a Memorial to Congress of the Agents of the New England Mississippi Land Company, With a Vindication of their title at Law* (Washington, 1805); U.S. Congress, Committee on Claims, *Report, from the Committee of Claims, to whom were referred the representation and memorials of sundry citizens of Massachusetts, purchasers . . .* (Washington, 1805); *Register of Debates*, Senate, 18th Cong., 2nd Sess., Ser. 1 (January 1825–3 March 1829), 487 (debate and Van Buren remarks, February 7, 1825).
49. Michael Witgen, *An Infinity of Nations: How the Native New World Shaped Early North America* (Philadelphia: University of Pennsylvania Press, 2011); Saler, *Settler's Empire*, chaps. 1–3.
50. White, *Middle Ground*, 516–523; Witgen, *Infinity of Nations;* Arthur Spirling, "U.S. Treaty Making with American Indians: Institutional Change and Relative Power, 1784–1911," *American Journal of Political Science* 56, no. 1 (2012): 84–97.

51. To His Excellency Gov. Harrison, Vincennes, Indiana Territory, August 6, 1810, box 1, folder 17, Harrison Papers, IHS; Harrison (endorsing petition) to Secretary of War, August 7, 1810, in Logan Esarey, ed., *Messages and Letters of William Henry Harrison* Volume I (Indianapolis: Indiana Historical Commission, 1922), 455–457.
52. Petition of Samuel T. Scott and others to Madison, July 31, 1811, in Esarey, *Messages and Letters*, 538–540.
53. "To James Madison from the Inhabitants of Knox County, Indiana Territory," July 31, 1811, *ASP-IA* (Washington, 1832), 4:802.
54. Adam Jortner, *The Gods of Prophetstown: The Battle of Tippecanoe and the Holy War for the American Frontier* (Oxford: Oxford University Press, 2012), 11, 183.
55. Resolutions of inhabitants of the county of St. Clair, 1811; memorial of the inhabitants of St. Clair County to Madison, December 1811; *ASP-IA*, 4:797, 803–804. On Sibley's election, overseen by Governor Lewis Cass, see Cass to Sibley, November 4, 1820, Solomon Sibley Papers, BHC-DPL; Cass to Sibley, November 4, 1820, box 6, Lewis Cass Papers, BHC-DPL.
56. Memorial of the Legislature of the Indiana Territory to the Senate and House of Representatives, September 10, 1814, box 2, folder 13, Harrison Papers, IHS; Memorial of Indiana legislature requesting purchase of Indian lands, presented in Waller Taylor to James Monroe, February 18, 1818, and James Noble (writing from the Senate Chamber) to Monroe, February 19, 1818, Letters Received by the War Department, RG 107, NARA.
57. *Report of the Joint Select Committee, Appointed by the Legislature of North Carolina to Memorialize Congress upon the Subject of The Cherokee Lands* (Raleigh: Lawrence and Leman, 1827); *ASP*, 32:393–394; considered by the House Committee on Indian Affairs; HR20A-D10.1, RG 233, NARA; Arkansas territorial memorial of 1823, *TP*, 19:671. Georgia legislative memorial of 1823: Thomas Stocks and David Adams to James Monroe, December 18 & December 20, 1823, Letters Received (copy, enclosed in George M. Troup to John Quincy Adams, 13 April 1825), Adams Family Papers, MHS; William W. Winn, *The Triumph of the Ecunnau-Nuxulgee: Land Speculators, George M. Troup, State Rights, and the Removal of the Creek Indians from Georgia and Alabama, 1825–38* (Macon: Mercer University Press, 2015).
58. *Ohio Archaeology and History Society Publications* 4:190, 199–230, esp. 228–229.
59. H. Dora Stecker, "Constructing a Navigation System in the West," *Ohio Archaeology and Historical Society Publications* 22 (January 1913):

18–25; Cox, Gibbons v. Ogden, 41–43; Charles W. Dahlinger, "The New Orleans, Being a Critical Account of the Beginning of Steamboat Navigation on the Western Rivers of the United States," *Pittsburg Legal Journal* 59, no. 42 (October 1911): 570–591; Alfred R. Maass, "The Right of Unrestricted Navigation on the Mississippi, 1812–1818," *American Neptune* 60 (2000): 49–59.

60. El Gobernador Interino de Californias, "Plan de Pitic," Año de 1794, Californias, in AGN, Tierras, vol. 2773, exp. 22, published in Guillermo Margadant S, "El Plan de Pitic," *Boletín Mexicano de Derecho Comparado* 21, no. 62 (May 1988): 699–715; Alexander de Humboldt, *Political Essay on the Kingdom of New Spain* (1814), 1:278–282; Michael C. Meyer, *Water in the Hispanic Southwest: A Social and Legal History, 1550–1850* (Tucson: University of Arizona Press, 1996), 30–37; José A. Rivera, *Acequia Culture: Water, Land and Community in the Southwest* (Albuquerque: University of New Mexico Press, 1998), 6–7.

61. "Haciéndose hallado en muchas marizcados contra los Indios Barbaros que hostilizan esta Provincia" and "alcanzando su espíritu intrépido a dar muerte par su propio brazo a quatro de los Barbaros Agresores," Capitan Joaquin Vidal de Lorca (writing of Sargento Pedro Garcia) to Felix Calleja, June 10, 1808 (my translations); Calleja approval of request (propuesta), August 18, 1808, AGN, Provincias Internas, Tomo 253 (Provincias Internas de Oriente y Occidente 1808–1817), 2–4; Capitan Joseph Miguel Espriella to Calleja, requesting *licencia absoluta,* February 8, 1808; Calleja response, March 24, 1808, AGN, Provincias Internas, Tomo 253, 9–12; Ignacio de Morelos, request for retirement with right of *fuero militar,* to Calleja, May 5, 1806, August 29, 1807, AGN, Provincias Internas, Tomo 257, 25–29; Joseph Florencio Barragan letters to Calleja, September 14, 1805, to December 21, 1805, AGN, Provincias Internas, Tomo 257, 222–230.

62. On *genízaros*, consult Brooks, *Captives and Cousins,* 121–142; Malcolm Ebright and Rick Hendricks, *The Witches of Abiquiu: The Governor, the Priest, the Genízaro Indians and the Devil* (Albuquerque: University of New Mexico Press, 2006). Land grant petitions featuring *genízaro* names were common in the early nineteenth century: San Miguel del Vado (1803), San José del Vado (1803), Mora (1818), and Anton Chico (1822); Brooks, *Captives and Cousins,* 198, 210.

63. Eloisa L. Bergere, "Brief for the Petitioner" (*Bergere v. United States*), Bergere Family Papers, NMSRCA; Rivera, *Acequia Culture,* 8–12; Malcolm Ebright, *Land Grants and Lawsuits in Northern New Mexico* (Albuquerque: University of New Mexico Press, 2008), 23–24, 33, 64–65; John R. Van Ness and Christine Van Ness, eds., *Spanish and Mexican*

Land Grants in New Mexico and Colorado (Santa Fe: Sunflower, 1980), 22–39.

64. The basic laws governing land grants were summarized in the *Recopilación de Leyes de los Reynos de las Indias, Las Siete Partidas,* book 4, title 3, law 24 (describing the role of the *poblador principal*), and the Mexican Colonization Law of 1824 and its concomitant Regulations of 1828; Malcolm Ebright, *The Tierra Amarilla Grant: A History of Chicanery* (Santa Fe: Center for Land Grant Studies, 1993), 4–6; David L. Caffey, *Chasing the Santa Fe Ring: Power and Privilege in Territorial New Mexico* (Albuquerque: University of New Mexico Press, 2014), 114.
65. Brooks, *Captives and Cousins,* 220–229, 250–257, 260–261; Center for Land Grant Studies, "The Abiquiu Genizaro Land Grant," New Mexico Office of the State Historian (Santa Fe, 2010); Ebright, *Tierra Amarilla Grant,* 6–10; Eloisa L. Bergere, "Brief for the Petitioner" (*Bergere v. United States*), Bergere Family Papers, NMSRCA.
66. Ebright, *Tierra Amarilla Grant,* 6–10.
67. Melgares, grant of land to Baca, signed September 12, 1819, copy in Bergere Family Papers, NMSRCA, cited in parts by Justice Peckham in Bergere v. United States, 168 U.S. 66 (1897), 71–72. Melgares served from 1818 to 1822, and his status appears to have been provisional, a fact that may have heightened land petitioning at the time. Eloisa L. Bergere, "Brief for the Petitioner" (*Bergere v. United States*), Bergere Family Papers, NMSRCA; Mark Thompson, "Para Nada! War (and Litigation) over the Baca and Sandoval Land Grants," *New Mexico State Bar Bulletin,* September 10, 2007. Peckham opinions in *Bergere,* 168 U.S. 66, and Whitney v. United States, 181 U.S. 104 (1901); Michael Miller, "Land Violence and Death: The Bartolome Baca Grant" (New Mexico Office of the State Historian, Santa Fe, 2010).
68. The *alcalde* supervising the Baca land grant of 1819 in New Mexico, José Garcia de la Mora, was simultaneously the largest petitioner and investor in Abiquiu pueblo lands. Miller, "Land, Violence and Death"; Center for Land Grant Studies, "Abiquiu Genizaro Land Grant"; Howard Roberts Lamar, *The Far Southwest, 1846–1912: A Territorial History* (Albuquerque: University of New Mexico Press, 2000), 35, 44; Denise Damico, "'*El Agua es la Vida*' (Water Is Life): Water Conflict and Conquest in Nineteenth-Century New Mexico" (PhD diss., Brandeis University, 2008)," chap. 2 (on the Martínez family, 37–38); E. A. Mares, "The Many Faces of Padre Antonio José Martínez: A Historiographic Essay," in Mares et al., *Padre Martínez: New Perspectives from Taos* (Taos: Millicent Rogers Museum, 1988), 18–47; Brooks, *Captives and Cousins,* 220–221, 228–229; Adolfo Steen, petition for land grant, 1832–1833, ID 1969–027,

box 1, folder 31; and Stephen Nicholson, petition for land and for citizenship, 1835–1836, box 1, folder 36, ID 1969–027, Mexico Documents Collection, 1570–1913, UH; Frymer, *Building an American Empire,* 172–174, 184–187. On Mexican slavery debates and petitions, see Chapter 6.

69. On Canadian institutions, see Chapter 7.

5. FIRST NATIONS, FIRST WAVE PETITIONERS

1. John Ross, "The Contrast" [date unclear but text is accompanied by a clerical marking suggesting 1835]; John Ross Papers, TLSA.
2. Ross, "The Contrast."
3. Ross, "The Contrast."
4. Ross, "The Contrast"; Ross (writing at Red Clay) to Cherokee Nation, August 15, 1837; John Ross Papers, TLSA.
5. Ross, "The Contrast."
6. On the question of remaining, I consciously follow the Anishinaabe writer Gerald Vizenor, *Survivance: Narratives of Native Presence* (Lincoln: University of Nebraska Press, 2008), esp. chap. 1.
7. Maxime Gohier, *La Pratique Pétitionnaire des Amérindiens de la Vallée Saint-Laurent sous le Régime Britannique: Pouvoir, Représentation et Légitimité* (1760–1860) (PhD thesis, Université de Québec à Montréal, 2013); Gregory Evans Dowd, "Indigenous Peoples without the Republic," *Journal of American History* 104, no. 1 (June 2017): 19–41.
8. Lisa Brooks, *Our Beloved Kin: A New History of King Philip's War* (New Haven, Conn.: Yale University Press, 2018); Gordon Day, *The Identity of the Saint Francis Indians* (Ottawa: National Museums of Canada, 1981), 104–105, 110–111. Requisition lists place the number of Natives receiving gifts in 1828 at 348. "Requisition for the Annual Presents to be given to 108 Men, 123 Women and 123 Children of the Abenaqui Indians of St. Francis for the year 1828," LAC RG10, vol. 483, 174509, bob. C-13338.
9. Petition of Abenaki chiefs, February 7, 1802; Pétition des Abénaquis de Saint-François à Robert Hunter, December 9, 1799, in Gohier, *La Pratique Pétitionnaire,* 228, 316. Lenior and Annance had combined to make claims on settled lands a week earlier. Petition of Abenaki chiefs, February 1, 1802, LAC, RG10, vol. 486, 3913, bob. C-13338. On invocations of nation, see Pétition de Thomas Martin ("première chef des Hurons") à Robert Mills [1803?], LAC, RG10, vol. 486, 3924, bob. C-13338; "Pétition des Chefs des trois Nations Sauvages, les Abénaquis, les Micmacs et les Malécites à James Kempt, July 9, 1830, LAC, RG10, vol. 25, 26202–26204, bob. C-11006; Jean Barman, *Abenaki Daring: The*

Life and Writings of Noel Annance, 1792–1869 (Montréal: McGill-Queen's University Press, 2016), 69–72 (petition and Long Island), 235–238; Lisa Brooks, The *Common Pot: The Recovery of Native Space in the Northeast* (Minneapolis: University of Minnesota Press, 2008), 136–139.

10. Barman, *Abenaki Daring*, 68–71, 104 (Noel Annance as Captain during War); L. Homfray Irving, *Canadian Military Institute: Officers of the British Forces in Canada during the War of 1812–1815* (Toronto: Canadian Military Institute, 1908), 218–219; Day, *Identity*, 71 (war service).
11. "Pétition des Abénakis et Sokokis du Village de St. François" to Plessis, July 1, 1819, BANQ-Montréal, E4, S1, SS1, D178. Signatories appear in Day, *Identity*, 72 (Figure 1).
12. *JCABC* 1820–1821, 142 (assembly vote on appropriation bill).
13. Pétition des Abénaquis de Saint-François à John Johnson, December 14, 1824, BAC, RG10, vol. 16, 12886–12891, bob. C-11003; Gohier, *La Pratique Pétitionnaire*, 417–418; Philippe Charland, *Les Abénakis d'Odanak* (Montréal: Éditions du Lévrier, 1964), 186–192, 194, 221.
14. I acknowledge Lisa Brooks (Mississquoi Abenaki) for this point.
15. Gerald Taiaiake Alfred, *To Right Certain Wrongs: A Report on Research into Lands Known as the Seigniory of Sault St. Louis* (Kahnawake: Kahnawake Seigneury Office, 1995), 40, 153–154; Gerald Taiaiake Alfred, *Heeding the Voices of Our Ancestors: Kahnawake Mohawk Politics and the Rise of Native Nationalism* (Oxford: Oxford University Press, 1995); Audra Simpson, *Mohawk Interruptus: Political Life across the Borders of Settler States* (Durham, N.C.: Duke University Press, 2014), 39. On voting rights, see Petition of Augustin Cuviller to the Legislative Assembly of Lower Canada, February 9, 1810, *JCABC* 1810, 89–101; Daniel Rueck, *Enclosing the Mohawk Commons: A History of Use Rights, Landownership and Boundary-Making in Kahnawá:ke Mohawk Territory* (PhD diss., McGill University, 2013).
16. Plaintes contre M. Rinfret par quelques femmes de la confrérie de la Sainte-Famille du Sault St. Louis à Joseph-Octave Plessis, July 29, 1809, in Marie Lise Vien, "'Un mélange aussi redouté qu'il est à craindre': Race, genre et conflit identitaire à Kahnawake, 1810–1851" (master's thesis, UQAM, 2013), 78–79.
17. Pétition des guerriers et femmes du Sault St. Louis à Joseph Fleury Deschambault, October 1816, in Vien, "Un mélange," 98.
18. In Gohier, *La pratique pétitionnaire*, 375 (see also 360–361, 373–374 on women's participation in councils).
19. Kateri Tekakwitha was canonized by the Roman Catholic Church in 2012. Nancy Shoemaker, "Kateri Tekakwitha's Tortuous Path to Sainthood," in *Negotiators of Change: Historical Perspectives on Native American Women*, ed. Nancy Shoemaker (New York: Routledge, 1995), 67.

20. Pauline Turner Strong, "Feminist Theory and the Invasion of the Heart in North America," *Ethnohistory* 43, no. 4 (1996): 694.
21. Gohier, *La pratique pétitionnaire,* 354–355.
22. Mathieu Chaurette, "L'opposition des missionnaires catholiques à la scolarisation des Autochtones au Bas-Canada, 1826–1845," *Revue d'histoire de l'Amérique française* 65, no. 4 (2012): 482–485, 490–493.
23. Louis Garoniatsigowa et al., à Plessis, November 3, 1825 (my translation).
24. Mathieu Sossoyan, *The Kahnawake Iroquois and the Lower-Canadian Rebellions, 1837–1838* (master's thesis, McGill University, 1999), 27 (see also 28, 40).
25. Sossoyan, *Kahnawake Iroquois,* 84 (intermarriage and its concomitant tensions), 82–91 (Lorimier and the Kahnawakehro:non); Pétition des guerriers et femmes du Sault SI-Louis à Joseph Fleury Deschambault, October 1816, BAC, RG10, vol. 12, 10851–10853 (bob. C-11001), in Vien, "Un Melange Aussi Redouté," 97–98.
26. Chefs et habitants de Kahnawake à Lord Gosford, September 21, 1835 (my translation), in Sossoyan, *Kahnawake Iroquois,* 93.
27. Pétition des Iroquois du Sault St. Louis à Jean-Jacques Lartigue, June 21, 1835, BAC, RG10, vol. 90, 36283–36286, bob. C-11467.
28. Sossoyan, *Kahnawake Iroquois,* 103–104.
29. Daniel R. Mandell, *Tribe, Race, History: Native Americans in Southern New England, 1780–1880* (Baltimore: Johns Hopkins University Press, 2008), chap. 3, esp. 72–91.
30. Mandell, *Tribe, Race, History,* 76–81.
31. Passed acts, 1775–1997 (SC1-229), St. 1807, c. 109, MAC. The petition has been digitized and is part of the Digital Archive of Native American Petitions in Massachusetts, https://iiif.lib.harvard.edu/manifests/view/drs:48612875$1i.
32. Passed acts, 1775–1997 (SC1-229), St. 1807, c. 109, MAC.
33. Mandell, *Tribe, Race, History,* 81–82.
34. Counterpetition at Passed acts, 1775–1997 (SC1-229), St. 1807, c. 109, MAC; digitized at https://iiif.lib.harvard.edu/manifests/view/drs:48612875$9i; Mandell, *Tribe, Race, History,* 81–82.
35. Mandell, *Tribe, Race, History,* 91. See the end of this chapter for the Mashpee Revolt.
36. See, for instance, Petition of Chippewas of Colborne on the River Thames (Credit Mission) to Lieutenant-Governor of Upper Canada, August 20, 1836, CHM, ICHi-31906; Gohier, *La pratique pétitionnaire,* 429–436; Cary Miller, *Ogimaag: Anishinaabe Leadership, 1760–1845* (Lincoln: University of Nebraska Press, 2010).
37. Daniel Carpenter, "On the Origins of the Administrative Petition: Innovations in Nineteenth-Century North America," in *Administrative*

Law from the Inside Out: Themes in the Work of Jerry L. Mashaw, ed. Nicholas Parrillo (New York: Cambridge University Press, 2017); Gohier, *La pratique petitionnaire,* 320.

38. Roland Viau, *Femmes de personne: sexe, genres et pouvoirs en Iroquoisie* (Montréal: Éditions du Boréal, 2000), 102; Deborah Doxtator, What Happened to the Iroquois Clans? A Study of Clans in Three Nineteenth-Century Rotinonhsyonni Communities (PhD thesis, University of Western Ontario, 1996), 70.
39. *JCABC* 1820–1821, 94, 104–105, 114–115; Gohier, *La pratique pétitionnaire,* 200 (newspapers publishing petitions), 222–226 (educated indigenous elite), 231–232 (missionaries and petitions).
40. Theda Perdue, "The Legacy of Indian Removal," *Journal of Southern History* 78, no. 1 (February 2012): 3–36; Frymer, *Building an American Empire;* Claudio Saunt, *Unworthy Republic: The Dispossession of Native Americans and the Road to Indian Territory* (New York: Norton, 2020), chaps. 1, 3–5; Theda Perdue and Michael D. Green, *The Cherokee Nation and the Trail of Tears* (New York: Penguin, 2007); Jeffrey Ostler, *Surviving Genocide: Native Nations and the United States from the American Revolution to Bleeding Kansas* (New Haven, Conn.: Yale University Press, 2019), chaps. 8–10; Laurence M. Hauptman, *Conspiracy of Interests: Iroquois Dispossession and the Rise of New York State* (Syracuse: Syracuse University Press, 1999); Michael Witgen, *An Infinity of Nations: How the Native New World Shaped Early North America* (Philadelphia: University of Pennsylvania Press, 2011).
41. Karim M. Tiro, *The People of the Standing Stone: the Oneida Nation from the Revolution Through the Era of Removal* (Amherst: University of Massachusetts Press, 2011), chap. 4, esp. 84, 92–95, 96–102 (1795 treaty); Brooks, *The Common Pot,* 137 (New Stockbridge as a center of Native New England identity); David J. Silverman, *Red Brethren: The Brothertown and Stockbridge Indians and the Problem of Race in Early America* (Ithaca: Cornell University Press, 2010), 34–37, 94–95 (Native New England link with Oneida); Tiro, *People of the Standing Stone,* 82, 112–114 (1805 partition), 114–118 (differences between the parties), 119–120 (warring petitions); Oneida petition to Taylor, February 27, 1806 (two council fires), Ayer MS 658, f. 3, Newberry.
42. Oneida (Christian Party) petition to NYS Legislature, February 7, 1814, Ayer MS 658, f. 4, Newberry; Pagan Party deputation, February 19, 1814, Ayer MS 658, f. 5, Newberry; Tiro, *People of the Standing Stone,* 135.
43. Stockbridge Tribe of Indians to New York, November 16, 1847, Ayer MS 836, f. 11, Newberry; *JHRUS,* 13th Congress, 32 (January 17, 1820), 33 (January 18, 1820); Silverman, *Red Brethren,* 160–163, 167–168, 172–174, chaps. 8–9; Tiro, *People,* 135, 148–149, 152–153.

44. Hauptman, *Conspiracy of Interests,* 92, 97, 128 (Porter frustration).
45. Richard White, *Middle Ground: Indians, Empires and Republics in the Great Lakes Region, 1650–1815* (Cambridge: Cambridge University Press), chap. 11; Bethel Saler, *The Settler's Empire: Colonialism and State Formation in America's Old Northwest* (Philadelphia: University of Pennsylvania Press, 2015), 80; Hauptman, *Conspiracy of Interests,* 49–50; John Sugden, *Tecumseh: A Life* (New York: Henry Holt, 1999).
46. Granville Ganter, *The Collected Speeches of Sagoyewatha, or Red Jacket* (Syracuse: Syracuse University Press, 2006), 162–163, 177, 183–184; Alyssa Mount Pleasant, "After the Whirlwind: Maintaining a Haudenosaunee Place at Buffalo Creek, 1780–1825" (PhD thesis, Cornell University, 2007).
47. Ganter, *Collected Speeches,* 192; Daniel Carpenter, "On the Origins of the Administrative Petition: Innovations in Nineteenth-Century Native America," in Nicholas Parrillo, ed., *Administrative Law from the Inside Out: Essays on Themes in the Work of Jerry L. Mashaw* (Cambridge: Cambridge University Press, 2017), 349–372; Maggie Blackhawk, "Federal Indian Law as Paradigm within Public Law," *Harvard Law Review* 132, no. 7 (May 2019): 1811.
48. Cass to Calhoun, December 16, 1820, box 6, Lewis Cass Papers, BHC-DPL.
49. Cass to Calhoun, December 16, 1820.
50. Cass to Solomon Sibley, January 26, 1822, box 6, Lewis Cass Papers, BHC-DPL. Ganter, *Collected Speeches,* 192 (approaching Indian agent as protocol); Carpenter, "Emergence of the Administrative Petition"; Blackhawk, "Federal Indian Law," 1811.
51. Colin G. Calloway, *Pen and Ink Witchcraft: Treaties and Treaty Making in American Indian History* (Oxford: Oxford University Press, 2013), 7, 31–33, 43–48 (council fire oration), 70.
52. Ganter, *Collected Speeches,* 192–195.
53. Petition for Protection to Governor Clinton, February 14, 1818, in Ganter, *Collected Speeches of Sagoyewatha,* 196–197 (including signatures of Red Jacket [signing first], Big Kettle, and other chiefs).
54. Sachems, Chiefs and Warriors of the Seneca Nation to Calhoun, December 10, 1823, NARA, RG 75, M234, r. 832. "And one of the girls, Mary, came to the council with the Chief called Red Jacket and made known her claims and protested against any part of that land being sold." Copy of deed of cession by the Seneca Nation to Mary and Chloe Allen, July 15, 1791, Jasper Parrish Papers, Vassar.
55. Matthew Dennis, *Seneca Possessed: Indians, Witchcraft, and Power in the Early American Republic* (Philadelphia: University of Pennsylvania Press, 2012), 188.

56. Hauptman, *Conspiracy of Interests,* 155–158 (fraud in 1826), 156–160 (role of Livingston report and Seneca, and the failure of the 1826 "treaty").
57. Malcolm Ebright, Rick Hendricks, and Richard W. Hughes, *Four Square Leagues: Pueblo Indian Land in New Mexico* (Albuquerque: University of New Mexico Press, 2014), chap. 1; G. Emlen Hall and David J. Weber, "Mexican Liberals and the Pueblo Indians, 1821–1829," *New Mexico Historical Review* 59, no. 1 (1984): 5–32.
58. Ebright, Hendricks, and Hughes, *Four Square Leagues,* 12–17 (Ordinance of May 1567 and subsequent laws), 32–33, 152–153.
59. Ebright, Hendricks, and Hughes, *Four Square Leagues,* 36–40.
60. Ebright, Hendricks, and Hughes, *Four Square Leagues,* 38–43; Rafael Aguilar, Lucas Domingo Vigil, and José Manuel Armenta, Petition of "the principal citizens of Pecos Pueblo," March 12, 1826, SANM I, 1370; Hall, *Four Leagues of Pecos: A Legal History of the Pecos Grant, 1800–1933* (Albuquerque: University of New Mexico Press, 1984), 49–50; John L. Kessell, *Kiva, Cross and Crown: The Pecos Indians and New Mexico, 1540–1840* (Albuquerque: University of New Mexico Press, 1987), 445–446; David J. Weber, *The Spanish Frontier in North America* (New Haven, Conn.: Yale University Press, 1992), 221–222.
61. Ebright, Hendricks, and Hughes, *Four Square Leagues,* 42–43. On the 1829 petition, see Rafael Aguilar and José Cota, representing Pecos Pueblo, to the Santa Fe deputation, March 9, 1829, SANM I, 288.
62. Cortés had tried to sell some of her pueblo lands as early as 1808. Cortés petition to Maynez, Santa Fe, August 26, 1808, SANM I, 208, doc. 1; Deed of Cortés land sale, January 15, 1812, SANM I, 208, doc. 6; Maynez decree, May 22, 1815, SANM I, 208.
63. Petition to the *ayuntamiento* complaining of Father Alcina, October 1, 1820, SANM II, 2934; Malcolm Ebright and Rich Hendricks, *The Witches of Abiquiu: The Governor, the Priest, the Genízaro Indians, and the Devil* (Albuquerque: University of New Mexico Press, 2006), 251–261, 318–319; Center for Land Grant Studies, "The Abiquiú Genízaro Land Grant" (Santa Fe, n.d.).
64. Petition of Francisco Trujillo et al., [*genízaros* of Abiquiú], April 20, 1824, SANM I, 208, doc. 18 (*los principales hijos de la congregación,* which does not necessarily carry a religious connotation but likely did here as they represented Santo Tomás Apóstol de Abiquiú).
65. Petition of people of San Jose de la Laguna to the Governor, July 16, 1830, folder 1, docs. 1, 3, Bureau of Indian Affairs Collection, 1689–1859, FACL; James A. Vlasich, *Pueblo Indian Agriculture* (Albuquerque: University of New Mexico Press, 2005), 75–77; Maurice S. Crandall,

These People Have Always Been a Republic: Indigenous Electorates in the U.S.-Mexico Borderlands, 1598–1912 (Chapel Hill: University of North Carolina Press, 2019), 138–143.

66. Crandall, *These People*, chap. 3; Vlasich, *Pueblo Indian Agriculture*, 75–77.
67. People of Santo Domingo, petition for justice to Gov. Albino Perez, February 18, 1836; League measurement document in statement by Miguel Antonio Lobato to Governor, January 25, 1841, folder 6, docs. 3, 5, 6, Bureau of Indian Affairs Collection, 1689–1859, FACL; Lobato, petition to Mariano Martínez, August 23, 1844, SANM I, 1380; Ebright, Hendrick, and Hughes, *Four Square Leagues*, 45–46.
68. Juan Manuel Lucero and others, Petition against the Vigil claim to land along Río Lucero, August 13, 1836, SANM I, 628, reel 4, frames 142–145 ("que de tiempo immemorial"), reel 5, frame 310 (English translation), NMSRCA; Denise Damico, "'*El agua es la vida*' (Water Is Life): Water Conflict and Conquest in Nineteenth-Century New Mexico" (PhD diss., Brandeis University, 2008), 35n72, 50–53.
69. Ebright, Hendricks, and Hughes, *Four Square Leagues*, 152; Ebright, *Advocates for the Oppressed: Hispanos, Genízaros, and Their Land in New Mexico* (Albuquerque: University of New Mexico Press, 2015), 3–4.
70. The conclusion that pueblos survived in part because of Natives' insistence on their league rights, expressed and organized through the Spanish and Mexican petitioning process, comes from Ebright, Hendricks, and Hughes, *Four Square Leagues*, 36, 45–47. See also Damico, "*El agua es la vida*," chap. 2.
71. Theda Perdue and Michael D. Green, *The Cherokee Removal: A Brief History with Documents* (Boston: Little, Brown, 2005). Like the Choctaw, the relative stability of the Cherokee meant that many in the nation were remnants of other, less fortunate tribes and villages. Richard White, *The Roots of Dependency: Subsistence, Environment, and Social Change among the Choctaws, Pawnees, and Navajos* (Lincoln: University of Nebraska Press, 1983), chaps. 4, 5.
72. Perdue and Green, *Cherokee Removal*, 129–131; Theda Perdue, *Cherokee Women: Gender and Culture Change, 1700–1835* (Lincoln: University of Nebraska Press, 1998); Tiya Miles, "'Circular Reasoning': Recentering Cherokee Women in the Antiremoval Campaigns," *American Quarterly* 61, no. 2 (June 2009): 221–243; Michelene E. Pesantubbee, "Nancy Ward: American Patriot or Cherokee Nationalist?" *American Indian Quarterly* 38, no. 2 (Spring 2014): 177–206; Duane Champagne, "Institutional and Cultural Order in Early Cherokee Society," *Journal of Cherokee Studies* 15 (1990): 3–26; Theda Perdue, "Nancy Ward," in *Portraits of American*

Women: From Settlement to the Present, ed. G. J. Barker-Benfield and Catherine Clinton (New York: St. Martin's, 1991).

73. In 1822, McIntosh would petition, ambiguously but earnestly, for the rights of a White woman, and her petition was signed with a separate testimonial by Return J. Meigs. Petition #44, 1822, Legislative Petitions Collection, TSLA. On Margaret Ann Scott, see Miles, "Circular Reasoning," 228–229; Laura E. Donaldson, "'But We Are Your Mothers, You Are Our Sons': Gender, Sovereignty and the Nation in Early Cherokee Women's Writing," in *Indigenous Women and Feminism: Politics, Activism, Culture,* ed. Cheryl Suzach et al. (Vancouver: UBC Press, 2010), 43–50; Cynthia Cumfer, *Separate Peoples, One Land: The Minds of Cherokees, Blacks, and Whites on the Tennessee Frontier* (Chapel Hill: University of North Carolina Press, 2007), 34–39.
74. Petition of Cherokee Women, May 2, 1817, Andrew Jackson Papers, book 29, no. 17, vol. 14, 6452–6453, in Presidential Papers Microfilm: Andrew Jackson (Washington, 1961, series 1, reel 22).
75. Petition of Cherokee Women, May 2, 1817.
76. Petition of Cherokee Women, May 2, 1817. For more on voluntary removal as matricide, see Miles, "Circular Reasoning," 226.
77. Petition of Cherokee Women, June 30, 1818, Papers of the American Board of Commissioners for Foreign Missions, Houghton-Harvard, reprinted in Perdue and Green, *Cherokee Removal,* 131–133.
78. Petition of Cherokee Women, June 30, 1818.
79. Petition of Cherokee Women, June 30, 1818.
80. Perdue and Green, *Cherokee Removal,* 18–23.
81. McMinn to Cherokee, November 18, 1818.
82. Cherokee to McMinn, June 30, 1818, including extract of a letter to Col. Return Meigs (November 21, 1811), NARA, RG75, in "Cherokee Treaty, February 27, 1819. Composite document," 24, B4, F17, Paul M. Niebell Collection, OUSC. Ross's was the final signature listed on the memorial to McMinn, but he also listed the title "President of the National Committee."
83. Andrew Denson, *Demanding the Cherokee Nation: Indian Autonomy and American Culture, 1830–1900* (Lincoln: University of Nebraska Press, 2004), 32–35.
84. Cherokee Deputation to George Graham (acting Secretary of War), October 28, 1817; Cherokee Deputation to Monroe, November 22, 1817; Cherokee Deputation (led by Going Snake) to Secretary of War, December 11 and 13, 1817; Cherokee Deputation to State of Tennessee (presented at Knoxville), January 4, 1818, M271, reel 002, NARA, RG75. Cherokee delegation (on behalf of Path Killer) to Calhoun, July 23, 1818,

NARA, RG 75, copy in B4, F17, Paul M. Niebell Collection, OUSC. On the legal team, see Cherokee Nation (Ross) to David Irwin and Thomas G. Barron, October 3, 1830, Cherokee Collection, B1, F23, TSLA.

85. Steve Inskeep, *Jacksonland: President Andrew Jackson, Cherokee Chief John Ross, and a Great American Land Grab* (New York: Penguin, 2015), 86–88 (delegations), 108–111 (Ross writing Jackson), 117–119 (delegation to Washington); "Caution to Travelers," February 17, 1837, signed by Ross and other Cherokee, attaching reprint in *Washington Globe* (February 13) of letter/petition (original of February 9), in Records of the Virginia House of Delegates, Speaker, Executive Communications, box 15, folder 25, Misc., reel 5392, LOV.
86. David A. Nichols, "Land, Republicanism and Indians: Power and Policy in Early National Georgia, 1780–1825," *Georgia Historical Quarterly* 85, no. 2 (Summer 2001): 199–226.
87. Memorial of John Ross, Geo. Lowrey, Major Ridge, and Elijah Hicks, Delegates from the Cherokee Nation of Indians, April 16, 1824, U.S. Congress, House of Representatives, 18th Cong., 1st Sess. (Washington: Gales & Seaton, 1824), HR 18A-F21.4, box 1, folder 2, RG 233, NARA (manuscript version).
88. Memorial of John Ross, Geo. Lowrey, Major Ridge, and Elijah Hicks.
89. Memorial of John Ross, Geo. Lowrey, Major Ridge, and Elijah Hicks.
90. Perdue and Green, *Cherokee Removal,* 7–15. On gold, see *Athenian* (Athens), September 15, 1829, 3; October 13, 1829, 2; February 9, 1830, 2; May 14, 1830, 3.
91. See the insightful analysis of Saunt, *Unworthy Republic,* 54–59.
92. Forsyth-Clay exchange in *Register of Debates* 23 (1), 1773; *Globe,* 23 (1), 396. *Papers of Henry Clay,* 726–777; S. Cooper (Acting Secretary of War) to Hon. John Bell (Committee on Indian Affairs), May 19, 1838, HR25A-D11.2 (Committee on Indian Affairs), RG 233, NARA.
93. Catherine Beecher, "Circular Addressed to the Benevolent Ladies of the U. States," *Christian Advocate and Journal and Zion's Herald* (New York), December 25, 1829, 65.
94. *National Intelligencer,* August 5, 1829.
95. Alisse Portnoy, *Their Right to Speak: Women's Activism in the Indian and Slave Debates* (Cambridge, Mass.: Harvard University Press, 2005), chap. 1. Portnoy's characterization (53–54) of the January 1830 petition as "the first time in United States history that a group of women petitioned the national legislature regarding an issue of national consequence" is plausibly true for White women, but given the announced presence of fourteen women's signatures on a Cherokee petition of December 1829, it also stands in need of some modification or context ("Memorial of the

Cherokees," December 1829, HR21A-G23.3, tray 1 of 4). See also Mary Hershberger, "Mobilizing Women, Anticipating Abolition: The Struggle against Indian Removal in the 1830s," *Journal of American History* 86, no. 1 (June 1999).

96. Portnoy, *Their Right to Speak*, chap. 1.
97. Miles, "Circular Reasoning"; Theresa Strouth Gaul, editor's introduction to *Cherokee Sister: The Collected Writings of Catharine Brown, 1818–1823* ed. Theresa Strouth Gaul (Lincoln: University of Nebraska Press, 2014), 36; Saunt, *Unworthy Republic*, 66–68.
98. Richard petition, *JHRUS*, 10th Congress (January 19, 1809), 6:221; SPG petition, *JHRUS* 15th Congress (February 5, 1817) 10:166; Friends' petition, *JHRUS* 15th Congress (December 16, 1818), 12:24; Religious denominations of New York City, *JHRUS* 15th Congress (January 20, 1819), 12:48; Baptist Board of Foreign Missions, *JHRUS* 15th Congress (February 15, 1819), 12:70.
99. *Cherokee Phoenix* 5, no. 20 (1833) reprints the signed resolution of Seneca leaders (Big Kettle et al.) refusing to leave their lands.
100. Petition of John Ross and Other Representatives of the Cherokee Nation, HR25A-G7.2, Memorial of the Cherokee Nation, HR25A-H1.3 (folder 1 of 6), RG233, NARA, http://recordsofrights.org/events/47/cherokee-removal.
101. Ministers of the Gospel in Somerset and Franklin Counties (Maine) to House; Citizens of Oxford (Maine) to House; Inhabitants of Chesterville (Maine) (April 1838) to House; Inhabitants of Newburyport (Massachusetts) to House, all undated but probably April 1838, HR25A-H1.3, RG 233, NARA.
102. *National Gazette* (Philadelphia), January 29, 1831; *Southern Banner* (Athens), February 5, 1835, 2; *Southern Banner*, April 14, 1838, 2.
103. Ross, "The Contrast," Ross Papers, TSLA. The prayers of Ross-authored petitions to the U.S. Congress match the writing of "The Contrast"; see Petition from a delegation from the Cherokee Nation now on a visit at the Seat of Government of the United States (April 15, 1824), HR 18A-F21.4, B1, F2; Memorial of the Cherokees (December 1829), HR21A-G8.2, B2; RG233.
104. Petition to Harvard Corporation, May 21, 1833, reprinted in William Apess, *On Our Own Ground: The Complete Writings of William Apess, a Pequot*, ed. Barry O'Connell (Amherst: University of Massachusetts Press, 1992), 174–175.
105. Petition to Harvard Corporation, May 21, 1833, 176.
106. Petition to Harvard Corporation, May 21, 1833, 177.
107. Apess, *On Our Own Ground*, 205–206, 218–219. The petition was presented in January 1834 (220–221).

108. Mashpee petition, December 1833, http://nrs.harvard.edu/urn-3:FHCL:13481281.
109. Mashpee petition, December 1833.
110. D. L. Child, H. Stebbins, and D. Fellows Jr., "Report [on the condition of the native Indians and descendants of native Indians, in this Commonwealth]," *Massachusetts House Reports*, no. 68 (Boston, 1827); Daniel R. Mandell, *Tribe, Race, History: Native Americans in Southern New England, 1780–1880* (Baltimore: Johns Hopkins University Press), 97.
111. Jill Lepore, *The Name of War: King Philip's War and the Origins of American Identity* (New York: Knopf, 1998), 215–220.
112. Mashpee petition, December 1833.
113. *Liberator*, January 25, 1834; in Apess, *On Our Own Ground*, 220–223.
114. *Liberator*, January 25, 1834; in Apess, *On Our Own Ground*, 223.
115. Apess, *On Our Own Ground*, 206–208 (legislators' remarks).

6. SLAVERY, SKIN, AND BLACK STRATEGY

1. Memorial of Jean Baptiste Philip, Doctor of Medicine, and John J. Congnet, Esquire, to the Right Honorable The Earl Bathhurst (1823); Reply of the Committee of the Coloured Inhabitants of Trinidad, to the Answer of His Majesty's Attorney General of that Island on the Subject of their Claims (1824); Commissioners of Legal Enquiry in the West Indies, 1822–1828, 243ff. (memorial), 364 (Reply; Philippe's is the fifth signature), CO 318/76, NAUK; Philippe [pseudonymous], *An Address to the Right Hon. Earl Bathhurst, His Majesty's Principal Secretary of State for the Colonies, Relative to the Claims which the Coloured Population of Trinidad have to the same Civil and Political Privileges with their White Fellow Subjects, by a Free Mulatto of the Island* (London: S. Gosnell, 1824).
2. The free Black petitioners of the Caribbean surge of 1823 to 1825 were, as far as records indicate, almost entirely male, a fact that reflects the political gender hierarchy of the British Empire. "Free People of Color of St. Augustine to Florida Legislative Council, 1823," in *The Southern Debate over Slavery*, vol. 1, *Petitions to Southern Legislatures, 1778–1864*, ed. Loren Schweninger (Urbana: University of Illinois Press, 2001), 75.

   The complicated relationship between race, ancestry, and skin color in this period requires a cautious approach to terminology. I generally use "Black" to describe persons of African descent but without European descent, and "mixed-race" and person "of color" to describe those with joint European and African ancestry. When referring to a specific context in which participants deployed racial categories of the time—"free colored," "mulatto" and "quadroon," for example—I will use these while recognizing their contingent nature. See Daniel Livesay, *Children of Uncertain Fortune: Mixed-Race Jamaicans in Britain and the Atlantic Family, 1733–1833* (Chapel Hill: University of North Carolina Press, 2018), 17–18.

3. Petitions for freedom from "Felix" (Unknown) to Hutchison, January 6, 1773; from Peter Bestes and other slaves (April 20, 1773), both in *A Documentary History of the Negro People in the United States*, ed. Herbert Aptheker (New York: Citadel, 1951), 1:6–8; Christopher Cameron, *To Plead Our Own Cause: African Americans in Massachusetts and the Making of the Antislavery Movement* (Kent: Kent State University Press, 2014), 55–58; Ira V. Brown, "Pennsylvania's Antislavery Pioneers," *Pennsylvania History* 55, no. 2 (April 1988): 59–77; Sean Wilentz, "American Slavery and the Relentless Unforeseen," *New York Review of Books* (Daily), November 19, 2019.
4. "Petition of a Grate Number of Blackes" to Thomas Gage (May 25, 1774); "Petition of a Great Number of Negroes" to the Massachusetts House (January 13, 1777), both in Aptheker, *Documentary History*, 1:8–10; Cameron, *To Plead Our Own Cause*, 58–63.
5. Aptheker, *Documentary History*, 1:9–10.
6. Daniel Mandell, "Petition of Prince Hall and Other African Americans to the Massachusetts General Court," in *Milestone Documents in African American History: Exploring the Essential Primary Sources*, ed. Paul Finkelman (Dallas: Schlager, 2010), 74–75, 77 (coalition with elites). Mandell remarks that "the 1777 petition was the first effort by African Americans to improve their situation after the country had declared itself free of British rule" (78).
7. Alan Gilbert, *Black Patriots and Loyalists: Fighting for Emancipation in the War for Independence* (Chicago: University of Chicago Press, 2013); Cameron, *To Plead Our Own Cause*, 65–66.
8. Manisha Sinha, *The Slave's Cause: A History of Abolition* (New Haven, Conn.: Yale University Press, 2016), 65–69.
9. Sinha, *Slave's Cause*, 71.
10. Sinha, *Slave's Cause*, 71.
11. Paul J. Polgar, *Standard-Bearers of Equality: America's First Abolition Movement* (Chapel Hill: University of North Carolina Press, 2019); Richard S. Newman, *The Transformation of American Abolitionism: Fighting Slavery in the Early Republic* (Chapel Hill: University of North Carolina Press, 2002), esp. chap. 3; Sinha, *Slave's Cause*, 71–75; Gary Nash, *Forging Freedom: The Formation of Philadelphia's Black Commu-*

nity, 1720–1840 (Cambridge, Mass.: Harvard University Press, 1988), 102–109.

12. Petition of Cato Hanker, June 9, 1794, House unpassed legislation, 1775–1996 (SC1-230), 1794, Docket 4052, MAC; digitized at APMD, https://doi.org/10.7910/DVN/DOQ82. Over three decades earlier, Hanker had petitioned from Cambridge, protesting discrimination against him in commissary purchases. Petition of Hanker, February 23, 1760, Massachusetts Archives Collection, 1629–1799 (SC1-45x), vol. 78–Military, 1758–1760, MAC; APMD, https://doi.org/10.7910/DVN/PGHE7.
13. Petition of Belinda, February 14, 1783, Massachusetts Archives Collection, 1629–1799 (SC1-45x), vol. 239–Revolution Resolves, 1783, 11–14, MAC; digitized at APMD, http://nrs.harvard.edu/urn-3:FHCL:13906083; Roy E. Finkenbine, "Belinda's Petition: Reparations for Slavery in Revolutionary Massachusetts," *William and Mary Quarterly* 64, no. 1 (2007): 99. On the changes in Black print culture at this time, consult Newman, *The Transformation of American Abolitionism*; Joanna Brooks, "The Early American Public Sphere and the Emergence of a Black Print Counterpublic," *William and Mary Quarterly* 62, no. 1 (2005): 67–92; Patrick Rael, *Black Identity and Black Protest in the Antebellum North* (Chapel Hill: University of North Carolina Press, 2002); Daniel Carpenter and Nicole Topich, "Contested Boundaries of Representation: Patterns of Transformation in Black Petitioning in Massachusetts, 1770–1850," in *Democracy, Participation and Contestation: Civil Society, Governance and the Future of Liberal Democracy*, ed. Emmanuelle Avril and Johann N. Neem (New York: Routledge, 2015), 201–222.
14. Nicholas P. Wood, "A 'Class of Citizens': The Earliest Black Petitioners to Congress and Their Quaker Allies," *William and Mary Quarterly* 74, no. 1 (January 2017): 109–144.
15. Absalom Jones and others, "The Petition of the People of Colour, Freemen within the City and Suburbs of Philadelphia," December 30, 1799, Slave Trade Committee Records, HR 6A-F4.2, RG 233, NARA, reprinted in Sidney Kaplan, *The Black Presence in the Era of the American Revolution* (Washington, D.C.: National Gallery of Art, 1973), 273–275.
16. Gary B. Nash, *Forging Freedom: The Formation of Philadelphia's Black Community, 1720–1840* (Cambridge, Mass.: Harvard University Press, 1988), 188.
17. Wood, "Class of Citizens," 130, 135–139.
18. Seymour Drescher, *Capitalism and Antislavery: British Mobilization in Comparative Perspective* (London: Basingstoke, 1986); "Whose Abolition? Popular Pressure and the Ending British Slave Trade," *Past and Present*

143 (1994): 136–166. On Plymouth, consult Richard Huzzey, "A Microhistory of British Antislavery Petitioning," *Social Science History* 43, no. 3 (2019): 599–623; Christopher Leslie Brown, *Moral Capital: Foundations of British Abolitionism* (Chapel Hill: University of North Carolina Press, 2006), esp. chaps. 6 and 7; Adam Hochschild, *Bury the Chains: Prophets and Rebels in the Fight to Free an Empire's Slaves* (New York: Houghton Mifflin Harcourt, 2005), 137–139, 230–231; Sinha, *Slave's Cause,* 100–102.

19. Newman, *The Transformation of American Abolitionism,* chap. 3 (deferential culture). While Wood ("Class of Citizens") qualifies Newman's judgment, the absence of immediatist rhetoric and the limited signatory lists of these petitions support Newman's characterization that the late 1820s and early 1830s saw substantial changes.
20. Arthur O. White, "The Black Leadership Class and Education in Antebellum Boston," *Journal of Negro Education* 42, no. 4 (1973): 508–509, 511; Rael, *Black Protest Identity and Black Protest in the Antebellum North,* 45, 48–49, esp. chap. 3, "'The Sign of Things': Names Controversy and Black Identity" (summary on 83, 115–116); "Petition of Daniel Wild and Others for a Lottery to Finish the African Meeting House School Room," House unpassed legislation, 1775–1996 (SC1-230), 1807, Docket 5977, MAC; "Petition of Daniel Wild," House unpassed legislation, 1775–1996 (SC1-230), 1808, Docket 6174, MAC; digitized at APMD, https://doi.org/10.7910/DVN/ZDJTR.
21. Nash, *Forging Freedom,* 181. Petition of James Carmichael et al. to the South Carolina House of Representatives, December 12, 1812, PAR #11381203; Petition of Citizens of Tennessee to the General Assembly, October 8, 1813, PAR #11481305; Petition of Sanders Glover et al. to the South Carolina Senate and House of Representatives, December 4, 1816, PAR #11381601; Schweninger, *Southern Debate over Slavery,* 47–49, 55–56, also 59–61, 62–63.
22. Andrew K. Diemer, *The Politics of Black Citizenship: Free African Americans in the Mid-Atlantic Borderland, 1817–1863* (Athens: University of Georgia Press, 2016), 56–60; Newman, *Transformation of American Abolitionism,* 18–31, 43, 60–85; *The History of the New-York-African free-schools, from their establishment in 1787, to the present time . . .* (New York: Mahlon Day, 1830), 19–20, 30–33; Thomas R. Moseley, A History of the New-York Manumission Society, 1785–1849 (PhD thesis, New York University, 1963), 107–108, 114–119, 128–138, 164–170, 293–294; Martha S. Jones, "Time, Space, and Jurisdiction in Atlantic World Slavery: The Volunbrun Household in Gradual Emancipation New York," *Law and History Review* 29, no. 4 (November 2011):

1048–1060; Polgar, *Standard-Bearers of Equality,* 168–172; Sinha, *Slave's Cause,* 116–122.

23. Philip Lawson, *The Imperial Challenge: Quebec and Britain in the Age of the American Revolution* (Montreal: McGill-Queen's University Press, 1989); Bridget Brereton, *A History of Modern Trinidad, 1783–1962* (Kingston: University of the West Indies, 1981), chaps. 4, 5, esp. 82–88; Livesay, *Children of Uncertain Fortune,* 370–371.
24. Jeremy D. Popkin, *You Are All Free: The Haitian Revolution and the Abolition of Slavery* (Cambridge: Cambridge University Press, 2010); Sinha, *Slave's Cause,* 54–56.
25. Livesay, *Children of Uncertain Fortune,* 24–25, 45–47; B. W. Higman, *Slave Population and Economy in Jamaica, 1807–1834* (Kingston: University of the West Indies, 1995), 141; Richard S. Dunn, *A Tale of Two Plantations: Slave Life and Labor in Jamaica and Virginia* (Cambridge, Mass.: Harvard University Press, 2014), 169. On barriers to manumission, see Colleen A. Vasconcellos, *Slavery, Childhood and Abolition in Jamaica, 1788–1838* (Athens: University of Georgia Press, 2015), 52–57; Sheila Duncker, "The Free Coloured and Their Fight for Civil Rights in Jamaica, 1800–1830" (master's thesis, University of London, 1956); Gad J. Heuman, *Between Black and White: Race, Politics and the Free Coloreds in Jamaica, 1792–1865* (Westport, Conn.: Greenwood, 1981); Livesay, *Children of Uncertain Fortune.* See also Jerome Handler, *The Unappropriated People: Freedmen in the Slave Society of Barbados* (Baltimore: Johns Hopkins University Press, 1974); Edward L. Cox, *Free Coloreds in the Slave Societies of St. Kitts and Grenada, 1763–1833* (Knoxville: University of Tennessee Press, 1984); Melanie J. Newton, *The Children of Africa in the Colonies: Free People of Color in Barbados in the Age of Emancipation* (Baton Rouge: Louisiana State University Press, 2008).
26. Livesay, *Children of Uncertain Fortune,* 38–39.
27. On restrictions placed on free people of color, consult Commissioners of Legal Enquiry in the West Indies, 1822–1828, folios 6–7 (free coloured of Dominica), 24–25 (Dominica), 61–71 (Jamaica), CO 318/76, NAUK; Livesay, *Children of Uncertain Fortune,* 38–39, 370–72.
28. Jane Austen, *Sanditon,* reprinted in Austen, *Northanger Abbey, Lady Susan, the Watsons, Sanditon* (Oxford, UK: Oxford University Press, 2008), chaps. 9, 11 (Miss Lambe); also chap. 6 (West Indian families who "fancy themselves equal"); Sarah Salah, "The Silence of Miss Lambe: Sanditon and Contextual Fictions of 'Race' in the Abolition Era," *Eighteenth Century Fiction* 18, no. 3 (Spring 2006): 334–338 (on Lambe), 339–344 (on persons of color in other novels of the time); Livesay,

Children of Uncertain Fortune, 370–375, 401–403 (disappearance of privilege petitions).

29. Brereton, *History of Modern Trinidad,* 43–44; Newton, *Children of Africa in the Colonies,* 43–45.
30. Vasconcello, *Slavery, Childhood and Abolition in Jamaica, 1788–1838,* 57–58; Commissioners of Legal Enquiry in the West Indies, 1822–1828, folio 49, CO 318/76, NAUK; Heuman, *Between Black and White,* 7. The 1813 Jamaica petition, *JAJ* 12 (November 5, 1813), 506; Commissioners of Legal Enquiry in the West Indies, 1822–1828, folio 50, CO 318/76, NAUK; Livesay, "The Decline of Jamaica's Interracial Households and the Fall of the Planter Class, 1733–1823," *Atlantic Studies* 9 (2012): 107–23, esp. 116–117; Livesay, *Children of Uncertain Fortune,* 401–403; Heuman, *Between Black and White,* 27–28.
31. The term "political disabilities" reflects common usage at the time; see "The Humble Petition and Memorial of the Coloured Inhabitants of His Majesty's Island of Dominica," July 11, 1823, folio 5, CO 318/76, NAUK.
32. Hansard, *House of Commons Debates,* July 25, 1822, vol. 7, 1801–1844.
33. *Substance of the Three Reports of the Commissioner of Inquiry into the Administration of Civil and Criminal Justice in the West Indies* (London: Joseph Butterworth, 1827); Brereton, *History,* 72; Lauren Benton and Lisa Ford, *The Rage for Order: The British Empire and the Origins of International Law, 1800–1850* (Cambridge, Mass.: Harvard University Press, 2016), 71–75, 215.
34. *Statement of Proceedings of the People of Colour of Jamaica in an Intended Appeal to the House of Assembly of 1823, for the Removal of their Political Disabilities,* Commissioners of Legal Enquiry in the West Indies, 1822–1828, 109–114 (signatory list on 114), CO 318/76, NAUK. "On the Policy of Conferring Additional Privileges on the People of Colour," *Jamaica Journal,* September 27, 1823; "Proceedings in the House of Assembly, Friday, November 14, Petition of the Free People of Colour," *Jamaica Journal,* November 22, 1823, 493–494; Livesay, *Children of Uncertain Fortune,* 370–372, 401–403. On Lecesne and Escoffery and their petition and trial, see *Hansard—House of Commons Debates,* May 21, 1824, vol. 11, 796–804; June 16, 1825, vol. 13, 1195–1196 (reference to 1823 petition); Heuman, *Between Black and White,* 36–41.
35. John Campbell, John Manderson, and Thomas Reaburn (Montego Bay), on behalf of the People of Color of the Parish of Saint James, to Commissioners of Legal Enquiry (Montego Bay, December 1825), Commissioners of Legal Enquiry, folio 47, CO 318/76, NAUK.

36. Livesay, *Children of Uncertain Fortune,* 401–403 (on increase of privilege petitions); Memorial of the Free Coloured Inhabitants of Jamaica, in Commissioners of Legal Enquiry, folio 71, CO 318/76, NAUK.
37. Memorial of the Free Coloured Inhabitants of Jamaica, in Commissioners of Legal Enquiry, folio 55 (also 53), CO 318/76, NAUK.
38. Memorial of the Free Coloured Inhabitants of Jamaica, in Commissioners of Legal Enquiry, folio 55 (also 53), CO 318/76, NAUK.
39. Memorial of the Free Coloured Inhabitants of Jamaica, in Commissioners of Legal Enquiry, folio 60, CO 318/76, NAUK.
40. "Trinidad, May 15," *Jamaica Journal,* June 19, 1824; "Trinidad," *Saint Christopher Advertiser,* January 31, 1826; *Grenada Free Press and Weekly Gazette,* February 14, 1827; *Antigua Weekly Register,* July 31, 1827, and August 7, 1827; "Jamaica," *Grenada Free Press and Public Gazette,* January 26, 1828.
41. Newton, *Children of Africa in the Colonies,* 58–62.
42. Commissioners of Legal Enquiry, folios 5–8 ("Coloured Inhabitants of His Majesty's Island of Dominica" to Bathhurst), 9–11 ("Coloured Inhabitants" to Maddock and Dwarris, 11 July 1823), 22–31 (289 signatories to His Majesty's Council and the House of Assembly of Dominica), 38–43 ("Coloured Inhabitants of Grenada" to Maddock and Dwarris), 122–125 ("Coloured Inhabitants" of Antigua to Maddock and Dwarris, October 8, 1823), 126–131 ("Coloured Inhabitants" to Assembly, September 4, 1823), 153–160 ("Memorial of His Majesty's Subjects of Color of the Island of Saint Christopher" to Maddock and Dwarris, November 24, 1823), CO 318/76, NAUK.
43. Selwyn Reginald Cudjoe, *Beyond Boundaries: The Intellectual Tradition of Trinidad and Tobago in the Nineteenth Century* (Amherst: University of Massachusetts Press, 2003), 23 (Philippe's writing "the first sustained act of resistance" on the island) and 59–62 (abundance of petitions); Brereton, *History of Modern Trinidad,* 34–40 (Picton), 60–62 (Philippe's memorial and later petitions), 63–67 (statutory discrimination); Carl Campbell, *Cedulants and Capitulants: The Politics of the Coloured Opposition in the Slave Society of Trinidad, 1783–1838* (Trinidad: Paria, 1992), 242.
44. Memorial of Philip and Congnet to Bathhurst, folios 243–244, in Commissioners of Legal Enquiry, CO 318/76, NAUK.
45. "Coloured Inhabitants of His Majesty's Island of Dominica" to Maddock and Dwarris, July 11, 1823, folios 9–11, and "Papers from the Free Coloured Inhabitants of Dominica," folios 20–21; "Memorial of Jean Baptiste Philip Doctor of Medicine and John J. Congnet Esquire" to

Bathhurst, June 7, 1824, folio 243, in Commissioners of Legal Enquiry, CO 318/76, NAUK.

46. Charles H. Wesley, "The Emancipation of the Free Colored Population in the British Empire," *Journal of Negro History* 19, no. 2 (April 1934): 137–170, esp. 156–157 (Lecesne and Escoffery trial and petitions from free people of color discussed in same sessions), 158–159 (government orders for Saint Lucia and Trinidad), 159–166 (other Caribbean islands from December 1830 to July 1832).
47. The conclusion about 1833 is Wesley's (166–167). See also Whittington B. Johnston, "The Amelioration Acts in the Bahamas, 1823–1833: A Middle Ground Between Freedom and Antebellum Slave Codes," *Journal of the Bahamas Historical Society* 18 (October 1996): 25–27; *Race Relations in the Bahamas, 1784–1834: The Nonviolent Transformation from a Slave to a Free Society* (Fayetteville: University of Arkansas Press, 2000), esp. chaps. 4–6.
48. Barry R. Weingast, "Political Stability and Civil War: Institutions, Commitment, and American Democracy," in Robert H. Bates, Avner Greif, Margaret Levi, Jean-Laurent Rosenthal, and Barry R. Weingast, *Analytic Narratives* (Princeton, N.J.: Princeton University Press, 1999); Gregory Wawro, "Peculiar Institutions: Slavery, Sectionalism, and Minority Obstruction in the Antebellum Senate," *Legislative Studies Quarterly* 30, no. 2 (May 2005): 163–191.
49. Sean Wilentz, *The Rise of American Democracy: Jefferson to Lincoln* (Oxford: Oxford University Press, 2005), 220–221; Sven Beckert, *Empire of Cotton: A Global History* (New York: Random House, 2014); Andrew J. Torget, *Seeds of Empire: Cotton, Slavery, and the Transformation of the Texas Borderlands, 1800–1850* (Chapel Hill: University of North Carolina Press, 2015), 82–83.
50. William E. Foley, *The Genesis of Missouri: From Wilderness Outpost to Statehood* (Columbia: University of Missouri Press, 1987).
51. Memorial of the Citizens of Missouri Territory, 1817, Missouri Collection, C3982, folio 560, SHSMO, http://digital.shsmo.org/cdm/ref/collection/GovColl/id/20762.
52. On land claimant petitioners, consult, for instance, the claims of Samuel Thompson and Burwell J. Thompson, *JHRUS*, February 10, 1817, 226; Papers of Original Claimants, 1785–1857, Second Board of Land Commissioners, U.S. Recorder of Land Titles, B1, folders 9–10 (Thomas Maddin, Amable Partenay, and Vallé families), B5, folders 9–10 (John Hawkins and Vallé family members), RG 951, MSA.
53. *JHRUS*, 15th Cong., 1st Sess., January 26, 1818, 180. See also Foley, *Genesis*, 248–249.

54. Taylor speech reprinted in *NWR,* March 4, 1820, 24. See also Sinha, *Slave's Cause,* 186–187; Weingast, "Political Stability and Civil War"; Wilentz, *Rise of American Democracy,* 223–224.
55. Wilentz, *Rise of American Democracy,* 224–225, 229–231.
56. Wilentz, *Rise of American Democracy,* 223, 232–237.
57. *House of Commons Debates,* May 15, 1823), vol. 9, 257–287 (Buxton); David Brion Davis, "James Cropper and the British Anti-Slavery Movement, 1823–1833," *Journal of Negro History,* 46, no. 3 (April 1961): 154–173; Wilentz, *Rise of American Democracy,* 237–239.
58. "South Carolina Association to Senate, ca. 1823," in Schweninger, *Southern Debate over Slavery,* 80, 78.
59. "South Carolina Association to Senate, ca. 1823," 80. See also Edward L. Cox, *Free Coloreds in the Slave Societies of St. Kitts and Grenada, 1763–1833* (Knoxville: University of Tennessee Press, 1984), 101–102.
60. "South Carolina Association to Senate, ca. 1823," 82.
61. "South Carolina Association to Senate, ca. 1823," 80.
62. "Citizens of Rutherford County to Tennessee Assembly, ca. 1825," in Schweninger, *Southern Debate over Slavery,* 93.
63. "Wilmington Union Colonization Society to Delaware Assembly, ca. 1827," in Schweninger, *Southern Debate over Slavery,* 96, 98.
64. "Charleston City Council to South Carolina Senate, ca. 1828," in Schweninger, *Southern Debate over Slavery,* 104.
65. "Charleston City Council to South Carolina Senate, ca. 1828," 104.
66. Nikki M. Taylor, *Frontiers of Freedom: Cincinnati's Black Community, 1802–1868* (Athens: Ohio University Press, 2005), chap. 3, esp. 54–55.
67. Petition of the Inhabitants of Sampson, Bladen, New Hanover, and Duplin Counties to the North Carolina General Assembly (ca. 1830), PAR #11283004; *Acts Passed at the General Assembly of the State of North Carolina, at the Session of 1830–1831* (Raleigh, 1831), 12, 17–18; Schweninger, *Southern Debate over Slavery,* 117–122.
68. Petition of the Inhabitants of Sampson, Bladen, New Hanover, and Duplin Counties to the North Carolina General Assembly (ca. 1830), PAR #11283004; Walter Johnson, *River of Dark Dreams: Slavery and Empire in the Cotton Kingdom* (Cambridge, Mass.: Harvard University Press, 2013), chaps. 6–8.
69. Manisha Sinha, *The Counterrevolution of Slavery: Politics and Ideology in Antebellum South Carolina* (Chapel Hill: University of North Carolina Press, 2000), 18–19, 33–35; Wilentz, *Rise of American Democracy,* 298–299.
70. Sinha, *Slave's Cause,* 173–174. For purposes of this calculation, procolonization memorials include ACS memorials, petitions from state and

local colonization societies, as well as petitions from the American Convention before 1821.

71. District slavery regulation and abolition petitions from CPD.
72. Andrés Reséndez, *Changing National Identities at the Frontier: Texas and New Mexico, 1800–1850* (Cambridge: Cambridge University Press, 2005); Torget, *Seeds of Empire,* 69–73, 82–83.
73. Torget, *Seeds of Empire,* 61–72.
74. Torget, *Seeds of Empire,* 73–75.
75. Reséndez, *Changing National Identities,* 93–95; Torget, *Seeds of Empire,* 75–79.
76. Reséndez, *Changing National Identities,* 93–95; Torget, *Seeds of Empire,* 80–92.
77. Reséndez, *Changing National Identities,* 93–95.
78. Reséndez, *Changing National Identities,* 95–98.
79. Torget, *Seeds of Empire,* 110, 116–117, 134 ("Through petitions, protests, negotiations, backroom wrangling, and outright threats, [Anglos and Tejanos] succeeded in pushing state legislatures away from immediately freeing the enslaved people toiling on Texas plantations").
80. Torget, *Seeds of Empire,* 116, 145–150, 154–156,161–164, 206.

7. *PATRIOTES* AND REBELS: PETITIONING AND PARLIAMENTARY SOVEREIGNTY IN FRENCH CANADA

1. Jean Dessaulles à Louis-Joseph Papineau (hereafter LJP), Saint-Hyacinthe, 12 April 1827, Fonds Papineau, LAC. Original language appears in Daniel Carpenter and Doris Brossard, "*L'éruption patriote:* The Revolt against Dalhousie and the Petitioning Explosion in French Canada," *Social Science History* 43, no. 3 (Fall 2019): 453–485, from which parts of this chapter are adapted. Tocqueville, remarks of September 2, 1831, in Jacques Vallée, ed., *Tocqueville au Bas-Canada* (Montréal, Éditions du Jour, 1973), 74 (my translation).
2. On self-rule, consult James T. Kloppenberg, *Toward Democracy: The Struggle for Self-Rule in European and American Thought* (New York: Oxford University Press, 2016); Seyla Benhabib, *The Rights of Others: Aliens, Residents, and Citizens* (Cambridge: Cambridge University Press, 2004); Ian Shapiro, *Democratic Justice* (New Haven, Conn.: Yale University Press, 2001), 37. On lawmaking and representation, consult Nadia Urbinati, *Representative Democracy: Principles and Genealogy* (Chicago: University of Chicago Press, 2006); Gordon S. Wood, *The Creation of the American Republic, 1776–1787* (Chapel Hill: University of North Carolina Press, 1998), esp. chap. 2.

3. Allan Greer, *The Patriots and the People: The Rebellion of 1837 in Rural Lower Canada* (Toronto: University of Toronto Press, 1993), esp. 323–329 (ideas of "habitant-militiamen"). For further discussion of Upper Canadian politics, consult Chapters 8 and 9 of this book. Gilles Gallichan suggests that the political unrest of the Dalhousie crisis would "culminate" in the Rebellions of 1837–1838 ("Le crise parlementaire de 1827 au Bas-Canada," *Les Cahiers des dix* 66 [2012]: 134).
4. For explicit democratization readings of Canada in this period, consult Gallichan, "Le crise parlementaire," esp. 96–97, 100, 137; Allan Greer, "Historical Roots of Canadian Democracy," *Journal of Canadian Studies* 34, no. 1 (Spring 1999): 7–26; Greer, *Patriots and the People*, 137–141. See also Henri Brun, *La formation des institutions parlementaires québécoises, 1791–1838* (Québec: Presses de l'Université de Laval, 1970); Philip Buckner, *The Transition to Responsible Government: British Policy in British North America, 1815–1850* (Westport, Conn.: Greenwood, 1985); Louis-Georges Harvey, *Le Printemps de l'Amérique Française: Américanité, anticolonialisme et républicanisme dans le discours politique québécois, 1805–1837* (Montréal: Boréal, 2005). The Lower Canada population totaled 423,373 in 1827, according to the Select Committee report occasioned by the 1827–1828 anti-Dalhousie petition. *Rapport du Comité choisi sur le gouvernement civil du Canada* (Québec: Neilson & Cowan, 1829), 363.
5. William Henry Atherton, *Montreal 1535–1914: Under British Rule, 1760–1914* (Montréal: S. J. Clarke, 1914), 139; Gallichan, "Le crise parlementaire de 1827 au Bas-Canada," 131–133; Peter Burroughs, "Ramsay, George, 9th Earl of Dalhousie," *Dictionary of Canadian Biography*, vol. 7 (Toronto: University of Toronto Press, 1988) (hereafter *DCB*).
6. Further discussion of Durham's *Report* and its aftermath appears in Chapter 9.
7. Hannah Weiss-Muller's perceptive essay ("From *Requête* to Petition: Petitioning the Monarch between Empires," *Historical Journal* 60, no. 3 [2017]: 659–686) shows that the difference between these terms extended well beyond mechanistic translation. In reading memorials as *requêtes* and not merely petitions, French Canadians were invoking an older tradition of supplication. See also the patterns of supplication described in Arlette Farge and Michel Foucault, *Disorderly Families: Infamous Letters from the Bastille Archives*, ed. Nancy Luxon (Minneapolis: University of Minnesota Press, 2016).
8. Philip Lawson, *The Imperial Challenge: Quebec and Britain in the Age of the American Revolution* (Montreal: McGill-Queen's University Press,

1989), 37–41; *Report from the Select Committee on the Civil Government of Canada* (Reprinted, House of Assembly of Lower Canada) (Québec, 1829), 29 (hereafter *Report SCCGC*).

9. Lawson, *Imperial Challenge,* 37 (question of assembly representation given French majority over English); *Rapport du comité choisi* (1829), 11; *Report SCCGC,* 3, 29; Greer, *Patriots and the People,* 113–115; Brun, *La formation des institutions parlementaires québécoises,* 231; Gallichan, "Le crise parlementaire," 96.
10. Michel Ducharme, *Le Concept de Liberté au Canada à L'Epoque des Révolutions Atlantiques, 1776–1838* (Montréal: McGill-Queen's University Press, 2010), 69–78, 82.
11. [Bédard], *Mémoire au soutien de la requête des habitans du Bas-Canada, à son Altesse Royale le Prince Régent* (Quebec: n.a., 1814): ". . . ils ont été terrassés, comme opposés au gouvernement" (reprinted in Yvan Lamonde and Claude Corro, *Le rouge et le bleu: Une anthologie de la pensée politique au Québec de la Conquête à la Révolution tranquille* [Montréal: Presses de l'Université de Montréal, 1999], 71–79, quote on 72). On Bédard and his influence, consult Gilles Gallichan, "Pierre Bédard, le devoir et la justice: 2e partie—La politique et la magistrature," *Les Cahiers des dix* 64 (2010): 145–207; Ducharme, *Le Concept de Liberté.*
12. Gallichan "Le crise parlementaire," 109; Ducharme, *Le Concept de Liberté au Canada,* 89.
13. Greer, *Patriots and the People,* 60–68 (parish). The phrase *la constitution de cette province* was used in the 1828 anti-Dalhousie petition as well as in the Ninety-Two Resolutions of the Legislative Assembly of Lower Canada (see Resolutions 8, 39, and 88); William Paul McClure Kennedy, *Statutes, Treaties, and Documents of the Canadian Constitution* (Toronto: Oxford University Press, 1930); Maxime Dagenais, "92 Resolutions," *The Canadian Encyclopedia* (Toronto: Historica Canada, 2017); Harvey, *Le Printemps de l'Amérique Française,* 100–101 (embrace and critique of British constitutionalism).
14. In Lower Canada, the union bill was known as "Bill de l'Union des Législatures du Haut et du Bas-Canada, tel que projeté et amendé par un Comité de la Chambre des Communes, le 31 juillet 1822."
15. Gilles Chaussé and Lucien Lemieux, "Lartigue, Jean-Jacques," *DCB,* vol. 7; Lucien Lemieux, "Les évêques canadiens contre le projet d'Union des deux Canadas (1822–1824)," *Revue d'histoire de l'Amérique française* 22, no. 3 (December 1968): 393–400. Lartigue was a disciple of the ultramontane Abbé Félicité de Lammenais. John W. O'Malley, *Vatican I: The Council and the Making of the Ultramontane Church* (Cambridge, Mass.: Harvard University Press, 2018), chaps. 1–2, esp. 66–69.

16. "Copie de la Pétition dressée et arrêtée par les comtés des districts de Québec et de Montréal, contre l'Union," *Le Canadien,* November 27, 1822, 357–359 ("toutes les classes du people de cette Province ont constamment manifesté un attachement inviolable à cette Constitution"). See also *Le Canadien,* January 1, 1823, 353–357 (another anti-Union petition), 357–358 (pro-Union memorial). On ancien régime language in nineteenth-century France labor, see the classic account of William Sewell Jr., *Work and Revolution in France: The Language of Labor from the Old Regime to 1848* (Cambridge: Cambridge University Press, 1980).
17. On Bathhurst, see Chapter 6 in this book. Jacques Viger kept detailed records of the 1822 committee meetings that launched the petition. *Procédés des habitants de la Cité et du District de Montréal, amis de la Constitution des Canadas de 1791, aux fins de concerter des moyens de la conserver intacte et de prévenir, si possible, la passation du "Bill d'Union des Législatures du Haut et du Bas-Canada, tel que projeté et amendé par un Comité de la Chambre des Communes, le 31 juillet 1822"; contenant la correspondance du Comité Général de ce District avec ceux des districts de Québec et des Trois-Rivières, et plusieurs des Comités Constitutionnels du Haut-Canada. Avec Appendices* (Montréal, 1822). On Viger and Bathhurst, see Lemieux, "Les évêques canadiens," 397–398; Gallichan, "Le crise parlementaire," 96–97; Harvey, *Le Printemps de l'Amérique Française,* 10; Buckner, *The Transition to Responsible Government,* 112–121; Helen Taft Manning, *The Revolt of French Canada: A Chapter in the History of the British Commonwealth* (New York: St. Martin's, 1962), 151–170; Fernand Ouellet, *Le Bas-Canada, 1791–1840* (Ottawa: Éditions de l'Université d'Ottawa 1976).
18. Ducharme, *Le Concept de Liberté,* chap. 3; Gallichan "Le crise parlementaire," 100–101, 103–104.
19. Francois Blanchet, *Appel au Parlement impérial et aux habitans des colonies anglaises dans L'Amérique du Nord sur les prétentions exorbitants du Gouvernement exécutif et du Conseil législatif de la Province du Bas-Canada. Par un membre de la Chambre d'assemblée* (Québec, 1824), esp. 11–12, 21–22; Viger, *Analyse d'un entretien sur la conservation des établissements du Bas-Canada, des loix, des usages &c de ses habitans: Par un canadien dans une lettre a un de ses amis* (Montréal, 1826); *JCABC,* 1823, 30. See also l'Assemblée, *adresse au roi; JCABC,* 1823–1824, 239 (cited in Ducharme, *Le Concept de Liberté,* 262n57); "Copie de la Pétition dressée et arrêtée par les comtés des districts de Québec et de Montréal, contre l'Union," in *Le Canadien,* November 27, 1822, 357–359.

20. Gallichan, "Le crise parlementaire," 97, 104n26; Ducharme, *Le Concept de Liberté,* 83.
21. Gallichan, "Le crise parlementaire," 97–98; Ducharme, *Le Concept de Liberté,* 84–85.
22. Gallichan, "Le crise parlementaire," 99–100, 114–115; Ducharme, *Le Concept de Liberté,* 87 (the elections "swung essentially on the question of *Assemblée* control of revenues and of the civil list").
23. *Report SCCGC,* 66.
24. *Report SCCGC,* 1.
25. Greer, *Patriots and the People; Report SCCGC,* 11–40, 49–52.
26. *Report SCCGC,* 23–24; Bettina Bradbury, *Wife to Widow: Lives, Laws and Politics in Nineteenth-Century Montreal* (Vancouver, 2011).
27. *Report SCCGC,* 38–39; Greer, *Patriots and the People.*
28. *Rapport du comité choisi* (1829), 343–344 ("Ainsi le Conseil Législatif n'est en effet que l'exécutif sous un autre nom . . ."); *Report SCCGC,* 31.
29. For an examination of sixty-two officers dismissed from the district of Montréal and another twenty-eight in the *comté* of York, see Christian Dessureault, "La crise sous Dalhousie: Conception de la milice et conscience élitaire des réformistes bas-canadiens, 1827–1828," *Revue d'histoire de l'Amérique française* 61 (2007): 176–178, 183, 190. Lee protestation of Québec, October 29, 1827, quoted in "Extracts from the *Canadian Spectator* of the 3d Novr. 1827, containing the libelous matter, for which an Indictment was found by the Grand Jury against the Editor and Printer of that Paper, in a Court of Oyer and Terminer and General Goal Delivery, held at Montreal in Novr. 1827," file 30, no. 2, Records of the Colonial Office, LAC. In other cases, protesting militia officers sent their complaints directly to colonial ministers such as William Huskinson; see the case of M. Mondelet of Montréal in Murray (Dalhousie) to unnamed recipient, 6th September 1828, Fonds Dalhousie, LAC, 215a5. See also Greer, *Patriots and the People,* 100–107.
30. Burroughs, "Ramsay, George, 9th Earl of Dalhousie"; Ducharme, *Le Concept de Liberté,* 75; Gallichan, "Le crise parlementaire," 107–108, 125.
31. *Report SCCGC,* 66–67.
32. In a letter to his daughter Julie in 1828, Papineau wrote of "La Requête des Citoyens de Montréal se plaignant des abus de la dernière Administration. . . ." LJP à Julie Papineau, December 8, 1828, Fonds Papineau, LAC [microforme p. 1031]. The *assemblée* of Sainte-Anne d'Yamachiche spoke of not of the petition but of "le projet de Requête, adoptée à l'assemblée du 22 Décembre dernier "; rapport de M. Valere Guillete, January 1, 1828, folios 225–226, Fonds Papineau, LAC. On "la Requête de Mon-

tréal," consult A. N. Moran to John Neilson, Denis Benjamin Viger et Augustin Cuvillier (écuyers), Montréal February 17, 1828, Fonds Neilson, LAC. Extrait des registres d'un Comité nommé par une Assemblée Générale des Electeurs de la Ville et Faubourgs de Québec, tenu à Québec le 13 décembre 1827 touchant les abus qui existent en cette Province, Fonds Neilson, LAC. On the terminology of the period, see Muller, "From Requete to Petition," and Benoit Agnès, *L'appel au pouvoir: Les pétitions aux parlements en France et au Royaume-Uni (1814–1848)* (Rennes: Presses Universitaires de Rennes, 2018); Carpenter and Brossard, *"L'éruption patriote,"* 466–467 (links to older French *assemblée* practices).

33. "A une assemblée de la paroisse Ste-Anne d'Yamachiche, tenue après avis public, donné à la porte de l'église, en la Salle Publique, mardi le premier janvier 1828," in rapport de M. Valére Guillete, January 1, 1828, folios 225–226, Fonds Papineau, LAC. The assemblée of Sainte-Anne d'Yamachiche spoke not of the petition but of "le projet de Requête, adopte à l'assemblée du 22 Décembre dernier." For a similar rubric used at St. Charles, see unsigned letter, St. Charles, December 27, 1827, folio 88, [microforme, p. 788], Fonds Papineau, LAC.
34. Brouillon de pétition de L'Abbe Pierre Dominique Debartzsch et Louis C Duvert, 24 ou 26 Déc. 1827, Assemblée St. Denis; fonds Papineau, folios 85, 87 [microforme, pp. 785, 787]. In some cases, the *paroisse*-level efforts relied heavily on local notables, such as the case of Pierre St. Ours in the *paroisse* of L'Assomption. H. W. Ryland to Dalhousie, undated (probably early 1828), Fonds Dalhousie, LAC, 213a.
35. Because only part of the petition appears in Figure 7.1, the visual impression it made was at least as large as it would appear from the museum display.
36. Bradbury, *Wife to Widow*. For a statistical encoding and analysis of French versus English surnames and surname clustering, consult Carpenter and Brossard, *"L'éruption patriote,"* 469–471. For other evidence from Canada on hierarchically organized signatory lists, consult Watt, "'Duty Bound and Ever Praying'," 135, 191, 197. On Galt, see Atherton, *Montreal 1535–1914*, 3:254.
37. *Rapport du comité choisi*, 343, 355.
38. George Moffatt to Sir George Murray, 1827, 7, Fonds Papineau, LAC.
39. Porteous's statement appears in *Addresses to His Excellency the Governor in Chief from Different Parts of Lower-Canada, with His Excellency's Answers* (Montréal, 1828), 27.
40. Signature List from Pétition des comtés des districts de Montréal et des Trois Rivières; numéro d'inventaire 1957.6, Musée Stewart, Montréal.

Consult Carpenter and Brossard, "*L'éruption patriote*," 469–471, for analysis. See also Bradbury, *Wife to Widow*, 260–275; Watt, "Duty Bound and Every Praying," 123.

41. *Addresses to His Excellency the Governor in Chief*, 25–26.
42. *Report of a Select Committee of the House of Assembly Appointed to Enquire into the State of Education in this Province* (Quebec: House of Assembly, 1824).
43. *Addresses to His Excellency the Governor in Chief*, 28–29; Special Committee of the House of Assembly of Lower-Canada, *Reports and Evidence of the Special Committee of the House of Assembly of Lower-Canada: To Whom Were Referred the Petition of the Inhabitants of the County of York, That of the Inhabitants of the City of Montreal, and Other Petitions Praying the Redress of Grievances* (Québec: House of Assembly, 1829), 6–7, 189.
44. Abbé Lionel Groulx, *Quelques causes de nos insuffisances* (Montréal: Cercle Universitaire de Montréal, 1930), 11.
45. Watt, "Duty Bound and Ever Praying," 135–38; Zaeske, *Signatures of Citizenship;* Richard Franklin Bensel, *The American Ballot Box in the Mid-Nineteenth Century* (Cambridge: Cambridge University Press, 2004).
46. The organizers' testament on marks having represented informed consent appeared as follows: "Nous soussignés certifions que les signatures ci-dessus auxquelles des croix sont apposées ont été données volontairement en notre présence par les personnes y nommées, après communication de l'objet de cette requête"; Montréal signature page 1, Faubourg Saint Laurent page 4, Signature List from Pétition des comtés des districts de Montréal et des Trois Rivières; numéro d'inventaire 1957.6, Musée Stewart, Montréal.
47. The biographer was L'Abbé Auguste Gosselin: *Le Docteur Labrie: un bon patriote d'autrefois* (Québec, 1903), 140.
48. Gallichan, "Le crise parlementaire," 134, citing Ouellet, *Le Bas-Canada*, 327. "Presque partout l'exaltation politique 'avait gagné les devants'": Michel Bibaud, *Histoire du Canada et des Canadiens sous la domination Anglaise* (Montréal: Lovell et Gibson, 1844), 307. Petition for widows of Québec; see Chapter 11 this volume.
49. "Que tous les membres de la Comite principal qu'adjoint, s'emploient de toutes leurs forces pour recueillir des souscriptions volontaires et des signatures à la Requête a sa Majesté"; "A une assemblée de la paroisse Ste Anne de Yamachiche . . . donnée à la porte de l'église, en la salle publique" (January 1827), Fonds Papineau, 225–226 [microforme, 7022–7023], LAC; Brouillon de pétition de L'Abbe Pierre Dominique Debartzsch et Louis C. Duvert, 24 ou 26 Déc. 1827, Assemblée St. Denis;

fonds Papineau, folios 85, 87 [microforme, 785, 787], LAC; Thomas Chapais, "Le Comité des Griefs de 1828," *Canada français* 3 (1920): 326.

50. Mondelet remarks in *JCABC* 1828–1829, February 21, 1829, 519–520 (petitions and counterpetition, 521–523); Francis J. Audet, *Les Députés de Trois-Rivières, 1808–1838* (Trois-Rivières: E. Fabre Surveyer, 1934), 34–42; Gallichan, "Le crise parlementaire," 126.
51. Carpenter and Brossard, *"L'éruption patriote,"* 469–471, 475–476 (detailed statistical analysis of the Montréal and Faubourgs sample).
52. Greer, *Patriots and the People.*
53. Jean Dessaulles à LJP, St. Hyacinth, April 12, 1827, Fonds Papineau, LAC.
54. *Report SCCGC* 1829, 52.
55. On the petition's transmission, consult Fonds comité de pétition de 1828, BAnQ, Québec. See also *Messrs Nelson, Viger & Cuvillier, Delegates from the inhabitants of Lower Canada, with Petitions of Grievances;* CO 42/218, including Viger to Huskisson, March 31, 1828, NAUK.
56. *The Petition of the undersigned Chiefs and Warriors of the Huron and Wyandot Indians, residing at Lorette in the Province of Lower Canada,* Lorette, February 1, 1828; CO 42/218, NAUK. On the surge of petitioning from the Saint Lawrence valley Indigenous populations, consult Maxime Gohier, "La pratique petitionnaire." On Kahnawá:ke women voting for Cuvillier, consult Bradbury, *Wife to Widow,* 263.
57. "Canada," *NWR,* April 21, 1827, 129.
58. "Canada," *NWR,* April 21, 1827, 129.
59. "Canada," *NWR,* December 22, 1827, 272.
60. "Fortifications of Canada," *NWR,* July 7, 1828, 29–30, 32.
61. "Fortifications of Canada."
62. "Fortifications of Canada."
63. *Report SCCGC* (1829); Bruce Curtis, *Ruling by Schooling Quebec: Conquest to Liberal Governmentality: A Historical Sociology* (Toronto: University of Toronto Press, 2012), 61; Atherton, *Montreal Under British Rule, 1760–1914,* 139; Burroughs, "Ramsay, George, 9th Earl of Dalhousie"; John J. McCusker and Russell R. Menard, *The Economy of British America, 1607–1789* (Chapel Hill: University of North Carolina Press, 1985).
64. On the breadth of the transfer of budgetary power, see the judgment of J. A. MacLean, "In 1831, on the recommendation of the Canada Committee of 1828, the proceeds of the Quebec Revenue Act were surrendered without reserve or condition to the control of the Provincial Legislature" ("Crown Revenues in Lower Canada (1763–1847)," in *Report of the Sixty-Seventh Meeting of the British Association for the Advancement of Science* (1897) (London: British Association for the Advancement

of Science, 1898), 743. See also Hansard's *House of Commons Debates*, February 18, 1831, 2:686–693. On the statement admitting that the 1831 act gave the provincial assembly vast powers over colonial revenues, see the remarks of Lord Stanley in Hansard's *House of Commons Debates*, April 14, 1837, 37:1234 (and more generally 1209–1293). Similar judgments on the growth of provincial assembly authority abound; see John Henry Barrow, *The Mirror of Parliament for the First Session of the Thirteenth Parliament of Great Britain and Ireland*, 2nd series, vol. 2 (1837–1838) (London, 1838), 1331–1332; Charles Richard Tuttle, *Tuttle's Popular History of the Dominion of Canada*, vol. 1 (Montréal and Boston: Downie, 1877), 371–372; J. A. McLean; Sir Spencer Walpole, *A History of England from the Conclusion of the Great War in 1815*, vol. 4 (London: Longmans, Green, 1910), 116–117; Brun, *La formation des institutions parlementaires québécoises*, 231, 247–249; Gallichan, "Le crise parlementaire," 123, 134.

On another petition from the assembly and reportedly 24,500 colonists in 1834, consult John Alexander Boyd, *A Summary of Canadian History* (Toronto: James Campbell and Son, 1869), 101; *Petition from Lower Canada with Explanatory Remarks* (London: William Clowes, 1835).

65. Greer, *Patriots and the People*, 138–141.
66. Malcolm Chase, "'Brothers under Oppression': Chartists and the Canadian Rebellions of 1837–8," in Chase, *The Chartists: Perspectives and Legacies* (London: Merlin Press, 2015), 28–46.
67. See Chapter 11 this volume.
68. Viger, *Analyse d'un entretien sur la conservation des établissements du Bas-Canada, des loix, des usages &c de ses habitans;* Harvey, *Le Printemps de l'Amérique Française.*
69. Greer, *Patriots and the People*, 128–131, 137–141.
70. Gallichan, "Le crise parlementaire, 134. "Without intending to, Governor Dalhousie, through his aristocratic stubbornness, induced the advancement of a fledgling Lower Canadian democracy, the first time in pushing the project of colonial fusion in 1822 and a second time in rejecting the choice of Papineau as Speaker." Gallichan, "Le crise parlementaire, 134–135 (my translation).

8. PRODUCERS, ELECTORS, CITY DEMOCRATS

1. Alfred Chandler, *The Visible Hand: the Managerial Revolution in American Business* (Cambridge, Mass.: Harvard University Press, 1977); Sven Beckert, *Empire of Cotton: A Global History* (New York: Random House, 2014); David Montgomery, *Citizen Worker: The Experience of*

Workers in the United States with Democracy and the Free Market during the Nineteenth Century (Cambridge: Cambridge University Press, 1993); Christine Stansell, *City of Women: Sex and Class in New York, 1789–1860* (New York: Knopf, 2012); David R. Roediger, *The Wages of Whiteness: Race and the Making of the American Working Class* (New York: Verso, 1991); Seth Rockman, *Scraping By: Wage Labor, Slavery and Survival in Early Baltimore* (Baltimore: Johns Hopkins University Press, 2009); Anne Boylan, *The Origins of Women's Activism: New York and Boston, 1797–1840* (Chapel Hill: University of North Carolina Press, 2002); Paul Boyer, *Urban Masses and Moral Order in America, 1820–1920* (Cambridge, Mass.: Harvard University Press, 1978).

2. Sean Wilentz, *Chants Democratic: New York City and the Rise of the American Working Class, 1788–1850* (Oxford: Oxford University Press, 1984; Sean Wilentz, *The Rise of American Democracy: Jefferson to Lincoln* (Oxford: Oxford University Press, 2005); John Aldrich, *Why Parties? The Origin and Transformation of Political Parties in America* (Chicago: University of Chicago Press, 1995); Robert V. Remini, *Andrew Jackson and the Course of American Freedom, 1822–1832* (Baltimore: Johns Hopkins University Press, 2013); Remini, *Andrew Jackson: The Course of American Democracy, 1833–1845* (Baltimore: Johns Hopkins University Press, 1988); Arthur Schlesinger Jr., *The Age of Jackson* (New York: New American Library, 1945); Matthew H. Crocker, *The Magic of the Many: Josiah Quincy and the Rise of Mass Politics in Boston, 1800–1830* (Amherst: University of Massachusetts Press, 1999).
3. Wood, *Creation of the American Republic*, esp. chap. 2; J. G. A. Pocock, *The Machiavellian Moment: Florentine Political Thought and the Atlantic Republican Tradition* (Princeton, N.J.: Princeton University Press, 1975); Daniel T. Rodgers, *The Work Ethic in Industrial America, 1850–1920* (Chicago: University of Chicago Press, 1979).
4. Edmund Morgan, *Inventing the People*, 107–121; Jack Rakove, *Original Meanings: Politics and Ideas in the Making of the Constitution* (New York: Vintage, 1996), chaps. 2–4; Richard Tuck, *The Sleeping Sovereign: The Invention of Modern Democracy* (Cambridge: Cambridge University Press, 2015).
5. David A. Bateman, *Disenfranchising Democracy: Constructing the Electorate in the United States, the United Kingdom and France* (Cambridge: Cambridge University Press, 2018).
6. Kloppenburg, *Toward Democracy*, chaps. 10–14; *Reports of the Proceedings and Debates of the Convention of 1821, Assembled for the Purpose of Amending the Constitution of the State of New York* (Albany: Hosford, 1821), 224 (French republican models); hereafter *RPDC-1821-NY.*

7. Richard Purcell, *Connecticut in Transition, 1775–1818* (Middletown: Wesleyan University Press, 1963), 195–199, 340–41, 364–366; Wilentz, *Rise of American Democracy,* 185.
8. Tocqueville did in fact notice associations petitioning; *Democracy in America,* chap. 12, "On Political Associations in the United States." The *Hartford Times* observed: "Every bill which passed the House, intended either to remove popular complaints or redress public grievances, was neglected by the Council." Quoted in *Niles' Weekly Register* 12:240.
9. *Journal of the Proceedings of the Convention of Delegates, Convened at Hartford, August 26, 1818, for the Purpose of Forming a New Constitution of Civil Government for the People of the State of Connecticut* (Hartford, 1901); Constitution of Connecticut, 1818, Article III, Legislative Branch; Purcell, *Connecticut in Transition,* 341, 357–58, 388–89; Wilentz, *Rise of American Democracy,* 186–87.
10. Alfred B. Street, *The Council of Revision of the State of New York* (Albany, 1859); Hulsebosch, *Constituting the Empire State,* chap. 8; Wilentz, *Rise of American Democracy,* 189.
11. *JSSNY,* 34th Session (March 21, 1811), 126 (petition of Ezra Wait, David Eddy and John C. Spencer, delegates from Ontario County townships convened at Canandaigua); Lincoln, *Constitutional History of the State of New York, 1,* 615 (petitions as evidence of popular pressure for general suffrage); Wilentz, *Rise of American Democracy,* 190–191 (factional divisions and the Clintonians' demise).
12. *RPDC-1821-NY,* 224.
13. *RPDC-1821-NY,* 246.
14. *RPDC-1821-NY,* 246.
15. *RPDC-1821-NY,* 249, 254 (demands, specter of France); Street, *Council of Revision,* 467–68.
16. Keyssar, *Right to Vote,* 37 and appendix, 328–342; Wilentz, *Rise of American Democracy,* 192–95; Howe, *WHGW,* 489–93; *RPDC-1821-NY,* 180 (Ross), 183 (Col. Young amendment).
17. Memorial of Thomas Sipkin, introduced September 12, 1821, in *Journal of the Convention of the State of New-York, Begun and Held at the Capitol in the City of Albany, on the Twenty-Eighth Day of August, 1821* (Albany: Cantine & Leake, 1821), 49. Other records have the surname as Sipkins, and I follow this spelling.
18. Will and Testament of Thomas Sipkins, *Record of Wills and Probates, 1796–1879* (J1043–92), vol. 67–68 (John Jervis Ingersoll, 23 Dec. 1830; Enoch Dunn, 22 Oct. 1831), 25–28; New York County, Wills and Probate Records, NYSL; Leslie M. Harris, *In the Shadow of Slavery: African-Americans in New York City, 1626–1863* (Chicago: University of Chicago

Press, 2003), 85. Charles H. Wesley, "The Negroes of New York in the Emancipation Movement," *Journal of Negro History* 24, no. 1 (January 1939): 74–75 (Henry Sipkins); Daniel Perlman, "Organizations of the Free Negro in New York City, 1800–1860," *Journal of Negro History* 56, no. 3 (July 1971): 194–195.

19. *RPDC-1821-NY,* 180–81.
20. *RPDC-1821-NY,* 189–191.
21. *RPDC-1821-NY,* 193–194 (Van Vechten), 376 (Van Buren), 186–187 (Robert Clarke); Wilentz, *Rise of American Democracy,* 192–193.
22. Wilentz, *Rise of American Democracy,* 189 (New York held "the greatest reform convention held anywhere in the country during the decade after 1815"), 196, 840n34.
23. Petition of the Freeholders and Inhabitants of Henry County, December 18, 1805, Legislative Petitions of the General Assembly, 1776–1865, Accession Number 36121, box 119, folder 59, LOV.
24. Jefferson, *Notes on the State of Virginia,* Query XIII, "Constitution."
25. Petition of the Freeholders and Inhabitants of Henry County, December 18, 1805; Legislative Petitions of the General Assembly, 1776–1865, Accession Number 36121, box 119, folder 59, LOV. Henry County residents had raised these concerns nine years earlier. See Petition from Inhabitants of Henry County, November 12, 1795; Accession Number 36121, box 329, folder 20, LOV.
26. "Petition of Sundry Inhabitants and Freeholders of the County of Accomack," December 10, 1810, Petitions in Legislative Petitions of the General Assembly, 1776–1865, Accession Number 36121, box 1, folder 43, LOV.
27. Petition introduction and disposition (vote) appear in *JHODV,* 1810–1811 (December 10, 1810), 15 (January 29, 1811), 84–85.
28. J. A. C. Chandler, *Representation in Virginia* (Baltimore, 1896), 22–23.
29. Assembled memorials of the freemen of Rockingham County, Petitions in Legislative Petitions of the General Assembly, 1776–1865, Accession Number 36121, box 224, folder 64, LOV. Pro-convention petitions also came in the session from Brooke, Frederick, Greenbrier, Hampshire, Ohio, Patrick, and Shenandoah Counties, *JHODV,* 1815–1816, 33, 37; Chandler, *Representation,* 23–24; *Journal of the proceedings of a convention, begun and held in Staunton, the 19th day of August in the year 1816* (Staunton, 1816), including "Memorial of the Staunton Convention, to the Legislature of the State of Virginia"; also in *NWR* 40, no. 2 (September 7, 1816): 17–23.
30. Chandler, *Representation,* 24–25; Wilentz, *Rise of American Democracy,* 200–201.

31. Chandler, *Representation in Virginia,* 24–44. Chandler's calculations on the number of signatures follow the report of the select committee; *JHODV* (1825–26), 15, 17, 103, 104. For an example from the pro-reform side, see Inhabitants of Berkeley County, December 8, 1825, Accession Number 36121, box 27, folder 64, LOV. The counterpetition campaign explicitly targeted the memorial of the Staunton convention; see, for instance, the petition of New Kent County, December 12, 1825; Accession Number 36121, box 179, folder 62, LOV.
32. Wilentz, *Rise of American Democracy,* 197, quoting *AC,* 11th Congress, 3rd Session, 1347–1348. Jack Ericson Eblen, *The First and Second United States Empires: Governors and Territorial Government, 1784–1912* (Pittsburgh: University of Pittsburgh Press, 1968), 61–63, 160–65. Floyd Calvin Shoemaker, *Missouri's Struggle for Statehood, 1804–1821* (Jefferson City: Hugh Stevens, 1916), 119–120.
33. Wilentz remarks that "in no state did reform come easily, or without agitation and pressure from below," and that "in no instance did reforms occur simply because of the calculations of existing ruling groups" (*Rise of American Democracy,* 201). Contrast Daron Acemoglu and James A. Robinson, "Why Did the West Extend the Franchise? Democracy, Inequality, and Growth in Historical Perspective," *Quarterly Journal of Economics,* November 2000, 1167–1199.
34. Richard Hofstadter, *The Idea of a Party System,* 47 (deference); Wood, *Creation of the American Republic,* chaps. 10–13.
35. Wilentz, *Chants Democratic,* 25–27; Murphy, *Building the Empire State.*
36. Wilentz, *Chants Democratic,* chap. 2 ("artisan republicanism," see also 25–31, 35, 67); Amy Bridges, *A City in the Republic: Antebellum New York and the Origins of Machine Politics* (Cambridge: Cambridge University Press, 1984), chaps. 1–3; Naomi Lamoreaux, *Insider Lending: Banks, Personal Connections and Economic Development in Industrial New England* (Cambridge: Cambridge University Press, 1994), esp. chap. 1 (networks of credit).
37. *Annals of the General Society of Mechanics and Tradesmen of New York, from 1785–1880* (New York: General Society, 1882), 7–61; Wilentz, *Chants Democratic,* 38–41; Bridges, *City in the Republic,* 104–105; Lawrence A. Peskin, "From Protection to Encouragement: Manufacturing and Mercantilism in the York City's Public Sphere, 1783–1795," *Journal of the Early Republic* 18, no. 4 (Winter 1998), 589–615. Society's petitions in *JASNY* 34th Session (1811), 18, 40, 136.
38. Ray Bert Westerfield, "Early History of American Auctions: A Chapter in Commercial History," *Transactions of the Connecticut Academy of Arts and Sciences* 23 (May 1920): 159–210 (aggregate figures, 172); Horace

Secrist, "The Anti-Auction Movement and the New York Workingmen's Party of 1829," *Transactions of the Wisconsin Academy of Arts, Sciences and Letters* 17, no. 1 (1911): 149–166; Wilentz, *Chants Democratic,* 150–151; Memorial of the auctioneers of New York (parroting anti-auctioneer arguments) in *AC,* 16th Cong., 2nd Sess., 1529–1530 (debate at 2173–2176); Joanna Cohen, *Luxurious Citizens* (Philadelphia: University of Pennsylvania Press, 2017), chap. 3.

39. Memorial of sundry merchants, manufacturers, &c., of Baltimore, January 19, 1824; *AC* 18 (1): 3127–3130; "Anti-Auction Meeting: Memorial," *NWR* 35 (December 6, 1828), 228, "Great Anti-Auction Meeting," *NWR* 36 (May 16, 1829), 184; Secrist, "The Anti-Auction Movement of 1828," 153; *New York Evening Post,* December 23, 1828, 3; "Antiauction Meeting: The Memorial of the Mechanics, Merchants, Manufacturers and Others, of the City of New York," in *Workingmen's Advocate* 1, no. 7 (December 12, 1829).
40. Memorial of the farmers, manufacturers, mechanics, and merchants, of the county of Renssalaer . . . praying for a revision of the Tariff, January 26, 1824; *AC* 18 (1): 3132–3139.
41. Jonathan J. Pincus, *Pressure Groups & Politics in Antebellum Tariffs* (New York: Columbia University Press, 1977), 53; Daniel Peart, "Looking Beyond Parties and Elections: The Making of United States Tariff Policy during the Early 1820s," *JER* 33, no. 1 (Spring 2013): 87–108. Peart concludes that "petitioning was by far the most common mode through which protectionists sought to influence the decision of the Sixteenth Congress" in the spring of 1820 (99).
42. *JSUS,* December 27, 1819, 50; *JHRUS,* November 21, 1820, 24–25; *JSUS,* January 4, 1821, 94; Petition in *ASP* III (Finance) III (1832), 462; Peart, "Looking Beyond Parties and Elections," 100; John W. Maxon Jr., "American Papermakers in the Great Tariff Debate," *Paper Maker* 31, no. 1 (1962): 23–24. On the coalescing nature of tariff politics, see Rock, *Artisans of the New Republic,* 172–177; Wilentz, *Chants Democratic,* 47; City petitions in *ASP* Finance, vol. 3 (Protection to Manufactures, 16th Cong., 1st Sess.), 441. Joshua R. Greenberg, *Advocating the Man: Masculinity, Organized Labor, and the Household in New York, 1800–1840* (New York: Columbia University Press, 2008), chaps. 4–5.
43. Pincus, "Pressure Groups and the Pattern of Tariffs," *Journal of Political Economy* 83, no. 4 (1975): 757–778.
44. The Vote on the House Tariff Bill of 1828 was 105–94 in support. New England provided a negative margin (16–23 against), but the mid-Atlantic states voted for the measure 56–6 and the northwestern states of Ohio, Indiana, Illinois, Missouri, and Kentucky voted 29–1 in favor. F. W.

Taussig, *The Tariff History of the United States,* pt. 1, 5th ed. (New York, 1910), 70–74.

45. Wilentz, *Chants Democratic,* 40, 54, 140, 145–151 (Society as a "stalwart friend of religion and morality," 149); Peter M. Kenny, *Duncan Phyfe: Master Cabinetmaker in New York* (New York, 2011), 45–47; Rock, *Artisans,* 184–189, 196–197; Teresa Anne Murphy, *Ten Hours' Labor: Religion, Reform, and Gender in Early New England* (Ithaca: Cornell University Press, 1992), 49–50; Rockman, *Scraping By.* Tavern complaints in "Complaints, Taverns, April 1822," B1, F3, Stephen Allen Papers, NYHS; Richard R. John, *Spreading the News: The American Postal System from Franklin to Morse* (Cambridge, Mass.: Harvard University Press, 1995), 186–187.
46. Wilentz, *Chants Democratic,* 82.
47. Allen, "The memoirs of Stephen Allen (1757–1852): sometime Mayor of New York City . . ." (typescript, edited, with an introduction by John C. Travis), 41–104; NYPL; Paul A. Gilje, *The Road to Mobocracy: Popular Disorder in New York City, 1763–1834* (Chapel Hill: University of North Carolina Press, 1987), 270; Wilentz, *Chants Democratic,* 72–73.
48. Allen to Rev. Gardner Spring, June 17, 1823 (re Sabbath regulations); to Charles Town (February 24, 1824; on poor laws and pauperism); to John Morss (February 29, 1824); to Gideon Lee (February 7, 1823); to Walter Borone (March 27, 1823 (enclosing and endorsing a General Society petition), April 4, 1823, and March 17, 1824 (relaying General Society petition), B1, F7, Allen Papers, NYHS; Novak, *People's Welfare,* chaps. 3, 5.
49. Crocker, *Magic of the Many,* 49.
50. Crocker, *Magic of the Many,* 25–27, 47–51.
51. Crocker, *Magic,* 24–25 (expanded work areas for debt-prisoners' furloughs), 27–28 (militia reform), 29–33; "Militia Law," *New England Galaxy and Masonic Magazine* 3 (June 23, 1820), 146. On the debt-prisoners' petition, see *The Debtors' Journal* 1, no. 1 (September 23, 1820); the article directly reports 2,500 signatures, whereas Crocker separately reports 4,000 or more. Crocker, *Magic of the Many,* 65–69 (mass petitions in 1822). General court responses appear in *Acts and Resolves, 1819–1824,* 136, 359, 412, 446. No such examples of discharge appear in the 1815 to 1819 period. Ronald Formisano, *The Transformation of Political Culture: Massachusetts Parties, 1790s–1840s* (Oxford: Oxford University Press, 1983), 187–190; Wilentz, *Rise of American Democracy,* 187–189.
52. Crocker, *Magic,* 27–29.
53. Crocker, *Magic,* 64–67.

54. Crocker, *Magic,* 67 (Central Committee's handling of the issue as "a direct violation of the principles of democracy").
55. Crocker, *Magic,* 68–69.
56. Crocker, *Magic,* 68–69, 78.
57. Crocker, *Magic,* Chapter 4, 71, 77–78, 81–82, 150, 161–63.
58. David Colden Cadwallader, *Memoir . . . in Celebration of the Completion of the New York Canals,* Volume 1 (New York, 1825), 222. Wilentz writes that "Independence, in 1825 as in 1788," signified "in the first place, independence from Britain." Wilentz, *Chants Democratic,* 86, 89–90 (Erie Canal parade and Saint Clement), 92, 145.
59. Wilentz, *Chants Democratic,* 39–40, 152, 172; *Memorial of the General Society of Mechanics and Tradesmen for the Renewal of the Charter of the Mechanics' Bank* (New York: General Society, 1829), Stephen Allen Papers, NYHS.
60. Joanna Innes, "Origins of the Factory Acts: The Health and Morals of Apprentices Act, 1802," in *Law, Crime and English Society, 1660–1830,* ed. Norma Landau (Cambridge: Cambridge University Press, 2002), 230–255; Samuel Kydd, *The History of the Factory Movement: From the Year 1802, to the Enactment of the Ten Hours' Bill in 1847,* 2 vols. (London: Simpkin, Marshall, 1857); Eileen Groth Lyon, *Christian Radicalism in Britain from the Fall of the Bastille to the Disintegration of Chartism* (London: Ashgate, 1999), 125–150.
61. *The Artisan,* February 22, 1832; April 5, April 19, and August 16, 1832 (petitions); Murphy, *Ten Hours' Labor,* 49–50.
62. Martha S. Jones, *Birthright Citizens: A History of Race and Rights in Antebellum America* (Cambridge: Cambridge University Press, 2018), chaps. 1, 4; Rockman, *Scraping By,* 3, 28, chap. 5 (starting at 132), 148–152.
63. Rockman, *Scraping By,* 1–3, 253–55; Jones, *Birthright Citizens,* chaps. 4, 6, 7.
64. "Of jails, penitentiaries and prisons, and the government and discipline thereof," *JASNY* 1828, 101–102; Jonathan Gosman and Elijah Atwater (County of Tompkins), "Petition," *JASNY,* January 6, 1830; Greenberg, *Advocating the Man,* chap. 3; Petition of Thomas Stokes to employ a Matron for the female prisoners at Bellevue, and Report, *Minutes of the Common Council of New York,* March 21, 1831, 576–77. See the "spirited memorial" prepared for the Pennsylvania House, *Reports of the Prison Discipline Society of Boston v. 1 (1826–1835)* (Boston: Prison Discipline Society, 1836), 495 (Sixth Report—1831), 572–73 (Seventh Report, 1832), 723 (Eighth Report—1833).

65. Gerald Craig, *Upper Canada: The Formative Years, 1784–1841* (Toronto: McClelland and Stewart, 1963), 42–65; David Mills, *The Idea of Loyalty in Upper Canada, 1784–1850* (Montreal: McGill-Queen's University Press, 1988), chaps. 1–2; Carol Wilton, *Popular Politics and Political Culture in Upper Canada, 1800–1850* (Montreal: McGill-Queen's University Press, 2000), chap. 1.
66. Schrauers, *"Union Is Strength,"* 61–63.
67. *Dictionary of Canadian Biography*, "Weekes, William"; Wilton, *Popular Politics*, 11–12, 24–27.
68. Wilton, Popular Politics, 27–28; "Gourlay, Robert," *Dictionary of Canadian Biography.*
69. Gourlay, Robert, *Dictionary of Canadian Biography.*
70. Gourlay, Robert, *Dictionary of Canadian Biography;* Wilton, *Popular Politics*, 29.
71. Wilton, *Popular Politics*, 29–31.
72. Wilton, *Popular Politics*, 31.
73. Wilton, *Popular Politics*, 29–31.
74. Wilton, *Popular Politics*, 34.
75. Wilton, *Popular Politics*, 34.
76. Gourlay, *Statistical Account of Upper Canada, Compiled with a View to a Grand System of Emigration* (London: Simpkin and Marshall, 1822); Wilton, *Popular Politics*, 34–36.
77. Schrauers, '"*Union Is Strength,*" 177–179; Wilton, *Popular Politics*, 36–40; Lillian F. Gates, "Ketchum, Jesse," in *Dictionary of Canadian Biography*, vol. 9 (Toronto, 1976).
78. Fred Coyne Hamil, "The Reform Movement in Upper Canada," in *Profiles of a Province: Studies in the History of Ontario*, ed. Edith G. Firth (Toronto: Ontario Historical Society, 1967), 9–19; Wilton, *Popular Politics*, 27.
79. Wilton, *Popular Politics*, 37–41.
80. Wilton, *Popular Politics*, 43.
81. Wilton, *Popular Politics*, 11, 42–43.
82. Mills, *Idea of Loyalty in Upper Canada*, chaps. 1–2; Wilton, *Popular Politics*, 44–52.
83. According to Paul Romney (*Mr. Attorney: The Attorney General for Ontario in Court, Cabinet, and Legislature 1791–1899* [Toronto, 1986]), the petition was "the most comprehensive public declaration yet made of Upper Canadians' grievances against the form and style of their government" (145–146); Wilton, *Popular Politics*, 44–46, 61.
84. As Wilton summarizes, "The petitioning movement of 1831 was the most important outburst of popular political activity in the entire Upper

Canadian period. [I]t mobilized the greatest number of people yet in the cause of general political reform. Beyond this, the petitioning movement of 1831 acted as a catalyst that transformed Upper Canadian politics in fundamental ways" (*Popular Politics,* 55; see generally chap. 2). Lillian F. Gates, "Ketchum, Jesse," *Dictionary of Canadian Biography,* vol. 9 (Toronto: University of Toronto Press, 1976).

85. Wilton, *Popular Politics,* 57.
86. The conclusion is from Wilton: "The most widespread and effective form of extraparliamentary organization since the late 1820s had been not electoral organization but petitioning." Wilton, *Popular Politics,* 60.
87. Wilton, *Popular Politics,* 56–59.
88. Wilton, *Popular Politics,* 55–62.
89. S. F Wise, ed., *Sir Francis Bond Head, A Narrative with Notes by William Lyon Mackenzie* (London, 1839; reprint: Toronto, 1969), 2; Wilton *Popular Politics,* 65–67.
90. Wilton, *Popular Politics,* 64.
91. Wilton, *Popular Politics,* 66–69.
92. Wilton, *Popular Politics,* chap. 3, esp. 85–93.
93. Wilton, *Popular Politics,* 93–104, 108–112.
94. Wilton, *Popular Politics,* 6 ("a much higher percentage of the population signed petitions than voted in provincial elections"), 112–13, appendix B.
95. Wilton, *Popular Politics,* 124–129, appendix A.
96. I discuss electoral mobilizations of the 1840s and 1850s in Chapters 10 and 11.

9. THE COALESCENCE OF OPPOSITION: FROM THE BANK WAR TO CANADIAN REFORM

1. Hofstadter, *The Idea of a Party System: The Rise of Legitimate Opposition in the United States, 1780–1840* (Berkeley: University of California Press, 1969); Aldrich, *Why Parties?;* Sean Wilentz, *The Politicians and the Egalitarians: The Hidden History of American Politics* (New York: Norton, 2016), esp. introduction and chap. 1; Nadia Urbinati, *Representative Democracy: Principles and Genealogy* (Chicago: University of Chicago Press, 2006), chap. 1.
2. Daniel Walker Howe emphasizes skepticism of a strong executive as an important and enduring element of Whig political culture in *The Political Culture of the American Whigs* (Chicago: University of Chicago Press, 1979), 90–95. Michael Holt locates important origins of anti-Jackson coalescence in Congress in December 1833 (with some southern politicians adopting the label "Whig" around that time), but the first meetings

and newspapers organized under "Whig" auspices did not emerge until the spring of 1834, well after the petition campaign had started. Holt, *The Rise and Fall of the American Whig Party: Jacksonian Politics and the Onset of the Civil War* (New York, 1999), 19–30.

3. I concur with Sean Wilentz's moderated reading of Whig antislavery. Wilentz, *The Rise of American Democracy: Jefferson to Lincoln* (Oxford: Oxford University Press, 2005, 491–493. See also his discussion of the corruption agenda (486–487) and, on new dynamics of party competition, chap. 16. On the Whigs and Seneca, consult chap.12 and Laurence M. Hauptman, *Conspiracy of Interests Iroquois Dispossession and the Rise of New York State* (Syracuse: Syracuse University Press, 1999).
4. On the older homogeneity of the people, consult Gordon S. Wood, *The Creation of the American Republic, 1776–1787* (Chapel Hill: University of North Carolina Press, 1998), chaps. 1–2.
5. Wilentz, *Rise of American Democracy*, 493.
6. Robert V. Remini, *The Election of Andrew Jackson* (Philadelphia: J. B. Lippincott, 1963), 64–67, 85–86, 94–97. On the centrality of Green to the building of a patronage-based strategy—even as his rivalry with Jackson grew (Wilentz, *Rise of American Democracy*, 303, 318)—consult Richard R. John, *Spreading the News: The American Postal System from Franklin to Morse* (Cambridge, Mass.: Harvard University Press, 1995), 209–215.
7. Eric Lomazoff, "Turning (Into) "The Great Regulating Wheel": The Conversion of the Bank of the United States, 1791–1811," *Studies in American Political Development* 26 (March 2012): 1–23; Howe, *WHGW*, 81–85; Bray Hammond, *Banks and Politics in America from the Revolution to the Civil War* (Princeton, N.J.: Princeton University Press, 1957).
8. Arthur Meier Schlesinger Jr., *The Age of Jackson* (Boston: Little, Brown, 1945), 111–114; Howe, *WHGW*.
9. Holt, *Rise and Fall*, 25.
10. Clay and Biddle initially thought that the Bank recharter veto would turn the country against Jackson; Biddle to Clay, August 1, 1832, in Henry Clay, *The Papers of Henry Clay*, vol. 8, *Candidate, Compromiser, Whig, March 5, 1829–December 31, 1836* (Lexington, 1984), 556–557 (hereafter *PHC*); Erastus T. Montague (Waltham, Virginia) to Clay, April 4, 1832, *PHC*, 487; Clay to Thurlow Weed, April 14, 1832, *PHC*, 492. On the tenuous state of alliance between Anti-Masons and National Republicans in New York, see also Clay to John H. Ewing, April 14, 1832, *PHC*; Clay to Peter B. Porter, May 1, 1832, *PHC*, 556–557 ("I greatly fear that the co-operation between the Anti Masons and N. Republicans in N. York is

far from certain"); Clay to Porter, April 26, 1832, *PHC,* 499–500; Ambrose Spencer (New Albany, N.Y.), to Clay, April 28, 1832, *PHC,* 500–501; Hiram Ketchum to Clay, May 12, 1832 (putting hopes in an alliance of anti-Masons and NRs), *PHC,* 510; William Preston Vaughn, *The Anti-Masonic Party in the United States: 1826–1843* (Lexington: University Press of Kentucky, 2014), 42–45. On Kentucky, see Thomas Metcalfe (Frankfort, Kentucky) to Clay, May 7, 1832, *PHC,* 506.

11. Clay to Charles Hammond, November 17, 1832, *PHC,* 599.
12. Samuel L. Southard to Clay, December 1, 1832, and Robert W. Stoddard to Clay, November 12, 1832, *PHC,* 601.
13. Charles Shaler (Pittsburgh) to Clay, February 6, 1833, *PHC,* 618.
14. Wilentz, *Rise of American Democracy,* 487–488.
15. Holt, *Rise and Fall,* 83; *PHC,* 687. Taney's report of December 30, 1833, was also distributed as a pamphlet.
16. Holt, *Rise and Fall,* 26.
17. Clay to Biddle, December 21, 1833, *PHC,* 681. Clay adds that "if the local Banks could be induced to concur in such a movement so much the better."
18. Clay to Henry Clay Jr., January 23, 1834, *PHC,* 692.
19. Memorials in favor of the restoration of the deposits arrived from Philadelphia and were received in the Senate on March 4, 7, 14, 19, 25, 26, and June 19, 1834. Holt, *Rise and Fall,* 25.
20. For the speech of December 26, consult *Register of Debates,* 23rd *Cong., 1st Sess.,* vol. 1 (January 1834), 58–94 (hereafter *RD*); *PHC,* 684; Holt, *Rise and Fall,* 26–27. Southard's speech, more technical and elaborate than Clay's, appears in *RD* 23:1, vol. 1, January 8, 1834, 143–198.
21. *RD* 23:1, vol. 1, December 26, 1833, 67–68.
22. *RD* 23:1, vol. 1, December 26, 1833, 67–68.
23. *RD* 23:1, vol. 1, December 26, 1833, 75.
24. Clay, *PHC,* 691.
25. *Scioto Gazette,* March 19, 1834: "Gen. Duncan McArthur was called to the Chair, Col. Abraham Hagler, George Will, Esq. and Gen. James Manary chosen Vice Presidents." Peter B. Porter (writing from Black Rock, N.Y.) to Clay, January 5, 1834, *PHC,* 686: "Every day's discussion [of the deposits] aided by manifestations of public sentiment, and evidences of public distress, cannot, I think, fail to produce some effect on the Jackson men in Congress who have not abjured every sentiment of patriotism." On transformations of political discourse in these years, see Howe, *Political Culture,* and *WHGW;* Gustafson, *Imagining Deliberative Democracy in the Early American Republic,* esp. chap. 4.

26. Memorial of the Subscribers, Citizens of the State of Pennsylvania, residing in the Third Congressional District, in the County of Philadelphia, March 24, 1834; 23A-H1.1, RG 233, NA.
27. *Spectator*, January 16, 1834.
28. Lomazoff, "Turning (Into) 'The Great Regulating Wheel.'"
29. Clay to Biddle, February 2, 1834, *PHC*, 694.
30. *PHC*, 705, 710.
31. Porter to Clay, January 5, 1834, *PHC*, 685–686.
32. Porter to Clay, February 15, 1834, *PHC*, 698.
33. Clay to Littleton W. Tazewell, February 1, 1834, *PHC*, 693. See also Clay to Clay Jr., February 19, 1834, *PHC*, 699. On Virginia's resolutions against removal of the deposits, consult *NWR*, January 4, 1834, 309, and February 1, 1834, 388.
34. Clay offered remarks on petitions from Troy, New York, and Berks County, Pennsylvania, and noted that the support went well beyond the anti-Jackson vote in the 1832 election. *RD* 23:1 vol. 1, 681, 718. For similar remarks on a petition from Louisville, Kentucky, consult *RD* 23:1 vol. 1, 719–724.
35. For remarks on four hundred signers of a petition being "Administration men" and "Jackson men," see *RD* 23:1 vol. 1, March 4, 1834, 802–803, 860–862.
36. On the Erie County petition with between four thousand and five thousand signatures, see Porter to Clay, March 30, 1834, Clay, *PHC*, 1, 709. For Clay's suggestion that the Senate compile and analyze all petitions and memorials presented to Congress on the issue, see *RD* 23:1, vol. 1, 1302–1305, 1310–1315; *PHC* 713–715, 733.
37. For remarks on petition totals and their representation and measurement of public opinion, see Clay's Comment in Senate, April 11, 1834, and Remark in Senate, June 9, 1834, *RD* 23:1 vol. 1, 2036–2037; *Congressional Globe: 23rd Congress* (1834), 464.
38. "Common opposition to Jackson therefore was, at least initially, the strongest bond uniting incipient Whigs" (Holt, *Rise and Fall*, 28).
39. On the contours of the sample of 715 petitions, consult Carpenter and Schneer, "Party Formation through Petitions." Validation of local and state samples from research in the National Archives (RG 233) suggests that the clerks were not selectively aggregating numbers. Hammond, *Banks and Politics in America from the Revolution to the Civil War*, 356–357.
40. Holt (*Rise and Fall*, 27), notes the plausible role of the bank's local supporters but also argues that the petitions did reflect "genuine economic suffering."

41. The full text of the memorial, along with meeting minutes and a list of citizens attending, was printed in the *Scioto Gazette,* March 19, 1834.
42. This passage came from an account of a public meeting of the people of Loudoun County. The report remarked that it was a "very numerous Meeting." *Alexandria Gazette,* January 21, 1834.
43. *Alexandria Gazette,* January 21, 1834; *Portland Advertiser,* March 18, 1834; *Enquirer,* January 16, 1834.
44. Self-referenced occupations include farmers, merchants, mechanics, traders, boot and shoe makers, cordwainers, tin-plate workers, sheet-iron workers, chair-makers, upholsterers, authors, publishers, bookbinders, watchmakers, silversmiths, and jewelers.
45. One important piece of evidence comes from the fact that the persistent correlation of 1832–1834 petitioning at the county level with Whig voting in the subsequent two decades is not diminished by controlling for previous National Republican vote patterns. See Carpenter and Schneer, "Party Formation through Petitions."
46. On the statistical evidence here, see Carpenter and Schneer, "Party Formation through Petitions." Table 9.1 shows the relationships for Whig presidential voting and similar patterns obtained for congressional voting. The regressions control for state fixed effects and thus evince patterns within states rather than across them. Holt, *Rise and Fall,* 49–59, 111–113; Richard McCormick, *The Second American Party System: Party Formation in the Jacksonian Era* (Chapel Hill: University of North Carolina Press, 1966), 208–209, 276–277, 346–356.
47. On opposition to strong executives as a central element of Whig culture, consult Howe, *Political Culture of the American Whigs,* 90–95.
48. Holt, *Rise and Fall,* 43, 52–55, 75 (Table 6). Cleveland was a smaller town at this time, with a population of just above six thousand in 1840, about equal to that of Columbus and with far less political activity.
49. On later Whig evolution, consult Howe (*Political Culture,* chaps. 7–11), Holt (*Rise and Fall,* chaps. 13–23), and Wilentz (*Rise of American Democracy,* 483–493).
50. *Report on the Affairs of British North America from the Earl of Durham, Her Majesty's High Commissioner* (4th Sess., 13th Parliament, 2nd Victoria, London, 1839) (Montréal: Morning courier office, 1839), 95 ("no history, and no literature"); Papineau, *Histoire de la résistance du Canada au gouvernement anglais,* published in *La Revue du progrès politique, social et littéraire* (May 1839).
51. David Mills and Richard Mills, "Durham Report," *Canadian Encyclopedia* (Ottawa: Historica Canada, 2017).

52. *Report on the Affairs of British North America from the Earl of Durham,* 52–56.
53. Wilton, *Popular Politics,* 194.
54. Wilton, *Popular Politics,* 164–165.
55. Wilton, *Popular Politics,* 204–206, 242–244.
56. Schrauwers, *"Union Is Strength,"* 347–352.
57. Wilton, *Popular Politics,* 196–197 (note the "continuity with the pre-Rebellion reform movement"); Powell's son would be better known as a lieutenant colonel and Indian superintendent in the late 1800s.
58. Wilton, *Popular Politics,* 215.
59. Wilton, *Popular Politics,* 217–219; Stephen Leacock, *Baldwin, Lafontaine, Hincks: Responsible Government (The Makers of Canada)* (Toronto: Morang, 1912), 273–294. On Lafontaine and his partial break with Papineau, see Leacock, *Baldwin, Lafontaine, Hincks,* 288–292, and Chapter 12 of this book.
60. Wilton, *Popular Politics,* chaps. 5, 219.
61. The assembly of unified Canada met in Kingston from 1841 to 1844, then in Montréal until 1849, where rioters' destruction of the parliamentary edifice resulted in a move to Toronto. Only in 1857 would Queen Victoria choose Ottawa as the new capital, and the last pre-Confederation Parliament met there in 1865. J. M. S. Careless, *The Union of the Canadas: The Growth of Canadian Institutions, 1841–1857* (Toronto: McClelland and Stewart, 1967).

10. ABOLITION AND THE TRANSFORMATION OF U.S. POLITICS

1. See, for instance, the petition of 142 "undersigned minors" of New York State (1837); HR 25A, LOC B 108, F2; RG 233, NARA. The median age of signatories for this petition was thirteen, twenty-seven signers listed their age as ten, and one listed his age as eight. On girls as young as eleven involved in canvassing, see Carpenter and Moore, "When Canvassers Became Activists: Antislavery Petitioning and the Political Mobilization of American Women," *American Political Science Review* 108 (3) (September 2014): 479–498.
2. Nathaniel Paul, *An Address, Delivered on the Celebration of the Abolition of Slavery, in the State of New-York* (Albany: John B. Van Steenburgh, 1827).
3. David Walker, *Walker's Appeal, in Four Articles; Together with a Preamble, to the Coloured Citizens of the World, but in Particular, and Very Expressly, to Those of the United States of America* (Boston: David Walker, 1830). See also Sinha, *Slave's Cause,* 199–208; David E. Swift,

Black Prophets of Justice: Activist Clergy before the Civil War (Baton Rouge: Louisiana State University Press, 1989), chap. 3.

4. Manish Sinha, *The Slave's Cause: A History of Abolition* (New Haven, Conn.: Yale University Press, 2016), 197–198, 213–214.
5. Elizabeth Heyrick, *Immediate, Not Gradual Abolition* (Boston: Isaac Knapp, 1824).
6. Benjamin Lundy, *Genius of Universal Emancipation*, December 24, 1825, 129–130.
7. Mary Prince, *The History of Mary Prince, a West Indian Slave. Related by Herself. With a Supplement by the Editor. . . .* (London: F. Westley and A. H. Davis, 1831).
8. Sinha, *Slave's Cause*, 213–214.
9. Sinha, *Slave's Cause*, 213.
10. *JASNY*, February 23, 1830, 270 (Paul petition); Mark Arkin, "A Convenient Seat in God's Temple: The Massachusetts General Colored Association and the Park Street Church Pew Controversy of 1830," *New England Quarterly* 89, no. 6 (2016): 39–42; Petition of Thomas Paul, Passed acts, 1775–1997 (SC1-229), St. 1819, c. 68, MAC; digitized at APMD https://dataverse.harvard.edu/dataset.xhtml?persistentId=doi:10.7910/DVN/6YKLQ; "Petition of John T. Hilton, Case of Washington Goode; Council; Files of Inactive Pardons and Pardons Not Granted (GC3-771), MAC; digitized at APMD http://nrs.harvard.edu/urn-3:FHCL:12208730.
11. "Petition of John T. Hilton, Case of Washington Goode."
12. "Great Anti-Slavery Meeting in England," *Genius of Universal Emancipation*, August 1, 1830, 69; see also 91 (discussion of petitioning); "British House of Parliament," *Genius*, April 15, 1826, 260; "Petitions, Petitions!," *Genius* 1, no. 10 (January 1831): 140–141.
13. "Abolition of Slavery . . . ," *Genius*, September 2, 1829, 3.
14. "District of Columbia," *Genius*, November 6, 1829, 67.
15. Henry Mayer, *All on Fire: William Lloyd Garrison and the Abolition of Slavery* (New York: St. Martin's, 1998), 75, (see also 72–74, 108–116).
16. Mayer, *All on Fire*, 112.
17. "District of Columbia" and "Petition to Congress for the Abolition of Slavery in the District of Columbia," *Liberator*, January 1, 1831, 5. See also "A Good Example," *Liberator*, January 29, 1831.
18. "To the Free Colored Population of the U.S.—No. II," *Liberator*, February 5, 1831, 22.
19. "District of Columbia" (1) and "To John Quincy Adams" (3), *Liberator*, January 21, 1832.
20. Lincoln, "Speech at Peoria, Illinois, in Reply to Douglas, October 16, 1854," in Lincoln, *Complete Works*, vol. 1, ed. John G. Nicolay and John

Hay (New York: Lamb, 1894), 185; Adam Goodheart, "A Capital Under Slavery's Shadow," *New York Times*, February 24, 2011; Sinha, *Slave's Cause*, 223.

21. "Notice," *Liberator*, November 24, 1832.
22. *First Annual Report of the Board of Managers of the New England Anti-slavery Society* (Boston, 1833), 4.
23. Roman J. Zorn, "The New England Anti-Slavery Society: Pioneer Abolitionist Organization," *Journal of Negro History* 52 (July 1957): 157–176; Valerie Cooper, *Word, Like Fire: Maria Stewart, the Bible, and the Rights of African Americans* (Charlottesville: University of Virginia Press, 2012); Gilbert Hobbs Barnes, *The Anti-Slavery Impulse 1830–1844* (New York: Peter Smith, 1964), 130–145; Sinha, *Slave's Cause*, 223–225.
24. *Declaration of Sentiments of the American Anti-Slavery Society, Adopted at the formation of said society, in Philadelphia, on the 4th day of December, 1833* (New York: William S. Dorr, 1833), 2.
25. *Declaration of Sentiments*, 2.
26. John Greenleaf Whittier, *Justice and Expediency, or Slavery, Considered with a View to its Rightful and Effectual Remedy, Abolition* (New York: C.P. Thayer, 1833), 51, 55; Sinha, *Slave's Cause*, 224–226.
27. *Declaration of Sentiments*, 2.
28. Samuel Thomas Pickard, *Life and Letters of John Greenleaf Whittier*, vol. 1 (London: Sampson, Low & Marston, 1895), 134–137.
29. Miller, *Arguing Against* Slavery, 108–112.
30. *Fifth Annual Report of the Board of Managers of the American Anti-Slavery Society* (Boston: American Anti-Slavery Society, 1837), 17. The remaining petitions and committee documents for these years can be found in NA, RG233, 22A-G5.2, 23A-G4.3 (Committee on the District); 23A-G21.6, 24A-G22.4 (select committee).
31. Miller, *Arguing against Slavery*, 109–111; Zaeske, *Signatures of Citizenship*, 55–59. Ohio tabulations for 23rd Congress from CPD.
32. Miller, *Arguing*, 110–111; Gilbert H. Barnes and Dwight L. Dumond, eds., *Letters of Theodore Dwight Weld, Angelina Grimke Weld and Sarah Grimke, 1822–1844*, vol. 1 (New York: D. Appleton-Century, 1934), 175–176; Zaeske, *Signatures*, 58.
33. *Fifth Annual Report of the Board of Managers*, 11–12.
34. Drew Gilpin Faust, *James Henry Hammond and the Old South: A Design for Mastery* (Baton Rouge: Louisiana State University Press, 1985), 166–167; Young, *Washington Community*, 98–106; Miller, *Arguing*, 116–117.
35. *Register of Debates*, 24-1, 4052–54; 24–2, 1412; Miller, *Arguing*, 143–145, 200–209. Jeffrey Jenkins and Charles Stewart III, "Causal Inference

and American Political Development: The Case of the Gag Rule," *Public Choice,* 2019, https://doi.org/10.1007/s11127-019-00754-9.

36. Before the Twenty-Fourth Congress, the chambers had tabled petitions at least 1,740 times (the House alone, 1,175 times) for 5.6 percent of the 30,822 petitions recorded as introduced to the chamber floors (analysis of CPD). Joanne Freeman, *The Field of Blood: Violence in Congress and the Road to the Civil War* (New York, Farrar, Straus and Giroux, 2018), 50, 90–91; Jenkins and Stewart, "The Gag Rule"; Scott R. Meinke, "Slavery, Partisanship, and Procedure in the U.S. House: The Gag Rule, 1836–1845," *Legislative Studies Quarterly* 32, no. 1 (February 2007): 33–57; Daniel Wirls, "'The Only Method of Avoiding Everlasting Debate': The Overlooked Senate Gag-Rule for Antislavery Petitions," *Journal of the Early Republic* 27 (2007), 115–138; Peter Charles Hoffer, *John Quincy Adams and the Gag Rule, 1835–1850* (Baltimore: Johns Hopkins University Press, 2018), chap. 2; John, *Spreading the News,* chap. 7; *Register of Debates,* 24-2, 1685, 1733–34; Sinha, *Slave's Cause,* 251.
37. Calhoun, "Speech on the Reception of Abolition Petitions, delivered in the Senate, February 6, 1837," in *The Works of John C. Calhoun,* vol. 2, ed. Richard K. Cralle (New York: D. Appleton, 1856), 625–633. Miller, *Arguing,* 124 (Calhoun prediction), 140–142, 146 (Pinckey read out of Nullifiers); Hoffer, *John Quincy Adams,* 35–38.
38. *JHRUS* vol. 30 (24-2, February 6, 1837), 347–351.
39. Miller, *Arguing,* 214–222, 225–230.
40. *Proceedings of the Antislavery Convention of American Women, Held in the City of New-York, May 9th, 10th, 11th, and 12th, 1837* (New York: William S. Dorr, 1837). Gamaliel Bailey to Joshua Giddings, February 7, 1839; Joshua R. Giddings and George Washington Julian Papers, LOC.
41. Anti-Slavery Convention of American Women, *An Appeal to the Women of the Nominally Free States* (Boston: Isaac Knapp, 1838), 10–13.
42. Anti-Slavery Convention, *Appeal to the Women of the Nominally Free States,* 58–60. On Grimké's authorship, consult Gerda Lerner, *The Grimké Sisters from South Carolina: Pioneers for Women's Rights and Abolition* (Chapel Hill: University of North Carolina Press, 2004), 214–215; Jean Fagan Yellin, *Women and Sisters: The Antislavery Feminists in American Culture* (New Haven, Conn.: Yale University Press, 1989), 34–36.
43. *Liberator,* July 9, 1836.
44. *Liberator,* June 23, 1837, 2.
45. Zaeske, *Signatures,* 72–74, and, in general, chap. 4; Freeman, *Field of Blood,* chap. 4, esp. 90–97; Miller, *Arguing,* 277; Howe, *WHGW,* 512–515.

46. Zaeske, *Signatures,* 118–119; Deborah Bingham Van Broekhoven, *The Devotion of These Women: Rhode Island in the Antislavery Network* (Amherst: University of Massachusetts Press, 2002), 28–31; Portnoy, *Their Right to Speak.*
47. *Liberator,* June 23, 1837, 2.
48. *Liberator,* June 23, 1837, 2.
49. *Liberator,* June 23, 1837, 2.
50. *Liberator,* June 23, 1837, 2. Petition of Nancy Richardson and fifteen hundred other women of Lynn, Massachusetts, for the abolition of slavery in the District of Columbia, February 5, 1838; HR25A-H1.8, RG233, NA.
51. Diary of Mary White, Boylston, Massachusetts, entries of June 30 and July 14, 1837, vol. 1, 1836–1844, Old Sturbridge Village.
52. Lerner, "Political Activities of Antislavery Women," in *The Majority Finds Its Past* (Chapel Hill: University of North Carolina Press, 2005), 112–128, esp. 120–121; Zaeske, *Signatures,* 110–111; Jeffrey, Great Silent Army, 46, 93; Lerner, Grimké Sisters, 113–119 (Grimké sisters' lecture tour); Deborah Bingham Van Broekhoven, "'Let Your Names Be Enrolled': Method and Ideology in Women's Antislavery Petitioning," in *The Abolitionist Sisterhood: Women's Political Culture in Antebellum America,* ed. Jean Fagan Yellin and John C. Van Horne (Ithaca: Cornell University Press, 1994), 179–200.
53. Caroline Weston to Deborah Weston, March 3, 1837; Deborah Weston to Anne Weston, February 29, 1840; Anne Weston to Deborah Weston, September 15, 1837; Weston-Chapman Papers, Anti-Slavery Collection, BPL. Mary Leavitt (Greenfield) to "Dear Cousin" Hooker, February 20, 1838, F2, Joshua Leavitt Family Correspondence, LOC.
54. Anne Weston to Deborah Weston, September 15, 1837, 4, Weston-Chapman Papers, BPL.
55. W. O. Duvall (Port Byron, New York) to Hon. William Slade, January 22, 1839; Petition of the Inhabitants of Mertz, Cayuga County, February 4, 1839; HR25A-H1.8, F34, RG233, NA. Antislavery women also sent copies and kept the originals for local display and organization; female citizens of Amherst, Massachusetts, to House (tabled February 14, 1838), HR25A-H1.7, F3, RG 233, NA.
56. Zaeske, *Signatures,* 63–64, 97 (Grimké signatures); Miller, *Arguing,* 230–232. Judith Wellman, *Grassroots Reform in the Burned-Over District of Upstate New York: Religion, Abolitionism and Democracy* (New York: Taylor and Francis, 2014), 140–141. Anti-dueling petitions also coursed into Congress after the Cilley-Graves duel; Freeman, *Field of Blood,* 90–91.

57. Carpenter and Moore, "When Canvassers Became Activists" (statistical analyses).
58. Caroline Weston (Boston) to Mrs. Roger Leavitt, Charlemont, Mass., July 17, 1837, F2, Leavitt Family Correspondence, LOC; Van Broekhoven, *The Devotion of These Women*, 28, 50–52, 74–75, 87–88, 90; Zaeske, *Signatures*, 97, 106–111.
59. Wellman, *Grassroots Reform*, 140–151.
60. Wellman, *Grassroots Reform*, 151; Jeffrey, *Great Silent Army*, 10 (Salem, NJ, petition drive precedes antislavery organization); Carpenter, "Recruitment by Petition," Table 1.
61. Jeffrey, *Great Silent Army*, 27, 48, 134–135; Carpenter, "Recruitment by Petition," 706–709.
62. "Angelina E. Grimké," *Liberator*, March 2, 1838, 3 (italics in original).
63. "Angelina E. Grimké," 3 (italics in original).
64. Lerner, *Grimké Sisters*, 127, 154, 167; Lerner, "The Political Activities of Antislavery Women," 120–125; Zaeske, *Signatures*, 117–121, 201; Amy Benson Brown, "'A System of Complicated Crimes': The (Con)Fusion of Subjects in Angelina Grimké's Public Speeches," *Women's Studies: An Interdisciplinary Journal* 27, no. 1 (1998): 31–52.
65. "M. W. C." (probably Maria Weston Chapman) to Garrison, *Liberator*, March 2, 1838, 3.
66. "M. W. C." to Garrison, 3.
67. Beecher, *Essay on Slavery and Abolitionism, with Reference to the Duty of American Females* (Philadelphia: H. Perkins, 1837), 104.
68. Angelina Grimké, *Letters to Catherine E. Beecher in Reply to an Essay on Slavery and Abolitionism* (Boston, 1838), 112.
69. Grimké, *Letters to Catherine E. Beecher*, 112.
70. Zaeske, *Signatures*, 114–118; Van Broekhoven, "'Let Your Names Be Enrolled,'" 179; Jeffrey, *Great Silent Army*, 88; Sinha, *Slave's Cause*, 278–284; Portnoy, *Their Right to Speak*, 203–223, 240–241.
71. Dorothy Sterling, *Ahead of Her Time: Abby Kelley and the Politics of Antislavery* (New York: Norton, 1994), 33–34, 77–81; Mayer, *All on Fire*, 261–284 (on the schism more generally); Sinha, *Slave's Cause*, 186–188.
72. See the careful work of Jeffrey (*Great Silent Army*, 105–126; Garrison remark, 102), Von Broekhoven (*The Devotion of These Women*, 164–172, and chap. 7), and Sinha (*Slave's Cause*, chap. 9).
73. The inferences available are limited by the constraints of AASS chapter data, which mainly come from the 1838 *Annual Report*. Chapters did not uniformly report their month of founding, and comparable membership totals are best represented for the 1838 *Report*, which reflects total accumulation and attrition to that point (essentially May 1838).

74. Richard H. Sewell, *Ballots for Freedom: Antislavery Politics in the United States, 1837–1860* (New York: Oxford University Press, 1976), 107–117; Douglas M. Strong, *Perfectionist Politics: Abolitionism and the Religious Tensions of American Democracy* (Syracuse: Syracuse University Press, 2001), chaps. 4 and 5, esp. 124–131; Bruce Laurie, *Beyond Garrison: Antislavery and Social Reform* (Cambridge: Cambridge University Press, 2005), 117–120 (Liberty Party and Latimer mobilization); Vernon L. Volpe, "The Liberty Party and Polk's Election, 1844," *Historian* 53, no. 4 (1991): 691–710 (complications of Liberty Party contribution to Polk victory). On Stewart, see *Massachusetts Abolitionist* (Boston), July 4, 1839 (italics in original), in Sewell, *Ballots for Freedom,* 11.
75. Jonathan Earle, *Jacksonian Antislavery and the Politics of Free Soil, 1824–1854* (Chapel Hill: University of North Carolina Press, 2004), esp. 68–77, chap. 3, and 166–170 (Giddings and the 1848 election); Sewell, *Ballots,* 156–157, 165–169, 229; Jeffrey, *Great Silent Army,* 154–158 (Ohio).
76. Wellman, *Grassroots Reform,* 147; Sinha, *Slave's Cause,* 251; James M. MacPherson, "The Fight against the Gag Rule: Joshua Leavitt and Antislavery Insurgency in the Whig Party, 1838–1842," *Journal of Negro History* 48, no. 3 (July 1963): 177–195; Meinke, "Slavery, Partisanship and Procedure in the U.S. House"; Jenkins and Stewart, "The Gag Rule."
77. Sinha, *Slave's Cause,* 254.
78. On the class basis of signatures, consult Edward Magdol, *The Antislavery Rank and File: A Social Profile of the Abolitionists' Constituency* (Westport: Greenwood, 1986), chaps. 3, 6; John Jentz, "The Antislavery Constituency in Jacksonian New York City," *Civil War History* 27, no. 2 (June 1981): 101–122.
79. Stewart, "An Address Delivered at the African Masonic Hall, Boston, Feb. 27, 1833," *Liberator,* May 4, 1833, 72; Martha S. Jones, *All Bound Up Together: The Woman Question in African-American Political Culture, 1830–1900* (Chapel Hill: University of North Carolina Press, 2007), 34–38.
80. Undersigned citizens (signing as "colored people") of Jefferson County, Indiana, to House (three petitions), tabled February 4, 1839, HR25A-H1.8, F33, RG 233, NA. On DeBaptiste and the Andersons, consult Mark A. Furnish, "Black Hoosiers and the Formation of an Antislavery Stronghold in the Central Ohio Valley," *Ohio Valley History,* Fall 2016, 6–27.
81. *Journal of the House of Representatives of Ohio, 1836–1837,* 187, 198–99, 237, 263, 270, 284, 370–375 (Judiciary Committee report), 676, 696, 702; *Journal of the Senate of Ohio,* 38th General Assembly, First Session

(Columbus, 1839), 146, 168–69, 202. As the historian Nikki M. Taylor summarizes, "Ohio's African Americans had rarely petitioned the Legislature before 1830," but "between 1836 and 1841, the Ohio General Assembly was inundated with petitions and memorials by blacks and their allies throughout the state praying for the repeal of disabling laws" (*Frontiers of Freedom*, 114; also 176–77). Frank U. Quillin, *The Color Line in Ohio: A History of Race Prejudice in a Typical Northern State* (Ann Arbor: G. Wahr, 1913), chap. 3, 35–43 (1849 repeal was "a great consummation to those who had petitioned for it").

82. David E. Swift, *Black Prophets of Justice: Activist Clergy before the Civil War* (Baton Rouge: Louisiana State University Press, 1989), 83–84 ("Colored American" and its origins in petitioning campaigns), 102 (the "movement of political protest" launched by Cornish and Ray "was largely by petition"), 102 (the petition campaigns "were the occasion, especially in New York, of at least minimal political involvement on the part of hundreds of free black people who had never before known that such activity was possible or could perhaps make a difference"), 102–106, 107–108 (9,300 signatures and organizational momentum). Jones, *All Bound Up Together*, 61–63.

83. [Robert Purvis], *Appeal of Forty Thousand Citizens, Threatened with Disfranchisement, to the People of Pennsylvania* (Philadelphia, 1838), 4.

84. Eric Ledell Smith, "The End of Black Voting Rights in Pennsylvania: African Americans and the Pennsylvania Constitutional Convention of 1837–1838," *Pennsylvania History* 65, no. 3 (Summer 1988): 279–299; Bateman, *Disenfranchising Democracy*, 186–196.

85. Rael, *Black Identity and Black Protest in the Antebellum North*, 89, 102, chap. 3, 147; James Brewer Stewart, "The Emergence of Racial Modernity and the Rise of the White North, 1790–1840," *Journal of the Early Republic* 18, no. 2 (1998): 187–190.

86. Stewart, "The Emergence of Racial Modernity," 191; Anne Firor Scott, "Most Invisible of All: Black Women's Voluntary Associations," *Journal of Southern History* 56, no. 1 (1990): 6; Jeffrey, *Great Silent Army*, 35, 127–129; Petition of Ruth C. Johnson, House unpassed legislation, 1775–1996 (SC1-230), 1837, Docket 249, MAC; https://iiif.lib.harvard.edu/manifests/view/drs:46621075$1i in APMD. A Friend, "Shall Women Sign Our Petitions?," *Colored American*, November 13, 1841; Jones, *All Bound Up Together*, 53–58, 77–79.

87. Andrew Delbanco, *The War Before the War: Fugitive Slaves and the Struggle for America's Soul from the Revolution to the Civil War* (New York: Penguin, 2018),177–186; Kantrowitz, *More Than Freedom*, 70–74; Price and Stewart, "The Roberts Case, the Easton Family, & the

Dynamics of the Abolitionist Movement in Massachusetts, 1776–1870," 101–102.

88. "Petition of Lucia Weston and 113 other colored women of Boston, MA," ca. 1843–1844, 206 VU 89 T, House unpassed legislation, MAC; Amber Moulton, *The Fight for Interracial Marriage Rights in Antebellum Massachusetts* (Cambridge, Mass.: Harvard University Press, 2015), chap. 4; Newman, *The Transformation of American Abolitionism*, 106.

89. Remonstrance of Leonard A. Grimes and 168 other Colored Citizens of Boston against the repeal of the Personal Liberty Law; Remonstrance of William H. Logan and 149 other Colored Citizens of Boston against the repeal of the Personal Liberty Law; Remonstrance of Henry Mitchell and 413 other Colored Citizens of Boston against the repeal of the Personal Liberty Law; Acts 1861, c. 91, passed March 25, 1861, MAC; Graber, *Dred Scott and the Problem of Constitutional Evil;* Anti-Dred-Scott petition from Black Massachusetts citizens, 1858; Petition of John T. Hilton and 10 others, Resolves 1858, c. 44, MAC.

90. Sarah Gronningsater, "'On Behalf of His Race and the Lemmon Slaves': Louis Napoleon, Northern Black Legal Culture, and the Politics of Sectional Crisis," *Journal of the Civil War Era* 7, no. 2 (June 2017): 206–241; "'Expressly Recognized by Our Election Laws': Certificates of Freedom and the Multiple Fates of Black Citizenship in the Early Republic," *William and Mary Quarterly* 75, no. 3 (July 2018): 465–506; VanderVelde, *Mrs. Dred Scott;* Vandervelde, *Redemption Songs,* incl. chap. 4 ("Winny and Her Children"); Schweninger, *Appealing for Liberty.*

91. See, for example, Petition of Citizens of Augusta County, March 5, 1849, LOV-VLP; *Journal of House of Delegates of Virginia* (*JHODV*), *1848–49,* 40, 43 (special committee), 591–592 (bill); *JHODV, 1852,* 78 (joint committee), 185 (citizens of county of Culpeper, February 24), 224 (citizens of counties of Clarke and Warren, March 9); Petitions of Margaret Jane Lee, February 17, 1859, and of Mary Elizabeth, September 12, 1858; Rockbridge County Circuit Court, Free Negro and Slave Records, 1836–1864, LOV; Ted Maris Wolf, *Family Bonds: Free Blacks and Re-enslavement Law in Antebellum Virginia* (Chapel Hill: University of North Carolina Press, 2015), chaps. 1–2.

92. Jones, *Birthright Citizens,* 111–114, 161–164; J. W. Harry, "The Maryland Constitution of 1851," in *Johns Hopkins University Studies in Historical and Political Science,* 20 (Baltimore: Johns Hopkins University Press, 1902), 438–441. On the 1852 bills and petitions on free Blacks' licensing rights, see "Oppressive Legislation—Colonization," *National Era,* May 27, 1852; *Baltimore Sun,* April 3, April 15, May 3, 1852. Christopher Phillips, *Freedom's Port: The African American Community of Baltimore,*

1790–1860 (Champaign: University of Illinois Press, 1997), 232–234; William Freehling, *The Road to Disunion, II: Secessionists Triumphant, 1854–1861* (Oxford: Oxford University Press, 2007), 196–198.

11. WOMEN CONTESTING COLLECTIVELY: WORK, WAR, *IGLESIA*, AND THE BALLOT

1. Judith Apter Klinghoffer and Lois Elkis, "'The Petticoat Electors': Women's Suffrage in New Jersey, 1776–1807," *JER* 12, no. 2 (Summer 1992): 159–93; Bettina Bradbury, *Wife to Widow: Lives, Laws and Politics in Nineteenth-Century Montreal* (Vancouver: UBC Press, 2011), chap. 4; Nancy Isenberg, *Sex and Citizenship in Antebellum America* (Chapel Hill: University of North Carolina Press, 1998); Sylvia M. Arrom, *The Women of Mexico City, 1790–1857* (Stanford: Stanford University Press, 1985).
2. "Declaration of Sentiments," *Report of the Woman's Rights Convention, Held at Seneca Falls, N.Y., July 19th and 20th, 1848* (Rochester, 1848).
3. Ruth Bogin, "Petitioning and the Moral Economy of Post-Revolutionary America," *William and Mary Quarterly* 45, no. 3 (1988): 391–425; Bradbury, *Wife to Widow*.
4. Isenberg, *Sex and Citizenship*, 249, 253; Peter Guardino, "Gender, Soldiering, and Citizenship in the Mexican-American War of 1846–1848," *American Historical Review* 119, no. 1 (February 2014): 23–46.
5. Nancy F. Cott, *The Bonds of Womanhood: "Woman's Sphere" in New England, 1780–1835* (New Haven, Conn.: Yale University Press, 1977); Arrom, *Women of Mexico City, 1790–1857.*
6. Anne Boylan, *The Origins of Women's Activism: New York and Boston, 1797–1840* (Chapel Hill: University of North Carolina Press, 2002).
7. "Declaration of Sentiments and Resolutions," in Report of the Woman's Rights Convention, Held at Seneca Falls, N.Y., July 19th and 20th, 1848 (Rochester, N.Y.: John Dick, 1848), 5.
8. *JHALC, 1828–1829,* 81.
9. *JHALC, 1828–1829,* 81.
10. Montesquieu, *L'Esprit des Lois,* bk. 11, chap. 6 (De la constitution d'Angleterre).
11. *JHALC, 1828–1829,* 82.
12. *JHALC, 1828–1829,* 81.
13. *JHALC, 1828–1829,* 81.
14. Bradbury, *Wife to Widow,* 262–264; Greer, *The Patriots and the People: The Rebellion of 1837 in Rural Lower Canada* (Toronto: University of Toronto Press, 1993), 113–117.

15. Nathalie Picard, "Les femmes et le vote," *Montreal Gazette*; Bradbury, *Wife to Widow*, 260–64, 440.
16. Bradbury, *Wife to Widow*, 263.
17. Bradbury, *Wife to Widow*, 265–271.
18. Papineau remark in Denyse Baillargeon, "Les Quebecoises et le vote," *Bulletin d'histoire politique* 23, no. 2 (Winter 2015): 165–172.
19. Bradbury, *Wife to Widow*, 283–286.
20. Alan Greer, "La république des hommes: les patriotes de 1837 face aux femmes," *Revue d'histoire de l'Amérique française* 44, no. 4 (Spring 2007), 507–528.
21. Frances H. Early, "A Reappraisal of the New England Labour-Reform Movement of the 1840s: The Lowell Female Labor Reform Association and the New England Workingmen's Association," *Histoire Sociale / Social History* 13, no. 25 (1980): 33–54.
22. Joseph C. Rayback, *A History of American Labor* (New York: Macmillan, 1964), 62; Teresa Anne Murphy, *Ten Hours' Labor: Religion, Reform, and Gender in Early New England* (Ithaca: Cornell University Press, 1992), 203–212; Kathryn Kish Sklar, "'The Greater Part of the Petitioners are Female': The Reduction in Women's Working Hours in the Paid Labor Force, 1840–1917," in *Worktime and Industrialization: An International History*, ed. Gary Cross (Philadelphia: Temple University Press, 1988), 103–133; Thomas Dublin, *Women at Work: The Transformation of Work and Community in Lowell, Massachusetts, 1826–1860* (New York: Columbia University Press, 1979).
23. Lowell Female Labor Reform Association, "Ten Hours, Ten Hours!!," *Voice of Industry* (Fitchburg, Mass.), January 15, 1845, and December 26, 1845; in *Mill Girls in Nineteenth-Century Print*, AAS. "House . . . No. 50," *Documents Printed by the Order of the House of Representatives of the Commonwealth of Massachusetts during the Session of the General Court, A.D. 1845* (Boston: General Court, 1845), 1–6, 15–17; Yukako Hisada, "The Ten-Hour Movement and the Massachusetts State Legislative Election in 1845," *Journal of the Faculty of Foreign Studies, Aichi Prefectural University* 47 (2015): 274–275.
24. *Voice of Industry*, February 12, 1845; House No. 50, *Documents . . . A.D. 1845* (Boston, 1845), 2.
25. "House . . . No. 50," *Documents . . . A.D. 1845* (Boston, 1845), 1–6, 15–17; Hisada, 174–175.
26. *Voice of Industry*, July 10, 1845, and January 9, 1846; "Great Workingmen's Mass Meeting in Woburn," *Lowell Advertiser*, July 8, 1945; Early, "Reappraisal," 46.

27. *Voice of Industry,* June 12, 1845; Early, "Reappraisal," 46. Hisada, "Ten-Hour Movement"; Dublin, *Women at Work,* 122–126.
28. *Voice of Industry,* June 12, 1845.
29. "Last Call!" *Lowell Advertiser,* November 8, 1845, reprinted in Hisada, "Ten-Hour Movement," 281.
30. Hisada, "Ten-Hour Movement," 281 (emphasis in original).
31. Hisada, "Ten-Hour Movement," 281–282.
32. Early, "Reappraisal," 52–54; *Voice of Industry,* May 7, 1847, and June 11, 1847.
33. Thomas Dublin, "Women, Work and Protest in the Early Lowell Mills: 'The oppressing hand of avarice would enslave US,'" *Labor History* 16 (1975): 114–115; *Voice of Industry,* September 3, 1847 and September 17, 1847. U.S. Bureau of Labor, *Report on Condition of Woman and Child Wage-Earners in the United States, in 19 Volumes;* Senate Document No. 645 (61st Cong., 2nd Sess.) (Washington: Government Printing Office, 1910), 70–72.
34. Pekka Hämäläinen, *The Comanche Empire* (New Haven, Conn.: Yale University Press, 2008); Peter Guardino, *The Dead March: A History of the Mexican-American War* (Cambridge: Cambridge University Press, 2017); Lyon Rathbun, "The Debate Over Annexing Texas and the Emergence of Manifest Destiny," *Rhetoric and Public Affairs* 4, no. 3 (Fall 2001): 459–494.
35. Congressional Antislavery Petitions Database (Harvard Dataverse); Carpenter and Moore, "When Canvassers Became Activists."
36. Guardino, *The Dead March,* chap. 1.
37. Petition of John P. Andrews (Salem, Massachusetts), *JHRUS* 29, no. 2 (January 25, 1847): 227.
38. Guardino, "Gender, Soldiering, and Citizenship in the Mexican-American War of 1846–1848."
39. *Quakers Grossly Insulted: The Great Constitutional Rights of Petition Violated by the "War" Party in Congress* (Washington, 1848), CSL.
40. "To the Women of the city of Philadelphia, and of the United States generally, the friendly address of the undersigned women inhabitants of the City of Exeter in England," Pennsylvania Peace Society Records (restricted collection), SCPC.
41. "Peace Movements at Home and Abroad," *Advocate of Peace and Universal Brotherhood* 1, no. 7 (July 1846): 174–176.
42. "A Plea for Peace," *NWR* 70 (July 4, 1846): 274.
43. "Dr. Hollick's Lectures," *Pennsylvania Freeman,* March 12, 1846, 3; Isenberg, *Sex and Citizenship,* 69.

44. "History of the American Peace Society and Its Work," *Advocate of Peace* 69, no. 1 (January 1907): 15–20; James L. Tryon, "The Rise of the Peace Movement," *Yale Law Journal* 20, no. 5 (1911): 358–371; "New England Convention: Letter from Mary Grew," *Pennsylvania Freeman,* June 4, 1846.
45. *Anti-Slavery Bugle,* June 20, 1845; September 5, 1845; June 12, 1853 (women in school elections). See also Isenberg, *Sex and Citizenship,* 18–20, 215–216.
46. *JHRUS* 30, no. 1 (April 13, 1848): 679.
47. *JSUS* 30, no. 1 (February 29, 1848): 193–194.
48. Computations from data in Congressional Petitions Database and from Antislavery Congressional Petitions Dataverse (Carpenter and Moore, "When Canvassers Became Activists").
49. See Isenberg, *Sex and Citizenship,* 252; *Anti-Slavery Bugle,* July 10, 1846; *Practical Christian,* October 3, 1846.
50. "Petitions for Peace," *Pennsylvania Freeman,* September 23, 1847, 2.
51. "Petitions for Peace," 2.
52. José Antonio Serrano Ortega and Josefina Zoraida Vázquez, "El nuevo orden, 1821–1848," 423–442 (esp. 425–431 on the centralizing tendencies underway); Andrés Lira and Ann Staples, "Del desastre a la reconstrucción republicana, 1848–1876," 443–446, in *Nueva Historia General de México* (México City: Colegio de México, 2010).
53. Fernando Alanís Enciso, "Los extranjeros en México, la inmigración y el gobierno: ¿tolerancia o intolerancia religiosa?, 1821–1830," *Historia Mexicana* 45, no. 3 (1996): 539–566; Berninger, *La inmigración en México, 1821–1857,* 131; Charles Hale, *El liberalismo mexicano en la época de Mora, 1821–1853* (México: Siglo XXI, 1987), chaps. 1–3, 6, esp. 216–217.
54. *Pastoral que sobre Tolerancia Religiosa dirigió en 23 de septiembre de 1848 a los fieles de la Santa Iglesia de Señora Su Obispo el Dr. D. Lázaro de la Garza y Ballesteros, Actual Arzobispo de México, y que ahora reimprime y dedica a los de este arzobispado* (Sonora: Imprenta de J. M. Lara, 1855); *Representación que los habitantes de Puebla eleven al Soberano Congreso de la Unión contrariando los conatos que para establecer la tolerancia religiosa en nuestro país aparecen hoy desgraciadamente* (Puebla, 1848), reprinted in *La Voz de la Religión,* November 15, 1848, 577–580; Bieringer, *La inmigración en México,* 131.
55. The Oaxaca women's petition of 1849 was, according to historian Peter Guardino, "by far the largest collective intervention Oaxacan women made in early-nineteenth-century politics" (*The Time of Liberty,* 174–175). *El Guajalote Periodista,* April 12, 1849; translations are Guardino's.

56. "Representación que el bello secso de Orizaba hace al Soberano Congreso pidiendo que no so admita en la republica la libertad de cultos," *La Voz de la Religión,* January 31, 1849, 136–139; February 3, 1849, 156; cited in Berninger, *La inmigración,* 131.
57. On the Veracruz, consult *El Catolico* (Madrid), May 17, 1847, 300; Benjamín Maciel Gómez, *Síntesis cronológica,* 49–69, esp. 53–54.
58. Guardino, *The Time of Liberty,* 173–175; Jacqueline Covo, "Intolérance et fantasmes au Mexique: les pétitions contre la liberté des cultes de 1856," *América: Cahiers du CRICCAL* 21 (1998) (Polémiques et manifestes aux XIXe et XXe siècles en Amérique latine), 141–142.
59. Margaret Chowning, "The Catholic Church and the Ladies of the Vela Perpetua: Gender and Devotional Change in Nineteenth-Century Mexico," *Past and Present* 221, no. 1 (2013): 197–237, esp. 211–217.
60. While parish priests appear to have collaborated with these women, Chowning concludes that "the church hierarchy was not involved" in these petitions and Velas (215). See also the devotional model established in the Return of the Flowers (*El Regreso de la Flores*), *Álbum Mexicano,* t. II (México: Ignacio Cumplido, 1849), 553–555.
61. Translated by Guardino, "Gender, Soldiering and Citizenship," 23.
62. Signed *representaciones* came from the men of Autlán, Etzatlán, Córdova, Guachinango, Magdalena, Mascota, Orizaba, Puebla, Tala, and Teocuitlatán; many were published at Guadalajara's Imprenta de Rodríguez. *Exposición del ilustre ayuntamiento y vecinos de Córdova, contra la tolerancia de cultos* (Puebla: Imprenta de J. N. Valle, 1848), 1 ("la gran familia mexicana"); *Representación que el ayuntamiento y pueblo de Teocuitlatán hace al Excmo. Sr. Presidente de la Republica para que se oponga a la admisión de tolerancia de cultos* (Guadalajara: Imprenta de Manuel Brambila, 1849), 7; *Representación del ayuntamiento y vecindario de la villa de Etzatlán a las augustas Cámaras, contra la tolerancia de cultos* (Guadalajara: n.a., 1848), 3 ("la voluntad nacional"); *Representación que los vecinos de Autlán dirigen al supremo gobierno nacional contra la tolerancia de cultos en el país* (Guadalajara: Imprenta de Rodríguez, 1849), 4–5 ("!Legisladores Mexicanos! ¡Legisladores católicos!). Translations mine.
63. Guerrero, "Tolerancia religiosa e inmigración," 68–69.
64. *Representación del ayuntamiento y vecindario de la villa de Etzatlán,* 1–2.
65. *Representación que los vecinos de Autlan . . . ,* 3. See also Guerrero, "La tolerancia religiosa," 71–72.
66. Will Fowler, "El Pensamiento Político de los Santanistas, 1821–1855," in Luis Jáuregui and José Antonio Serrano Ortega, *Historia y nación (actas*

del Congreso en homenaje a Josefina Zoraida Vázquez), I: La política en el siglo XIX (México: Colegio de México, 1998), 183–226. *Principios y credo político del partido que hoy invoca el nombre del general Santa Anna* (19 de junio de 1849); Pedro Santoni and Will Fowler, *Mexico, 1848–1853: Los Años Olvidados* (London: Routledge, 2017). On the reform period, consult generally Richard N. Sinkin, *The Mexican Reform, 1855–1876: A Study in Liberal Nation-Building* (Austin: University of Texas Press, 1979), and Zachary Brittsan, *Popular Politics and Rebellion in Mexico: Manuel Lozada and La Reforma, 1855–1876* (Nashville: Vanderbilt University Press, 2015), chaps. 1–2.

67. Article 15 from Francisco Zarco, *Crónica del Congreso Extraordinario Constituyente, 1856*–1857 (reprint, México: Colegio de México, 1979), 319; my translation.

68. "Prospecto," *La Cruz: Periódico exclusivamente religioso, establecido exprofeso para difundir las doctrinas ortodoxas, y vindicarlas de los errores dominantes* [Ciudad de México] vol. 1, no. 1 (November 1855): 1–2. José David Cortés Guerrero, "'Viva la religión y mueran sus enemigos': Oposición a la tolerancia religiosa en México a mediados del siglo XIX," *Anuario Colombiano de Historia Social y de la Cultura* 33 (2006), 209–246. *La Cruz; Representación al soberano Congreso contra el art. 15 del proyecto de constitución sobre tolerancia religiosa* (México, 1856), 1 (*La Cruz* material copied in *representaciones*).

69. The number of memorials sent in 1856 is larger than the set available today due to a 1909 fire in the Mexican parliamentary archives; Covo, "Intolérance et fantasmes au Mexique," 140.

70. Guerrero, "'Viva la religión y mueran sus enemigas,'" 236; Mercedes de Vega, "Puros y moderados: Un obstáculo para la defensa nacional: Zacatecas, 1846–1848," in Josefina Zoraida Vásquez, *México al tiempo de su guerra con Estados Unidos (1846–1848)* (México: Colegio de México, 1997), 616–644; Pedro Santoni, *Mexicans at Arms: Puro Federalists and the Politics of War, 1845–1848* (Fort Worth: TCU Press, 1996).

71. *Representación que las señoras mexicanas elevaron al congreso constituyente, pidiendo no se establezca en la República la Tolerancia de Cultos* (México: Imprenta de Vicente Segura, 1856), 14, cited in Guerrero, 228.

72. San Luis Potosí representación from Antonio Martínez Báez, *Representaciones sobre la Tolerancia Religiosa* (México: 1959), 23 (my translation). See also, more generally, Sosenski, "Asomándose a la política"; Arrom, *Women of Mexico City*, 42–43.

73. *Representación que las Señoras de Guadalajara dirigen al Soberano Congreso Constituyente sobre que en la Carta Fundamental que se*

discute, no quede consignada la tolerancia de cultos en la Republica (Guadalajara: Tipografía de Rodríguez, 1856), 3–4.

74. *Representación que las Señoras de Guadalajara,* 5–6.
75. *Representación que las Señoras de Guadalajara,* 7–8.
76. Zarco, *Historia del Congreso Constituyente (1856–1857)* (México, 1956), 574; Covo, "Intolérance et fantasmes au Mexique," 141.
77. Arrom, *Volunteering for a Cause: Gender, Faith, and Charity in Mexico from the Reform to the Revolution* (Albuquerque: University of New Mexico Press, 2016), 57–58 (Table 2.1), and 97–99 (Table 3.2).
78. Chowning, "The Catholic Church and the Ladies of the Vela Perpetua," 223–226, 229–237; Arrom, *Volunteering for a Cause,* introduction and chaps. 1–3, and 141–143; on the "Catholic axis," see Manuel Ceballos Ramirez, *El catolicismo social: un tercero en discordia:* Rerum Novarum, *la "cuestión social" y la movilización de los católicos mexicanos (1891–1911)* (México: Colegio de México, 1991), 16.
79. See, for example, Peace Petition to Congress from the Inhabitants of Trumbull County, Ohio, 1847, U.S. House, Records of Committee on Foreign Affairs, RG 233, NA.
80. Extract from a letter addressed to *Louisville Courier,* dated October 17, 1847, in Abiel Abbot Livermore, *The War with Mexico Reviewed* (Boston: American Peace Society 1850), 129. See also "Woman on the War-field," *Emancipator and Republican,* April 28, 1847, cited in Isenberg, *Sex and Citizenship,* 253; Sylvia D. Hoffert, *When Hens Crow: The Woman's Rights Movement in Antebellum America* (Bloomington: Indiana University Press, 1995), 63–66; Amy S. Greenberg, *Manifest Manhood and the Antebellum American Empire* (Cambridge: Cambridge University Press, 2005), 88–90, 112–138. The *Intelligencer* article comes from Robert W. Johannsen, *To the Halls of the Montezumas: The Mexican War and the American Imagination* (Oxford: Oxford University Press, 1985), 138.
81. "Varias Mexicanas," *American Star,* October 5, 1847, 2, reprinted in "A Petition by Various Mexican Women," in Christopher Conway, ed., *The U.S. Mexican War: A Binational Reader* (Indianapolis: Hackett, 2010), 103–104.
82. Greenberg, *Manifest Manhood,* 19, 23 (how this imagery justified American aggression), 26, 55, 88–90.
83. Isenberg, *Sex and Citizenship,* 141–43, 253; Greenberg, *Manifest Manhood,* 88–90, 112–138.
84. Marie W. Horton to Martha P. Jones, February 21, 1847, Rubinstein Library, Duke University.

85. Isenberg, *Sex and Citizenship,* 129–130, 248, 252. Isenberg calls this petition-focused meeting "the initial step toward addressing women's rights and female criminals" (129).
86. Varon, "Tippecanoe and the Ladies, Too: White Women and Party Politics in Antebellum Virginia," *Journal of American History* 82 (September 1995): 495, 503.
87. "Liberty Party and Women's Rights," *National Anti-Slavery Standard,* August 6, 1846. See also Isenberg, *Sex and Citizenship,* 214–215.
88. Bishop and Attree, *Report of the Debates and Proceedings of the Convention for the Revision of the Constitution of the State of New-York, 1846,* 646, reprinted in Ginzberg, *Untidy Origins,* 2–3. See also Dawn Winter, "'The Ladies Are Coming!': A New History of Antebellum Temperance, Women's Rights, and Political Activism" (PhD thesis, Carnegie Mellon University, 2018).
89. Ginzberg *Untidy Origins,* 16 (citizenship as democracy); Isenberg, *Sex and Citizenship,* 133 ("democratic citizenship").
90. Isenberg, *Sex and Citizenship,* 69–70 (literary and political public spheres).
91. Judith Wellman, "The Seneca Falls Women's Rights Convention: A Study in Social Networks," *Women's History* 3, no. 1 (1991): 9–37; Wellman, *The Road to Seneca Falls: Elizabeth Cady Stanton and the First Women's Rights Convention* (Champaign-Urbana, 2004). Carpenter and Moore, "When Canvassers Became Activists," 493. I acknowledge Judith Wellman for her assistance in making these attributions. Winters, "'The Ladies Are Coming!'" (on links to temperance).
92. Isenberg (*Sex and Citizenship,* 252) rightly emphasizes the Salem, Ohio, convention of 1850. List of signatories of Randolph convention all from *Anti-Slavery Bugle,* September 17, 1847 (p. 3, column 5). For Ohio antislavery petitions, consult Petition of K. G. Thomas (Ohio), to House; 27A-H1.7; Petition of Joseph Dugdale, HR25A, LC box 127; Petition of Legal Voters of Madriver Township, Ohio, to the House (27th Congress, Dugdale is first name), 27A-H1.6, F2; Citizens of Ashtabula County to House (December 1839, Lyman Peek) and Women of Ashtabula County to house (probably December 1839, Peek), HR26A-H1.5, F1, F5; Citizens of Columbiana County to House (Garretson is lead signatory), HR 28A-G5.1, F2 of 4 (unnumbered); Inhabitants of Stark County, Ohio, to House (Brooke, where 41 of the 69 signatories were women), HR 25A, LC box 127; all in RG 233, NA. Flexner and Fitzpatrick, *A Century of Struggle,* 66–81.
93. Lucy Stone, "Suffrage for Women," *Liberator,* February 1, 1850, 19, cited in Joelle Million, "Seeking Simple Justice: Lucy Stone and Early Suffrage Petitioning in Massachusetts," manuscript (2018).

94. Million, *Woman's Voice, Woman's Place: Lucy Stone and the Birth of the Woman's Rights Movement* (Westport, Conn.: Praeger, 2003), esp. 103–110.
95. Petition of 41 men and women of Feltonville, Massachusetts, 1850; Digital Archive of Massachusetts Anti-Slavery and Anti-Segregation Petitions; House unpassed legislation, 1775–1996 (SC1-230), 1850, Docket 2577, MAC, http://nrs.harvard.edu/urn-3:FHCL:11029709.
96. Petition of 44 men and women of Plymouth, 1850; Digital Archive of Massachusetts Anti-Slavery and Anti-Segregation Petitions; House unpassed legislation, 1775–1996 (SC1-230), 1850, Docket 2577, MAC, http://nrs.harvard.edu/urn-3:FHCL:11029710; Rachel L. Einwohner, Jocelyn A. Hollander, and Toska Olsen, "Engendering Social Movements: Cultural Images and Movement Dynamics," *Gender and Society* 14, no. 5 (October 2000): 679–699.
97. Million, *Woman's Voice,* 105–110.
98. "Amendment of the Constitution," *Liberator,* February 4, 1853, 19.
99. *Journal of the Constitutional Convention of the Commonwealth of Massachusetts, begun and held in Boston, on the fourth day of May, 1853* (Boston: White & Potter, 1853), 35, 44, 61, 78, in Million, "Seeking Simple Justice," 14–19.
100. Hoffert, *When Hens Crow,* 74–75, 141.
101. "Abolitionists, Constitutional Convention . . . ," *New York Daily Tribune,* June 4, 1853, 1; *Anti-Slavery Bugle,* June 4, 1853, 2; *Pennsylvania Freeman* (*Liberator,* July 1, 1853, 104); *Una,* July 1, August 1, September 1, 1853; in Million, "Seeking Simple Justice," 25.
102. Channing letter in *Proceedings of the National Women's Rights Convention, Held at Cleveland, Ohio, Wednesday, Thursday, and Friday, October 5th, 6th, and 7th, 1853* (Cleveland: Gray, Beardsley, Spear & Co., 1854), 67–70.
103. "Miss Anthony's first campaign on behalf of her new cause was for signatures to a petition addressed to the New York legislature" (Flexner and Fitzpatrick, *A Century of Struggle,* 80); Susan Goodier and Karen Pastorello, *Women Will Vote: Winning Suffrage in New York State* (Ithaca: Cornell University Press, 2017), chap. 1; Million, "Seeking Simple Justice," 25–27.
104. *Address to the Legislature of New York, adopted by the State Woman's Rights Convention, held at Albany, Tuesday and Wednesday, February 14 & 15, 1854* (Albany: Weed, Parsons & Co., 1854). Petition of Sarah H. Earle and 137 others . . . ; House unpassed legislation, 1775–1996 (SC1-230), February 15, 1855, #4046; Petition of women from Nantucket, House unpassed legislation, 1775–1996 (SC1-230), 1858,

referred to special committee on voter qualifications, MAC, http://nrs.harvard.edu/urn-3:FHCL:11029839. *Report of the select committee of the Ohio Senate, on giving the rights of suffrage to females* (Columbus, 1858), earlier printed in *Anti-Slavery Bugle,* March 14, 1857, 1; *Report of the Majority of the Judiciary Committee, Made to the Assembly of Wisconsin, March 1, 1857* (Madison: Legislative Assembly, 1857); Million, "Seeking Simple Justice," 27–28

105. Isenberg, *Sex and Citizenship,* 172–174, 180, 188–190. *Remarks comprising in substance Judge Herttell's argument in the House of Assembly of the state of New York, in the session of 1837, in support of the bill to restore to married women "The Right of Property," as guaranteed by the constitution of this state* (New York, 1839; reprint Boston, 1867). Richard H. Chused, "Married Women's Property Law: 1800–1850," *Georgetown Law Journal* 71 (1983): 1359, 1366; New York statute at 1848 *New York Laws* 307, Ch. 200; Reva Seigel, "The Modernization of Marital Status Law: Adjudicating Wives' Right to Earning, 1860–1930," *Georgetown Law Journal* 82 (1995): 2127–2211.
106. Elizabeth Cady Stanton, ed., *History of Woman Suffrage* (New York: Fowler & Wells, 1881), 1:208–215; Elizabeth B. Warbasse, "Mary Upton Ferrin," *Notable American Women 1607–1950* (Cambridge, Mass.: Harvard University Press, 1971), 611–612; Glendyne R. Wergland, *The Daughters of Rural Massachusetts: Women and Autonomy, 1800–1860* (PhD thesis, University of Massachusetts, Amherst), 68–69, 104–111; John R. Mulkern, *The Know-Nothing Party in Massachusetts* (Boston: UPNE, 1990), 93, 107–108; Virginia Cadwell Purdy, *Portrait of a Know-Nothing Legislature: the Massachusetts General Court of 1855* (PhD thesis, George Washington University, 1970), 118–121, 220–235.
107. Kerber, *Women of the Republic,* esp. chaps. 3, 6, 9; Cott, "Divorce and the Changing Status of Women in Eighteenth-Century Massachusetts"; Amy Porter, "Tejanas and Ranching: María Calvillo and Her Ranching Enterprises," in *Texas Women and Ranching: On the Range, at the Rodeo, and in their Communities,* ed. Deborah M. Liles and Cecilia Gutiérrez Venable (College Station: Texas A&M University Press, 2019), esp. 16–17. Collins, "'Petitions without Number': Widows' Petitions and the Early Nineteenth-Century Origins of Marriage-Based Entitlements."
108. On committee hearings as demonstrative of access sought by organized interests, consult John Mark Hansen, *Gaining Access: Congress and the Farm Lobby, 1919–1981* (Chicago, 1992).

12. THE ECLIPSE OF LORDSHIP: PETITIONING AND LAND TENURE IN THE UNITED STATES AND CANADA

1. Jefferson, *Notes on the State of Virginia,* Query XIX. Jefferson's *Summary of the Rights of British North America* (1774) took a similar view, and its embodied justification for rebellion was located in the allodial and antifeudal nature of American property.
2. John Locke, *Second Treatise of Government,* Section 27.
3. Louis Hartz, *The Liberal Tradition in America: An Interpretation of Political Thought since the Revolution* (New York: Harcourt, Brace, 1955), esp. pt. 1, chap. 1; Stephen Skowronek, *Building a New American State: The Expansion of National Administrative Capacities, 1877–1920* (New York: Cambridge University Press, 1982), chaps. 1–2; Naomi R. Lamoreaux, "The Mystery of Property Rights: A U.S. Perspective," *Journal of Economic History* 71, no. 2 (June 2011): 275–306.
4. Carol Wilton, *Popular Politics and Political Culture in Upper Canada, 1800–1850* (Montreal: McGill-Queen's University Press, 2000), 76, 78; Alexis de Tocqueville, "Conversation avec Mr. Quiblier, supérieur du Séminaire de Montréal," Voyages I, 77–78, in *Tocqueville au Bas-Canada,* 56.
5. Reeve Huston, *Land and Freedom: Rural Society, Popular Protest and Party Politics in Antebellum New York* (Oxford: Oxford University Press, 2000); Charles W. McCurdy, The *Anti-Rent Era in New York Law and Politics, 1839–1865* (Chapel Hill: University of North Carolina Press, 2001). As with others writing on the rent debate, I am deeply indebted to Huston's and McCurdy's masterful accounts.
6. Colette Michaud, "Les Censitaires et le Régime Seigneurial Canadien (1791–1854): Étude des Requêtes Anti-Seigneuriales" (thesis, Université de Montréal, 1982), Tableau IV, 140–142.
7. The conclusion that "law and politics"—including party competition, electoral forces and judicial interpretation—could not solve a problem that modernity, capitalism, and liberalism wanted corrected is McCurdy's (*Anti-Rent Era,* xiv–xvi, chap. 13).
8. McCurdy, *Anti-Rent Era,* 12–17.
9. *Report of the Committee on so much of the Governor's Message as relates to the difficulties between the landlord and tenants of the Manor of Rensselaerwyck* (Assembly Doc. No. 271, 1840), 4–6; David Maldwyn Ellis, *Landlords and Farmers in the Hudson-Mohawk Region, 1790–1850* (Ithaca: Cornell University Press, 2018 [reprint]), chaps. 2, 7; McCurdy, *Anti-Rent Era,* 15–29.

10. *Report of the select committee, to whom were referred the petitions from numerous tenants of the manor of Rensselaerwyck* (March 26, 1844), NYAD No. 189 (1844), 3.
11. Seward remarks in "Annual Message" to the Legislature (63rd Sess.), January 7, 1840, in *Messages from the Governors: Comprising Executive Communications to the Legislature . . . with Notes* (Albany: J. B. Lyon, 1909), 3:776. See also Laurence M. Hauptman, *Conspiracy of Interests: Iroquois Dispossession and the Rise of New York State* (Syracuse: Syracuse University Press, 1999); Daniel Walker Howe, *The Political Culture of the American Whigs* (Chicago: University of Chicago Press, 1979), introduction and chap. 1; Michael Holt, *The Rise and Fall of the American Whig Party* (Oxford: Oxford University Press, 1999), chaps. 2, 5–7.
12. *Jackson ex. Dem. Lewis & Wife v. Schutz* (1820); McCurdy, *Anti-Rent Era*, 25–30.
13. McCurdy, *Anti-Rent Era*, 17.
14. The anti-renters' Declaration of Independence was also a convention, a mutual pledge of assistance and loyalty, which underscored its contrast with a feudal pledge of loyalty to a lord. Huston, *Land and Freedom*, 91–92. Pauline Maier, *American Scripture: Making the Declaration of Independence* (New York: Penguin, 1997), 151–153; David Armitage, *The Declaration of Independence: A Global History* (Cambridge, Mass.: Harvard University Press, 2007), esp. 36–62; Seward, "Annual Message," 774–76.
15. New Scotland anti-renter letter excerpted in *Message from the Governor, in relation to the difficulties in the Manor of Rensselaerwyck*, New York Senate Document 70 (63rd Sess., 1840), 22–26. See also McCurdy, *Anti-Rent Era*, 18–22.
16. *JASNY*, 63rd Session (1840), 170 (January 21, 1840), 247 (Albany County, 744 signatures, January 31), 292 (Knox and Bern townships, 152 signatures, February 5), 448 (February 25), 504 (March 3), 515 (March 4). The Albany Capitol fire of 1911 destroyed the state's legislative records. *Report of the Committee . . . Rensselaerwyck*, 3–4; McCurdy, *Anti-Rent Era*, 42–43.
17. *Report of the Committee . . . the Manor of Rensselaerwyck* (Assembly Doc. No. 271), 3.
18. *Report of the Committee . . . the Manor of Rensselaerwyck* (Assembly Doc. No. 271), 3.
19. *Report of the Committee . . . the Manor of Rensselaerwyck* (Assembly Doc. No. 271), 3–4; McCurdy, *Anti-Rent Era*, 34–53; John Joseph Wallis, "The Depression of 1839 to 1843: States, Debts and Banks" (NBER Working Paper, 2005).

20. Bern Declaration, printed in the Albany *Argus*, May 6, 1841.
21. McCurdy, *Anti-Rent Era*, 68–74. On the long history of White citizens performing an American identity through the projected adoption of Indigenous dress and rituals, see Phil Deloria, *Playing Indian* (New Haven, Conn.: Yale University Press, 2004).
22. McCurdy, *Anti-Rent Era*, 86, 96, chap. 5 (esp. 114–115).
23. *Report of the committee on the judiciary, on several petitions for a law to extend the exemption of personal property from sale on execution or distress for rent,* New York Senate Document 81 (April 22, 1841), 1, reprinted in *Albany Evening Journal*, April 26, 1841.
24. *Report of the committee on the judiciary*, New York Senate Document 81, 2.
25. "Exemption of Furniture," *Albany Evening Journal*, April 28, 1841, 3.
26. On $150 exemption in Sibley bill, see *Albany Evening Journal*, May 4, 1841, 2.
27. McCurdy, *Anti-Rent Era*, 66.
28. *JASNY* 1841, 387 (May 3, petition from Seneca Falls), 416 (May 11, Rochester), 423 (May 13, Summitt, Schoharie County), 428 (May 15, two petitions from Tompkins County), 432 (May 17, five petitions), 476 (May 22, Greene County), 486 (May 24, Onondaga and Kings counties), 492 (May 25, petitions from Onondaga County, Weedsport, Madison County, New York, and Canajoharie); *Report of the committee on the judiciary in relation to the exemption of property from levy or sale, on execution, or distress for rent;* DSNY (1842), no. 76, 3.
29. Josiah T. Marshall, *The Farmers and Emigrants Complete Guide, or, A handbook with copious hints, recipes, and tables, designed for the Farmer and Emigrant* (Cincinnati, 1856), 16; Carroll D. Wright, *Comparative wages, prices and cost of living* (Boston, 1889), 148, 150; McCurdy, *Anti-Rent Era*, 87–89.
30. McCurdy, *Anti-Rent Era*, 87–93.
31. In his otherwise masterful summary of this episode, McCurdy (*Anti-Rent Era*, 96) appears to conflate petition signatures with petitions themselves. He writes, "The merchants redoubled their effort that fall and bombarded the legislature with 7,127 petitions during the 1843 session," but in using the number 7,127, the Strong report was clearly referring to "The number of those who have petitioned" (6), meaning signatories. A study of the New York State Assembly *Journal* for 1843 confirms this reading.
32. *JASNY* 1843, 283, 447. Ward population figures from *The New-York State Register for 1845* (Albany: C. Van Benthuysen and Company, 1845), 45; *Proceedings of a Number of Democratic Citizens of the Eighth Ward in Opposition to the Secret Clique System* (New York, 1843); Sean Wilentz,

Chants Democratic: New York City and the Rise of the American Working Class, 1788–1850 (Oxford: Oxford University Press, 1984), 221–222, 382.

33. Petition of residents of the County of Schoharie to the Assembly and Senate of New York, February 14, 1844, in *Report of the select committee, to whom was referred the petitions from numerous tenants of the manor of Rensselaerwyck,* March 26, 1844; NYAD No. 189 (1844); McCurdy, *Anti-Rent Era,* 96–103, 124–127.
34. *Report of the select committee, to whom was referred the petitions from numerous tenants of the manor of Rensselaerwyck,* March 26, 1844, NYAD 189 (1844), 3.
35. *Report of the select committee,* March 26, 1844, 3. See also McCurdy, *Anti-Rent Era,* 131–133.
36. Huston, *Land and Freedom,* 101–102; McCurdy, *Anti-Rent Era,* 171–177.
37. *Report of the minority of the select committee on landlord and tenant,* NYAD No. 247 (1845), 68th Sess., 1 (no signatory enumeration). On Scott Patent, consult Ellis, *Landlords and Farmers,* 57–58, 243 (on how Rensselaer and Schoharie County tenants petitioned instead of rent-striking); McCurdy, *Anti-Rent Era,* 89–90.
38. *Report of the Comptroller, in answer to a resolution of the Assembly of 1844, in relation to taxing rents, quarter sales, interests in water right reservations, &c.,* NYAD No. 228 (68th Session, April 18, 1845), 1–7; *Report of the majority of the select committee on numerous petitions from the manor tenants in several counties of this State for relief,* NYAD No. 231, 68th Session 91845); *Report of the minority of the select committee on landlord and tenant,* NYAD No. 247, 4–9; McCurdy, *Anti-Rent Era,* 194–196.
39. James D. Livingston and Sherry H. Penney, "The Breakup of Livingston Manor," in *The Livingston Legacy: Three Centuries of American History,* ed. Richard T. Wiles (Annandale-on-Hudson: Bard College, 1987). The King purchase contract is reprinted in the *Jefferson Courier and Schoharie County Chronicle,* July 27, 1905; McCurdy, *Anti-Rent Era,* 196–200.
40. McCurdy, *Anti-Rent Era,* 256–60.
41. Huston, *Land and Freedom,* 87–93, 119–120 (anti-renters "fervently believed in the redemptive power of the ballot box and the petition").
42. Marcel Trudel, *Les débuts du régime seigneurial au Canada* (Montréal: Fides, 1974), 72–74 (royal *Arrêts de Révocation* in 1672, 1675 and 1679 limiting speculation, and another in 1732 limiting timber land sales); Ouellet, *Histoire sociale et économique du Québec, 1760–1850.* Louise Dechêne, *Habitants et marchands de Montréal au XVII*[e] *siècle* (Montréal:

Plon, 1974); Allan Greer, *Peasant, Lord and Merchant: Rural Society in Three Quebec Parishes, 1740–1840* (Toronto: University of Toronto Press, 1985).

43. Jean-Pierre Wallot, *Un Québec qui bougeait: Trame socio-politique du Québec au tournant du XIXe siècle* (Québec: Boréal Express, 1973), 10; Lawson, *The Imperial Challenge.*

44. Fernand Ouellet, *Histoire Économique et sociale du Québec, 1760–1850;* Ouellet, "Le régime seigneurial dans le Québec, 1760–1854," in *France et Canada français du XVIe siècle au XXe,* ed. Claude Galarneau and Elzéar Lavoie (Québec: cahiers de l'Institut d'histoire, 1966), 167–169.

45. Amury Girod, *Notes Diverses sur le Bas-Canada* (Village Debartzch: L'Imprimerie de J. P. Boucher-Belleville, 1835), 121; Georges Baillargeon, "La tenure seigneuriale a-t-elle été abolie par suite des plaintes des censitaires?" *Revue d'histoire de l'Amérique française* 21, no. 1 (1967): 65–66. André La Rose, "Objectif: commutation de tenure—Edward Ellice et le régime seigneurial (1820–1840)," *Revue d'histoire de l'Amérique française* 66, no. 3–4 (2013): 365–393. The Canada Tenures Act (6 Geo. IV, Ch. 59) corrected features of the 1822 Commerce law that Ellice and others found frustrating.

46. *Journaux de l'Assemblée législative de la Province du Canada,* 1er session (June 28, 1841), 103–104 (Motion of M. Dunscomb); Baillargeon, "La tenure seigneuriale a-t-elle été abolie . . . ," 68–70; Petitions from data in Michaud, *Les Censitaires et le Régime Seigneurial Canadian (1791–1854): Étude des Requêtes Anti-Seigneuriales* (Ottawa, 1982), Tableau XVI, 247.

47. *Journaux de l'Assemblée législative de la Province du Canada,* 1er session (July 28, 1841), 273–274 (resolutions and vote). The assembly formed a Committee of the Whole at least 190 times in the first session, but voting on resolutions was rare in part because of the unanimity with which they were usually received. Baillargeon, "La tenure seigneuriale a-t-elle été abolie . . . ," 68–70.

48. Brian J. Young, *The Politics of Codification: The Lower Canadian Civil Code of 1866* (Montreal: McGill-Queen's University Press, 1994), 57–58, and, in general, Young's instructive chap. 4.

49. Pierre Davignon, "Aux Signataires de la Requête des Comtés du Rouville, Chambly et Laprairie demandant la réforme de la tenure seigneuriale," *La Minerve* 21, no. 95 (August 6, 1849): 2; "C'est le plus grand nombre de pétitionnaires qui se soit adressé à la chambre d'assemblée demandant le redressement d'un seul grief."

50. Davignon, "Aux Signataires de la Requête des Comtés de Rouville."

51. "Tenure seigneuriale," *La Minerve* 22, no. 1 (September 10, 1849): 3; "Tenure seigneuriale," *La Minerve* (October 11, 1849): 2; Baillargeon, "La

tenure seigneuriale a-t-elle été abolie . . . ," 70–72 (where some of the *La Minerve* issues are wrongly dated); "Tenure Seigneuriale," *La Minerve* 21, no. 14 (October 26, 1848).

52. Lafontaine argued that "l'agitation continuelle contre la tenure seigneuriale a eu l'effet de diminuer de plus en plus les propriétés seigneuriales" (remarks reported in "Chambre de l'Assemblée," *La Minerve,* June 20, 1850, 2). The difference of 240 names across the signatory lists of commutation and abolition prayers is statistically significant ($F = 8.85$, $p = 0.0041$); data collected and analyzed from Michaud; Baillargeon, "La tenure seigneuriale a-t-elle été abolie . . . ," 71–73.
53. "Chambre de l'Assemblée," *La Minerve,* June 20, 1850, 2; Baillargeon, "La tenure seigneuriale a-t-elle été abolie . . . ," 71–73; Pétition de Simon Bertrand et autres, du Comté de Rouville, demandant l'abolition du Conseil Législatif, que la charge du Gouverneur soit rendue élective, et que Gouvernement de cette Province soit fait semblable autant que possible à celui des États-Unis, *Journaux de l'Assemblée législative de la province du Canada* (1854–55), partie première, 279 (November 6, 1854).
54. Baillargeon, "La tenure seigneuriale a-t-elle été abolie . . . ," 74.
55. *Journaux de l'Assemblée législative de la province du Canada* (1854–55), partie première, 208 (October 20, 1854), 255 (October 30, 1854), 208. The abolition of *retrait conventionnel* was not, however, judged to be retroactive; see the case of "Garon et Casgrain," in *Lower Canada Reports: Décisions Des Tribunaux du Bas Canada* (Québec: E. R. Fréchette, 1858), 8:397–400, 535. The final statute was titled l'*Acte pour l'abolition des droits et devoirs féodaux dans le Bas-Canada;* Benoit Grenier, "A propos de l'extinction des rentes seigneuriales au Québec, 1854–1974," *Revue d'histoire de l'Amérique française* 64, no. 2 (Automne 2010): 75–98.
56. Huston, *Land and Freedom,* 197–207; McCurdy, *Anti-Rent Era,* chap. 13, "The End of an Era," esp. 331–336. *Statuts refondus du Bas Canada* (Montréal, 1861), chap. 41 and articles 30, 33, 91; George Baillargeon, "A propos de l'abolition du régime seigneurial," *Revue d'histoire de l'Amérique française* 22, no. 3 (December 1968): 365–366; Grenier, "A propos de l'extinction des rentes seigneuriales," 80–83.

13. NATIVE CONTINUANCE, NATIVE GOVERNANCE

1. For rich insights on the following narrative of the Seneca Nation, which is dedicated to the late Rick Jemison, I thank Seneca Nation historians Jaré Cardinal, Rick Jemison, and Randy Jones, and Professor Alyssa Mount-Pleasant (Tuscarora). Laurence M. Hauptman, *Conspiracy of Interests:*

Iroquois Dispossession and the Rise of New York State (Syracuse: Syracuse University Press, 1999), 176–178.

2. Protest of Seneca Chiefs (Big Kettle et al.) to President, October 16, 1837. Onondaga and Oneida chiefs had also written and signed protests in August; Hauptman, *Conspiracy*, 185. Undersigned chiefs of the Seneca Nation, assembled on the Buffalo Creek reservation, to Prentiss, February 28, 1838; Big Kettle, William Kronse and John Kennedy to Prentiss, March 3, 1838; Joint Committee on Indian Affairs, *The Case of Seneca Indians in the State of New York* (Philadelphia, 1840), 112–121.
3. Hauptman, *Conspiracy*, 186–188. The alliance between the Seneca and Hicksite Quakers was deep and enduring, but a number of sources indicate that the Seneca petitioned and protested before the Quakers did. The House, for instance, records the first protest against the Treaty of 1838 as coming from Governor Blacksnake (a chief warrior) and others (*JHRUS* 31 [September 27, 1837]: 21), with another arriving some eight months later (*JHRUS* 33 [May 21, 1838]: 15), whereas the first relevant Quaker petition recorded in House proceedings came in June 1838 (*JHRUS* 32 [June 18, 1838]: 159) (archived in HR25A-G7.1, RG 233, NARA).
4. Undersigned sachems, chiefs and residents of the Seneca Nation of Indians (at Buffalo Creek reservation) to the President, September 7, 1838; and Undersigned chiefs and residents of the Seneca nation of Indians to Van Buren, September 28, 1838, transmitted January 24, 1839, in Joint Committee, *Case of the Seneca*, app. 9, 122–135. Israel Jemison, Seneca White, Maris B. Pierce, and John Kennedy to Van Buren, February 7, 1839, in Joint Committee, *Case of the Seneca*, app. 10, 136–137. Claudia Haake, "Iroquois Use of Customary Haudenosaunee and United States Law in Opposing Removal," *American Indian Culture and Research Journal* 36, no. 4 (2012): 29–56.
5. Petitions of warriors and residents from Tonawanda, Erie County (Buffalo Creek), and Cattaraugus, respectively, appear in Joint Committee, *Case of the Seneca*, app. 10, 139–143.
6. Undersigned Chief Warriors, Sachems and Chiefs of the Seneca Nation of Indians to U.S. Senate, December 16, 1839, SEN 26A-G7, RG 46, NARA; Thomas S. Abler, "Seneca Moieties and Hereditary Chieftainships: The Early-Nineteenth-Century Political Organization of an Iroquois Nation," *Ethnohistory* 51, no. 3 (Summer 2004): 459–488.
7. H. A. Vernon, "Maris Bryant Pierce: The Making of a Seneca Leader," in *Indian Lives: Essays on Nineteenth- and Twentieth-Century Native American Leaders* (Albuquerque: University of New Mexico Press, 1985), 19–42; "Maris Bryant Pierce: A Seneca Chief at Dartmouth," *Dartmouth*

Alumni Magazine, December 1983, 38–41; Colin Calloway, *The Indian History of an American Institution: Native Americans at Dartmouth* (Hanover, N.H.: Dartmouth College Press, 2010).

8. This petition, like others asking for delay, was tabled or rejected, and the 1838 Treaty was ratified by the Senate in January 1840. Executive Proceedings of the U.S. Senate, January 3, 1840, *Congressional Series of United States Public Documents* 353:563.
9. On the use of censuses for Indigenous removal in the South, consult Claudio Saunt, *Unworthy Republic: The Dispossession of Native Americans and the Road to Indian Territory* (New York: Norton, 2020), 182–184; Joint Committee, *Case of the Seneca,* app. 10, 159–164.
10. Joint Committee, *Case of the Seneca,* app. 10, 135.
11. Petition of Tonawanda Seneca Clan Mothers to President, March 14, 1841, OIA, M234 (reel 584), RG75, NARA, reprinted in Laurence M. Hauptman, *The Tonawanda Senecas' Heroic Battle against Removal: Conservative Activist Indians* (Albany: Excelsior, 2011), 127–128. See also Nancy A. Hewitt, *Radical Friend: Amy Kirby Post and Her Activist Worlds* (Chapel Hill: University of North Carolina Press, 2018), 114–116; Judith Wellman, *The Road to Seneca Falls Elizabeth Cady Stanton and the First Woman's Rights Convention* (Urbana: University of Illinois Press, 2004), 107.
12. On payments, see James Stryker, Orlando Allen, Henry P. Wilcox, Thomas L. Ogden, et al., Account book kept from May 1837–1844, folder 16, Transactions between the Ogden Land Company and the Seneca Indians, 1826–1871 (Mss. A2016–35), BHM. Of those who had signed the 1839 Senate petition (Figure 13.1), only Samuel Gordon appears in these books. Seneca chieftains (at Cattaraugus) to New York Governor William Seward, October 28, 1841; GLC05487 [digital], GLC, NYHS.
13. Memorial of the Genesee Yearly Meeting of the Society of Friends of the State of New York to the Senate and House, June 1838, HR25A-G7.1, RG 233, NARA; recorded in *House Journal* 32 (June 18, 1838): 159. The petition was signed by Thomas J. Alsop and Anna R. Brown, clerks of the Men's and Women's Yearly Meeting. Memorial of the Presbytery of Buffalo to the House and Senate, January 28, 1841; Petition of the Citizens of the Town of Alexander (New York) to Congress, Petition of the Citizens of the County of Erie (New York) to Congress, Petition of the Citizens of Napoli (New York to Congress (all undated but referred to committee in February 1841), SEN26A-G7, RG 46, NARA; Hauptman, *Conspiracy,* 188, 191–196.
14. Hauptman, *Conspiracy,* 207–211; Hauptman *Tonawanda Senecas,* 45–58.

15. Hauptman, *Conspiracy*, 211. Hauptmann sees Pierce as having been duped, having "had no clue about the implications of the Supplemental Treaty" (211).
16. On Blacksmith, see Hauptman, *Tonawanda Senecas*, chap. 5.
17. Memorial of the Seneca Women (Cattaraugus Reservation) to (Friend) Philip E. Thomas, October 12, 1848, in *Documents and Official Reports Illustrating the Causes Which Led to the Revolution in the Government of the Seneca Indians* (Baltimore: W. Wooddy & Son, 1857), 20–24.
18. Another petition signed by nineteen Seneca women in 1849 countered the approach of Pierce himself. Memorial of Seneca Women to the President of the United States, April 2, 1849, in *Documents and Official Reports Illustrating the Causes Which Led to the Revolution in the Government of the Seneca Indians* (Baltimore: W. Wooddy & Son, 1857), 20–24. While the Quaker authors of this document reported selectively on the Seneca, the petitions they reported were real. Consult *Constitution of the "Government by Chiefs" of the Seneca Nation of Indians: Adopted Nov. 30, 1854, by the National Council, Subject to the Approval of the Electors of the Nation*; Thomas Abler, "Friends, Factions and the Seneca Revolution of 1848," *Niagara History* 21 (1974): 74–79.
19. Pierce to Taylor, March 13, 1849, Maris Bryant Pierce Papers, Mss. B00-9, box 2, folder 7, BHM; Abler, "Friends, Factions and the Seneca Revolution of 1848."
20. Hauptman, *Tonawanda Seneca;* C. Joseph Genetin-Pilawa, *Crooked Path to Removal: The Fight over Federal Indian Policy after the Civil War* (Chapel Hill: University of North Carolina Press, 2012), chap. 2.
21. The Eastern Cherokee reservation in North Carolina is larger in population, and it is slightly smaller geographically than these two reservations in New York. (This is without counting Oil Spring.)
22. Augustin Hamelin, conveying Memorial of united Ottawa and Chippewa to Lewis Cass, December 5, 1835, Letters Received by the Office of Indian Affairs, Michigan Superintendency, 1832–1835, NARA, RG 75, M 234, reel 421, 724. See also Elizabeth Neumeyer, "Michigan Indians Battle against Removal," *Michigan History* 55, no. 4 (1971): 279; Theodore J. Karamanski, *Blackbird's Song: Andrew J. Blackbird and the Odawa People* (East Lansing: Michigan State University Press, 2012), 74–76; Michael Witgen, "Seeing Red: Race, Citizenship, and Indigeneity in the Old Northwest," *Journal of the Early Republic* 38, no. 4 (Winter 2018): 596–597, 600–601.
23. Petition of Ottawas to Andrew Jackson, Rapids of Grand River, January 27, 1836, Letters Received by the Office of Indian Affairs, Michigan Superintendency, 1836–1837, NA M234, reel 422, 146.

24. Neumeyer, "Michigan Indians Battle against Removal," 279; Richard White, "Ethnohistorical Report on the Grand Traverse Ottawas" (unpublished manuscript, 1991), chaps. 3–4 (esp. 89–90, 111–112).
25. The 1835 memorial and its delegation were funded in part by Bishop Frederic Rese of Detroit. For the request-petition of 1816, see William H. Puthuff to Lewis Cass, *Wisconsin Historical Collections*, 19:413; Karamanski, *Blackbird's Song*, 36–37, 74; *Annales de l'association de la propagation de la foi: recueil périodique des lettres des évêques et des missionnaires des missions des deux mondes, et de tous les documens relatifs aux missions et à l'Association de la propagation de la foi*, Tome Second (Lyon: *L'Association de la propagation de la foi*, 1834), 102–103 (*requêtes* of 1823 and 1824). I acknowledge Eric Hemenway of the Little Traverse Bands of Odawa Indians for valuable conversations on Hamelin. White, "Ethnohistorical Report," 101–102 (representation); Cary Miller, *Ogimaag: Anishaabeg Leadership, 1760–1845* (Lincoln: University of Nebraska Press, 2010).
26. Matthew L. M. Fletcher, *The Eagle Returns: The Legal History of the Grand Traverse Band of Ottawa and Chippewa Indians* (East Lansing: Michigan State University Press, 2012), chaps. 1–2; White, "Ethnohistorical Report," chaps. 4–5; Neumeyer, "Michigan Indians Battle against Removal," 281–282; Francis Pierz (L'Arbre Croche) to President of the U.S., July 20, 1843; NA, RG 75, M234, reel 425.
27. As White summarizes, "Looked at in one way, the story of Indian Removal in Michigan for the Ottawas and Chippewas is an account of something that never happened"; "Ethnohistorical Report," 79. Neumeyer, "Michigan Indians Battle Removal," 282–284; Fletcher, *Eagle Returns*.
28. Consistent with practice at the time (see, for instance, the statute books during the third year of Victoria onward until at least the fifteenth), I use "Lower Canada" and "Upper Canada" to describe Canadian lands east and west of the Ottawa River, respectively.
29. Alain Beaulieu, *La question des terres autochtones au Québec, 1760–1860: Rapport préparé pour le Ministère de la Justice et le Ministère des Ressources naturelles du Québec* (Varennes, MNRQ, 2002), 431 (Napier's claim as to potential claims of Indigenous in Canada East). Durocher (Lac des Deux Montagnes) à Bourget (Évêque de Montréal), July 12, 1839 (255.110, 839–16); Durocher à Bourget, July 30, 1839 (255.110, 839–20); Durocher à Bourget, July 13, 1840 (255.110, 840–5), AAM.
30. Jacques Frenette, "Note de recherche: La pétition montagnaise du 1er février 1843: chasse, pêche et agriculture à la baie des Escoumins," *Recherches Amérindiennes au Québec* 33, no. 1 (2003): 105–114; "Peti-

tion of Monteigneirs" (Montagnais/Innu), August 9, 1844, E.20/1, folios 240–241, Ile Jérémie miscellaneous records, Hudson's Bay Company Records, AOM.

31. The Innu expression is *eku etsheskakuiats esku mauats pek shipu nika ianan tshe pistuaiats,* and the French interpretation of *mauats* is "pas même." The left-hand column of the prayer displays hallmarks of Innu handwriting of the mid-nineteenth century, which usually lacked majuscules and did not hyphenate words or mark paragraphs or sentences from one another as European handwriting and print did. I am greatly indebted for these observations to a consultation with the Institut Tshakapesh of the Innu First Nations (Uashat mak Mani-Utenam), as well as Professor Lynn Drapeau.

    The exact number of petitions sent to colonial authorities is unknown, but Frenette ("Note de recherche," 105) remarks that it was nearly twelve from 1844 to 1850.

32. "Note du Rév. P. Boucher, accompagnant la requête des Sauvages Montagnais à la Législature Provinciale," *Le Journal de Québec,* July 3, 1847, 2–3; Durocher, "Notes explicatives accompagnant la requête des Montagnais," Dossier 295.098, 847–4, AAM.

33. See the summary of Indigenous petitions to the assembly in Alfred Todd, *General Index to the Journals of the Legislative Assembly of Canada in the 1st, 2nd and 3rd Parliaments. 1841–1851* (Montréal: Legislative Assembly, 1855), 290–291. Petition of A. Campbell, Esq. and others, Merchants, Ship Owners and Others to Assembly, read March 15, 1849; *Journal,* 1849, 156–157; Frenette, "L'original de la pétition montagnaise du 8 avril 1847," 86–88.

34. Dumesnil, "De l'état déplorable des descendants des anciens naturels du Canada, et du moyen de les civiliser," in *De L'Abolition des Droits Féodaux et Seigneuriaux au Canada* (Montréal: Starke, 1849), 49–52. See also Baillargeon, "La tenure seigneuriale a-t-elle été abolie par des plaintes des censitaires?," *Revue d'histoire de l'Amérique française* 21, no. 1 (June 1967): 64–80.

35. *Act for the better protection of the lands and property of the Indians in Lower Canada* (1850), 13 & 14 Victoria, chap. 42.

36. Pétition des Indiens du Sault-Saint-Louis, de Saint-Régis, du Lac-des-Deux-Montagnes et de Saint-François à lord Elgin, September 18, 1850; LAC, RG 10, bob. C-13383, vol. 607, 51856–51858, in Beaulieu, *Rapport,* 495–496 (my translation).

37. Beaulieu, *Rapport,* 495–496.

38. *JAPC* (1847), 56, 66 (Innu); (1849), 77 (Innu); (1848), 7 (Abénakis and Maliseets); (1848) 31 (Odanak); (1849), 20 (Odanak); (1849), 187 Algon-

quins on the Gatineau River); (1851), 20 (Kahnawake, Odanak, etc.); (1851), 20 (Algonquins and Nipissings).

39. *JAPC* (1851), 207, 359; 14 & 15 Victoria, chap. 59. The conclusion that Indigenous petitioning occasioned the 1851 repeal of, and revisions to, the Act of 1850 is not mine but Beaulieu's (*Rapport*, 496). See also Gohier, *La pratique petitionnaire,* 41. Anthropologist and Kahnawá:ke citizen Audra Simpson recounts a set of conversations at Kahnawá:ke in the 1990s, to the effect that "the beginning of the argument" for local control over membership and spaces "are here" in the Native complaints of the 1850s. Simpson, *Mohawk Interruptus: Political Life across the Borders of Settler States* (Durham, N.C.: Duke University Press, 2014), 58).
40. Schedule of lands set apart and appropriated to and for the use of certain Indian Tribes, in Lower Canada, in *An Act to set apart certain Lands in Lower Canada for the use of the Indians in that part of the Province,* 4th Sess., 3rd Parliament, 14 Victoria 1851.

14. THE CLOSURE OF PETITION DEMOCRACY IN THE U.S. SOUTH, 1839–1860

1. Macon, quoted in Sean Wilentz, *The Rise of American Democracy: Jefferson to Lincoln* (Oxford: Oxford University Press, 2005), 231–232; William A. Link, *Roots of Secession: Slavery and Politics in Antebellum Virginia* (Chapel Hill: University of North Carolina Press, 2003), 108–110.
2. The decline of southern democracy in the two decades before the Civil War has been noted before, though not connected to petitioning. Wilentz, *Rise of American Democracy,* 576; Jonathan Wells, *The Origins of the Southern Middle Class, 1800–1861* (Chapel Hill: University of North Carolina Press, 2004), including chap. 4 (on voluntary associations); Johann Neem, *Democracy's Schools: The Rise of Public Education in America* (Baltimore: Johns Hopkins University Press, 2017).
3. *Journal of the House of Representatives of the State of Georgia, at the Annual Session of the General Assembly, Commenced at Milledgeville, November 2d, 1859* (Milledgeville, 1859), 54 (November 7), 96 (November 14).
4. Author's calculations from the Legislative Petitions Digital Collection, LOV. Legislative journals from the 1850s and 1860s also record a decline in in the 1850s and 1860s. William G. Shade, *Democratizing the Old Dominion: Virginia and the Second Party System, 1824–1861* (Charlottesville: University of Virginia Press, 1996), esp. chap. 8.
5. *JHDOV, 1855–1856* (December 15, 1855), 112 (committee inquiry into bill for giving married women control over "absolute and real personal

property"). See Petition of Citizens of Ohio County for a law to forbid the making and selling of spiritous liquors, March 12, 1852; Legislative Petitions of the General Assembly, 1776–1865, Accession Number 36121, box 191, folder 38, LOV; *Documentary History of the Maine Law: Comprising the Original Maine Law, the New-York Prohibitory Liquor Law, Legislative Debates, . . .* (New York: Hall and Brother, 1855).

6. *Journal of the House of Representatives of North Carolina, 1853*, 13, 60, 148.
7. Pamunkey Indians, Protest against the petition for the sale of land occupied by the Pamunkey Indians, January 21, 1843, Legislative Petitions of the General Assembly, 1776–1865, Accession Number 36121, box 135, folder 3, LOV.
8. William Smith, Governor's Address, December 4, 1848, *JHDOV 1848–1849*, 20–23.
9. "An Act Providing for the Voluntary Enslavement of the Free Negroes of the Commonwealth" (February 18, 1856), in *Acts of the General Assembly of Virginia Passed in 1855–56 in the Eightieth Year of the Commonwealth* (Richmond, 1856), 37–38. See also Maris-Wolf, *Family Bonds*, esp. chap. 3; William A. Link, *Roots of Secession: Slavery and Politics in Antebellum Virginia* (Chapel Hill: University of North Carolina Press, 2003), 174–179.
10. Petition of Citizens of Rockbridge County to Honorable County Court, July 2, 1835, requesting denial of free Blacks' privilege to remain in the state; Sally Henry and Children, Application to Remain in Rockbridge County, August 4, 1845; Application of Jacob ("Jake") Madison to Remain in Rockbridge County, June 20, 1845 (rejected August 4); Petition of Joseph Lee for reenslavement, April 14, 1860; Rockbridge County Free Negro and Slave Records, 1836–1864, LOV.
11. Wells, *he Origins of the Southern Middle Class*, 204–209.
12. For the Bill to reorganize Transylvania University (initially rejected), see *Journal of the House of the General Assembly of the Commonwealth of Kentucky, 1855–1856*, February 29, 1856 (544–549). Passage later in the 1856 session would be revisited in the 1857–1858 session. *Journal of the House of the General Assembly of the Commonwealth of Kentucky, 1857–1858*, 25 (December 8); Harold D. Tallant, *Evil Necessity: Slavery and Political Culture in Antebellum Kentucky* (Lexington: University Press of Kentucky, 2003), 137–142, chap. 8 (esp. 193–196 on Fee and colonization).
13. Manisha Sinha, *The Counterrevolution of Slavery: Politics and Ideology in Antebellum South Carolina* (Chapel Hill: University of North Carolina Press, 2000), 30–31, 76–78, 166–167, 225–230.

14. *Journal of the House of Representatives of the State of South Carolina,* 1853, 1854, 1857–1858, 1859, various indices. Women's petitions in the 1850s came from the Mason Female Institute (1853) and the German Ladies' Benevolent Society (1854); the Trustees of the Spartansburg Female College also petitioned (1857–58 session, November 29, 1857, *House Journal,* 83), but these eleven officers were men, seven of whom were reverends. Clement Eaton, *Freedom of Thought in the Old South* (Durham, N.C.: Duke University Press, 1940), 323.
15. Jonathan Daniel Wells, *The Origins of the Southern Middle Class, 1800–1861* (Chapel Hill: University of North Carolina Press, 2005), Tables 6 and 7, and 190–191 (citing scholarship by J. Mills Thornton III and Lacy K. Ford); Clement Eaton, *A History of the Old South* (Durham, N.C.: Duke University Press, 1949). On women journalists, consult Jonathan Daniel Wells, "A Voice in the Nation: Women Journalists in the Early Nineteenth-Century South," *American Nineteenth Century History* 9, no. 2 (2008): 165–182.
16. The claim that electoral democracy flourished in the South during the 1850s is quite old, going back at least to Clement Eaton's *Freedom of Thought in the Old South,* in which, pointing to growing electoral participation, he argues, "After 1850 a large measure of political democracy was achieved in the Southern states" (ix). Even after pausing to note that planters continued to dominate state legislative politics in South Carolina, Mississippi, and Louisiana, he asks, "What was the effect upon the thought of the Old South of this rise of the common man to greater economic and political democracy?"
17. *Journal of the House of Representatives of the State of Michigan* (1853), petitions against general railroad law (219), for and against a general railroad law (283), acts for regulating the crossing of farms by railroads (26), and remonstrances against amendments to railroad charters (272). Petition of undersigned citizens of Butte County to Gov. J. Neely Johnson (1856); Petition of undersigned citizens of Sacramento to Gov. J. Neely Johnson (1856); Petition of undersigned draymen and expressmen of the city and county of San Francisco to Gov. J. G. Downey (1860); B1, Petitions to the Governor, 1850–1909, Governor's Office Records, CSA.
18. Petition of the Citizens of Alexandria and Adjoining Counties for a test of the validity of the Baltimore & Ohio Railroad charter of 1847, February 5, 1853; Legislative Petitions of the General Assembly, 1776–1865, Accession Number 36121, box 355, folder 13, LOV; *Journal of the House of Representatives of the State of South Carolina, Being the Annual Session of 1853* (Columbia, 1853), 48, 68, 182 (South Carolina Railroad Company), 57 (Savannah River Valley Railroad Company); *Journal of the House of*

Representatives of the State of South Carolina, Being the Annual Session of 1854 (Columbia, 1854), 93 (December 6, Blue Ridge Railroad Company).

19. Laura F. Edwards, *The People and Their Peace: Legal Culture and the Transformation of Inequality in the Post-Revolutionary South,* (Chapel Hill: University of North Carolina Press, 2009), chaps. 7, 8, 257–266.
20. Governor Joseph E. Brown, "Governor's Message," in *Journal of the House of Representatives of the State of Georgia, 1859,* 12–13.
21. Joseph H. Parks, *Joseph E. Brown of Georgia* (Baton Rouge, 1977); Charles B. Dew, *Apostles of Disunion: Southern Secession Commissioners and the Causes of the Civil War* (Charlottesville: University of Virginia Press, 2017); Ralph Wooster, "The Georgia Secession Convention," *Georgia Historical Quarterly* 40, no. 1 (March 1956): 21–55.

15. FREEDOM AND THE PETITIONER'S DEMOCRACY

1. "Petition of the Colored Free & Freed Citizens of Savannah, Ga.," [1865], Andrew Johnson Papers, Duke-Rubenstein.
2. Eric Foner, *Reconstruction: America's Unfinished Revolution, 1863–1877* (New York: Harper Collins, 2011); Eric Foner, *Forever Free: The Story of Emancipation and Reconstruction* (New York: Vintage, 2005); Eric Foner, *The Second Founding: How the Civil War and Reconstruction Remade the Constitution* (New York: Norton, 2019); Heather Cox Richardson, *The Death of Reconstruction* (Cambridge, Mass.: Harvard University Press, 2001), esp. chaps. 1–2; Sean Wilentz, *The Rise of American Democracy: Jefferson to Lincoln* (Oxford: Oxford University Press, 2005), chap. 25; Manisha Sinha, *The Slave's Cause: A History of Abolition* (New Haven, Conn.: Yale University Press, 2016), chap. 16, epilogue.
3. James M. McPherson, *Battle Cry of Freedom: The Civil War Era* (New York: Oxford University Press, 1988), 254. See, for example, *JHRUS* 36:2, 213 (January 22, 1861), 230 (January 28), 243 (January 29); action was often postponed on these memorials under House Rule 24.
4. For examples, consult *CG*, February 5, 1861, 740; *JHRUS* 37:2, 275 (February 6), *JSUS* 37:2, 192 (February 6). The difference of two additional petition introductions among days where women's petitions were introduced is statistically significant, controlling for calendar date. Analysis of petitions in RG233 and RG 46 (NARA) supports this conclusion.
5. *JSUS* 36:2, 192 (February 6, 1861); *JHRUS* 37:1, 52 (petitions of citizens of Williams county, July 9), 152 (Summit County, July 26), 164 (petitions from Summit County and Stark County, Ohio, July 29); *JSUS* 37:1 (citizens

of Jewett City, Connecticut, July 12); Fawn Brodie, *Thaddeus Stevens: Scourge of the South* (New York: Norton, 1959), 154. Foner, *Forever Free,* 83–86.

6. *JHRUS* 37:2, 46 ("war power," "slaves of rebels," "total abolition," December 9, 1861); *JSUS* 37:2, 457 (citizens of Florida for confiscation, May 8). Petition of the Citizens of Walworth, Wisconsin, praying Congress to enact the War Power to abolish slavery, January 29, 1862, HR37A-G7.2, RG 233, NARA. My dating of this document differs from that of Zaeske (*Signatures of Citizenship,* 167–168); *JHRUS* 37:2, 241. McPherson, *The Struggle for Equality: Abolitionists and the Negro in the Civil War* (Princeton, N.J.: Princeton University Press, 2014), 112–115 (canvasser remark).
7. *Liberator,* March 14, 1862; Stanley Harrold, *American Abolitionism: Its Direct Impact from Colonial Times into Reconstruction* (Charlottesville: University of Virginia Press, 2019), 254–255.
8. Portage County Ohio Citizens to Abraham Lincoln, 1862; Benjamin H. West to Lincoln, August 27, 1862; Washington County, Pennsylvania Citizens to Lincoln, August 28, 1862; Boston Clergymen to Lincoln, September 1862; Illinois Citizens to Abraham Lincoln [1862]; all in Series 1, General Correspondence, 1833–1916, Lincoln Papers, LOC (digitized). The Chicago ministers' story was related by Schuyler Colfax; William Eleroy Curtis, *Abraham Lincoln* (Philadelphia: J. B. Lippincott, 1903), 329–330; McPherson, *Struggle for Equality,* 75–86, 93–94; John R. McKivigan, *The War against Proslavery Religion: Abolitionism and the Northern Churches, 1830–1865* (Ithaca: Cornell University Press, 1984), 186–196.
9. Foner, *Fiery Trial;* "The Emancipation of Abe Lincoln," *New York Times,* December 31, 2012. Richard H. Parham, Sr., to Lincoln, December 16, 1862, in Lincoln Papers, LOC (digitized). On the 1862 setbacks, consult Foner, *Forever Free,* 84–86.
10. Resolution of April 7, 1862, *Report of the Select Committee on Emancipation and Colonization* (Washington, 1862), esp. 19–33 (colonization plan). See disposition of H.R. 683, A Bill to establish a Bureau of Emancipation, referred to the Select Committee on emancipation on January 19, 1863; Leonard Richards, *Who Freed the Slaves? The Fight over the Thirteenth Amendment* (Chicago: University of Chicago Press, 2015), 134–137; Records of the Select Committee on Emancipation, 38A-E23.2, 38A-G25.1, RG 233, NARA.
11. *JSUS* 38:1, 30 (black soldiers in fourth and sixth regiments, and Maine petitioners, December 16, 1863); *JHRUS* 38:1, 134 (Michigan citizens, January 13, 1864), 121 (Brig. Gen. Burney petition, January 11, 1864).

Rick Beard, "Black Union Soldiers Fought a Costly Battle for Equal Pay," *Military Times,* February 12, 2018.

12. Albert I. Slomovitz, *The Fighting Rabbis: Jewish Military Chaplains and American History* (New York: NYU Press, 1999), 16–17.
13. On thousands of Jews in the war military, consult Simon Wolf, *The American Jew as Patriot, Soldier and Citizen* (Philadelphia: Levytype, 1895). Isaac Markens, "Lincoln and the Jews," *American Jewish Historical Society* 17 (1909): 109; Gary Phillip Zola, *We Called Him Rabbi Abraham: Lincoln and American Jewry, a Documentary History* (Carbondale: Southern Illinois University Press, 2014), 72.
14. Jonathan Sarna, *When General Grant Expelled the Jews* (New York: Knopf Doubleday, 2012), 16–17 (including discussion of B'nai B'rith petition of 1863); Sarna and Benjamin Shapell, *Lincoln and the Jews: A History* (New York: Macmillan, 2015), 118; Zola, *We Called Him Rabbi Abraham,* 100.
15. *JHRUS* 38:2, 52 (memorial of "employees in the various departments at Washington," December 19, 1864); Dudley T. Cornish, *The Sable Arm: Negro Troops in the Union Army, 1861–1865* (Lawrence: University Press of Kansas, 1956), 1–12; Richard H. Abbott, "Massachusetts and the Recruitment of Negro Soldiers, 1863–1865," *Civil War History* 14 (1968): 197–210; *JSUS* 38:1, 304 (April 7, 1864); *JHRUS* 38:1, 67 (Greene County, December 16, 1863); *JHRUS* 38:1, 331 ("1,065 citizens" and Massachusetts, March 2, 1864); *JSUS* 38:2, 20 (Col. Thomas Wentworth Higginson, December 12, 1864), 83 ("colored soldiers at Camp Casey," January 19, 1865).
16. *JHRUS* 38:1, 145 (January 15), 151 (1,305 men and women of Knox County, Illinois, January 18), 181 (Vermont citizens, "abolish African slavery," January 25), 67 (Greene County, December 16, 1863), 220 (four Ohio petitions, February 4, 1864); *JSUS* 38:1, 244 (1,000 black Louisiana petitioners, March 15, 1864), 315 (women, April 11). Women's petitions were three percentage points more likely to use the language of "African descent" and seven percentage points more likely to call for "universal emancipation" (statistical comparisons conducted in CPD within legislative calendar days using a fixed-effects regression with standard errors clustered on legislative calendar days; $p < 0.001$). Concord, Massachusetts, children to Lincoln, April 1864, Series 1 (General Correspondence, 1833–1916), Lincoln Papers, LOC [digitized]; "Women's Emancipation Petition" (with "African descent" in prayer), January 25, 1864, SEN 38A-H20, RG 46, NARA; Sumner, "Refusal to Colored Persons of Right of Petition," undelivered speech (June 15, 1860), in *Charles Sumner: His Complete Works,* vol. 6 (Boston, 1900), 288–290.

17. Records from the Sumner committee suggest that an initial aggregation compiled 90,062 names, with more women than men but not in quite the ratio suggested by the official count of Anthony and Stanton; "38 Congress: Petitions of men & women in the United states asking for the abolition of Slavery in the United States ("store room" comment), SEN 38A-H20, RG 46, NARA. Whether this reflects a campaign separate from that of Anthony and Stanton is unclear. Sumner, "The Prayer of One Hundred Thousand: Speech . . . on the presentation of the first installment of the emancipation petition of the women's national league" (New York, 1864), portfolio 125, folder 10, Printed Ephemera Collection, LOC; Sinha, *Slave's Cause,* 587–89; Zaeske, *Signatures of Citizenship,* 147, 170–72; McPherson, *Struggle for Equality,* 143–147.
18. "Women's Emancipation Petition" and "To the Women of the Republic," January 25, 1864, SEN 38A-H20, RG 46, NARA; Richards, *Who Freed the Slaves?,* 187–190, 201–202; Moorfield Storey, *Charles Sumner* (Boston, 1900), 259–260.
19. Carpenter and Moore, "When Canvassers Became Activists," 493–495 and Table 5.
20. *Oration, by Frederick Douglass, Delivered on the Occasion of the Unveiling of the Freedmen's Monument in Memory of Abraham Lincoln,* April 14, 1876 (Washington, D.C., 1876), 4.
21. Annette Gordon-Reed, *Andrew Johnson* (New York: Henry Holt, 2011), chap. 8; Brenda Wineapple, *The Impeachers: The Trial of Andrew Johnson and the Dream of a Just Nation* (New York: Random House, 2019), 54–59, 90–92 (Confederate murder of black child); Gregory P. Downs, *After Appomattox: Military Occupation and the Ends of War* (Cambridge, Mass.: Harvard University Press, 2015), 149–150, 156–159, 177–178, 199–203.
22. Petition of "The Colored free & freed citizens of Savannah, Ga." [1865], Andrew Johnson Papers, Duke-Rubenstein.
23. The colloquy has been reprinted in Ira Berlin, et al., eds., *Free at Last: A Documentary History of Slavery, Freedom and Civil War* (New York: New Press, 2007), 310–318; Foner, *Forever, Free,* 37–42. Petition of "The Colored free & freed citizens of Savannah, Ga." [1865]; "Roster of the Fifty-Fourth Massachusetts Infantry," in Luis F. Emilio, *A Brave Black Regiment: History of the Fifty-Fourth Regiment of Massachusetts Volunteer Infantry, 1863–1865* (Boston: Boston Book Company, 1891), 383–388 (Company K Roster).
24. Storey, *Sumner,* 294–295.
25. "The petition of the subscribers being colored citizens of the State of South Carolina" to Johnson, June 29, 1865, 55 pages, series 1, reel 15,

Johnson Papers, LOC, partially reprinted in *Papers of Andrew Johnson*, 8:31; Wineapple, *The Impeachers*, chap. 10.

26. Steven Hahn et al., eds., *Freedom: A Documentary History of Emancipation, 1861–1867, Series 3, Volume 1, Land and Labor 1865–1867* (Chapel Hill: University of North Carolina Press, 2017), 440–442; these petitions and other related documents have been published digitally in the Freedmen and Southern Society Project by the University of Maryland History Department. Foner, *Forever Free*, 112–114.
27. A nuanced argument for an emergent form of equality at Freedmen's Bureau offices appears in Antoinette Van Zelm, "On the Front Lines of Freedom: Black and White Women Shape Emancipation in Virginia, 1861–1890" (PhD thesis, College of William and Mary, 1998), 137–139; Julie Saville, *The Work of Reconstruction: From Slave to Wage Laborer in South Carolina, 1860–1870* (New York: Cambridge University Press, 1994), 90–96, 109–110.
28. *Proceedings of the Colored Men's Association of the State of Michigan . . .*, September 12–13, 1865 (Adrian, 1865); "The Mississippi Protest," *Liberator*, October 27, 1865; "Report on the Convention of the Colored People of North Carolina," *Liberator*, October 20, 1865; *Proceedings of a Convention of the Colored Men of Ohio, Held in Xenia*, January 10–12, 1865 (Cincinnati, 1865).
29. *Proceedings of the Colored People's Convention of the State of South Carolina, Held in Zion Church, Charleston, November, 1865* (Charleston, 1865). The conventions are the subject of a classic article by Herbert Aptheker, "South Carolina Negro Conventions, 1865," *Journal of Negro History* 31, no. 1 (1946): 91–97.
30. Wineapple, *The Impeachers*, 151–167.
31. *JSUS* 39:2, 100 (Norfolk, Virginia, January 15), 103 (North Carolina, January 16), 129 (Georgia, January 23).
32. The first impeachment petitions in 1867 appear at *JHRUS* 39:2, 106–107 (January 3, 1867), 110 (January 4, 1867). Ashley's speech occurred on January 7; Wineapple, *Impeachers*, 198–99. *JHRUS* 39:2, 251 (January 24, Wilson introduction), 40:1, 420 (February 27, 1868, committee appointment).
33. Reggie L. Pearson, "'There Are Many Sick, Feeble, and Suffering Freedmen': The Freedmen's Bureau's Health-Care Activities during Reconstruction in North Carolina, 1865–1868," *North Carolina Historical Review* 79, no. 2 (April 2002): 141–181.
34. *Narrative of Sojourner Truth; a Bondswoman of Olden Time, . . .* (Battle Creek, Michigan, 1884), 199–200, 205–207, 219–220, 225–227, 236–253. *Emporia* (Kansas) *News*, October 27, 1871, 3; Nell Irvin Painter, "Truth,

Sojourner," *American National Biography.* Margaret Washington, *Sojourner Truth's America* (Champaign: University of Illinois Press, 2011), 357–371.

35. Washington, *Sojourner Truth's America,* 357–358; Carleton Mabee, "Sojourner Truth, Bold Prophet: Why Did She Never Learn to Read?" *New York History* 69, no. 1 (January 1988): 55–77.
36. Petition of William F. Parker and others, calling for the abolition of capital punishment (undated but tabled on March 6, 1844), House unpassed legislation, 1775–1996 (SC1-230), 1844, Docket 1410, MAC; Petition of Eliza P. Hammond and others for the removal of Edward Greeley Loring (date unknown but probably January/February 1855); Senate unpassed legislation, 1780–1996 (SC1-231), 1855, Docket 18373, MAC (APMD); Washington, *Sojourner Truth's America,* 360–362, chaps. 13–14.
37. W. E. B. DuBois, *Black Reconstruction* (New York: Harcourt, Brace, 1935), 230; quoted in Aptheker, "South Carolina Negro Conventions, 1865," 91.

AFTERWORD

1. Adams's remarks concerned "the Qualifications of Voters," but as he knew, the debates over those qualifications were being made in petitions as well as pamphlets and speeches. "From John Adams to James Sullivan, 26 May 1776," *Founders Online,* National Archives, https://founders.archives.gov/documents/Adams/06-04-02-0091. Prince Hall's January 1777 petition appears in Massachusetts Archives Collection, 1629–1799 (SC1-45x), vol. 212–Revolution Resolves, 1777, MAC; digitized at APMD.
2. Nadia Urbinati, *Representative Democracy: Principles and Genealogy* (Chicago: University of Chicago Press, 2006), chap. 1; John Kingdon, *Agendas, Alternative and Public Policies* (New York: Longman, 2011); Baumgartner and Jones, *Agendas and Instability in American Politics,* 2nd ed. (Chicago: University of Chicago Press, 2009); Deva R. Woodly, *The Politics of Common Sense: How Social Movements Use Public Discourse to Change Politics and Win Acceptance* (Oxford: Oxford University Press, 2015), esp. chaps. 5–6.

Acknowledgments

This book opens with the transcribed words of six Innu chiefs and their 125 cosignatories, and my study of their petition, like every other part of this endeavor, was deeply collaborative. I visited Uashat mak Mani-Utenam (Sept-Îles and Maliotenam) in the summer of 2019 for a collective, compensated consultation with the Institut Tshakapesh of the Innu First Nations. Marjolaine Tshernish, Jérémie Ambroisie, Kathleen André, and many others walked me around their lands, fished with me on the *mishta shipu* (Great River, or Rivière Moisie) that has sustained their people for millennia, fed me meals traditional and modern, and shared their remarkable language and culture with me. To the Institut and the Innu, *Tshinashkumitinau!*

My work with Institut Tshakapesh and the communities at Uashat mak Mani-Utenam was something of a template for my work with other Indigenous nations. My aspiration was to visit authoring Indigenous communities, collaborate with other Indigenous scholars, listen to the readings of the document by community elders, pay these communities for their time, and promise to return and collaborate further. I approached and requested permission from tribal Institutional Review Boards where they exist, such as the Cherokee Nation of Indians IRB, to ensure conformity with appropriate protocols. The full set of relationships and procedures merits a separate methodological treatment, but I was influenced by Duane Champagne, "Centering Indigenous Nations within Indigenous Methodologies," *Wicazo Sa Review* (2015) and Alyssa Mount Pleasant, Caroline Wigginton, and Kelly Wisecup, "Materials and Methods in Native American and Indigenous Studies: Completing the Turn," *William and Mary Quarterly* (2018). It goes without saying that nothing in these collaborations commits these Indigenous communities to any concordance with or endorsement of what I have written, and that the same is true for any other consultation in the writing of this book. All errors and omissions remain mine alone.

Nya:weh to Jaré Cardinal and Randy Jones of the Seneca Nation of Indians, and Alyssa Mount Pleasant (Tuscarora). The late Rick Jemison, a Seneca Nation elder and historian, helped with many references and conversations; he is dearly missed. Thanks also to Ramona Peters and Stephen Curley of the Mashpee Wampanoag, and Elizabeth James-Perry of the Wampanoag Tribe of Gay Head (Aquinnah); Eric Hemenway of the Little Traverse Bands of Odawa Indians; Matthew L. M. Fletcher of the Grand Traverse Band of Chippewa and Ottawa Indians; Paul Buckner, David Cornsilk, and Honor Keeler of Cherokee Nation and Cherokee National Historical Society; Richard Smith of Laguna Pueblo; and Vina Begay of the Pueblo Indian Cultural Center. And my deep gratitude to Lisa Brooks (Missisquoi Abenaki), James Francis (Penobscot Indian Nation), Bonney Hartley (Stockbridge-Munsee Band of Mohican Indians), Elizabeth Solomon (Massachusett), and Cheryl Toney-Holley (Nipmuc), who with Elizabeth James-Perry serve as the Tribal Advisory Council for the Digital Archive of Native American Petitions in Massachusetts.

Other communities of petitioner descendants are not organized in the same way as Indigenous North Americans, but in a number of cases I tried to glean perspectives from descendants of petitioning communities. I learned much from Christle Rawlins-Jackson and Beverly Hector-Smith of the Beacon Hill Scholars, whose ancestors appear in the Black petitions of antebellum Boston. Joanne Haynes of Trinidad and Tobago, a descendant and biographer of Jean-Baptiste Philippe (see Chapter 6), exchanged papers and data and taught me about the complicated racial politics of Philippe's world.

It was Paul Pierson who, after hearing me present an early paper on antislavery petitioning, suggested that I think about what a "political technology" might be. Two decades later I haven't fully done justice to his question, but his query still animates me, and I hope to continue addressing it. Thanks to Paul and other scholars in the remarkable network of institutional political scientists who have discussed this project with me, including Chris Achen, Steve Ansolabehere, Larry Bartels, Angie Bautista-Chavez, Richard Bensel, Barry Burden, Nancy Burns, Melani Cammett, Tim Colton, Jean-Gabriel Contamin, Ryan Enos, Paul Frymer, Gerald Gamm, Claudine Gay,

Daniel Gillion, Jacob Hacker, Peter Hall, Rick Hall, Hahrie Han, John Mark Hansen, Don Herzog, Jennifer Hochschild, Will Howell, Scott James, Jeffrey Jenkins, Ira Katznelson, Desmond King, Margaret Levi, Steve Levitsky, David Lewis, Jane Mansbridge, Shom Mazumder, Tali Mendelberg, Suzanne Mettler, Rob Mickey, Eric Nelson, Karen Orren, John Padgett, Christopher Parker, Susan Pharr, Jon Rogowski, Michael Rosen, Ruth Bloch Rubin, Elizabeth Sanders, Eric Schickler, Wendy Schiller, Theda Skocpol, Stephen Skowronek, Rogers Smith, Jim Snyder, Charles Stewart III, Dawn Teele, Kathleen Thelen, Gregory Wawro, Barry Weingast, Keith Whittington, and Daniel Ziblatt. A number of economists, sociologists, and other scholars have also contributed their insights, including Daron Acemoglu, Elisabeth Clemens, Robert Gibbons, Michèle Lamont, John Manning, Doug McAdam, Orlando Patterson, Daphna Renan, Woody Powell, John Wallis, Susan Zaeske, and David Zaret.

Historians at Harvard and around the world have shared their careful readings of this manuscript and their ideas in conversation about it. The many people to thank include Benoit Agnès, Sven Beckert, Alain Beaulieu, Thomas Bisson, Ned Blackhawk, Diego Palacios Cerezales, Nancy Cott, Phil Deloria, Christine Desan, Maxime Gohier, David Golove, Allan Greer, Robert Gross, Daniel Hulsebosch, Romain Huret, Richard Huzzey, Joanna Innes, Maartje Janse, Walter Johnson, Martha Jones, Mark Knights, James Kloppenberg, Naomi Lamoreaux, Tiya Miles, Henry Miller, David Moss, Johann Neem, William Novak, Nick Parrillo, Noah Rosenblum, Claudio Saunt, Dan Smail, and Paul Grant-Costa and Tobias Glaza of the New England Indian Papers Series. Reeve Huston shared his insights and his remarkable new manuscript on antebellum American political practices. Anne Boylan, Nancy Hewitt, Jane Kamensky, Joelle Million, and Judith Wellman suggested materials and taught me much about women's history. Eric Foner, Martha Jones, and Manisha Sinha were especially helpful in studying the petition that begins Chapter 15. Malcolm Ebright and Rick Hendricks lent their expertise and their archival references on nineteenth-century New Mexican pueblos.

Scholars Gregory Ablavsky, Maggie Blackhawk, Paul Frymer, Alex Keyssar, Kate Masur, Ruth Bloch Rubin, Eric Schickler, Manisha Sinha, Charles Stewart III, Gregory Wawro, and Richard White read the entire manuscript and gave withering and constructive commentary. Richard also shared some of his unpublished materials on Great Lakes history. He has been an inspiration and a great critic for over two decades.

Among the many research collaborators who assisted with different facets of this project, I want to thank Christopher Carden, Colleen Driscoll, Justin Curtis, Kaneesha Johnson, D. J. Lacy, Alina Scott, Mark Scott, Elizabeth Thompson, and Tess Wise.

Other collaborators have also served as coauthors, including Doris Brossard, Colin Moore, Clayton Nall, Tobias Resch, and Ben Schneer. The remarkable Nicole Topich and Garth Griffin joined in creating new petition databases that, I hope, will assist students and scholars for decades to come. I have learned so much from working with Maggie Blackhawk (Fond du Lac Band of Lake Superior Ojibwe) on petitioning that I cannot possibly repay the debt. Many citations, further collaboration, and a heartfelt *Miigwech* will have to do for now.

The book began with support from the Center for Advanced Study in the Behavioral Sciences and the rare experience of camaraderie there. A Guggenheim Fellowship gave me critical support at a time when I needed the momentum. The National Endowment for the Humanities and the Mellon Foundation (through the Council on Library and Information Resources) provided critical grants to build new petition databases. David Moss and John Cisternino and the wonderful group at the Tobin Project provided a supportive and critical community.

The Radcliffe Institute for Advanced Study, where I was fortunate enough to have a fellowship in 2007–2008 and where I gratefully served as faculty director of the social sciences for seven years, provided an unparalleled interdisciplinary home. This project would not have come to fruition without the institute's guidance and support. Hearty thanks to Dean Lizabeth Cohen, Dean Tomiko Brown-Nagin, Rebecca Wassarman, Sean Taft O'Donnell, Jennifer Birkett, Kristen Kravet, and Maura Madden.

Archivists too numerous to mention here facilitated much of my research. Let me acknowledge in particular Richard Hunt and his staff at the Legislative Archives Center of the U.S. National Archives, Rick Hendricks of the New Mexico State Archives and Records Center, and Michael Comeau and Martha Clark of the Massachusetts Archives.

Much of Chapter 7 was first published as an article I coauthored with Doris Brossard titled "*L'éruption patriote:* The Revolt against Dalhousie and the Petitioning Explosion in Nineteenth-Century French Canada," *Social Science History* 43 (Fall 2019): 453–485. Portions of Chapter 9 were first published in "Party Formation through Petitions: The Whigs and the Bank War of 1832–1834," coauthored with Benjamin Schneer, *Studies in Amer-*

ican Political Development 29 (October 2015): 213–234. Chapter 13 builds on ideas first presented in "On the Origins of the Administrative Petition: Innovations in Nineteenth-Century Native America," a chapter I contributed to *Administrative Law from the Inside Out,* edited by Jerry Mashaw and Nicholas Parrillo (Yale University Press, 2017).

At Harvard University Press, James Brandt and Emily Silk shepherded my ideas with enthusiasm and exercised their remarkable acumen to render my argument more legible and direct. Deep thanks as well to Mihaela Pacurar and Stephanie Vyce. Press Syndic Michael Rosen offered his ever sage guidance on developing the ideas.

Friends, family, and supporters have sustained me over decades. My love and thanks to Tim Chafos, Mark Gammons, David Hooper, Chris Jordan, Dan Kirsch, David Savio, and Chris Yannelli, and to the late and beloved John Breslin, S. J. I am ever grateful for the love of my parents, Kathleen Carpenter and John (Jack) Carpenter, and my sister, Rebecca Peterson. My partner in life, Rita Butzer, continues to inspire, care, and sustain. Laurel Bernice Carpenter and Leo Edward Carpenter, I love you beyond words. This world is now yours. Bring justice.

Index